The Right Honourable W. L. Mackenzie King:
a portrait by Frank O. Salisbury, unveiled in the Rotunda
of the Parliament Buildings, June 1947

# THE
# MACKENZIE KING
# RECORD

### VOLUME 4
### 1947-1948

J. W. Pickersgill

and

D. F. Forster

UNIVERSITY OF TORONTO PRESS

ISBN-0-8020-1686-3

# Preface

IN THIS FINAL VOLUME of the Mackenzie King Record, there is no need to repeat what the interested reader can find in the prefaces to the first three volumes. We simply wish to renew our thanks to the University of Toronto Press and, in particular, to Miss Francess Halpenny who supervised the preparation of these volumes. In common with many other Canadian authors and editors, we owe a great debt to Miss Halpenny for her patience, skill and understanding.
J.W.P.
D.F.F.

*Ottawa and Toronto, October 1969*

The Index to volumes 3 and 4 has been prepared by Mr. and Mrs. John Bryden.

# Contents

# Illustrations

---

# THE MACKENZIE KING RECORD

## Volume 4

## THE MACKENZIE KING MINISTRY, JANUARY 1947

| | |
|---|---|
| *Prime Minister and President of the Privy Council* | W. L. Mackenzie King |
| *Minister of Veterans Affairs* | Ian A. Mackenzie |
| *Minister of Justice and Attorney General* | J. L. Ilsley |
| *Minister of Reconstruction and Supply* | C. D. Howe |
| *Minister of Agriculture* | James G. Gardiner |
| *Minister of Trade and Commerce* | James A. MacKinnon |
| *Secretary of State of Canada* | Colin W. G. Gibson |
| *Secretary of State for External Affairs* | Louis S. St. Laurent |
| *Minister of Labour* | Humphrey Mitchell |
| *Minister of Public Works* | Alphonse Fournier |
| *Postmaster General* | Ernest Bertrand |
| *Minister of National Defence* | Brooke Claxton |
| *Minister of Mines and Resources* | James A. Glen |
| *Solicitor General* | Joseph Jean |
| *Minister of Transport* | Lionel Chevrier |
| *Minister of National Health and Welfare* | Paul Martin |
| *Minister of Finance and Receiver General* | Douglas C. Abbott |
| *Minister of National Revenue and Minister of National War Services* | J. J. McCann |
| *Minister of Fisheries* | H. F. G. Bridges |
| *Minister without Portfolio and Leader of the Government in the Senate* | Wishart McL. Robertson |

# CHAPTER ONE

# Introduction

LIKE THE PRECEDING THREE VOLUMES in this series, this volume is basically a record prepared by Mackenzie King outlining and interpreting his activities as leader of the Liberal party and Prime Minister of Canada during the period from January 1, 1947, until his retirement as Prime Minister on November 15, 1948.

Often plagued by ill health and feeling the accumulated burdens of his record term of office, Mackenzie King became absorbed during this period by plans for his retirement and arrangements for choosing his successor. Among his cabinet colleagues, Louis St. Laurent continued to enjoy a close personal relationship with the Prime Minister and clearly became his choice for the leadership of the party even though the two men occasionally differed over details in the conduct of Canada's external relations. The pressures of war, postwar reconstruction and financial relations between the federal and provincial governments had affected J. L. Ilsley's health and his effectiveness in the Cabinet was reduced. C. D. Howe continued to carry heavy responsibilities in the postwar government but personal relations between him and Mackenzie King became no closer. Despite many strains, the personal bond between the Prime Minister and Ian Mackenzie remained strong and earned Mackenzie an appointment to the Senate after he finally left the Cabinet. The irrepressible Minister of Agriculture, J. G. Gardiner, continued to be a powerful force in the Cabinet but the Prime Minister's suspicion of him increased, particularly when Gardiner seemed to threaten Mackenzie King's plans for the succession. Both Humphrey Mitchell and J. A. MacKinnon remained on friendly terms with Mackenzie King though their influence in Cabinet was never great.

Among his younger colleagues, Brooke Claxton continued to have a close relationship with the Prime Minister though Mackenzie King had serious doubts about Claxton's political and administrative style. D. C. Abbott, as Minister of Finance, had great influence in the Cabinet and

Paul Martin and Lionel Chevrier assumed heavier responsibilities during this period.

J. E. Handy remained the central figure in the Prime Minister's staff at Laurier House. In the East Block, Lester Pearson, as Undersecretary of State for External Affairs, had frequent contact with Mackenzie King. Despite often acute disagreements over external policy, Mackenzie King continued to admire Pearson and, at every opportunity, encouraged his political interests. The Prime Minister had the satisfaction of seeing Pearson enter the Cabinet shortly before his retirement. Arnold Heeney continued in the office of Clerk of the Privy Council and Secretary to the Cabinet and J. W. Pickersgill was head of the Prime Minister's office with the title of Special Assistant during this period.

At the beginning of 1947, Mackenzie King faced a task he always dreaded, preparing for a session of Parliament opening on January 30. There were details of new tax agreements between some of the provinces and the federal government to attend to and a range of problems connected with readjustment of the Canadian economy to a peacetime environment. Problems of reconstruction and inflation, balance of payment difficulties and commodity trade arrangements occupied an increasing amount of the Cabinet's time. In international affairs, growing tension between the West and the Soviet Union was the Canadian government's main preoccupation and forced it to move towards a new role and develop a new relationship with the United States, Britain and Europe. In the House of Commons, the government's majority remained slim and Mackenzie King was forced to devote a great deal of time to relations between cabinet and caucus and party organization. John Bracken continued to lead the Progressive Conservative opposition; M. J. Coldwell and Solon Low led the C.C.F. and Social Credit parties respectively.

# CHAPTER TWO

# The Search for a Successor

MACKENZIE KING'S diary entry for January 1, 1947, was an accurate forecast of his mood through most of the year. "I have at different times felt," he wrote, "that if a memorial to myself should be erected at any time by the country, I would like to have it on the little triangle between the War Memorial, the Langevin Block and Parliament Hill. Perhaps a sort of reproduction of the standing one with little Pat which was given me on my 25th anniversary as Leader of the Party. It would be out in the open thoroughfare in immediate contact with the traffic and the people of the City and in a part of the Capital which I have helped to beautify.

"Curiously enough, this thought seemed to be revived with the thought of being known as a man of the people; as one who has tried to further the well-being of those we speak of as citizens of a country. To raise their standards rather than to create or maintain standards of difference."

There was a kind of Indian Summer at the end of the year, but, during most of 1947, the Prime Minister seemed to have lost his sense of purpose and to be concerned mainly with his place in history, his successor and, above all, his failing health and strength. Though he had no new initiatives to promote, he did not relax his grip on policy and was increasingly jealous of his prerogatives as Prime Minister and as leader of the Liberal party. In particular, he insisted on having final authority in the conduct of Canada's external relations.

On the evening of January 3 he attended a ceremony, organized by the Secretary of State, where he received the first citizenship certificate issued under the Canadian Citizenship Act which had been passed in 1946 and came into force on January 1. The Prime Minister found the whole ceremony deeply moving. "Later, when giving the address of the evening, I was given a wonderful reception, both at the beginning and at the close. I was quite surprised how quickly the audience applauded, when I began by saying 'I speak as a citizen of Canada.' There was instantaneous applause and I had to wait before getting on to the next sentence. I noticed too quite a response when I referred to Canada being founded on the fusion of two proud races. One could have heard a pin drop, excepting when the movie machines were continually at work. The applause at the end was so long that I had to rise and acknowledge it with a bow to the audience and the Chief Justice."

When he returned to Laurier House that night he "placed the little certificate in front of my grandfather's portrait and then read the papers before turning out the lights. I really have experienced a greater joy today and a sense of greater honour than the time of receiving the freedom of cities elsewhere and other marks of recognition. To be the first citizen of Canada in the two senses of the word: 1) in the position I enjoy and 2) in the certificate of the fuller citizenship which has come about as a result of legislation enacted by [the] administration of which I am the head makes me very happy indeed."

With a slim majority, one of Mackenzie King's chief preoccupations throughout the year was party organization in and out of the House of Commons. At the first Cabinet meeting of the year, on January 3, he spoke "about the most important thing for the year being proper party organization. Unless some means could be found to this end, we were certain to encounter defeat, possibly in the House before an election and defeat at any election which could wipe out the Liberal party perchance altogether. Might result in coalition with either C.C.F. or Tory at the head. I then spoke of the most important thing being the relations with the provinces. It is an appalling fact that we opened the year with all practically against us, having antagonized them one way or another. Left things in shape that those we had pleased would be eventually disappointed. Then spoke of the Defence services and the problem that they presented as being the next great question.

"Glen said something about needing a message as well as organization. I said I thought the message would come clear enough when we reached the time of election. What we needed now was to get back to the old Liberal principles of economy, reduction of taxation, anti-militarism, etc." He added that he "thought we would have to decide whether we were going in for increased military expenditures or to seek to carry out our programme of social legislation. We could not have both. We would have to have a definite policy."

As Mackenzie King indicated, a first priority in the new year was the problem of tax rental negotiations with the provinces which were close to complete collapse at the end of 1946. The governments of New Brunswick and Manitoba, which had already accepted agreements, were upset by what they regarded as more favourable terms given to British Columbia. Premier Garson had protested privately but Premier McNair of New Brunswick had sent a strongly worded telegram to the Prime Minister which he proposed to make public. On January 6 Mackenzie King telephoned McNair to see if he would hold back publication of the telegram only to find that it had already been released. "I was careful to be extremely polite, knowing McNair's temperament. Really feeling a bit that our people had not been wholly fair and square with him. He was the first to put the agreement into shape. He said the only solution he now saw was a completely fresh restatement of everything." To the Prime Minister, "the whole business is certainly a terrible muddle and all because of the rigidity of the Finance Department not yielding a few minor taxes in the last Conference."

On January 9, after a talk with Abbott, St. Laurent and Claxton, Mackenzie King was somewhat more optimistic about reaching a solution to the problem. The next day he telephoned McNair again to let him know that the Premiers of Manitoba and Saskatchewan had agreed to come to Ottawa for further discussions and that he hoped McNair would come too. The Premier of New Brunswick was reluctant but promised to give an answer the next day. He was assured that "it was the intention from the start to protect the interests of the provinces who were the first to negotiate with [the] federal government."

In the event, McNair did join his colleagues from Manitoba and Saskatchewan in Ottawa to examine a new federal offer. Under the revised formula, the guaranteed minimum payment to a province could be calculated on the basis of one of two options. The first, which was designed to appeal to Nova Scotia and Saskatchewan particularly, provided $15.00 per capita on the provincial population of 1942 plus all subsidies due to the province as a result of past constitutional or statutory action. The second option offered $12.75 per capita on the 1942 population of the province plus 50 per cent of the personal and corporate income tax revenue raised in the province during the fiscal year ending nearest to December 31, 1940, and all previous statutory subsidies. Whichever option was chosen, all provincial payments were subject to annual increase over the five years of the agreements through the application of a complicated adjustment formula which related changes in provincial population and per capita gross national product during the three years preceding the year of payment to the base year 1942. It was estimated that the new scheme potentially involved an increase of some $25,100,000 in annual payments to the provinces. On January 15 the Prime Minister "talked at some length with Abbott and St. Laurent over negotiations with three of the provinces. Abbott feels that agreements will be reached. I certainly think the formula worked out is a quite remarkable one and should appeal to the several provinces."

Angus Macdonald was in Ottawa on other business and on January 16 he and Mackenzie King had a talk about the new federal proposals. He reported that Macdonald "seemed most interested in talking of the annual meeting of the provinces and the Dominion. I told him there were times and seasons for all things – he could hardly expect, recalling the way Duplessis had behaved at the last Conference and the way he talked, and of Drew speaking about the Government being incompetent, etc., that men like St. Laurent, Ilsley, Abbott and myself could be expected to want to have annual conferences with them. Besides I thought the Government should be free of any one commitment that would bind us. There were far too many conferences today. We could not get on with our work. Ministers and officials abroad were busy on Committees. The last two conferences had added to the confusion of the unsettled state in the public mind. I thought people wanted a rest from conferences for awhile. We could get on far better with the individual agreements. I said later when we meet to consider the health and welfare problem, if all went smoothly, we might then consider when another conference might be called. I said Duplessis and Drew as Conservative Governments were trying to defeat our Government. I did not think we were in any way responsible to provincial governments. We were responsible to members that came from the provinces in our own Dominion Parliament. I felt that Macdonald was not pressing the matter far but putting himself in a position where he could tell Drew there could be no chance of a conference. I said I was glad he happened to come to Ottawa at this moment. Not having been asked to come especially but finding a new agreement here all worked out, I thought it was fortunate he was here at the moment.

"He told me Abbott had given him the figures and he was looking over them. I agreed that the Finance Department had in its original programme gone too far in what appeared to be taking from the provinces certain fiscal rights and leading to centralization in expenditure. I agreed too that it was desirable to discuss quietly with the provinces matters affecting them before announcing to the country that plans had been agreed upon but made no commitment as to any annual conference.

"As he was leaving, he spoke nicely about my looking well, etc., and in parting said: good luck – which is quite different than it has been for some time. I shall be surprised if he does not accept the agreements which the five other provinces have virtually already accepted.

"In Council, Abbott gave an account of what was being proposed,

There is no doubt as he said we are paying out much more than we originally would have, had we, at the outset, thought of the formula we now have or made certain concessions of sources of revenue we are now prepared to make."

On January 22, the Minister of Finance told the Cabinet that "he had had a very satisfactory talk with Manning of Alberta who he thinks will accept the proposed agreement. It looks as if all but Ontario and Quebec will do so. The general feeling is that Ontario will find a way to do so. Duplessis may do nothing so as to have an election first with centralization an issue. As St. Laurent sees it, Duplessis will be making an appeal solely to racial prejudice. Will claim that if eight provinces signed agreements in Canada it would be evidence of English-speaking provinces ganging against the French.

"In Council I did my best to keep everything on an even keel and in good humour. I think I succeeded fairly well. Remarkably well considering the differences of view that had to be reconciled. St. Laurent is an immense help; is so clear-sighted and far-sighted."

Mackenzie King continued to be almost as anxious about the political impact of defence expenditures as he was about federal-provincial relations. On January 9 there was a long discussion in the Defence Committee about the size of the defence estimates and the Chiefs of Staff were given instructions to keep them below a certain ceiling. Reporting on the meeting of the Defence Committee on January 14, the Prime Minister wrote that "Claxton has done wonderful work in compelling the defence forces to cut down different establishments, effecting a saving of something like $100,000,000. I listened with great interest to Solandt's account of the work of the proposal for army research at Valcartier. I feel in the long run research will do much more than aught else, but find the present proposed outlay pretty heavy. I suggested cutting down more on army estimates and allowing research estimates to stand. Matter to be considered further. I found that the Defence Council swung around to my point of view of getting rid of one of the aircraft carriers. This afternoon the Cabinet was about decided to get rid of both. I am inclined to believe one aircraft carrier may be advisable. If war should come at any time flying from the northern regions would be an important factor. Having a Defence Committee of the Cabinet and presiding over it is all important in effecting saving of public money."

At the Cabinet meeting on February 5, "a great deal of time was taken up discussing defence estimates. I pointed out that at the time Abbott had made a statement to the House promising a certain size of service, army, navy and air, I had been to see Truman and Attlee and attending a

Prime Minister's Conference. Had I been here I would certainly not have countenanced statements being made that these figures were other than for planning purposes as had been understood when I left. I also pointed out that when Gibson had made his statement regarding the navy I had again been absent at the Paris Peace Conference. Had I been here I would have opposed very strongly some of the undertakings then given. I pointed out particularly that the Committee had intended to build a lot of armouries for reserve purposes. I would have fought that tooth and nail. After the last war we decided to get rid of armouries and use them as community halls. I told the colleagues to review that at the moment. Their thoughts may have been formed in part by fears of Russian aggression growing out of Communistic revelations. I did not think there was any justification for having large numbers in the defence forces, where money was needed for a reduction of taxation and for social services.

"Claxton made out a very good case for what he had done in trying to cut down so that the Minister of Finance might bring in a budget that would be under two billion dollars – something almost unthinkable. Claxton held to his position that he could not possibly go further in view of what had been understood originally and keep responsibility for the Department. I felt he was on the whole right on what he had been saying though I told Council that I believed the C.C.F. would come along and produce a motion to cut expenditures in half – to reduce them by a third or one-half and they would have no better political capital throughout the country. I also, in reply to Claxton's statement, asked if he had not received communications expressing favour for reduction of army, etc. I said if not, he had better see the communications that came to my office and if he wanted to test the Liberal feeling let us have the matter discussed at party Caucus. That was the place to get the views. Not as sent in by persons interested in army to the Minister of War."

In fact, there was relatively little criticism of the size of the defence estimates in the House but the government did come close to defeat on the Militia Bill during the evening of February 13. The bill embodied the Cabinet's decisions on the peace-time size of the three armed services and the reserve units. The Prime Minister was at Laurier House that evening and Ian Mackenzie, who was leading the House, telephoned "to say they were expecting a discussion on the military bill. That there were not enough of our Members present to carry the bill. Asked what he should do in the event of the Government being defeated. I said to adjourn the House at once and, if asked about tomorrow's business, to say that would depend on the decision the Government might take as a result of the vote just registered.

"I was relieved when I learned at 11 that the House had just adjourned and that Claxton had been wise enough to say that he was prepared to consider suggestion from the Opposition as to Parliament controlling the size of the militia. This is something that ought, it seems to me, to have been done by our own people in advance and not to have left anything of the kind to be done by Order-in-Council. In some way or another, it seems impossible to get Ministers to give up this little authority which they have exercised during times of war and leave it to the body to which it belongs, namely Parliament. I do not object to the Opposition forcing our people to fall properly into line on the supremacy of Parliament."

Anticipating the tensions of the new session, Mackenzie King had more than his usual case of pre-session depression in 1947. In addition, he was not feeling at all well. On January 17 he had expressed worry "about feeling so exhausted and fatigued; also with pain in my left eye, which continues to be inflamed. Having, too, a renewal of the dread of the approaching session, in order to be in readiness for the debate on the Address – this is something I never seem to be able to overcome." His physical condition had led again to thoughts of retirement. "During the early morning I thought a good deal about what I should do as to continuing on as Prime Minister, having in mind, first of all, my present age; second, what has to be done in disposing of my letters, properties, etc.; and third, arranging my own life in the light of advancing years, with possible loss of strength and health, should I be spared to live on for some little time. Looking into these things before one becomes too infirm in mind and body to give them the proper consideration they should have. I felt the first thing to be perfectly positive about was, on no account, to contest another election. That would be a great mistake. It would probably be too great a tax on my health. Also I think it would leave the way open to the mistake which I find so many public men have made in remaining too long on the stage of public affairs, helping thereby to destroy such record as one has made. It certainly would affect one's after years. The position of the Party has, of course, to be considered. I think the Party should go to the country with the Leader who will have to carry on either in office or in opposition after the election.

"There are two dates which I think I should keep in mind. One, June 10, when I will have completed twenty years in the office of Prime Minister; and August 7th, when I will have completed twenty-eight years as Leader of the Party. Should the coming session prove too great a tax on my health, I should I think make one or other of these dates, provided I am spared, if not giving up office, at least of announcing definitely my intention of so doing forthwith and of arranging for a Convention to be held before the year is out. A Convention some time in the autumn would probably be best, were I to give up this year.

"The other alternative, conditional on my health and strength permitting it, and the support of the party in the House, would be to seek to carry over until 1948 to these dates at the latest. Were I to continue in office until June 10, 1948, I would have completed 21 years in office and would also have exceeded Walpole's record, which means not only the record in all parts of the world today, but a record as far as is known for all time thus far. If that were to come about, I would seek I think to have a Party Convention held, choose a new Leader on August the 7th, giving up office on what would be the 29th anniversary of the day on which I had been given the Leadership of the Party and when I would be in my 22nd year in the office of Prime Minister. That, it seems to me as I dictate, is continuing in both positions too long. On no consideration, should I consider going beyond either of these dates, unless it were that, experiencing a real [improvement in] health that I can hardly believe would be possible, [I could] announce on the date that I was chosen Leader, a date for a Convention to appoint a new Leader later in the year. It is perhaps wrong to even speculate on these possibilities as what is for the best is alone known to Providence but, even more, what may be possible. The most I feel I should aim at at the present is to hold on for certain until June the 10th as Prime Minister when my portrait might be then hung in the Halls of Parliament in the presence of the Members and keeping in mind a possible Convention in August depending, of course, on the length of the session or arranging in August for a Convention later in the year. I thought the last time I worked on the Speech from the Throne, it would be the last I would work on. Naturally many thoughts come to my mind as I begin the one for the Opening of this Session. I can see where I may have to do, if spared, with the writing of the closing speech of the coming session. I can hardly contemplate at this time working on the speech in a session of 1948, though I would like if it were the will of Providence to perhaps hold on long enough to have surpassed Walpole's record which would be April 14, 1948. Walpole, however, was not really a Prime Minister as that office is understood today in relation to the confidence of the people rather than the will of the Sovereign."

He had returned to the theme of retirement on January 28 after reading an article by C. G. Power "on what is the matter with the Liberals. No doubt he is taking this means of getting even with the Government in appointing Bouffard to the Senate instead of himself and not having made him organizer of the party in Quebec. The article is a very good one and I confess I pretty well agree with the whole of it. He could not have been fairer or kinder in his references to myself. I am beginning to wonder if the article is intended to bring on a movement for a National Convention, aiming at getting Gardiner or someone else in as Leader, who will bring Power back into the Ministry. I feel that McGeer and one or two others may be in correspondence with Power over the matter. Of this I am not sure. They may be arranging for a National Convention some time in the autumn. I am not at all sure that this would not be the best time rather than waiting until the following year.

"Power says in his article that I would be offered the Leadership anew by acclamation. He thinks it would be difficult for me not to accept it because of the pressure there would be for me to hold on. I am determined, however, at all costs not to lead the party through another election. I can see that I have not the strength for that. I tire too quickly. When I get fatigued, my memory is not what it used to be. I cannot keep up throughout long stretches of the day."

On January 30, the day the session had opened, Mackenzie King found it "unfortunate beyond words that I should be at the lowest depth of depression before beginning the session. This remains one of the mysteries that I cannot comprehend. I can only trust to the grace and power of God to see me through. These feelings make me more resolved than ever not to attempt to carry on as Leader of the Party beyond the present year. My mind is now strongly focussing on calling a National Convention, sometime in November or October, at which a new Leader can be chosen and the Government's policy outlined. Should this be arranged, I might be able to get some of the summer months and early autumn quietly to prepare a farewell to public life – that is if my lot should not be that of Sir Wilfrid, which was to himself be present at a Convention which was to choose his successor, but was deprived of this by the end coming sooner than he had anticipated. As I dictate I have less heart or hope than I believe I have had at any time at the beginning of a new session, though until last night I had felt that in more respects than one I was in better shape than I had been for the opening of any session for some years past. Again, I can only pray that I may be given strength to endure what has to be endured in the next few weeks."

Actually the preparations for the session had not been particularly strenuous. On January 21 the Prime Minister had spent about three hours "going over the Speech from the Throne with the Cabinet, making it the occasion of discussing many matters of which the policy had still to be settled. Ilsley thought the Speech had not much in it. I told him that was exactly what I was looking for – something to put in it. Would he tell me what, or some of the others. I found, as I went around the table, that no one had anything to add. As I went over it the second time, picking it up clause by clause, they found that there was more in it than they had anticipated. There were sixteen Members of Cabinet present; each in turn had his chance to suggest anything. They finally approved the drafts with such slight changes as I had indicated might be made in the light of discussion.

"I then took up some commitments made at the last session and outlined the line to be taken in reference to them. It was a most profitable afternoon and one which on the whole I much enjoyed. I felt real progress was being made, but we did not get beyond the first item of today's agenda. I do not think ever before did I have the Speech from the Throne in galley proof ten days in advance of the opening. There are still, however, many knotty questions to be decided. Most difficult of all things were those that arise out of the kind of thing that the Finance Department let us in for in its first proposals – green book, etc."

One question which had to be settled before Parliament met was procedure for handling House representation in Cartier constituency since Fred Rose's conviction and sentencing the year before. The Cabinet had discussed the problem on January 9. It "involved the necessity of having him expelled as a Member of Parliament," Mackenzie King explained. "I drew attention of Cabinet to fact that I might have to be careful about what was said of rights of Members and their being expelled when I recalled that among opponents of the family compact, my own grandfather, in his day, was expelled five times from the House."

In discussion with leaders of the opposition parties on January 28, a procedure was agreed upon and on the first day of the session "the Speaker tabled the judgment he had received in the Court with respect to Rose's indictment. I rose immediately and read a resolution which we had prepared which was to the effect that . . . Rose had been found guilty of an indictable offence and sentenced to six years' imprisonment. He was, therefore, under the criminal law unable to vote or take his seat and ordering that the Speaker should issue a warrant for a new writ and an election ordered in the constituency of Cartier. When I finished reading the resolution, I said this resolution speaks for itself. I have nothing to add. It was read by the Speaker and passed unanimously. Not a soul saying a word." With the seat declared vacant, a by-election was called for March 31.

For once, the Prime Minister was satisfied by his contribution to the debate on the Address on February 3. "Bracken," in his opinion, "made a frightful exhibition of himself. Whoever prepared the material for him, and a good deal of it was done by himself, seems to have sought to scrape together everything in the nature of a petty criticism that it is possible to gather against the Government, and myself in particular. A lot of hackneyed phrases and characterizations of one kind or another, platitudes, etc. All written out and read from different sets of papers. I really could not help feeling sorry for Bracken. He seemed so completely at sea. Between trying on one hand to say something without the manuscript and when he had manuscript reading material that was anything but graceful in expression. There was no flow, nothing natural about the whole business. He kept on until twenty minutes to six.

"I was very tired, but decided to get into the debate at once and clear the slate of one or two topics. Much to my surprise I found that I had more energy and fire than I believed I would have after sitting still so long.

"I hurried home from the House and got a good forty minutes rest before having dinner. Then I merely glanced at some of the notes I had made, returned to the House and spoke for a little over an hour without any notes whatever and without any difficulty in bringing out the points that I wished to make. I deliberately discarded a lot of the material that I might have used so as to shorten the speech. There were a few interruptions which gave me a chance to come back pretty hard, much to the delight of our party.

"What gave vim to the whole speech was that Bracken's amendment had declared that the Government had lost the confidence of the House which brought to the fore the possibility of an immediate general election.

"I did not lose an instant in taking up the challenge but I confess I have felt very concerned about our exceedingly limited majority and what may be the consequence of it if we cannot get our men to realize how serious the situation is. It is a little short of tragedy that we have lost the by-elections we have through lack of organization. The tragedy lies in the fact that one does not know what would follow a defeat of the Liberal party at the polls, with the kind of devices that are used in campaigning by Communists, Socialists, and others. This may bring this beautiful country into a serious state of affairs in the not too distant future. I was delighted to find that my cold seemed to leave me almost entirely while speaking, though I was still a little husky. I found our men followed with tremendous enthusiasm and I was impressed with the way in which the Opposition seemed to follow, almost approvingly, much that I said that helped to ridicule Bracken's behaviour.

"I spoke tonight in the House as I usually do in Caucus. It is the method I should have adopted from the very beginning of my public career. It has been a great mistake, wasting time writing out speeches and working over them with meticulous care, especially when one has a natural talent for expressing one's self on one's feet. The right thing to do is to master a subject and then trust to one's memory and gift for expression to do justice to it in the light of the conditions under which one is speaking. It is only now at the end of my public career that I am really beginning to do some of the things that I should have followed throughout. I was given a great reception when I got up to speak and a real ovation at the close. It delighted me to see our men so generally pleased. I felt grateful to God that I had had the strength to get through as well as I did and naturally not knowing whether I might ever be speaking again on a Speech from the Throne. I was pleased that the record left by this one is one of which I need not be ashamed."

Next day Mackenzie King spoke to the Liberal caucus "pretty much straight from the shoulder. I referred to the very critical position in which the party has found itself. I spoke of having lost the seats we had simply through lack of organization. I reminded the Members I had repeatedly asked that the by-elections be brought on at once and this had been ignored, and I thought it was responsible for the loss of the seats. I said that what was needed was organization but that frankly that was not the task I could undertake with the responsibilities I had as Prime Minister and should not be expected to. I went on to say that unless Members themselves and Ministers and others could find a way of bringing into being a really effective organization, I would ask them to allow me to retire from the Leadership. I said that it saddened me at heart to see a great political party that had the record that ours had had over a century gradually disintegrating and getting to the point where it would totally disappear as the Liberal party in Britain had disappeared, just because there were not in the party men who were prepared to see to it that we had an effective organization. I spoke about the need for Members of the Senate doing a little more to help in campaigning and organization work instead of making some situations more difficult for the Government. I reminded them that every one of them had been appointed from the party and owed the party an obligation as long as they were there.

"I then took up in turn the immediate situation in the House, which I said might well, unless all Members were present in their seats, result in the defeat of the Government. I asked the Caucus what I should do if the Government were defeated – did I have any alternative but to tender my resignation to the Governor?

"I did not know who I could ask to be sent for but I told them to realize that that was a situation that we were now facing whereas had we organized as we should have we might have carried the by-elections and our strength be such that from now on we would have had nothing to be worried about, with the possibility of staying in until 1950 if we wished to. I begged of the Members to see that none of them made engagements which would take them away. If they had already made engagements, I suggested they should cancel them, pointing out that the Opposition might not grant pairs. I next took up the necessity of winning the next two by-elections, Cartier and Halifax. I discussed the responsibilities there. Finally I took up the need for organization generally so as to be able to carry on. I urged that the Whips get together and arrange matters in the House and that Ministers and Members decide on what could be done by way of organization. I said nothing about not contesting the next election but I did make clear that unless there was some evidence of support in organization, I would ask to get out without much further delay."

At the Cabinet meeting on February 5 Mackenzie King told his colleagues that, if the by-elections in Cartier and Halifax were lost, he would "have no alternative but to call a convention of the party in the autumn and review the whole situation. The colleagues well understood that this meant that I will also tender my resignation as leader at that time."

The Prime Minister had a talk about his future with Howe on February 11 and told him "I really felt I must not try another general election. That I was now considering just when it would be best to have a convention called. He said to me that he thought it would be expecting a good deal of me to stay on through another campaign with the risk of being defeated, etc. Much better to get out right away or get out some time before an election. I said it was not the defeat I was concerned about. It was what was fair to the party and the country. If I did not intend to stay on after an election and I knew I could not, because of my strength and years, I thought it would be unfair to the country to run the campaign with myself as Leader.

"Howe said it would naturally be wise to give whoever was coming on a chance before a campaign. I said I agreed with that and was debating whether to have a convention this year or some time next – certainly not later. He himself has no intention of running again. Says he gathers that after the first six months of retirement, a man begins to find a joy in life that he has not known before. I told him that my life had been so completely given to work that I had to, in some way, get a little time to attend to my own affairs before the end came if that was possible and also that it was, I thought, advisable to leave the story of the party to the country. Howe said: you have a very remarkable record to give. I told him it was one that was of tremendous credit to Liberalism and I felt I owed it to the party to leave the story on record, if possible."

Earlier that day Gardiner had spoken to Mackenzie King, urging him to remain as leader on the grounds that "it would make a considerable difference in the campaign. That he knew the country would support me more strongly than anyone else. I said to him I was not equal to a campaign. The Government must be in the hands of younger men. I know he is ambitious for the leadership himself. I don't know how he might interpret my reference to younger men. He seemed, however, quite anxious that, if I could be induced to stay on, I should.

"All of this is very comforting in one way. I confess, however, that I am already beginning to feel the sadness of separation from the associations in which I have lived so completely for at least the last thirty years and in large measure the last fifty. It will be unpleasant in a way as well as saddening to separate from men who have been as loyal as practically all of my followers have been. I do not mind the selfish individuals here and there but it is the great body who have trusted me so completely. However these things will work out in due course but my eyes are in no way shut to the fact of what it will mean once one goes into the Parliament Buildings and has not a room of one's own in which to hang his coat and hat. However I believe there is another part of life which more than compensates for what will be lost in the strain and stress and incessant anxiety of politics. If I did not worry so greatly, and felt equal to travelling about, addressing audiences, etc., it might be another matter."

On February 12 there was a good deal of discussion in Cabinet about the risks of defeat in the House because some of the members, particularly from British Columbia, could not be counted on in a vote. The Prime Minister told his colleagues that he "had come to the conclusion that if we were to be rewarded in this way all along through the session, we might as well let others take a hold at once. I thought the best thing to do was to call a Caucus for Friday at which I would tell the Members directly that the party was in a precarious position. If we could not get the support of our own followers without being perpetually held up in this way, I was not prepared to take responsibility for attempting to carry on Government any longer. They must decide themselves what, as a consequence, they might wish to do. The Cabinet at once agreed with me it was the only thing that would bring them into line and it was the thing to do. I accordingly sent out word at once that Caucus was to be called for Friday."

He added that as he "listened to the different matters discussed in Council today and what we were facing of certain discussion on them in Parliament, I confess I felt it was going to be impossible to get these things through. Where there is no spirit of co-operation between the Opposition and the Government, having regard to the national situation, government in these difficult matters becomes well nigh impossible. If there was any likelihood of an election clearing the air, and not making the situation still more difficult, there would be everything to be said for an immediate appeal. The tragedy is that if our own people were only solidly behind us we could run on despite everything else until 1950. That, however, is out of the question. It looks more and more to me as though I shall have a convention some time in the autumn. A possible alternative is a general election in June without a convention meanwhile, but having our party in the House of Commons choose its own Leader."

In reading the *Ottawa Journal* on February 14, Mackenzie King saw "a reference to some article Bruce Hutchison had written in which he was trying to interpret the secret of my twenty years of Prime Ministership and did so in terms of a deliberate policy on my part of mediocrity. He meant I think a deliberate effort to be just average citizen – not a superman. He contrasted this attitude with that of Roosevelt as the Great Guy, and Churchill's attitude as John Bull. The whole business disclosed an appreciation of human values on the basis of exhibitionism. A pretty low standard and one which is not very complimentary to the electorate. It is the kind of standard that I, myself, personally loathe; the pretence of superman, etc.

"What neither he nor the *Journal* seemed to grasp at all was that what is implied of political sagacity and political wisdom as helping to account for success in leadership was an entirely different kind of standard.

"The Opposition papers are fond of calling it: political astuteness. It has the further factor of belief in what is right as the course most likely of itself to defend itself."

At the party caucus that afternoon, the Prime Minister devoted considerable time to the organization of the party in the House, a particularly appropriate subject after the potentially close call on the Militia Act the night before. He "then went on to say that no government could carry on business satisfactorily, where there was uncertainty as to just what existed in the minds of its supporters; how far it was being supported by its own Members; where there was some difference of opinion among Members of the party as to what it was best to do, I said I thought the first thing to be ascertained is what the party itself wished.

"I wanted to point out to them that we had been returned in June 1945 and that it would be August 9, 1950, before the term for which we had been elected would expire. If we keep our majority up to that time, we had that length of period to continue in office, if we so desire. More than that, the election need not take place until September or October or even November, 1950, if it were thought wise so to do. I doubted the wisdom of any government staying in office until the very end though one or two Conservative Governments had and held on to office until the expiration of time.

"A Liberal Administration prior to last election had occupied the full five years with the exception of a few hours and then itself had voluntarily asked for a dissolution and had come back. This was something that had never happened in Canadian history before and I doubted if it would ever happen again. I then said the party might not wish to wait until 1950 but have the election in 1949. That was another objective. Again some might think that 1948 would be preferable. There were some I knew who were talking about 1947 which was this year. Thinking of an election either for August or Autumn. Again there might be some who might think it would be best to have an election at once and not wait through the session at all. What I wanted to know was what the party wanted in this particular as I would arrange my plans accordingly. I was anxious to meet the party's wishes to the greatest extent possible so long as I believed they were in the public interest. I then said I wished to know their wishes for the reason that I had a responsibility not only as Prime Minister to my colleagues and to Parliament but as Leader of the Party I had responsibility also to the Members of both Houses and to the Liberals of the country who had given us such power as we had and whose representatives we were. If an election were desired this year, I thought I ought to take steps immediately to have a Convention called for the Autumn. If an election might come next year or the year after, it might be preferable to wait until the session was well under way or over before deciding when to call a Convention. I thought, however, that a Convention should be called before a general election and that the Convention should decide what was needed in the way of organization for a campaign. Should get fresh statements of the Government's principles and policies on which appeal would be made and a question of future leadership also determined. I pointed out that this was not something new on my part. That Sir Wilfrid Laurier after the election of 1917, had, in 1918, decided there should be a Convention in 1919. . . .

"I then said that I thought the greatest care should be taken as to circumstances under which the party went to the country. That if we went as a result of a defeat in the House of Commons either at the instance of Opposition through our own numbers not being represented in divisions as well as they should be, or because of some of our own people voting with the Opposition, or not giving us the support that was needed, we might expect that the party would be wiped out thoroughly in the country. People would say that not being able to carry support in the Commons with our own following, we did not deserve their support any longer. That would be one of the appalling political tragedies if it ever took place. A party with the noble record we had over the years finding itself practically wiped out as it certainly would be. It would be a terrible thing. On the other hand, if we performed our duties satisfactorily, built up our strength, we would some day, at the appropriate moment, in June or elsewhere, go to the people and give them stronger reasons than ever why we should continue to have their support. That our road was perfectly clear. It was to oppose Toryism on one side, Socialism on the other; and by enacting laws which would preserve freedom of enterprise and freedom generally, continue to shape the future of the country."

Mackenzie King then referred to the changed complexion of the Cabinet. "That of the first Cabinet I had formed in 1921, I was the only one who continued to be in office today. There was applause at this which seemed to me rather doubtful as to what it might signify. It was, of course, well meant. I said that they might be more surprised to know that of those who were with me in the first Cabinet when I came to form a Cabinet after Bennett had been in from 1930 to '35, Senator Dandurand and Lapointe were the only two of the first Cabinet who were Members of it. They had both since passed away.

"I then said that of the Cabinet formed in 1935, there were only, at the present time, five of us who continued to be Members. I did not mean to say that others were not alive but these were the only ones who continued to be in the Ministry. I would go further and say that if we went to the country, that probably after [the election], the Cabinet would be changed. I followed this by saying that I thought younger men ought to realize that while it was irksome to sit on what was called 'back benches,' etc., there were exceptional opportunities for men who had initiative themselves to undertake duties themselves, thereby making themselves indispensable in government and leadership."

Before the caucus broke up, the Prime Minister referred to those members who were "talking of having an election immediately, saying they believed the party would win if we did. Personally I attached a good deal of importance to the old saying that a bird in hand is worth two in the bush. I said I wanted the party to realize we had been returned in June 1945. We had been in office for only a year and a half. We had still three and a half years to run. That I very much doubted there was anything to be gained by risking the next three and a half years if so long as we had our majority we could hold office for that time. Furthermore, I said what would be gained supposing we did win; could we expect in next Parliament that we, the Liberals, would be in for a longer period than the three and a half years that we still have now before us without any election? I said I thought to many people the Government existed for the sake of an election instead of an election being the method by which the Government would discuss certain duties to perform. I said our duty was to keep right on strengthening our ranks; while we had opportunity, to get as much Liberal legislation on the Statutes as we could, keeping other forces that were reactionary or extreme out of power. I pointed out this was a very difficult year. If we got over this year all right, I thought questions of relations with the provinces would be out of the way. Housing problem out of the way. Conditions in the world would be more settled than they are. We will look for a period of almost a boom in building as Howe had prophesied it would be, and further great prosperity and trade. There was time to look forward to appealing to the people."

Mackenzie King was convinced that his speech had had "a very sobering effect." To him, the caucus meeting "was an historic one. It is the first time that I have spoken of the step which must inevitably lead to my giving up the leadership of the party and public life. I made it wholly plain that I intended to discharge my duties to the party and the country to the full. To have a convention, organization and platform settled, and then the question of leadership."

In a casual conversation the day after caucus, Paul Martin told the Prime Minister that he had given the members considerable concern. Mackenzie King assured him that he was "wholly in earnest about not on any account going through another general election. That I was concerned about the best time to call a convention. Would look to him and others to help to guide me in that matter. I said I certainly felt that without organization throughout the country and in the House, the sooner I got out of the leadership, the better. This caused Martin to say that Claxton and he and others have been talking over matters and that Claxton, he thought, would be willing to take on the organization if I asked him. I feel this is putting a pretty heavy burden on his shoulders but I certainly will take that step."

Still in an introspective mood on Sunday, February 16, Mackenzie King read another article by Bruce Hutchison in the *American Mercury* which he thought was "meant to be kindly but with some wholly unwarranted statements such as, for example, being a 'throat cutter' growing out of reference to Ralston's resignation. Also never having had any popularity, etc. How they work out these things in the light of general election returns puzzles me.

"Most surprising of all was the reference to not being liked by one's colleagues though they stood in awe. I don't know to whom he can refer lest possibly Angus Macdonald and some others who may have been temporarily disappointed on not being made Imperial Privy Councillors as soon as anticipated. I doubt, however, if any Prime Minister has ever had friendlier colleagues than I have had over the period that I have been in office. The kind of stuff that the press has spread through not having accurate information makes it, I believe, more necessary than ever that one should seek to get the truth out before life itself is over."

The Prime Minister became ill with bronchitis and influenza on February 18 and two days later acute pneumonia developed. Characteristically, he took an extraordinary interest in his symptoms and the opinions of his doctors, all of which are fully recorded in the diary. He was particularly distressed at being put under the care of trained nurses and quite concerned about the cost. On February 23 he wrote that "the day has gone by fairly quickly, but, oh, what a waste of time it all seems." The next day his colleague, Dr. McCann, came to see him with his regular doctor. McCann told him that he had been seriously ill, should plan to stay indoors until he was completely recovered, and then go south for a rest. Mackenzie King noted in his diary on February 26 that he felt it would be "unwise to try and keep on with heavy work indefinitely. What surprises me most is the complete lack of interest I feel in anything related to what is happening in Parliament or for that matter in the country. It is a state of exhaustion and fatigue." He added that "there can be little doubt that this illness is helping to prepare the minds of Members of the House for my handing the task of leadership to others, in all probability, before the year is out."

During his illness, the Prime Minister finished reading Feiling's biography of Chamberlain and on March 3 he read reviews of the book in the London *Times* and the *New Statesman*. It seemed to him "they were rather cruel in what they had to say of Chamberlain and the use they made of material Feiling had prepared. Much of it most unjust. In reading these reviews, I felt it might almost be a mistake to try to write anything of one's own life and work. One's political and personal opponents always manage to distort whatever is said. On the other hand, not to leave a true record and interpretation oneself, is to allow one's life to be misinterpreted and misrepresented to future generations. No one in Canada has suffered more from that than my grandfather. I wish I could find the time and means and the energy to get his life re-written and my own before the end of my days."

In reading on March 6, he found an article by Harold Dingman in *Liberty* magazine "complimentary and generous enough" but could not understand "how these writers keep putting forward the idea, first of all, that I am lonely and solitary, aloof and monastic, etc., and what I understand less is that my colleagues regard me as a sort of autocrat. Many of them have not kindly feelings. They are afraid of opposing me in my successor, etc. These are all things as contrary to the truth as they can be. All these writers seem to assume that men in public life were actuated by ambition alone, desire for power for power's sake, motivated by vanity, etc. As a matter of fact in appointments and everything else, I have sought only what I thought was the highest good for the public. In the same way with regard to measures before the House, etc., I have not tried at any time to assert myself against what I believe to be the best interest of the country and the party. It would be ludicrous to think that one could have carried on for twenty years with the kind of motives which so many of these reporters who don't really know one at all keep attributing to one."

The day before his doctor had told the Prime Minister that he would not recover fully "until after I had been somewhere where I could get a couple of weeks of sunshine. He strongly advised taking not two weeks but three in some warm place and recuperating for all I was worth. He thought I should loaf. The only way I would get back my strength was by taking things very easy. It was clear my nervous energy was largely depleted through fatigue. . . . He did not think it would be necessary for him to come again. He suggested I should go out for a walk when it was sunny, but not to take too much in the way of exercise for a while. He saw no reason once I got properly rested that I should not live for many years to come. He thought I had a good constitution but that I needed rest. He repeated again his belief that it would be wise not to stay on in public life much longer."

Mackenzie King returned to the House of Commons on March 10. He was given a great ovation. It "was really quite a memorable moment in one's life to encounter so fine an expression of good-will from all sides," he wrote. "For the moment I felt as though I would like to stay on in politics indefinitely if I could feel my strength as in previous years."

During his absence, the debate on the Address had continued and the House had begun consideration of a number of government bills, including amendments to the Canadian Wheat Board Act. However, some time had been devoted to external affairs, both relations between Canada and the United States and the problems of peace-making. A few days before his illness, the Prime Minister had read a statement in the House outlining the general principles on which defence co-operation between Canada and the United States would be based. It was "an important document," he wrote on February 12, "and a far-reaching sequel to the meetings with Roosevelt, at Ivy Lea and later at Ogdensburg. It seems to me that Canada itself is getting to be not merely the interpreter between United States and Britain but the pivot – the pivotal point of union between these two great countries." Mackenzie King announced that the Permanent Joint Board on Defence would continue to exist and that, under its auspices, more exchanges of military personnel would be organized and standardization of arms, equipment, and methods of training would be encouraged. The two countries would co-operate fully in defence planning, he indicated, without limiting the control by either of military activities within its territory and steps would be taken to ensure "mutual and reciprocal availability of military and naval and air facilities in each country." He stressed that no treaty or executive agreement had been signed and that each country remained free to determine the full extent of its practical collaboration. A step in implementing these principles was the announcement that American personnel would participate in the activities carried on at a small experimental station in Churchill, opened in 1946 on the recommendation of the Board. The non-military character of the work at Churchill was stressed and Mackenzie King denied again that the United States had asked for bases in northern Canada. In an attempt to divert Russian criticism, Claxton indicated in the House the next day that all foreign military attachés in Ottawa had been invited to visit the station and, during the visit later in the month, a Soviet major joined the party.

Another step in the programme, the establishment within the next three years of nine Arctic weather stations, was announced by Howe on March 4. Later the number was reduced to five and, under the joint arrangements, Canada provided all permanent buildings and installations and the United States most of the equipment. Each station was commanded by a Canadian and the staff was half Canadian and half American.

These steps were taken against the background of increasing east-west tension. During the meetings in New York in December 1946, the Council of Foreign Ministers had finally reached agreement on drafts of the minor peace treaties although several important issues remained outstanding. In Paris on February 10, 1947, General Vanier signed on behalf of Canada the treaties with Italy, Rumania, Hungary and Finland. Canada had not been at war with Bulgaria. Copies of the treaty texts were tabled in the House the same day, with a report on the Paris Conference prepared by Claxton. Exhausted and embittered by their labours, the Council made little progress on a peace settlement with Germany and Austria and, at New York, only agreed to appoint deputies to complete detailed preliminary work on the treaties for presentation to the next meeting, in Moscow on March 10. The deputies, who met in London from January 14 to February 25, were instructed to hear the views of Germany's neighbours and other allied states which had actively participated in the war and, in fact, much of their time was spent in debate on the extent and type of participation the smaller states should have. On January 4, through the Ambassador in Washington, Canada received an invitation to submit its views to the deputies "at its earliest convenience . . . on those aspects of the German problem which are of interest to it." There was no indication that Canada would be permitted to discuss procedure or to participate in the actual drafting of the treaties at any stage short of a final peace conference. On January 14 the Canadian High Commissioner in London presented a memorandum to the deputies arguing for a continuing association of Canada and other small states with the preparation of the treaties and two days later the text of this mild protest was published. The deputies made no direct reply to the Canadian note but, a few days later, Canada was asked to present its views to a meeting on January 25. Despite many reservations, the government did decide to prepare a preliminary submission; it was presented on January 30 and tabled in the House that day.

Australia, Belgium and the Netherlands joined Canada in protesting the procedures which had been adopted by the great powers but the deputies remained unimpressed. Both General Marshall and Ernest Bevin made gestures of support for the position of the smaller powers in February and during the abortive Moscow Conference but neither the Soviet Union nor France were prepared to make significant concessions. On the initiative of Gordon Graydon, the House had debated the issue on March 3 and many speakers made a connection between the minor role assigned to Canada in peace-making and the decision to withdraw Canadian occupation forces from Germany in mid-1946 which, it was argued, had weakened Canada's position. Speaking for the government, both Claxton and St. Laurent tended to brush aside these arguments and, during the debate, the Secretary of State for External Affairs was quoted in Hansard as saying Canada had been "left out" while the press version read that Canadian troops had been "kicked out" of Germany. His statement, however interpreted, simply added fuel to the debate which, when Mackenzie King returned to the House on March 10, was still at full boil, centring on a motion by General Pearkes for the production of all correspondence with the British government concerning the decision to withdraw. The government had decided to oppose the motion but had agreed to disclose as much information as possible. In a statement when the House opened, the Prime Minister repeated that the decision had been taken because of administrative difficulties in maintaining the small Canadian force and also because of reluctance to replace men who had already had long years of overseas service with N.R.M.A. conscripts. The Prime Minister had felt "all along that the Government was making a mistake in holding back on a full statement." To him there had been no "question, the Tories would make much of our having refused to keep an army on indefinitely. On the other hand, I have felt right along that the country would approve our action once they knew the exact nature of it and the ground for it."

The statement itself, he thought, "read exceptionally well. While I know the use the Tories will make of it, as I said to St. Laurent, that is their stock in trade, we have everything to gain and nothing to lose by having them take the position that we ought to do anything we are asked to do by Britain by way of supplying men, money, etc., at any and all times, instead of having some regard for being misunderstood in our own country – the nation having its own responsibilities to its own taxpayers. Also some regard for what has been done, what it is wise to do, and how far it is possible to go. I felt the statement would clear the air and I could see that all sides of the House were satisfied. I had stated the position very clearly.

"General Pearkes, in withdrawing the motion, admitted that that was the case. I am sure I saved the Government a very embarrassing situation and have helped to free us from a lot of nagging for information which, subsequently, would have been extracted anyway. I think the statement went to show that it was only to our credit instead of being a source of embarrassment.

"It made clear that years before the war was over we were taking care to try and get our men back at the earliest date possible. I shall be surprised if the veterans will find any fault with this."

Mackenzie King discussed the issue with the Governor-General on March 13. Alexander "volunteered the statement that he thought what Mr. St. Laurent had said [in the House on March 3] was quite right – whether kicked out or left out; that as a matter of fact it might be put that we had been asked to do certain things under terms it was impossible to accept. I said to him that he had been at Yalta and would recall that, at the conference there, the big powers decided to divide Germany into zones which they themselves would control; that they also would have representatives on the German Control Commission. We were given no voice at all in the period between the end of the war and the settlement of peace.

"His Excellency said that the reason we had been left out was that each time the question was brought up of Dominion representation, Russia would press for representation of the Ukraine and of one or two other Soviet Republics which had been agreed to as separate entities. This again involved repercussions with the United States. I said I understood all that. What I had felt at the time was strange was that we had been told nothing of the proceedings of Yalta. Had not been kept informed of what was going on. Told nothing until after the whole business was over. I stated I had not at the time made any issue publicly because we were still at war. I had drawn attention of both Britain and the United States to the fact that we had received no word or recognition. This was something we hoped would not be repeated in relation to other situations which might arise. I said now comes the exact parallel in the making of the peace. We would hardly be expected, at the instance of four powers today, to send a division for any purpose, being left out as we were in the voice of and the making of the peace. He also said and volunteered the statement that he thought we were quite right in recognizing that we would be creating a serious problem for ourselves, having our troops subject to the officers of Britain; that while they would naturally welcome the men he could see wherein there were difficulties if we agreed to terms under which we had to hand over our own people to others in times of peace. He said he had felt at the time of the withdrawal of our troops from Italy to join the others – to make one army in the north of Europe – a little put out at losing his men, but he felt it was perfectly right that Canadians should be together under their own command. I told him as far as we were concerned we had to consider in Canada that our troops had been two years longer in the war than the Americans; that if we had not done what we had to get them back as rapidly as we were and certainly as rapidly as the Americans were getting theirs back we would have a terrible problem on our hands. [I said] . . . to him I knew my personal friendship with Roosevelt had had its effects. It was on his insistence that full justice should be done our men in the matter of their return and recognition given to the fact of length of time of service overseas that arrangements had been made. I also explained that we had gone over the whole situation with Churchill. He understood we were withdrawing our people. Attlee's Government had come in and asked for a reconsideration. If we had changed our decision and agreed to let our men stay for Attlee, after refusing to have them stay for Churchill, it would immediately have been said we were prepared to assist a Socialist Government in its experiment, but not help a Government that had had all the fighting to do during the war.

"I also spoke of our men being pretty restless in Germany at the time. I found Alexander very understanding, as well as alert to the whole situation in a keen way."

In this connection, the Prime Minister was impressed on March 15 by a statement prepared by Pat Sullivan, the Secretary of the Trades and Labour Congress, on communist penetration in the trade union movement. He thought "it ought to have an effect on the election in Cartier. What, however, is more to the point is that it will help to silence some of these people who have been trying to make light of the steps taken by the Government to reveal the Communist menace. The whole action of the United States Government is based on its determination to prevent Communism spreading to this continent and over Europe. The fact is the line is being pretty sharply drawn between the Communists and the anti-Communist peoples of the world. The United States and Russia are lining up against each other.

"These exposures are all to the good. I think in this particular as in many others, Canada has really led the way. I still believe that making known our conditions in this country was one of the outstanding acts of real courage on the part of any Government."

Heeding his doctor's advice, Mackenzie King decided on March 26 to go to Virginia Beach and Williamsburg for a holiday. He was still concerned about the succession and his own future. The Governor-General had inquired during their conversation on March 13 whether he intended to get Pearson into politics. Mackenzie King wrote that he "would rather have Pearson succeed me than anyone, when the time came, but I did not know whether it would be possible for the party to accept him – not knowing his ability, and his not having had any part in public life. If he could be in the House for a session, it would be sufficient, I thought, but I did not see a chance meanwhile." In a conversation with St. Laurent two days before he left Ottawa, he told him he did not know which of them was going to find it hardest to leave public life. St. Laurent replied: "perhaps I can show you the way." Mackenzie King added: "I am most anxious not to leave in a way that will embarrass anyone. Must have time to think the situation out clearly and then act decisively."

The Prime Minister received the news of the Liberal victory in the Cartier by-election on March 31 at Virginia Beach. Since he had not expected the Liberal candidate to win, he was greatly relieved and pleased that the Communist candidate had placed third. Writing on April 2, he reflected that "Each day emphasizes anew the appalling alignment that is shaping up between Capitalist and Communistic countries. The insidious nature of the Communist movement is its worst feature. It is the dragon in action. Destructive of all that is constructive. Undermining standards of morality, beauty and truth; religion and all else that makes for enduring peace, happiness and prosperity."

The by-election victory was only a momentary encouragement and, throughout his holiday, Mackenzie King was obsessed with his health problems. He did have a slight relapse at Virginia Beach but a thorough medical examination at Williamsburg showed considerable improvement in his general condition. He stayed in Williamsburg until April 21 and then went to Washington to stay at Blair House as a guest of President Truman. The next day he went to the Naval Hospital to see his old friend Cordell Hull who was looking much better than he had expected. The Prime Minister was particularly gratified when Hull greeted him by saying: "of all the men, from this or any other planet, you are the one that I am most pleased of all to see." Later in the day he had Wrong and Acheson to lunch and dined with them and their wives at the Canadian embassy residence in the evening.

Mackenzie King was received by the President at noon on April 23. "As I entered the President's Office," he wrote, "I noticed his Secretary in the outer room beckoned to Mr. Woodward to go in with me. This is something I did not altogether like. Wrong had asked me if he should come along and I had told him I thought I would prefer to see the President by myself. Some of the members of the American Government have a way of having a third person in the room. I do not think that as between the President and the Prime Minister that sort of thing is necessary. However, it made no difference in my conversation."

They first talked about the President's proposed visit to Ottawa on June 10, 11 and 12. Mackenzie King told Truman that "on the 10th of June, I would have fulfilled twenty years in the office of Prime Minister. He said that he would make every effort to come on that day. I said I thought if he did I could regard it as a crowning event and thereafter be prepared to part in peace. I expressed the hope he would be accompanied by Mrs. Truman and his daughter. He replied that Mrs. Truman was coming and he hoped his daughter might also come. He was writing to her to New York to see if she could come with them. Said we would make the announcement at both centres at the same time later on.

"I told him that the plain people wanted not only a chance to see him but to cheer for him. They thought he had been very courageous and fearless and carried out his convictions in a splendid way. His reply to that was: I only try to do what is right; not to trouble about anything else.

"He has a very happy smile which never leaves him.

"I spoke appreciatively of Marshall's attitude in seeking to get Canada her rightful place in the making of the peace; of what Marshall had said in London and in Moscow. I said it was something we had considered was due to our country having fought as she did from the start. Made sacrifices. The President said we had made sacrifices of men, money and material, etc., and certainly no country had, in proportion to its size, made a greater contribution. He said they would continue to press for Canada having her rightful opportunity.

"I said we understood that some of the Latin-American countries had to be thought of. They had wished to enter the war and perhaps had to be promised they would have their share in peace-making, notwithstanding that they did not make any contribution in men or treasure. But I thought there should be a distinction between those countries like Mexico and Cuba, etc., and others that had made a real sacrifice. The President himself mentioned different countries of the British Empire and said he agreed very strongly. I said that the drafting [of the peace treaties] could be done by committees on some very important questions. Others forming other committees. I thought our country might be put on some of the larger committees. Others could be satisfied with lesser committees. The President agreed with this.

"I said to the President that he would doubtless be pleased with the result of yesterday's vote in the Senate on the aid to Greece and Turkey. He said we took that over for Britain. He said that the United States had done everything they could to be friendly with Russia, further her interests in past year, and had no desire for anything other than friendly relations. She was too weak at present to attempt anything in the way of fighting. He felt it must be made clear to her that while the United States had only peace in mind, she was determined to remain strong, to see that that peace was maintained."

Discussion then turned to trade policy, particularly the conference currently under way in Geneva. In February 1946 the Economic and Social Council of the United Nations had adopted an American resolution calling for an International Conference on Trade and Employment and a preparatory commission, to which Canada was named, was instructed to prepare an agenda for the conference and a draft charter for an International Trade Organization. The commission, which met between October 15 and November 26, 1946, in London, made unexpectedly quick progress and consensus was reached on most of the provisions of an agreement which was finally completed at the Geneva conference in August 1947. At the conference which opened on April 10, the Canadian delegation, led by L. D. Wilgress, the Canadian Minister to Switzerland, took an active part in final work on the agreement as well as in detailed multilateral tariff negotiations with seven of the twenty-three participating countries, principally the United States. With Truman, Mackenzie King pointed out that "our people attached a great deal of importance to the Imperial preferences. That we would be prepared to lessen preferences, but only for some specific tariff reductions on the part of the United States. That long-term agreements with promises would not be enough. There would have to be specific things done. The President said he fully agreed with that point of view. That we should do all we could to make trade as general as possible. I spoke next of the depreciation of our currency and the need for American dollars. I said there would be a demand to restrict commodities coming in. I hoped we would not begin tariff restrictions if some other means could be found whereby we could get currencies more on a basis of par. Suggested the United States might wish to purchase some of our metals, aluminum, etc. The President said they had a pretty good supply of aluminum but he thought that zinc and lead and others were short. I spoke too of the policy on the part of the States which would help to relieve Europe in a way to enable some of the countries there to purchase our goods with American dollars. I said this was a subject the departments would have to be taking up themselves. He said he thought the State Department was giving consideration to this matter.

"I spoke about the Pan-American Union. I said I thought it was just as well not to have that pressed too strongly at present and hoped there would be no official invitations sent without a word with our Government first. That in debate in a large way there were those who seemed to think that Canada might be drawn aloof – away from the British Commonwealth into a Western hemisphere orbit. That some thought we ought to be consolidating our position more strongly in the British Empire. I thought it was best not to have unnecessary debate on that question at present. The truth was we wanted to be part of the British Commonwealth of Nations and also part of the Western hemisphere. . . . We had our interests with both and were in a position to be helpful in relations between both.

"The President said he understood that. I felt he was anxious to have us come into the Pan-American Union. . . .

"I was particularly impressed with the compact, healthy appearance of the President. He is now sixty-five years of age and was most friendly in his whole manner.

"I also spoke of the Defence matters that we had talked of the last time and said I thought the joint developments would work out fairly well and would continue to do so so long as there was not too much pressure or haste – or for the size of the undertakings. The President said he was very pleased in the way in which that relationship had worked out. He did not bring forward any subjects himself. . . .

"I had a few words with the press, almost exclusively in reference to the President's visit."

The Prime Minister left later that day for New York and returned to Ottawa on April 26, still far from satisfied with the state of his health and firmly resolved to make definite plans for his retirement. In the House on April 28 he was welcomed by the leaders of the opposition parties and "was pleased to notice how the different speakers referred to the splendid way in which St. Laurent had managed. In acknowledging the other thanks, I extended my thanks to him. He is an exceedingly valuable addition to Parliament. I think there is no doubt in the world that the party would accept him as its leader at this or any time in the future, should I retire and should he be willing to accept. I am more than pleased at this fact, as having succeeded Sir Wilfrid, to have a French Canadian succeed myself would be in the nature of poetic justice."

The following day Abbott delivered his first budget speech. In Mackenzie King's opinion "the House was astounded at the size of the surplus announced and it was interesting to watch the increasing eagerness with which members of all parties waited for the announcement on taxation. When the figures were given, the entire House applauded the reductions. Our own men were tremendously enthused. I said to Abbott when he had concluded that I had thought the speech would go down as one of the highlights in budget addresses in the history of Canada. That excepting only the Robb budgets which brought in great reductions in tariffs in the duties on the implements of production, I did not think there had been comparable budgets in relieving burdens of taxation directly or indirectly, in the history of our country. It is a budget which has brought real relief to the people of Canada, taking a tremendous burden off the shoulders of many."

The Prime Minister returned to Ottawa just in time to share in the final stages of the shaping of post-war immigration policy. A number of changes had been under consideration since January 1947. On January 23 the Cabinet had decided to seek legislation repealing the Chinese Immigration Act and approval was also given to the "principles regarding admission . . . of labourers for primary industries which I think is a needed opening of the immigration door; also some further latitude where relatives are prepared to look after those admitted. There was a considerable discussion on immigration policy – very interesting and many sided. Council agreed that no immediate opening of doors should be decided upon as transportation is not available, nor is housing available, but all were agreed that in the long range view Canada would certainly need to have a large population if she hoped to hold the country for herself against the ambitions of other countries and to build her strength."

As could be expected the details of the new policy were not easy to settle. On February 13 the Cabinet had " a rather long and desultory discussion on immigration problems. A good deal of confusion in the minds of all of us as to where to draw the line and how to draw it in the matter of discrimination between different races and peoples who wish to come to Canada. There should be no exclusion of any particular race. That I think has really been wiped out against the Chinese but a country should surely have the right to determine what strains of blood it wishes to have in its population and how its people coming from outside have to be selected."

At the party caucus the next day, the Prime Minister "spoke out pretty feelingly about what was involved in the question of no discrimination against races and what this might give rise to later when the people of the Orient, Japan, China, India, etc., felt they were entitled to this part of the earth and its resources and should not be discriminated against in coming in numbers to this country. I tried to have caucus see we could not move too cautiously. What we did on one hand by way of admitting numbers, and on the other, by way of exclusion against any particular races. This telegram on India made me sad at heart. It left open the way for India to run completely outside of the Commonwealth which she probably will do. Should it unite with other countries of Asia in common attack upon some other parts of the world, this old globe may come to witness the most appalling of disasters with which it has yet been faced." The telegram, which was from Attlee, indicated that the British Government had decided to fix a definite date for Indian independence.

The Cabinet resumed study of the new immigration policy on March 17. "Glen," the Prime Minister wrote, "had been very secretive about what is to be said on that question and has evidently been planning to make a speech on his own and fight the measure through. I told Cabinet I thought it was perhaps as important as any measure we would have at this session. It was one over which we were likely to get into difficulty with our own people more readily than with any other.

"Fortunately St. Laurent came in while we were discussing the matter and in the course of the discussion said he thought the statement should be made by the P.M. before any debate took place at all. I knew he had in mind the feeling which a lot of our own men have against Glen and the difficulties he will have in piloting the measure. I said I did not mind making the statement if it were carefully prepared in advance but that I could not do more than that. I was not in shape to enter into a debate. I agreed it would be wise to have a general statement made in the light of the world situation.

"It was then decided that the Cabinet Committee would get together at once and try to have matters definitely framed up. Would have some of the officials assist."

Mackenzie King was convinced that "if we can get this jumble straightened out, it will mean more in the way of shortening up of the session than almost anything else."

The revision of the statement on immigration policy was the Prime Minister's first major job after he returned to Ottawa from his holiday. He was still working on it on May 1, the day the statement was to be delivered in the House. That morning he "made one very important change in what had been drafted. The draft had indicated that the Japanese were never to be allowed to enter Canada. I was able to quote what I had said during the war would be done after the war. Mentioned that we held to that policy. That it represented the present position of the Government, namely, not to admit Japanese. I had, however, said this was not to be an indefinite policy, so in the statement I inserted the words that it would be for future Parliaments to decide what, if any, change should be made in this regard. That makes it clear to the U.N. and to the Japanese that it is not a policy of permanent exclusion we have asserted. I mentioned to Council that nothing could be worse than that we should allow the Japanese to say that they were permanently excluded, and find them possibly united with Russia at some future time in their resentment with Canada. As a matter of fact, I do not know any greater danger that our country faces than this possibility and indeed almost probable possibility. The nations of the Orient with their crowded populations will resent a small population here with the almost unlimited resources of this country and its relatively small population seeking to hold part of the globe exclusively to itself. I am sure my experience in these matters will have saved a very difficult situation as regards the future.

"I went as far as I could in indicating the danger facing us by saying that in a world of shrinking distances and international uncertainties, a small population could not expect to hold the heritage we have."

The statement was approved by the Cabinet that afternoon and shortly after 3.00 P.M. the Prime Minister read it in the House. The new policy recognized the need for a larger population through the encouragement of selective immigration, the flow related to the economy's absorptive capacity. He stressed that entry to Canada was not a fundamental right but rather a privilege; the government had no intention of fundamentally altering the character of the Canadian population. Consequently, immigration from Asia would continue to be strictly limited. Initially, admission of relatives of persons already in Canada would receive first priority because of a shortage of transportation facilities. A second priority was the resettlement of refugees. The Prime Minister made it clear that the Immigration Act of 1927, as amended, would remain in force and that policy would be adjusted to meet changing circumstances through alterations in the regulations made under the Act.

Mackenzie King felt the statement "was well received by the Members. Had I given them time, they would have applauded more between paragraphs. I could see the Conservatives were much interested in what I was saying about getting population; also that our people were greatly pleased at the definite statement about there being no fundamental human right which caused us to admit people that we did not think could be assimilated and which would change the composition of our country. It was clear, too, that our men approved strongly of what was said in relation to the Orient as helping to meet the situation in British Columbia.

"Of all the problems ahead of us, at the moment, it is about the thorniest. I am glad it was held over until my return. I am glad that it has now been made."

Next afternoon, the Chinese Immigration Act repeal was introduced in the House. "I stayed in the House throughout the entire afternoon," Mackenzie King wrote, "really enjoying the proceedings. The statement I made yesterday on the Government's policy semed to have cleared the air completely and to have met with all but complete approval on the part of the different groups in the House, so much so that I doubt if there will be a division on the second reading.

"Some weeks ago, it seemed in the Cabinet as if this would be the most difficult measure of the session. It certainly has been worth all the time and effort that has been given over to discussion, revisions, etc., of the statement as finally shaped.

"I was greatly pleased to find speakers of different groups one after the other commending yesterday's statement. What there was of criticism seemed to me wholly reasonable. The one thing I would like to have had us go a step further on would be allowing Chinese in Canda to send at once for their wives and dependent children as in the case with persons from Europe.

"I doubt if, having regard to shipping, it would have made any appreciable difference in the numbers who would come. However, there is that fear of an influx and there has been a situation in British Columbia to meet."

A problem which absorbed much of his energy for the next two weeks first came to the Prime Minister's attention on May 1. At the Cabinet meeting that day the Minister of National Revenue raised "the question of refunding taxation to the Niagara Falls Bridge Commission for carillon bells to be placed at Niagara. They have just been imported and are all, at present, lined up in the open at Niagara Falls. McCann said he was not prepared to recommend any refund particularly in the light of the inscription on the bells. What appears there is simply amazing. The largest bell is labelled 'Churchill' in raised letters. Then there is a poem, as follows:

'CHURCHILL

Even as a bird
    Out of the fowler's snare

Escapes away.
    So is our soul set free.
Broke are their nets,
    And thus escaped we.

Therefore our help
   Is in the Lord's great name

Who Heav'n and earth
   By His great power did frame.

To God's glory and in grateful memory of our nation's leaders, Winston Spencer Churchill and Franklin Delano Roosevelt.'

"This is all part of the campaign that was started against me in the middle of the war because I would not agree to a National Government. It was engineered in connection with the War Loan when advertising boards carried words similar to those on the inscription. Carried the names of Churchill and Roosevelt to the exclusion of my own as our country's leaders. I never could get over the indifference of our own party to that insult to their leader and to our country but said nothing at the time. If the Liberals of Canada now permit these bells to be put in position and a ceremony held in connection with the inauguration of the Carillon without making a nation-wide protest, it will be a strange sort of thing indeed and a pretty serious reflection on members of a party who have a leader who has carried six general elections out of seven. One of them after the war, and after this cruel campaign had been waged for all its worth. I was a little surprised that Dr. McCann should have said that, of course, this could not be changed now; to alter the lettering would change the tone of the bell. It never occurred to him that by permitting this inscription, they are seeking to change the tone of the nation down through the ages to come. It will be a black blot on the escutcheon of chivalry so far as Canada is concerned if a record of that kind is permitted to exist. A reflection on the Canadian people as a whole if a memorial bearing words of that kind is permitted to be erected and remain as a part of our country's history."

By May 7, Mackenzie King was even more indignant and felt that "if the Liberals of Canada were indifferent to an insult of the kind to myself, I should consider very carefully whether, as the party's leader, I should immediately drop out or not. I said personally I was willing to do anything to commemorate the services of Churchill and Roosevelt in the war, but I would never admit that 'they were our nation's leaders.' That, as Prime Minister of Canada, I could not do that." He asked Martin and Chevrier to see what could be done. Characteristically, he suspected that George Drew had been responsible for the whole affair but on May 8 he discovered that the inscription "had been written by McQuesten who was in Hepburn's Cabinet and who was Chairman of the Canadian section of the Commission. A New York–Ontario Commission controls the bridge.

"I confess I felt a sense of relief that Drew had not lent himself to anything so extreme though he undoubtedly knows of what has been done and is countenancing the action. I would not be surprised if there had been a combination of Hepburn, Drew and others to get me out of public life, even in those early days, but that McQuesten was, of course, a mere creature of Hepburn's – poorest affair imaginable. Why he should have been so bitter against me except that I opposed him on the liquor issue – he was a tool of their interests – I cannot understand. He has been venomous in his attitude but roundly defeated when it came to elections.

"The inscription had been written in 1941 which was after the general elections but at a time when the effort was made to get me out because I would not support conscription or a coalition Government.

"Still later today, Paul Martin found out that the representatives on the Commission were from the Niagara Parks [*sic*] Commission. That Mr. Haines is the Chairman and is a Liberal and is to preside at the Ontario meeting next meeting. Two other members of the Commission are also Liberal appointees and are men like Haines who are real friends and supporters of mine. Harstone, of Hamilton, is one of them. They have simply paid no attention to the inscription themselves. Haines said that he had not thought anything of it at the time though he had since worried a good deal about it. That shows the sort of men we have in our entrusted positions in public life. Is it any wonder that the Liberal party has gone to pieces in Ontario? This makes a pretty embarrassing situation for our friends. If Drew understood the first thing about politics, he would be the one to say that he had noticed this thing and would not permit it."

Mackenzie King also learned that Humphrey Mitchell, as the Member of Parliament for Welland, had written the letter asking for the tax remission. On May 9 he decided to "speak out to the Cabinet as a whole about the matter. I re-read the inscription and then said how I had felt when I had thought Drew and the Tories were responsible for it. I then said I had now found it was the Liberals all along the way who were responsible. I said to Mitchell: Your letter to the Minister of National Revenue is the one that asks that the taxes be remitted and the letter of the Parks [*sic*] Commission says that these are our nation's leaders. I then said I wished not to be considered in the matter at all but when we spoke of Canada's national leaders in the war, I thought of the colleagues who were around me at the table. Who had helped Canada's war effort. Mentioned what Ilsley had done in Finance. What Howe had done in Munitions and Supply. What Gardiner had done for Agriculture. What others had done and said these men were Canada's national leaders, not Mr. Roosevelt nor Mr. Churchill. That, as Prime Minister of Canada, I did not propose to allow any false inscription to go up.

"Chevrier then said he had talked with Harstone who was shocked to learn that there was such an inscription. Said there had never been a meeting of the Board who authorized it. One or two other members of the Board had spoken similarly. I said I thought it was for the Ministers to see that action was taken which would prevent all of this coming out at the meeting of the Ontario Liberal Convention on Thursday next. That Haines who would be presiding was one of those who was on the Parks [*sic*] Board. Chevrier said something about my name being added. I said that I did not want my name on any memorial of the kind; that did not correct the error which was that Canada's leaders were just not Englishmen nor Americans. This memorial was being put on Canada's soil. So far as I was concerned, I was quite content to leave my service to Canada over the years I had been in public life to the keeping of the people in future generations. That I feel that the Liberal party was apt to get itself in a very false position, if this matter could not be remedied or straightened out before the meeting."

During the afternoon, Humphrey Mitchell, who had learned that the bell had actually been installed, suggested that it be melted down. To Mackenzie King this suggestion was foolish; "the thing to do was to have the bell down and have the inscription removed. They had to get the Commission together; both on the American side and the Canadian and have that inscription immediately removed. Mitchell did not seem to see the seriousness of the situation so I reminded him that it might be particularly embarrassing to some of the party if the correspondence was asked for in the House and it was discovered that he was the one who was asking for remission of duty at the instance of the Commission. He then said he would go and have another talk with Kaumeyer about action being taken. He later told me there was some talk of having an architect come to the meeting on Thursday to explain the situation. That the architect's name was William Lyon Lovering. What they wanted the architect for, Mitchell was unable to say. Knowing how absolutely lacking in any full appreciation of the situation [they were] and thinking they might allow it to drift, I felt later I should speak again to one or two about it. So I rang up Chevrier and let him know of my talk with Mitchell. Suggested action should be taken at once, not left until Monday or later. He was astounded when he heard that the bell was up. Said Harstone had assured him it was not up. He finally said that he thought the Ontario Ministers should get together and decide what to do. I told him I thought that was a wise course. He 'phoned me after 6 that they had had a meeting and he was to contact Harstone. Someone else would contact Haines. Somebody else, somebody else and that they were all to say that they expected the Board should meet together with the members on the American Board and that the bell was to come down and the inscription taken off or changed.

"Later I got into contact with Paul Martin at Windsor who told me that Atkinson had gone to no end of pains about working out the matter. That it was after getting in touch with Kaumeyer and Percival Price in the States that they had learned the sources; how the inscription came to be put on the bell. That brought the thing to McQuesten as the one who was responsible for the inscription. Price is coming to Windsor to see Martin about the effect of changing the inscription.

"I also had a talk with Roebuck. Told him what had happened. He rang up Archie Haines and 'phoned me later that he had done so. He said Haines was very much upset about the whole thing. Said he had had no knowledge of the matter. Had driven over to Niagara to see what steps could be taken, etc. Haines did not tell the truth in this because he said yesterday it was the first he had known about it, he was very worried, but he told Roebuck he had had no knowledge of the inscription at all, until the last day.

"Roebuck mentioned he had brought Senator Bench into the matter (that was a good sign). Bench had said he would look into the situation and impress Haines with the seriousness of it. Roebuck had told him he had a resolution prepared for Thursday which would be brought before the whole convention if the whole matter was not settled before then and would ask Haines how he would square himself presiding at the Convention. Really the whole business is the greatest comedy of errors I have witnessed in my lifetime. Would be a most amusing affair throughout if it did not reflect so very much on such a large number of supposed Liberal followers and friends."

The next day (May 10) the Prime Minister was relieved that "latest word on the bells is that Haines and Harstone are meeting two American Commissioners on Monday. They are also to have Kaumeyer and an architect present. If the inscription can be taken off the bell, that will be done. If not, the bell will be taken down and recast. If necessary, they will have the entire Committee meet and pass the necessary resolution."

The Prime Minister received word from Chevrier on May 12 that "the Niagara body had had a meeting that afternoon at which, unfortunately, there was not a quorum. There were three Canadian members: McQuesten, Haines and Harstone, and one American. McQuesten had agreed that the words around the rim of the big bell should be deleted or altered in a way that would be perfectly satisfactory. He, Chevrier, was not told how this was to be brought about. It was, however, subsequently learned that a cable was being sent to a firm in London, or in Croydon, evidently to ascertain what could be done without affecting the tone of the bell or whether it would have to be re-cast. It was learned too, subsequently, that McQuesten had protested very strongly at the start, but when he saw all the others, including the American contingent, were against him, he acquiesced. He said he agreed it was best to have the inscription removed. The truth of the matter is that McQuesten sees where he will land if it once becomes known that he is responsible for the inscription.

"I have since learned that the Board had authorized the bells. It is possible they also authorized an inscription, but apparently there is no record of any inscription having been submitted to the Board and no member apparently had seen the inscription except McQuesten. Chevrier was assured that I would be perfectly satisfied with what would be finally arranged. Another meeting had to be called, at which all members of the Board are to be present and a Minute of the Board recorded."

On May 29 Mackenzie King "had a talk with Harstone of Hamilton who assured me that they proposed to take the name of 'Churchill' off the big bell and the names of 'Churchill' and 'Roosevelt' from the inscription around the base, leaving only the verse which is all right. . . . He said I could count on that being done with certainty within a short time. That, of course, is wholly satisfactory if it is done. I told him I regarded the whole business as a comedy of errors."

Lionel Chevrier made a statement in the House on June 16 "putting the matter in its true light." Mackenzie King found it "interesting to watch the faces of the Tories while Chevrier made his statement – not one of them so much as smiled or moved. Not one of them said a word when he had concluded." Later that day he wrote that "the record on Hansard giving the truth regarding the Niagara Bells brings to a conclusion a long battle; opposing political forces; treachery in one's own ranks but of the Right triumphing in the end."

The final act in the drama of the bells took place two days later when the Prime Minister learned that Premier Drew had "dismissed the Canadian members of the Niagara Commission. Senator Bench came in to have a talk.

"Bench thinks Drew has not the power to do this. I have been fully expecting that all along. For that reason, I was anxious the change in the inscription should be made before this was done. However, the whole business will create more in the way of controversy than ever; at the same time, Chevrier's statement has exposed the whole business. It is interesting to note how mistakes were made: (1) in my name not being inserted at the outset; (2) that it should be inserted in addition to Roosevelt, Churchill instead of obliterating their names. What pleases me very much is that it is now evident that the country – even the Tories – dare not say a word against my name as a national war leader.

"When I come to write of this, I shall be careful to mention the inscription which is placed on the big bell in our main Tower, and contrast it as being in keeping with the Glory of God – as against motives which lay behind McQuesten's inscription."

On May 13 Nova Scotia became the seventh province to accept a tax rental agreement with the federal government. In the Prime Minister's opinion, Macdonald's "speech in the Nova Scotia legislature made an awful lot out of a mole hill and evidenced, I thought, both a narrow outlook and a vain mind. Macdonald is both very conceited and dour." Both Ontario and Quebec refused to sign agreements, the former because it had enough tax potential to make the final federal offer questionable financially, and Quebec's rejection being based on a traditional distrust of centralization. Neither province chose to levy a provincial income tax and the 7 per cent corporation income tax imposed by both was largely offset by the extra 5 per cent tax levied by the federal government in the agreeing provinces. As far as Mackenzie King was concerned, the subject of federal-provincial relations faded well into the background.

During this period, the Prime Minister took a good deal of interest in the question of self-government for India. Late in May the government was asked for its views on possible Canadian participation in an aid programme for the two states into which India was to be partitioned. On May 28 St. Laurent consulted Mackenzie King on the text of a statement prepared by External Affairs in reply to the British government's request. The Prime Minister "opened out pretty strongly against Canada pretending to advise on matters we know nothing about" and "said quite openly that there was not a single member of the Cabinet who was in a position to advise in regard to India, who understood the situation there or realized what implications there might be in tendering advice in a matter of this kind. St. Laurent admitted it would mean an obligation of mutual assistance. I said yes, and if Canada's decision pleases one part of India and displeases another, we may find that the other may join in with Russia to form a common cause with her and that, in addition, we would be pulled into some of the civil war that may result from an action which may be taken at this time by Britain. I pointed out that India was a dependency of Britain. She should deal with the matter herself. That this was part of an effort on Britain's part to get rid of her burdens and to throw them on to the Dominions. I thought we ought to help bear burdens that were legitimate, but should not go out of our way to load Canada with obligations that we could not see the beginning or the end of."

The Prime Minister added that he "felt at the end of the discussion that, if matters of this kind were to carry forward, I would feel the responsibilities we were assuming in this blindfold fashion were much too great to be responsible for. I don't know whether St. Laurent will bring the matter forward again but I intend to fight it to the end. I can see pretty clearly that what the British have in the back of their minds is, as I pointed out, to create a Commonwealth policy here which we were all to follow; they found it impossible to do that under the name of Empire. They are going to try to do the same thing under the name of Commonwealth. I have fought all through my public life for Canada as a nation. I do not intend, at this stage of my career, to become a mere echo of any department or government in London."

This issue was the first evidence of a serious divergence in outlook between Mackenzie King and St. Laurent on Canada's role and responsibility in external affairs, a division which was to become more acute by the end of 1947. On this occasion, the gap was bridged without too much difficulty. The Prime Minister noted on May 30 that he had "spent some time both last night and this morning going over a despatch of Attlee regarding India. I did not think Canada should commit itself one way or the other to anything arising in the present situation beyond indicating that our attitude would be, as far as possible, helpful. We were not consulted about India's independence. We had nothing to do with negotiations, nor do any members of the Government or the people of Canada know anything about India.

"I feel the utmost caution has to be used in saying anything that may convey wrong impressions in Britain, in India, or in Canada. However, to assist the situation somewhat, I revised considerably the statement which Pearson had prepared and, during the afternoon, went over it with both Mr. St. Laurent and Pearson. We all agreed on the changes which I had suggested and which were in the nature of abbreviations and avoidance of raising any question about independence within the Commonwealth, vs. Dominion status, etc., at this time."

The British government announced on June 3 that the two new states, India and Pakistan, would become independent on August 15. During the day, the Prime Minister "drafted a short message regarding P.M. Attlee's announcement re self-government in India, thinking that perhaps to make no comment might be misconstrued and to say what I had in mind, might be helpful." In the statement, the "peoples of India" were assured "of the sympathetic understanding and good will of the government and people of Canada."

In the House of Commons on June 4, Graydon asked Mackenzie King to make a statement on the situation in India. He replied that it was "one of the most critical and difficult of the situations of the world. I doubted if anyone could get a statement on it. I certainly could not venture to do so. That I had made a comment in the press yesterday and would give to the House in answer to his question what I had already given to the press and which had appeared in the papers. I also brought out some material that St. Laurent had put on Hansard in answer to previous questions from Church [Conservative M.P. for Toronto-Broadview]. I also drew attention at once to the fact that we had not been consulted. We had been informed and had been asked for an opinion. I had said this morning to St. Laurent that there would certainly have been trouble over a despatch from a high official in England saying we had been consulted.

"The House received well what I said and Coldwell followed it up by saying that he thought the House should confirm the position that the Government had taken. All of this shows the importance of the position I took in the Cabinet the other day in refusing to let our Government tell the British Government what we thought ought to be done and giving to ourselves an importance in this matter which we were not justified in giving. I think I have helped to save a major difficulty there."

On July 3 the British High Commissioner sought the Prime Minister's opinion on whether the bill respecting India should be entitled the Indian Independence Act. Mackenzie King felt the use of the word independence "would imply complete separation from the British Commonwealth" and advised against it, stressing that this was merely a personal opinion.

Mackenzie King, greatly distressed on June 4 by news of Norman Robertson's serious illness, saw his own doctor again on June 6 and 7. The doctor warned him that he must get plenty of rest and avoid excitement. This advice was quite appropriate because he had become agitated about arrangements for the visit of President Truman and the obligations of hospitality for his friends, the Salisburys, who were staying at Laurier House. Their visit had been arranged to coincide with the unveiling of Salisbury's portrait of Mackenzie King which he had arranged to present to Parliament on June 10, the day on which he would complete twenty years of service as Prime Minister.

Mackenzie King had actually drafted his letter to the Speaker, offering the portrait as a gift to Parliament, as early as January 10. On May 19, during a discussion about arrangements for the formal presentation, the Speaker told him that a Forbes portrait of Sir Robert Borden had arrived. Fauteux said "he had told Beauchesne to put it away in a locker. Say nothing about its receipt. Did not wish to be worried or troubled about it for the present. He said to me he did not want to be worried about that portrait until after mine was in place. He thought Sir Robert's might be hung in the summer time. He did not wish to have a ceremony preceding mine. If it were known the portrait was there, there might be some comment as to why there was no ceremony when it was being hung. I told him he had better not trust Beauchesne in any particular. I went on, however, to suggest myself that it might be well to have both portraits hung at the same time.

"I had not thought of the fact that Sir Robert was Prime Minister during the first Great War. The Speaker followed with a thought that would mean if they were hanging the portraits of the two war Prime Ministers at the same time, this would protect me from any criticism by the Tories. He had told Bracken they were getting a painting of Sir Robert. This would fit in splendidly. I said there would be no hesitation on the Governor General's part to unveil both portraits he having been a General in the last Great War, and Field Marshal now. It would make it particularly appropriate that he should do the unveiling as the King's representative. If the President were here, so much the better.

"The Speaker seemed to take very cordially to this idea as one which would remove any possible criticism or unfavourable comment. The more I think of it, the more I feel it would be in every way the right thing to do and would, if anything, make the occasion still more significant. Having it on the 10th of June would, of course, be the significant thing so far as I am concerned. Borden was Prime Minister for eight years – four of which were years of the Great War. I have been Prime Minister for twenty years, six of which were years of war."

The Governor-General had already been approached informally, but, on June 4, the Speakers of the two Houses went to Government House to ask Lord Alexander officially to unveil the two portraits on June 10 shortly after President Truman's arrival in Ottawa. The Prime Minister was told that "when it was suggested to the Governor that he might come after Truman's arrival, his first reaction had been it would interfere with showing Mr. Truman his garden. However, when it was explained that the unveiling related to the twenty years and had been settled long before there had been any knowledge of the date Truman was going to be here, the Governor said he would be prepared to come.

"Earlier in the day, I had suggested to the Speaker it might be well to have Pearson tell the United States Ambassador, who was going to Washington, that this unveiling would take place in the afternoon of the day of his arrival, and leave it to Mr. Truman to say himself whether he would like to come. I know he would instantly say he would because at Washington he said to me that as on the 10th – as I told him – I would have completed twenty years, he said he would make it a point without fail to come. It hurts me a little to think there should have been a moment's hesitation on the Governor General's part on coming to unveil the portrait of myself, no matter what the circumstances were. After all, he owes his appointment as Governor General unreservedly to myself and as his Prime Minister, I think he should have gone out of his way to welcome the opportunity. However, the fact he had known nothing of the twenty year aspect of the situation may well have accounted for his attitude. After all, the President's visit is to Canada primarily on the invitation of the Government. . . . It recalls the incident in regard to the visit to the United States of the King and Queen. The determination of the British Government to have Lord Halifax and not the Prime Minister of Canada accompany the King to that country. It was the President who insisted on my going to the United States with the King and Queen rather than having the then British Ambassador be the one to act as Foreign Minister at the time. Again I say is it any wonder that those who really understand the situation in Canada feel as they do about the selfishness of the British in some things as contrasted with the brotherly and friendly attitude of the United States. Self-conscious superiority of the British contrasted with the friendly and co-operative, even brotherly attitude of the Americans. I may be doing Lord Alexander an injustice in this as I have not had a very direct statement on what took place in the interview."

On June 10 the House of Commons met at 2.45 P.M. and as soon as prayers were over, Ian Mackenzie made "quite an oration." "It was a biographical sketch," the Prime Minister wrote. "He brought in influences that had meant much in my life. Referred to mother's picture, grandfather, Laurier, Pasteur. He had quite a hard struggle speaking and it was just his Highland loyalty that made him go ahead with it.

"Mackenzie was followed by Bracken, Coldwell and Low. Low got off first rate. He said it was a poor horse I was riding – meaning political party but said I made a hell of a good ride. He was followed by Fournier who spoke very nicely and at some length in French, St. Laurent having gone to Rouse's Point to meet the President.

"Breithaupt made a little speech as well, referring to Waterloo County. I had not been able to really get my mind on to anything to say beyond extending a word of acknowledgment to Ministers and Members of the Public Service. Mackenzie's speech threw me a little off what I had in mind, by his references. I perhaps took the matter a little more personally than I otherwise would have. However, I was glad this record was there on Hansard for today.

"I hurried through what I had to say as it was after 3 when I began to speak. President Truman was coming in at 3.30 P.M. I got through by 3.15 and then asked that I be allowed to leave the Chamber; shook hands with the Speaker. Got my hat and cane, and then drove pretty fast to Island Park Drive. The train was just coming in. The Governor General and others were waiting. They said they got pretty anxious. They thought the President would arrive and no Prime Minister. I told them what happened.

"There was just time to be at the step of the train to greet the President and Mrs. Truman. The President was very hearty and natural in his greeting. Photographs were taken and then we started in to the City."

Mackenzie King accompanied the President to Government House and then hurried back to the Parliament Buildings to prepare for the unveiling ceremony. He was very tired and found the arrangements somewhat confusing. In this, he was by no means alone. When Truman, Alexander and the others in the official party were seated "Fauteux started off proceedings very well by reading his preliminary statement. Dr. King then called on the Governor General to unveil Borden's portrait and led him across the rotunda to where my portrait was placed. That was a bad slip. The Governor drew the cord; instead of Borden's portrait revealing itself, mine was shown. Dr. King had then to take the Governor across to the opposite side to where Borden's portrait was unveiled. Poor King, I felt very sorry for him. He was deadly white and apologized for his error. Said he was sorry. I thought he met the situation with great dignity. Fauteux tells me there had been a rehearsal during the day, and he should have known which side to go to.

"Dr. King then read some word from Borden's nephew [Henry Borden], not being present. This was unexpected but wise [Borden was ill]. He then called on [Senator] Ballantyne to speak which was not in accordance with the programme. His Excellency should have been called on next. Ballantyne read his speech very nicely. I was amused that he included all the titles and degrees that Borden had. His Excellency then spoke very clearly, briefly and most effectively. I liked immensely the references he made. It was a tremendous moment for me when I heard Alexander himself refer to the two war-time leaders – the recognition that was due them, and their portraits being for all time in the very part of the country which they had served so well, etc., and this in the presence of the President of the United States. If anyone would have me believe that there was not behind all this a plan that was being worked out by invisible forces representing Divine Providence, and something of the inevitable Justice, I should tell him that he lacked ordinary intelligence. To speak of this as coincidence is just perfect nonsense.

"It is evidence of a moral order based on Righteousness and Justice which in the end rules the world and determines the final issues.

"Fauteux then read his statement in regard to my own portrait.

"After the Governor unveiled the portrait, [Kenneth] Forbes was called upon to bow. Fauteux then asked the Governor to unveil my portrait and went with him to the portrait itself. There was a fine round of applause. I was really surprised as well as touched at how sustained it was, seeing the Members of all Parties were gathered together there.

"Salisbury was then called upon to present himself which he did in a very nice way, bowing to the President, the Governor General and myself. After this, Ballantyne was called on. The Governor should have spoken at this point. Then the Governor General made his speech. When His Excellency had finished, Fauteux read his statement. When Fauteux had finished, I came forward and spoke without looking at a note. All the others had read what they had to say. While I was frightfully tired and wondered if I would get through without losing the thread of what I had to say, I nevertheless stuck it out. Made a few impromptu remarks, speaking both of the President and the Governor General and in the case of the latter, speaking of the happy intimacy of our association and thanking him personally for coming. In the same way, speaking direct to the President and what it had meant to me that he should have come immediately to the ceremony.

"When it came to the concluding paragraph of what I had to say, for a moment or two, I could not think of the first line. I then said 'associations melt into memories' instead of 'associations of the present soon melt into memories of the past.' When I could not think of those lines, I became a bit alarmed. However, I had the thought of the paragraph in my mind and managed to express it pretty much I think as it had been prepared. Immediately after this, the band played 'O Canada' and those of us who were seated at the end of the hall, formed a procession beyond the Hall of Fame. The Governor General was to one side, the President next to him and I was next to the President. I should have, of course, been to the Governor's left but there was no chance to get over to that far side.

"As we talked on, the President spoke of the Hall of Fame resembling very much a cathedral. It certainly presented a fine appearance. We then went on to the Speaker's apartments. Had a little refreshment there and the Governor General then drove off."

Most of the next day was spent with the President and Mackenzie King found it much more enjoyable. He thought Truman's address to Parliament "was a splendid one, admirably suited for the occasion and good as a world utterance." The whole visit was a great success, but the Prime Minister obviously felt there was nothing of the intimate personal relationship with Truman that he had enjoyed with Roosevelt.

Another important event in June 1947 was the arrival in Ottawa of a delegation from the Newfoundland National Convention. An earlier delegation had been sent to London to determine what financial help Newfoundland could receive from the United Kingdom in re-establishing responsible government. The British government's response had been unsatisfactory and in March the Convention decided to send a delegation to Ottawa to ascertain "what fair and equitable basis may exist for federal union of Newfoundland and Canada." On March 25 Mackenzie King had "had a talk with Mr. St. Laurent about the answer to be given the Newfoundland Government which is planning to have a delegation come to Ottawa regarding having Newfoundland come into Canadian federation. I told St. Laurent I thought we ought to be very careful in what was said; that we would be raising questions with the provinces as to their right as to what was to be done; also that the other parties in the House would have to be considered. We could not regard this as a party matter but [it] must be regarded as a national one. I said I thought we ought to get our own provincial affairs straightened out before attempting anything else. Indeed, I can see only trouble ahead in having to deal with this question at this time. Newfoundland is certain to be a great financial responsibility. . . . I warned Abbott later as to being on the watch about any commitments."

The Prime Minister raised the problem in Cabinet the next day and said he "thought it was all important that we should see clearly the factors that had to be considered in advance. I pointed out first that we could not, as a Liberal party, seek to bring another country into Canada as part of the Dominion. That we would have to take other parties in the House into our confidence and have them work with us. They must realize that will not be an easy situation. Second, and more important, is the fact that they could be perfectly sure that other provinces of Canada would want to have their say in the matter, as well, inasmuch as Newfoundland would be brought in as a liability, and that the provinces of Ontario and Quebec would be sure to take exception to ours – as a central Government – because of taxation, increasing their liabilities, without consulting them.

"I repeated these thoughts over the 'phone to Pearson this afternoon. He told me that the B.N.A. Act provides for the Canadian Parliament bringing Newfoundland into the Confederation by resolution of both Houses so that we had the constitutional right. I said that would not meet the situation at all. That what we were attempting with provinces now, over taxation agreements, was certainly within the rights of the Constitution but that did not make any difference. We had run counter to a feeling generally in the provinces, that we were taking away some of their rights. This [to bring Newfoundland into Confederation by resolution] would only emphasize all of that kind of reasoning and would be very dangerous. Third, the thing was that there was that question of what it would involve later in having added that liability to others that we have in Canada at the present time. That Macdonald, of Nova Scotia, was not friendly. McNair was a difficult man. Jones, a crazy man. These Maritime provinces would all want their say; unless we were pretty sure we would get a solid backing with them, we better not raise a Maritime issue. That it would hurt us there. I could see from Pearson's eagerness and have seen from St. Laurent's presentation that External Affairs will want to have Newfoundland brought in at once. Every effort made to have Newfoundland brought in at once.

"Pearson said we will have to watch to see that the United States do not get too great a control through what they have in there of airfields in Newfoundland. To that I replied I was not at all sure that, having regard to the future, we would gain rather than lose in having the United States assume a certain military responsibility for the protection of this Continent rather than our taking on the whole thing ourselves in that Island. I agreed, of course, that all this would have to be carefully studied." Despite Mackenzie King's reservations, the government agreed on April 1 to receive the delegation.

During a conversation with the Governor-General on April 30, Mackenzie King "spoke about Newfoundland coming into Confederation. The Governor said of course it was plain that Newfoundland belonged to Canada. It would never do to have it a part of the United States. I told him I fully agreed as to this but that great care had to be taken with the timing and the method of approach. I thought our party should consider getting the goodwill of the other provinces and the other parties.

"I said I would like to clear up differences between the provinces and our Government before quitting my career and if that could be satisfactorily arranged to have the way prepared to bringing Newfoundland into Confederation. I did not want to create a fresh problem before others were satisfactorily settled. I said I might ask him later on to give us a hand when we might wish to bring all the Premiers together for conference purposes. He might be willing to have a dinner at which he might develop some matters in a friendly and informal way. This I could see met with his instant approval. He said he would be delighted to do anything of the kind."

The Prime Minister and St. Laurent had a talk with Pearson on June 2 about the reception of the Newfoundland delegation. "The three of us agreed that it would be best for me to preside at a dinner at which the delegates would be welcomed and also at the first conference. Then to have a Cabinet Committee meet the delegates to discuss matters on which they wished to receive information. I suggested that St. Laurent should be

Chairman of that Committee and other members should include Ilsley, Abbott, Claxton, Bridges and Howe. I agreed to having the leaders of the Opposition parties told confidentially of the background of the meeting. That a statement be prepared to be given in the House. We might let leaders know we were anxious that the matter should not be a party affair. That we might call them into conference later. That there would be an official committee to gather data, etc."

On June 23 the Cabinet discussed Newfoundland again and Mackenzie King observed that it was "going to be very difficult to give Newfoundland terms which will be sufficient to bring them into Confederation and at the same time not make a serious problem with each one of our provinces."

The delegation, which was led by F. G. Bradley, the Chairman of the Convention, and included J. R. Smallwood as secretary, arrived in Ottawa on June 24. The Prime Minister spent most of the day revising his speech for the opening meeting and preparing his remarks for the government dinner at the Country Club that evening.

At the dinner, Mackenzie King had a long talk with Bradley whom he found "exceedingly pleasant." "We seemed to be of one mind on every subject we touched on. He himself is a Liberal and was the leader of the Liberal party of Newfoundland though, at one time, he had only one follower. He, himself, is strongly for the confederation of Newfoundland with Canada and has been fighting that battle pretty much alone part of the time. He told me that the delegation that went to London was not a good delegation. There were unfortunate circumstances as well in that they arrived two days ahead of time. Had to be put up in a make-shift hotel first night and another place, the next night. Altogether arrangements very poor. He spoke in the highest possible terms of Lord Addison. Was very reasonable about the position of the delegation. Said they knew we had our problems as well as they, themselves. He spoke of what happened in '69. New Dominion being little known and the agitation being waged against it. Merchants particularly who wanted to hold on to tariffs. Had control of the polls. There was open voting and poor fishermen and others who wanted to vote for Confederation were told they would get no credit or gratuities, etc., if they did. Also of how when the delegation came to Ottawa in 1895, Sir Mackenzie Bowell was Prime Minister. The whole proceedings were rushed and they could get nowhere. Of course, the Tory Government of that day was dying. . . . He thought our greatest difficulty would come in dealing with other Maritime Provinces. Lester Burry was also, I found, most pleasant. . . .

"A very nice dinner was served. When it came to the toast to Newfoundland, I found it very easy to speak. I began by making references to recent conferences we had had, where we all had to be on our good behaviour, watch our steps, etc. Said it was a relief to me and my colleagues that we were now able, all of us, to talk together like ordinary folk. That was the way we felt toward our friends from Newfoundland. Referred to our owing allegiance to the same Crown and being members of the Commonwealth.

"I spoke of this being particularly the 450th Anniversary of the discovery of Newfoundland. Said I wanted them to have their friends in Newfoundland know we were celebrating this anniversary with them. I then mentioned that we had at the table not only Ministers of the Crown and Members of the Government but leaders of the Opposition of all parties in the Commons and the Senate. That they need not imagine those gentlemen had come to do any honour to me. They would be glad to get me out of office, but they all wished to do honour to our friends from Newfoundland. Also I was anxious that we all should realize the question we were about to consider was altogether above party and one on which we would wish to have all parties united. In speaking about my own knowledge of Newfoundland, I referred to the flights that I had had over the Island but spoke more particularly of having gained my knowledge in associations which made both Labrador and Newfoundland very dear to me.

"I then referred to Norman Duncan's books and mentioned that Duncan and I had roomed together at College in 1891–92, and that Grenfell and I had been great personal friends. Referring to Duncan's story of fishermen and all, I said that these memories lent, as it were, a soft glow over all the Island and its romantic beauty, etc. This thought came to me while speaking and had not been in my mind before at all. It really was quite touching, even to myself, while speaking. I had also not thought of anything about the leaders until I was on my feet. In fact, one's best thoughts all come in these ways.

"When I came to the mission, I said my colleagues had told me I would have to be very careful of what I said. I then mentioned that I believed some day – the dream of a great country – a British country, extending from the waters of the Atlantic to the Pacific, all one, united, etc., would come to pass. Whether this was the moment or later, one could not say. I was sure, however, that our present gathering would bring us one step nearer that result. I then spoke of the only basis on which a solution could be found was one which would be satisfactory to the people both of Newfoundland and Canada. It was of course for Newfoundland itself to decide whether they wished to come in. I then proposed the toast to Newfoundland, coupling it with Mr. Bradley's name, and asking that our warmest greetings be brought back to our friends in Newfoundland. I spoke feelingly of the hospitality extended by Newfoundlanders to our troops in the course of the war."

The Prime Minister enjoyed the evening very much and on the way home from the Club reflected that he would not be surprised "if it might yet be that my part would help to bring about the rounding out of Canada as a nation in a manner which would take in all the territory from the waters of the Atlantic to those of the Pacific. To this end I would be tempted to remain a little longer in public life than otherwise I would wish to be. I am, however, not at all sure that it will be possible to make an agreement which Newfoundland would regard as satisfactory. There would then have to be a referendum.

"To my surprise this delegation is likely to be here for a month at least. From what Scott Macdonald tells me they hope to manoeuvre things so as not to make their recommendations to the British Government until October, when it will be too late to have a referendum this year, and it might come some time next year. I realize that we are all at the moment writing a real page of history."

The next morning Mackenzie King arrived at the Parliament Buildings a little before 10.30 A.M. and met the Newfoundland delegation in the Hall of Fame. "As we were going into the Railway Committee Room, shook hands with them all and had a pleasant word. In the Railway Committee Room, many photos were taken after we were seated. Members of the delegation were to my right. St. Laurent and our delegation to the left around a sort of square. Advisers along both sides. The press ranged in two rows further to the right. After numerous photographs were taken, I read my opening address. It was replied to by Bradley in a very carefully prepared address, remarkably friendly. After, more photographs were taken. Significantly enough, a huge map of Canada was immediately behind where we were sitting and a picture of the Fathers of Confederation on the walls to the left. Bradley reminded the gathering that two of the Newfoundland representatives were among the Fathers of Confederation. St. Laurent proposed that Bradley and I should be photographed in front of the picture. It seemed to me, however, that was going a little too far. The picture was very high up on the wall. I told the photographers that Mr. St. Laurent was a man of high ideals. Mr. Bradley and I then went together over to the C.B.C. to record our speeches."

The Prime Minister did not participate in the detailed negotiations with the delegation but on July 11, St. Laurent reported that confederation "would mean an added obligation of fifteen million dollars every year in cash apart from many other obligations that would have to be overtaken – above anything we could do for the Maritime provinces. He was afraid this would at once create a Maritime province problem; also that other provinces would wish to have their positions strengthened from the federal treasury. He did not see how we could at this time, without political disaster, attempt anything of the kind. I pointed out this is exactly what I had said to the Cabinet at the time it was proposed we should receive the delegation. He asked me if he should see Mr. Bradley privately and let him know the situation. They would go back and report that they were well received, etc., but had not found it possible to get an agreement that was mutually acceptable. Everything would be done in a nice spirit. He said every person meeting the delegation seemed to take it for granted that Newfoundland is coming into Confederation."

This suggestion was not, in fact, pursued; instead, at the Cabinet meeting on July 18 it seemed "pretty much the unanimous view . . . that Canada would wish Newfoundland in Confederation and that if a way were not found at this time, future generations might feel that the Government was at fault in taking chances in the changed relationships that might develop, for example, between Newfoundland and the United States. It is true that a Union cannot be brought about without our assuming a considerable liability and one which may make some of the other provinces, particularly the Maritimes, resentful, at giving better terms to a bankrupt colony than we would give to our own provinces. However, the feeling was that there were larger national and Commonwealth considerations of which full account should be taken, and we decided therefore to continue the meetings with the Newfoundland representatives though, as St. Laurent said, this would mean they would have a stronger feeling than ever that we were determined to have them brought into Confederation. It may even be that terms cannot be arranged but it is worth while going as far as we can. The two points that came up were, first of all, bringing the other parties of the House into the knowledge of what we were doing. The ground was laid for that in the Country Club but we felt that they would probably just take advantage of the information we gave them. Would not accept any responsiblity and might use the information later in ways that would suit their own purposes.

"The other was the question of the wisdom of having a conference with the provinces, specifically on this point, and the possibility of letting that Conference help to solve the larger questions that are still outstanding. On discussion, it was thought that McNair and Macdonald would say that they would reserve judgment; probably not commit themselves to anything, while Drew and Duplessis would make matters increasingly difficult. I made the suggestion that the best way to proceed would be by a resolution in Parliament. That we should go as far as we felt we could go, and then place a resolution on the order paper stating that the Government was of the opinion that we should offer these terms to Newfoundland with a view to bringing the colony into Confederation. The effect of that would be to put each political party on the spot. If the parties voted against the resolution, they would have to share the responsibility for not having Newfoundland come in. I am not at all sure that to take that attitude would not make a first-class national issue in the campaign. I am sure the Canadian people will wish to see our Dominion rounded out from the outward waters of the Atlantic to those of the Pacific. Of course, it may be that the delegates here will wish something too exorbitant. That would alter the situation.

"While I would gladly have preferred not having this question at this time, and until relations with our own provinces were settled, I have nevertheless come pretty well around to the view that the large, long-time aspect of the situation is the one that it is important, above all else, to consider. That we must work toward that end. The idea of the Resolution seemed to appeal pretty strongly to Council as avoiding the necessity of our taking other leaders into our confidence in advance or having any negotiations with the provinces."

In a conversation with Mackenzie King later that day, "St. Laurent stressed the value it would be to my name and to the future to have Newfoundland come into Confederation while I am still Prime Minister." Discussions with the Newfoundland delegation continued until the end of October but the Prime Minister took little direct interest in them for the next month.

During the last three weeks of June, Mackenzie King was often concerned about Norman Robertson's serious illness. On June 25 he discussed with Pearson the appointment of Dana Wilgress as acting High Commissioner in London and this led him to set out his views on "the position of the High Commissioner. I said it must be understood that the High Commissioner represented the Government of Canada, not any department of government, and that while the Department of External Affairs carried on the work of communication, etc., the High Commissioner was the appointee of the Prime Minister, not of the Secretary of State for External Affairs. That no government would ever sanction allowing one department to say who would be High Commissioner or what the High Commissioner's policies were to be. Pearson asked me if there was not a certain difference so far as London was concerned. I said it was more important that this should be recognized in relation to London than to any other centre. Were it otherwise, we would be establishing a bureaucracy beyond all question and would be having a permanent service that was telling the people's representatives what they were to do and who they were to appoint. I could not understand this for a moment. I appreciate his desire to keep these appointments free from partisan politics but as a matter of fact the position of High Commissioner ought, I thought, in many instances, to go to those who held the position of Minister of the Crown or to some person who enjoyed very closely the confidence of the Prime Minister. I said, for example, that as Prime Minister, I would have certain relations with the British Government and these I could never put into the hands of any department of government. It was a matter for the Government to say who would be the representatives. Pearson I could see was trying to find some way of taking a somewhat different view but he could not give any expression to it in words. I pointed out that if another party came into office they might very well wish to have an entirely different representative but must be free to have it so. I might have mentioned how both Ferguson and Perley had tendered their resignations as High Commissioners when we came into office knowing that the Government would wish to make its own appointments in a confidential relationship. This whole matter will have to be carefully explored."

The Prime Minister learned of Lord Bennett's death on June 27. He noted that "the feelings I had when I learned of his death were those of compassion. I can honestly say that I cherished no feeling of resentment though I imagine that there were few, if any, men in public life . . . [who] took a more contemptible and arrogant attitude than he did toward myself.

"I realized at once that I had a very difficult situation to meet in seeking to prepare something in the nature of a tribute in Parliament this afternoon."

In fact, it took him so long to prepare his remarks that he had only a glass of milk for lunch. He hurried to the House and when he came to read his tribute "found it quite difficult to get my breath and to go through the manuscript. I was pretty certain that the press would put this down to an emotional condition, which, however, is far from being the fact. It was simply the effect of the pressure of the morning in the light of all the doctors had told me I should seek above all else to avoid. While thinking over what I should say I recalled the letters exchanged between Bennett and myself when he resigned the Leadership of his party. I think they were the last communications exchanged between us. Indeed, excepting for the meeting at the Guildhall, at which he hesitated even to shake hands, I have not either seen or heard from him since the afternoon the session concluded in the House of Commons and I left for Kingston to speak at some important meeting."

However, he recognized one point in common with Bennett; "in the light of what I feel so strongly were wholly mistaken policies which have worked irreparable injury in many directions and his own attitude toward myself, in dictating I could not but recognize, however, how strange a parallel in at least one particular our lives were, namely, life devoted almost entirely to public affairs and very much alone with the result that much of what is richest and best in life, home and happiness, were missed altogether, and the last part of life become increasingly lonely."

After all the excitement and emotion of June 10, Mackenzie King began once more to think of retirement. On June 14 he wrote: "I am now in my twenty-first year of leadership in the Office of Prime Minister. On no consideration will I think of remaining in office to the end of another year. I have thought a little of seeking to outstrip Walpole's record but the parallel is not a fair one. There is, however, a natural feeling that one might, if one were strong enough, wish to stay on to that time, if one were sure of health, strength and ability to continue with work. My own feeling, however, is that I should seek to plan for a national convention some time before the autumn months are out. However, all this is in God's hands and in His own good time."

In a conversation on July 7, Brooke Claxton "brought up the question of St. Laurent staying on. He said he wondered if any pressure could be brought to bear to have him stay. He knew that the party would rather have him succeed me than anyone and that he hoped I would stay on as long as I could. [Claxton wondered] if St. Laurent could be persuaded to stay on by being promised he would be made Prime Minister even for a time, or made Chief Justice. I said I would make him Chief Justice in a moment in succession to Rinfret even if it meant following one French-Canadian by another on the Bench as Chief Justice. That there was no one I would rather have succeed me as Prime Minister. I said Sir Wilfrid had pointed out he had been in minority of race and religion himself and that that had been his cross. He doubted if there would ever be another French-Canadian Prime Minister. I told him my reply to Sir Wilfrid had been he had held the office for quite a while, etc.

"I then said to Claxton that if St. Laurent went, I would probably go myself and that there were one or two others who might also go at the same time. That if I felt like I had at the beginning of the session, I would resign now. On the other hand, I felt my health was coming back of late and I might be prepared to stay on for a time longer and possibly another year. It would all depend on my health and what the party wished. If the party wanted to change tomorrow, I would be quite agreeable. He said he knew the party wanted me to stay just as long as I could. What I know is in his mind is the desire to be made Secretary of State for External Affairs. He said he had been at the External Affairs picnic and was with St. Laurent. They had been talking over their future together. St. Laurent had told me of the talk and had spoken about the possibility of Claxton having External Affairs. We were speaking about the best person to send to Australia. I told Claxton that the length of my further stay in office was in the hands of the party. That especially with the situation as critical as it is in Europe today, I did not like to appear to be pulling out. Everything, however, would depend on my strength and the support I had around me, both in the Government, in the office and in my home. I certainly would not allow myself – if I could avoid it – to come down with any break through staying too long. I said, however, with the House over now I thought I would take the summer to decide when it was best to have a Convention called and get the party's affairs so shaped that I could leave at the time that it was best."

On July 11 the Prime Minister was approached by two of St. Laurent's friends from Quebec who were anxious to discover how eager he was to keep his Quebec lieutenant in public life. "I told them that if St. Laurent went that I myself would have to go. I did not think I could carry the burden there would be if St. Laurent were no longer in the Government. This seemed to startle them. They both said that the country would not let me out of this position at the present time. They really seemed quite crest-fallen. I told them it was simply a matter of health. Today I was enjoying public life much more, having regained my strength, but if it gave way again I would have to withdraw. I did not wish to risk things too long. They left with the intention, I think, of doing their utmost to have St. Laurent stay, but I can see from different sources it is becoming apparent that his mind is definitely made up not to remain much longer. I told them I would like to have him succeed me as Prime Minister if he could be persuaded to remain. I thought our party would support that absolutely."

Mackenzie King had a talk with Howe on July 17 to make sure that he was willing to stay on in the government. He also spoke of his own plans. "Said had I not felt so much better, I would have been arranging to get out at once. Howe said to me that he understood my position and indeed if he were in it, he would get out while one was at the top of things and before a break came in the conditions. I told him I had not thought of that. It was my health that I was really concerned about. I did not like to leave while there were great problems. I did feel that perhaps it might be well to stay on if one were spared by Providence, to beat Walpole's record. That I thought from letters I had received, expressions of different persons, that it would please Canada if the Prime Minister of Canada had the world record for the longest service in that office and it was perhaps worth arranging to stay that long at least but that I would not think of going much beyond that time and would have to arrange accordingly. I said I would like to see St. Laurent succeed me if he could be kept in. Howe said that would please everyone. There was not a member of the party that would not welcome St. Laurent staying on.

"I have been told that the thing that might keep him on is the knowledge that I wanted him to stay and that I, myself, might not stay if he went which, of course, would mean a very serious situation for the party. One thing that has occurred to me and this might help him to stay – is that I might arrange to give up the office of Prime Minister about Easter of next year; have a Convention about that time and then if St. Laurent would take over, I might agree to continue to hold the office of President of the Council at the wish of the Ministers, so as not to lose my seat in the House which would mean the difference of a vote. Also be in a position to give the Ministry the benefit of my experience which I know they would all wish to have.

"In some ways, it might be best to drop out altogether but this arrangement is one that might be allowed to continue as long as the Party was in office which would mean that I could hold that post even while an election was on. This, however, is all too far ahead yet to decide.

"I am thinking over what might induce St. Laurent to stay and also what would enable me to have still an additional income which I will need and to render the service that I would be capable of rendering though being freed of the heavier load."

After the Cabinet meeting next day (July 18), the Prime Minister took St. Laurent to the Country Club for dinner to talk over "what he really had in mind and wished to do." St. Laurent's reply convinced Mackenzie King that he wished to retire "before the end of the year. My immediate reply to that was that if he dropped out, I felt I would have to drop out as well. That I doubted if I had either the strength or the ability to carry on as leader without his support. I spoke of the need of a leader from Quebec as well as from Ontario. Said I had always tried to govern in that way. He said that had not always been necessary and pointed to Sir John's time. But I drew attention to the fact that in that day, there were strong men both from Ontario and Quebec who matched each other.

"He then said that Sir Wilfrid did not have an English leader. I pointed out his Ministers from Ontario were strong men – like Mulock and others. While there might not have been one individual, there were several of them. I told him that I could not have got through this session without the consideration shown by all colleagues. He said he supposed I had felt a certain confidence in what was going on in Council as long as he was there and had felt free to stay away at times which I told him was absolutely the case. That I needed the rest. I then spoke of just how sick I had been and of the difference I was experiencing at the moment. He said it was notice-able to all that I had in the last little while, come back to my old self again in a very real way. I said that would not last if I were over-powered with too much responsibility and it would be better for me in every way to give up before any break came. I mentioned having seen Fielding lie on his back for a couple of years; Rowell, the same. Referred to Bennett's heart condition which had kept him apparently out of much effort, and of others. I could not and would not risk incurring paralysis or anything of the kind. . . .

"St. Laurent said to me that he had had a talk with Chief Justice Duff and asked him whether he thought the people would feel that he was not doing right if he got out. That he had come in just to help in the war period, and would they think that he was not worthy of the place that he had won. Before he told me what Duff said, I replied that no one would think that for a moment. That everyone realized that his part had been not only a tremendous part, but the country would be everlastingly indebted to him. That he must not feel that his going out would occasion any such feeling. People could realize he had done his full share. I said to him quite frankly that what I would like to do would be to have it definitely understood he would succeed me as Prime Minister and I would give up the office any time that he might wish to take on its duties. I said I had felt now that I had gone so far along the road – if it was the will of Providence, I would like to outdistance Walpole's record, and this not because of anything other than that I felt the people of Canada would like that honour to come to our country, and also I thought many of our friends in the Empire would be pleased to see one of our day and under a democratic regime, make that record. He, at once, said that that certainly ought to be done and turned around to say that it would not be possible to arrange a convention in time – to have any change made at an earlier date. I said my thought had been to have a convention called for Easter of next year. Have a vacation of two or three weeks. I would pass Walpole's record by that time, and he could continue on from there with the session. He then said to me that he could not, on any account, think of taking on the office of Prime Minister. That he did not think it would be fair to Quebec. I asked him in what way. His reply was that he thought the country was today more prosperous than it had ever been. This prosperity might continue another two years. After that time, there was bound to be a decline and the country might fall on some of the hardest times it had known. That if he were in office, the public would say that was the responsibility of having a French-Canadian at the head of the nation. I said to him that was utter nonsense and wholly untrue. People did not think that way of Bennett in hard times. They realized that was part of a world depression. I said Sir Wilfrid used to say that being in the minority of race and religion was the cross he had to bear. But I had told him that fifteen years in office continuously, unbroken, was a pretty good record, and that I thought he, St. Laurent, could hold a place second to none if he was to take on the duties.

"He then spoke about his own position financially. Told me there were certain monies coming to him from his legal work for which payment had not been made when he came into the Government. That he had been using these monies to help to supplement what he got as a Minister of the Crown, etc., but that with the taxation what it was, his expenses of family in Quebec, and living in Ottawa, he was able to save each year only about the amount of the car allowance – which was $2,000. That he felt he ought to get back to his practice before it was too late. His earning power would grow less and less, but he would be able to make enough to ensure himself security in the end. That the other way, were he to attempt to go on in public life, he might become embarrassed before long. He mentioned that friends were ready to help him. I said if it had not been for the help I got from friends, I could not have got through. I did not feel any embarrassment on that score, nor had I been embarrassed in any way by what had been done. I thought he could feel the same."

St. Laurent was concerned about his own health and pointed out "that the years in office had been quite a strain to him. He was pretty tired. I said that I knew. I could sympathize entirely with him in what he said in that. He then mentioned that he was beginning to feel a pain in his right leg, very often; I know exactly what that is. He said he was afraid of these things developing. I told him that I thoroughly understood all that. The only thing would be he would have to arrange to get plenty of rest, etc. He thought that Easter would be too soon for a convention. He said it took Murphy a long time arranging the other convention. It would take about a year, he thought. I said I did not see why it should be that long but he thought the time to arrange a convention would be some time next autumn – over a year hence. I said to him nothing would induce me to try to go through another session and wait over until the autumn for a change. His feeling was if that time were taken, the new leader could then come in and have a year in office before going to the people. That would bring us to the latter part of '49. He doubted whether it would be wise to wait out the full five years, not knowing what the conditions might be when the moment came. I told him I had felt that way about the penitential year but that I thought one of the great achievements we had done marvellously, was when we brought the House to its full five years during the war and yet dissolved without efflux of time or being defeated in any way.

"I then said to him if we were to fit into an arrangement of the kind, would you be willing to take on the position of leadership and the office of Prime Minister. That I knew every member of the House of Commons wanted that and would wish it more than anything else. He then said to me in a very definite way that he would not. He did not wish to assume that position at his years – he is now 65, and with the times what they were and for the reasons he had given me. I said to him: must I take it as definite that nothing would induce you to stay on, with a definite understanding that you would have the leadership and Prime Ministership at any time that you might wish it. He then said, quite firmly, that he would not. He did not feel that he could. I asked him who he thought would be the best one to take on. He gave me the name he thought would be best as one that the country would feel would not be too extreme in some of the measures that otherwise might be introduced. I think that he thought the country would feel toward him as they had, in a way, toward myself and also himself.

"Speaking of Quebec, he said I may tell you that I think there is more affection for you in Quebec than even in the English provinces. I said I was perfectly sure of that and said that it was because I had stood by Sir Wilfrid. He said: no, that was true but the real reason was French-Canada felt that I wanted to have an absolutely square deal between the English and the French. That I had protected their rights all along the way. He thought we would carry the next election with the new leader if an election were to come at the time he has mentioned and he was given the year's opportunity. He did not think it would be wise to have a new leader appointed too long before election. He might show certain weaknesses which the Opposition would seize on. If the term was short, this kind of criticism would not develop."

To Mackenzie King, it was quite clear that "St. Laurent's mind is made up not to consider the Prime Ministership. I think it is made up to leave at the end of the year though I believe the chivalry in his nature might cause him to stay on through the next session and until the time of a convention if one were definitely fixed before the moment for his withdrawal would come.

"I told him I had spoken to Howe who was prepared to stay on. He said he was glad to hear that. I said I thought Ilsley also would stay on if he could get a Judgeship later in Nova Scotia. That if we were all together for some little time yet, I felt the party would be in a good position. I told him at the end we could regard this conversation as an overture; beginning of chapter one in a series of talks. That I would not regard what he had said as being final in any way. I would have to have talks with others as well."

Next day Mackenzie King dictated a letter "to be sent to each of my colleagues telling them that I wanted them to keep me informed of their movements and definitely fixing early weeks of September as those in which I wanted special meetings of the Cabinet to discuss matters pertaining to the position of the party in Parliament and in the country. It is the first definite step toward my own retirement from the leadership and the Prime Ministership. I intend in September to definitely fix a time for a convention and to have it called either in September or later in the year, as matters may shape themselves in these discussions.

"The letter will let the Ministers know that there is now no longer any speculation or doubt as to my staying on beyond another year. Everything, of course, will depend on my health and who remains with me. If St. Laurent goes, I may stick it out until after Easter of next year. If he does not go, I might leave the convention until a year from the date of the convention in which I became leader of the party myself – somewhere around August the 7th. That would be the outside limit, come what may, if it is God's wish that I should [be] in health and strength that long.

"I felt an immense relief when I had dictated this letter and had this date line definitely established. It naturally grew out of my conversation with St. Laurent last night."

The Prime Minister also gave some further thought to the disposition of his property during this period. On July 31 he discussed the future use of Laurier House with a friend who "was strongly of the view that the best thing would be its being kept as it is and given to the nation, allowing visitors to be shown through. He told me that since Hyde Park had been given to the United States, already the number of visitors had been so great that they would either have to stop attempting any more or reconstruct whole foundations. The house was unable to carry the weight. I pointed out how fortunate I was that steel girders and all had been put in before I went into the house. He kept saying one must look ahead – 50, 100 years. The whole meaning of everything would be much greater to younger generations."

That day, in Cabinet, Mackenzie King was annoyed to discover how many Ministers were planning to be out of the country in the fall. He decided, therefore, to anticipate what he had proposed to say about his retirement but "took up first the question of the number of Ministers who would want to cross the ocean. Pointed out that the number was going up to 8 or 10. It was a mistake – half of our number going abroad. I said I did not want to impose my will. Let each man answer his own conscience. If young men were doing these things, it was going to tell against them when it came to a general election. If those who had come more recently to the Cabinet were taking on these trips, etc., I thought it would hurt them very much in the elections. That I also thought they should instead of going abroad be speaking in different parts of our country. I could not get any response from any of the Ministers as they did not wish to say anything that was likely to reflect on colleagues but I could see they were in agreement with me."

He then told them the real reason he had asked for a special series of meetings in September was to decide on the date for the calling of a convention. He pointed out that "a convention would have to be called to choose a new leader; also to prepare the platform of the party. I said one of the most serious things was the way in which organization had been neglected altogether. If we had had a decent organization, I would feel a little different about trying to continue on but I thought with the Conservatives, the C.C.F. developing their organization as they have, and our people doing nothing, that we would find that would cost the success of the party at a general election.

"I reminded my colleagues how often I had spoken of the matter, both in the Cabinet and in Caucus. There was quite a silence when I said I was determined on the matter. I had been studying the time it took and had been looking up procedure in regard to previous conventions – Sir Wilfrid, 1893 and our own, with a view to seeing the time it would take.

"St. Laurent then spoke of it taking a considerable time – he thought, part of a year – at least six months. I said we would move faster in these days."

After a good deal of discussion, the Prime Minister concluded that a meeting of the National Liberal Federation should be held in mid-December, with Parliament called for a month or six weeks later. "At the time of the Federation meeting, mention made of the date of the convention and its purpose. That will have a steadying effect. It was clear that that seemed to be the general view of all who were present. I could see that what McCann had in mind was the possibility of St. Laurent carrying on, acting in an interim capacity. A convention a year or two later. What St. Laurent himself has told me caused me to realize there was no sense in this. Also I pointed out it would be a disadvantage to whoever ultimately became the leader. Men are very short sighted.

"Very few can take the long view. See things years ahead. When I saw that we could not get further, not likely to get any more out of discussion, I emphasized anew my determination when we met in September, to consider whether I would stay longer than December, this depending on results of discussion and how I may feel in September."

Mackenzie King was still quite uncertain about how long St. Laurent could be persuaded to stay in the Cabinet. He noted that St. Laurent had agreed "to go to the meeting of the U.N. Open proceedings there which he did not want to do a week or two ago. He has also promised me to stay until after the [Royal] wedding, if only six months ahead. He might agree to stay on if I did. I told the Ministers I was anxious whatever I did was done in a way that would help the party most and show my appreciation of their confidence over the years. I mentioned about Sir Wilfrid having thought of staying in the House [after retirement as leader] and lending a hand. I did not know whether I could be of any help in that way. There was general expression at once: by all means.

"What I have in mind is the possibility of staying on as President of the Council which would give me at least a Minister's salary but that again would depend on what can be accomplished between now and that time. I must get my correspondence cleared; cases of it at Laurier House. Will made and one or two other things.

"I felt when I had finished the talk that the air had been cleared somewhat and that Ministers were feeling the reality of the position, knowing what it would mean."

On August 1 Mackenzie King wrote to his colleagues about absences abroad. "I wanted them to know," he noted, "that as I told Council the other day, my authority in these matters must be observed. A circular letter is perhaps the best form of securing this and of meeting situations which may arise a little later on."

Almost all the Prime Minister's time for the first ten days of August was taken up with the illness of his dog "Pat II." His colleague Frank Bridges, the Minister of Fisheries, was also critically ill at this time. "I was really shocked and deeply pained today," Mackenzie King wrote on August 8, "when I rang up the Civic Hospital today to be told by Bridges' nurse that he was quite seriously ill, not allowed to see anyone. His brother is here, but was only permitted to see him for a moment. Tonight Mitchell went out to see him but just allowed to look in. He phoned me to say Bridges' throat is paralysed. This is all most serious, and I feel more deeply than I can say. Strange one should pay the attention and concern one does to a little animal, and not feel the same deep concern for a Minister of the Crown who is a colleague. I write this way to show to myself how much our lives are centred on interests that are immediate to ourselves."

Bridges died on August 10 and this simply increased Mackenzie King's feelings of guilt. "I cannot reproach myself too keenly for not having gone in to the hospital at once when I heard Bridges was there. This is all very sad – Bridges so much alone, so promising and fine a man. It means too another by-election. There may be others. We can ill afford our majority being reduced. Bridges too was pretty much the only one we could rely upon from the Maritimes for organization work."

Just after he had returned from Bridges' funeral the next day, the Prime Minister received word of the death of Senator McGeer. He actually revised his tribute to McGeer at the veterinary hospital where "Pat" had been taken to be operated on or destroyed, depending on the result of the examination. An operation was not possible and the loss of the little dog was a severe blow to his master.

The question of retirement came up in a conversation with Howe and Gardiner on August 21. "Gardiner said he thought the party's best chance was for me to stay with it through the next campaign. Howe replied that that was true but he thought I had done my full duty by the party. If I felt I should retire, I would be entitled to it. I said much depended on what St. Laurent would do. The time of the Convention would have to be announced before the end of the present year."

At the Cabinet meeting on September 11, just before St. Laurent left for the United Nations, Mackenzie King repeated "what I had said before as to desirability of having a meeting of the Federation in December and at the Federation meeting, announce my intention to ask for a Convention to select a new leader and to outline the party's programme. Wishart Robertson thought that the meeting of the Federation should be just after Parliament assembled. That, of course, means another jam as we had before the opening of Parliament last year and will have to be carefully considered.

"I stated I would be prepared to stay on if spared at least until after Walpole's record had been beaten but that I thought the thing I should do was to hand back on that day, if possible – at the end of 29 years – the trust that had been given me that many years ago.

"All members sat perfectly quiet while I was making this statement. I could see in the faces of some of them, a look of anxiety and of disappointment that was wholly apparent. Naturally they could not but feel what this change might mean to their own fortunes. I told them, however, that I did not wish to continue on at a time that I might become decrepit. That I would have fulfilled my full duty by the party after serving in the office of Prime Minister over 21 years, and in the leadership, for 29 years."

After the meeting, the Prime Minister had an encouraging talk with St. Laurent. "We stopped in the ante-room by the Council Chamber. Discussed one or two matters about the U.N. meeting. I said to him I would have a further talk with him later on about other matters. He, himself, then said to me that he had been very worried over the last few years about some losses that he had met with, and had not been able to overtake. That some of his friends had told him that these had been wiped off and met in a manner which left him under obligation to no one but which they were glad to have him know were in recognition of services he had rendered in the last few years in staying in the Government, instead of continuing on with his profession. He said I might easily have met these amounts in a short time, had I continued my practice, and suppose I could do so very soon by withdrawing at once. I can see, however, that if you leave the party and if I leave, everything will go to pieces. It will be a very serious matter for the party and I think I feel now that I am in a position to stay on or words to that effect. I cannot describe the relief this brought to my mind. St. Laurent had a very peaceful, happy look in his face. Indeed I have not seen a more serene expression on his countenance. I thanked him warmly and said I would now decide to stay on through the session. He told me that Howe had, in speaking to him, strongly urged that he should stay. That he, Howe, would stay. St. Laurent then said he thought I should work things out whereby Howe could be given the direction of industrial development – along with resources. Also that we might have a lot of trouble over the appointment of Parliamentary Assistants. I said I was in favour of arranging for some changes in portfolios. Something to use Howe's abilities to the utmost. Also I thought we would fill all Parliamentary Assistants positions.

"I said to him that at the Convention, there would be a terrific drive to have him take the office of Prime Minister. He said he did not think that would be so. He then mentioned a recent Gallup poll in which he and Ilsley had received the same vote. I said that did not represent the feeling of the House or of the country. He then said he thought we would win the next election but it would mean someone else would have to be chosen in another five years as he was now 65. I said we could let those matters stand and see how things develop within a year but that I was immensely relieved at his decision to stay on. He said that what had been done would enable him to live more as he had lived in Quebec. Up to the present he had not felt he was at all at home in Ottawa. This has meant more to me and the party than anything else possibly could."

On September 19 Mackenzie King had a long talk with Pearson who had received another offer of a post outside Canada. The Prime Minister "thought he ought to stay in Canada; that his future was here. Curiously enough, I was speaking to him now the way Laurier had spoken to me. . . . Sir Wilfrid had said my place was in Canada and he thought I should look forward to a career in our Parliament. I told Pearson I thought he should do the same. I told him about Mr. St. Laurent agreeing to stay on for another year and that there would be strong pressure on him to accept the Prime Ministership. He had told me even if he were chosen it would mean another Convention in five years as he could not run on after 70. I said it might well be that a year hence he would be sufficiently in the minds of Members of the party to be nominated, even though he had not been in Parliament. The only difference between himself and myself in that regard was that I had been in Parliament a couple of years and in the Ministry before the Convention. He, I know, continues to feel that public life in this country has a strong attraction for him.

"I am wholly convinced, having regard to the future and its problems, he would be the best man to succeed myself though this I do not wish to breathe to others. Conditions may change between now and the time of a Convention. I shall take no step which would be in any way disloyal to any of my colleagues or to lessen the chances of any one of them becoming the choice of the Convention."

The Prime Minister repeated his advice to Pearson on October 9 when he drove him home from a dinner at Government House. On October 14 Pearson told him "he had decided to hold to his present position, not leave Canada. He said he was grateful to me for having had a chance to talk matters over with him. It had made the situation much easier. I told him I thought he had made the right decision and would live not to regret it."

Greatly relieved by St. Laurent's decision to stay in the Cabinet, the Prime Minister was further encouraged by some evidence which emerged during a conversation with him on October 1 that he might be interested in seeking the party leadership. First they reopened the question of a new portfolio for Howe. "He suggested Trade and Commerce. I told him I thought Howe was so identified in the minds of the people with manufacturers that he might be expected to be of protectionist leanings which would not be helpful in the West. I thought a better arrangement would be a Department of National Development to take the place of Mines and Resources. This could include Immigration and would permit of shaping lines of development. This could easily take in housing, etc. I felt that Glen was not equal to any real work. St. Laurent strongly agreed.

"We both also felt that Mackenzie's day was pretty nearly over and, if possible, we should get and have Gregg later take over that portfolio. Let Fisheries go to B.C. I promised to go into this work of reconstruction before leaving for England.

"I pointed out the difficulty in regard to by-elections. That, however, will have to be surmounted somehow. To my real surprise, St. Laurent gave the first indication of his not merely readiness but apparent desire to succeed myself in my present office. He spoke of his friends wishing this very much; of his feeling a certain obligation to meet their wishes in standing for the position. He said, however, that he would want to be perfectly sure that it would not raise a racial or religious issue. He was afraid that the Western delegates might have a feeling that there would be a Quebec bloc that would control. If anything of the kind existed, he would not allow his name to go forward. He thought that the ground would have to be felt out thoroughly by Fogo in advance. I could see, however, that he himself has been talking matters over with both Howe and Claxton who are bringing what persuasion they can upon him. I said I was perfectly sure of the solid support of the Parliamentary party. I thought, too, their influence would go far with other representatives of constituencies. Agreed that the matter should be explored.

"I told him I was immensely relieved to know how he felt. I think what was in his mind in part was that in the interval, I should perhaps try to get Howe's position and that of one or two others straightened out in advance. He went over with me a list of places he has been asked to speak. I told him the ones I thought he should accept and urged him to take on only the most important meetings; not to tire himself out."

On October 6, Mackenzie King noted in his diary that "the Montreal Gazette of this morning contained an article which would indicate someone has been talking pretty freely about what I had said in the Cabinet about arranging to retire next year. (The article is from Vineberg, its Quebec correspondent.)

"It brought in mention of my having the Federation meet when I return from the visit to Europe but was wrong in stating that I would have St. Laurent be acting Prime Minister until the Convention which would be held in the fall of next year. I feel the article may do St. Laurent great harm. It is bound to at once create opposition to his appointment on the part of persons in other provinces. No doubt it has been through some of St. Laurent's friends that this position has been disclosed but it is truly most unfortunate."

After the Cabinet meeting on October 9, the Prime Minister "had a talk of some length with Mr. St. Laurent. I spoke to him of the despatch from Quebec. . . . He said he felt strongly as regards the Convention that Fogo should, in making a trip through the West, to arrange for it, sound out our people and make sure that his being a candidate would not result in some racial division between Quebec and the rest of the provinces. I told him my fears were not on the racial but on the religious score. I referred to the experiences Gardiner and others had with the Ku Klux Klan in Saskatchewan and the intolerance of many Protestants. I said to him quite frankly that the feeling was gaining ground throughout Canada that the Catholic Church was seeking to make Canada its future stronghold. That the Marian Congress [held in Ottawa, June 18–22] had fostered this idea and it was a circumstance that had to be reckoned with. This I believe to be true."

By the time Mackenzie King left to go overseas for the Royal wedding, he had found his successor.

# CHAPTER THREE

# The Royal Wedding and the Dollar Crisis

MACKENZIE KING's planning for and preoccupation with retirement was interrupted early in July 1947 by the betrothal of Princess Elizabeth and the prospect of attending the Royal wedding in London. It had been proposed by the King that a meeting of the Imperial Privy Council "at which Canadians and others would be present" should be held in connection with the ceremony, a suggestion which almost precipitated a constitutional crisis in Canada. On July 11 the Prime Minister discussed the King's request with St. Laurent who "agreed absolutely we would have to take our stand on the position of the Dominions as set out in the Westminster Act. We could not be represented as Canada in a meeting of the U.K. Council. I said I was sure we would find tremendous pressure on this score. That was Britain's way of seeking to gain her end, to bring all the social pressure to bear that was possible. This event, connected with Elizabeth's marriage, will be made a means of trying to create something new in the way of Commonwealth – with one government or cabinet. That was running wholly contrary to all that from the beginning we had sought to effect in the way of recognition of the Dominions as nations within the Commonwealth.

"I spoke to Pearson too about the importance of our getting a carefully drafted reply to a message which came from Lascelles [the King's Private Secretary] which indicated that we were at the beginning of a controversy. It was clear we were going to have considerable controversy before we would get our position rightly established. Once again trying to do the thing that would help to save the imperialists, etc., from themselves, in a manner which would help to preserve the Commonwealth, the only way in which it can be preserved as a community of nations. It seems to fall to my lot at every turn to continue this battle, though I imagine no one has done more to help keep matters relating to the Commonwealth on an even keel, even if I say this myself."

Later in the day he discussed the question with the British High Commissioner who told him that he had received a message from London indicating that the King "attached very much importance to personal touch with Ministers and was very hopeful that a Minister from Canada would be present. I explained to him fully the position we were in, with respect to the Statute of Westminster. Asked him if he noticed how in the U.S. the American Government was gaining the impression that through all attending a meeting in Canberra [of Commonwealth governments, August 26 to September 2, to discuss the Japanese peace treaty], we were ganging up against the U.S. I said great care would have to be taken in a matter that was so all important as the position of the British Commonwealth of Nations, as had developed. I could see that the British are determined to make a real fight on this. It was very unpleasant for all as it brings me into direct contact in a controversy with the King himself and that, over a matter that is so distinctly personal and social as something connected with the marriage of his daughter who will be the future Queen."

Next day Mackenzie King received from Lascelles "a communication telling me that the King was distressed at the thought of there being no Canadian at the meeting of the Council. That he was very much concerned himself. Pretty anxious to make this one of the great events of his whole reign, etc., etc. Of course all of this is simply Lascelles and other Imperialists around the Throne using the King to further Imperialistic ends."

The Prime Minister spent most of the evening on July 13 writing a reply to Lascelles' telegram. His objective was to assure the recognition of "absolute equality between all the nations of the Commonwealth in the matter of representation of their Councils at any meeting of the nations of the Commonwealth over which the King may preside. Lascelles and company are striving to create, out of the U.K. Privy Council, an Imperial Privy Council which to appearances would be over all the nations of the Commonwealth. It is a very delicate business as the King himself is immediately involved as the central figure. Lascelles has sought to have it appear – and it may be so – that it is His Majesty's wish that what he has suggested should at all costs be done. That he, himself, has written out the names of those he wished present so far as the U.K. Council is concerned, etc. It seems to be my lot to be brought endlessly into apparent conflict with the Crown in those steps which, if followed, would lead to controversy in the Commonwealth and which if avoided would help to keep the Commonwealth together."

A reply was received from Lascelles on July 14 "saying that the King, on further reflection, had agreed with my proposal of having the Councils of the different nations of the Commonwealth appoint their representatives to go to London. It did not, however, touch the main crux of the situation as to whether the gathering over which the King is to preside is to be a meeting of these representatives or a Council which in reality will be the U.K. Privy Council."

On July 16 another telegram from Lascelles "pointed out the difficulty of Canadian P.C.s other than those that were members of the U.K. Privy Council being able to attend the meeting in London.

"In the message the King had sent to the Governor General, the word 'Imperial' was dropped out in reference to the meeting of the Council, and the word 'meeting' was used instead. I said to St. Laurent I did not think we should seek to embarrass the situation by doing other than seeking to meet the King's wishes – and having a Canadian P.C. who is also a U.K. P.C. present at the meeting, seeing we had registered our position quite clearly. Telegrams were sent off to this effect today." The next day Mackenzie King asked Howe to attend the proposed meeting as the Canadian representative.

A meeting of Canadian Privy Councillors was held in Ottawa on July 31 to receive the formal announcement of the King's consent to the marriage of Princess Elizabeth. Sir Allan Aylesworth and Sir Thomas White had been summoned to the meeting and Mackenzie King observed that "it was the first occasion on which a group of Privy Councillors for Canada had met I think since Confederation in any official way." He added that "at Quebec, I recalled having arranged to bring all the Privy Council together to meet the King on his arrival in Canada. I had thought that the Duke of Connaught had brought the Privy Council together when the first war was declared but I recollect later that he presided at the Council. It was the Cabinet and not the Privy Council. When war came in our own case, I could see it was not possible to bring all the Privy Councillors together at that time. This, however, was an historical occasion as creating a new precedent. I confess I was amazed at the correspondence that there had been back and forth over keeping secret the word that was to come from the King when I saw what it was.

"I read over to Judge Kerwin what it seemed appropriate for him to say. He was very pleasant and unassuming. Had never been in the Cabinet Council before so we walked in together. I told him in advance about invitations to Aylesworth and White and who might be expected in the Cabinet.

"There were present: Ilsley, St. Laurent, MacKinnon, McCann, Abbott, Claxton and Bertrand. As I recall the seating, Ilsley was in his accustomed seat to the right of the Prime Minister's chair. Abbott was next to him. Further along, immediately opposite, was MacKinnon. On the other side,

Bertrand and McCann. St. Laurent gave up his seat for me. He was seated to my right when I took a seat to the right of the Deputy Governor General.

"In a few words, I explained to my colleagues the purpose of the presence of the Deputy Governor General who had a personal message sent through to the Governor General which the King wished to have given personally to the Privy Council. Mr. Justice Kerwin then read the statement, a copy of which will be in my papers.

"When Mr. Justice Kerwin concluded, I thanked him for the message and said I thought he knew all the members of the Government. Mentioned each one in turn. He made a few rather pleasant remarks saying it was quite a privilege to him to meet them all. He had never seen the Council Chamber before and it was a pleasure to be participating in an event of historic significance.

"I then left with Mr. Justice Kerwin. Told him to keep the statement which he had read which he seemed interested to retain as being historic. After he had made the statement in Council, I signed it as I would a minute of Council and he put his signature where the Governor General would sign – as approving. There was no precedent for this but it seemed wise to establish it as a record."

The Prime Minister welcomed the prospect of attending the wedding and visiting the Continent before the ceremony but he was firmly resolved at this point not to become involved in any formal meetings while in London. He received word in Cabinet on July 31 that the wedding would take place on November 20 and told his colleagues "I supposed I would be invited and would have to go to the wedding. I would bet anything to nothing that they would work in some kind of a conference of Prime Ministers or Imperial Conference. There was nothing I disliked as much or which was so trying or exhausting each time I had to take issue with the British Government itself in their own Council Chamber."

Once the date for the wedding was set Mackenzie King began making plans for his trip. On September 30 he "had an interview of some length with Sir Alexander Clutterbuck in regard to a memo from the British Government which seemed to involve – while not a full meeting – at least a partial meeting of Prime Ministers. I told him I would agree to informal, individual conversations but would not agree to attend any meeting at which proceedings were to be recorded. That I was not in a position to discuss under a general heading of European conditions anything involving defence and trade, etc. I was not taking experts with me and would make no commitment without opportunity to consult with colleagues. I mentioned I was going to Holland the week prior to that of the wedding. Would be remaining over for a short time after. Would welcome opportunity of getting information but said there must be no misunderstanding about what might be regarded as participation in a meeting of Prime Ministers. Prime Ministers of neither Australia nor New Zealand nor India nor Pakistan can be present.

"I made clear I was not in a position to undertake any heavy obligations at present. Sir Alexander said he understood and would advise the British Government accordingly. . . .

"What annoys me is the way the British begin by saying one thing and end up by implying another as for example not having full meeting where they should say no formal meeting, etc."

There were many things to cheer the Prime Minister during the latter half of 1947. He was delighted by the Liberal candidate's overwhelming victory in the Halifax by-election on July 14. "Taken in connection with the victories in Richelieu-Verchères just before Christmas, and Montreal Cartier just before Easter, this victory at the moment of the conclusion of the session, when Members are leaving for the next six months" he felt had "redeemed the three losses which took place last year and which, had they been victories instead of losses, with the present results, would have more or less completely broken up the strength, certainly, of some of the third parties and would have resulted in men from the third parties coming over to our side, and making perfectly secure the Government's position for the next couple of years.

"Today's victory in Halifax places an additional obligation to stay in public life for a while longer, but I must get some more rest if I am to do this. It makes me happy to think of how these results will read in the U.K. and the U.S. as well as in Canada. It is a marvellous thing on top of the record of the Liberal party in office at a moment when the world is in the state of unrest that it is at this time."

After Bridges' death on August 10, Mackenzie King lost no time in trying to arrange to fill the vacancy from New Brunswick in the House and in the Cabinet. Despite the party's success in the Halifax by-election, he was far from optimistic about the prospects in New Brunswick and about the political effect of the negotiations with Newfoundland in the Maritimes. At the Cabinet meeting on August 14, there was "a long discussion on Newfoundland matters. Mr. St. Laurent reported the point at which he . . . and McCann had reached with the Newfoundland delegates, indicating the extent of the undertakings we would have to give in order to meet what the Newfoundland delegation believed would alone enable them to carry their people in favour of the federation.

"On hearing from Mr. St. Laurent that the delegation would like to make the suggested terms known as soon as possible, and that probably within the next couple of weeks at the latest, I raised at once the situation which had arisen because of the death of Mr. Bridges. I pointed out that we no longer had in the Cabinet a direct link with Mr. McNair, the Premier of New Brunswick, and that I felt a very serious situation would arise if the Newfoundland federation became the subject of debate in the by-election in York-Sunbury.

"I strongly advocated bringing on the by-election at the earliest date possible. . . . I said I thought we would have to let McNair know confidentially what was being proposed and ascertain whether he would be prepared to support our Government in its proposals if the question came up in the by-election.

"St. Laurent was a bit hesitant about this, saying that the question of the federation of Newfoundland should be settled on its merits. McCann supported this view, saying we had to look ahead and see how the future would view what we had done. Ilsley, too, presented a similar point of view.

"This caused me to speak very frankly about just how the matter was to be dealt with and who was to take responsibility for the course that might be decided upon. St. Laurent had said that he was sure the Gallup poll would show that 80% of the country was for Newfoundland coming in. I replied that was perfectly true, until they knew the terms. Once the terms were known, the different provinces would begin to take exception to them. This, more especially, as St. Laurent had pointed out we would have to give terms better to Newfoundland than we were giving to New Brunswick. We would be asked why we were treating strangers better than our own people and supporters. It was suggested that the matter might be met in some other way, but everyone admitted that Macdonald, as well as McNair, might prove very difficult in agreeing to the terms being suggested. . . . They all would question the terms. We would have utter chaos in Canada, and the Government would be beaten, and we would be further away from federation with Newfoundland than ever. Unless we could make perfectly sure of winning the forthcoming by-election, I felt it would be much better to let the present delegation go back and tell their people that we could not agree to their terms.

"There was then some further debate, and I thought it well to put the situation as a practical problem clearly before the Cabinet. I then said: now let us consider the situation. We have the by-election. Who is going to handle this by-election? Mr. Ilsley will have to take that responsibility. He is at present the only Minister in the Maritimes. Did Quebec ministers think they could carry the by-election, and they said no. I then asked who was to carry it? I suggested myself, with Fogo, to take some responsibility and work with Mr. Ilsley, but if the question of the federation of New-foundland would come up and the terms of the Maritime provinces discussed, Ilsley would be left alone in this. I then said we ought to go a step further and ask how are we going to get this matter through Parliament? . . .

"I then said that I was calling a meeting in September to ask my colleagues to let me know the date which should be settled for a convention. That I might ask my party to select a successor. I wanted a decision in September, so that I could plan accordingly. I then said I had not the heart to ask Ilsley or St. Laurent to continue for another year as they had gone much beyond anything intended, but that I must tell Council frankly if they were both out before the New Year it would be just folly for me to attempt to carry through another session of Parliament.

"I then asked pointedly who was going to handle this Newfoundland matter in the Commons. That better be carefully thought out before any pronouncements were publicly made as to what terms were being proposed. This seemed to have a real sobering effect in the discussion and to bring the Ministers down to earth instead of looking at some future which may turn out to be in the approach a mere mirage. I pointed out how hopeless it was to do anything that Mr. McNair himself would not become responsible for."

St. Laurent then suggested that McNair should be invited to come to Ottawa to discuss the political situation, both the question of a candidate in the by-election and the Newfoundland proposals. "Some colleagues thought that McNair himself wished to come to Ottawa, with a view to going later on the Bench. I said that I could not believe but that he would wish to stay where he is and, if it was his wish to go to the Bench, to go from there.

"I found, too, that some of the Ministers had discovered Bridges' brother would make a very good candidate. I told them I had the highest opinion of him personally and even spoke to him about the possibility without consulting anyone. He had said that McNair would settle everything. . . .

"I pointed out to the Cabinet that Hanson had held the seat for twenty years and that the man whom Bridges had defeated had since become political organizer for the province and had things pretty well in his own hands. I said the constituency was probably very corrupt and that the Tories would make every attempt to win the seat, and to lose that seat would be very unfortunate. All agreed that there was nothing to be gained by postponing the by-election. I agreed to ask McNair to come as soon as he could.

"It seems to me that the Newfoundland business is going to be almost impossible for us to put over, with the Government in the shape it is – a majority none too certain, and the provinces at sixes and sevens in their attitude towards the Ottawa Government. I think all of the Ministers have begun to see that now.

"Mr. St. Laurent summed up the situation by saying he thought the only thing he could do was to continue discussions with the Newfoundland delegates, get to the point where they agreed, and then ourselves decide whether we could offer them those particular terms. If no, let them know and have the matter dropped.

"Losing Bridges at this moment is one of the hardest hits the Government has had. It may mean failure in bringing the Newfoundland matter to a satisfactory conclusion and also mean the loss of a seat. However, whatever it means, we have to face the situation and go ahead and meet it the best we can. It certainly shows up the weak position in which the Administration is in regard to its representation as it at present exists in the Maritimes. No one dislikes organization matters more than Ilsley, and knows less about them. Wishart Robertson might be of some help, but he has not been over-enthusiastic."

Premier McNair came to Ottawa on August 25 and the Prime Minister met with him, St. Laurent, Ilsley, Howe and Abbott. He "told McNair we would all be delighted to have him come into our Government but he felt he had his duty to New Brunswick and did not think he should come into the federal field at this time. He may be seeking a Judgeship in New Brunswick later on. He had canvassed the situation as to candidates. Admitted quite frankly that the best of all candidates would be Taylor, a member of his own Government but feels it would be unfair to Taylor himself to press him to enter the federal field as it might cost him heavily on his own farm and business. Also McNair looks to Taylor as a successor for the Premiership should he leave at any time but he says Taylor could be forced to come. We could get no better candidate.

"He spoke next of Milton Gregg, former Sergeant-at-Arms and Principal of New Brunswick University. He had seen Gregg who apparently is willing to come if no other acceptable candidate can be found though he would prefer to remain at the University. McNair says that we can win with either of these two candidates though a by-election in New Brunswick is sure to be costly. We might, however, with either of these men taken in the Cabinet be able to get an acclamation. He feels that both are better than Bridges, the brother of the late Frank Bridges who, however, he thinks, would make an excellent candidate at Moncton at the next federal elections. He is not too sure that we could win in this by-election with Bridges. Both St. Laurent and I pressed rather strongly for Taylor on the score of the need to give the Maritimes the best man available, outstanding leader in relation to the problems of the future. I thought McNair showed great perspicacity in the way he spoke of the different men and situations. His manner, moreover, is much freer than it has been previously. He has a degree of confidence and a much pleasanter air than I have known him to have at any time.

"We discussed a little the question of Newfoundland. McNair was of the view that generally speaking, the Maritimes would favour bringing Newfoundland in but, if the terms were to be better than those given the other provinces, might raise serious issues. He was very strongly of the view that it would be well to avoid that issue being raised."

At the Cabinet meeting that day, Mackenzie King reviewed the discussion which had taken place in Cabinet on August 14. He also "spoke of the possibility of merchants of Newfoundland using their money to win their point by defeating the Government's candidate in York-Sunbury which I think is true. Also the folly of attempting to debate an issue of the kind with arguments being used in Newfoundland which would be used against us in the Maritimes. The only place for debate, I said, was in Parliament where our opponents could be met in arguments in the open and bound to answer, and not on the hustings.

"I think all came to feel that it was well to get McNair's impression as to what was desirable. McNair made it quite clear that he thought it would be a great mistake to have this question dealt with pending the election. It was practically agreed that St. Laurent and others would let Bradley of the Newfoundland delegation know that until we got a Minister for the province of New Brunswick who would be responsible, we would have to let the matter await final decision."

When the Ministers met the Premier again after Cabinet, he argued strongly for Milton Gregg as a candidate and predicted that the constituency could be carried by a majority of between one and two thousand votes. Fearful of Gregg's lack of political experience, the Prime Minister made some further efforts next day to convine Taylor to run. On August 29 McNair telephoned to say that Taylor would not accept nomination but that Gregg was willing to run. Mackenzie King arranged to have Gregg come to Ottawa on September 2 to be sworn in as Minister of Fisheries. News of his appointment had leaked to the press and some Liberals charged that the new Minister was really a Conservative. Gregg told the Prime Minister "during the day that his father had been a strong Conservative. He had never taken any active part in politics. His appointment as Sergeant-at-Arms was simply due to his being a V.C. That his sympathies had always been Liberal and he had felt our Government had the right policy toward the army and toward the country. He was also liberal in his own attitude – liberal with a small 'l,' and was certainly in favour of our Government."

At the Cabinet meeting on September 11, the question of Newfoundland was discussed again. According to Mackenzie King, "everyone fell in line eventually with my view that the truth of the situation should be given as the reasons for discontinuing discussions for the present, namely, that they concerned New Brunswick.

"We did not wish to continue anything until we had a Minister from that province present in Council. I could hardly understand the wish of St. Laurent and some of the others to not let the Newfoundland people break off at this time. It begins, however, now to be apparent that whatever we agree to as reasonable, they will want many more things in addition, etc. It will be all to the good if it became increasingly apparent that nothing came of the negotiations at present. It may be infinitely better to have nothing done until Newfoundland has a responsible government of its own. We are dealing with one section of the people only."

Mackenzie King's enthusiasm for the project was certainly not increased when he read a memorandum on September 28 outlining the proposed terms of the federal offer to Newfoundland. He felt "that we were giving Newfoundland pretty much everything that she wanted without adequately weighing what Canada would be getting in return. I also felt strongly that we should give no guarantee of the time at which our decisions would be made known to the Newfoundland Government." Next morning, he had a telephone conversation with St. Laurent about "the Newfoundland report which he [St. Laurent] had gone over and eliminated everything that made for a committal. Spoke of an article in the Gazette which was mischievous to which he proposed to reply this afternoon. Went over what he intended to say. I cautioned strongly against saying anything that might lead the provinces to assume we were not to consult them; also anything that might give the electors of York-Sunbury a chance to feel that we were determined to get through the annexation of Newfoundland, once the election was over. I told him that I believed New Brunswick was dead against Newfoundland coming in on practically any terms and it would only help Sansom [General Sansom was the Conservative candidate in York-Sunbury] if anything were said which indicated we were keen on having Newfoundland brought in. He agreed to make wholly clear that there was no commitment of any kind.

"I also spoke against giving any assurance to the delegates that the Government's decision would be made known at a specific date. I told him at most to say that it would be given as expeditiously as circumstances would permit after Cabinet had a chance to consider what was a mere factual report."

In Cabinet on October 1, the Prime Minister "made it clear that the Cabinet had not yet considered the report of the Committee; also pointed out it was inadvisable we should discuss the matter in the Cabinet until Newfoundland itself had passed upon what we were proposing. St. Laurent pointed out that the opposition might move a resolution that the terms were not satisfactory – either too much or too little. That is true but I doubted if they would. The real danger will be the Maritime provinces becoming aroused when they see the terms and some objection being raised to any terms being offered without further consideration of Maritime claims.

"I was glad to get Gardiner's strong support on the view that the British Government should take our terms as those on which the referendum would take place. That we should not discuss matters in Parliament until after the referendum.

"I took strongly the view that we had gone as far as we could be expected to go, virtually confining ourselves to their terms if they were acceptable to Newfoundland. If they were not acceptable, the matter would end there. If acceptable, the Government would then stake its existence on putting them through. I am sure if the Newfoundland Government accepted the terms, the Canadian feeling generally would favour their acceptance."

Gregg's victory in York-Sunbury on October 20 with a majority of over 3,000 votes, "a source of great relief and joy" to Mackenzie King, removed one major obstacle to the negotiations and, at the Cabinet meeting on October 28, the "discussion on Newfoundland passed off very pleasantly and with complete unanimity. Understanding being the people of Newfoundland would have to approve terms of basis of settlement before resolution respecting same would be introduced in our House. Gregg reported that Premier McNair was agreeable to what was being proposed. Ilsley was present at the meeting."

A document summarizing the federal government's proposals, "Proposed Arrangements for the Entry of Newfoundland into Confederation" was submitted to the Newfoundland government the next day and made public on November 6. Under the terms, the island, including the territory of Labrador, was guaranteed status as a province and appropriate representation in the Senate and House of Commons. All federal welfare services were to be extended to Newfoundland and the federal government agreed to take over the island's railway and Gander airport, both of which operated at a substantial loss. Canada undertook to assume the bulk of the colony's debt, $63 million; Newfoundland would retain the accumulated surplus of some $30 million to use for development purposes and the maintenance and improvement of various provincial public services.

Annual statutory subsidies of $180,000 and 80 cents per capita, together with a flat payment of $1,100,000 in lieu of grants made to the Maritime provinces, were proposed. If Newfoundland agreed to rent its major tax fields to the federal government after confederation, it would be entitled to receive a minimum of $6,200,000 annually, including the statutory subsidies. In addition, a series of transitional grants were promised, amounting to $3,500,000 for the first three years, scaling down to $350,000 in the twelfth year. Finally, the federal government agreed to appoint a royal commission within eight years after confederation to review the terms. In his letter which accompanied the formal terms, the Prime Minister made it quite clear that the federal government would not consider any amendments to the offer which would impose larger financial responsibilities on Canada. In the National Convention which had reconvened in St. John's on October 10, the Canadian offer touched off a bitter debate which raged for the next three months between the Confederate Association and the Responsible Government League.

An event which gave Mackenzie King great pleasure in September was a visit to Kitchener and Waterloo County. He received an enthusiastic welcome on September 8 and "was astonished to find myself feeling much more belonging to Kitchener and Waterloo County than either to Ottawa, in which I have lived for the last forty-seven years, or Toronto. Indeed I have nothing like the same sense. I felt infinitely more at home in Kitchener than I do in the Capital, that is as to being a part of a community. My life in Ottawa has been really more a part of government and special work with Dominion-wide and world associations. The other was different. It was like a large home life." During the second day of his visit, he spent some time at his old home, "Woodside," and with personal friends.

An honour which gave him even greater satisfaction was his election as a Bencher of the Law Society of Upper Canada. In a letter from the Society's treasurer on June 24, he had been informed that his election would recognize "one my long years as Prime Minister, the other my father's long association with the Law Society. This delights me very much as I know how it would have delighted the heart of my father. It is a great honour to be a bencher of the Law Society of Upper Canada, as well as Bencher of Gray's Inn in London, England." On August 13, he wrote: "What I had not known and never realized or thought of till I read it in the letter was that I am to be made a barrister-at-law, admitted to the bar of Ontario. I confess it frightened me a little when I read this. I did not feel I merited anything so great." Again, he thought of his father. "How marvellous this is, his wish fulfilled and what has been perhaps the wish I have felt most deeply to share with him membership in his profession fulfilled." The description of the ceremonies at Osgoode Hall on September 18 filled five pages of Mackenzie King's diary and, for the rest of his life, he regarded his admission to the Ontario bar as the greatest honour he had ever received.

The most serious problem the government faced during the autumn of 1947 was a drastic decline in Canada's foreign exchange reserves. One contributing factor was heavy drawings on the loan to the United Kingdom and other foreign aid appropriations, reflecting the slow rate of European recovery. In addition, the decision taken in 1946 to restore the Canadian dollar to parity with the American had contributed to a sharp reduction in the inflow of capital from the United States while a high rate of domestic capital and consumer spending caused large increases in Canadian imports of American goods. Canada's current account deficit in transactions with the United States doubled during 1947 to a total of $1,134 million and, by the end of the year, foreign exchange reserves had dropped to $500 million. For help in meeting the problem, the Canadian government first turned to the United Kingdom, herself suffering serious balance of payments difficulties. On May 13 the Prime Minister had reviewed the situation with Abbott, Towers and Gordon. He had noted that "Towers is to visit England tomorrow and wished to lay before me the position he proposed to take as to the desirability of the British Government helping us in the matter of our need for more in the way of American dollars, either by agreeing not to use our credit for some time to come or continuing it only for a certain time. This to avoid the necessity of placing restrictions on trade from the United States to Canada, which would discriminate between trade from the United States and trade from the other countries. I agreed that the latter would be most unfortunate both in relation to the [trade] conference at Geneva and the future relations between Canada and the United States. The whole problem is extremely intricate. I could not but be impressed by what Towers said as to the very serious condition of affairs which may arise two years hence unless some of these matters are straightened out. The United States is taking a very generous attitude in the matter of spending millions abroad. It would enable more American dollars to be used in purchasing commodities from Canada. . . ."

General Marshall's speech at Harvard University on June 5, in which he invited the nations of western Europe to draft a plan for economic reconstruction underwritten by the United States, held out some prospect for an eventual solution of Canada's short-term balance of payments problems if the traditional surplus with the United Kingdom and Europe could be restored and used to offset the growing deficit in transactions with the United States. Another hopeful sign was the establishment in

July of the Committee of European Economic Cooperation and the completion in September of a four-year economic recovery programme, both essential prerequisites to the further development of the Marshall Plan. On August 7 Towers and Pearson dined with the Prime Minister at Kingsmere. Towers said, according to Mackenzie King, that "we have moved much more rapidly towards the crisis – financial – than anticipated. What was expected by him and others in this circle for next March now comes about Sept. necessitating some import restrictions and a loan of several hundred millions from the U.S. I could see he was leading up to a possible special session [of Parliament] . . . but I spoke strongly against this. He thought if we got the loan, the special session might not be needed. I pointed out it would have an alarming effect in country and might precipitate harmful discussion in parlt. He wanted my authority to talk with an assistant of Snyder [Secretary of the Treasury of the United States] . . . or Snyder himself before he goes to Eng. to prepare him for possibility of our needing a loan, that preparations might be made for such a request. I gave it with understanding Abbott approved at end of week. I pointed out, once we borrowed, we would find it increasingly difficult to loan abroad or make further advances for relief, etc. This may not be a misfortune. The sooner the country or more the Gov't realizes that we can't go on spending at will the better. It looks, with Br. restrictions, etc. as if a breakdown all round might come in the winter season or early spring of next year. The war has made nations, except the U.S. and ourselves, largely bankrupt and this has to be realized. . . ."

On August 18 the British High Commissioner brought a message to the Prime Minister regarding Britain's financial situation. "The Cabinet has taken a decision regarding currency matters which means unilateral treatment and which Clutterbuck himself privately was inclined to doubt the wisdom of, specially as [Sir William] Eady had just reached Washington and was to meet the Secretary of the Treasury, this morning, to see what would come from further negotiations with the States. It is all very involved but what it resembles in the matter of Britain's supply of American dollars is a run on the bank by other countries that wish to get American dollars. It threatens to have a serious result in many parts of the world. I am afraid this winter is going to be exceedingly difficult for the British people in the matter of getting supplies of food and necessities of life."

The Canadian foreign exchange problem became acute just before Mackenzie King left for Europe and just as the multilateral trade negotiations in Geneva were concluding. On October 16 Abbott showed him a memorandum from Towers on the "alarming position of our gold reserves." The Bank of Canada Governor forecast the need for restrictions on imports from the United States and possibly on travel abroad. "A line of policy," the Prime Minister wrote, "in large part just the reverse of what, as Liberals, we would wish to follow. In addition, there is the agreement that is being reached at Geneva which may be helpful toward developing multilateral treaties, insuring greater freedom of trade. It is all exceedingly secret. My own feeling is that Clayton's resignation [from the Truman cabinet] in the U.S. at this time is not due so much to his wife's health as it is to his unwillingness to yield anything to Britain re lowering of United States tariffs without complete sacrifice of British preferences, and that the American agitation is not prepared to go that far in breaking relations – undoing all the work that has been accomplished to date in seeking to bring about lowering of tariffs, etc. I shall know when Hector McKinnon [the chief Canadian negotiator] arrives from Geneva tomorrow just what has been secured and the time at which the announcement is to be made.

"This all led, as I expected it would, to Abbott's statement that it would be absolutely necessary to have a session of Parliament before Christmas. He thought of a special session early in December. The Government will try to reach finality on all essential decisions before I leave for England on the 30th. I can see this is going to be an almost impossible task. It may even mean that I shall have to, at the last moment, cancel the trip to Belgium, Paris and Holland and go by the Queen Mary instead of the Elizabeth. That, however, I think, I should avoid if at all possible in view of the jam  that will come later on. What it will mean at the other end is that my stay in England will have to be shortened to a very few days and that I will have to return on the New Amsterdam instead of on the Queen Mary, a week or ten days later. . . . The third alternative is that the House would meet without my being present, letting St. Laurent take on the task of Acting Prime Minister. This I think is also possible and may be advisable. It will let some of the others see what is involved in arranging for a session. It is going to be difficult, however, for whoever has the task to get the Speech from the Throne prepared, and all our policies in readiness for a meeting of Parliament.

"Abbott was strongly for a special session. He thought matters could be jammed through because of a desire of the parties to get home for Christmas. He thought we should carry on the day after Christmas, if need be, so as to get through by the new year. My present view is against that. If a session is to be held, I would have it a regular session. Opening in December with an adjournment over the Christmas Season into at least the middle of January, provided we can get through the special legislation before Christmas. This would mean continuing the debate on the address in January. Getting down to business in February. It would all work toward an earlier adjournment of Parliament, possibly by July 1, and perhaps lead to future sessions being opened in the Autumn as they used to be instead of the beginning of the New Year. This, however, is all very sudden and I confess the mere thought of what it means of pressure made me feel a bit older almost instantly. Thank God, I have been protecting my health by staying at Kingsmere as much as I have. I wish, however, I had seen more of the out of doors in the course of the summer days. The point, however, that I feel now most strongly is that I must bend my will to the tasks of Parliament, first, foremost, and as largely as possible, altogether. Letting no personal desires stand in the way of doing my utmost to make my contribution to the great problems that are facing the world today. I have got most matters cleared up to date."

Four days later, on October 20, the Prime Minister received Hector McKinnon and John Deutsch at Kingsmere to review the results of the negotiations at Geneva. "I have not spent a more interesting day in the course of my years in office in so far as getting a clear and complete picture of all important negotiations and problems of world significance. For two hours, I listened to McKinnon explain the nature of the negotiations. What they involved in the way of concessions by Canada and gains by Canada in agreements which cover seventeen nations in all as contrasted with the noble eighteen or sixteen which helped to defeat the Reciprocity Agreements in Sir Wilfrid's day. I was genuinely amazed at the outcome of the negotiations. They are much more far reaching than any reciprocity agreements in the past. In many ways, really epoch-making agreements since they may lead to greater freedom of trade throughout Europe and America and Canada which are bound also to influence other countries of the world. I shall not try to record what is set forth in the agreements since the matter is so wholly secret. McKinnon has brought with him only one copy from Geneva. He and Deutsch up to the present time have matters practically exclusively in their hands. They came to report to me before taking up matters with either the Minister of Finance or the Minister of Justice or any member of the Cabinet in order to have my reaction as to the best course to be pursued.

"I agreed it would be wiser to have the entire Cabinet told at one and the same time and that beginning tomorrow – not to have any committee of Council to consider the matter first. The agreements suggested have to be accepted all in all or not at all.

"I 'phoned Abbott later in the day. He said he was relieved to know that I thought it best not to have any committee. After discussing the tariff agreements, I was told of an article which appeared in the New York Times of yesterday which indicated a leak from the United States and which rather suggested that they had won a victory and that we were doing away with fixed margins [between preferential and most-favoured-nation tariff rates] and [Commonwealth] preferences. This may prove embarrassing but it is a hurdle that will have to be gotten over. Most unfortunate, however, that the leak should come just at this time. It is certain to give rise to many questions in the British House when it meets a short time from now."

To him "what McKinnon and Deutsch have achieved along with their staffs is truly amazing. It presents a programme that will take all of next session and which is one that we could sweep the country on were we to encounter too much opposition to it. It made me almost wish that I had said nothing about not leading the party through another general election. However, if this agreement goes through, it will be ending a session of Parliament in a blaze of glory and putting the Liberal party once again far in the van. I believe it is a programme we can carry out."

Mackenzie King was particularly pleased "to hear McKinnon say that he would rather have negotiations before all the Cabinet at once with myself in the chair than any course that could be pursued. This indicates the confidence he has in my management of negotiations of the kind. It was most interesting to see how much our talk today revived of the negotiations of the Reciprocity Tariff Agreements with the President [Roosevelt]. If these new agreements go through, it will be the largest achievement on trade matters ever put through in the history of our country and indeed, in some respects, in negotiations between any countries in the world.

"I was interested in hearing McKinnon and Deutsch both say that though Canada was a small country, we were looked on as one of the leaders in world negotiations. . . . McKinnon stressed it was my letter to Attlee telling him that I hoped negotiations would not be permitted to break down that caused this change in the attitude of the British at the end and saved the day. He said Australia and New Zealand and Britain had all been keeping quiet on the question of fixed margins. Finally were not going to allow anything which meant sacrificing fixed margins to go through. My telegram caused the word to come from Attlee that negotiations were not to be allowed to fail. There were . . . [two occasions] when it looked as though everything was up. Once with disagreement between Britain and the United States on preference matters, and another time between Australia and United States. However, there is now no question about agreements having been reached."

In the Cabinet meeting on October 21, the Prime Minister reported, "there was a fine attendance . . . to hear the outcome of Geneva discussions. I counted seventeen Ministers in all including myself. Had chairs moved back to allow McKinnon and Deutsch along with [Norman] Robertson to sit on the sofa while McKinnon outlined to the Cabinet the results of the discussions which began formally in Geneva in March last and continued to within the day that McKinnon left for Canada. The last agreements reached re doing away with fixed margins were brought to the plane in typewritten form by one of his staff as he was leaving for Canada. He arrived on Saturday last. It was, therefore, not possible to give Council an earlier account of the agreements. Twice in the last little while they almost fell through completely.

"I outlined to the Cabinet the beginnings of the discussion and negotiations. Explained why we were getting the first full information; also that I, alone, had up to that moment, any knowledge of what had been finally arrived at. In all probability, the agreements would have to be signed on the 28th of this month. Made public about the 18th of November. Let the Cabinet know they would have to be agreed to all in all or not at all. Also they affected seventeen nations in agreement with ourselves.

"McKinnon began speaking about 11.30. Spoke without any interruption from anyone, except an occasional word from myself, to keep the sequence before the Cabinet, until one o'clock, when we adjourned till 3.

"It was a quarter past when I came in. He continued for another half hour. Then Deutsch spoke for another three-quarters of an hour. Also without interruption. Both he and McKinnon made an excellent presentation. I congratulated and thanked them individually on behalf of the Government. Stated that we felt we could not have been better represented in the negotiations and complimented them on their presentation. They have really achieved a marvellous result.

"As Ilsley is likely to be more affected than any other Minister, I was careful to invite him to speak and to mention any matters he was concerned about. He had previously asked by what authority we had done away with fixed margins. McKinnon took the matter on his own shoulders at once saying he had to decide in an instant what it was wisest to do and acting on his knowledge of discussions in tariff negotiations at Washington, had stated what he believed to be the policy of the Government and what he was sure the Ministers would support.

"I followed McKinnon immediately by stating he had set forth accurately what had always been our policy. Backed him up one hundred percent. Later when Ilsley spoke, he referred to the agreement as a whole and said there perhaps was nothing to do. He would have difficulty perhaps in making clear why of all others, his interests should have been the ones to be sacrificed but I think he felt as we did that the changes that are taking place in Europe made the step wise and that what had been done in other particulars had helped to make the situation equal to, if not better than what it would have been, had it remained what it was.

"Howe said he did not think that a single manufacturing interest would suffer at all with the changes that were being made. It was apparent that the agriculturists ought materially to gain by the wider markets achieved. I think others felt as I did that if there was an attempt to block proceedings in Parliament, an appeal to the country would bring the present administration back to office. It really was as impressive a meeting of the Cabinet as I have known in the years that I have been at the table."

Consideration of the looming exchange crisis resumed in the Cabinet on October 24. Mackenzie King noted that "the time of Council was taken up in the morning by a recital by Abbott of the position of our reserves, rapidity with which they are being depleted and the need, in order to restore our purchasing power, to devise measures of trade restriction against the United States and to keep down the excess of spending in Canada in directions which are helping to create a flow of our money to the United States. It is a grim picture. The measures required the very opposite of those which, as Liberals, one would wish to advocate, but apparently are more or less inevitable. Great care will have to be taken to see that they are not regarded as and do not become protectionist measures.

"The afternoon was devoted to going over what Abbott had discussed with officials and receiving from them reasons, etc. for the course proposed. There were seventeen Ministers besides myself present, MacKinnon and Gardiner, I think, the only absentees. The experts included Robertson, McKinnon, Deutsch, [K. L.] Taylor of Finance, Towers and Gordon, of the Bank of Canada. Discussion lasted from 2.30 till 6.00 P.M. A most interesting afternoon."

It was announced on October 30 that the regular session of Parliament would meet in early December rather than in January of the new year.

Measures to meet the exchange crisis were announced by the Minister of Finance on November 17 while the Prime Minister was in London. Under the authority of the Foreign Exchange Control Act, the new restrictions were imposed by order-in-council the next day. A limit of $150 per person per annum was imposed on funds for pleasure travel in the American dollar area and a special 25 per cent excise tax was placed on a number of consumer durable goods to discourage imports of such commodities from the United States. Imports of some products were prohibited except in cases of hardship and others were made subject to quota restrictions.

Sweeping authority to control imports of capital goods was vested in the Minister of Reconstruction and Supply, C. D. Howe. In addition, the government arranged for a loan of $300 million from the Export-Import Bank in Washington.

Ironically, Abbott's statement immediately followed a radio broadcast from London in which the Prime Minister announced the results of the negotiations in Geneva and the signing by Canada of the General Agreement on Tariffs and Trade on October 30. During the negotiations, Canada agreed to reduce rates or make other concessions on some 1,000 tariff items. In return, 75 per cent of Canada's export trade was guaranteed better access to foreign markets. Of greatest importance to Canada were the negotiations with the United States. Approximately 70 per cent of Canadian exports to the United States were expected to benefit from tariff reductions and rates on a number of other commodities were bound against increase. Canada agreed to reduce or bind rates on 70 per cent of American imports, on the basis of 1939 trade statistics. With Canada's concurrence, fixed margins of preference on trade among the Commonwealth countries were ended although most important Commonwealth preferences in the Canadian tariff were retained.

Meanwhile, Mackenzie King's planning for his trip had been complicated by another communication from the King. After the Cabinet meeting on October 21, he had been handed a letter from Lascelles which he thought "might have to do with the Royal Wedding. To my great surprise, it was to the effect that the King wished to confer on me at the time of the wedding, the honour of the Order of Merit which is from himself personally. Not on the advice of any Minister, and which is limited to a very few. As a matter of fact, the Order which was founded by King Edward VII and which cannot exceed twenty-four in all. . . . It does not carry any title with it and the persons who have been thus honoured in the past are by no means limited to men who have been prominent in public affairs but include literary men like Trevelyan. John Morley, I think, received the distinction as an historian. Lord Oxford and Churchill; also Lloyd George; Smuts, I think, has been given the same honour. It is perhaps the most distinguished of all the Honours in the British Empire. Naturally I have been occasioned much concern over what it is best to do. At the moment of receiving the letter, the feeling uppermost was to decline the honour lest the stand I have been taking on Titles might be misunderstood. Also what I feel about one person being honoured, numbers more deserving are passed over. There is, however, another side which I shall have to consider very carefully. It is what might be owing to the King himself at the time of the marriage of his daughter and to our long relationship. What is owing to the memory of my grandfather and my father and mother. It will be a remarkable rounding out of the circle which links the reward placed on Mackenzie's head by the Crown, with the highest award from the Crown to his grandson who has been carrying on his work.

"Much, too, is owing to the names of my Father and Mother. I asked myself what they would have wished. I am quite sure that each of them would have desired not to accept a title but to accept this special honour from the Crown. I would be the only one in Canada having the distinction which is given for eminent services and certainly having been Prime Minister longer than any Prime Minister in the British Empire, it might well be felt that a mark of this kind which would bring distinction to Canada in this connection is something that I should also consider. I can honestly say, however, that my thoughts, singular as it may appear, went later [more] to my little dog Pat II than anything else. I felt that that little creature deserved an O.M. a thousand times more than I do myself and then came the thought of the other little Pat who also merited more than I do, and the loyalty of his nature, fidelity and all that counts for most."

"I keep thinking increasingly of what may be due to the name of my grandfather and my father and mother, and indeed also to the Liberal party," the Prime Minister wrote the next day. "This action on the part of the King would be a very strong answer to all that the Tory party has sought to do to monopolize Royalty and to seek to make out that my grandfather was disloyal and that I have been anti-British, etc. My stand with Sir Wilfrid in 1917, my stand on the conscription issue, etc. – to all of this would be an answer of about the only kind which the Tory party would really have to recognize. They would find it difficult to blame the King. This is really an important consideration in the light of history.

"I had thought after receiving the Honours that have come since the dinner at Downing Street, with all that has come from Greece, from our own M.P.s, etc., Law Society, welcome in North Waterloo, etc., thought that nothing further could possibly be bestowed in the way of honour. This would be truly a crowning event and might well be considered in relation to my giving up the leadership of the party and Prime Ministership next year.

"The King and Queen might well think that I had been ungracious to have declined such an Honour extended at such a time. The country would be no wiser until after I had passed away. They would then see that I had declined to accept any honour from the Crown. Whether this would be viewed as something worthy on my part or something that might be regarded as continuing a certain churlishness toward Royalty, etc., is questionable."

Mackenzie King was still pondering the problem on October 23 but felt that he "must not delay beyond tonight to send some word to the King as to acceptance of the Order of Merit. The more I have thought of the matter, the more strongly I have felt I should not decline but should accept the Award. I keep thinking of the names of my grandfather, my father and mother and my own career and what certain elements of the Tory party and some venomous enemies of our own party, have sought to do to belittle and destroy what has been done. I think, for example, of the kind of inscription placed on the bells at Niagara which my Liberal colleagues and friends have been too indifferent to have removed and which Drew and his Government have allowed to remain as they were and which seemingly some of my own colleagues were too indifferent to have removed.

"The Royal recognition by the King of the Order of Merit at this stage of my own career will give something to them which cannot be gainsaid. It is not an Honour that brings one into the category of aristocracy except to be in the aristocracy of knowledge, but what is finer, it is the aristocracy of public service.

"The record speaks for itself and to have it as an expression of confidence on the part of both the people and the Crown is something that makes the circle complete. I have told J. [Mrs. Patteson] of what has been proposed. She feels very strongly I should accept. That it would be quite wrong to decline. My decision, however, has been made apart altogether from influences without, though having R. and P. both take the same view, knowing their attitude toward matters of the kind, confirms me that I have exercised the right judgment in the decision I have reached. Accordingly, tonight, I drafted a telegram to Sir Alan Lascelles to say that an affirmative reply to his letter of the 17th was being sent by air bag."

Before leaving Ottawa, the Prime Minister dined with the Governor General on October 29. They were "quite alone – a delightful little dinner party in the small blue room. Talked about embarrassments of dining with others present, particularly formal A.D.C.s. . . . Told His Excellency about the proposed Honour. He again spoke most appreciatively. Talked a good deal of Churchill. Told of the night he and Eisenhower and Smuts and I spent on the train before we crossed over the Channel. Asked the Governor General about statement for morning press about Patton attacking Montgomery. Alexander said Montgomery wanted a plan like shooting an arrow into the heart of Germany. Patton wanted to do the same. But Montgomery wanted it from his part of Europe. Patton from his part. Eisenhower very wisely was opposed to either adopting that plan. Felt the way to attack Germany was on a broad front. Not to let armies get into points and then close in both sides. Alexander told me an extraordinary thing about Montgomery. After he had stayed with him at the Citadel, had gone to much trouble to make everything pleasant, after leaving, instead of writing a letter himself to the Governor General, Montgomery had one of his aides write a word of thanks. One who recalls that both were Generals in the war, and Montgomery was writing the King's representative, it shows how self-centred and vain the man must be.

"Vanier told me that when he had been dining with the Captain on the ship coming over, Montgomery said it was ten o'clock. He must leave. The Captain had said he would see him tomorrow. Montgomery had said: Why would you want to see me? I gave you my autographed photograph this afternoon.

"After dinner, we talked a little about the Opening of Parliament and events related to Europe. Persons to be remembered in London."

In New York on October 31, Mackenzie King had lunch with Mr. and Mrs. J. D. Rockefeller and was further reassured about his decision to accept the Order of Merit. Later that day he was "horrified" when he learned that the charge for his suite on the *Queen Elizabeth* would amount to $2,200. "I had not been told about it and believe there would have been enough in the incident to cause me to lose confidence with the entire Canadian people and that the Government would have suffered tremendously as a consequence. I said at once I would give up the rooms for a room anywhere in the ship before I would allow that amount to be paid up. It caused me some distress of mind at night and really was a terrible blow at the starting point. This morning, fortunately, Gardiner of the C.N.R. who came down, was at breakfast with us. It occurred to me he might be a helpful person in dealing with the situation. I told him what had happened. He saw at once the force of what I was saying and asked to be allowed to get busy on the matter. He went to the offices of the Cunard people; explained the situation but could not get any final arrangement until Mr. Borer, the Manager, who was meeting some people who had just come off the Queen Elizabeth, returned to the office. Later in the day, having seen Borer, Gardiner sent word that Mr. Borer had said the Company would like to place the sitting room, which is much more expensive than the bedroom, at my disposal, and would charge nothing for it. That all I would need to take was one bedroom. There had been great pressure on the Company to yield up this space. There certainly was a Providence watching over me, to have saved this situation. I cannot be too grateful to H. [Handy] for having spoken to me of it. It has shaken my confidence terribly in my office, more particularly as I have spoken over and over again about letting me know matters before anything is settled finally, and having spoken particularly about finances of this trip, and wishing to be careful in expenditures. As it is, I am rather afraid that a paper like Time or some other journal may advertise the fact that I have a suite de luxe on the Queen Elizabeth and will publish cost, etc. These things destroy one's happiness in public life and help to destroy one's own credit before the public. It would be a tragic business were, after all the years I have been in public life, the nation left with the impression that I really cared for luxury and extravagance. Things that I have fought against all my life and which everyone who knows me, knows how I feel about it."

During the trip, the Prime Minister was accompanied by Norman Robertson, who was returning to London after his illness, Pickersgill and Handy. General and Mrs. Vanier and their daughter were also on board and the voyage passed agreeably and without incident. Mackenzie King arrived in London on the morning of November 7, settled himself in his customary suite at the Dorchester, and then made a few formal calls. That afternoon Attlee came to call. "I had him take off his coat. Take out his pipe and smoke while we had a talk. He looks older and rather hurried. Seemed like a man who was almost shrinking in size and internal tension. He had a curious characteristic of twisting one or two bits of hair at the back of his head while talking. He spoke of the situation in PAKISTAN and INDIA being quite serious. Would probably get worse. Said that his Government would have been blamed had self government not been given. PALESTINE too was a source of considerable anxiety. He admitted that the results in the municipal elections showed a changed feeling which he said was the reaction from the large vote received in previous elections, and blaming the Government in the interval for all difficulties. I asked if Canada had failed him in any way – have we in any way failed him in co-operation? He said: No, in everything we had been most helpful. Felt strongly about Churchill making the difficulty he had in regard to colleagues who had left the Government. Virtually all had recognized the situation and co-operated with him. Told him of the King's offer. He instantly said: I am very glad that you have accepted, and I said I was much concerned whether I should. He said it would have been a mistake, not to do that. It carried no title. . . . He spoke of its significance being greater than that of any other. It was a real relief to my mind to see how instantly he reacted and how strongly he approved. . . . I told him I had sent him a message realizing that in regard to finance that the one which had come to me was written by someone who did not understand how to communicate. Had not yet learned the position of Canada. I sympathized with him in his problems. I confess that I felt inwardly that they might crush him in the end. The present Government have attempted too much in too short a time."

Mrs. Gooch, the cook at Laurier House, had also been a passenger on the *Queen Elizabeth* and, between Southampton and London, her trunk had been lost. Mackenzie King "felt a real sadness at word that Mrs. Gooch had lost her trunk. Had been waiting at the station for three trains. Nothing turned up. Luckily H. went to look after her. While the trunk was not secured, he was able to bring her to the hotel for the night and see that she had dinner and a place to rest. It really saddened my heart very much to think that coats and all in her possession had been lost in this way. I cannot believe that her trunk is stolen. I think it will still turn up. Very fortunate that we were here at the time. I should have taken her baggage in my car along with my baggage to London."

The Prime Minister remained preoccupied with the search for Mrs. Gooch's trunk after he arrived in Paris the next day but word reached him on November 9 that the trunk had been found. Unfortunately, Mrs. Gooch's trunk was not the only luggage to go astray during the trip. After a pleasant weekend in Paris, Mackenzie King left for Brussels on the morning of Monday, November 10. He had a rest on the train and "was horrified on getting up to learn from Nicol that our baggage had not been put on the special train and was still in Paris. Would not arrive till 5 tonight which meant that I had no proper clothes for the afternoon's ceremony at the university. Moreover, I was put out altogether by discovering that the ceremony was during the afternoon. I thought it had been fixed for another day and that I had most of today free. By the time I got to Brussels, I was nearly distracted at the thought of how I would manage at the University."

The Canadian party was met by the Belgian Prime Minister and, while Mackenzie King was having a rather agitated lunch with the Canadian Ambassador, Handy and Nicol were scouring Brussels for a suit he could wear at the honorary degree ceremony that afternoon. "Immediately after luncheon," he wrote, "I took a rest of fifteen minutes. When H. and Nicol arrived with a suit of clothes which they had secured at a shop in Brussels, I got up. Fortunately the trousers fitted perfectly though a little tight around the waist. A wonderful fit about the shoulders but almost touching the floor. Shirt a little narrow but Nicol managed to cut buttons. I felt instant relief to be at least dressed properly; also a silk hat, novel shape but right size. Instead of taking a longer rest, I dressed and then tried to think of sequence of thoughts which would serve for remarks at the University. . . .

"At 4.15 P.M., we went to the University where I was presented to the President and the Rector, and introduced to members of the Faculty – a formidable looking body.

"To add to my dismay, before the time arrived, I was informed that the Queen of the Belgians [Elizabeth, widow of Albert] had just this morning expressed a wish to be present which was an additional note of distinction to the occasion, and an appropriate tribute to Canada."

After the introductions, "a procession was formed into a large hall. The President and Rector of the University and members of the Faculty sat on the stage. Immediately opposite . . . the Queen sat, with the audience behind her and the Gallery. Other members of the Faculty were to the right of the Queen. Immediately opposite to the left was a little dais with two seats; I was given the seat nearest the platform with Doré [the Canadian Ambassador] to my right. I then listened to a long address in French which fortunately I had had a chance of glancing at. I just had a chance to read it and found three or four mistakes which I thought were unfortunate.

"I was credited in a paragraph with defining the status of British Dominions, etc., instead of being stated that I had helped to draft. Also a statement that Canada had moved toward independence under my control. I changed that to full nationhood; also twenty-three years Prime Minister instead of over twenty. These were evidently slips that Doré had made in preparing the speech for the President of the University. He, by the way, reminded me we had met at a dinner in Brussels in 1910 which was at the time of the Exhibition year and the conference on technical education. I hope these corrections got to the press in time. Doré made them in conversation with the President while we were going toward the room where the Party assembled.

"I thought the Rector made a very fine address though I could understand very little of it. It had some fine quotations from *Industry and Humanity* and other writings.

"I then came down from the dais. One of the professors then read a diploma which was being presented – all in Latin. I doubt if anyone except a very few could understand. I was then given the hood which was in the nature of some decoration which I wore over the left shoulder and which fell off while I was speaking but which was put on. Once I began to speak, I felt more at ease. I apologized for not speaking in French, specially where French was one of our official languages. I then asked permission to thank Mr. Spaak for his invitation which accounted for my being present. Made a reference to the presence of the Queen. Referred to having met the late King Albert in 1910, which was a risky step seeing that the Royal Family situation in Belgium is a particularly difficult one at the moment. The audience, I think, applauded that remark. I then spoke of the degree itself and my feeling that receiving it reminded me of the time I received a degree from my own University. That I had accepted it because my father was not there to accept it.

"I then spoke of feeling this time it was not my father but the country that was being honoured. Canada would appreciate the tribute which was being expressed in this way to her fighting men. I then referred to the purpose of my visit – strengthen the bonds of friendship among our countries, to honour our dead. Further good-will. Then concluded by saying a word to the students in relation to the importance of public service.

"What I had seen of Embassies and Legations, Foreign Offices, etc. That we were now at a point where we could either move on toward higher things, or where mankind would suffer destruction. I believed that the spiritual forces would mean that those fighting for Right, Truth and Justice, had the moral law on their side, and were keeping me in accord with realities. I said I wished to say a word on Universities as custodians of tradition, of common ideals and ideas, of our common aspirations and hopes. That University men the world over in meeting with each other could help to formulate public opinion. Advised the students to keep public service before them as one of the outstanding traditions of some of the Universities, each keeping a certain amount of public service before them. They would help to create public opinion that would control in the direction of affairs. Felt so grateful as I came near the end and finding I was able to give expression to one long sentence, of what was really most in my heart.

"The words of my speech were given a really enthusiastic reception after which the national anthems were played. First, O Canada and then God Save the King, and the Belgian National Anthem. We then adjourned to an adjoining room where the Queen was receiving a number of Ministers and University members, and met there quite a number of persons who had been in Canada before. Among others present, there was Brugère [a French Minister to Canada before the War] whom I was delighted to see. I hear that some unfortunate difference between him and Bidault at something that he said, has caused him to leave the diplomatic service.

"After quite a little time in conversation and a very pleasant word with the Queen in which she again spoke very feelingly about what Canada had done – what Belgium owed to Canada . . . I returned to the Hotel Astoria and went immediately to bed. Had a good hour's rest. Up to that time, the baggage had not arrived but it came while I was asleep."

The rest of the visit to Belgium and Holland was a great success and Mackenzie King enjoyed himself thoroughly. He returned to England on Sunday, November 16, and at noon the next day "went to Buckingham Palace and was shown into Mr. Colville's office. He was one of Mr.

Churchill's secretaries at Quebec. The fur coat and token gift had been sent in his keeping. While I was waiting to be received by Princess Elizabeth, he spoke about coming to Canada next year. He said he wanted to speak quite confidentially. Hoped I would not mention the matter to Lascelles as he might not like it which I thought was extraordinary. He went on to say that he knew the Princess and Mountbatten would like to come to Canada but it would be well not to press the invitation longer than a week's stay – in the months of April or May. Would go over on a ship. Rest that way and perhaps take in Toronto and Ottawa. Rather hinted that events might be forthcoming and then went on to say he doubted if the King would wish them to go and might be a little hesitant. He would feel they should settle down and have family life first. I had to smile as he was talking as that was repeating exactly what King George V said to me when I asked to have the present King and Queen come out to Canada, shortly after they were married. Colville was working with two secretaries clearing up piles of correspondence. Said Churchill is making good headway with his book. Has over a million words written.

"The Princess received me in one of the drawing rooms alone. She was very pleasant, looking quite happy and smiling. We spoke first of meeting anew and I said I had come to bring her all possible good wishes from the Government and people of Canada, and also to present her the wedding gifts which our country would be pleased if she would receive with our good wishes. I then handed to her the mink coat which was over my arm.

"She said at once she had been delighted when she learned that she was to receive a mink coat. She made some comment on how beautiful it was and how pleased she was to have it. I then handed to her the silver cup (227 years old) as a token gift. I said we were all so pleased she had selected the candelabra and other pieces wholly to her own liking. She said it had been so kind to allow her to make a selection. Said they were very beautiful. Asked if I had seen the photographs of those that had been photographed. I then said we would have certain pieces suitably inscribed later as from the Government and the people 'With Every Good Wish.' I then said that the Legion had honoured me by asking me if I would present her with the brooch which its officers and members were making at the time of her marriage. I then read to her the illuminated scroll and handed it to her. She said something about how beautifully it was inscribed, illuminated and how kind it was of the veterans to have made the gift they did. Their acknowledgements were all made in a very informal, natural way. She looked much what she is – quite a young girl. Obviously happy and not too tired.

"I wore my own Legion membership badge at the time of these presentations. I then said there was one more invitation which I would wish to convey personally, which was that she and Lieut. Philip Mountbatten might honour us with a visit to Canada in the very near future, at whatever time would be convenient to them. She said that she would very much like to make the visit but did not mention any particular time. After renewing good wishes, I withdrew."

Before leaving the Palace, the Prime Minister had a talk with Lascelles and reviewed his objections in July to the proposed meeting of the Privy Council. He stated that "what we were wishing was to be sure there was not some new Council being created. That the P.C. for the Commonwealth, I thought, should not be brought into being – if it were to be brought at all – without agreement by all governments of the Commonwealth, etc. He spoke of a situation which might arise where, for example, the Government of India might advise the King one way, and the King of South Africa, another. There must be some way that the King could get advice as to what should be done other than by his British Ministers. He thought perhaps something might be worked out whereby the King might cable Ministers in different parts of the Commonwealth and have them come to London and advise him. I said I could see the problem that might arise. It would have to be given much careful thought. Lascelles was really exceedingly nice and particularly in the way in which he referred to the significance of the Order and, as he said, how pleased he had been when the King had asked him to write as he had written."

After his talk with Lascelles, the Prime Minister was presented to the King who "Spoke of the pleasure it was to see me again and then walked over to the little table on which the Insignia of the Order of Merit was in its case.

"The King picked it up and said that it gave him great pleasure to confer this Order upon me. He was pleased I had been willing to accept it. Spoke of its numbers being limited. Mentioned it was an Order his grandfather Edward VII had created. I said to His Majesty that I was deeply touched by his having felt me worthy of so great an Honour and what pleased me particularly was that it was a personal gift from himself. That I had debated in my own mind whether it might not be in the interests of such service as I might still be able to render to my country and other nations of the Commonwealth, for me not to accept any honour. That in no way could any motive of mine be misconstrued. The King then said something about knowing personally of my services over many years. Asked me exactly the length of time, saying something of over twenty years. I spoke of the years as Leader of the Party and as Prime Minister. Said that he personally knew from what he had seen for himself in Canada, what my services had been over many years. And since. In presenting the Order, the King said he hoped he would be seeing me wearing it at the evening party at the Palace tomorrow night.

"The King referred to Churchill and Smuts having the Order and said something about the three of us being outstanding in the Commonwealth in the service we had rendered. I said I valued very much the association with both Mr. Churchill and Field Marshal Smuts in the membership of the Order.

"The King then asked me to be seated and began to speak of different subjects. The trip to South Africa. Was most enjoyable but found that while trains were comfortable, they were very slow. Considerable distances between localities. People in motors could travel as fast as a train. He would meet the same people over and over again at the different stops. He thought it was a promising country with good opportunities of settlement.

"We spoke about the weather. The King said things were very unsettled here, not pleasant. Very troubled conditions in the world. One could see he rather felt the discord and unrest. He did not ask many questions about Canada. I spoke about our present position in trade relations.

"We talked of the Communist disclosures. He said that what Canada had brought out had certainly helped to reveal what was a very far reaching movement. He also spoke to me about the trip on the Continent of which I gave him a brief account.

"I then withdrew to have a few minutes before luncheon. Was shown again into that same room. Shortly before one, I was taken upstairs to another drawing room just off the drawing room. There were two persons at the end of the room. I could not be sure with the light in my eyes just who they were. First I thought they might be the King and Queen. It turned out it was the Queen of the Hellenes and Lieutenant Philip Mountbatten. They both came forward together. The Queen shook hands and then said: This is my cousin (or nephew) but did not mention any name. I saw at once it was Mountbatten. I was most favourably impressed with his appearance and manner.

"The Queen then began to speak of how pleased they all were with General LaFlèche and what a fine Ambassador he had made. We were engaged in this conversation when the King and Queen followed by Princess Elizabeth and Princess Margaret came into the room. The Queen first of all greeted the Queen of the Hellenes, kissing her on the cheek. I then came forward and she shook hands with me. The King also did the same.

"After shaking hands, the Queen extended to me her congratulations upon the Order and said how well it was merited. How pleased she and the

King were that I had received it. Her Majesty asked me to show it to her. The others then came forward and extended their congratulations. The Party then went on into the room in which luncheon was served at a round table. The King was seated with his back to the door that we had come in at. To his right was the Queen of Greece, Lord Mountbatten to her right and then the Queen. I was seated to the right of the Queen. Princess Elizabeth was to my right. Princess Margaret Rose to the right of Princess Elizabeth and next to the King.

"After the conversation began, I remarked that I was seated as I had been at Balmoral when I might have added dinner at Buckingham Palace, to the right of the Queen, with Princess Elizabeth to my right.

"I spoke of Margaret Rose and how the King had tried to stop her from trying to look cross-eyed at Balmoral. The Queen said she still tries to do that. I then spoke of the time I first met the two Princesses on Piccadilly. The Queen immediately referred to how small they were.

"The conversation at times was general and everyone seemed very happy. There was nothing in the least formal. Much was said of the gifts to Princess Elizabeth. . . . The Princess spoke particularly of the wild mink. Also said she had received some protest about accepting anything which involved the killing of animals. . . . The Princess said the most extraordinary gift which had been made to her was I think she said, from Trinidad. It was a lunatic asylum. The people there wanted an asylum and had raised the money for the purpose of a gift for the wedding. . . . The Queen spoke about how publicity had been in the last few weeks. Would be glad when the wedding would be over. . . .

"In conversation, the Queen recalled some of the incidents of the trip to America. We talked a good deal about Roosevelt. How he had looked forward to coming to London. I told the Queen the story of the search the King and I had for our rooms after our long talk with the President. Later in front of the window as we were all looking out, the King asked me if Houde was still about. Said something about having seen that he had been re-elected. . . .

"At the table, the Queen mentioned she thought there ought to be a fountain of Honour. Looking again at the Order, and thanking the King for it, the King said something about wearing it tomorrow night. I mentioned that the side bearing the words for MERIT should appear in front. He then took the Order out of the box and said that Smuts when he had first worn it, had worn it the wrong side foremost. I asked about the position at which it should be worn. The King told me and then took the ribbons himself and put them around my neck, to show me just about where this should be placed.

"I then said I have the additional honour of having had the Order placed around my neck by the King himself. At one time the King explained there was no miniature to be worn on any lapel.

"The King and Queen were standing together as I withdrew. The Order was lying open in my hand. I said that for such a time as I might be spared to continue public life, I should value any opportunities of service to Their Majesties which might present themselves.

"After luncheon, watching for time for the cars going to St. James Palace, there was a short conversation in the room from which we came and I referred again to the Honour the King had bestowed upon me.

"I should have mentioned as I went into the room to meet the King, the names which were in my mind and which I went over by myself were the names of the family and grandparents who are the ones who were being honoured today. The Queen standing by one door about to enter in the other room waited there until I had reached the hall when she smiled and when I said good-bye.

"I must say I found it very easy and very pleasant talking at the table, infinitely more so than I had almost feared as a strain specially with the heavy cold I still have."

From Buckingham Palace, Mackenzie King went directly to St. James Palace to meet the Robertsons and view Elizabeth's gifts. "I enjoyed very much going with them through the different rooms. It was more like holding a reception as one went along meeting so many old friends. . . ."

Next morning (November 18) Field Marshal Smuts called on the Prime Minister to congratulate him on receiving the Order of Merit. "He said he would be here only a few days," Mackenzie King wrote. "He has his Parliament opening and has a general election next year. He is going to run another election and thinks he will win but says he is determined to allow the younger men to have their chance after that. He said what had been bothering him was whether when he got out, when he ceased to be Prime Minister, whether he should stay on in Parliament or not. His own preference would be to leave completely. He said he would get out now only the Party would not let him and their five years would be up next year which made it necessary for him to contest the election. I told him what I had planned to do and said as to staying on in the Government, I was debating that point, etc., but really felt it was best to get out altogether.

"Smuts said he thought it was a mistake for a man to stay on until he was in his dotage. I asked him if he did not have a lot of splendid information – material which he could leave to the country for advantage. He said you must have a lot of the same. I think you ought to give your time to writing. He talked of the King's trip [to South Africa]. He said they took on much more than they should have but it was their own fault. They were anxious to see so many things. The trip had been most enjoyable. I told him he looked exceedingly happy in some of the pictures. Spoke about 50th wedding anniversary. He did not think the Government would expect us to discuss any matters seriously here. He said they might wish to tell us some things of their own they would like us to know but that certainly he was not prepared to discuss things. Everything was so confused at this time. I said to him it was amusing that each of us, two Prime Ministers, at the wedding, should be at the head of countries that had divided races and were each rebels. Descendants of rebels. He kept remarking about the Order. That it showed how wise the King was. He said they have been keeping these things too much in their own little circle here. He thought it was most wise they had extended the Honours as they had. He was exceedingly pleasant. Looked quite vigorous though thin. Nothing could have been kinder than his manner."

On the day of the wedding, November 20, Mackenzie King "reached the Abbey in good time – about 10.30. The sight on coming in was very similar to that of the days of the Coronation. Coming in the Abbey . . ., I was surprised to find that part of the Abbey already filled. On the way, recognized Anthony Eden. It seemed strange to see him in that part of the Abbey. Conservatives must find it very trying to be in second place at a time like this. I was shown to the seat next to the one occupied by the Prime Minister. The Prime Minister's seat was at the corner of the transept facing the Altar. The best seat in the Abbey to see the ceremony.

"General Smuts came in shortly after and was seated to my right. A little later Churchill came in and was seated to Smuts' right. As we talked together, Smuts spoke of what a world is this! And then added: We shall not see the like of this again. We shall soon be passing away.

"Throughout the service, he kept on his overcoat and I did the same. I noticed though he wore high boots. Churchill seemed to be quite frail. I noticed his legs trembled a little. He had difficulty stooping down.

"Attlee looked wonderfully well, calm and quiet. Mrs. Attlee and Mrs. Churchill and others were in seats immediately in front. I did not find the time long, waiting for the procession. I enjoyed looking at the people; formation of the pageant. Listened to the music, enjoyed seeing choir boys in their crimson robes. The procession itself was very well. The sight of Royalty, quite a picture. The King and Queen looked very well. So did the bride and groom. The group at the altar made a fine scene. I could hear the responses of both Elizabeth and Philip; also the address by the Archbishop of York. There was a series of lovely tableaux but one felt that all this pomp was a demonstration of power and ceremonial – something that is really helping to foment the unrest of the day, and that in the nature of things would not last long. It will some day be swept away in a great class struggle.

"I have become increasingly impressed with what I see and learn of the different countries. What is taking place to destroy the so-called middle class and leave the battle between masses and the upper classes with a view to the destruction of the latter. What is really needed one feels is a strong middle class with numbers on either side becoming increasingly limited. These thoughts were much in my mind during the service. I thought the Queen looked very beautiful, quite happy and smiling, natural. The King himself very quiet and refined in all his actions and movements – one of the finest moments of all was when the bride and groom, after the Register had been signed, came forward hand in hand and bowed to Queen Mary. She is a wonderful old woman. Looked very regal.

"The Service was the regular one of the English Church. The words well selected seemed to take on almost a new meaning. I enjoyed seeing [Norman] Robertson sitting in one of the stalls on the opposite side. I keep puzzling over the position of High Commissioners. The trouble they are likely to give the British Government and the need of careful control by the Dominion Government over their position in London. The British are seeking to court the Dominions, bringing them into the centre of the Commonwealth arena and will find themselves much embarrassed and may be increasingly so as time goes on.

"On leaving the Abbey, I said to Smuts that as Attlee had his wife and Winston had his wife, he, Smuts, had left his wife at home and I had no wife, he and I ought to walk together which we did following Miss Attlee and Mrs. Attlee. . . ."

The Prime Minister drove alone from the Abbey to Buckingham Palace. "A short route had been selected. At the Palace, met Lord Athlone and Bevin and walked with them into where they met their respective wives and went together upstairs to the hall where Royalties were all assembled.

"While they were being photographed, I had a nice talk with the Queen's brother Lord Bowes-Lyon and later with several of the Royalties themselves. Prince Charles of Belgium was very pleasant. King Peter, of Yugoslavia, introduced his wife. We had a nice talk and later shook hands with the Queen and had a short talk with Her Majesty, Smuts and I sharing those moments together.

"When it came to the wedding breakfast, I was given the honour of taking in Princess Alice and had the Princess of Greece to my right. The latter told me she was a Bonaparte. After luncheon, she introduced me to her husband. I found her an exceedingly clever and pleasant person to talk with. Princess Alice was exceptionally cheerful and pleasant. At the same table, was the Dowager Marchioness of Milford-Haven, the grandmother of Prince Philip. A most entertaining person. I had a long talk with her before breakfast. She told me some amusing stories about Royalty of earlier days. She is the lady who was Lady-in-Waiting at Badminton when I was there.

"The King spoke nicely in proposing the bride's health. Lieutenant Philip made a short but pleasant reply. Later the bride cut her wedding cake with his sword. There was considerable conversation after the luncheon, and in the large hall where, among others, I had a long talk with the Queen of Spain. She told me she was a grand-daughter of Queen Victoria.

"Still later a talk with the Dowager Duchess of Devonshire who used to be in Canada. She was very pleasant. She told me that she had secured from Queen Mary the seat for Violet Markham which she had in the Abbey. Also invited me to come and spend some days at her home in the country. I had made the mistake, last night, of sitting up a little too late and finding it difficult to get to sleep. I should not have got so overtired and then would have remembered better the details of the day.

"There were many persons I might have met and much I might have heard which I passed by because of a feeling more or less of fatigue and indifference. However the scene is one which, with the aid of the press, I shall ever recall with interest.

"Before coming away from the Palace, at 4, I was present among others when the bride and groom left. They each shook hands and I asked God's blessing on each of them. They looked very happy and were wholly natural. Indeed the whole proceedings at the Palace were much more dignified, quiet and natural than most weddings that I have attended. There was not a note of boisterousness or excessive talking that I heard. One felt what a marvellous family the Royal family really is.

"I kept some of the paper petals. One of the Royalties said to keep some of the petals instead of throwing them after the bride."

Mackenzie King dined with the Attlees that evening. "It was a small dinner but an exceedingly pleasant and memorable one. Other guests present were Mr. and Mrs. Bevin, Mr. and Mrs. Noel Baker, Smuts and I. Unfortunately, I was a little late in arriving. Knowing everyone had had a busy day, I made a move early and went away a little before 10.30. It happened to be Mrs. Attlee's birthday. Later in the evening, I proposed her health and said I wished for many happy returns of the day. Conversation had much to do with the European situation. The seriousness of the position in France and the critical nature of the conferences about to begin with the Foreign Ministers. Bevin spoke quite freely to Smuts and myself." This conversation with Bevin and Attlee appeared to set the mood for the rest of the Prime Minister's stay in London. The Council of Foreign Ministers was about to begin another set of meetings in a few days but almost no one believed that any real progress would be made on the German and Austrian peace settlements. The Moscow Conference in March, angry debates about Greece and Korea during the Second Assembly of the United Nations in the fall, and communist exploitation of political difficulties in France and Italy, had all contributed to a dangerous increase in tension between the West and the Soviet Union.

The Prime Minister spent the weekend at Chequers and, after lunch on Sunday, November 23, he had a long talk with Attlee, Lord Addison, and Patrick Gordon Walker, the Parliamentary Under Secretary of State for Commonwealth Relations. One question discussed was the future role of the Commonwealth High Commissioners. According to Mackenzie King "the British Government is much embarrassed by their position. My own advice was that whatever should be done for them should be as a matter of courtesy. It would be a mistake to try and give them a place on the Table of Precedence which would precede that of members of the British Government themselves. I pointed out that our representative in Canada of the King was the Governor General. The King was our King when we were here. The High Commissioners were agents of the Government, not representatives of the King. Care must be taken not to give them a status which would be above that of representatives of the people who were in the Ministry and who had to determine policy. I could see that the High Commissioners themselves have been urging more prominence for their posts. More recognition. There is a real danger in this – to the Government in London and the Governments of the Dominions. I stressed the necessity of keeping decisions of Ministers themselves in the Cabinet. When one sees some of the types that are being appointed High Commissioners; also new men coming from Pakistan and India, and later probably from other parts, the need for caution at this time is very great.

"I brought up the question of the Governor General's title, desirability of having it changed. Spoke of the difficulty of another name such as King's representative as being wrong. Would try to get something much better. All agreed Vice-roy would not do because of its significance in India. Walker thought of the term – King's Lieutenant – which made a strong appeal to all concerned – to all of us. It carried the name of the King; makes clear that the occupant is not a Sovereign himself or Governor General but is someone associated with the King in an official relationship. I should not be surprised if this title might not be adopted.

"There was a good deal of talk about my years of office and importance of having something done when I have outrun Walpole's record which would attract attention in all countries. One suggestion was that some arrangements should be made for endowment of a house, Laurier House, to be preserved for historical purposes. I mentioned my thought of turning it over to the State keeping it as a memorial for Sir Wilfrid and myself. Our more than sixty years of leadership between us. His sixteen years as Prime Minister and mine now, over twenty. I had not thought of this nor did I suggest anything but it is quite evident that the British Government would like to do something when the Walpole record is beaten. They are wise in seeking to give recognition to the significance of the event, keeping it as a part of the history of the British Commonwealth. I can see that everything is being done for Britain to hold within the Commonwealth, the great position which she has held before as leading centre of the Empire – position she is losing as a nation by herself."

On November 24 the Prime Minister attended a briefing on the international situation at 10 Downing Street with Attlee, Smuts, several ministers of the British government, and the Commonwealth High Commissioners in London. Attlee "opened proceedings with a short word of welcome saying they were pleased to take advantage of the presence of Smuts and myself to have us and other High Commissioners meet with members of the Government that were together in the room. The Prime Minister stressed the necessity for great secrecy in regard to what might be said. Bevin had a meeting at the Palace at 4 and he had agreed to give us a brief review of the present situation.

"Earlier in the day, I had received a printed paper containing a review which was the one on which Bevin based what he had to say. The earlier part of his statement paralleled what was printed there. It had to do with the progress and failures of the United Nations to date. The failures of the peace negotiations, and led up to the meeting of Foreign Secretaries which was being held the day following. I do not recollect in detail what Bevin said as he reached the subject of the conference. It was something to this effect: that Europe at the moment was in a very serious condition. A very large part of the working population in France was on strike. France was honeycombed with Communists who were seeking to upset the Government and create as much trouble as would be possible. There was no strong person to lead the Government. There was not authority necessary to maintain the Government or order. The Marxian doctrine was to destroy the middle class so that there would be left only the ruling classes on the one side, the proletariat, on the other, and the clash would be inevitable. It was war against the middle classes that the Communists were doing their utmost to foment.

"In Roumania, hundreds of thousands of the middle classes had been ruthlessly murdered. The King of Roumania was in England now. The Communists were fomenting trouble in Italy. It was not as serious as in France but might lead to an overthrow of Government there with civil war in Italy and civil war developing in France. That, however, was not the worst. At the present conference, the Russians might make it impossible to get a settlement – a peace settlement with either Austria or as regards Germany. He, Bevin, himself, felt more pessimistic than he had felt at any time in his life. He feared that the conference would not be successful. That the Russians would keep up the attitude they had assumed. He felt that the Americans and British and French must make a stand to save Western Europe. The Russians would try to make this impossible. Matters might even come to the point where in three weeks' time, Russia might seek to keep within her zone, the part of Berlin which she now controls. This would mean that the British would be cut off from getting into the part of Berlin which they control. This also true of the Americans. (I am not sure that I have this wholly correct.)

"Bevin then said that if matters reached that stage, he feared there would be conflict. At that stage, I asked a question: what do you mean by conflict? Do you mean conflict within the conference or without? Between the countries which are represented at the conference. Bevin then said: I mean without. We could never allow ourselves to be prohibited by any nation from free access to Berlin and to other parts of Western Europe. The Russians might seek to make this impossible. What he feared was not an open declaration of war, or the intention on the part of Russia to bring on a war immediately, but rather that the Americans with their sense of power might become impatient at Russia's behaviour and that matters would drift unintentionally but quickly into overt acts which would lead to war. I said this was a most serious statement – the most serious statement I had ever heard in the years I had been in Downing Street.

"I then asked what has become of the theory that Russia would continue to bleed from the effects of the last war for at least five years. That it would take the following five years to build up her strength. Her industries, etc., and that war might come in the following five years but could not be expected to come sooner. To this Bevin replied: that I know is the theory of the Americans. I replied it was what was said at this table. Bevin followed by saying: it is the army's view. They are always working out plans but these matters are not governed by army plans. They are the result of human action. People acting in a certain way under certain stresses. He stressed again that the war would not begin intentionally but replied that he himself had to admit that he feared that that is what was coming. He said something about: How would you like to have my job? That is what I see – I believe is what I am facing or words to that effect.

"Smuts then joined in and said that he did not think there would be war. The Russians would undoubtedly do all they could to foment unrest to prevent the success of the Marshall Plan. Bevin had stressed the progress that was being made in the production of coal, in transport, etc., and spoke of the handicaps there still were to real recovery in the French zone and some of the other countries. Bevin continued to combat Smuts' attitude and asked point blank the question as to whether, if the Russians sought to prevent free access between Britain and the British zone in Berlin, Britain could afford to allow them to do so. I made no reply to this but Smuts said he agreed they could not. Britain would be allowing Communism to spread over all of Europe and brought to her very door if that were to take place. He thought the Russians would have to be told that that could not be permitted to happen, at any cost. I said I thought that Marshall would be cautious. Also it was to be remembered that next year was a Presidential [election] year. It was not the Republicans who were in office. It was the Democrats. That the Democrats had never sought to make war an issue in a general election. That I doubted very much if Marshall and the President would take any quick action."

Bevin replied that "the action might be forced on them. I said I agreed that both were military men. Men who were fearless and courageous and far-sighted. That they would certainly not allow the whole of Europe to come under the control of Russia. That if that were the alternative, the United States might find themselves prepared to go to war. Bevin repeated the situation was exactly parallel to what it had been when Hitler went into the Ruhr. That if he had been checked then, a great war would not have taken place.

"The question now was that it was better to stop the Russians at this stage effectively or to seek appeasement which would inevitably bring another war in a very short time. It was the view of the British Government, regardless of everything, that appeasement should not be allowed at this stage. Russia must be told that the question of geography – boundaries of territories, the question of ocean ports, etc., could easily be settled; that what Britain and Western Europe wanted to know was whether Russia herself was prepared to stop fomenting in Europe. Stop trying to destroy the Marshall plan, and that if she were unwilling to do this, she would have to be told that measures would be taken immediately to prevent further aggression on her part. There was some discussion on Communism in America and how live the Americans had recently become to its undermining influences in their own country. I was asked about Canada and said that I thought we had got the better of that movement. That our early exposure had caused people not only in America but elsewhere to see what was really going on, and that the Communists had lost very great ground."

At this point, Mackenzie King noted that the high commissioners for India and Pakistan were present. "I had been told privately earlier by Noel Baker that there were some things Bevin could not tell as they were afraid whatever went back to India, there being no real provisions for security there, that much might be passed on to the Russians. They are not too sure yet as to where India stands. One theory might be that Bevin spoke as he did in the expectation of the word reaching the Russians in this round about way. That Britain and America were determined to stand up to them at this time. I do not hold this view. Bevin gave no reasons in private conversations or in other talks with me to lend support to that belief. Indeed his whole manner both at the dinner at Downing Street and at this meeting of the Cabinet was that of a man who was firmly convinced of the truth of what he was saying and saw in it a situation that was more appalling or terrible than he himself believed he could face though he felt he must.

"I confess after listening to the discussion, I began to review anew the kind of controversy that has taken place in previous meetings of the Foreign Ministers and of their deputies. What had taken place at Paris and particularly the controversies at the United Nations and above all so much talk of war and readiness for war in America. If one looks at these events in the light not of mere bluff but of the actual fear which Russia and America entertain respectively of each other's designs, that they are along world conquest lines, one can help to account for the whole programme. Otherwise it is hard to see why there need be on the part of either country so much indulging in extreme language of abuse, hatred, etc. . . . .

"I asked the question how will it be possible for the Americans to begin war in Europe, were not most of their troops withdrawn, etc. The answer given was that military preparations have been such they would quickly be put into operation but nothing definite was said. Perhaps for a special reason. I got the answer really the next day when at luncheon with Churchill, and I will record this later.

"When the Cabinet was over, Alexander [First Lord of the Admiralty], the Prime Minister, Robertson and myself met together in one corner of the room. Alexander had been wishing to have a special interview with me. I was not too anxious to discuss defence matters with him at this time. They had sent me a memo on defence on Saturday. Alexander then said that what I had said about the army plans, etc., – five year periods – were true. All this had had to be changed in the light of recently acquired knowledge. There were two factors: one was they had learned on good authority that the Russians had a trained army of Germans running into hundreds of thousands, all prepared for war, and which could be moved into Germany to fight for German freedom. They were, at the present time, in Russia but could be moved into Berlin in no time. That the people might rise in their support. Russia would give the assurances of complete freedom to Germany if she would come over to the Russian regime.

"Another surprise that the defence people had had was the extent of the air force which Russia now possesses. A demonstration over Moscow on the anniversary of the revolution had disclosed a power in the air much greater than the defence forces had realized Russia could possess. She had been collecting materials and manufacturing, and there was reason to believe these planes were very powerful. Could do terrific damage. What, of course, was to be most feared was the use of other forms of warfare, bacteriological, etc. It was not known how far this had developed in Russia, nor did the allied powers know how far she had really got on with the bombing warfare, atomic bomb, etc. At any rate, there were very strong evidences that she was preparing for war and that, soon. What she was waiting for was the unrest in other nations in Europe and the hope of depression in the States.

"I am not sure that Alexander spoke of the bacteriological warfare. Someone else in authority did so in some conversation with me. It was admitted that Britain was very weak in attempting to prepare to fight another war but Attlee and Alexander both agreed they felt the British people would fight rather than suffer the encroachment of Russian power over the whole of Europe which would mean their own extinction in a short time."

Robertson and the Prime Minister left the meeting together. "We each agreed it was the most serious situation that we could possibly have imagined and indeed was altogether beyond anything I had hitherto thought possible. In a word, it came down to this: that within three weeks, there may be another world war. This world war will grow out of the unwillingness of the Russians to make any peace settlement with respect to Germany at this time, and their determination to go on fomenting unrest in all countries. Carrying on the Marxian doctrine of class struggle as a prelude to the rule of the working classes throughout the world – world revolution prophesied by Marx. The whole thing based on the materialistic interpretation of history. I felt that instead of going on to a dinner at night with High Commissioners and others, we should all be on our knees praying for guidance. Frequently throughout this period, I have felt that the Royal Wedding might be in relation to future events, what the Coronation was to the war which followed immediately. . . . It has . . . been worth while coming over to the wedding. I got information which could not be secured any other way and which both Attlee and Alexander and myself could not be guarding too carefully.

"I had better add here immediately what I heard Churchill say, on the day following, which answered the question that I asked as to just how America could meet a situation against Europe, at this time, against Russia. Churchill had been speaking of the possibility of war along lines very similar to those followed by Bevin. So much so that Smuts who was sitting at the same table, looking over at me, said that is very like what we heard yesterday or words to that effect. I turned to Churchill and asked him how America could possibly mobilize forces at this time for another war. He turned to me sharply, his eyes bulging out of his head, and said: they would, of course, begin the attack in Russia itself. You must know they have had plans all laid for this, for over a year. What the Russians should be told at the present conference, if they are unwilling to co-operate, is that the nations that have fought the last war for freedom, have had enough of this war of nerves and intimidation. We do not intend to have this sort of thing continue indefinitely. No progress could be made and life is not worth living. We fought for liberty and are determined to maintain it. We will give you what you want and is reasonable in the matter of boundaries. We will give you ports in the North. We will meet you in regard to conditions generally. What we will not allow you to do is to destroy Western Europe; to extend your regime further there. If you do not agree to that here and now, within so many days, we will attack Moscow and your other cities and destroy them with atomic bombs from the air. We will not allow tyranny to be continued.

"This came as a revelation to me. I had not thought of plans being already in existence for war against Russia by bombing from the air. I know of course how America has continued to stock piles of atomic bombs and that her supply is very great. That she has also planes for the purpose and men trained. But from Churchill's words, it would seem as if his inside information was to the effect that America was expecting that she might have to act in a short time and had made her plans accordingly. Churchill said he believed if Molotov and Stalin and others were told that this is what would happen, they would yield and put an end to their bluff. He really believed they were hoping to increase their territories as Hitler had sought to increase his by bluff, etc. He sat back and said that war can be saved if we stand up to them now. I can see as clearly as can be, that if that stand is not taken within the next few weeks, that within five years or a much shorter time, there would be another world war in which we shall all be finished. His whole face and eyes were like those of a man whose whole being was filled with the belief which he had. He turned to me and he said: I told you many, many years before this last war, . . . that England would be at war within five years, and that she ran the risk of not possessing our own island at the end of that time. You remember this? I told him that I indeed remembered it, and had made a memo of it at the time. He said: I am telling you now what I see in the future. . . . I confess that while he was talking, I myself had a sort of vision of a welter of the world. It might just be the effect of his own words but they were strong and powerful and deeply felt. This statement gave me what seemed to supply what had been left out in the statements at Downing Street. I could see that of necessity, it would be so with the Indian delegates present; also I cannot see the wisdom of entrusting matters of this kind to types of men that some of the High Commissioners are and may be from time to time.

"So much for the meeting at Downing Street."

Next day (November 25) Ernest Bevin called on Mackenzie King at the Dorchester. They spent half an hour discussing the international situation and Bevin told him about a talk he had had with Molotov the previous evening. Molotov had returned to his favourite theme that Russia was "being threatened, indicating that nothing would be done while they were being threatened – he meant with war. Bevin said, I replied: threatened by whom? Certainly not the British. We have been fighting for freedom for ten and a half years past. We certainly are not threatening anyone. All we want is peace and peace in Europe. He said: I then went on to say to him that we could not afford to go beyond the present Conference without making some advance in that direction. That Britain could not allow herself to be put into a perilous position after all they had done. I do not remember his exact words but he added: I went as far as it was possible to go without actual words, and letting him see that we meant business at this time. That the Americans and ourselves were together in our determination to see Western Europe put into a position where she could again get on her feet. I took particular pains to find out from Bevin whether what he had said at Downing Street was for consumption on the part of others, for possible passing along, or were his own convictions. He was quite emphatic about it being his own convictions and beliefs. He told me he also had a talk with Marshall. It was along the line of necessity of seeing that precipitous actions of any kind do not take place. Assuring him of the wish of the British to work closely with the Americans in all the problems that had to be worked out."

Bevin said he had told Marshall that "if they, the United States, were going to be the ruling country of the world which they now were, – it sounded painfully to my ears to hear the Foreign Minister in London tell me that he had to admit that Britain had to take second place to the United States – that the United States could not hope to have that position and not put men into Europe to defend it. That, in other words, we could not look to Britain to do the shooting that was necessary and have her own people keep out of it."

Discussion then turned to the situation in the Middle East. Acting under the mandate, the United Kingdom had been unable to persuade the Arabs and Jews to agree on an acceptable political settlement and earlier in the year had turned the whole Palestine problem over to the United Nations. In May a special assembly of the UN had agreed to the appointment of a committee to investigate the situation. Mr. Justice Ivan C. Rand was the Canadian representative on the UN Special Committee of Observation in Palestine (UNSCOP) and played a prominent part in its work. Ignoring advice that partition of Palestine would provoke a war between Arabs and Jews, the committee's majority recommended a complicated plan for partition qualified by an economic union and this scheme won Canada's reluctant support in consideration of the UNSCOP report by an ad hoc committee appointed by the Second Assembly. In November Pearson became deeply involved in securing agreement to a compromise plan under which the British mandate would terminate, British forces would be withdrawn and new Arab and Jewish states would come into existence by July 1, 1948. In reporting his conversation with Bevin, Mackenzie King admitted that he "was not familiar enough with the Eastern situation to follow much of what Bevin said but the impression gathered in a general way was that so far as the Palestine question was concerned, it might have been settled, had not Wiseman's position been changed. (As I think of it, Noel Baker was strongly of the view that the Greek trouble might have been avoided but for Winston's insistence on fighting there.)

"That Britain had her agreements with the Arabs, etc. That he was afraid that before very long, a clash would come and 'shooting' would take place." Bevin went on to speak of the "appalling position" he had to deal with in Berlin. He gave Mackenzie King to understand the British might "have to order the shooting." Bevin "said there had been a perfect understanding with the Americans as to their being back of the British, but that Stalin had told him at Moscow that the Russians would not interfere with the British policy in regard to some of the matters in the Near East. As the translator was at work, he had him note carefully where the emphasis was put, and it being put on the word 'British,' he could see that if a policy were known to be British-American or Anglo-American, that Stalin could say he was free of his agreement. It was for this reason that he felt it was necessary for the British to be in the foreground or in the show-window as he expressed it, and the Americans themselves keep in the background.

"He certainly gave me the impression that we could expect civil war in that part before very long. He then spoke of how serious the situation was in some other parts of the world. Spoke of the Americans having great trouble in Manchuria, Korea. He spoke regarding the peace settlement offer re Japan that the Americans had originally agreed to. Unanimity on the part of the Five Powers but that they had since changed and were ready to support a view which did not permit of the use of the veto. Spoke of Evatt having made some situation difficult. Just what was said here, I do not know.

"In looking over the memo made in reference to the Near East, immediately after the conversation, I find the following notes:

"Stalin had agreed that he would not interfere with British Power but by inference, interpretation was British – not Anglo-American. This made it necessary for Britain to keep in the show-window, the United States to be behind to assist the military if need be.

"Marshall had told Bevin: you have an Empire but will not put in soldiers. Bevin said that the army always wanted to fight. Instead of putting in soldiers in some of the Near East countries, when they were expecting there would be civil strife, they had put in civil servants who were trained and who would take hold militarily, if necessary. Britain may have to do some shooting.

"Russia had backed up the Jews but once the British shoot, Russia will turn over and support the other side. When Wiseman collapsed, the Extremists got hold; till then they might have settled the question. Britain had agreements with the Arabs which they would have to hold to.

"*Re Japan*: First there was unanimity of the Great Powers. He, Bevin, had agreed to this and spoken on it. The Americans now had changed their position and agreed with those who said there should be no veto. Britain may have to join with Americans on this but he, Bevin, would be in a most difficult position to explain the complete change around.

"Evatt would not have the Five Power unanimity. Bevin says he is a strange fellow. Speaking of the relations with the Russians, geography, he says, is not a question. He had asked if the Conference were to get anywhere. Molotov had said: we are the people threatened. Bevin replied: You cannot say it is the British. We have fought ten and a half years for liberty. We cannot allow ourselves to lose our freedom now. In connection with these words, Bevin said: I spoke pretty straight.

"Bevin again said: Russia cannot fight a war but might bring on a situation to which the United States would react quickly. That was the great danger in the course of the next three months. He said he was anxious to work with the United States as much as possible but they could not be subservient to the United States. This was in reference to what Smuts had said at Downing Street that at all costs the Americans and the British must keep a united front in their dealings with Russians.

"I had agreed strongly with that view.

"Unfortunately, after Bevin's talk with me, I had, after making a few notes, to leave to go to Sir John Anderson's. Being very tired, found it difficult to make the record as clear as I should have liked. I feel I have the main points here which are:

"We may expect trouble in the Near East shortly;

"The British will be in the foreground, and the Americans will be behind;

"So far as oil-well situation, supplies, and the like are concerned, that has all been worked out satisfactorily.

"As Bevin went away, I told him I deeply sympathize with the great load he was carrying. Would welcome any opportunity to lighten his burden where I was sure the Canadian people would understand the situation well enough to cause the influence of our country to be felt."

After Bevin left, the Prime Minister went to lunch with Sir John and Lady Anderson. One of the guests was Winston Churchill. Mackenzie King reported that "during the luncheon, Winston did most of the talking. He looked wonderfully well. Complexion as fresh as that of a child and really quite different in appearance at St. Paul's and the Abbey. He was in a very pleasant though earnest mood. Got on to the present situation in Europe. After having talked strongly against Socialism and the ruination it was bound to bring to the people of the British Isles, I confess I shared his views on what made Britain what she is through initiative, self reliance, etc. However, she is paying the penalty today of permitting the conditions under which the masses worked in laissez-faire days.

"Getting on to the European situation, he pointed out that he believed we were today where we were at the time Hitler threatened to go into the Ruhr. He said had Britain and the other countries stood up to Hitler at that time, there would have been no war. They allowed him to pass and he started his series of encroachments. He believed that at this time, Russia would seek to enlarge her zone in Germany. Would seek to defeat the Marshall Plan. If she were permitted to do this, another world war was an absolute certainty. It might come very soon. It might be delayed a few years but not very many. He felt that the next three weeks might, in some ways, be the most critical of any, in that, they would show how far America was prepared to stand up against Russia. He believed that she would not continue to put up with Russia's effort to communize the balance of Europe and to communize America. I am inclined to think that Churchill has inside information regarding America's intention and goes further than appears on the surface. He thought America would, as indeed she should, tell the Russians just what the United States and the United Kingdom were prepared to do in meeting them in the matter of political boundaries, seaports, etc., but let them understand that if they were not prepared to accept this, their cities would be bombed within a certain number of days. He said if they were told this plainly enough, he thought they would retreat. If they were not given to understand that the countries had tolerated as much as they could, there was no hope for the world. . . .

"As I was sitting to his left, watching that side of his face, his eyes seemed to be bulging out of his head. So much so that one could see the greater part of the white of the eyes as well as the pupils, which looked as though they would come out of his head altogether. When he turned and looked and spoke as he firmly did, to me direct, his look was an earnest beseeching one. The gleam in his eyes was like fire. There was something in his whole appearance and delivery which gave me the impression of a sort of volcano at work in his brain. . . .

"Churchill admitted we did not know how great their [Russia's] power was. He thought the difficulty in dealing with the forthcoming war was greater than that of the one with Hitler in that the Russian ideology had made a religion of the issue. Hitler did not have that side. Churchill's statements being made in the presence of Smuts and myself as well as Sir John Anderson and Harold Macmillan made them much more significant."

He added that "after luncheon, there was an interesting moment when Winston, Smuts and I were together. The only three of the allied men who had co-operated actively in the war, who were now left. It must have been in the minds of the others as it was in my mind, that we might never be together again or . . . see each other again.

"It was pleasant to feel a deeply friendly atmosphere. Winston told me his first volume was complete now. Would be out next year – 1948. He had had to write the history of the preceding ten years to bring it up to the beginning of the war. I think, if I recollect aright, he indicated that while it would go to 1941, the whole would be out in the course of four years. He said to me I will send you the volumes as they come out. I told him he had been so kind in doing that with respect to nearly all of his books. He spoke as if he had been working very hard, writing.

"I confess that as I looked at him at the table, I felt that perhaps in more respects than one, he was the greatest man of our times. Not by any means the greatest in any one field but rather in a combination of fields – in the aggregate. I felt that his great knowledge of history which gave him a great outlook would cause him to speak with authority, causing other men to realize how little their knowledge and vision really was. The form with which he expressed his views was what gave him his great influence.

"Smuts, for example, mentioned of the Abbey scene, that it brought together all that was best at this time. Winston had used the expression – all that is best for all time – or something to that effect.

"I also heard him say to Mrs. Churchill that they were dining together that night. A sidelight on how little there is of home and family life when one is so completely given over to public affairs."

That afternoon, the Prime Minister called at Buckingham Palace to say good-bye to the King. He "first of all had a few minutes' talk with Lascelles thanking him anew for his many courtesies. He was exceedingly pleasant. Spoke of how well the wedding had gone, etc. Was shown upstairs to the room in which the King was alone standing a few steps away from the fire, as I went in. He asked me to sit down. . . . He brought up anew the question of the little opportunity he had for talking with different people about affairs. He said that while Europe was in a very serious situation, and England was in a difficult situation, what he regretted was there was so little that he himself could personally do to help. I said I thought he and the Queen had been wonderful in what they had done in keeping all parties working smoothly together. He went on to say there was really nothing he could do and he wished he could. . . .

"I brought up again the subject of possible visit of Princess Elizabeth and the Duke of Edinburgh to Canada. He said to me: is not the baby the important thing after all. Would they be wise to travel about before settling down in their own home. He said people try to pull you here and there, and you get no chance to get any home life. Then said something about taking a little holiday if he could, at his home in the country. There was nowhere to go to just now.

"I smiled as the King was talking about not encouraging them to come out thinking of what King George had said to me, when at the suggestion of Edward, I had asked if he, the present King – then Duke of York – might not come out. The King told me that I did not know anything about young people being married and what should be considered first. . . .

"We shook hands very warmly and in saying good-bye, I said that I hoped that God's richest blessings might be his.

"When I came downstairs – at the foot of the stairs – standing where two sides of an inverted wishbone would be – Smuts was standing, coming in for his interview. He said: Mackenzie, you are always getting ahead of me. I replied: you are always getting on my back. We had a happy little laugh together. I then spoke of the pleasure it had been to share the hours we had had together, and our interesting hour's talk at lunch with Winston. We agreed it would be perhaps the last chance we would have to shake hands before parting for our respective countries. I think nothing could have been friendlier than our meeting and parting at that moment. It is interesting that it should have been in the Palace of the King himself, when we consider the story of the past and our two countries and their relations with the Crown."

The following day Mackenzie King and his party boarded the *Nieuw Amsterdam* at Southampton and on December 3 they reached New York. In Ottawa the next afternoon, the Prime Minister gave his Cabinet colleagues an outline of his visit. He "told them perhaps more than I should about inside of situation in Europe as I knew it and believe is about to break. I could see what I said had a very sobering effect among all the Members. They were not surprised about conditions in France, but they seemed stunned at the thought of a possible conflict coming on immediately between Russia and the other nations. It is just too terrible to contemplate, but it does look to me increasingly as if the men at the head of affairs in Russia have got into their minds that they can conquer the world. What they may have in the way of secret weapons and missiles and poisons, no one knows."

Later in the afternoon he saw the Governor-General and "told him what had impressed me most in the visit overseas. I gave him the information I had received in conversation at Downing Street, and also from Bevin in our talk at the Dorchester. He agreed that the situation was very dangerous. He had not been expecting a possible outbreak of hostilities until next summer. He says he has been reading carefully everything he can. Had come to the conclusion that something might happen then and was surprised and a bit stunned at the thought of anything happening the next week or two. He did feel that a real effort would be made by the Russians to get the oil fields; that a serious situation was developing there. I told him Churchill's views and the thought of blasting gangsters out of Moscow. He said no doubt they had made preparations for all that and probably planned to conceal themselves behind the Urals or elsewhere. He believes it would not be difficult for the Russians to take the whole of Europe in no time and sweep right across to the coast. He did think that there might be some of the smaller powers which did not like Russia that would rise up if the situation got under way. My own feeling, however, is that those in authority are thinking of their own lives and that nothing of the kind is likely to be possible."

After a luncheon at Government House on December 6, their conversation resumed. Alexander said that since their talk "the other day he had read with renewed interest and a fuller understanding of the remarks that were passing between Molotov and Marshall. He had noted too Churchill's statement about all parties being united on foreign policy. Confessed matters had moved on more rapidly than he had anticipated they would. I said to him my understanding was that Marshall and Bevin, perhaps together, would finally say to Molotov that they wanted to know at once whether there was to be an end of this frustration and stirring up of Communism in Europe at the instance of Russia. Unless there were, the two countries would have to say at once that the moment had come when they could not allow matters to proceed further and to give Molotov to understand that Moscow would be destroyed within a certain number of hours if there were further delay.

"Alexander walked back and forth for a moment and then he turned and said: 'By Jove if they take that stand I believe the Russians will climb down.' He said he believed it was better to take that stand at once than to allow things to go on indefinitely. If the latter course were followed we would all be destroyed. He himself would rather be dead than deprived of his liberty at the instance of the Communists. It was a terrible situation to have to face. I told him I thought Attlee and Bevin were prepared to face it. I was quite sure that Marshall and the States were prepared. What I did fear most was the bacteriological warfare – the use of gas and germs. We did not know what Russia possessed in that way. Alexander was inclined to discount their having gone very far in that direction. I told him I was inclined to feel the contrary. They had brought in many scientists. We ourselves had known from our own experiments what could be done in the way of destroying crops and herds. Suggested to him he might some day have a confidential talk with Dr. Mitchell of the Research Department on what he knew of these matters.

"I much enjoyed luncheon and felt a certain freedom in the conversation both before and after luncheon, and at the table than I felt at any time. One thing the trip abroad has done for me is to give me more confidence in myself through what it has disclosed of the appreciation of other peoples and nations. Also I have seen wherein my own vision and judgment has not had to take second place to that of anyone else. I am most anxious to make the most of every moment and be prepared to speak fearlessly on the present day issues."

One of these issues, in Mackenzie King's opinion, was Canada's role in discussions about the future of Palestine. "The more I think of it," he wrote on December 6, "the more I regret that I have ever consented even to have Rand take part. I remember trying to persuade St. Laurent it was better for us to keep out. I know if I had been Secretary of State for External Affairs, I would not have permitted our side to take any steps.

"I am glad I stood firmly against allowing Pearson to become Chairman [of the ad hoc committee established by the Second Assembly of the UN]. Apparently they all use him in New York to be prominent in the Palestine affair, and he being young and no doubt feeling his ability in these matters, I think lent himself perhaps too wholly to the desires of others. . . . I told Pearson in talking with him, this afternoon, that I thought he should put his emphasis now on developing his own staff at home. I am terribly afraid we have gone too far in the prominent part we have allowed our own people to play at the expense of our own affairs. I believe we are going to have a difficult time in the House of Commons because of the length to which matters at home have been allowed to drift with the Americans. Too much has been left on Clark's shoulders and there has been too great a readiness to accept anything he might suggest. I must take my share of blame for all this; where I have given in has been the result of fatigue and over-weariness and exhaustion."

Parliament had met on December 5 and, as he was walking into the Senate Chamber, Mackenzie King "said to Wishart Robertson who was beside me: this will be the last time I will walk in this procession at an opening of Parliament." Later, he added: "I am sure I am right in not trying to continue on in public life after the present session, if spared through it all." When the House met, the Prime Minister explained that the session had been called earlier than usual to deal with urgent legislation approving the steps which had been announced on November 17 to meet the exchange crisis, implementing the trade agreements which had been negotiated at Geneva, and extending the Transitional Measures Act. His attempt to secure consent to introduce a motion making the debate on the address the first order of business on Monday, December 8, and giving precedence to government motions and orders touched off a prolonged procedural wrangle. "The Tories at once began a real filibuster," he wrote, "Bracken taking the line that the real questions were cost of living, etc. Matter of treaties could stand over.

"The whole proceedings were indeed an effort to block progress. I thought Coldwell spoke well. Low's speech amounted to nothing. It was the Tories that were most bellicose. I drew attention to the fact that all the fuss was over a motion dealing with procedure. That the Government was going to take that part into its own hands and not trouble about seeking to make agreements if we were to be taken to task every time an effort in this direction was made. We must make our own decisions and stand or fall by them.

"The filibustering took up quite a long time to no effect. It may have helped to save a debate of the same kind on Monday. At any rate, it has let us have the arguments in advance of further discussion."

When the House met on December 8, the procedural debate continued. "The Opposition had intended to amend my motion by striking out the last part of it and confining the motion itself to procedure for today only. I had learned of this and, in speaking, suggested that the House give its assent to my striking out the latter part [the reference to precedence for orders and motions]. The Opposition were in this position that all the speakers they had prepared were for purposes of obstruction, etc. They were knocked endways. However, they were bound to obstruct and they made them anyway – a disgusting sort of scene, but in the end they put themselves in a corner by my saying I would let the motion go as it was and the motion was so worded as to give the Government all the time for the rest of the session without even granting the customary right to answer questions and produce papers, etc. I never saw a whole army routed more effectively – turned back in their own steps.

"The debate on this motion kept on until 5 and then there was a division – a most foolish step on the part of the Opposition. It gave the Government a majority of something like 70 [the motion carried 139 to 69] in the first division of the session, the C.C.F. voting with the Government; the other people, the S.C.'s, with the Opposition."

With the procedural problem settled, the mover and seconder of the address "got through their speeches. . . . Providence seemed to be on my side to give me what was needed in the way of rest for preparing for the evening." After the dinner adjournment, Mackenzie King reported, "Bracken made a terrible speech. Had far too much material which had been prepared for him; was ill at ease through it all. He did, however, make a very kindly reference to the honour the King had conferred and to my trip abroad.

"In following Bracken I made the mistake of being a little too sharp with him at the start. I don't know exactly what occasioned this except that his vote of want of confidence in the Government rather annoyed me. I made a reference to his position in the leadership which I think I would have been wiser to have left unsaid. I managed however to express some appreciation of the honour having been well received by fellow-citizens and particularly by fellow-members in the House. Most of the day was taken up in a description of the trip abroad and something on the state of Europe.

"Matters worked out so that I had exactly between 10 and 11 to speak, which left me without having had to do any dallying and enabled me to get on record something that was pleasing and appropriate, and avoid much discussion on other questions. In other words, I went through marvellously well considering everything had come so suddenly with little or no time for preparation."

The opening days of the session were fully occupied by consideration of the exchange crisis and procedure for approving the trade agreements which, in any event, were to be implemented by order-in-council on January 1, 1948. On both issues, the Progressive Conservatives were prepared to mount major attacks on the government. In addition to specific complaints about concessions Canada had made during the Geneva negotiations, Bracken particularly objected to the weakening of the system of Commonwealth preferences implied by the exchange of notes between Canada and the United Kingdom annexed to the agreements. The Prime Minister moved acceptance of the General Agreement on Tariffs and Trade during the evening of December 9. The following day he "talked with Abbott, St. Laurent and one or two others about changing the resolution which had been framed for approval of Geneva agreements, pointing out I thought we should strike out approval of exchange of notes. It was unfair to expect the Tory party to approve those notes and besides it was not necessary. They were not an essential part of the agreement.

"When the House met at 3, I at once said publicly I thought we should amend the Bill in that particular; also drew attention to the fact that I had agreed to have resolution considered by a committee before asking the House to approve it. Had I been here when the resolutions were being prepared I would perhaps have been able to have the resolution drafted differently and saved the necessity of making the changes, but the wisdom of what I had suggested became apparent when Bracken stated that they themselves were proposing an amendment to the resolution on the lines I had suggested. I am glad to have gotten this stroke ahead of the Tories. I also I think scored on the matter of holding to the procedure which will help us most in the end to conclude business rapidly. . . .

"Merritt, of Vancouver, spoke for the Tories. He criticized me for having made a partisan speech on the Geneva agreements when I should have just brought out their bold outlines. I thought this was fair comment, and I would perhaps, had I had time, have taken a little different line, one that would have gained the co-operation of all parties in the House. There were other criticisms which seemed to me fair enough."

The debate on the resolution was not proceeded with after the Christmas recess and, though the Minister of Finance suggested that it would be re-introduced during the 1949 session, the GATT arrangements never received formal parliamentary approval.

The opposition parties were also very critical of the government's handling of the exchange crisis, both the remedies proposed and the long delay in dealing with the decline in reserves. Bracken argued that devaluation of the Canadian dollar would have been a more appropriate remedy and attacked the extraordinary powers given to the Minister of Reconstruction and Supply to regulate imports of capital goods. With part of the criticism, Mackenzie King agreed. In Cabinet on December 11, he "spoke out strongly against one of Abbott's measures giving Howe practically sole discretion to decide on the admission of certain commodities and the like. I stated there ought to be some Board that would have these powers from which there might be an appeal to the Minister but that it was a mistake to have a Minister of the Crown in the front line, and any one man given these powers specially a Minister of the Crown. It was pointed out we would have to organize a wholly new Board and measures were temporary. That we would be accused of establishing a bureaucracy, etc. It was obvious that there was no chance to alter the situation as the Bill was printed and was to be introduced this afternoon. This whole business was done with far too much of a rush. Before I left for England, I suggested the formation of a Board and pointed out this aspect as one far from Liberal in its character. I asked Council how we would act if we were in Opposition and the Government of the day was given arbitrary powers to decide on anything. I am afraid we may have to back away from a good many of the clauses that have been inserted. There is no doubt that wrong exercise of powers makes Ministers less willing to part with any power which they feel they might be able to exercise.

"I record this now as evidence of what I believe will follow and what will prove to be a weak spot in our armour. One very difficult to defend."

In the House that afternoon, business "got under way more rapidly and peacefully. . . . There will be little trouble over the continuation of powers given under the Transitional Measures Act and the Agricultural Products Act but I can see that we are in for a session that will be a very stormy and unpleasant one. An effort will be made to have us put down as a Government that is seeking and taking absolute powers. The executive usurping Parliament, etc. My own speeches against Bennett's will be widely used by the Opposition. I believe they will from the start oppose practically everything we are proposing on the score that it is arbitrary power we are exercising."

On December 16 the Prime Minister "stayed in the House throughout the afternoon, listening to Abbott's statement on the Emergency Measures which was an excellently prepared statement but one which he read throughout. He was replied to by Macdonnell who made I thought a pretty telling reply. The best speech I have heard Macdonnell make. He is right in his criticism of powers being given Howe under the Act. They are far too arbitrary and quite contrary to the Liberal method of preceedings.

"I made my protest as strongly as I could in the Cabinet. Howe could not have continued on unless he had had the powers and there was no use trying, at the last moment, to get the Bill differently prepared. I had spoken of the matter before I left for England. Council had settled it all meanwhile but I think both he and the Government will regret these features of the Bill. I said so quite frankly to Abbott as we sat together later in the afternoon."

Just after he returned from London, Mackenzie King became involved in negotiations between Canada and the United Kingdom on revised food contracts for 1948. A mission, headed by Sir Percivale Liesching, the Permanent Secretary of the Ministry of Food, had been in Ottawa since November and, in discussions with Canadian officials, had proposed a selective purchasing programme which involved release from further commitments to purchase Canadian bacon, beef and eggs. After hearing a review of the negotiations in Cabinet on December 9, the Prime Minister was "thoroughly shocked and disgusted at the British attitude; after we have made a long term contract for wheat, contract for bacon, eggs, we find the British Government prepared to cancel the latter altogether. Begin to purchase same commodities from other countries in the sterling area, just as if there was no obligation toward Canada in the light of all the credit she has given and all the help. I have said repeatedly in the Cabinet that I thought we were foolish in extending the credits we were to so many countries. That we would never be paid back but the Finance Department still would persist in giving additional credits. Also we were making a mistake in expecting that the British Government would show any thanks for what has been done. That has all now come to pass and the men who are more responsible than anyone else for letting us into that position are now finding it necessary to tell Britain that Canada cannot grant anything more in the way of credit to her, and that if she goes back on some of her contracts, we will have to cancel all and let our farmers and others sell wherever they wish, to whatever countries they wish.

"I think the Finance Department are most to blame for having gone too far. I think Gardiner is, too, much to blame in having made the contracts he did, going pretty much against the wish of the Cabinet as a whole, in entering into some of these without a proper discussion in advance. I recalled earlier discussions when almost everyone felt that Gardiner was putting us into wrong position on agricultural matters. Even he, himself, now says he has been deceived by the British as far as their keeping their word is concerned."

At the Cabinet meeting on December 11, the problem was discussed again. "The British Government apparently are quite unwilling to purchase more than a fraction of what they have contracted to take from Canada – bacon, eggs and the like. We had to consider carefully what the alternative should be.

"The decision was reached to allow a certain amount of extra credits – ten millions for the following three months, and then change to sales in the open market for our agricultural products. Reference to the debate will show in the past that I was opposed to long term agreements. Said I believed Britain would not find it possible to carry them out and thought it would be perhaps another year or two. They have already nearly exhausted our credit. It will be found too that I strongly opposed the extent to which they were giving credits to Britain and to the other countries but was overruled. Now we are rapidly getting toward a bankrupt condition because our credit is nearly exhausted.

"All these extra taxes and restrictions have had to be put on because of expenditures of public monies in many directions, not merely credits but for defence purposes, etc., running back to the days of the end of the war. Purchase of ships and the like which, if my advice had been heeded, would not have been necessary today. That is one of the advantages of keeping a daily record. One can see whether one was right or not."

That evening the Prime Minister met St. Laurent, Abbott, Pearson, Towers and Clark at his office in the House of Commons "to discuss what it is best to do with respect to trade arrangements with Britain. We concluded that because of the British decision not to purchase certain commodities: cheese, bacon, eggs, etc., also a limited amount for wheat, we might have to end the present contract and have our supplies sold in the open market. We agreed that it was desirable there should be an agreed announcement that the new arrangement had been come to because of the shortage in Britain and in Canada of American dollars and for the present at least, another three or four months, the following arrangement had been come to. Here we decided to allow a larger amount of additional credit to Britain than had been thought of at first – 20 millions a month instead of 10 millions a month, for three months, as we would derive more revenue from the sale of our wheat at market rates. Towers thought that we would be able to do this. He also asked if I would agree to our indicating that we might in the course of the next three or four years be able to do something in co-operation with the Marshall Plan, this in order to help gain support for the Plan in the States in Congress, and also to assist in bringing stabilization in Europe. I felt it was only right we should do this but that it should be conditional upon our finding it possible to do something. It should be pointed out that we had already done more than other countries; that for the present we could not assist, but might later.

"It was left to the three members of the service to talk to Liesching and Sir Alexander Clutterbuck to see if an agreed statement could be arranged with Britain."

On December 13 Pearson gave Mackenzie King a telegram from Norman Robertson "which indicated that the British were as anxious as we were not to break off completely the contracts between Britain and Canada over the purchase of goods, and were prepared to make another effort to review the situation. That has come through our standing firm and letting them see that we did not intend to bankrupt ourselves any more than they intended to bankrupt themselves. Had we not stood firmly and allowed ourselves to be driven through pressure into further credits being given which we are not in a position to afford, this would not have come about.

"What the Government is experiencing today is what I said so often would come fairly soon and that is, that a day of reckoning for our unnecessary expenditures during the latter part of the war and post-war period, particularly the too extensive credits granted and gifts made, is now upon us, and is facing us with a situation which we may find it impossible to meet. I am most anxious that for the next three months, at least, we do not break any contracts with Britain or Britain with us. At the end of that time, things will be either so much better, or so much worse, that they will find necessary revision one way or the other."

Late that afternoon the Prime Minister met Abbott, St. Laurent and Pearson in his office. "Abbott was pretty strong against allowing any additional credit to Britain. St. Laurent seemed to favour the last suggestion that had come from the British negotiators and which involved only an additional five million dollars a month for what had been suggested we might concede for three months. The figure previously understood being 20 million instead of 10 million dollars.

"I stated that I believed very strongly we should avoid, if possible, a total break in the contracts and substituting therefor the open market. This at least for the first three months of the new year. I said by that time conditions would be either so much worse or so much better that the situation could then be reviewed and meanwhile the Russians would not be able to say that there is a break between the United Kingdom and the Dominion, or our political opponents, that we were turning from Britain to the United States to be controlled by the latter country. We sent for Sir Percival Liesching and Sir Alexander Clutterbuck and I told them what we had been discussing. What I felt the Government would be prepared to agree to. I said that for my part I thought the Minister of Finance was right in not believing it right to give any more credit. I, myself, would not agree to go beyond what he had suggested except for the talks I had had while in England with Attlee and Bevin and the condition which I felt the United Kingdom and ourselves were facing as a possible result of failure of the conference of Foreign Ministers. . . .

"Liesching indicated that he would be prepared to recommend what we had indicated we would be prepared to reach agreement on. He could not, of course, say what his Government might do. He and Sir Alexander Clutterbuck seemed appreciative of the fact that we, as Ministers, had met late in the afternoon to go into the matter further and had sent for them at this particular time."

The problem came up again at the Cabinet meeting on December 15. "Gardiner brought out wherein the British Government were paying very high prices to the Australians and New Zealanders for wheat but that the Governments of those countries were giving the farmers only about one third or one quarter of the price but giving them as a subsidy for feeding purposes, part of the extra amount paid by the British Government. In this way, they were able to supply bacon and eggs, etc., to the British. Gardiner pointed out that England was able to pay this high rate to Australia and New Zealand by our letting her have grain at the low figure we have agreed to sell it to her. This seemed to change considerably the picture discussed on Saturday afternoon.

"Gardiner himself, I think, is at fault in not having known of this information and brought it out some days ago. Also distinctly at fault in not having had any written agreements about what was to be done by the British in payment for grain, beef, etc., in 1949. That apparently was all left at loose ends. Agreed to by departments but no signed agreement or written memo. The situation most involved."

During the Cabinet meeting on December 17, Mackenzie King read a message from Attlee "saying the British Government had accepted suggested basis of settlement which had been come to in my office on Saturday afternoon and which they continue to refer to as my proposals. It was a very fine letter and I am quite sure that my words on the afternoon of Saturday had their effect on bringing about their settlement in accordance with its terms. I am sure that it has saved a situation that would have been most harmful politically and in intra-Imperial relations, had the food contracts between Britain and Canada severed completely and had we gone on the open market as, at one moment, the Cabinet was on the verge of deciding to do. I held strongly from the start that while financially that might be the thing to do, that I knew of conditions as I had learned of them in Europe and felt it would be a terrible mistake politically. I think, too, it would have set a whole trend of criticism against the Government on the score of our separating from Britain and seeking to join up with the United States.

"I then had Mr. St. Laurent give to the Cabinet an account of negotiations. He was inclined to have a statement left to myself but I insisted that the Cabinet, as a whole, should know exactly what we were agreeing to. I had him go over twice the different features of the agreement so that there could be no mistake as to everyone agreeing to it."

Under the agreement, the wheat contract signed in 1946 was continued and Britain agreed to purchase somewhat smaller amounts of other food products at higher prices. The Prime Minister indicated in the House on December 18 that the purchases would be financed by drawings of $45 million on the Canadian loan to the United Kingdom up to March 31, 1948, and the payment of $100 million in dollars. He felt that the statement was "well received. Managed to get the afternoon's programme under way without another real row between the Opposition and ourselves." Details of the new food contracts for 1948 were released on January 2, 1948.

The House of Commons adjourned on December 19. Two days earlier the members had organized an enthusiastic demonstration in honour of Mackenzie King's birthday. He had been "careful to be in my seat as soon as the first bell rang to avoid any demonstration. However, even before the opening of the doors and prayers, as the Members came in on our side of the House, they began to sing: Happy Birthday and to applaud very warmly. They were joined by Members opposite.

"Immediately after prayers and the galleries then filled up, Bracken rose to extend congratulations. He was followed by Mackenzie and then Coldwell and Solon Low, Mr. St. Laurent, Pouliot, [J. H.] Harris [Danforth] and Homuth [M.P. for Waterloo South]. I was really surprised at the outspoken feelings of friendship on the part of Harris and Homuth and the way their remarks were received by the Conservatives.

"It was the 30th anniversary of Chubby Power's coming into the House. (This reminds me that it was the anniversary of my defeat in North Waterloo and the day before my mother's death. Perhaps the hardest moment in my life.)

"Power came in after the House had assembled. There was a great demonstration from Quebec Liberals who are doing all in their power to bring him again strongly to the fore. There was a basket of 73 roses in front of my desk and 30 roses on his desk. We were both brought naturally into the speaking. It was only while the others were speaking that I thought of the simile about speech being light upon the depth of the unspoken. It helped me to have the right kind of introduction and avoid making reference to individual speeches. I managed to say all that I had in mind and that, without confusion. The House was very silent and sympathetic while I was speaking. I could feel that the Members were realizing that the speech was one which they might have occasion to recall in future years. The last I would be making as Prime Minister on a birthday anniversary. I was quite surprised and touched by the evidence of great friendliness and appreciation of my attitude toward him on the part of Power. His words could not have shown more in the way of real appreciation of the true nature of our relationships.

"Before the speaking, John MacNicol came over and shook hands most warmly with me. After speaking, Homuth came over and extended congratulations. Tommy Church came and sat beside me. Spoke most affectionately and appreciatively. Irvine [Cariboo] came over from the C.C.F. group and said he might have spoken publicly but wished to say he felt I was a really great man. That he had a great regard for me and everything he might say, criticism in public would not relate to any personal feelings. . . .

"I went over myself and thanked Bracken. Shook hands with those seated near him and then the same with Coldwell. Later asked Solon Low to come to my room. Thanked him there and had a short talk with him. Received a charming letter from the Speaker. There were many other incidents and evidences of friendship and good-will. I felt immensely relieved when everything was over."

As the end of the year approached, Mackenzie King again began to think of arrangements for his retirement. On December 16 he "attended luncheon given by Fogo to Executive of National Liberal Federation. Several Ministers present. Made a few brief remarks. Thanked Executive for their part. Touched briefly at close on reference to passing of the years and the serious situation in Europe. Need for a Liberal party in these days which will keep to the middle of the road, avoiding extremes, regarding the general interest. Spoke of this hope that I cherished for the future.

"I confess I felt a little emotional as I made the references I did, having in mind that this was the beginning of the preparation of the Federation meeting at which I would ask that a Convention be called to consider the position of leadership, etc. I am at the moment greatly enjoying my work in Parliament and feel a new zeal and strength for it but I realize that time is passing, that I shall soon begin to feel the wear and tear and strain of long sittings in the House, etc. As I remember a year ago, I was feeling in the best of shape near the end of the year but the pressure that came in the early part of the year brought on the attack of influenza which brought me down more quickly and further than I had believed possible. I do not wish to encounter anything like this again. I keep feeling that I must hold firmly to the decision I have reached and not be tempted to continue on though I notice in today's Citizen, an article in which the members appear to have been discussing the situation and to have reached the conclusion that if times were difficult I would stay on."

The next day at the Cabinet meeting Mackenzie King's colleagues "all rose and remained standing until I was seated.

"Mackenzie then rose and said that the entire Cabinet wished to extend to me warmest birthday greetings. Referred to the regard and affection which they had for me. Hoped that I will continue on in public life in years to come. Spoke of the pleasure of seeing me looking so well, etc.

"He then referred to the gift which they had for me and Mr. St. Laurent thereupon presented me with a marble desk set which Mackenzie said they hoped I would find useful when I came to write my Memoirs. St. Laurent also spoke very feelingly and eloquently of the regard which they all had and the good wishes which they extended. I told my colleagues that it was difficult for me to express what I felt of gratitude for the beautiful gift they had presented and the inscription it carried. I spoke of there having been many interesting scenes in the rooms in which they were but I doubted if, at any time in the history of Canada, there had been a like expression of loyalty and friendship toward any member of the Government on the part of all his colleagues. I said that I did have a desire to write something of the history of the Liberal party in Canada but I hoped that the rays of light from the gift they had presented to me would help to lend its tone to what I might have to say. That, like them, I did not have a wife or children. That my life had been centred very much in that room and the circle around the table with the exception of father's own family and one or two old intimate friends. The lives of their family had meant more to me than those of any others. That I had only the happiest remembrances of the associations in that Chamber through the years. I thought the record had been a remarkable one in the interests of our country and the world, and should like to have time to leave it. Spoke of retaining the gift through my days and having it become later a national possession.

"I then said that I hardly expected or hoped that I would be occupying this seat on another birthday anniversary. That that lent a double significance to the present gathering. That I wanted each one of them to feel that I was grateful for their friendship and co-operation. That I had and would continue to have an abiding interest in their lives.

"I spoke of the meeting of the Federation in January and said I hoped there would be a large attendance at the meeting which would take place on the 20th of January. I hinted that I would then make public what I felt about a Convention in the summer."

On December 30 the Prime Minister noted "an effort of Fogo of the National Liberal Federation to change the date of their meeting and dinner to a time when Parliament was in session. I made it clear to P. [Pickersgill] to say in reply tonight to Fogo that it was attempting to deal with both the Federation and Parliament at the same time which brought on my illness last year. On the doctor's advice, I would not repeat that folly. Also I had the strongest of reasons for wishing to make a statement to the Federation before Parliament met rather than after. I have expressed a preference for the 20th as the date for the dinner but have agreed to the 23rd if that will help to relieve embarrassment in the matter of Members attending. Here again I intend to stand firm."

# CHAPTER FOUR

# The Crisis over Korea, Palestine and North Atlantic Security

MACKENZIE KING had returned from Europe in December 1947 almost convinced that a third world war was imminent. His apprehension was not diminished when he learned on December 15 that the meeting of the Council of Foreign Ministers in London had broken up without reaching agreement on either Austria or Germany. "We have now reached the point that Bevin feared might lead to war," he wrote. "It is clear that the United Kingdom, the United States and France intend to work together to save Western Europe and to further her recovery under the Marshall plan. It is equally clear that Russia intends to hold all her satellite powers together to seek to become the Master of Europe. The issue will reach its critical point when the three countries begin to plan an organization of Western Europe from their zones in Berlin. Russia may seek to prevent them going through the Russian zone. Should she do this, and threaten to enforce her position by threat of arms, war will be inevitable. It seems incredible to believe but it is a very real possibility. At a time like this, one can understand how Baldwin might well have felt that to speak of war again after the end of the first world war would have meant the defeat of his Administration and, on the other hand, to have given this as a reason for not disclosing to the British House of Commons, the real situation in Germany, while honest in statement, was a terrible mistake politically."

It was against this background of fear, frustration and international tension that the Prime Minister approached a question which in mid-December almost wrecked the Liberal government. After prolonged debate in the second session of the United Nations General Assembly, a resolution sponsored by the United States was adopted on November 14 which called for free elections in Korea observed by a UN temporary commission which would also arrange for the withdrawal of foreign troops. J. A. Bradette, the chairman of the House of Commons Standing Committee on External Affairs and a member of the Canadian delegation, had strongly supported the creation of the UN commission during the debate while Mr. Gromyko, speaking for the Soviet Union, had strongly opposed it. The delegate for the Ukraine had found particularly objectionable Canada's appointment to the commission.

At the Cabinet meeting on December 18, St. Laurent sought approval for the appointment of Dr. G. S. Patterson, Counsellor of the Embassy in Nanking, as Canada's representative on the UN Temporary Commission for Korea. The other nations represented were Australia, China, El Salvador, France, India, the Philippines, Syria and the Ukrainian S.S.R. Mackenzie King decided that "the time had come to speak out. I said that I did not see how I could support the recommendation. That I thought I ought to say I felt a great mistake was being made by Canada being brought into situations in Asia and Europe of which she knew nothing whatever, of interfering with Great Powers without realizing what consequences might be.

"I said I did not think there was a member in the Cabinet who could begin to say he knew anything about either the real situation in the Near East and much less about the situation in Korea and Manchuria. That President Truman had told me at the time of his visit that America was more worried over conditions in Korea and Manchuria than over anything else. They were fearful of the conflict that would come with the Russians there. I asked why should we attempt to go in and settle a situation as had arisen in Korea. Have our country drawn into or possible consequences that would come from war, if it broke out, as it well might, over interference with relations between Russia and the U.S. I pointed out that there was not one of the Big Powers on the Commission excepting France which could be said to possess any real power today; neither the U.S. nor the U.K. were on the Commission. Canada was most important of the powers. We would be made the spearhead of whatever arose. Ilsley remarked that Australia was one. I pointed out that Australia was not comparable to Canada in the eyes of the world. Someone mentioned they were Pacific powers. I said it did not matter who they were. We knew nothing about the situation and should keep out of it.

"St. Laurent said that he thought practically all members of the Council felt pretty much as I did; that we could, of course, withdraw from the United Nations if we wished, but that, being a member of it, we were now going to take a seat on the Security Council and we had to assume other obligations, etc. I replied that I thought the United Nations counted for nothing so far as any help in the world was concerned and, up to the present, had been really [impotent] and served mostly the purpose of the

Russians who used it for propaganda purposes and the like. If we had made a mistake in getting on to the Commission, I thought the sooner we were off, the better, rather than to go on getting into deeper water all the time. I said that I had heard nothing about Canada taking any part in Korean affairs until I read the speech Bradette had made, speaking for Canada at the United Nations on Korea. I asked what possible knowledge Bradette could have of that situation. I also asked if the matter had ever come before the Cabinet. St. Laurent said he did not think that it had; I said, if it had, it had never come out when I was there. Of course, I would have to be responsible if it had come up when I was not there. He went on to say he did not think it had come before the Cabinet at all. Ilsley said something about not knowing how it came up. He had been absent for a week or so when the matter was considered in New York.

"St. Laurent really had no knowledge of the sponsors of the matter at all. I said I would have objected very strongly to our taking any sudden part. That I did not see how I could place on my soul the burden of being responsible in any way for bringing Canada into a situation that might make this country partly responsible for war, for which we should in no way be responsible or involved. I also said that I did not think we had any business to be interfering with the Middle East. That Bevin, Foreign Minister, had told me that if Britain fell out with the Arabs, and our people took a position against the Arabs at the United Nations, that Britain and America have lost control of the oil-fields, that if they did and Russia became possessed of them, nothing could prevent Russia from dominating the entire world. The supply there would last a thousand years. I said what right had we to throw our country into a situation of the kind. It all arose from being unwilling to say we did not know anything about these matters and therefore would not assume responsibility in connection with them. Canada's role was not that of Sir Galahad to save the whole world unless we were in a position to do it. Ilsley then said that he disagreed with the view that I was taking. That he did not see why we should not go on a Commission there; that we had assumed responsibility and should carry it out, etc. I saw that the situation was getting rather intense so I said that obviously we could not decide the matter today and we would have a day in Council in reference to it, but I certainly wished to make my position very clear and, that, at the first moment that the subject had been brought up.

"I imagine that the truth is that Pearson with his youth and inexperience and influenced by the persuasion of others around him, had been anxious to have Canada's External Affairs figure prominently in world affairs and has really directed affairs in New York when he should have been in Ottawa, and without any real control by Ministers of the Crown and proper consideration of these questions.

"All meant well but very much the inexperience of youth. I am sure if [O. D.] Skelton had been alive, he would not have advocated our going afield in that fashion. Also in England, Robertson told me he thought it was a great mistake for External Affairs to be touching matters in Korea. I feel the same about Palestine."

The Prime Minister was resolved "to make a very strong fight on this question and to take the position that even if we have to get out of the League [*sic*], we must not stay in it if it means we are risking being drawn into wars; put into a position where we might become ostensibly responsible for a pretext for war. I said that all members of Council would have to take that responsibility.

"None of them spoke except Gardiner who agreed with me. Matters were then left over.

"I find Ilsley very difficult at times. I well recall that before this last great war, he could not be brought to believe that there was going to be war. Put all his faith in the League of Nations. Fought everything that looked like preparing for war. When war came, he was more fanatical than the rest."

On December 21, a quick reading of a memorandum prepared by the Department of External Affairs on Canada's representation on the Korean commission, simply made Mackenzie King feel "more strongly than ever that we should not proceed with that appointment."

At the Cabinet meeting the next day, there was another long discussion of the question. "I had refused a day or two ago to sign an Order-in-Council appointing Patterson in China as Canada's member on the Commission. . . . Mr. St. Laurent outlined the situation pretty much as it is set forth in a memo which Pearson had prepared. He concluded by saying that the question to be decided was whether we would boycott the Commission. . . . I did not think the question was one of boycotting the Commission. It was a very much larger question as to whether Canada was to be placed in a position where she might well be made the spearhead of an attack for having made more difficult the situation between the United States and Russia, and being drawn into a war because of the part she had taken against Russia. I pointed out that the question went back to conference at Cairo and Potsdam where it was a Great Power that was to act on the Commission. . . . The situation was quite different now where one of those powers had refused to have anything to do with the Korean situation beyond taking the position that both parties should withdraw their troops altogether. That I felt the United States was anxious to have Canada on the Commission. That we would thereby become inevitably allied with her as against Russia. Obviously there was nothing that the Commission could do to support the ends of the Resolution under which it had been appointed. The United Nations had no forces to carry out any of their decisions. That we thanked the Lord we had not gone on the Palestine Commission though, if a pretty positive stand had not been taken, we might well have been. The same was true of the Balkan Commission – that we kept off it. Why we should get into the Korean situation, I did not know. I said I was considering the matter, not from the point of view of any stand taken up to the present, least of all reflecting on any colleague or official but solely because of the conditions as I knew them to exist at the present time in Europe, as between the United States and Russia – both in Europe and in Korea. That we had seen the Council of Foreign Ministers break up over a question of one government for Germany. It was exactly the same question as in Germany – one government for Korea. That we knew that war was threatening out of the German situation. Even this morning's papers stated that Russia was interpreting the Marshall Plan as an invitation to war, saying that it meant war. Marshall himself had said that, until this struggle between the United States and Russia was ended, there would be no making of peace. That for us to go into Korea and tell Russia what to do was just an impossible thing. I pointed out that, of the countries named, Canada was only one that counted for anything. I said I considered the matter from the point of view of my responsibility as a Minister of the Crown to Parliament and through Parliament to the people. I was perfectly certain that debate on this question in Parliament would show that members of all parties did not wish us to intervene into the internal affairs of Korea. I was equally sure that the Canadian people as a whole did not want it at this time. Believing that, I might just as well say at once that I would not sign the Order-in-Council appointing a Commissioner. I was perfectly agreeable to have the whole responsibility put on myself and having the United States and United Nations told that I would not sign the Order for the reasons I had mentioned."

The Prime Minister reported that "Ilsley took pretty much the kind of attitude I expected. He was dour; hard as a rock. Took the whole question as a reflection on himself. He had not even been at the United Nations until the day that they were virtually forced, at the instance of the United States, [into] saying they would be on the Commission. He said that he was present when they had come to the point that Canada would have to stand up publicly to say she would not go on the Commission. He had agreed with those who thought it would be unwise to take that position and had sanctioned going on the Commission though up to that moment, our people had done all they could to keep off. St. Laurent admitted he knew nothing of the matter. It was also stated that the Cabinet had known nothing of it. . . . As I said to the Cabinet, I thought I was the only man in Parliament who had ever been in Korea. Our people knew nothing about the country and its problems. I know that in their hearts, every member of the Cabinet agreed with me. I got very little help from any colleague. Indeed one or two were somewhat embarrassing.

"Mitchell was outspoken and helpful, pointing out some of the utter folly of the whole business. That nothing could be accomplished anyway. Some had suggested we should go on to the Commission and have it report that nothing could be done. Claxton raised the argument that Russia would take advantage of Canada not proceeding with the Commission to point out that we were not united and the United States were afraid to go on with what had been suggested at the United Nations. He rather defended the action of supporting the Resolution when members of the delegations found themselves in an awkward place. I took strongly the position that no government should surrender its power of issuing instructions as to what was to be done on these matters that involved the possibility of war.

"I said that, personally, I felt that the Russians had made use of the Council of the Foreign Ministers and of the United Nations only as a basis for their own propaganda and to give themselves time to continue arming for a war of world domination and to stir up all the Communistic unrest that was possible meanwhile. That they had been doing this, not since the war only, but actually years before the war, and in an active way at the time that they were allies. That the United Nations had no power of any kind. They were people without responsibility. Were telling others what should be done in world affairs. For my part, before I would sanction a step that would throw Canada into another world war, where this could be avoided in any way, I would go out on a crusade myself against the United Nations and let the people see the mistake that was being made. That I would not, of course, do it as a member of the Government but would not wish to be in a government that would commit us to errors of the kind. I said I had not spoken as openly to the Cabinet as I had, excepting at the time of Munich. Then I had to speak out. Had said we would go to war if need be. I know that this involved the Cabinet being completely divided. I hoped we could save a situation of that kind at present. Certainly I did not intend in the last years of my public life to have the accusation brought against me that was brought against Baldwin. That I had hesitated to warn the people of a situation that I knew and to tell the truth concerning it because it might be politically injurious. That I would never do.

"Abbott asked a question or two which did not show much appreciation of the real issue that was involved. A sort of question that might have led Ilsley to feel that he was siding with him. Gardiner had already spoken against the business and did again today but all the rest of the Cabinet sat silent and said nothing.

"The question then came as to the form in which the matter was to be settled. Ilsley said all he wanted to know was what the decision of the Cabinet would be. Rather hinted if it went against his view, he would resign though he did not use those words but I could see that Mitchell and others seemed to take that meaning in what he was saying. It was finally agreed that the United States should be told that the Government had considered the matter and was of the opinion that in the light of the present world situation, as it had developed since the resolution was passed appointing the Korean Commission, that we were of the opinion that the establishing of the Commission should be reconsidered. Let it be known that I felt strongly, in the light of what I had learned in Europe, it was a mistake to go on with this Commission at this time."

Apparently "St. Laurent was for having the Americans told that I would decline to sign the Order-in-Council. I said I was wholly agreeable that Marshall should be told that, and also the President. I thought perhaps they might welcome it. If they did not, it might help to bring them and others to their senses. Certainly I would not sign the Order, feeling as I did. I had searched both my mind and soul to find grounds for so doing, but could make no other decision. I said perhaps all that was necessary was to bring up the question of reconsidering the Commission at present though they could be told confidentially what my attitude was. I took this last position largely because of Ilsley's attitude. If it was to relate to a decision which had been made, I could see he was going to resign on that score. He was going to take responsibility for the decision, having been the one who was supposed to be there and watching Canada's interests in the matter. . . . Ilsley said he wanted to see the despatch before it was sent. Was most insistent in his whole attitude. That, of course, was agreed to."

Ilsley's position in the debate simply confirmed the Prime Minister's opinion of him. "Nothing could better illustrate than his attitude in today's discussion how ill suited Ilsley is for leadership. I think toward myself he has a very bitter feeling and had it ever since [the] Ralston episode. He has since believed or imagined that my feelings toward him are either indifferent or antagonistic. . . . Running back into the years, he has been protectionist in the matter of apples. I think he was annoyed at the decision in Geneva to do away with any preferences. Probably feels that I have had to do with that. Apart from all else, in his overtaxed condition from time to time, his judgment has become far from sound. However, I see no necessity for having a break in the Government at this stage and will go a long way to avoid it but I certainly would go much longer to avoid Canada being drawn into war where everything associated with it would be utter folly. The truth is our country has no business trying to play a world role in the affairs of nations, the very location of some of which our people know little or nothing about. So far as External Affairs is concerned, they have been allowed to be run far too much on Pearson's sole say so, and Pearson himself moved far too much by the kind of influences that are brought to bear upon him. He is young, idealistic, etc., but has not responsibility. I am thankful I held responsibility for External Affairs as long as I did. At least, I did not get the country into trouble by keeping it out of things it had no business to interfere with. . . . I think, too, there is wisdom in the knowledge that, as one gets older, younger men begin to feel that the views of older men are out of date. I would not wish to be in a Cabinet that had any kind of opinion [of that sort] prevail. This all helps to make me believe that my decision to be out within another few months is a wholly wise one.

"Wishart Robertson was on the whole helpful. Howe, MacKinnon, McCann and others had nothing to say. It was an occasion where they should have made their voices heard. I am coming increasingly to feel that Claxton would not be a wise man for leader of the party. He is far too much given to an assertion of power (even where power does not exist – far too extravagant), though he has real ability. Abbott is more careful in the latter respect but, on many matters, still lacks depth and understanding of world questions."

On December 23 Mackenzie King revised the "External Affairs telegrams being sent to Washington re Korean Commission, so as to indicate the Commission had not yet been constituted and desirable to consider whether present situation would not make its work so ineffective as to render it undesirable to have it proceeded with."

During the morning of December 27, Pearson telephoned "about a message from Wrong in reply to his representations regarding the Korean Commission. I let him know at once that there was nothing in the representations that differed from what we already knew and understood.

Pearson suggested that perhaps the next step should be to tell them [the United States] to send the Commission without a Canadian representative. I replied I did not think we should tell them anything or give them any instructions but to let them know we felt the work would be futile and that conditions had changed in recent months. They [External Affairs] might as well let them know I would be quite opposed to signing any order. As I more or less expected, before 6 this evening, the [American] Ambassador said he had received a message from the President to deliver to me personally. It was to the effect that the President hoped we would not make any final decision in the absence of Mr. Marshall until the Under-Secretary had a chance to send us some representations. Atherton had offered to come to Laurier House on his way home with the message. I received him in my library. He let me read the message. I then said at once I would not make any final decision pending the communication which the President had mentioned. I then went on to give him my own views about the unwisdom of having Canada take any part in the Commission in the light of conditions as we now knew them. . . . The only points Atherton brought out were that their armies were in Korea and they might like to withdraw them. It was understood the Commission has given them a chance to do that. On the other hand, if the Commission did not go over, they might have to reconsider whether they should keep them there. He also said that Canada was on the Security Council and for us to withdraw from the Commission, would be quite serious. He further said that the Commission was a very weak one and that Canada was the one strong country on it. That, as we were going forward in our place in the world, taking the prominent part we were, that our voice would be the one that would count. I said at once that was the reason I did not want our people on the Commission. I felt we would become the spearhead of all the attack against the Commission, and I would never be forgiven by Parliament for allowing us to be placed in that position as long as it was possible to prevent it. Told him, as he knew, that Pearson had been crowded into agreeing to go on the Commission.

"The Cabinet had never known anything about our taking part. That we would have opposed it strenuously if it had come to us. . . . I told him also that I was very much concerned about the way things were shaping up between the States and Russia. I certainly did not want Canada to be put into any position which would throw her into any situation that we ought to have stayed out of from the start. I said the Commission originally was to have been between Russia and the United States. The view seemed to be that, when Russia had backed out, there was nothing for the United States to do but throw it over to the United Nations. I spoke of it being an indignity for Canada to be associated with other Powers that were named on the Commission; also that the man we were suggesting [Patterson] could not be expected to know anything about the situation. That he was the only person they could think of in the Orient who even pretended to know remotely about conditions there. The more I talked with Atherton and listened to what he felt, the more I felt very strongly that Pearson had been thrown into the situation under pressure from the United States and had yielded in order to help them out, so to speak. Not realizing how serious the whole business was. I then told Atherton what I felt about the United Nations itself. That it was becoming a menace. He could mark my words that the day would come when Russia would withdraw from the United Nations and give as her reasons that it had become a mere tool or instrument for the United States. Served United States policies as she and Germany and Japan had said about the League of Nations being made by France to further her policies in Europe. That they would get out just as they had gotten out of the Council of Foreign Ministers when that body had ceased to be of further use to them as a forum for their propaganda.

"Atherton was careful in what he said but spoke about the wisdom that I had – sense of security that he felt all North America gained in part through my having to do with these foreign relations. I went on to tell him I was getting out in August. Would be announcing a Convention in January. I certainly did not want my last act of importance to be one of having allowed our country to be drawn into a situation it should never have been brought into. In other words, I did not wish history to say of me, as it had of Baldwin, that I had known of a situation but had not told the people how dangerous it was for fear of not getting the support of the country. For my part, I was prepared to get out of the Government and of Parliament if need be and express the danger of the United Nations if I found things going on for some time as they had gone on in the last year or two. It was all nonsense for the United Nations to talk of making other countries independent when they had not forces of any kind to enforce any of their demands. I said to him I was afraid at no cost could I be persuaded to sign an Order-in-Council to send a Canadian representative to Korea. Better let the Commission go without him or find a way to stay at home but that I hoped I would not have to refuse any request from the President or the Secretary of State of the United States. This was one case when I felt much too strongly to yield against my judgment. One reason I was glad to get out was that I was getting over-concerned about what some of these younger men feel should be done in world affairs. When I had been at the head of the Department, I had kept a check on things, though they had gone in some directions much further than I thought they should. But since

I had given over the post, I had felt no longer having restraining hand. I felt we were getting involved in ways we should not begin to, as to our position on the Council [Canada had accepted appointment to the UN Security Council as of January 1, 1948]. Everything was said in the pleasantest way but very firmly and with Atherton saying that, living here in Canada, knowing Canada as he did, he was not surprised that I should take the attitude I did and feel as I did. . . .

"I said to Atherton I sometimes felt I should stay and try to prevent some of these things happening where I saw danger. On the other hand, when a man got to the point that his younger colleagues looked on him as old-fashioned and not to be taken too seriously, it was time that he should cease to continue to take responsibility."

Mackenzie King spent an hour talking with St. Laurent and Pearson on December 30 about a communication which had come from the American Under-Secretary of State. "When I looked at the clock at the end of the conversation, the hands were in a perfectly straight line – 25 to 1. . . . Mr. Atherton had sent over a long communication from the Under-Secretary. . . . I took it from the envelope and read it aloud to both Mr. St. Laurent and Pearson. I then repeated to them with emphasis what I had previously said and added that the document I had just read made me feel stronger than ever on the course I had decided upon. I could not agree to appointing any member of the Commission for Korea. I thought the document itself gave very strong reasons for no Commission being appointed and even for the United States, in its own interests, avoiding that step, if possible. I told them what I had said to Atherton the other day and mentioned he had spoken about the United States having to consider whether they would have to keep their troops on or [take] them out or add to the number. I said that was exactly what I feared, that Canada's support would be held responsible in one case for troops staying or, in another case, for the troops staying out. I said the whole thing was to put us into a position where we would be made the main reason for the future Korean developments. Also put in a position where we could not escape from sharing responsibilities with the United States for any resentment that Russia might exert. I pointed out, too, that, as the letter said, we were very prominent as a country. That for that very reason, I objected to our being put into a false position in a world situation which was nothing of our creation. I stressed, too, the absolute futility of the Commission's work. Sending a body of men on a fool's errand. That we knew absolutely it was impossible to achieve what the resolution asked for. I said I agreed with His Holiness the Pope's statement re insincerity. That all that was represented by the communication was so much paper; that so far as the United

Nations was concerned, they were absolutely helpless to do anything. Had no force to back up their decision. Had no business for that reason to be interfering in domestic affairs of other nations. I said that if members of the Cabinet felt we ought to take responsibility, I was quite prepared to resign immediately and leave those who took that view to assume responsibility but I would not stand in their way for a moment. That, indeed, if, as was hinted the other day by Ilsley, he intended to resign unless we acted in accordance with the resolution, I would much prefer I, myself, to take that step first as I had no desire to end my long career in public life through a difference with a colleague which would cause his resignation. I added that I did not think, with the exception of St. Laurent and Ilsley, each of whom took the position they did to defend what had been done at New York when it was done, that there was another single member of the Cabinet who did not agree with me about the unwisdom of our making any appointment at this time. I also said I resented, in part, some of the arguments in the letter addressed to me; that I did not think it was part of the duties of any official of the United States Government to begin to tell me what should or should not be done by the Canadian Government.

"I said nothing as to the course to be taken until Mr. St. Laurent said he thought perhaps Pearson had better go down and have a word with the Secretary of State and the President. I said Pearson had been good enough to suggest that course last week. I thought perhaps it would be most helpful all around. St. Laurent said he would go himself if necessary but said perhaps if Pearson went first that would leave him free to go later if necessary. He had begun to argue as to what would happen if I dropped out. That a coalition government would have to be formed – Conservatives and Liberals. I said it was ridiculous to have to even think of possibility of a government having to break up over a matter of this kind which was not of our concern at all. The truth of the matter is that those who have had to do with External Affairs have become so infatuated with having to do with world conditions that they are fast losing all perspective in regard to national affairs. . . . I said possibly it might be my destiny to have to do something at the end of my career which might seem a mistake, but I felt so strongly on the risks that the world was running with the United Nations, that I might find it necessary to step out and let my fears be known to the world. . . . There was some argument about what would be consequences if there seemed to be a division between Canada and the United States, etc. I said the United States itself would have to consider they had forced us into the position we were in, and they would just have to do what they thought best. Much better to have an immediate minor issue than to be blamed for all time for having made a colossal mistake in regard to one's own country. . . .

"Pearson then spoke of taking up with the United States some other grounds [on] which we were a bit concerned about the extent of their interference. Taking this up with the Secretary of State and the President. I told him by all means. He mentioned particularly the way in which they are seeking to control the situation in the Orient, etc. I mentioned at the outset of my remarks that terrible pressure had been brought to bear on me before the last Great War, that Canada would go in if Britain were attacked. That, to the last day, I resisted on the ground we would not go in unless we knew the cause, and secondly would not go in until Parliament said so. In this way, I had brought Canada successfully as a united country into the war. He could tell the United States they might need our assistance, co-operation actively at some critical time, and I did not propose to destroy our opportunity for usefulness at this time by taking a step that would have it said I was under the domination of the United States. I told Pearson to note that was the cry the Conservatives were making and would make with increased emphasis at the coming session; that that should be pointed out. I also added I would be very surprised if either Marshall or Truman would ever have me placed in a position where a crisis would be precipitated in our Cabinet involving the risk of existence of the Government itself."

The Prime Minister began work the next day "by writing out a letter to Mr. Ray Atherton in acknowledgment of one received yesterday from him enclosing a memo from the Under-Secretary of State at Washington re Canada and the Korean Commission. I sent copies of this communication along with documents pertaining thereto to Pearson with whom I had a talk of some length, over the 'phone. I counselled him strongly about the appeal of India to the United Nations for intervention. I drew his attention to the fact that Attlee and other members of the Commonwealth of Nations had declined to entertain a similar appeal on the score that they could not accomplish anything. I thought our attitude at the United Nations ought to have this circumstance kept much in mind.

"I said it was foolish for the United Nations to keep sending out commissions for observations, etc., where they really could do nothing. He had better realize they had been formed for the purpose of establishing an international police. Until this had been accomplished, they should limit as much as possible their activities by way of intervention in foreign lands. Conciliation was all right when both Parties agreed but was useless where one refused to conciliate.

"Later I spoke to him about what he might have to say in Washington and went over with him some observations of his own as to the need of more care being exercised by the United States and not taking for granted that Canada will always agree with them. That we could wish to maintain independence in all things. Also the need for more caution by the United Nations as respects their Commissions and greater care with regard to some of the things that they [the United States] are attempting to do in Northern Canada.

"While Pearson is very able and quick, he still lacks experience and, to some degree, distant vision but, next to Robertson and Wrong, is undoubtedly the best man in the diplomatic service."

After lunch on January 4, 1948, the Prime Minister "spent considerable time reading despatches that have come this year from External Affairs, including a splendid address by Smuts delivered after his return from the United Kingdom. Very simple; very direct. Completely in accord with my own views. Only expressed in terms even stronger than I have expressed them in regard to the possibility of war, and as to the uselessness of the United Nations as affording any security.

"Later in the afternoon, I received a long teletype from Pearson through the Consul General's Office in New York, from Lovett [the Under-Secretary of State] and the President. It was just a repetition of what had been said in Lovett's memo to me. Only it contained suggestions which made me feel more strongly than ever that I was right, and that the State Department was simply using the United Nations as an arm of that office to further its own policies. The memo even went so far as to suggest that our own representative might keep in the background as a member of the Commission. Take responsibility without any government direction, etc. To think of this in relation to a matter concerned with possibilities of war, causes one's hair almost to rise in amazement. I confess this whole business has considerably shaken my faith in Pearson's judgment. It has made me feel that he is much too immature. Much too ready to be influenced by American opinion. That in this, he has been more concerned with squaring a mistake that was made at the outset and saving the face of others than really seeing to the protecting of the interests of our own country. That is one of the dangers that comes from the United Nations. Men attending its meetings with great power because of their associations with government but with no real responsibility and acting much too much on their own. Mistaking the sources from which power comes and what it involves in the way of responsibility."

He reached Pearson by telephone late that afternoon and "told him of my feeling regarding the memo and of my fixed determination not to sign the Order. He told me that the President would be writing me a letter as well and he had suggested the possibility of the President 'phoning me. I told him I did not like the idea of a 'phone message and would refrain from discussing matters with the President over the 'phone but would answer any letter he might write. He explained that Lovett had his officials with him when he, Pearson, and Wrong were together seeing him; also that Lovett came with him to the White House. That he did not tell either Lovett or the President that the matter was one which concerned a situation which was developing in the Cabinet. That he thought this might lead to an assertion that we were taking a certain stand in an international matter because of embarrassment in a domestic affair. My reply to this, of course, would be that the whole matter is one that the State Department should have nothing whatever to do with.

"Our two Governments should have nothing whatever to do with it beyond trying to limit as much as possible the consequences of an original mistake for which our Government was not responsible. That it was really a matter for the United Nations itself to cope with.

"I told Pearson that I thought, from now on, I should not be concerned further with the matter. That I ought to leave it I thought to the Department of the Secretary of State for External Affairs and it would be for that Department to deal with the situation as it thought best in the light of the knowledge that I would not sign the Order appointing Patterson. The man suggested, as our representative on the Korean Commission. The United States statement even says that the Commission would probably get the United Nations to arrange for setting up of independence in one half of Korea. If they could do that with the aid of a milk and water Commission, they could certainly do it without any such fictitious support. The whole thing more clearly than ever comes to be an effort on the part of the United States to put us into sharing the responsibility vis-à-vis Russia in the action taken or against the acceptance of the Russian suggestion. Pearson said he thought the United States were now being sorry they had ever established a Commission. Thought it was a mistake but were now mainly concerned over propaganda use that the radio might make of a difference between Canada and the United States in not going ahead with the Commission. Also as giving reasons why their original proposals of . . . withdrawing their armed forces, should have been accepted. I am not sure, because I know nothing about it, why the Russian suggestion should not have been accepted. It certainly was in the nature of something that would appeal to the people generally where the whole effort relates to the withdrawal of Russian-American forces as a preliminary step to the independence of Korea.

"I said to Pearson the suggestion made to him that this would give the

Koreans hope for independence and encourage them in that hope, was I thought one of the worst statements of all. He and I knew that would be false hopes. That it was wrong to lend the hand of our Government in raising false hopes of the kind. That was making the last situation worse than the first. The truth is Pearson should not have yielded nor should Ilsley have yielded to the pressure from the United States for Canada to be a member of the Commission without any possible reference to the Cabinet or authority from the Cabinet and only because they were embarrassed in not taking a stand that would not meet the United States wishes and pressures at the moment.

"As I said to Pearson, the Russian policy at least was realistic and sound for its delegates did not hesitate to let it be known that they did not act without the authority of their Government.

"It is really outrageous that I should be expected to take my time as Prime Minister of Canada having stated my position in dealing with officials of the two Governments. I have gone as far as I have, seeing the embarrassment it has occasioned, to make the consequences as light as possible but I do not intend to let them exhaust my vitality any more than I can help."

On January 6 Mackenzie King received a letter from President Truman "evidently written for him to which I began to draft a reply. I 'phoned Pearson in New York to tell him what I intended to say to the President and which will be along lines already put forward. I feel very strongly impressed that it is necessary to make these matters quite clear.

"I have not been altogether satisfied with the way External Affairs have handled this matter. They seemed determined to bring pressure on me through the President to hold to what I don't believe rather than that of making clear to the President and others that my decision on certain lines has been made."

The Prime Minister completed revision of his letter to Truman the next morning. "It is I think the first time I have quite emphatically declined to meet a wish expressed by any President of the United States," he wrote. "In fact, one of the few letters written in the course of my life in which I have refused requests from the head of any country. There have been a number of occasions where I have had to differ with the British Government on matters that I thought required a different attitude on the part of the United Kingdom. This one is the first in which I had, by implication, to take a more or less open exception to a course adopted by the United States but which I feel is full of danger.

"I read over the letter I had written to the President to Pearson on his return from New York today. He said he would take no exception to the wording of the letter or to the statements that were in it, but he wondered whether I should send the letter before the Cabinet saw it. I said the President had written me himself – and I might have added without reference to any colleagues other than the acting Secretary of State. . . . I did not see that the letter was one which needed to go before our Cabinet, though I would wish Mr. St. Laurent to see it before it was sent. St. Laurent later 'phoned me that he had seen the letter and would like to have a word with me. I invited him to come to dinner with me tonight so that we could talk over this and other matters together. What was worrying Pearson most was his obligation to let the United Nations know that we were not going to be represented on the Commission. I told him that I had rung him up yesterday specifically to suggest to him that it would be well definitely to let the United Nations people know that I would not sign an Order appointing a Canadian. He said he had not liked to state definitely what would or would not be done, though he indicated that there were difficulties or something to that effect. The truth of the matter is that External Affairs have made up their mind from the start that they would rather bring pressure on me than agree with a course which I think is full of future embarrassment and defend the position taken at the Assembly of the United Nations where Canada's consent was given without any reference to the Government. The point always raised is the publicity that this may receive. My reply to that is that while I would for some reasons wish to avoid publicity on matters of the kind, on other scores I would welcome it. Someone is needed to sound a warning as to the vortex into which the United Nations is bringing its various neighbour nations, and the unwisdom of its procedure in many directions. Also the need for calling a halt to taking a course of public action which is a mere pretence and which cannot lead to a successful conclusion, but may lead to dangerous embarrassment."

That evening Mackenzie King and St. Laurent "had a very pleasant talk together in the dining room, and then came up to the library. He opened the conversation by recalling that six years ago he had been sitting just in the opposite corner in the library when we had our conversation together and he agreed to come into the Cabinet. He then said that if Canada was not to be represented on the Korean Commission he thought he and Ilsley would have to go. My reply was that I did not know why. Personally, I did not care what Ilsley might wish to do, but I would not like to lose him and certainly would take care to see that this would not happen. I said if there was to be any going from the Government I would be the one who would take that step and would take it at the forthcoming meeting of the National Liberal Federation. I had hoped to stay on until at least after I had outdistanced Walpole's record. That was not a matter of consequence, but was of interest to myself personally, and would be of interest as a Canadian record. St. Laurent said it would never do for me to go. That would mean a complete break-up of the Government. I said that, on the contrary, that would leave himself, Ilsley and others free to take responsibility which I was not prepared to take of risking Canada being made an enemy of Russia because of joining with the United States to seek to put over something at this time which we knew could not be accomplished. I said that the last thing I wanted was at the end of my career to have any difference with my colleagues. If I did not have the support I needed there was no sense in my trying to stay on. Mr. St. Laurent said there was no one of my experience at this time; there was more need of that than ever. To this I replied that my experience apparently did not count with either him or Ilsley, if they were seeking to resign because of my not feeling I could support a recommendation to appoint a representative on the Korean Commission. St. Laurent then began to speak at some length about being responsible for the mistake which was made in the appointment of a Commission; that, first of all, he was the Minister, but that he had not thought of the matter as being as serious as I had pointed out it was. I said to him that he had not been there and really did not know of the matters, which was what I had understood from him before. He then said that on the contrary he had a memo on the subject for a couple of months; there had been time to consider the action.

"(A reference to Pearson's memo on the matter will show that Pearson said that he [Pearson] had protested two or three times against Canada going on the Commission. Then the matter was brought up suddenly and they only had a few hours to consider it and then voted on it.)

"Ilsley also said in Council that he must take full responsibility as he had been there the morning of voting, though he had not been there on previous days. I think both he and Mr. St. Laurent had been up here [in Ottawa] and that it was the week we were discussing the Geneva Agreements. I said to St. Laurent that so far as Ilsley was concerned he could do what he liked. I realized he disliked me and I would give him, St. Laurent, some of the reasons. I hoped he would forgive my mentioning the first which was that I had asked St. Laurent to take my place each time I had been away of late; that he, Ilsley, was not without his aspirations for the office of Prime Minister and, undoubtedly, felt I was passing him over; that he had thought I had double-crossed him in the matter of doing away with fixed preference on apples, which was the centre of much of his thought. As he, St. Laurent, knew I had had nothing to do with this at all. He had been against me at the time Ralston left the Cabinet. That he, Macdonald, Ralston, together with Alex Johnston and one or two others, had determined at that time that there would be conscription and that I would be supplanted. I said I had been pretty decent to Ilsley in keeping him in the Government; that he would not be there today – except against his own mistaken judgment at times – I let him stay with vacations, etc., and then had given him the portfolio of Justice. St. Laurent said he thought Ilsley had been very well treated. He urged that he himself would not be able to go to the United Nations and take any part there if after being Minister of External Affairs the policy of the United Nations with regard to a Commission which he had supported was not carried out. This was said a little later in the evening. What he said immediately was that he did agree with me about the Commission not being able likely to accomplish anything; also that the situation had changed since the Commission itself was appointed; also he agreed that unless the Russians were agreeable to their so doing, the Commission should not attempt to do anything. He said that his construction of the resolution of the Assembly was that whatever the Commission [recommended] was likely to be for the whole of Korea. In other words, they were not to hold an election in South Korea, where the Americans are, unless the Russians were agreeable to holding an election in the North, where their armed forces were. He felt perfectly sure that the Russians would not agree to the latter step. That, in those circumstances, our position would be perfectly clear and that we would not be leaving ourselves open to unnecessarily antagonizing the Russians. I had in mind what appears in the American memo and what was previously suggested by our External Affairs if the Russians objected to the election in the North. We could go ahead and have elections in the South and go as far as we could. Something of this kind is suggested in a memo from the Acting Secretary of State in Washington, which was sent to me, pointing out that the biggest part of the population was there.

"When St. Laurent said that he himself could honestly say in Parliament that his construction of the resolution was that it meant that the Commission should only act where it could act over the whole of Korea, which would mean that it would be acting with the consent of the Russians as well as the consent of the Americans, I said at once that I thought if that could be definitely understood and so stated that it would be a matter of record to which we could appeal. I would not object in going that far in supporting allowing a Canadian representative on the Commission, particularly because of the President's letter and what he pointed out as the larger question that would arise and might give grounds for very considerable discussion if Canada had no one on the Commission, namely, the propaganda that Russia would make of it, etc. St. Laurent said he was quite prepared to take that position now and take it in Parliament and have our representative so instructed. I said to him if he would let me have in the morning the instructions that External Affairs proposed to send to our representative in accordance with what he had indicated I would then write the President and in my letter would quote from what were to be the instructions so that there could be no misunderstanding about our position, either in the American mind or any other. Also we would have to record, should the Russians take any exception to what the Commission might do, that our man had been instructed to remain on the Commission only so long as he had been receiving the co-operation of the Russians as well as of the Americans.

"It seemed to me that with that position asserted, the grounds of my refusal to sign an Order-in-Council with matters left open as to what the Commission and our representative in particular might do, no longer carried any weight and that our position would be even the stronger for making clear to everyone that we were only acting with the full consent and co-operation of both the Russians and the Americans and taking no step which would allow only one to profit at the expense of the other in relation to what was proposed for Korea. I pointed out to St. Laurent that I had given a good deal of attention to industrial disputes. The principles were exactly the same in international disputes. Without the consent of both parties there was little chance for success by conciliation. To go beyond conciliation meant the reliance not on good offices through mediation but on force. Power to compel one party or the other to fall in with what was done. The United Nations had no power of the kind and it was sheer hypocrisy to pretend that it would settle these international problems without having first made the provision for international force on which its whole power was to rest. I stressed over again how the Americans were seeking to make the United Nations a political arm of the Secretary of State's Department. I pointed out that was actually confirmed by the President going the length in writing me as he had. That, really, except for the desire not to embarrass the Americans, this whole matter was one that should have been dealt with only between ourselves and the United Nations. The Americans have shifted their whole original ground of desiring Canada because she was so prominent and would be so influential, to agreeing to have her stay in the background, and do nothing so long as we did not take her off the Commission. I said to St. Laurent I thought he would find that perhaps the United Nations would be glad to pull out of Palestine before actual war takes place there as a result of their interference and I also said I thought we should keep away from the India dispute. He himself had mentioned that earlier. That we had the best of reasons for not interfering there as they were members of the Commonwealth in which we were interested, etc. I found it, and St. Laurent found it, a relief, to have been able to find this really sound ground on which to overcome the impasse which has existed thus far. I think my firmness in the matter up to the point of the letter I had written yesterday will cause the Department of External affairs not to treat these matters so lightly or want to be figuring in world affairs too much regardless of consequences to our own country. I think, too, it will let the Americans see that we have a judgment of our own and are not a mere echo of themselves and of their policies."

Mackenzie King "was surprised to hear St. Laurent say that he thought Quebec would back up our going on with the Korean Commission just because we were members of the United Nations. I told him that four-fifths of Canada would be against anything of the kind. I doubted if, in the House of Commons, he could get a single supporter from Quebec if I were to present what I see of the situation. I cannot understand St. Laurent not seeing that side of it. I can understand his taking the view that, in a court of civil law, we would be bound by the agreement that we had made at New York and that being the Minister responsible for the agreement himself, he would have to resign if it were not carried out. I confess my confidence has been tremendously shaken in External Affairs in the last six months."

With this compromise and somewhat tortuous interpretation of the Commission's role, the immediate crisis was over and UNTCOK met for the first time in Seoul on January 12, 1948, with the Canadian representative present, but without the participation of the Ukrainian S.S.R. or the co-operation of the local Soviet commander and North Korean political leaders. However, the Prime Minister's lack of confidence in the direction of Canada's foreign policy persisted. On January 9 he wrote that St. Laurent did "not expect ever to see another world war, nor does he think it will come in fifty years," adding that he wished he "could share his optimism."

The day before, he reported on January 9, he had had "a good talk" with General McNaughton who had been appointed as Canada's representative on the UN Security Council. The Prime Minister had told McNaughton "the line I will expect him to take at the United Nations, to prevent repetition of folly such as we have witnessed over some of the Commissions, and necessity of the United Nations organizing an international force before doing much more in the way of interference. I told him also I thought he should watch the extent to which the Americans were seeking to use the United Nations as an arm of their foreign office. That he should exert himself to keeping us out of war – keeping Canada and other nations out of the possibility of war instead of being drawn into situations. I feel much [more] security in having him on the Security Commission [*sic*] than a man who would have had lesser experience, in standing up to those of adverse opinions to their own."

On January 14 Mackenzie King "was shocked . . . on reading a speech made by Claxton yesterday at Annapolis in which he is reported as having said: 'Our efforts now must be directed to preventing war if that is at all possible. But if war comes, we in Canada in co-operation with you in the United States must be prepared to defend our Continent and our way of living.' This without a shadow of doubt will be construed as meaning that we are committed to go to war if the United States is involved in war. Indeed it might be construed as applying even to Mexico and this without knowing from what quarter war may come or what the cause of the war may be. It is a commitment in advance to join with the United States whenever it is involved in war. I declined, with respect to Britain, to adopt any such policy, even to the hour that Poland was invaded. Claxton has left nothing for Parliament's decision. Has given a decision in the name of the Government in advance. I can only hope that those interested in making trouble for the Government do not notice the implications of this statement and that it may get by without open criticism. Otherwise we may have, when Parliament reassembles, one of the most difficult debates we have ever had, throwing into the open fire the fat of Canada's commitment to war in advance, and that not as a part of the Commonwealth but along with the United States on the mere ground of our sharing a continent in common. It is these sorts of things that fill me with terror. Claxton's whole trip to Washington at this time and the publicity connected with it is as unfortunate as anything could be. I noticed in another part of the paper that Swanson of the Citizen attacks me on the ground that I do not allow the Ministers a chance to speak or do anything in the way of further publicity. I cannot but think that all this is part of an engineered scheme to let some of these younger ambitious men play a role which their ambitions may feel it is their duty to play but which, if they were more experienced, they would hesitate to essay."

Later that day the Prime Minister had a long talk with Sir Alexander Clutterbuck, the British High Commissioner, "who came with a note from the Prime Minister to me on the policy of the British Government with regard to the situation which had arisen vis-à-vis the Russians and their efforts to spread Communism in western Europe. I went over the note with Clutterbuck, and pointed out that I was in general sympathy with the point of view expressed, but took decided exception to one paragraph which could be read as implying that through use of the words 'the power and resources of the Commonwealth to be devoted to the defence of civilization' might mean military power, finance, resources, etc., but I thought it was quite wrong that any paragraph should be so framed. Clutterbuck admitted it was badly drafted and that the meaning was not clear. I said they knew how to [make a] clear statement in England as well as we do.

What annoyed me with their Government was that paragraphs of the kind were framed deliberately so as to carry whatever meaning they wished to place upon it later. I wished he would tell his Government that I would not accept that paragraph – that it was objectionable to me. As to what referred to a spiritual outlook and co-operation, etc. I was in full accord but did not like the use of the word Commonwealth as though it was one entity instead of several nations. This message and the telegram that accompanied it are very important documents, the nearest thing to a statement of a possible approaching conflict between East and West that I have yet seen from the British Government in writing."

Conversation turned to the dispute between India and Pakistan over Kashmir which was threatening to become a full-scale war. Clutterbuck "spoke of a message he had received from Noel Baker, who is at the United Nations over India and Pakistan. It was to the effect that the British Government did not think they ought to interfere, as they had recently given India self-government. They had been disappointed that Americans who were professing to want to help were not wanting to do anything in reality. Not to take any side. They had tried different countries to try to get one to draft a formula. Finally had succeeded in getting Belgium. The Minister of Belgium, while ready to do his best, felt he would like to have Pearson come to New York to help if that could be arranged. They all liked Pearson there and felt he would be of great assistance. What they really wanted him for was, so to speak, to dot the 'i's and cross the 't's. I spoke frankly to Clutterbuck; said I thought the United Nations was doing more to draw us into war than to keep us out. That it was a mere façade. It had no powers. The sooner it got to work creating an international force, that would give meaning to its words, and leave other things meanwhile, the better. I told him in a general way what I had done in regard to the Korean situation, in writing the President, and said that I intended to adopt the same attitude in regard to India. That I did not think the United Nations ought to interfere in that matter at all unless they could get consent of both parties to voluntary conciliation. There was no use starting enquiries that they would not follow up. There was no use pretending to have power where they did not have it. Also that I did not intend to have Canada forced into this and that. He had said our position was so high and outstanding. I said that was exactly what the Americans had said, and finally told us it would be all right for us to take a minor role as long as we came in. I said I would not, for the rest of my days, allow that sort of thing for Canada if it could be avoided. I told him so far as Pearson was concerned, I would be strongly opposed to his going down. If necessary, our officials would have to choose between positions they held in Ottawa and positions they would like to have in the United Nations. They could not serve two masters. I thought Pearson was needed here and should be kept out of the United Nations in matters of the kind. Besides McNaughton had been appointed as our representative on the Security Council. I said I thought instructions had already gone to McNaughton to tell him the line that should be followed as that of Canada. This was done two days ago. I was shown the telegram which was drafted by External Affairs along the lines that I had indicated I thought should be done."

The next day (January 15) Mackenzie King spoke to St. Laurent about the letter and telegram from Attlee which Clutterbuck had delivered. St. Laurent "did not like the Commonwealth references. I spoke to him pretty strongly about the stand External Affairs should take in not being drawn into these difficult situations in other parts of the world. I think he is beginning to realize what it means; that the Department has gone much too far."

The Prime Minister returned to this problem three weeks later. At the Cabinet meeting on February 5, there was a discussion of "directions to be given our representative on the Security Council at New York, as to seeking to see that the Government got a chance to consider important matters before we were committed to them.

"I spoke out quite strongly about the possible consequences of action that might be taken in New York which would throw the Government, without having had any real chance to consider implications, into the possible expenditure of millions and even to involvement of war. I said that all democratic governments were founded on no taxation without representation. That we had no representation in New York in the sense that was implied by people's representatives in Parliament. We might have a civil servant or might even have a Minister or member, but matters were decided there frequently without giving a chance of having them referred back to the Cabinet. I drew attention to the fact that the memo itself stated that such was the case. I thought additions should be made to it to the effect that our representative should seek to get time to bring the situation fully to the attention of the Government here. That failing that, he should abstain from voting. I thought the attitude taken by the delegates from Russia of not being afraid to say they were waiting for instructions from their own Government was, in the circumstances, the realistic and right one, if done sincerely from that motive. St. Laurent mentioned that a budget had to be made up and that we would not be bound by more than what was allotted by the budget. I pointed out, however, that any course that we committed ourselves to at the outset would necessarily involve us in everything that grew out of that course. I did not think we should commit ourselves to anything. By 'ourselves,' I meant Canada without knowing where it was going to lead in the end.

"Some remark was made that that danger was not likely to arise. It caused me to say it had already arisen in the case of Korea. St. Laurent took this as a sort of personal reflection and said he might have made a mistake there, it was his mistake, etc. I at once said that I would not have mentioned the matter if I thought it would be interpreted in that way. All that I was anxious to do was to illustrate how we might become involved in a way beyond anything that our own representatives might regard as being implied. I mentioned the exchange of letters I had had with the President and said that the Russian attitude had borne out just what I said it was, namely that the United Nations had met with a further rebuff – and a needless rebuff. It was fortunate we had put our representative in a position where he could withdraw from continuing on the Commission along lines that the United States seemed determined to have us take. I then said to the Cabinet that I just wished to say to them as in all probability I would not be in the Cabinet some little time hence, that I hoped they would remember my words – that I believed the United Nations would get Canada into no end of trouble before very long. That we would be drawn into situations . . . that our own people would not wish to be drawn into, and we would find out only when it was too late, where we had landed our country. That I wanted to say that now and would like members of the Cabinet to keep in mind these words, when my voice might no longer be heard in Council. I could see that every member of Cabinet was strongly with me.

"Gardiner stressed very much the dangers we were getting into and involvements through being too entirely under the control of the United States, etc.

"This afternoon, in talking with Tucker, he told me that he had been terribly afraid of situations in New York. Had spoken out against Pearson being made Chairman of the Palestine Commission, though others seemed to hesitate to say anything because Pearson himself wanted it, he thought, and others were pressing for him. I told Tucker confidentially that as Prime Minister, I had said he could not, as Under-Secretary of State, take on that obligation. That word had been sent to him in emphatic terms. I think today Pearson himself as well as every member of the Government are mighty thankful that he was not made Chairman of the Commission. I really feel that, in these international affairs, matters of government, there is far too much left to a man like Pearson, or A. Heeney and one or two others, just as in Finance, far too much is left to the Deputy Minister and one or two others, and that the real function of the Cabinet is being sacrificed to some of the ambitions of younger men. It is one of the reasons that make me feel that I should not stay any longer than I have decided to, in the Cabinet. It would simply mean having to carry responsibilities for policies that I had no sympathy in, and which I would have to oppose though I would be overridden. It is much the same kind of feeling that, as St. Laurent says, Ilsley has about staying on where he feels that his voice would become negatived by that of the majority of others. He does not wish to encounter that situation."

The Prime Minister continued to fear that another world war was imminent. An explosive situation in Palestine, where sporadic fighting had broken out between Jews and Arabs, particularly concerned him and, at the Cabinet meeting on February 16, he spoke "quite earnestly about my deep concern with regard to the possibility of war within the next three months or sooner. I do believe that there will be terrible fighting between the Jews and the Arabs. That Russia will come in at some stage ostensibly to help the Jews and that Britain and the United States will be lined together to hold the oil fields in the Middle East and to save the Mediterranean area from the Russians. That may lead to anything in any part of the world.

"What brought the matter up today was Croll, Jewish Member of Toronto [Spadina], wishing me to make an appointment with Dr. Goldman, Jewish Leader, to see him tomorrow. Goldman wanted to come down to talk with me. What the Jews are after is for the United States to furnish arms to the Jews but not allow any to the Arabs. Secondly, to arrange for some Jewish Council under auspices of the United Nations. Thirdly, to have the United Nations form an international police force to keep order in the Middle East. I am terrified that further interference by the United Nations has to end by setting the heather wholly on fire. I shall be strongly opposed to Canada contributing to any force unless the contribution came to what was agreed under the Charter with Great Powers taking their full share. That, of course, Russia will not agree to do at all. England is refusing to do anything by way of force. The United States alone will not be able to meet the situation. Was glad that St. Laurent agreed it would be unwise for me to see Goldman which would only lead to the press asserting there was some relationship between our Government and the Jews, and this at a time when the Chairman of the Security Council at New York was an appointee of our Government.

"I had Croll come into my office this afternoon and explained the situation. He saw it. Talked a little while and thanked me for having him come in. He told me privately that the Jews had all the rifles and ammunition they needed. They would fight to the death.

"Between 5 and 6, tonight, I went down to Government House. Discussed this matter, among others, with the Governor General. Expressed my feelings to him. Drew his attention to what Eisenhower had said this morning about war being constant danger. I told him I would like him to read private memo from Wrong re Claxton's visit which I had gone over yesterday quite carefully again. That I thought he would be amazed at what it disclosed of fears and of inadequacies of the United States. I showed him, too, a letter that I got today from General Montgomery in which, among other things, Montgomery says that he is not at all happy about Europe.

"Lord Alexander tried to sum up, as he saw them, the points on both sides. He felt the Jews had large numbers. Will get help from outside to a very considerable extent. Had a few trained battalions who were pretty well disciplined and organized. The disadvantage was their coast line restricted their power of retreat. The Arabs, he did not think, were well organized – not organized at all for battle. Would not have the same numbers. Might keep up fighting some time. He spoke of the fighting lasting possibly two years. Said it would be in the nature of sniping.

"When I pointed out that Russia might come in on the side of one, namely the Jews, and that Britain and America might be drafted to help, assisting the Arabs to save the oilfields, Heaven alone knew what else, he agreed that that was an appalling possibility. I had told Pearson to send him the Wrong memos. Also suggested that Claxton should go down and tell him what he had heard at Washington. It was arranged he should go down in the morning."

Two days later Mackenzie King had a long talk with St. Laurent and with Pearson, who was about to leave for the United Nations, "first to deal with the Korean question at the meeting of the Assembly, and later with the Palestine question at the Security Council. In the Korean matter, St. Laurent and Pearson both had come to the point of view which I urged was the right one from the start, and the position to be taken will be that, as one of the two parties has refused to allow the Commission to enter its territory, the United Nations would not be justified in supporting a motion that the Commission should go ahead and set up a government in the one part of Korea in which the United States army of occupation is at present. If the latter course is to be adopted, the United States must do it as a matter of its own concern, not as one which carries with it an obligation on the part of the United Nations.

"Pearson said he thought the United States were worried a good deal themselves about the matter. He thought our position, and St. Laurent thought our position could be supported by law, and hoped that this might prove a way out of having to vote against the United States in their effort to take the further step. He, I believe, felt that they might find it necessary to take refuge in that method of retreat. Pearson seemed particularly anxious to avoid, if possible, Canada dividing itself from the States in the face of Russia. St. Laurent joined me in being adamant about our not letting ourselves in for further obligation which related to only the American part of Korea.

"In respect to Palestine, it was apparent that Pearson was considerably concerned. St. Laurent yesterday had given an answer in the House that we would fulfill our obligations under the Charter. I underlined those words 'under the Charter.' Said I thought his answer was correct, but this must never be interpreted that a similar power would be the one to send an international force into Palestine. It was agreed that we could not think of becoming a party to an international force to which the Big Powers were not contributing their proportion; also we would have to make clear that the Canadian Parliament itself would have to agree to any force that would be sent before we could be committed to intervene. I told Pearson in all his discussions to keep in mind what Parliament would do in Canada. I did not think for one moment that our House of Commons would vote to send troops from this country into Palestine. Pearson seemed greatly concerned lest the Russians would help the Jews in the event of all others backing out. They would take the ground that they were the ones that were supporting the United Nations. That may be so but it is necessary to consider what the consequences of some other course might be. I took strongly the position I mentioned in talking with the Governor General. He, a military man, had taken the same position. It would be better to send no force at all than an inadequate force.

"I was personally against trying to crowd the people into Palestine. Pearson suggested they might try to do more in the way of conciliation, bringing Arabs and Jews to the United Nations and discussing with them in private; reaching some settlement by way of voluntary conciliation. Carrying conciliation further in this way. Britain might be prepared to take a little different course and the U.S. also. The present position is that the United Kingdom and the United States took opposing views. Britain has taken the same view from the start. United States rushed in but since has been very indifferent and now is not ready to do very much."

On February 20 the Prime Minister spent some time reading over External Affairs material on Palestine. "It is interesting to me to see how our own Department of External Affairs is suddenly coming around wholly to my point of view with the folly of the United Nations attempting anything by force and the wisdom of proceeding in international affairs along the lines laid down in my 'Industry and Humanity' for a settlement of industrial differences. Conciliation is about as far as the United Nations can hope effectively to go at this time." Later that day Mackenzie King had Norman Robertson to lunch at Laurier House. "We had a pleasant talk together about the situation in the Middle East," he wrote. "Also about the financial situation in Britain. About his own work in the United Kingdom. With regard to the last mentioned, he did not hesitate to make clear to me his preference to be back in Canada and to hold the position here that he had before. I really think Robertson's judgment is sounder than Pearson's on these international affairs, and that he would be better at the head of the Department here. Is less fond of speaking or of travelling or of participating in the United Nations, etc. Less likely to get the Government into trouble. I feel the Department has been skating on very thin ice and I think Mr. St. Laurent is coming to feel that way himself, as it comes to the question of supplying troops from Canada to go and fight in the Holy Land. Ministers are beginning to take a little more seriously some of the consequences of commitments into which our country is being drawn – all unknown to themselves. I suggested to Robertson to stay on another week. Indeed rather insisted on this as I feel there may be some far reaching developments next week."

Mackenzie King spent the morning on February 25 looking through communications from Pearson about the Korean situation. "It does seem to me the height of absurdity that we should be drawn into these situations, wasting our time on those situations in remote parts of the world, where all we can do is to get our nation tangled up with others in situations in which we should be wholly free.

"I feel a good deal of concern with the part Pearson takes in New York. I think he is much too active in the name of Canada. His own report shows he does not hesitate to advise both the United Kingdom and the United States as to what it is wisest for them to do. He likes the international arena but some day it will land us in an obligation from which we will find a great difficulty in being freed. I have held firm in not being drawn any further in the Korean situation without the consent of both parties until at least the United Nations has its situations pending agreements necessary for an international organization."

Next day he went through some more External Affairs despatches which, he felt, illustrated again "what an enormous amount of time we are devoting to countries of the world when we should be giving our thought and time to our own country. I thought of this when I saw that St. Laurent had, in addressing the Rhodes gathering in Toronto, chosen support of the United Nations as his subject. He would have been much wiser to have explained our determination regarding prices, or necessity to save dollars with the United States. Something that our own people were more immediately interested in. It is a sort of escapist position to be continuing taking up matters relating to other countries than our own. . . ."

Disagreement over Canada's position in the Security Council debate on Palestine revived on March 1 when Pearson showed Mackenzie King "a statement which he thought ought to be in the nature of instructions to McNaughton at the Security Council tomorrow to support an American resolution which urges the United Nations to support the American position partitioning Palestine and doing so with force, if need be. The Belgians have an amendment which would do away with this and confine further efforts on the part of the United Nations to conciliation by the Great Powers.

"Pearson's memo seems to be based on the belief that a compromise could be worked out which would let us vote with the Americans on the main issue but which would, in the course of discussion, lead to the American position being voted down by others and thereby avoid our being drawn into necessity of supplying troops, etc.

"I went over his memo carefully twice this evening. Finally 'phoned and said I found it difficult to agree with his position. That I thought the Belgian one was the sound one. It was facing realities. While it might cost the United Nations some prestige, that was better than having their view endorsed to the point where partition would be attempted by force which might lead to a world war. I said I thought the only thing that would save the situation was if both the Americans and the British found they had been left to themselves to work out some solution that would prevent a war. I did not think they would come together on this until they found neither of them were getting the support from others that would favour their particular position. They would both find it to their self interest to carry on the work of conciliation. I told Pearson I thought we always had to look at what was possible eventually through Parliament. I did not believe the House of Commons would support any measure which meant that partition of Palestine would have to be brought about with the aid of Canadian troops. If we were not prepared to send troops, we should not support any measure which would logically place us in the position where we would have no escape from so doing. I thought the position could be taken that all that was meant was that the American resolution was supported by us; but subsequent events had shown that it had gone too far and that the United Nations themselves were not in a position to implement by force what was expected in that way. I told Pearson I thought the matter should be decided by the Cabinet later this week. He then said he would prepare a statement setting out the argument as I had presented it, giving the other side of what the Cabinet should consider.

"Mr. St. Laurent could then bring it forward in the morning. I told Pearson I thought it would be well for him to be at Cabinet at the same time. He accepted the whole position very nicely. I think in some ways it was a bit of a relief to him to have me take the stand I was taking, though it was contrary to what he was proposing to advise his Minister. In the meantime, he said he would communicate with McNaughton at once and let him know the position I was taking and there was a possibility of the Cabinet sharing my view.

"Pearson's proposal means supporting the United States in a resolution which means determining to enforce the partition by force. It means equally a refusal to support Britain in her determination not to attempt partition by force. As I said to Pearson, we would raise a very serious question in Canada if it came to be seen that what we were doing was requiring war in Palestine in order to support the United States in an attitude which was being wholly and strongly opposed by Britain. In this case, I thought we should do as Britain proposed to do, namely abstain from voting altogether. I stressed the point that if, in addition to it being alleged that we were being dominated by the United States on economic matters, we were being dominated as well on military matters, we would have a hard battle to face in our country. I have really become increasingly alarmed at what may grow out of the Department of External Affairs."

At the Cabinet meeting on March 2, Mackenzie King felt that St. Laurent "had come around very much to the point of view I have been emphasizing to Pearson. Indeed he emphasized in the Cabinet that the Belgian amendment which advocated the Big Five making further conciliatory efforts, etc., should have priority over any American motion which sought to endorse the position the United States would like to have taken, namely, a decision to follow up the partition of Palestine by instructing the Security Council to find means of enforcing the partition of Palestine. Ilsley, as I expected, was quite prepared, because he had taken the stand for partition, to insist on Canada going ahead on this line though he hedged about a good deal and was not too positive. However, no one else in the Cabinet supported that view. I said very little beyond mentioning that there was a wise saying in the Scriptures that before one went to war, it was well to count your men and your strength. That I wanted Council to know that in the decision of the United Nations might lie the way to war, and that any commitment we made to enforce partition by force would commit this country in that direction. That I personally did not believe we could get any support in Parliament for sending armed forces to Palestine. I pointed out, too, what it would mean politically for our representative to evoke the American resolution and in so doing, to take a different stand than the British who do not intend to vote for the American resolution and have intimated that they will abstain from voting altogether.

"As matters were under discussion for some time, St. Laurent finally came forward with a suggestion to instruct our representative to support the Belgian point of view. Try to get its motion introduced first. If not successful in that, to abstain from voting for the American resolution. To take the position that the Big Four should use their good offices first to try and get a settlement before any final settlement was reached on what should be done in regard to partition. I would like to have seen a direct opposition to supporting any idea of partition but felt it would be better to keep the Cabinet united and to fight that issue later if the course taken with the United Nations should render that necessary."

In addition to the problems in the Middle East and Korea, there were other dangerous and complex issues in Europe. The Communist coup in Czechoslovakia late in February, a traumatic shock to the nations of the West, again emphasized the division of the world into two hostile and suspicious camps and the powerful thrust of Soviet expansionism in eastern Europe. On March 3 St. Laurent showed Mackenzie King a statement, prepared by the Department of External Affairs, which "he thought excellent" and intended to use in the House in reply to a question by Graydon as to whether the government endorsed the strong condemnation of the events in Czechoslovakia expressed by the United States, France and the United Kingdom. "I read the statement aloud to P. [Pickersgill] to see what his reaction would be. I confess I was perfectly horrified if not terrified at the thought of anything of the kind read in the House of Commons at this time. It was a long story of what the press had contained of how the Government had changed. To me, it was a real interference with the domestic affairs of Czechoslovakia in an unpardonable way. Would certainly if cabled to Czechoslovakia create very bitter feeling against Canada at once. What was worse, its reference to such things as not allowing – or requiring Stalin's picture to be on the walls, etc. It was almost equivalent to an open declaration against Russia on the part of Canada. I confess that I get increasingly alarmed at the lack of judgment on the part of External Affairs in these matters and am beginning to mistrust St. Laurent's judgment in them. I think he has been carried away with the clerical feeling against Communists which has caused him to lose judgment on how these matters when expressed in Parliament in a certain way, may affect our own international relations.

"P.'s reaction was exactly the same. Perhaps the best example of the folly of what was written was the way in which the statement referred to John Hus as the great liberator and emancipator. St. Laurent had evidently not seen that John Hus was the reformer who fought Roman Catholicism and was responsible for Czechoslovakia becoming Protestant. I don't know where this statement made in Parliament might have landed him in the Province of Quebec. It is this kind of thing that fills me with concern."

On March 10 the Prime Minister was shocked "on listening to the radio to hear that Jan Masaryk had lost his life by jumping from second story window in the Foreign Office. Time may tell whether this was a suicide or whether that means was taken by the Communists to destroy his life. One thing is certain. It has proven there can be no collaboration with Communists. His role has been a very distinguished one for some time past. I could not but reflect that Kato, Japanese Ambassador in Paris, at the time of the war, who was also a personal friend of mine, had met his death in a similar way. Then, there is Winant, a very fine public man whose life ended by a suicide. All three were real personal friends and three of the best men I have known. What an age we are living in!"

The following morning Mackenzie King received word that the British High Commissioner had just received an urgent message from Attlee which he wished to deliver personally. Clutterbuck, who had been in London at the time of the coup d'état in Czechoslovakia, arrived shortly before noon. He reported that the British government had had no hint of what was coming and that "almost overnight, the whole situation changed from a democratic republic to a Communistic dictatorship controlled from Russia. That it demonstrated that a free country could be peacefully penetrated with Communists who could carry matters to the point where, without the knowledge of the authorities of the country, save those deliberately in the know, the whole power of government could pass under the control of another power. This had alarmed the Ministers greatly as to what might take place in other countries, for example, Italy, etc.

"He then said to me he assumed I had read the memo from the Secretary of State, Noel Baker's memo on the background in Europe which had been sent up yesterday. I said I had it at Laurier House but did not reply further. He gave me an extra copy. He then said he had received that morning two important communications. That the first was in the nature of a memo from the Ambassador of one of the countries of Europe to Bevin, the Foreign Minister, which made an important disclosure. . . .

"He then handed me what was marked as a personal letter from Attlee to myself which pointed out the need for a united front on the part of free nations. The importance of assistance from the United States. Necessity to organize collective security groups – one now being worked out in the Benelux group [nations associated under the Treaty of Brussels signed on March 17]. The other one to be worked out for the French-U.K.-U.S. and Canada in particular. Another, a Mediterranean group. The message stated that they had sent that information to Marshall . . . and this copy to me, and wanted to know if I would be agreeable to having the situation regarding Atlantic regional security group explored by British officials, United States and ourselves.

"I made no mention of this to any of my colleagues though I had Pearson come in and have a word. I had told Clutterbuck to leave copies with him. Pearson regarded the situation as grave. I arranged for him, St. Laurent and Claxton to meet me in my office after the Orders of the Day [in the House]."

In the meeting that afternoon, "all agreed that collective security was essential to preservation of safety and preservation of Canada. That no time should be lost in seeking to bring this about. That it was desirable to agree to explore the situation vis-à-vis the Regional Atlantic Pact of Mutual Assistance under Section 51 of the [United Nations] Charter and that I should so advise Attlee. Pearson drafted something as we were conversing. He had had something in part in readiness and we discussed the draft together. Later he sent me a revision which I further revised in my library at Laurier House tonight. Gave him the revision over the 'phone about 8 o'clock. The message went off to Attlee tonight. I stated that, in order to get the information necessary to discuss the information with the Cabinet, I would send one of our officials to Washington to meet the British and Americans to explore the situation. I was careful to make no commitment. To make clear that the Cabinet would have a knowledge of what was proposed before any final decision is reached as to what we would do. I am quite positive that we were right in not delaying an hour in getting off our reply to the British Government; also that if Britain and the United States were drawn into the war with Russia, nothing could keep our country out. If we did not join in at once with the United Kingdom and the United States in seeking to arrange a situation that might help to preserve peace, we would certainly be destroyed in no time.

"Indeed we would be a mark for the Russians almost instantly. In discussing the situation, I asked St. Laurent if he thought the Pope was right or wise in telling the electors in Italy that if they did not vote against the Communists, they would be committing a sin. Telling them how they must vote when the elections come in April. St. Laurent said he could not say. He thought the people took the religious aspect much more lightly in Italy than they did in our own country. I said to him I feared that a new issue was being created which might witness a conflict between that part of the population which did not wish the Church to interfere in politics and the Church itself, and that the Communists might really be helped as a result. I am afraid we will witness out of this whole situation, in all probability, a serious religious war. At this moment, there is the almost certainty of war in the present conflict between Arabs and the Jews developing into what might well be the beginning of a world war. There is a conflict between Russia and the Greeks. . . . The elections in Italy may upset the Government there and put a Communist Government in power. France would not last a day were the Russian armies or German armies to cross her territory. Spain is not to be relied on at the moment. Portugal is a weak power. All other countries pretty much look to the United States and Britain for assistance, rather than being in a position to assist them – except perhaps to help to prevent the Russians getting bases too easily.

"Then there is war being fomented in Manchuria and again in Korea. This is being done by Russia. The whole world may be in flames before very long. Conflagration in any one part may set all the rest afire. I do not recall prior to the last great war reading any despatches that seemed to me as serious and solemn as those I have received today.

"After talking with St. Laurent, Pearson and Claxton, I felt I should tell the leaders of the three main parties – read to them what was in a statement of the background of the situation in Europe – not tell them more than that. I could not read the other messages but I would like them to know they were very grave. I would some day let them see them. Could not do so now.

"Coldwell was not in the House but I had Bracken come in for a talk first, and later Solon Low. I read the statement to Bracken regarding the European background. He said that they were getting information from different sources which seemed to bear out what I had read. I gave him to understand this was a talk entirely between ourselves. No reference to be made to it in public." Later the Prime Minister saw Low who "regarded the situation as very serious" and, the next day, M. J. Coldwell who "felt very strongly that things were in bad shape."

On March 13 Mackenzie King was surprised "to see some of the things that had been said by St. Laurent in regard to our men having to be prepared to fight. This was in reply to the Catholic Union meeting and to their reference to conscription. I am afraid he may find he is raising a question it would have been better to have said nothing about. I become increasingly alarmed at the extent to which both he and Claxton are apt to talk of the international problem." Later that day he went to Government

House to show Alexander the exchange of messages with Attlee. The Governor-General "thought the situation was very serious. He again commented on how accurately I had reported the situation to him when I got back from Europe. I pointed out that then our attention was being focused on Berlin. I said I thought it looked now as if the Russians had deliberately sought to focus attention there so that attention might be drawn off what they were doing in Greece, Italy and Czechoslovakia, and also what they were doing in Finland, Norway, etc.

"Alexander said: I think you are probably entirely right. That is good military strategy. The encircling movement. He said: How skilful they are. They are doing all that Hitler tried to do but succeeding in ways beyond what he could. He thought the only thing to do was to face right up to them. Let them see that they would get the worst of it if they went any further. He said they are an Oriental people. Time is a secondary consideration to them. They might stop but will keep on their penetration patiently. Hitler was different. He wanted to get things done at once and do them himself. He feels we might have several years of very difficult time. Believes that a united front and strength are the only thing to meet the situation."

At the Cabinet meeting on March 15 the Prime Minister told his colleagues that "the situation in Europe was very serious and threatened to become more so. Not only in Europe but in Asia as well. I then said I would read to them statement of background from which matters should be considered. This had been sent to me by Noel-Baker, Secretary of State for Commonwealth Relations. . . . Told them I had called in the leaders individually and had read over this statement to them. I thought they should know the situation and share responsibility, especially as the behaviour in Parliament might have a serious bearing on what a little later would have to be considered. Members listened very attentively and looked in some way deeply concerned."

The Prime Minister and the Minister of National Defence then saw the leaders of the other three parties and told them that "We may be faced with a serious crisis at any moment. You have read what Marshall has said. Of the situation being very, very serious. You have heard what the President has said. You have read what Byrnes, ex-Secretary, has said. The President and the Secretary of State would never have made the statements they did if the situation were not very grave. Perhaps you have seen in this morning's paper the statement that de Gasperi, the Italian Prime Minister, had made in which he speaks of the possibility of Italy coming under a dictatorship controlled by a foreign power and that even before the 18th of April [the date of the Italian election].

"There is a rumour in papers of Friday that even before negotiations [on border redrawing and reparations] with Finland are concluded, Communists may make considerable headway in Norway and Sweden. There is every possibility of some repetition of Czechoslovakia in some other country, almost at any time during the next couple of weeks.

"You will remember that when I returned from Europe and made a pretty strong statement about the danger as I saw it, based on what I had gathered at Downing Street, that any attempt at control of Europe might proceed from Berlin outward across the Atlantic. That I had since come to believe the Russians had purposely brought things where attention was focussed on Berlin while they were busy with Czechoslovakia and also perhaps with Italy and perhaps also Norway and Sweden to the North. That we might easily see trouble break forth at both ends and even in the centre when the moment they thought to advance had come. I thought we had from now on to reckon with that possibility. You also know that already Manchuria is largely under the control of the Soviets. Also one part of Korea. That China is divided. There might be further outbreaks there. Instead of half a circle around Europe, we might begin with the situation what it has been in India and what it is now in Greece. Also between the Jews and the Arabs in the Holy Land. We might see fire around the world before very long. I did not wish to say these things in public. It was not possible to say that war was certain; equally it was not possible to say that with the horizon as we saw it, there was not immediately danger of war. This led me to believe that we ought to try to get our own house in order in the Commons as rapidly as possible. Get through as much work as we can. Get ready for any emergency that may arise. What I felt more strongly was that we must get a different spirit into the House than we have had up to the present. I had come now pretty well to the conclusion that a longer recess would be better than a short one though risking happenings in the interval."

Mackenzie King reflected that the government would look pretty foolish away from Parliament if war broke out in Europe, and "would be criticized as having known that war was imminent. It would be said that I knew and I allowed the House of Commons to go on a holiday. At the same time, I felt if we had only the short recess with the agitation that has been stirred up, we would find members resentful. If there had been a chance to breathe a little more freely, they would come back to a fresh start and by that time, we would know pretty much what the situation was likely to be immediately thereafter and all might be prepared to work together.

"The three leaders more or less simultaneously indicated they were of that mind. They believed that perhaps I was right." Some discussion then followed about the Parliamentary programme and the length of the Easter recess and general agreement was reached that a longer recess was desirable, particular if they "were heading into a world crisis."

Mackenzie King's diary entry for March 17, 1948, begins: "This has been one of the most anxious days of my life. It has also been a memorable day in the world's history."

There was a Liberal caucus that morning and arrangements had been made to adjourn in time for the Prime Minister to listen to a broadcast by President Truman. Mackenzie King spoke briefly before the broadcast outlining his views on the international situation. He told caucus that he would not be "in the least surprised" if Truman threatened war if Soviet militancy and expansion continued. "I had to conclude quite hurriedly for us all to reach the lounge at 12.30. I shall never forget the picture in that room – of myself seated at the side of a large table in the centre with back to some of the members, facing others who were seated round about on sofas, chairs and then at the table, all listening to the radio. The ensemble would have made a striking picture."

Truman's speech "was much along the lines that were expected," the Prime Minister wrote. "It really was an exceptionally fine, manly, courageous, direct speech. Claxton had told me as we went into the lounge that the press had had a flash that Truman had advocated compulsory military training. St. Laurent, he and I were walking together. I said that will, of course, at once raise the old issue of conscription here. I am afraid if conscription becomes an issue in Canada, we will find in some parts, large numbers joining the Communists. They will say if we are to risk our lives fighting Communism, we better save our heads by joining with them. I could see at a moment the appalling problem we would have again to face in Parliament. When Truman had concluded his speech announcing military service, etc., I knew that something would be expected at the opening of Parliament, so I stood up in the room and said I would ask that members of the Cabinet come to meet me at once in my room 401 upstairs. On the way, I stopped over in my own downstairs office and prayed very earnestly for strength and guidance. The scene in my office upstairs was another that will long be imprinted in my mind. Ministers were slow in coming together; some of them had not been at the broadcast; others had left before they got my call. No one but myself thought of arranging to have a stenographer there to type a statement. No one thought of sending for Heeney, getting him to get the Ministers together. Even after Heeney and others were there, no one thought of getting Pearson. No one thought of what was obviously needed to deal with grave situations in so short a time."

St. Laurent and Claxton entered the room first. "They were seated over near where my grandfather's bust is placed. When I came into the room, I went at once to Claxton and said to him I think you should cancel your trip to the Arctic. I repeated that a second time. I really think you should do that. We do not know what the situation is we are facing. I could see he was disappointed but he accepted my request. It seems to me showing complete lack of judgment on his part to have thought of going off at this time on such an expedition when he is needed in Council and when he knows anything might require his presence and instructions. He had said he could get back in a day by plane.

"Gibson and Gregg were the next two to come in. Then Martin, McCann, and a little later Gardiner, Mitchell, Bertrand, Fournier, Chevrier, Wishart Robertson and MacKinnon. I do not think Howe was present. Abbott was not. I had a talk with Abbott yesterday. The Ministers were grouped around the four walls.

"I said nothing until six or seven were present. I then said: You have heard what President Truman has proposed. We are now faced with a very real situation. All the old questions will come up. The last war will be revived. I shall have to make a statement of some kind when I get into the House this afternoon. I want the advice of the Cabinet; one of the first questions likely to be asked is what we intend to do about the matter of conscription. Claxton said the Chiefs of Staff would not favour that step at this time. They would regard it as a hindrance to our effective effort. I have already asked them to consider this matter and they have given me a report against it. I also spoke about Selective Service. Claxton thought that what we should do at present is to seek to fill up the gaps in our forces. St. Laurent pointed out that the real problem was how we could best make our contribution to the maintenance of world peace. We had always been prepared to take our share of duties. I said I assumed that we would stand behind the Western Union – but I imagined there would be no difference of view in the Cabinet as to our being prepared to do our part in helping to support the Western Powers from Europe. St. Laurent said the question of the methods of implementation was something that we would have to give further thought to. He mentioned the joint defence of the Continent was already something that had been worked out. Our generous attitude had always been to do our full part. We would be ready to do that now in ways that seemed best. Someone said something about a league of free people and we either had to be in it or out of it. I said I was sure there could be no doubt on the part of anyone as to our being in.

"Claxton read the words which he had taken down from the President's address to the effect that the United States was prepared to help the Western Nations of Europe with the same determination as they might show themselves. I asked in order to get consensus of opinion of the Cabinet whether we might not take that definite stand ourselves as the basis of our policy. We could say that we assumed our attitude would be the same. St. Laurent used the expression the rest was a matter of implementation. It need not follow that we would take exactly the same steps or at the same time. We would be governed by the conditions as we had an opportunity to review and study them."

After some discussion about the Communist threat in Canada, the Prime Minister suggested to Ilsley that "he have the officials of his Department see if they could not frame up legislation that would be more effective. For example, that we take the statement of the President as a basis of our policy and make it an offence for anyone to go contrary to what was basic in that policy.

"Ilsley then said he thought perhaps we might get some enactment that would give us considerable power. I told him to have his officials go into the matter.

"Heeney presented a statement which he had prepared of what was being done in our civil service. I read the memo. It was a little long, not suitable for use at this time. We left the Communist business for a time. The President's message had helped to prepare the way for action being taken in Parliament where to have moved earlier would have made the position very difficult.

"Gardiner I think it was who said he thought in any statement we issued it would be better to line up with the English rather than with the United States. The best thing would be to take Bevin's statement of January [urging unity among the Western nations] and show how the Brussels agreement had grown out of the Bevin plan, and that our attitude would be to help to implement the purposes of the Bevin plan. I at once said I agreed with them.

"In discussing the question of Communists, the position in Italy was referred to. That is, whether we should legislate against the Communists as such. The discussion then turned on Attlee's statement to the British House which we all felt was rather weak. It allowed Communists to remain in the public service while not being in key positions. If they are for the overthrow of the State in a manner in which this has been done in Czechoslovakia, they certainly should not be allowed in the public service.

"Claxton came forward with the idea that it might be an advantage to have someone sent from Canada to the Vatican, not as a permanent delegate but as Roosevelt did – sending some special emissary. Those present were obviously for the most part strongly opposed. I said I myself hoped that question would not arise. That Sir Wilfrid Laurier had said to me never in his life again would he allow a religious question to rise in Canada if he could prevent it. I said if we have Orange Lodges begin fighting us on the score of being a Catholic government, and with a war on our hands at the same time, we will have a bad mix-up in Canada. I did not say it but I felt strongly that it would be the end to St. Laurent's chances of being made the leader of the party. I said quite openly that I felt that His Holiness the Pope had made a mistake in telling the people how they should vote and making it a sin for any of them to vote for the Communist ticket. That would not gain a Communist vote but it would bring thousands of other votes to the Communist side on the part of those who want political freedom and religious freedom. I believe that we shall see ere long a real war between the Church and the State in southern Europe and other parts. Specially will this be the case if it comes to be Communists versus Catholics. That business is full of dynamite.

"I felt that the moment had come to tell the Cabinet of communications I had received from Attlee and of the statement which I had read to Council and also the substance of the messages which followed the day after. I told them of having read the background material to the leaders of the Opposition. I then said we would be faced with a question of being prepared to join a regional security pact of which the United Kingdom, the United States and ourselves would be the principal persons. I gave them the substance of the reports and said that I had urged one of our officials (Pearson) to go to Washington to meet the British and United States representatives purely for exploratory purposes; would have no power for commitment but I assumed that all parliament would feel that we should join in such a security pact for the Atlantic. There was agreement on the part of all. I brought up the question three or four times. Each time saying I wanted to be sure we were all in agreement. Used the expression one time, there is no dissenting voice. Gardiner spoke of not wishing to agree to military service, conscription, at once. Saw no need for it at present. I said certainly there would be no commitment of any kind. What we would want to know would be what would be expected; who the parties would be, etc. That when we got this information, Pearson would return and I would then give the Cabinet the particulars. We could reach a decision. I stated I really intended to wait until I got the result of the explorations before saying anything of the matter. Was so exceedingly secret but in view of the President's statement, I thought I should let them know immediately what the situation was so that when Pearson (I did not mention his name) went to Washington, he would go with the knowledge that, on the general principle, we were all agreed."

The Prime Minister then sent for Pearson. "We were just discussing this point. I went over it again in his presence. I then said we must get to work at once on a statement for the House. As Pearson and Heeney were comparatively fresh, I suggested they might start and draft something. St. Laurent, Claxton and I were waiting to assist but they thought they would get along better alone. I went down to my room, rested for about five minutes and then had a sandwich and a cup of tea and came back to my room [upstairs]. Went over what had been prepared. Made some modifications. The last paragraph of all I thought was drafted exceedingly poorly so I changed it in considerable part but it still appeared to be rather involved; to have a heavy sort of appearance. Much less clear type of statement than I would like to have made. My head, however, was much too tired. I was worrying over many questions that might be asked me on the Orders of the Day. The bells were ringing for the opening of the House before we could get the last of the statement typed. I just had to take what had been prepared as it was.

"My head was too weary for me, and the time too short, to think up clear, concise statement of the kind I would like to have given.

"Members were already seated when I got into the House. As soon as motions were carried, I read the statement. Fortunately I did this on motions and before any questioning had come from the Opposition. Bracken followed having evidently intended to move for the adjournment of the House to discuss the question of the Government's action re Communism. This the Opposition have had under way for some little time but had evidently planned to spring it as a surprise today. It was really an act of Providence that caused them to do this. It avoided any questions being asked about the Government's attitude toward Truman's statement and its proposals. That was what had been worrying me most, realizing how serious even the slightest comment was likely to be. I was then able to make some reference to Truman's speech. Also let it be seen that Canada was in line with the United Kingdom and the United States in the matter of security pacts. At the same time, without disclosing anything ahead – more or less prepare the House as I had the Cabinet for a Security Pact and, to all intents and purposes, secure their tacit assent to Canada becoming a party thereto. Fortunately, too, we had had the earlier discussion on Communism in the Cabinet in my office. I was, however, so very tired and my mind not working freely that, for the life of me, I hardly knew what to say in immediate reply to Bracken. While he was speaking, I asked St. Laurent to get something in readiness as I felt I should follow Bracken at once and express appreciation of the subject being brought up at this time. I could see the Tories had expected we would decline to regard the matter as one of urgent importance and hoped to force a division. Indeed after I had indicated to the Speaker to allow the motion, Graydon and one or two others rose to their feet.

"Had I had a clear mind, and not had so much anxiety in the preceding hours, I would have welcomed a chance to speak. As it was, I found my mind just a bit cloudy and difficult to get the exact words I wished to use. However, the minute Bracken concluded, I rose and took the opportunity before Coldwell also rose, for a chance to speak, and made clear that I welcomed the statement that Bracken had made and that all parties should unite together. The Tories as usual tried to provoke me while I was speaking and to make political capital. They did not succeed, however. I was able to register the fact that it was our Government that had really exposed the espionage business. That I, myself, had brought the matter to the attention of the authorities in the United States and the United Kingdom. That our Government had been blamed by the Tories for what we had done in the only effective way to round up the Communists and were now taking an attitude diametrically opposite to that which they had been taking, nominally, in the defence of civil liberties, etc. I could have said much more but was tired and a little afraid of saying something that might be just a slip. Therefore, thought better not to go further but I have felt very put out since that I did not avail myself of the occasion to speak upon the dangerous situation in the world. Have not done that, thus far, in Parliament with regard to the situation as I see it at the moment. What I had worked out several days ago would have been just the thing to have said, this afternoon. However, that has gone.

"Ilsley made a most effective speech. I thought it would be really preferable for him to speak as Minister of Justice ahead of St. Laurent. It deprived St. Laurent of getting into the debate in the afternoon which may have been a disappointment to him as I had asked him to participate. I had also asked Mitchell to speak but held him back, which was wise; as they had introduced their motion on the worst possible day – Wednesday being a half day – the whole afternoon went by without my having to make any references beyond what I did, references to Truman's speech and embarrassing questions arising therefrom. It really was as if the hand of Providence itself – as I believe it is – had guided the whole affair in a manner that saved me what would have been a moment in my life almost as difficult as at the time of Munich – or when the war came on and the beginning of the invasion of Poland. I found myself perspiring from sheer anxiety."

At the end of the day, Mackenzie King was convinced that "this was a day that had its place in History. It really is the line of demarcation between the past and efforts to adjust difficulties with the U.S.S.R. by conciliation and beginning of settlement by force, should the U.S.S.R. not back down immediately. I personally am afraid that fires are set in too many parts of the world to save conflagration on a terrible scale."

On March 18 the Prime Minister saw St. Laurent and Pearson to discuss Canada's stance in the UN Security Council debate on the future of Palestine. He had already "said to the Cabinet I still felt very strongly that we should not adopt an attitude of direct opposition to Britain. That I would not agree to the use of force in settlement of that question. Among other reasons, I was quite certain that our Parliament would not agree to the use of force there nor would they implement any agreements that implied use of force. I also felt there were interests that concerned all of the British peoples which Britain knew only too well. That I would not allow Canada to be put in a position of responsibility for having made British policy impossible, with consequences what they might well become.

"It is very trying to have to be the only one to speak out on these matters in Cabinet. In regard to Korea, I agreed to have our Commissioners act as observers of American troops making their own attempt at an election but on the ground that they were not to interfere in any way. St. Laurent stated anew the mission had agreed that our interpretation was right as to their not having the authority to conduct elections certainly in the whole of Korea.

"I do not know how deep a pit it might have been in which Canada would have fallen had I not taken the stand I did on this matter at the time I did. What everyone is forgetting is that simple words not backed with necessary power are meaningless in the world of today. Pearson had heard what was said in Council yesterday, so needed no further instructions. He did say that it might be suggested that a conference of nations should be held in considering a regional Atlantic Pact, and it might be suggested that this would be held in Quebec or Ottawa. Without much consideration, Mr. St. Laurent and I said we would be prepared to think the matter over. There was nothing settled."

By the next morning, the Prime Minister had become convinced that the proposed conference should not be held in Canada. He wrote that "during the night, I was thinking of what might be involved in having countries concerned with Atlantic Pact meet in Canada, at Quebec or elsewhere, as suggested by Pearson. I felt that St. Laurent and I had made a mistake in the evening countenancing the idea. First of all, External Affairs has more to attend to than it can attend to now. While this is true of other Departments, St. Laurent and myself would just be loading ourselves unnecessarily with another big obligation, but the real reason was what it would lead to of discussion in Quebec, throughout Canada generally of such questions as compulsory service, focussing in addition on immediate prospects of war, uncertainty of affairs, etc. Also I feel strongly that the big powers, particularly the United States, should be kept prominently in the van. It would be a mistake to make Canada a sort of apex to a movement which would be linking together United States and United Kingdom and other nations in a project that is intended to offset the possibility of immediate war with Russia. This is one of the dangers of having Pearson take too sudden a lead in any matters of the kind. He can get us much more deeply involved with world situations than we should ever be. He likes keeping Canada at the head of everything, in the forefront in connection with United Nations affairs. He does not see that the Big Powers are using us. That we will count for little or nothing once the struggle comes and we have served their purpose. He does not see at all what is involved in the way of getting Parliament to provide what would be necessary in the way of forces or money, etc. These things fill me with a sense of trepidation and fear. I tried first thing to get Mr. St. Laurent to 'phone Pearson but he was on his way to Montreal. So I 'phoned Pearson myself in New York. I gave him to understand I thought it would be unwise to countenance anything of the kind. He understood exactly what I meant and said he would watch that very carefully. I said I thought on no account should we allow the meeting here. I thought it ought to be kept in the United States."

Later that day, Mackenzie King wrote: "It is truly appalling how far the Russians have been permitted and have been able to get ahead in the four years since the war. I cannot but have the feeling that the United Nations with its fiddling and fussing and interfering in everything and affording them the platform they have had, has been responsible as was the League of Nations for enabling the situation to develop to the point it has. A perfectly appalling menace."

The Prime Minister felt "a sense of immense relief" on March 20 when he heard a radio report that "the United States had reversed its policy with regard to the partition of Palestine. Secretary Marshall had decided that it was preferable there should be a temporary trusteeship under the United Nations to give an opportunity for the Arabs and the Jews to work out their problem, by some arrangement other than that of forcible partition in accordance with the previous policy. All along I have opposed strongly the policy of seeking to settle the question of the Jews and Arabs by partitioning of Palestine at the instance of the United Nations. I have felt that the British were right in not attempting to have their problem settled in that way. My last word in the Cabinet on Thursday before Pearson left on Friday was that our representative should not vote in support of continuing the policy of the United States; to try to settle Palestine partition by force.

That he should, if need be, abstain altogether from voting rather than oppose the British. I was alone in speaking. Not another member of the Cabinet said a word other than St. Laurent who said he would pass on that view to Pearson but I know that Ilsley, Pearson and others felt that I was quite in the wrong in this. I don't know what view they will take now when they discover that the United States itself has felt that the policy was one which might set the world on fire and has deliberately changed. There is now a possibility of the United Kingdom and the United States working together.

"I might add in Korea as well the situation has come to where the present position makes perfectly clear that I was right in opposing our representative undertaking to join with the United States in undertaking to establish and conduct elections throughout the whole of Korea in order to establish a Korean state under the auspices of the United Nations. The purpose of the United States being to draw us into a situation where if force were needed, we would be thereby compelled to join at once with the United States. The way matters are now, the United Nations Commission are out of the picture altogether except as experts. It has become admitted that the elections cannot be carried on over the whole of Korea. It is now going to be one simply of United States army of occupation undertaking to see that elections are fairly conducted in the half of Korea controlled by the United States army.

"The Russian area is left outside the scope of the Army or United Nations Commission. It is sheer madness and wanton folly the way in which the United Nations have rushed into these commitments in different places of the world, and, worst of all, the way in which Canada has tagged along at their tail, cheering them on the way as though they were a world power which could effect miracles."

The Palestine problem came before the Cabinet again on March 23. According to Mackenzie King, the Department of External Affairs had recommended supporting "what the Americans are now proposing. Notwithstanding that Britain is holding rigidly aloof, I believe, on the sound basic theory that while speech is silver, silence is golden. I had talked privately with St. Laurent very strongly about our not again committing ourselves on matters that we knew nothing about. He explained the situation to Council from the memo that had been given him. As he came to the end, his own personal views began to shade toward his expressing himself as really not knowing sufficiently about the situation for us to express an opinion.

"Ilsley at once began to argue for our taking a stand and supporting the American attitude which was against the British; being annoyed at the British not saying what they would do, etc. I took strongly the position that the British had been a much longer time in their consideration of foreign policy than the Americans. That they were much wiser in regard to European affairs than the Americans, specially the Middle East, and the peoples there. I said, if they were refraining from deciding as between the Jews and the Arabs, it unquestionably was for the strongest reasons of policy – reasons which would undoubtedly affect the whole future of the British Commonwealth and possibly of the world but now that the Americans themselves had confessed through the Secretary of State that they were wrong in the policy they had proposed of partitioning Palestine, implying thereby that the British were right in not countenancing force to that end, we should not be led to supporting the American position again, specially where they were representing this time that they were sure they could do this and that and get a country to agree to this and this, when it was due to that kind of representation that we were misled in the first instance. I stated there might well be reasons that the members of the United Nations knew nothing about which causes the United States to take the stand that Marshall did at this time, in repudiating the partition. That I thought the only honest thing for Canada to do was to say that she did not know enough about the situation to side with either the United States or the United Kingdom and that she would therefore abstain from voting on a question that involved siding with one side or the other. This Ilsley strongly resented.

"Martin spoke up in good fashion about how he felt and what he had observed at the United Nations. Our people were taking their position as a result of pressure, others were advocating policies that they knew nothing about. He thought my stand was the only one which was right and wise. St. Laurent himself came along with words that at this juncture, it was all important that the Americans and the British should be got to work together and shape their policies as they would have to in the interests of both, so as to keep the Russians out of the control of Palestine and surrounding areas. He again took the position that our representative should be instructed not to take sides.

"Ilsley gave way reluctantly when everyone else in Council was either silent or had spoken along the line of St. Laurent and myself."

Next afternoon, the Prime Minister "read the statement McNaughton had made at the United Nations saying he would refrain from voting until we really knew where the larger countries stood. It seemed to me quite the most sensible statement that has been made yet. When A. H. [Arnold Heeney] made a broadcast, he rather indicated that the advisers made the policy – one would have thought the Government had little to do with the matter. When this matter came up yesterday, the advice given by experts was all the other way. The Cabinet turned it down and decided along the line McNaughton took today. I saw later a telegram which had been sent by External Affairs to Robertson in London which I thought was quite wrong. They talked about England's attitude being negative re Arabs and the Jews. I think it is a sensible positive attitude based on maintaining silence, not making enemies – holding strongly the position that was the only tenable one. Their position has been shown to be right."

In Cabinet on March 25 "St. Laurent took up the question of Palestine. Read McNaughton's statement but seemed to come back again to possibility later of supporting the Americans in their idea of a trusteeship with the use of force. I said I thought we had agreed that on no account were we to even consider supporting the United Nations in the use of force with partition still in view. The Cabinet agreed with this. What put me on my mettle was word that Robertson had rather indicated that he thought Bevin wished us to support the United States in their proposal. We would be getting more deeply into a difficult situation. I said it was an entirely wrong interpretation put on what Bevin might have said. I then said I thought External Affairs had been entirely wrong in talking about Britain's attitude as negative. I regarded it as positive, based on the sound maxim that while speech was silver, silence was golden. The British knew the difficulty would not be settled by partition. Had taken care neither to side with the Arabs or the Jews. They had not now, in the light of the American action, lost the friendship of either. The Americans in the light of their determination to forge ahead with force when it was impossible, had succeeded in making enemies both of Arabs and Jews alike. I did not think we should follow them into a further impossible position.

"I also said I thought we were wrong to assume that Britain, whose interests are more affected than the others, not only the Government but Parliament, could possibly have less knowledge of the situation than we had. I thought we had better hold pretty strongly by Britain. I asked the Cabinet if they had ever considered whether there might be some relationship between the Arabs and the British in protecting oil supplies which involved the whole future of the Commonwealth which the British Foreign Minister could not disclose to anyone who asked him questions concerning the matter. That I did not think it was fair to address to Bevin the question which put him into a position where he had to say yes or no, knowing that whichever he said, the whole business would sooner or later be on the street everywhere.

"I then spoke out very strongly about my feelings in regard to the United Nations acting as a super-government placing all real governments with their responsibilities under commitments which their Parliaments might not be prepared to carry out. I said to the Cabinet I would not be a member of the Government much longer. I would like them to remember my words. They would have serious problems over the next five years at least. They would find that the United Nations would be getting them into more and more trouble in different parts of the world. They had better exercise all the caution they could in not trying to set a pace on anything and everything that came up, but be content to take the honest straight-forward position, and of some of these questions we did not really know anything sufficiently, to say which of the Great Powers were in the right or in the wrong. To abstain rather than take a position that might be wholly wrong.

"I said to Mr. St. Laurent quite frankly that I thought the Department of External Affairs was much too positive in some of its views and were going much too far. I thought the foreign policy needed to be determined by the Cabinet as a whole with the utmost possible care."

On March 26 Pearson gave the Prime Minister a report on the progress of the talks in New York on the development of a security pact for the Atlantic region. "The form the scheme is now taking is a declaration by the President supporting his declaration of the other day [in the broadcast on March 17] in which the United States will offer to support the members of the Brussels Pact and invite other countries to join in mutual security around the Atlantic. Matters so arranged as to keep it in the Northern Atlantic zone. I liked the idea very much. Pearson thinks a conference will be held in about two or three weeks – possibly at Washington. . . . It seems to me in every way best that the whole matter should become one of United States leadership. It puts increasingly on the United States the obligation of maintaining peace in the Atlantic."

Although the coup in Czechoslovakia had galvanized the Western powers into serious consideration of mutual security arrangements, the situation in Germany, which had deteriorated steadily during the early months of 1948, was obviously more dangerous in terms of a direct con-frontation between the West and the Soviet Union. In February, the major Western powers had begun discussions on the future of west Germany with representatives of Belgium, the Netherlands and Luxembourg. Soviet pro-tests culminated in the withdrawal of Marshal Sokolovsky from the Allied Control Council on March 20 and Russian harassment of Allied traffic to and from Berlin. On April 1 all Allied trains scheduled to leave Berlin for the west were cancelled. Mackenzie King was in Williamsburg, Virginia, that day, with the Governor-General and President Truman, to receive an honorary degree from the College of William and Mary the following day.

He was very depressed by the international situation. "I cannot see how the world will escape a third great war," he wrote. "It may be postponed some little time. That will all depend on whether Russia possesses some terrible weapon of which we know very little. It looks as though they will rely mostly on capturing one country after another through internal strife. It does, however, begin to look as though the days of world revolution were already upon us and the present generation will know little, if anything, of real security and peace."

The Prime Minister had a chance for a short talk with Truman the next day. Truman "looked remarkably well," he wrote. "Appears to be in very good condition physically. When we were standing in the corridor about to come into the building, there was a choir of men and women marching past. There were just the Governor General, Governor Tuck and the Bishop and myself and Mr. Pomfret all talking together. The President said: conditions at the moment were very serious. As serious he thought as in 1939. He was referring to what had happened in Berlin last night where Americans had to bring food and passengers into their own zone by air and where incidents may occur at any moment that would set the whole of Europe on fire. . . . I feel terribly concerned about it all. Indeed I have come to the conclusion that if we escape war before this month is over or next at the latest, it will be a miracle. If the Communists feel sure of winning Italy, they will probably wait until after that event and may even avoid open war, having captured another country. On the other hand, if they think they are going to fail in this, they may well precipitate a move into Europe before the election itself takes place. I think, too, the situation in Manchuria and Korea is equally dangerous and in China. I did not think it necessary to ask Truman whether he thought the situation was very dangerous, very critical, because he had openly expressed that view to me and the others, as we were talking together. I did ask him when we were alone if there were any suggestions he would like to make to me. He said something to the effect that my judgment was sound in these matters. To just keep on as we were doing. He had in mind in this remark the negotiations re Atlantic Pact taking place in Washington just now. I was glad to hear him say before the others that he had seen my speech. This was before it was delivered. He was quite satisfied with it. I should be surprised if in his next pronouncement, he does not link up with what I said today. I told him that if, at any time, he wished to send message to me personally or otherwise, to feel that he could do so with perfect confidence. He thanked me warmly.

"I saw him alone in his room with Mrs. Truman and their daughter just before the Governor General came in as well for us both to shake hands with him and I said I admired the way he was keeping on with his fight [in the election campaign]. He said he was going to fight for all he was worth and he would lick these other fellows yet. I notice the sympathies about here seem to be Republican. At the meeting today [the convocation ceremonies], he was much crowded for time and he was faced with a thunderstorm coming in. However, he did manage to have three and a half minutes and to say a good deal extemporaneously. He said if they got back to the White House, he hoped I would come and pay him a visit there. Mrs. Truman said something about not waiting until another term. I thought Mrs. Truman looked very tired. Indeed quite changed but was very pleasant. Margaret was exceedingly nice."

After returning to Ottawa, the Prime Minister had a talk with the Governor-General on April 9 about the situation which had developed at Berlin and "the power that Russia might have. He spoke of the tremendous army they possessed. The many divisions they could put into the fields compared to those which could be put in by the United States or Britain. Moreover, the United States would have to transport its men. I pointed out how perilous this would be with the power of bombing from the skies. That in no time ships would be sunk. I spoke, too, of the concern the British had six months ago over the display of air power in Moscow. Of submarine power as recently developed and of the Germans that were trained by the Russians and under their direction for entering Berlin and sweeping on from there. I said what I felt most concerned about was the kind of weapons the Russians might be fighting with. The extent to which they might apply bacteriological warfare, gases and the like. Things that we had little or no knowledge of; what they might have been doing during recent years.

"I cannot but shudder each time I think of this enormous aircraft carrier which we are having brought out under the title of Magnificent. What Canada wants with the largest aircraft carrier afloat under a title like that, I don't know. It is just to invite an enemy's attack. I venture to say should war come soon, it would be about the first of the large vessels to disappear."

In Mackenzie King's judgment, "much depended on the developments in Italy. That if the Russians expected to have the Communists win, there would probably be no immediate fighting. If they thought the Communists might lose, we might expect a general movement in different places. He agreed that if the Russian armies had possession of Berlin, they would cross to the Atlantic coast in no time. Would soon have the whole of Europe under their control. He said it will go badly at first. Will be a hard fight – the United States and Britain would have to fight to get a base in

Europe and win back. This would come in the end. He said it would be very difficult landing men in numbers in Europe. I said I was glad he was going over at this moment. He said he would be able he thought to get the inside of the situation. Would let me know all that he could find out when he got back."

Mackenzie King's attention shifted back to the situation in the Middle East on April 13 when he and St. Laurent received Moshe Sharett, the Jewish representative in New York, at the Prime Minister's office in the House of Commons. "Mr. Sharett gave us a statement of the Jewish position in admirably concise and well expressed words. The point he was anxious to make was that, while the Jews were much opposed to trusteeship, we should not abandon the idea of partition in the end; also that he thought Jerusalem, being internationalized, could be protected for all religions by having forces of the United Nations undertake to administer its affairs. I asked him the question at the end, if instead of your coming to make the presentation you had, the Arabian leader had come. What would he have said and how would he [Sharett] answer what he said.

"His reply was equivalent to saying that the Arabs would misrepresent the situation. I told him that I thought it was inadvisable for Mr. St. Laurent and myself to express an opinion one way or the other. That would be understood by Mr. Croll. He accepted the situation in a frank and pleasant way.

"I must say I was immensely taken with his manner and his appearance; an exceptionally fine advocate. He told me at the end that he did not see why the situation in Palestine should embarrass the world situation. That it was really a local affair and should be kept as such. I said that was very promising. I hoped it was true."

In mid-April the Prince Regent of Belgium visited Ottawa accompanied by Paul-Henri Spaak. On April 17 St. Laurent brought Spaak to Laurier House for a talk with the Prime Minister who "spoke very frankly . . . about my fears as to the future. He had yesterday said that he was among those that were optimistic. I told him I supposed he had said that, feeling it was unwise to go further. That I really personally thought there was terrible danger of some incident precipitating some serious world crisis. He said he himself felt the latter danger was very great and that the situation was grave but had naturally not wished to say too much about that. He asked if anyone really knew the position of Russia. That he thought her people must be still suffering very much. That undoubtedly she could win a quick victory across Europe but it would mean destruction to Russia in the end. Surely her men would see that; that Stalin was a man who had reason and vision. He could see that the United States would

The National Liberal Convention, Ottawa, August 1948. Mackenzie King addresses
the delegates on August 6

*Above*: The unveiling of portraits of Sir Robert Borden and W. L. Mackenzie King, Canada's two wartime prime ministers, in the Rotunda of the Parliament Buildings, June 1947

*Above right*: President Truman speaking in the House of Commons, June 1947

*Right*: Mackenzie King with Mr. and Mrs. Frank Salisbury. Mr. Salisbury was the painter of the portrait shown in the frontispiece

*Below*: Mackenzie King with F. G. Bradley and Joseph Smallwood of Newfoundland, at the National Liberal Convention, August 1948

*Right*: Mackenzie King receiving congratulations after being given an honorary degree in Brussels, Belgium (*Photograph*, Actualité, *Brussels*)

*Below right*: Mackenzie King with dignitaries in Brussels, Belgium, November 1947 (*Photograph*, Actualité, *Brussels*)

*Above*: The National Liberal Convention, August 1948

*Above right*: Mackenzie King congratulates Louis St. Laurent on becoming leader of the Liberal party; Mme St. Laurent is with them

*Right*: The Governor-General, Viscount Alexander of Tunis, and Mackenzie King, with Louis St. Laurent and his first Cabinet (with Lester Pearson absent), Rideau Hall, November 15, 1948 (*Photograph, Star Newspaper Service*)

Mackenzie King leaves the National Liberal Convention, which has chosen his successor as leader of the party

defeat them in the end. He was not like Hitler who was a madman and could not be reckoned with on that account. He had not evidence that they were preparing for war in Russia. I mentioned, however, what Bevin had told me of the strength of the Russian air force; their submarine power and the German troops that they had brought under their influence, etc. These things he seemed to know of and I noticed that his face changed colour as we talked. Flushes coming at different times. He felt, however, that the European countries might be able to develop some military strength of their own and that if it became certain that the United States would resent further aggression in Europe, the Russians would not trust matters for at least some time to come. I again expressed my surprise, regarding the use by the Russians of weapons unknown at present to us. The form of gases, bacteriological warfare, etc. I must say reports coming from different sources, as for example Vanier, after talks with the Chief of the Air Staff, are all quite alarming as to what may happen in Berlin. The truth is that the situation is like what it was with Japan prior to Pearl Harbor. How near we may be to a Pearl Harbor, no one can say. I myself think that the danger is very real.

"I found that Spaak agreed very much about the United Nations not being what it appeared to be and the necessity of agreements being made independently of it altogether, using the United Nations [Charter] as a frame. Basing action on its principles but not counting on it for strength. When I spoke about the situation in Palestine, he put his head down to one side and threw up his hands. Said he had come to the conclusion he had made a mistake when he voted for partition at the start. He seemed to think that these Jews and Arabs might have to be left to fight out their differences together. He agreed that there was a good deal that was unrealistic in regard to the United Nations as to what they could do in the way of implementing matters that they undertook.

"The talk with Mr. Spaak was very much worth while. He seemed to enjoy the quiet of the library and spoke appreciatively of the House which he seemed pleased to see."

The Governor-General returned from a brief visit to England on April 29 and saw the Prime Minister later that day. Alexander, Mackenzie King reported, "had the impression that people did not begin to be as nearly aware as they should of the critical situation that might develop at any moment in Berlin. That the Russians were evidently determined to crowd the British and Americans out of Berlin. Some slip might happen that would precipitate a terrible situation. On the other hand, he found a good sign in that the Russian officers in Berlin were, on the whole, very friendly with the English and Americans. They got along well by themselves but there was always the direction from Moscow which made the situation very difficult. He had rather gathered that if the Marshall Plan got under way, in two years, things could be settled but between now and then there would be much uncertainty." President Truman had signed the Economic Cooperation Act on April 3 and, under its terms, appropriations totalling $5,300 million were authorized for the first year of the European Recovery Program.

In the Palestine debate at the United Nations, Canada's position continued to be cautious but the Canadian delegation endorsed a call for a truce in the fighting on April 1 and the appointment on April 23 of a UN Truce Commission. Events in May made much of the UN discussion academic. Formation of the state of Israel took place on May 14, one day before the British mandate ended formally. Within minutes of the Israeli announcement, the new state was recognized by the United States and the partition of Palestine became a political reality. The Arab countries immediately went to war and the UN General Asembly reacted by approving the appointment of a mediator, a post filled by Count Folke Bernadotte on May 20. Writing about the formation of Israel on May 15, Mackenzie King felt that it was fortunate "things have calmed down a bit in the larger international arena and I believe the nations will think twice before they start to allow the present conflict to enlarge to too great an extent. There is, however, a grave possibility of very serious developments which might bring great peril to the world. Somehow or another, I feel nevertheless much less concerned than I did some months ago."

Sir Alexander Clutterbuck called on May 17 to give the Prime Minister the views of the British government on the question of recognizing Israel "and the considerations of which they have to take account with the Arabs. It is all in accord with the views that I myself have fought for in Cabinet from the start, and believe to be the wisest today. The American action in taking the course they did without conferring with the British Government is evidence of the impetuousness and lack of real wisdom on occasions in American diplomacy. I can look back with a good deal of satisfaction on what I did to save our Government from falling into a pit in difficult times. . . . I think they must all see today that my judgment was right and sound though only they and certainly not British and others will ever know what has been saved in the situation.

"I talked with a good deal of freedom to Sir Alexander who I thought should know how difficult the situation had been in some particulars. Also suggested to Pearson that he and Mr. St. Laurent should allow Clutterbuck to come and talk directly with them and tell them what he had given to me in confidence."

On May 20 Mackenzie King discussed the situation in the Middle East with St. Laurent and Pearson. "Pearson made it clear that the United States were trying to gain our support in the Security Council for a motion of theirs which would declare that Egypt was guilty of aggression but which would lead to sanctions – possibly economic sanctions as a means of dealing with her.

"It was also stated that the United Kingdom intended to have a Resolution which would press for mediation but nothing that would lead to an attempt to enforce any position by force.

"I told Pearson at once that I thought he should support the United Kingdom in their motion and that our representative should abstain from voting on the United States motion. That I held to the belief that mediation was right and possible and should be continued to the limit but I did not think that force on the part of the United Nations would lead anywhere except to trouble. Especially as they were not in a position to give guarantees as to what force would be used. Whether they could carry out what they proposed. It was clear from what Pearson said that Wrong had been unable to get any clear idea of what the United States was able to do. The United States was much upset over the declaration yesterday by the British that they intended to have their officers and others help the Arabs. I, myself, was much amazed at this statement to be made at this time, but I am sure it is not without reason on the part of Britain. I have little confidence in the judgment of Americans in regard to matters in the Middle East. Equally I feel that the British have the best of reasons, having the most to lose for the course they have pursued.

"I was pleased to learn after I had stated my position that word had already been sent by External Affairs to McNaughton which was to support the British motion and to abstain from voting on the American.

"Pearson added he thought he should suggest to McNaughton to use all the power possible to get the situation such that, while the British motion will be carried, the American motion would not have to be defeated. I was glad to find St. Laurent feeling equally strongly on not attempting to recognize Israel at the moment, but to allow time to make clear the course of development we should take. It seems to me utter folly that it should be left to a new organization like the United Nations to settle this problem of peace and war with neither experience nor responsibility in taking these matters practically out of the hands of governments and countries that have great responsibilities all over the world.

"I pointed out what I think is most important that, as both the Russians and Americans were together in their attitude of recognizing the Jewish State, we need not fear anything serious in the way of general war developing as might have been the case had the Russians and Americans been opposing each other in that field as in so many other parts of the world."

On May 24 Clutterbuck showed Mackenzie King messages "that had passed between the United States and the United Kingdom. Pretty straight talking between the two. Mention by the United Kingdom that if the United States furnished arms to the Jews, the United Kingdom would have to furnish arms to the Arabs. There was a strong plea that both try to get together to come to some means of helping to save the situation. I thought the British view of urging strongly that nothing be done, [through] committing the United Nations to force, was very sound, particularly as it mentioned that they did not know how force could be applied. They should keep on joint efforts at conciliation. Also very wisely urging that nothing should be said about defining the limits of the State of Israel. If a settlement was to be made, it might be on some compromise of boundaries. If England loses the friendship of Arab states, it might mean these States are joining the Russian circle with possible loss of the Far East to British interests. This is what the Americans would never see and which some of our own people have been unwilling to see. Russia, of course, is the [beneficiary] of this dispute."

At the Cabinet meeting on May 26, the Prime Minister, feeling that the British case on developments in the Middle East should be put strongly, "took the matter in hand myself . . . and read British despatches to Africa, Australia, etc., making clear that the real issue involved was whether the whole Arab states were likely to swing into the Russian orbit, if Britain went back on her obligation to the Arabs, and a break up of British Empire followed in consequence, if Russia ever got control of areas now held by the Arabs. . . . Today the Arabs have declined to obey the cease fire truce of bombing Jerusalem. It may be that great destruction will be wrought in the Holy Land before the fighting is brought to a close. Thank God, it looked as though Russia, while she may hope [to] and probably will profit by the differences between Britain and the United States, hardly is prepared to go to war at once. But one cannot look very far ahead with any degree of certainty."

On June 2 the Prime Minister discussed the situation with General McNaughton, who was in Ottawa for a few days and "who was more than 100% behind me in my attitude against attempting to embarrass a settlement in Palestine by force. He said all it would succeed in doing would be to turn over the Middle East to the Soviets and probably the Mediterranean as well. I had to fight like a tiger in Council against External Affairs on this, Ilsley and some others in the Cabinet. That organization [External Affairs] is a dangerous institution. McNaughton thinks it will be some time before a truce is recognized. They will want to kill a lot more of each other before they agree to a truce."

A truce, ordered by the Security Council on May 29, went into effect on June 11 but all efforts to prolong it failed. A threat by the Council on July 15 to impose sanctions on the belligerents brought another temporary halt to the fighting but no real solution.

Meanwhile, Russian pressure on Berlin had steadily increased. On June 10 all German traffic on the Autobahn was halted and further restrictions were placed on British rail freight movements to and from the city. The blockade tightened on June 22 when all rail traffic between Berlin and the Western occupation zones was stopped; only the air corridors remained open. Three days later, Mackenzie King expressed "a deep concern" about the situation. "One can only pray that so-called 'cold' war may continue cold but ultimately cease and let nothing too precipitate take place as a result of constant goading and irritation by Russians in Berlin."

On June 26 the Prime Minister continued "to feel great concern over the Berlin situation and possible developments there, specially in the light of a communication from Robertson which says the British Government rather expect a clash in Berlin but do not think it will result in war.

"My own feeling is, if men are killed, American and British soldiers, the resentment will be so strong that nothing will avert a situation that might soon become one affecting the whole of Europe, if not also the whole of the world. Of those around me, no one seems to give this appalling possibility so much as a thought. They just reason that anything so terrible cannot be. With strikes in France and Italy, upset conditions of the United States in a general election and much else, the signs are ominous to say the least."

On the last day of the 1948 session, June 30, the Prime Minister received a message from Robertson "which stated how serious the situation was in Berlin. That Bevin had stated it might mean war but what concerned me most was its reference to a chance remark that Bevin had made to Robertson and other High Commissioners not only as to food from the Dominions but as to air transport to assist in overcoming the Russian blockade into Berlin.

"It was fortunate I saw this at that time as I was confronted by a question by Green at the opening of the day which disclosed that he had received some word of this matter. Later I learned that the Standard in London had published a sensational article which had been born of a leak that had come from Bevin's confidence in the High Commissioners and which stated in definite terms that request had been made to Canada, Australia, etc., naming the different Dominions for air transport. When Green asked this question, I felt how careful I should be in reply so as to avoid a stampede in the country or anything being said that the Russians might take as some evidence of the over-concern on the part of the three other nations occupying Berlin, so I simply said I had no answer to the question at the moment but would wish to confer with my colleagues about it. I made it clear that any answer that might be made, not having the whole situation carefully reviewed first, would necessarily carry with it implications that might be serious in a very critical situation.

"I was sent in the course of the morning two other telegrams from External Affairs which also emphasized the grave danger of the situation but one of which fortunately made clear, in reference to the repairing of railways and their possible use later, [an] indication that the real crisis would be surmounted. That Russia would not want war. However, the British Government, I think wisely, feel that an attitude of the kind might be wholly misleading or a part of the same tactics that Hitler employed in putting other countries off their guard."

The situation in Berlin was discussed in Cabinet later in the day. To Mackenzie King, the matter would "require the most careful thought that it is possible for us to give. I then spoke of the question that Hackett [Conservative M.P. for Stanstead] had put to me in the morning about a request from Britain for air transport to assist in taking food to Berlin because of the Russian blockade. I outlined in a sketchy way what the telegrams stated, drawing attention to the fact that Bevin, the Foreign Secretary, had used the expression that the situation was such that it might mean war. That the British, Americans and French had decided to face that possibility and would not leave Berlin, even if attacked. I described the city in a state of seige by Russians. Also referred to the presence of troops and tanks in the streets of Berlin, and what might be expected at any moment, if some precipitate action were taken. I said I could not understand the reference Bevin had earlier made, that there might be a clash in Berlin, but not war. My own view was if a clash came, war would be next to inevitable.

"I then spoke of what I had said when I came back last December. Pointed to the dangers of Berlin. Spoke of the crisis that nearly came at Easter and of the larger crisis now imminent. Said that I recalled some of the Ministers in the United Kingdom had thought that, if the crisis did not come at Easter, it would probably come in June. I then said I thought members of Council as a whole should all know exactly what was in the despatches. Decisions to be made were a responsibility which rested on all the members of the Government, not only on one or two and they must be prepared to take their share.

"I said to Mr. St. Laurent that I thought the despatches ought to be read. If he would not mind, I would perhaps read them myself. He was getting the copies out of his portfolio at the time. I did this because I have noticed right along that St. Laurent seeks to avoid reading out communications and indeed has frequently said to me he did not think that we could get along, telling the Cabinet as a whole this and that. That is very much Pearson's way of acting. I know that Pearson, for many reasons perhaps, equally dislikes having the Cabinet as a whole have too much of a say, discuss foreign affairs more than is necessary. I had too in mind the memo which was attached to one of the despatches by Pearson and which advised the Minister that he should take the position that we would send transport and food at once. This, of course, is right along the lines that External Affairs has been taking for some time past, to get into every international situation and as much in the front of it as possible, not realizing what the appalling possibilities are."

The Prime Minister then read the despatches. "There was a dead silence in the room. Ministers looked anxious. St. Laurent, I could see, was deeply concerned. I have noticed in the last little while that he sees what it means to have these great decisions to make and stand by and fight for. He has begun to look much more anxious than formerly. Indeed at times, quite weary. His lot, if he comes into the leadership, as I believe he will, will be a very difficult one, particularly on these matters that relate to relations with the United Kingdom.

"In speaking to the Cabinet, I stressed mostly the feeling of indignation I had that on a matter as grave as this, it should be projected into the press of the world by some persons in Britain who, as I said, I believed would prefer Empire and war, to no war and separate nations of the Commonwealth. That was only an expression but rather reveals the view of many centralists in England who want the world control and hope to get it through centralization of Commonwealth problems in London. I said the whole position reminded me of the Chanak incident. Told of how I had been going into North York on a Saturday when the appeal was made from Chequers to the nations of the Commonwealth to send naval, military forces, etc. Recalled how Australia had responded. Meighen had said we should say: Ready, aye, ready. I had called the Cabinet together on Sunday. Asked Britain for more information and had said, if there was to be war, I would bring Parliament together and it would decide whether we should participate or not. I said that Asquith had said that some of the Dominion statesmen were wiser than some of the men who had sent the call were. I said that I thought we should proceed with great caution. I then looked to Claxton and asked him if his Department had received any request and the position we were in with respect to transportation. I had expected Claxton, in the light of the advertising that he is giving Canada's armed services, what he had been saying [about] what the defence forces could and would do, etc., . . . [to] immediately say something to the effect that they were ready to supply a certain number of planes with crew, etc., and that we should send word immediately as to what we were prepared to do. Instead of that, to my amazement, he took the very opposite view. He said he thought we should keep out of the situation altogether if we possibly could. He said if we were to send planes over and one of our planes were to be shot down, it might lead to war or we might be credited with having been responsible for shooting down some other planes. He thought the whole business was much too dangerous. Besides we had not been drawn into any of the councils respecting matters concerned with Berlin and had been left out. He did not think we should be drawn in if it could possibly be avoided. Immediately I heard a note of acquiescence from different parts of the room. Gardiner shook his head, nodded in the affirmative. Others were more or less silent. I repeatedly asked for expressions of opinion from others. Neither Ilsley nor Gregg nor any of those present excepting Mitchell really said anything. Mitchell said something about knowing Bevin and how careful we should be in dealing with anything he did say.

"When speaking of the supply of planes at the request of Britain, I was rather surprised to hear St. Laurent say we might have to consider the request. The United States might wish us to supply them and we have to consider that. There again I detected a note which is characteristic of Pearson with his close association with the United States. It all illustrates where St. Laurent is going to have great and grave difficulties if these questions, as they undoubtedly will, continue to come on. I think the Cabinet saw for the first time that I had been wise in the fight that I had been making right along against getting too quickly and easily and unnecessarily drawn into situations in all parts of the world which we should be extremely careful about assuming. They saw in a moment when faced with decision as to war just how grave that decision was.

"The second thoughts in these matters are often better than the first. Bertrand said that if war came, he assumed we would have to go into it; otherwise Communism. It would be a war against Communism, and his thoughts seemed to be centring on Quebec being ready for a fight against Communism. I said I felt it was quite certain that if war broke out, between the three great powers and Russia, Canada would wish to come in instantly. The Cabinet agreed with that. They felt that there could be no two views on that score. They were, however, pretty chary about how far they were prepared to go at this time.

"After some discussion, I asked Claxton and Heeney to go and draw up a statement which would express the word that should be sent to Robertson, our High Commissioner. Claxton had suggested that we should telegraph him to see Bevin at once and tell him that it would be a great embarrassment to us if any request were made for transport planes. That he hoped it would not be put forward. This coming from Claxton surprised me beyond words. He has been boasting of what we were ready to do."

When a draft statement for the House of Commons had been prepared, it was quickly approved by the Cabinet and Mackenzie King "pointed out that I thought I should let the House know at once, lest too much in the way of speculation and rumour got afloat, and I then went into a room to get additional copies. Found Pearson there. To my amazement, Pearson said the press was publishing a statement that the foreign office had proferred a request. My statement had just indicated that while there had been conversations, there had been no request. I told Pearson of Council's views in regard to what should be said to Robertson. He at once said he thought it would be best for him to 'phone. I agreed. I told him something of the views of the Cabinet. For the first time, I have seen Pearson look really frightened. He looked almost terrified. Quite evidently he had at last come to see what the decision was. Quite all right to be in on all these things; when it comes to actually have one's country involved in war, there were limits to what we might be able to do, and the commitments that it was wise to make. I think if anything he was relieved at the Government's attitude which really was quite the opposite of what his memo to St. Laurent had proposed earlier in the day as to the policy of External Affairs.

"I came back to the Cabinet and told them what had taken place; that I would have to postpone what I would have to say in the House. It was considerably after 2 and I felt I could not give more time to Cabinet matters, so we adjourned to meet possibly again tomorrow or earlier if the situation required."

This difficulty was straightened out and the Prime Minister "was glad at 6.00 P.M. before the House adjourned, to be able to give a statement finally agreed upon after conference with Pearson regarding the Berlin situation and the so-called request for planes. It helped I think to quiet matters." In the House, he declared that "no request had been received from the United Kingdom government either for food stocks or air transport" but admitted that Bevin, in informal talks with the Commonwealth High Commissioners in London, had "touched on the question of the adequacy of present air transport facilities for supplying the civilian population of Berlin." In the face of a great deal of domestic criticism, the government continued to maintain that no formal request for assistance of any kind had been received and, for the duration of the Berlin blockade, no Canadian assistance was given.

In a conversation with the Governor-General on July 7, Mackenzie King found him "deeply concerned" about the Berlin situation and reported that he "would not be in the least surprised if war came at any moment. Indeed will regard it as next to a miracle if it does not come. He said he was speaking very privately at the table. Said if he had to bet, he would 'reluctantly' place his money on there being no war, which laconic remark I took to mean, reluctantly that he would lose his money – but would rather lose it and have no war, than to win it and have war come.

"I said what I feared was an incident in Berlin which would give an excuse for an army of Germans under Russian control to walk in and take possession of the city. Claim that they now held Berlin as their own and make the next step one of the allies [attempting] to drive them out which, of course, would mean that they would then seek immediately to overrun the whole of Germany and possibly the whole of France as well and be ready for a world war. Everything depends on what the Russians have in the way of secret weapons and sources of destruction, such as gases, bacteria, etc. It is of the latter that I am terrified.

"Alexander thought if war came, there would be occasional air raids over Canada and the States, more to terrify than anything else. I pointed out this would probably help to arouse the nation to universal volunteering and justify conscription. The fact that the Communists have lost in the Finland election; that Tito is making it difficult for them in Yugoslavia – if that is not a blind – that there has been a demonstration in Czechoslovakia on behalf of Benes – this coming at the present time may cause the Russians to hold back a bit; forego perhaps for the present altogether any further attempt at aggression. On the other hand, there is confusion in the United States over national elections; almost a certainty of war in Palestine; China in a state of revolution; in Malaya, a Communist uprising. Heaven alone knows the real situation in India, etc., to offset the possibility. One can only pray that war will be kept off but certainly Lord Alexander and Her Excellency both were profoundly and deeply disturbed and really alarmed. What I think they felt very strongly was how exactly matters had developed along lines I had foretold on coming back from Europe, late Autumn."

Over the next two weeks, the situation in Berlin remained tense and, to Mackenzie King writing on July 20, "the significant thing of today has been the appreciation at last by the Cabinet and also by External Affairs that there is a real possibility of war, and that within the very near future. Indeed, it is coming nearer to a certainty every hour. St. Laurent and others in speeches have repeatedly said there would be no war, which I told them each time was a great mistake. Claxton, too, as War Minister, has talked in that way. What utter foolishness. Today he indicated what the numbers of our forces amounted to.

"It is generally conceded that France will not resist. At today's Cabinet I spoke of the possibility of Parliament having to be summoned at any time very soon. Also said it was to bring together the committees that have to do with the matters regarding the preparation of war. Claxton said people were at work on the War Book, and it would be another year before it was ready. I told him they had better have as much in the way of readiness within the next two weeks as possible. I told Claxton he should be able to report to us on different aspects relating to Canadian forces.

"Russia is determined to have Berlin. Once they have Berlin, and once it blazes up between Russia, America and Britain, it is likely to become another world war. The situation is indeed very, very serious. I have almost come to believe that Russia is quite decided on war, and if the Allied Powers do not yield to their demands upon Berlin war will come sooner than is expected."

Mackenzie King mentioned to his Cabinet colleagues the qualification he had made in the House about not necessarily retiring as Prime Minister immediately after the choice of the new party leader. He "told them I had regretted not having made this statement outright, that this depended on there being no emergency. I said if I am to hold on for reasons of state which no responsible Minister could ignore, certainly the Cabinet would want me to undertake responsibility of leading Parliament into war. It was a situation that one would have to face if one had the interests of the country at heart.

"While St. Laurent and I were talking in Council a message came from Wrong telling of the talk that he had had with Lovett about American feeling on the whole situation. That report convinced me more than ever of how very serious the situation is.

"The reasons that were set forth as to the grounds on which there might be some belief that Russia could draw back, or was bluffing, seemed to me in the nature of wishful thinking. On the other hand, the situation was so critical that it could not be regarded other than extremely serious. Notwithstanding this, there was a positive assertion that the States, Britain and France would not give up their position in Berlin without fighting. Against that, we have Montgomery's statement that troops were in the three zones. All would be driven out of Berlin in no time, and fighting would extend immediately to the banks of the Rhine, to continue there for how long God only knows."

# CHAPTER FIVE

# Cabinet Reconstruction and the Announcement of Retirement

MACKENZIE KING's diary entry for January 1, 1948, closed with these words: "I confess that I felt very happy all day long, in part because of not being over-fatigued; in part, the pleasure of meeting friends at the beginning of another year. In large part, however, and I believe mostly because of feeling that I was now in the year that would bring me relief from the burdens of office and give me a chance to complete the part of my life's work and life story which I should like to be able to finish, if so be it, the Will of God, before I die. I doubt if any man in Canada could look on more that he has to be thankful for, on this day, than myself. A more beautiful home; more in the way of friends whose friendship is worth possessing or more in the way of opportunity for continued public service."

The Prime Minister had already decided to announce his intention to retire at a meeting of the National Liberal Federation on Tuesday, January 20, and, on January 13, he had made a few notes "about what I should put in my speech for Tuesday night. I was thinking of what it was going to mean to me to sever connections with all colleagues. That my life has all been centred in Cabinet and Council and my own office in the East Block and Parliament. All of this will be gone once I retire.

"There will then be no place to go in connection with one's work other than one's own house. That it might occasion a sense of loneliness. Nevertheless my thought was that there were other things to be done which I have not done thus far. Nothing done towards Memoirs. I have to think of the interests of others who were going to follow on, etc., and must remember that 'the night cometh when no man can work.' That I wished to do while I still had health and strength as it should be done."

However, before announcing his own retirement, Mackenzie King had to give some consideration to an immediate reconstruction of the Cabinet. Ian Mackenzie was his senior colleague in terms of service but the state

of his health was such that the Prime Minister had been thinking of re-
placing him since October 1947. He tackled this problem, which was
bound to involve several shifts in the Cabinet, on January 2. That afternoon, he saw J. A. MacKinnon, the Minister of Trade and Commerce. He
told MacKinnon that "St. Laurent, Howe and Abbott had talked with me
about the necessity of having Howe take on the business of carrying on the
Government's policy with respect to the restrictive measures that we knew,
at the time, would have to be enacted to avoid depletion of American dollars. Howe had told me that unless he could get a Department with a staff
that could do this work, he would have to drop out. He and others had
suggested the Department of Trade and Commerce. I had said at once
that I did not wish to make any changes in a Minister's Department without a chance to confer with him first. That, as a matter of fact, my reaction
to the suggestion was that it was not a good one. I looked on Howe as a
protectionist and would be sorry to see our Trade and Commerce Department made an instrument for furthering protection.

"I had been assured by him and the others that such was not the case.
That he really felt strongly about greater freedom of trade. I had myself
suggested the possibility of his taking the Department of Mines and Resources, along with Immigration, etc., but the others had pressed for Trade
and Commerce. I said I had been amazed and distressed to find that the
conversation which we had had on these matters had been given to the
press in a statement which appeared after I had left Ottawa [for the United
Kingdom].

"I did not tell MacKinnon this but I think it was a statement given by
St. Laurent to Hume [a reporter for the *Ottawa Citizen*] at the time that
I was leaving. I saw them both conversing at some length together. Mac-
Kinnon himself, before I had referred to the Department of Mines and
Resources, volunteered the statement that he thought the Department of
Trade and Commerce was the one that could best carry out the Govern-
ment's policy on these restrictive measures. That Howe would be the best
person to do that work. He, himself, did not feel he had the toughness or
words to that effect – to administer the new regulations as they should be.
He said his own office had sent him a copy of the article.

"I said I had seen it myself only on looking through some of the newspapers which had been forwarded to me in London, and had been much
surprised and annoyed when I read it. MacKinnon himself said he thought
Howe would be really the best person for the Department of Trade and
Commerce. That it was all in good running order at present. He had enjoyed it very much and would welcome a lighter Department. He had
spoken of Howe as the one for Trade and Commerce before I had made

any reference to that myself. I at once said that I had taken a different view and had thought of the Department of Mines and Resources.

"I said to him I was pleased he had brought up this matter in part himself and volunteered the statements he had as it made it a little easier for me to work out the problems I had. He then said he hoped he could remain in the Government. I said to him I thought the change which should be made was to have Mackenzie give up Veterans Affairs. That I could put Gregg into that post which would leave Fisheries vacant. MacKinnon said that there were a good many inland fisheries. I said I did not think a man needed to be an expert on the work of the Department. What was needed was judgment of policies and administrative ability. He then asked what I thought of Gibson. He said nobody seemed to feel he was a real strength which I agree with though he has done much better as Secretary of State than in anything else. He is, however, a good deal of a play-boy and likes position, decorations, etc. I said nothing in reply to that suggestion.

"He then spoke about the Post Office Department. Asked whether I thought Bertrand should be kept on. My reply to that was he must not forget we had to keep the number of Quebec portfolios intact. For him to drop out meant finding another Minister from Quebec. MacKinnon had been speaking of the very large majority Bertrand had and the ease with which another person could be elected. I said I thought Bertrand would welcome the Senate any time but I doubted whether a change should be made at once."

The Prime Minister then referred to the impending by-election in Yale constituency in British Columbia. Grote Stirling, the sitting Progressive Conservative member, had resigned on October 8, 1947. "Pointed out how unfortunate it was for a by-election there. That with our Treaty – Geneva Agreements – apples was the one thing which had been more or less sacrificed. I was wondering whether some arrangement could be made if Mackenzie were to drop out to have someone chosen in his constituency who could be elected there. The difficulty was with our limited majority. I felt, however, that Mackenzie's behaviour was such it would not be right to continue him longer in the Ministry.

"[Senator] McKeen told me privately when Mackenzie had gone to the West to give six or seven meetings in British Columbia, he took the first meeting but was evidently quite the worse for liquor when speaking at it, and had to give up the others. . . . MacKinnon agreed that none of the Ministers had any respect for him. He had received more than enough consideration up to the present. He also said that Mackenzie seldom, if ever, paid any attention to his Department. My problem is with him in the House of Commons.

"I talked with MacKinnon a little about my own position. Recalled how I had spoken in the Cabinet about having the Federation Executive meet before the end of the year. That had had to be changed to the New Year. Told him my reason for not allowing the meeting to be held after the reopening of Parliament. I spoke about the worry that External Affairs policy was occasioning me and said if there came to be any disagreement over these policies, I would be wiser to announce at the Federation meeting that I was asking one of my colleagues to act as Prime Minister for a time, pending the time that I might resign as Prime Minister, and let St. Laurent have the responsibility of carrying out policies that he was responsible for but which I could not accept.

"I said I did not like Ilsley's attitude. Thought Ilsley thoroughly disliked me, etc. MacKinnon said he did not think Ilsley disliked me but he certainly did not show me the consideration I was entitled to have. . . . He said he really believed Ilsley still had it in mind he might become Prime Minister and was working toward that end.

"This may well be in the light of what some recent Gallup Polls have disclosed in ranking him ahead of St. Laurent as the popular choice. I said I felt sure he never would be chosen. That he was much too narrow in his outlook and views. That the policies of the Finance Department in this direction had not been wise. A younger man should be chosen unless St. Laurent himself should be the choice. I said I can understand Ilsley's opposition to me arising years ago through my attitude in the apple business. He thought I was responsible for the abandonment of fixed margins. That he had had antagonism ever since the time Ralston went out. Now again was feeling the apple business, etc. I told MacKinnon that what I had really in mind was the announcement of intention of the calling of a Convention to select a new leader. That I would, of course, say nothing about the Premiership as that was a matter between myself and the representative of the Crown. That I would wait and see what developed internationally before making any final decision in August. That I might consider remaining in the Government, if necessity arose without taking the responsibilities of Prime Minister but that on this I would decide later. I spoke, too, of the possibility of our party being defeated in the House if members were not present for divisions. He asked me what I would say if we were defeated in that way; would I not dissolve and go to the country. I said I would certainly not go to the country. That I had already stated that I would not lead the party through another election. I would be almost obliged to ask the Governor General to call on Bracken who has the largest following in the Opposition. That he might go to the country or ask that Coldwell be called on or that we be recalled. I thought he would be foolish enough to ask for a dissolution and go to the country. (If supply, however, could not be voted at the time, he would find himself in an impossible position there.) What I might do after conferring with the Governor General – this I did not say, but might say – was to point out that no party opposed could form an administration. We had been defeated but defeat was not expressive of the House and ask the House for a vote of confidence before actually tendering my resignation.

"MacKinnon was quite frank in saying he thought I was right in not trying to stay on indefinitely. He felt I had earned the right to rest. It might shorten my life were I to continue longer. On the other hand, I might have years of happy life still if I gave up the worry and responsibilities. I told him that was the way I myself felt.

"I wanted to do something more in the way of writing and also settling my own affairs, etc. He said he thought I was never stronger in the country than at the moment. Cabinet were one hundred percent loyal toward me and that the party were solidly behind me. That was a good position to be in.

"We reached no final decision in what was to be done in Cabinet reconstruction. He himself leaves on Monday for his constituency. Will be back on the 18th. I said that I wished he would be here instead of away; if he felt he must go, well and good. He said he had some meetings to address. He said he hoped I would make no announcement until he got back. I said I would not. I might possibly withhold everything by way of announcement until Parliament reassembles but what was best in that regard remained to be seen. MacKinnon said he naturally left himself entirely in my hands. Said he hoped I would find it possible to keep him in the Government. I said for personal reasons I was very anxious to keep him in the Government. He was always a very helpful supporter there. However, I might have to be controlled by circumstances beyond my control. He admitted that this was so. I, myself, felt a great relief at having him know he would not continue as Minister of Trade and Commerce but that that portfolio would go to Howe."

On January 7 the Prime Minister and St. Laurent, after reaching a compromise on the Korean problem, turned to the subject of cabinet reconstruction and Ian Mackenzie. "He agreed he was no strength. Indeed he is the one who is most anxious to get him out. He thought perhaps it would be best to have him go to the Senate. That if he were still in the House, he would be troublesome there which is very true.

"For Mackenzie to go to the Senate opens a seat in Vancouver [Centre] with possibility of our losing the seat – of C.C.F. being elected in his place which we can ill afford to do. There are three vacancies: Vancouver, Yale and Ont. [W. E. N. Sinclair, the sitting Liberal member in Ontario constituency had died on November 26, 1947], all difficult. If we could get an agreement not to have an election in Yale or Vancouver, I would be inclined to think Mackenzie might go to the Senate. It is something which will have to be settled in the next few days and which promises to be very difficult."

Two days later, Mackenzie King telephoned Senator McKeen "to tell him I thought Campney would be prepared to run without consideration of any kind and could carry the seat [Vancouver Centre]. Also [to ask] whether there was a chance of the constituency going by acclamation if we allowed Yale to go by acclamation. He was not too sure that Howard would agree to an acclamation in Vancouver. He said some of the local men might want to run someone in Yale just to give themselves prominence. He did not think we could win Yale though, at present, the apple growers had been doing exceedingly well. As to Mackenzie, he feared there would be quite a scene which would be costly to him, Mackenzie, in his health if I were not to call him and speak to him quite bluntly myself. That the ground ought to be prepared. He thought speaking to Matheson might be a good idea. He offered to come himself and have a word and it was arranged he would be here on Monday next. He said he is convinced he [Mackenzie] should get out. He said if he were to get the Senate right away, he would be exceedingly lucky. I am sure that is the best procedure to follow. He said he has talked to Mackenzie about his getting out – about the way he has neglected his pledges and promises. He thinks Mackenzie is sort of toying with the idea of going to the Senate. It would have to be, of course, without conditions and immediately."

The Prime Minister saw Senator McKeen on January 12. McKeen reported that he had had dinner with the Mackenzies and the Pickersgills the previous evening and had "told Mackenzie he felt very strongly he should not try to stay on any longer in the Commons. They had gone over different things that Mackenzie had suggested. McKeen brought along the suggestion that, if he could have a chance to go to the Senate at once, he should do so. Open an office here. He, McKeen, would help to get him retainers, which would supplement his income. He would have a surety for life in the Senate. If he postponed it, he might be left without anything. He had sought to impress this on Mackenzie's wife who had admitted to him she had been disappointed in his not being able to leave drinking. She thought she could reform him but realized it was going to be a great problem. . . .

"As a matter of fact, Mackenzie should be dropped completely. However, he is my oldest colleague. I doubt if he will live many months. There will, I think, be a feeling that for his years in public life, he is entitled to go into the Senate but once he is there, I am afraid it will not be long before there will only be the memory of his name in that House.

"It is necessary, however, for me to get a vacancy at once so as to move Howe into Trade and Commerce. I spoke to McKeen about Campney. He said Campney would be ready to take on at once but he thought some assurance that he might be taken into the Government would have to be given. I said I would give no such assurance. I had never given anyone promise of any appointments. My selection of men for office had been made on the basis of what they were prepared to do first. I told him of my own coming into public life. Giving up Deputy Ministership of Labour to go into a riding represented by Seagram, etc. I said what I wanted for the Government is what Canada wanted – men who were interested in serving Canada first and taking risks in so doing. We may lose the seat by opening it but I feel that the risk has to be taken.

"We spoke about Senatorships. He thought Mayhew deserved a Senatorship for British Columbia. I think he is right in that. I spoke of Hart's public service. He thought it merited recognition but Mayhew priority. I said I did not think we would be wise to fill the other vacancy until after the by-election. We could see then who would be most entitled to it. In the meanwhile, all groups would have to work for the election of our candidate. This would be a test of their right to recognition later."

After the Cabinet meeting on January 13, Mackenzie King told Howe that MacKinnon was prepared to give up Trade and Commerce and described "the problem I now had in having Mackenzie give up his portfolio. I could see nothing other than to offer him the Senate with no condition other than that he accept it immediately. That I would put Gregg in Veterans Affairs and MacKinnon for the time being at least in Fisheries. I mentioned MacKinnon's ambitions for other portfolios but, as he was not going to remain in the Government for the campaign, we must let younger men have their chance of becoming known to the people before it took place. I am hopeful that McKeen's talks with Mackenzie will save any real embarrassment in my talk with him which is being arranged for tomorrow. I rather believe it will."

The Prime Minister saw Mackenzie the next day and began by referring to "recommendations he had made of different persons for the Senate. I then referred to some of the suggestions he had made as, for example, his running again in a general election. I told him I doubted if he would be in shape for that and doubted, too, if he could be elected. I then referred to myself as being unequal to another general election and of my decision to announce on Tuesday night my desire to have a Convention called, that a new leader might be chosen.

"I then spoke of his desire for a post in the diplomatic service. I said I had no longer the filling of appointments in External Affairs but I doubted if there was any position there which would be available. I then referred to the Chairmanship of the International Joint Commission and said that reasons which would make some of these other posts impossible, would also govern there. I said that as regards an appointment to the Senate, I thought he was justified in feeling that he had a strong claim for preferment, in that regard. That several of the Ministers were anxious to go to the Senate. That as he knew a life appointment in the Senate was really in the nature of a reward for a long public service. That several of those who had been Ministers were now in the Senate. . . . That all were fortunate in having a life position in the Upper House. He knew, however, the objection I had to making an appointment which involved the opening of a seat. In his case, I could not be at all sure that we could carry the constituency in a by-election. I was, however, in the difficult position of myself getting out in a few months' time. When that moment came, I would have to consider carefully whether I should not leave existing vacancies to whoever might be selected as a new leader to assist him in organizing his Government.

"I could not say that if matters were left that long, there would be any guarantee of him getting an appointment. I then said that because of our long association, and his loyal support and work over the years, I would be prepared in order to see him secured, to take a chance which I had not taken with any other person, of risking the losing of a seat in order to make sure of his being appointed to the Senate. If I were to do that, however, it would have to be done at once and before Parliament reassembled. That I had to effect some reorganization. The Department of Munitions and Supply had served its day. Would have to be wound up. I would have to find another Department for Howe. There were other changes. I thought it best to make them all before the House met. Mackenzie was quite silent while I was speaking. Inclined to agree as I went along. Certainly not to disagree in any protesting way but to realize the seriousness of what I was saying. He looked pretty formidable when he came in. Ruddy complexion of yesterday, etc., but not combative.

"I then changed what I had to say and spoke of what it meant to be in the Senate – to have a life tenure. That none of us knew how long we could retain our health. That, at any moment, we might break down, suffer long illnesses and the like. That it was a great comfort to feel one was assured of an income as well as of a position in such circumstances. That he knew as well as I did what his physicians had said about the condition of his health. He also knew that he had not taken care of himself which . . . he had promised time and again he would do. . . . I pointed out that were he not to get into the Senate at once, he might be left without any position at all. That the Senate would give him $6,000 a year, also railway transportation, franking, etc. He would have opportunity for careful preparation of speeches, a platform to speak from, keep up his interest in politics, etc. In a word, what I wished for him was that he might continue in public life. If he were careful of his life, he might do so for some time to come, and be remembered in the future as one who perhaps had the longest career of anyone in Parliament in his day. He had been Minister of the Crown, might be a Senator for years, a member of the Imperial Privy Council, and would leave an honourable name – or find himself out of everything and forgotten and without friends or money. I would strongly advise him not to lose this opportunity. I said to him that he ought to reorient his life altogether, get in his mind the picture of the fireside in his own home, where he could read and write, and enjoy the companionship of his wife and their friends, and give up the other life altogether.

"Mackenzie thanked me, and asked me whether he might have twenty-four hours to think it over and could he mention what I had said to his wife. I certainly did not want to crowd him in any way, but give him plenty of time, and said by all means to talk it over with his wife. He not only could, but should, tell her everything I had said. He again thanked me and said he would do that and let me have an answer tomorrow. As he was leaving, I said to him to remember that I was his friend. And his reply was that he had always been my friend too."

That evening, the Prime Minister sent for Senator McKeen who told him that "as soon as Ian had left my office, he had phoned to him, Senator McKeen, to come to his Mackenzie's house, and there Mackenzie told both him and Mrs. Mackenzie what I had said. He said I had been very nice to him, had spoken very frankly. They both strongly advised him to take advantage of what I had proposed. Ian was to have gone to dinner at the Chateau with other B.C. Liberals who were dining there, but he said to McKeen that perhaps he should stay at home that night. McKeen did not advise him to come, but said he himself would come down and see him after his friends had left. He did go down later, and told me the following morning he thought I would receive during the day a letter from Mackenzie expressing his desire to go into the Senate; that he had accepted everything very nicely. It had been a considerable shock to him, but he had seen it was the only thing to do. . . . It was an immense relief to my mind to get this reply and to have all worked out without the necessity of talking with anyone other than Senator McKeen.

"I told McKeen he must now make the best arrangement possible about the Vancouver seat. Not to delay bringing on any by-election there."

The next afternoon (January 15) the Prime Minister received a "nicely written" letter from Mackenzie accepting a senatorship "and another letter in which he expressed desire to be relieved of administrative duties because of impairment of his health. A letter that I can table and to which I will reply in a way that should be helpful. I can say that by relieving him from duties, I would like to have him continue to give the country the benefit of his experience in the Upper Chamber.

"During the day, I 'phoned MacKinnon. Told him I might have to announce tonight his appointment to Fisheries. He was quite agreeable though he said he would have preferred one of the others but would not give me any trouble. I also spoke to Gregg about taking on Veterans Affairs. I was surprised he did not seem a bit eager about it. He said he had come to rather like the Fisheries Department and to be very much interested in its work. However, he was quite prepared to do whatever I wished him to do and said I might make him Minister of Veterans Affairs before the end of the week and might wait until he came back from the Maritimes for which he was leaving this afternoon.

"I had thought once of bringing Mayhew in without portfolio which would leave a vacancy in one of the Parliamentary Assistants and give that position to Reid [M.P. for New Westminster]. Mayhew would be glad, I think, to be a Minister for a short time. He is not going to run again. On second thought, however, I decided it would be unwise to fill any of the B.C. positions until the by-election is over."

It was not until January 19 that Mackenzie King told the full Cabinet about the changes in portfolios and Mackenzie's resignation and appointment to the Senate. "As he was in Council, I said I was sorry as he knew to lose so old a colleague. That all of us would miss him very much. I explained that I felt his long experience in public life and his knowledge of the soldiers' problems made it desirable that he should continue in Parliament. Mackenzie himself then spoke very nicely in reference to my kind consideration of him all the time in Council in the years we have been together. He regretted leaving. Spoke of the kindness of other members.

"I was a little surprised that no other member of Council said anything. When he was finished speaking, he asked if he should leave. I said: by no means – until the Governor General had signed the Order, he was not a Senator. However I could see he was a little moved and did not feel like staying. When he left, I stood up and rather expected other members of the Cabinet to do the same. One of the other members began to get up but he had left [the] Council chamber before there had been opportunity for others to rise. There is lots of room for reflection on Mackenzie's career. If I did not feel that he is so exceedingly fortunate in having a life position given him I might have been sorry to see him leave the Government. As it is, I feel that he has received much more than his deserts but I pray it may help to save his life and enable him to do public service in the time that may be left.

"I then spoke of appointing Gregg to War Veterans Affairs. Next, of Howe coming to Trade and Commerce. MacKinnon was in his seat. I told Cabinet of how he had been in saying that he thought the new conservation exchange policy made it desirable that Howe should come to the Trade and Commerce Department. He himself preferring to do whatever I wished. I said I had thought it was better to have him take Fisheries on for the present. MacKinnon said he thought there might be some feeling about Alberta, not being particularly interested in Fisheries, etc. That he had no qualifications for Fisheries. Had raised the question of the position of Minister not being an expert. I said he was there not as an expert but as an administrator. If we required men to be experts in different Departments, I did not know what the lawyers in the Cabinet would do. I had made it clear I wished him there only temporarily. There would have to be further adjustments. I said I thought we must give young men in the House a chance to come forward. Bertrand spoke of liking Fisheries and finding it a nice Department. I then asked him if he would like to take it over as a former Minister of Fisheries. He said he was prepared to do whatever I wished. I then had a talk with him privately. He was ready to do whatever I wished but felt it was wiser to hold on to the Post Office.

"Talked with MacKinnon and explained that Quebec might feel they were losing a certain portfolio. Also talked with St. Laurent who took that view. Decided then to put through what I had originally planned.

"MacKinnon told me that just as he got back, Mackenzie kept at him until he could see him and then told him he understood he was to be made Minister of Fisheries and advised to fight against that for all he was worth. It seemed to me that Mackenzie had been going in quarters trying to make a good fellow of himself. I am afraid he will find his influence has gone. It will be a relief to have him out of the Cabinet and out of the House of Commons.

"It is what we prevent often more than what we accomplish that tells for most in the end."

After the Cabinet meeting, Mackenzie King met the press to announce the changes. "Had a somewhat short interview. Not many questions asked."

Meanwhile, the Prime Minister had been making slow progress on his speech announcing his own retirement. On January 16 he wrote that he "found it heavy going to express my thoughts and did not feel too sure of the line I was taking. Whether getting too sentimental or not. It does not do to be sentimental before the public. However, I am seeking to give the facts. I am afraid it is going to be very unsettling – that the mere announcement of a Convention is going to be unsettling to the party, but it will be as nothing compared to what matters would be if I let matters run on without a Convention and found that I was unable, as I am, to tackle a general election when it comes, and without putting responsibility for its own leadership on the party in the first instance."

On January 20 he spent most of the day on final revisions. He felt he "was able to bring the emphasis onto a Convention and the reasons for calling the same, apart from the Liberal leadership and to give a truer perspective to its real significance. I was pleased with this part of the statement. I suppose because I was at last able to express in public what I have wished my own party and the public clearly to understand. But it was a quarter past five before I had finished with the revision of this section. My eyes were very weary. My left eye pained me quite a bit. . . .

"It was about 6.45 before I had again dressed and shaved. Came to the library. The dinner being 6.30 for 7, I had to leave Laurier House by 7. This I did almost exactly to the minute though it was some 10 minutes after 7 when I joined those at the head table in the ball room at the Chateau. Most of the members of the Government and their wives were present along with Angus Macdonald (Premier of N.S.); Stuart Garson (Premier of Manitoba) and Farquhar Oliver, the Ontario Leader. I was pleased that these three were present and made special mention of their presence when I came to speak. Several photos were taken. Procession formed to the head table. Arrangements of the head table had been made evidently before the announcement of Mackenzie's appointment to the Senate as Mrs. Mackenzie was given the seat to my right as the wife of the senior member of the Cabinet, Mackenzie himself holding a corresponding position on the other side of Mrs. Hodges, Vice-President who, at the end of the evening, thanked me for my address. Fogo presided.

"When we went into the ball room, I was really amazed at the size of the gathering. Every available bit of space was taken up but, in addition, the other dining room had also been brought in for the large numbers that had applied for tickets. The Hotel had at noon to refuse making reservations for any more but they allowed some of those that applied to be seated in the Galleries upstairs though not undertaking to provide them with a meal. It amused me somewhat, some weeks ago, when I had been pressing for a meeting all this time, that the Federation Office were afraid that there would not be enough present to make a showing and therefore wanted to hold the meeting off until after Parliament met. I knew perfectly well that there were enough members of the party [who would] appreciate that this was a significant meeting to cause a large gathering to assemble. I do confess that tonight's dinner or banquet as some called it was a much finer and larger demonstration than I had expected.

"The guests at the head table were piped into the room. I was given a great ovation. To tell the truth, being fatigued, I hardly noticed it. Mrs. Mackenzie asked me in the course of the evening if I was not greatly thrilled by the ovation. I had to admit to her that I had experienced no sensation beyond that of observing that there was quite a demonstration and feeling a considerable measure of surprise."

After dinner, Milton Gregg was the first speaker. "What he said was excellent [in] regard to the place of youth and Liberalism," the Prime Minister wrote. "A fine analytical, helpful study of the situation. He has not, however, a good delivery or too pleasing a voice but one felt the splendid quality of his mind.

"Paul Martin made I thought an exceptionally good speech. He spoke first in French. I really was surprised at his eloquence. In English, he was equally good. Struck exactly the right notes. If anything, was too laudatory of myself. By touching on the humanitarian side as being the one the Liberal party had furthered in the past, and needed to further still more in the future – he was exactly on the right line.

"When my turn came to speak, I was myself surprised to find how easy it was to speak off hand and how really vigorous I was in speaking. Also I felt exceedingly happy and quite enjoyed the introductory part of my remarks. I began by thanking Fogo and his executive for arranging the meeting. Extended greetings to delegates from different parts. Expressed pleasure at the size and character of the gathering. Made special mention of leaders from outside. Then made a reference to recent appointments of Mackenzie and Gregg. Congratulated latter also on his speech. Referred to Martin's speech and extended congratulations to Mackenzie on his appointment to the Senate. And Howe on his appointment to Trade and Commerce. MacKinnon on Fisheries and then came to the speech itself which I told the gathering I had had prepared in part before today and had hoped to deliver in most part without having it in written form but had spent today getting it into final shape. As there was no nationwide broadcast, I felt it was important to have the record made as exact as possible. Specially as members of the press had been kind enough to suggest they would welcome assistance in those lines. Once I began reading, there was intense silence. Indeed all the time that I was speaking about Communism, I could see that everyone was a bit surprised and quite clearly concerned. It was not until I had concluded the whole section that there was applause. The same was true of the second section, on Prices. There was a spontaneous burst of applause when I announced intention to appoint a House of Commons Committee to hold an investigation into causes of increases. It was clear that that was warmly welcomed by the gathering. This is the part of the speech that Ilsley would have ruled out altogether had he had his way and which I think he, Howe and Abbott would have preferred to have had omitted.

"It is fortunate for the Liberal party that I took the bull by the horns and determined to make a central feature of the session, the Government's determination to go into this whole question in a manner which would help to satisfy the public mind that we were doing all that could possibly be done. I think that part of the speech was excellent. There was pronounced applause at the close. I found, however, in the reading that my throat was a little dry on one or two occasions. I had perhaps spoken a little too loudly at the beginning.

"When I came to the third part which dealt with the Convention, I could feel the whole audience were really in a state of suspense and listening with rapt attention. Where I referred to my enjoying the confidence of the party more today than ever, I was given tremendous applause. Equally where I made reference to not using the kind of tactics that amounted to subterfuge but being straightforward with the party and the public.

"At the end of the speech, there was a tremendous ovation. Everyone in the room stood and cheered for some time. They had started cheering before I sat down. After remaining seated for some time, I stood again and acknowledge the ovation which again kept up for quite a little while. It was clear that the meeting had been all that one could possibly have wished; also that it was recognized as an historic occasion. I felt, too, that the audience realized that I had been taking the right and chivalrous role. It is not often that it is given to a man himself to ask to be allowed to retire from the leadership of a political party, and to press his own retirement, specially after many years of leadership and of office. Particularly when one is able to say as I said last night and was strongly applauded for saying it that in the twenty-nine years I had led the party, I had had the confidence throughout of the Cabinet and members of both Houses of Parliament and of the party throughout the country and that I had never enjoyed that confidence more than I do today. It is a marvellous statement to be able to make. Truly, as I said, it was the highest of all rewards in public life.

"After the dinner, I was interested in observing how many of those present referred to what was said. I stood near the door of the ballroom and shook hands with those who came up to greet me. It was clear that men and women alike were deeply moved and very genuine in their expressions of regret. There were tears in the eyes of a good many. I noticed that particularly in the case of Dr. and Mrs. King, Bertrand, and several others. Dr. McCann seemed to be particularly stirred. Mentioned it was the best speech that I had ever made, as several others did. Claxton was quite strong in his words, in a similar vein.

"Gardiner was not present, neither was Mitchell nor Glen. I have a feeling that Glen is not too well. The recent death of his mother may have kept him away.

"On passing Mackenzie and Howe on the way out, both were very cordial in their words. Ilsley did not make any appearance after the meeting, nor did he have anything to say. St. Laurent had to leave for Quebec. Colin Gibson and his wife seemed to feel the occasion; also Fournier and Jean and Chevrier. Paul Martin seemed particularly moved.

"Wishart Robertson and his wife also made their feelings felt. I did not see Abbott again after the dinner, nor did I see Angus Macdonald again. Garson came up to say good-bye as he was leaving for the train. I was told that Alex Johnston was at the dinner. Fogo seemed to think that this was quite a triumph. I have no use for him [Johnston]. Angus was in evidence and he is one of Angus's friends in the hope that when the Convention comes, Angus may be in the running for the leadership. He [Macdonald], himself, has spoiled his chances effectively. There is no question that, ere this, he had hoped to be the leader of the party. St. Laurent's name got a great reception when it was mentioned by Martin. It is interesting how the Journal and other papers keep mentioning at least half a dozen Ministers, any one of whom they say has the qualities of a Prime Minister and might well be chosen. This ought to be useful material when it comes to a campaign, telling the country we already have a Cabinet of men whose statures are those of Prime Ministers. I was quite disappointed at Fogo's remarks in regard to what I had said about the need for organization. I had told him while we were sitting at the table, what I was going to say and he agreed with me thoroughly. When he came to speak, he said he had exception to take to that part of my remarks and went on to say that the party had a first-rate organization throughout the country, of able men and women who were furthering the party's affairs in all parts of the country. What I think he was really trying to say was that he should not be given credit for what was being done. That the others were the ones entitled to it. That would have been all right. He lost a great chance in not telling the party that I had told him that the task was a much vaster one than they realized and that more effective organization was required if the party was to hope to win. I am glad I made what I felt about this aspect of the party's affairs so clear. If the party loses the next election, it will be due more to the inadequacy, insufficiency, etc., of the organization than to anything else. Indeed had I really had first class assistance in party organization and felt the strength of it, I might well have felt that I, myself, could carry on through another campaign. It has been the worry of this each election that has made the task so heavy. Men with the right vision might well have seen that there is a power and a joy in organizing a political party for victory which is equal to that of headquarters staff in fighting a battle. We have never had a Headquarters staff worthy of the name, as long as I can remember. Excepting one campaign where Massey and Lambert threw their energies into the situation, has the Party ever had what it should have had in the way of a first class organization?

"I am recording all these feelings as I have experienced them so that the story some day, if I am spared, can be told in its true light.

"I spoke for over an hour. It is a long time to stand and I found myself at the end of the time beginning to perspire, though I was amazed at the power and strength which I possessed." He added: "I must confess that I have felt a real sense of relief and of joy in having at last taken the first step in my retirement and being able to feel that I have been wise, in each move I have made toward reaching the stage which has been arrived at, at last, tonight. I am sure that the next six months will show the wisdom of what, thus far, has been done. I might have mentioned that I am resigning not at a moment when the party is in a bad way but rather as is said on all sides when the party, in the eyes of many of its own supporters and in the eyes of many of the M.P.'s, stands at the very zenith of its strength. My own feeling is that we are not as strong at the moment as many of the party believe.

"We should win the next election and can win it if care is taken from now on to leave no stones unturned, to hold to the path of a true Liberalism.

"Tonight after concluding what I had to say, and listening to the applause I could not but look a little wistfully over the gathering and think of how new developments might shape themselves.

"I could not but help thinking of how the scene was changing and of the significance of tonight's meeting as marking one of the milestones which bring one nearer to the end of life's journey. I cannot say that I had any real feelings either of sadness or regret. I felt really peacefully happy. Something tells me that the best is yet to be – if I can hold to all that is best. My father and mother, sisters and brother, Sir Wilfrid, Mr. Larkin and Sir William Mulock, Lapointe and others and my grandfather Mackenzie, in particular, were much in my thoughts tonight. They would have been more so had I not been so completely absorbed in the task of the speech itself. I am convinced that I have been helped and inspired in its preparation. What pleases me most is to see how it has all worked out and the way I more or less foresaw and believed it would. I thanked God for the guidance that has been vouchsafed to me along the way."

The Prime Minister telephoned Pickersgill after the meeting and was "surprised" to discover that he had not been present. "Apparently he has abstained from other meetings of the Federation. It amazes me very much that he should not have felt, because of its historic significance, it was an occasion he would somehow or another manage to be present, even if only from the Gallery. It was almost like not attending the Convention itself, this being the beginning of the end of the road of both my leadership and my Prime Ministership. No doubt his concern was that of someone taking exception to his being at a political meeting when acting in the capacity of adviser to the Prime Minister.

"I could not have imagined myself in a like relationship with Sir Wilfrid having missed on any account being a witness to what was actually taking place. It was one of the historic occasions and scenes in Canadian history."

At the meeting of the Cabinet on January 22, Mackenzie King was pleased to hear that his colleagues felt he had made "a strong and effective speech. I can see and feel, however, the note of regret and concern at my pending retirement. Having witnessed what a furore the announcement which the country looked for ever since the last campaign has created, this time I feel more convinced than ever that I am right in not having delayed longer the calling of a Convention. It is shocking, however, the manner in which the opposition press are seeking to distort the intention and still to blame a measure of bad faith on my part in regard to future intentions. The deliberate misrepresentation of motives is one of the worst features of public life. Perhaps the worst of all is the unpleasantness of public life.

"I was pleased to see that President Truman had expressed regret at my retirement and had referred in strong terms to the friendships I had enjoyed at the White House.

"Tonight I read an editorial from the Washington Post written evidently by some editor who had been loaded up on Tory propaganda and prejudices over the past years, making out that I was not suited for our times, etc., being a Victorian Liberal; not enough colour, etc., as though what the policies of today demanded was something in the nature of a cross between a monkey and a jack-ass to make one sufficiently interesting to hold the attention of the public. It has been because of Mussolini, Hitler and other exhibitionists that the world has gone through agony which it has suffered of late. The theory of these writers is that a political leader must accord with what the times demand, rather than having the quality which helps to get the times out of their difficulties into paths that are helpful and enduring."

Reading the morning newspapers the next day, Mackenzie King was shocked "to see that St. Laurent in speaking in Winnipeg, last night, had said that he was prepared to take on the duties of leader provided that they would not create a division on racial or religious grounds. In other words, he himself has raised the issue now which not only may help to defeat his own chances in the Convention but defeat the Liberal party itself at the next election. He has emphasized the fact that he is a French-Canadian and that he is an R.C. We may be perfectly sure that, from now on, in as many quarters as are possible, the bigoted elements in our country will begin to work under cover and above board as well, against the possibilities of Canada being governed in the next few years by a Roman Catholic and a French-Canadian. They will say they do not want the Province of Quebec to rule over the rest of the Dominion. It will be pointed out that there will be a solid Quebec and other elements of the country will take the view that they do not wish Canada to be governed by Quebec. If he had said nothing at all until the Convention elected him, there would have been little meanwhile in the way of organization against him. Sir Wilfrid was under the opinion, as he said himself, that his defeat was owing to his being a Catholic and French. He said to me his belief was that the French Catholics would never again be at the head of a Government in Canada for the reason that the French and the Catholics were in the minority. . . . I have succeeded in keeping it down in the years I have been Prime Minister by being in the majority myself and taking care to see that the Catholics and French-Canadians were given equal opportunity with others – in denouncing any attempt to create an issue on race and religious grounds and in upholding the rights of the minority. I thought, too, St. Laurent was making a mistake in his speech in bringing forward so strongly at this moment references to Sir Wilfrid. He did that I thought rather with undue emphasis in Quebec when he was speaking about the unity of Canada and the strongest evidence of national unity being the election of Laurier as Prime Minister when he was a Frenchman and a Catholic, but Sir Wilfrid got into the leadership by not having had that issue raised against him in advance.

"I do not think it was wise to raise that issue on the Prairies with the bigoted population they have, both in Manitoba and in the adjoining province of Saskatchewan and with Ontario and its Orangemen on the other side. I thought, too, it was a mistake that those who had charge of his visit had arranged for a special meeting with the French-Canadians of Winnipeg and St. Boniface, adjoining district.

"The fact that he is a French-Canadian should be kept in abeyance rather than thrown into the foreground and the emphasis placed upon his being an outstanding citizen whose vision is beyond that of any single province, any single race, or any single religion. When I read his Quebec speech, and when he told me of it, I felt he had been unwise. Had I known there was a possibility of his repeating in the West what he said in Quebec, in that regard, I would have counselled against it. Oddly enough, in seeking to defend me on the score of not telling finally whether I would continue on as Prime Minister or not, he said the very thing by which he should have governed his own utterances, namely, that Mr. King would not be Prime Minister today had he not had the wisdom to leave the decision on public matters until the moment at which all the facts were known in the light of which a decision should be made. I know in St. Laurent's case, it has all arisen from his own fine sense of integrity. He would not consider the position for a moment if he thought it would give rise to racial or religious differences. On the other hand, his lack of political experience and his intense desire to be scrupulously careful in seeing that that issue is not raised, has caused him to make an issue where none otherwise might have been raised; also in declaring his intention to stand as a leader. He is already inviting embarrassment for himself in Parliament and in the press.

"From now on, there will be an effort to draw him into difficult positions, to exploit every minor mistake, etc. He would have been much wiser to have discounted the possibility of being in the running and to have said that he thought the country might be well advised to take a younger man. The younger men would then have joined together to see that he was given a place. It is just too bad. I think, too, that Abbott is making a mistake in saying who he will support, etc. It is going to be hard to hold back French-Canadians in Parliament, in their press, etc., in their desire to see a French-Canadian again Prime Minister. Their aggressiveness in this regard is going to develop forces against them which may defeat their chances in this regard. On these as on most matters, people are very shortsighted. They become what they feel strongly in their personal likes and dislikes. They are apt to express these too freely and too loudly. I repeat again: few men have suffered in public life for what they did not say. Many have suffered for having spoken when it would have been much better to have been quiet. I doubt if I had been in Canada prior to the Liberal Convention – for the months preceding it – I would have been chosen. I was wise enough to be out of the country altogether until within a week of the Convention itself.

"I cannot say how distressed I feel; of all men in the world, I have greater regard for St. Laurent than I think for any of the others."

On January 26 Ilsley asked to see the Prime Minister after the Cabinet meeting to let him know that he had decided to leave politics and return to a law practice. According to Mackenzie King, Ilsley said: "I am thoroughly sick of having the papers say that I am waiting for the Chief Justice of Nova Scotia to die in order to get his position; and also to have them say that I am a sick man, etc. I have never felt better in my life than I do now. I will stay on for the session. It would not be right for me to get out without sufficiently long notice. I will watch everything carefully but at the end of the session I will get out. I want to make an announcement at once so that there will be an end to this talk about my going on to the Bench, etc. He then said, I have been thinking over this, the last couple of months . . .I have no doubt I could get the Criminal Code into shape, etc. I could do this and do that and leave a name as a good Minister of Justice but I am not ambitious for that nor do my wife and children care about that. I have to think about how I am to get along – get money to provide for the latter part of my life. If I am to earn money at all, I should do it – I should begin to practise at once. I have had no practice over a great many years. I know from those with whom I have talked privately and who are in the know that I could soon make a good deal of money. I shall probably, when I am out, think I have made a mistake and often wish I were back again but I know I can do well in law. My interest is in law. I have a judicial way of looking at matters and I am sure I could soon make a good sum. I then asked Ilsley how old he was. He said he was 53. I said, My Lord, that is 20 years younger than I am. I then said to him that I hoped he would not reach any hasty conclusion. Take plenty of time to think over matters. I said I thought his first consideration of all should be his health. That he had worked very hard. It might well be that some reaction would set in later. I felt he ought to be in a position which would secure him for life. I said he would recall that I had wanted him to keep open the Chief Justiceship in his province. He said that he remembered that but he had not wanted that to be done. I then said: there were other positions. . . . I said what about the Supreme Court of Canada. He said that we already had the best possible man from the Maritimes in Justice Rand. That he would not want to crowd Rand out though he told me confidentially that Rand had a little while ago been thinking of getting out. I said I did not see why the Supreme Court did not need enlargement and why there should not be two Judges from the Maritimes. That idea seemed to appeal to him. He said the Supreme Court would be a fine position. Would be interesting work there but, having made that comment, returned to his determination to get back into practice."

Mackenzie King assured Ilsley that "he would have no difficulty whatever in getting many retainers and in having a large, important and lucrative practice. He said: I have often wished I would be doing public service work. I said he would always have a chance for that. Governments would wish to retain his services. Many occasions would come up when they would be glad to retain him but I came back to what I had said about something in the nature of security for the rest of his life, having held the place he had had in public life and undergone the strain he had, was a desirable thing. He, however, came back to his definite decision to get out; to have matters known at once so that people and newspapers would no longer be saying the things they were. I said to him I had seen nothing of that. At any rate, papers were not worth listening to, at any time. He said: O yes, they had been at it this last week again. I then said to him I hoped he would not make any statement at present. What I would like him to do was to talk over the matter with St. Laurent. He then said he would talk it over with St. Laurent in the morning but would not talk it over with anybody else, as he wanted to make a statement very soon. He then spoke again about wanting to get out at the end of the session and he said: I suppose that will mean a by-election. He said he would not want to be staying on and sitting in the House. He went on to say that he would be leaving the party in the best of shape in the Maritimes; there would be no difficulty in carrying his riding; that the Liberals had done well in New Brunswick and Nova Scotia and Prince Edward Island. I then said if he was decided on the matter, I thought the time to take the step would be at the time of the Convention, when the new leader would be coming in. Would be wishing to reconstruct the Cabinet. He could put a younger man in the post of Minister of Justice. His reply to that was that he wanted to make the announcement at once and would talk the matter over with St. Laurent. He wanted to make clear his decision was not the result of any disagreement in the Cabinet; nor disagreement with any policy of the Government, or anything other than just his desire to make a living for himself and accumulate the wherewithal to provide for his after-years and his family. He said he supposed St. Laurent, Howe and other men had quite an income they could count on. He was differently situated. I replied I doubted that. I thought St. Laurent had become responsible for some other people's debts. I felt sure he had nothing for the future and I said he is a brave fellow to plan to stay on – he being now at the age of 66. Ilsley agreed with that and said he would be out of practice for some time.

"I could see there was not much use discussing matters at any length with Ilsley; though he does not know it himself, I imagine he has been upset at not being put into the forefront of the running for the position of Prime Minister. That he sees pretty well he could not be selected for that post. That St. Laurent is easily ahead of him and other names are mentioned, of younger men who might gain the post over him. That this has thwarted an ambition which he legitimately has had. I also imagine that my speech of the other night making clear my intention to get out, giving plenty of notice, has also had its effect specially in occasioning him to give notice for a considerable time ahead. I shall be surprised if he does not hold to his statement and come out with some statement very soon. That following on top of my determination to give up the leadership will have a considerable unsettling effect on the party. I wish St. Laurent could persuade him to at least defer his announcement until the time of the Convention. Ilsley is very headstrong; also proud and vain. He would not wish to be defeated in a Convention and he, I have no doubt, feels that the Government might be defeated in the next general elections in which event he will be only a private member in opposition. I think however that the fundamental aspect of the whole business is his own nervous upset condition. He has got into a condition of mind where he never feels quite sure of anything. Makes a decision and then wonders if it is the right one. Worries over it. . . . While he was very earnest and determined and a little excited while talking, he nevertheless was quite happy in his manner throughout, laughed occasionally at what he thought the consequences might be here and there. I thanked him for telling me what he had in mind. Said to him again I wanted him to know that any position he could think of that was available now or might be later, I was quite sure he could have. . . . He is impulsive but stubborn and I greatly fear his mind is now made up in a manner which will lead to some declaration fairly soon though he has, according to his own words, only been thinking of all this in the last three weeks. I told him to take at least three weeks longer before deciding but this he would not undertake to do."

The next afternoon Mackenzie King "had a long talk with St. Laurent who, on taking his seat today, received a great ovation from the French and other members. He had just got back from his visit to Winnipeg. He told me that Ilsley had had a talk with him this morning which he had promised me he would have. We discussed what lay at the root of it. St. Laurent said he, himself, had talked with Ilsley a couple of weeks ago about what he could probably make as a lawyer in practice, etc., though Ilsley had not indicated then any intention of resigning. Theirs was rather a general discussion about leading lawyers whose opinions were highly valued. . . . He thought Ilsley might perhaps feel that he had not been sufficiently appreciated. That was one of the motives he had. The other thought was that he doubtless felt that there would be uncertainties in conditions after the next election. He might be in opposition. That he would not want to be just a back bencher. Now was the time to strike out for himself. St. Laurent was even firmer of the view that Ilsley felt it was all right, while I was there, to stay on. That I could keep certain questions from arising but that some questions might arise which he, himself, would not wish to support but equally would not want to oppose. On asking what these were, St. Laurent said he thought and rather feared some of the matters that were being brought forward by the French-Canadian M.P.s. That so long as I was there, I could prevent these going too far. If I were away and particularly matters were under St. Laurent, he [Ilsley] might feel embarrassed in asserting his views. I said to St. Laurent that, to my mind, was a wholly new slant. I gave him as my view that Ilsley did not like the thought of facing a Convention and having a younger man chosen – not being the first choice. Though in this I was prepared to admit that I might be mistaken. I suggested to St. Laurent to try and have him see that the time to get out was at the time of the Convention. . . . He could say that he had spoken to him and to myself and possibly also to Howe. Refer to us as to having not made any public announcement at this time. That it was well to say then that he wanted a younger man to come into the Government, etc., and not allow his name to go before the Convention. St. Laurent seemed anxious to have him talk with Howe. He [Ilsley] had not wanted that but I advised strongly that both talk with him.

"I spoke to St. Laurent about his bringing up the matter of race and religion in reference to himself. I thought [it] was unwise to raise that issue. I could understand his feelings but I would leave it alone."

A Liberal caucus was held on January 28 and the Prime Minister used the occasion to discuss the proposed convention. "I was given a very fine reception when I got up. I began by saying that I had addressed the caucus on many occasions but never with feelings as mixed as mine were today. I imagined the same was true of the feelings of the Members. I went on to say that I thought it was perhaps advisable I should say a few things to them in the privacy of the Caucus which I had not wished to say in the statement I had made the other night. But I would like to say that I felt complimented, as I felt many times in the course of my career, at the attitude of the party but I had never felt more so at the expressions of regret which had come to me from the Members in so many quarters, at the possibility of my retirement. I said had there been cheers at the announcement that I was going, I should have felt very differently than I did this morning. As it was, I felt very deeply the responsibility of the trust which I was holding from the party and was anxious that no step on my part should be other than what would be most in the interest of the party. I added that if we discussed matters, we would discover that what was in my interest, for reasons that I would later mention, and what was most in the interest of the party, would be found to be pretty much the same. That our association had been so long that our interests had become irrevocably intertwined. I then said that they would realize that what I had said on Tuesday night last was not any sudden decision. They would recall my having mentioned that before the last election, I said it would be the last I would contest as leader. They would remember what I said publicly and at different times since. That if I were speaking to them, making this announcement for the first time today, I could understand what the shock would be. All would be wondering why I had not told them sooner. I said, however, it would be nothing to what the shock would be, a year or two hence, if on the eve of election, I found I was really unable to conduct the campaign and made announcement at the last moment. That I thought the party should secure someone else. . . .

"I then said that I was not reaching this decision without having had the best reasons as the result of advice that I had sought which was advice I could not afford to ignore. That I did not wish to share the fate that Mr. Fielding had . . . of being confined to bed for a couple of years as the result of a crash. One had to consider these things very carefully. I would be of no use to the party and myself if I allowed a situation like that to develop. I then said if anyone imagined that I was taking this decision lightly or without the best of reasons, I would ask him to put himself in my place and ask how he would feel if he had to give up the salary of Prime Minister, his indemnity as a Member of Parliament, allowance made for the car, his transportation pass, his franking privileges as well as his position, and then had neither pension nor profession for the rest of his days, and to have this come when one's earning power had gone with obligations notwithstanding to maintain a certain position. I said I had always had faith of ways being found in the future; that caused me the least concern. I believed all would work out but that I mentioned this that they would understand how much pleasanter it would be for me to look forward to holding the office of Prime Minister for a couple of years longer, etc. . . . I said I would like to give them something to think over which would help to show whether my attitude was the right one in the party's interests. I said I would like them to consider the careers of Sir John Macdonald and of Sir Wilfrid. That the party had held on to Sir John to his dying day. He was a very old man. No provision had been made for a successor. They used him to go through an election. He died immediately after. . . . With what result – that when it came to a general election, it was seen that the party had no real leader. That it had been disintegrating and went to pieces. Never got back into power until Sir Robert Borden came in in 1911 and was in only those few years but was out all the rest of the time and might be now out forever. That was something to keep in mind. I said if I was to run the next election, it would be said that I was just running it for the purpose of the campaign. That there was no one to succeed and it would be made clear I would be dropping out immediately after. That might cost the party the campaign, supposing I would be able to lead.

"I then took the position of Sir Wilfrid. Sir Wilfrid had said to me I am getting to be an old man. There is the calendar. This is what the years say. I have been through the strain of war though in Opposition. I think a Convention should be called to choose a successor. If spared, shall do what I can to help to assist him in the work and to establish him in his position. Unhappily Sir Wilfrid did not live until the Convention over which he had hoped to preside. I said that the same thing might happen to me though I was not expecting it. I hoped it would not happen. No one could say; at any rate there was a Convention already called. When the Convention was held, a new leader was chosen and a platform which he was to expound – I said the new leader then visited all parts of Canada, expounding the platform of the party. Had members with him wherever he went. He was loudly acclaimed by the Liberals with the result that when the election came later, the country had the impression that the Liberals were well organized. That their new leader had their confidence; had their platform and the result was that the party was returned to power. With the result also that the party had been in power with the exception of six years, all the time ever since.

"I asked them to look at the Convention and what it might stand for in that light. I added that no one had had less experience than I had had in the leadership of a political party when I was chosen but the Convention had helped to make that situation work itself out.

"I then said that I would like to give a word of counsel in regard to the Convention; what was going to happen at it. I said I had noticed Mr. St. Laurent who was sitting right beside me had said that he would be prepared to consider running providing it would not raise any question of race or religion. I said for Heaven's sake, let nobody raise the question of either race or religion at this time in connection with leadership. Surely we had reached the stage in our citizenship where we could base our rights on everything as Canadian citizens, and leave aside all reference to any governing possibility outside that – leave these other matters unsaid. My advice to all the members of the government was, when they were asked about the leadership, to say they were all in the running. They were going to wait and see what the Convention would decide and there would be time enough to say who is favoured. I said I would not confine it to members of the Government. I said the future leader may be in this room, in this audience today. More than that, he may be somewhere in the country, unthought of at the moment. Let them all say they were going to stand, but that they were going to abide by the Convention. They were saying nothing until the Convention itself. I said that that was the only sound position to take. I said I could understand Mr. St. Laurent's sensitive nature not wishing to do anything that would be other than in accord with his own conscience. I myself had made a break of the same kind when I was defeated in 1925, and was out of the House, though still Prime Minister, and Lapointe luckily was leading the Government. I said I wanted a vote of confidence from the House before I would agree to go back as Leader. Fortunately, old Sir Allen Aylesworth, who had great wisdom, had said he had never heard of such a thing; that I should not ask for an expression of confidence, it was for the Opposition to say they had no confidence; and for Parliament to say what they thought of the Motion. I said I am mighty glad that matters changed in that way. This led me to refer to what was said about commitments.

"I then said that the Journal had made comparisons between Disraeli and myself in regard to looking ahead as to what course should be taken, and had said that with long experience and long time in politics, and a certain political cunning, we were not making final commitments. What they ought to have said was not political cunning, but political wisdom. That was the kind of wisdom that was gained through experience – it was wisdom gained through experience that guided one. I said I myself had made a commitment that I would never support conscription. When it came to war and the situation changed, I decided to ask the people to relieve me of that pledge, and if they relieved me because of the situation, I would then decide what course I would take thereafter. I thought that was one of the finest things that was ever done by the party in the way of upholding a true democracy, though that fact had been little noticed. I pointed out that the discussion had brought out that so far as different Ministers were named, it was apparent that we had a Cabinet of Prime Ministers. I thought that of itself ought to give our party a pretty good start in any campaign. I then spoke about the talk of my continuing as Prime Minister, though not Leader. I said if all that I had said, the reasons I had given did not make plain that I wanted to be freed of responsibility altogether, I did not know what further words I could use. I wished, however, to point out to Caucus that I held my position as Leader of the party from the party, and was responsible to them in that capacity. It was to them that I naturally addressed myself, when deciding on whether a new Leader should be appointed or not. The reason was entirely different in regard to the Prime Minister, I did not hold that office from the party. I held it from the Crown.

"I was adviser to the Sovereign. I was sworn to give him the best advice that I could give at any time that it was necessary to tender advice. I did not feel, that being my obligation, I should say anything which might, in any way, impede the advice that I might be called upon to give at any time. I thought the people could draw their own conclusions as to what advice I would like to tender if I ceased to be Leader of the party because I wished to get out of public life but that I owed it to the Crown from which I had received the office, to let nothing interfere with that relationship which could, in any way, affect the relationship itself or make it open to question from any source.

"I had earlier spoken about keeping before the public mind that we had until mid-summer of 1950 to continue in office; not to think of election too soon. Be prepared for it at any time but keep on holding office until it seemed advisable to go to the people. . . .

"I was given very hearty applause when I had finished. Indeed, I think the Members felt that I was taking the right view, though they naturally, I think, continue to feel that while what I am doing may be in the interests of the party over the years, it may prejudice their individual chances at the next campaign. . . . My business is to the party as a whole over the years, not to what might lead more or less to its complete disruption meanwhile.

"The effect of the speech was apparent later when Members were asked to bring up any question they wanted to discuss. One Member from Charlottetown spoke about some wharf but no one else paid attention."

Mackenzie King continued to worry about the possibility of developing opposition to St. Laurent's succession on racial and religious grounds. At the Cabinet meeting on January 30, "Ilsley had brought forward a Bill to do away with the appeals to the Privy Council which is drafted in the form of a complete abolition of all appeals. He expressed anew his doubts as to the wisdom of the Bill, specially at this time.

"The morning papers contained a speech by one of the Members, Arsenault, of Quebec, in which he had paid the kindest of tributes to myself and had suggested that on my retirement and the expiration of the term of the present Governor General, I should be given the appointment of Governor General. Among other things, this would satisfy the ambition of many to have a Canadian. Personally I think it is one of the last positions that I would wish ever to hold. Certainly when I give up the responsibility of Prime Minister of the country, it will not be to accept the responsibilities of an office such as that of Governor General. These two things coming together in connection with others which I have been giving much thought to of late, caused me to say in Council that while perhaps I should not speak of the matter there at this time, that I nevertheless felt as the Liberal Convention would be along in August, our friends in Quebec would feel it to their own interests not to press a number of matters at this time which might when brought together, and used in ways political opponents would use them, might prejudice the very cause in which they were most interested, for example, there was the question of the flag and of Dominion Day. To these were added the abolition of appeals to the Privy Council and doing away with appointment of a Governor General from Britain, etc. It would almost certainly cause a number of Conservatives who were now supporting the Liberal party, and many old-fashioned Liberals, to fear that leadership from Quebec might mean all these things, and more in that direction if the Leader were to be chosen from Quebec. That I thought they would be well advised to allow these matters to stand until a later time and not have the public mind focussed on them in a way that might create prejudice in advance of another general election. I was rather surprised that St. Laurent, in whose interest I was speaking, seemed to take the suggestion as something that would cause him to feel he would not wish to be in the running for the position of leadership. He said he would never agree that Members from Quebec should not have the same right to speak, or to put forward their views as anyone else. That it would be intolerable to be in a position where he felt there was anything which he could not bring forward in the same way as anyone else. I explained, of course, that all I was referring to was the timing of situations. There was a time for everything. There was also a passage in the Scriptures which said it was well to be as wise as a serpent, and as harmless as a dove. That I thought in dealing with people whose stock-in-trade were prejudices and the like, it was well to be as wise as a serpent. Not to give them the opportunity for which they were looking, to destroy others.

"Ilsley remarked that Britain was receiving many hard blows at the present time, and that this would be a bad time for that reason to bring in the Bill regarding abolishing appeals. Also caused St. Laurent to express a certain resentment as to our being prevented from doing anything because of Britain. However, when the Bill was being discussed further, and Members were expressing their minds, Gregg, of New Brunswick said he thought the abolition of the appeals at this time would cost us heavily in New Brunswick. Other Members were more or less silent but I noticed that before discussion on the Bill had gone very far, all were glad including St. Laurent himself to have the measure reconsidered from the point of view of the wisdom of introducing it as drafted at this time, or as amended so as to still permit of appeals where provinces were concerned. (I personally think this most important.) Without it, Drew, Duplessis and

Angus Macdonald would all make an issue of the question, or linking up this measure with that of securing the right to amend our own constitution first. Personally I think to do the latter would be adding to the flame of prejudice rather than the opposite. I could not help thinking as I took in the situation generally, how completely different Sir Wilfrid Laurier would have been in dealing with a matter of the kind.

"Sir Wilfrid always recognized that there was a strong British feeling throughout Canada and that not to take full account of it, was to destroy his own power. Sir Wilfrid's success lay in his ability to know how far it was wise to go in achieving a particular end, and at looking at questions from a realistic point of view rather than through the eyes either of his race or his nationality.

"I am recording this matter because I feel that unless caution is shown in the directions I have indicated, St. Laurent's chances for leadership will be materially lessened, when it comes to the Convention, and that what is perhaps more to the point, the chances for the party winning the next election will be materially lessened. I think, for example, of a man like Aylesworth. Strong Liberal as he has been, all his life, he would vote against the party, I am sure, if a series of proposals of the kind were to be too prominently brought forward.

"We are heading in the direction of all the matters mentioned. They will come in time and in due course, but to allow them to become a sort of programme of the Province of Quebec as against the rest of Canada would be the most unfortunate of all possible situations. I shall never forget Sir Wilfrid having said to me he did not believe another French Canadian would ever be Prime Minister of Canada because of his being in the minority of race and religion. I told him that I did not agree with him on that. That I thought his own life disproved the fact that a French-Canadian could not have as long a lease of office as any English Canadian, which is true. It was not race or religion that defeated him in 1911. It was Sifton and his gang on the trade issue. I can see, however, that unless a French-Canadian leader exercises the same broad vision that Sir Wilfrid exercised in relation to national affairs, and as General Smuts has exercised in South Africa, the party may well find itself on shoals, if not upon the rocks. The unity of Canada is the problem of all problems for success in leadership. That success can be gained by the exercise of political wisdom. It cannot be made to endure if men allow personal feelings to override calm judgment.

"I noticed the Ottawa Journal has an editorial on St. Laurent exactly along the lines that I spoke of in Caucus, and which asks why does he continue to raise the question of race and religion. The very thing that should, above all others, be kept away altogether."

The question of abolishing appeals to the Privy Council came up again at the Cabinet meeting on February 3. "St. Laurent stated that the Quebec Caucus was quite prepared to back the Government in a Bill that would abolish all appeals except those where there were constitutional questions arising between provinces and the Government, where three of the provinces at least have asserted they would insist on having rights of appeal retained. Here again Ilsley was the only one who seemed to think differently or at all events wanted considerable time to consider, etc. He has drafted the present Bill. It seemed inconceivable that, as Minister of Justice, he should not have considered this important aspect. He said he had understood it was to be all or nothing which certainly is not true. St. Laurent has the right idea and it will prevail.

"The feeling of weariness at Council today after last night's late sitting made it clear to me that I had been wise in making up my mind not to continue beyond a certain time."

That afternoon in the House of Commons, Mackenzie King had "showed St. Laurent the letter from the Chief Whip indicating what a small margin we can count on in divisions in the House. I said I had been thinking over what I should do if we were defeated on a division that was important. I could not go to the Governor General and ask that we be retained, nor could I ask him to take any of the leaders opposite as no one of the three would be capable of forming a Government. I could only ask we should have a dissolution and allow the people to decide. It would be the Byng business all over again though I feel no question as to what the Governor would do, if he would accept the advice. St. Laurent then said to me that, in that case, he assumed I would stay on as Prime Minister through the campaign, exercising that office until the campaign was over, after which I would name a successor. I told him that was exactly what I would not do. Nothing would cause me to go through another campaign as Prime Minister. That on that, I was definitely decided. What would happen would be I would resign as Prime Minister and ask the Governor to call on him, St. Laurent. He certainly would be the one whom the party would wish to have lead. I thought I should make that very clear to him now. He said that he thought if we were to be beaten before a Convention, he expected they would look to him to lead if they had to choose another leader. I felt I wanted him to help the French Members to understand just how important it was that he should not be put into the position of leadership before being chosen at a Convention when all groups could unite around him and not at a time when the question of prices and cost of living was the main issue."

The question of appeals to the Privy Council did not come up again until March 5 when "Ilsley rather hinted he is not too keen about proceeding with legislation but if we did, it should be all or nothing. Not to reserve for the Privy Council the constitutional cases. Claxton had been strongest of any one, having all appeals abolished. St. Laurent himself held the wiser view of reserving constitutional questions by the Government. Bertrand was strong for abolishing – as indeed were all the Quebec Ministers, except St. Laurent.

"Martin took the view that constitutional questions should be reserved. There had been a suggestion that on constitutional questions the provinces might join in appointing certain judges to sit with the Supreme Court judges. This had made an appeal to some. Particularly Bertrand but Varcoe had got an opinion from Chief Justice Sir Lyman Duff who was much against the idea. He had wisely said that a Court was like a Cabinet; working together they developed a feeling of solidarity which was very desirable. Judges from different provinces brought in for an occasion would regard themselves as having to follow special lines. He had other reasons as well.

"It looked as though the Cabinet could not come to any real decision. I had purposely kept out as I had spoken before on the question and they knew my views. However, when I saw we were getting nowhere and they were leaving it to me, I said I would like to speak on a phase of the question which had not been mentioned and which I thought most important. I said it was clear that there were going to be provincial elections in the next few months: Quebec certainly; Ontario possibly, and maybe New Brunswick. Ilsley had said he had talked confidentially with Angus Macdonald who was, I thought, quite opposed to the abolition on the score of not being fair to the provinces. I said just what will we be doing if we make it possible for Duplessis, Drew and Macdonald to come together on another question, as an illustration of how the Liberal Government at Ottawa is trying to get everything in its own hands here; take away fair play from the provinces and concentrate it in a Court in Ottawa under their influence. I said you are only giving them one more chance to play us on the idea of centralization of control, etc., but I added [that a] much more important consideration was how we were going to get through with this session of Parliament. So much in the way of business. Hardly anything concluded thus far, that one would be getting into another long debate and one in which lawyers would become specially interested. It had been mentioned that Farris, of British Columbia, was strongly opposed to taking away the appeals. I said the battle would be led by Ayles-worth when we have many of our own leading lawyers taking sides, and making controversy. I thought it would be unfortunate for the work of the session. Much better to leave the question alone for the present and see what headway we made with the Government business.

"I then put forward the idea that we were having a Liberal Convention in August, among other reasons, to frame a programme for the Liberal party; by that time I said the provincial elections will be over and I saw no reasons why the party should not insert in its programme the abolition of appeals if that was in accord with the view of Liberals throughout the country. That would serve for purposes of election, any good that taking up the matter earlier would render." Mackenzie King added that "the Cabinet seemed relieved to get this line. St. Laurent favoured it. Ilsley did not oppose it. I think he was glad not to have to touch the matter. It was agreed at any rate to leave it all over for the present."

# CHAPTER SIX

# Marking Time

POSTPONING the issue of abolishing appeals to the Privy Council partly, as Mackenzie King saw it, in the interests of St. Laurent's prospects for the party leadership, was a good deal easier than dealing with some of the other controversial issues the government faced at the beginning of 1948. The matter of greatest domestic concern and importance was rapid price inflation, a subject the Prime Minister and St. Laurent discussed on January 7. They agreed on "the necessity of investigation into these high prices, price of butter in particular. St. Laurent said he did not see how he could avoid supporting oleomargarine if butter were to run up where ordinary people could not get it for their bread. I strongly urged, as I have in Council, the establishment of some body to find facts, not to fix penalties, but to give public opinion something to go on."

The Cabinet discussed the issue at length on January 13. Mackenzie King, particularly anxious to get a statement on price policy he could use in his speech at the meeting of the National Liberal Federation, felt "it was fortunate that the meeting was held when it was. Howe and most of the other Ministers were here, except Gardiner. All were feeling pretty fresh after the rest of their vacation. The result was we were able to make headway, with little in the way of contention. There was absolute agreement that the Wartime Prices and Trade Board should be extended for another year. Equal agreement that there should be control on the price of butter and other commodities. Also a strong plea made by St. Laurent and supported generally when it was decided that prosecutions should be commenced under the Wartime Prices and Trade Board at once. Further, the Combines Act should be used for prosecutions. Unfortunately, Mc-Gregor [the Commissioner under the Combines Investigation Act] is in Havana, and the man acting in his place is too timid to do anything. Here again the curse of these outside conferences taking away officials.

"Finally, Ilsley asked what council might think of having a Committee of the House of Commons investigate the whole question. I had been stressing right along the need for some body that would get at the facts:

give the information so that the public could judge for themselves. I kept pointing out that publicity was a better cure than penalty. The Prices Board had been suggested for this purpose. It was clear we would never get any department of government to organize some other Board. As soon as Ilsley made his suggestion, I seized on it at once and told Cabinet that Ilsley's suggestion appealed to me most strongly. I thought for many reasons it should be adopted. In the first place, I thought the high court of Parliament was the right place to try offenders, where the offence was one of profiteering at the expense of the community; that I had stressed the rights of the community as supreme, their interests being over and above all special interests. That they could not produce anything or distribute anything but for what service to the community it is rendering. That the M.P.s were the representatives of the people; it was the people who were demanding investigation, and now every Member of Parliament would have his chance to investigate. The attack no longer could be made on the Government. M.P.s would have to bear the attack themselves. I do not think people want others to be prosecuted or to exact penalties or to put people in gaol or to deny fair profits to anyone, but they want to know the facts. I said that I myself wanted to know why apples should be five cents a piece when there are quantities of apples in every community that should be sold for a very small price.

"St. Laurent wanted to know why the sudden rise of prices due to the action of packers. If they were right, the people should know it. They would not complain. I kept pressing these and other arguments and particularly that this would give to the Opposition lots to do during the session and would help to relieve the Government of some of the pressure that would come in connection with our restrictions, etc. . . . I kept at this before the whole Council until I felt I had everyone pretty well brought around to see the wisdom both from the political and economic side. I did this expecting that opposition would come from some quarter. It did come from Howe, who said he did not like the idea of bringing a lot of heads of big concerns before Parliament to be tormented, etc. My reply to that was, if they had a good case they ought to be willing to let people know it. Secondly, that Howe himself was going to be the subject of very strong attack for the arbitrary powers that had been given him. While there was no chance for investigation as to how these powers were being exercised, whether they were helping big interests, etc., that it would be a protection to him to be able to point to this Board and have the opportunity of full investigation. I thought that would become very necessary and we had better take this step before other parties made the suggestion themselves and made a demand for it in the House, which it would be difficult to prevent our people supporting. Howe then said he was not objecting, was only saying what difficulties he saw. Abbott had mentioned much the same thing. I pointed out, however, that nothing could be free of objections. It was a choice of what was the wisest course.

"I then reviewed the five points of our programme and had them endorsed distinctly by the Cabinet. Gardiner not being there, I had later a talk with him over the long distance phone. I had Abbott talk with him as well. And understanding was reached as to what Abbott would say in a statement which I had said should go to the press on Thursday night after Council. . . .

"The entire discussion took a couple of hours, during which time Taylor and Drysdale [Grisdale] were brought in as experts to answer questions. All went through with the best of feeling and practical unanimity."

At the Cabinet meeting on January 19, the Prime Minister read the portion of his proposed speech to the Federation dealing with inflation. "When I had finished, Ilsley at once raised objections to anything being done in the way of appointing a Committee of the House. Gave different grounds for this, etc. I pointed out that it was a little late to raise that question as the Cabinet had decided at its last meeting that it was to be a main feature of our prices policy and that I was to be the one to announce it at the meeting tomorrow night. Ilsley said that nothing was settled until it was actually made public. I replied that that hardly applied in this case. I would like to know if Council would agree that I should not say anything about prices tomorrow. The press were saying this was the one question they wanted to hear from the Government and from me in particular instead of my talking about signs and symbols, etc. I then said it was the one question that the people of Canada were interested in. Several Members of the Cabinet agreed with this statement very strongly, that the question of prices was the most important one. Ilsley then wanted to know who was to be Chairman of the Committee, and how it was to proceed. I replied that I thought no better one could be found than himself. As to proceeding, I thought the Committee could ask at least half a dozen Members of Parliament to join in indicating what should be investigated and that would put a certain responsibility on them. Ilsley said he had thought he would perhaps be the one since he had mentioned the subject in the first instance but that certainly he would not wish to be Chairman. He already had the human rights question. Did not know why we had taken that up, etc. Said that I thought Ilsley was right. It was no easy task. Also that if he did not feel he should take on this Committee, others could be found. I thought perhaps it would be well to have some of the young men in Parliament, one of the Parliamentary Assistants, to act as Chairman. To give these younger men a chance to show their ability. Also we would draft the terms ourselves and would have a majority on the Committee. Ilsley went on enlarging on the difficulties, supported by Abbott. When I began to point out what was in my speech, nothing but asking for information – Abbott modified his statements.

"Wishart Robertson came out strongly and said he thought that not only we should have a Committee, this year, but there should be a body that would be existing for all time whose duty it would be to get information on all these matters. I said I would be happy if Council preferred to establish a Permanent Court but I thought to begin with, it would be wise to have a Committee.

"Mackenzie spoke out quite strongly and well about how the people felt and that this was a very grave question. Said that I thought our party was losing ground steadily through not having grappled with this matter strongly enough. Moreover the situation was like a Prairie fire which if it was not stamped out soon, would consume the Government itself. It was time we should have attacks made on Members of Parliament of all parties instead of on the Government.

"St. Laurent thought we ought to emphasize a little more strongly that instructions had already been given to the Prices and Trade Board to prosecute.

"Some discussion also about McGregor's Combines Board. That McGregor should be back here, instead of at Havana or Switzerland or elsewhere, looking after his own department. St. Laurent was going to cable him to come back.

"Howe said nothing. When it was seen that practically every Member of Council except Ilsley favoured the Committee, I made it clear that I was going to be in a pretty embarrassing position if tomorrow night, I was going to be confined to speaking only of the need of a Convention when the National Liberal Federation was already meeting in the city. Ilsley ceased to say very much and I got the matter through with the understanding later that we would frame the terms of reference ourselves. I thought of McCann as a possible Chairman. St. Laurent later suggested Claxton to me. He would be very good."

Following the meeting, it was announced that butter had been brought back under price control effective immediately and that the government would seek legislation extending authority under the Continuation of Transitional Measures Act to continue price control until March 31, 1949. In his speech the next evening, Mackenzie King indicated that a Select Committee of the House of Commons would be appointed to inquire into the rising cost of living.

The Prime Minister spoke to Claxton on January 22 about becoming chairman of the committee. "That naturally I had an interest in all my colleagues and I did not wish to have him think I was saying anything to him as being more interested in his future than that of others but that I was interested in his future, and that I felt as Minister of Defence he had performed his duties so well, and had made such a name for himself, identified himself so strongly with all aspects of the Department's work that I felt that there was a danger of the public forgetting that his fundamental interest was in social problems and of thinking of him as one who was concerned with questions of defence, etc. He knew the latter would not make much of an appeal to the Canadian people whereas the problem of rising prices was the subject of greatest concern to them. I felt if he would take on the duties of Chairman of the Enquiry, he could make a strong position for himself in the country. He said he appreciated what I had said and would ask if he could have 24 hours to think it over. I said: by all means and had mentioned that St. Laurent also had thought he would be the best person. . . . He then spoke to me of doubting if he should think of taking on the Prices work with what he has. That his present job takes him twelve hours a day. That the other job would be a very difficult one and would keep him out of the House most of the time. I said I recognized this aspect but wanted him to have a chance to think matters over."

On reflection, Claxton decided not to accept the assignment and Paul Martin was appointed chairman. As could be expected, the opposition parties in the House were rather sceptical about the proposal and charged that the committee was a device by which the government hoped to evade its responsibilities. The Prime Minister closed the debate on February 10. He reported that "our men gave me a very warm reception when I rose to speak and terrific applause as I began to reply to some of the objections of the Opposition. They like combat. It is difficult to restrain one's feelings at the utter hypocrisy and insincerity of the Opposition and their tactics. Had I not been Prime Minister, I would have gone much further . . . in what I said than I did. I made very little use of the notes I had, and would have felt wholly content with the reply had I, in the closing words, not done the opposite of what I had all along felt I should not do, namely, say anything about the vote to come on division before the close of the debate itself. I do not think it made any difference in the final result as I believe that both Conservatives and C.C.F. had decided they would vote against the motion, though not withdraw from the Committee, and that would have come when the division was called. However, they might come to say that it was my challenge to them after the vote which had caused them to stand so solidly together. I think they have made a great mistake. They are doubtless banking on prices not falling and rather blaming the Government for having done nothing. They may be greatly surprised to see a fall in prices that will go much beyond anything the country desires, even before the year is out." Establishment of the committee accomplished the government's purpose and kept the issue of price inflation out of the House for most of the session.

With Mackenzie's retirement, the Prime Minister became concerned about the by-election in Vancouver and representation for British Columbia in the federal Cabinet. On January 28 he discussed the problem with Mayhew, Campney, and Senator Turgeon. "Campney brought up the subject of being possibly taken into the Cabinet. I said I could give no commitments but I would say I did not think I would have anyone come into the Cabinet until the session was over. Turgeon was of the view it might be well to take Mayhew in, specially as Minister of Fisheries. It would be known he would be in only for a time.

"Mayhew himself did not seem to know what was best to have done. He was pleased that Ian had been appointed to the Senate. Turgeon thought we could win Yale. The other two were not so clear on this. My feeling at the moment is that the best thing to do is to let Howe take charge of the situation to be advised by Turgeon who will get in touch with others."

Two days later, Mackenzie King had a long conversation with B.I. "Boss" Johnson who had succeeded John Hart as premier of British Columbia. "I was delighted with the conversation I had with him. A man who told me of his humble beginnings, struggle to gain a livelihood, difficulties in the family; how he had now become employer of Labour on a large scale. Of the measures he had introduced to help to make better the family conditions. He came down particularly to urge my rounding out the health hospitalization plan, if that was possible, as something that would fit in [with] my work, and rounding out the situation for the Liberals, both provincially and federally. This, needless to say, I should welcome doing and will endeavour to do something but here again I feel my lack of strength to force measures through the Government in the light of opposition I know this legislation will meet. I indicated to Johnson where I thought he could help me in making progress in that direction. He was very strong upon repealing the Orders-in-Council regarding the Japanese. He said we would lose the Vancouver seat with certainty if we did. He thought there was a chance of winning in Yale.

"I had a long talk with him. Believe him to be one of the best men I have met in public life. He tells me he has always been a total abstainer; does not smoke. Such trouble as he has experienced has been with men that drink."

On February 3 the Cabinet discussed the politically sensitive question of continuing the orders-in-council restricting the rights of Japanese-Canadians in British Columbia. "Johnson . . . had said there would be great trouble if these orders were removed within another year's time. All the British Columbia members feel the same way including Mayhew, who is the most reasonable of all. Mackenzie out in British Columbia stated publicly he would be against their removal which was quite outrageous on his part, having just received an appointment to the Senate. Campney, who was here, took the same view. All agreed there would not be a chance in the world to win either by-election . . . if the Government did not continue the orders. The Cabinet were agreed that they should be continued. Ilsley, however, made one of his characteristic outbursts in which he said he thought that History would denounce the party for having continued these orders. Without saying so, he replied that he would be prepared to lose both by-elections.

"I replied that I thought History would condemn a Government standing for certain principles if it allowed itself to be defeated and an enemy government take its place, when it was within its power to still carry on. These are the difficult decisions to make. One had to always take the larger view."

This question was also the major item on the agenda at the party caucus on February 18. Mackenzie King noted that "a great deal of feeling has been worked up by people who want full liberty for Canadian citizens in regard to the continuation of this measure as running wholly contrary to Liberal principles. Ilsley has taken the matter very much to heart and seems unwilling to bring the measure in. I was glad it came up this morning and there was a full discussion by those favourable and against. It made clear how completely divided the Caucus was. The Members did not seem to want to discuss anything else. When that discussion was ended, the Chairman called on me to speak. I felt it was one of the cases where if I did not take a very positive stand myself, we would find the party hopelessly divided in the House of Commons. I tried to meet the situation by saying that at the last Caucus, everyone had been unanimous as to the continuation of the Order. That I had expressed surprise at that. Was glad that someone had come along and reopened the question today. I then mentioned that Crerar and others had spoken about fundamental Liberal principles; what I had stood for in opposing Wartime Elections Act; discrimination, etc. I answered this by saying that Crerar himself believed free trade was a Liberal principle. Yet he had never voted for free trade all the time he was in Parliament. Other Members claimed that non-interference with industry, private initiative, etc., was another Liberal principle. Yet all of them today were more or less favouring controls to a certain extent. It was so with other principles. It was necessary to have the fundamental principles but their application in relation to both time and space was of the essence of politics.

"I then took up the question of the rights of minorities. That had been stressed very strongly in favour of the Japanese. I said I agreed with the question of the rights of minorities and the liberal principle that it should be applied at this time but I wanted to know which minority it was we intended to protect. Was it the minority constituted by a handful of Japanese, or was it the minority constituted by the entire population of British Columbia. I pointed out that the population so far as the Liberal representation in this Parliament was concerned, included all the Liberal Members of the House of Commons and the Senate. Everyone of whom felt that the Order should be extended and that if it were not, the consequences would be very serious for the party in British Columbia. I asked if the other provinces of Canada could afford to be indifferent to what were the wishes of every Liberal Member of our Parliament with regard to a question that was vital to British Columbia. I then spoke of the by-election and said it was all right to talk of not caring whether we lost a by-election; I was not too sure that we would win either but I felt a great deal depended also on the issue on which the by-election was raised. If we lost because we were indifferent to the wishes of every Member of our party in that province, I thought it was just opening the door to our opponents walking into the Parliament of Canada from that province at the next general election. I mentioned Grover Cleveland's favourite expression – that it was not a theory but a condition that we were concerned with, and I had to meet. I hoped that certainly no action would be taken in our Parliament in the few months that remained while I was Leader of the party which would be responsible for our losing an entire province in a general election.

"Senator Gouin told me this afternoon he thought the speech was one of the best I had ever made. . . . Ross Macdonald, of Brantford, said he had felt strongly the other way but thought I was right. Senator Turgeon said British Columbia Members were very pleased and felt I had done the only right thing that could be done. I got a great reception at the end of the speech and think it made a real impression and will help to save the situation for us in one of the most difficult problems we have before us. I really sometimes wonder what is going to happen to the party later." The orders-in-council were not rescinded at this time.

Another difficult question the Cabinet had to face was whether to bring oats and barley under the Wheat Board's marketing arrangements. At the meeting on February 12, Gardiner, MacKinnon and Glen "were all strongly of the opinion that if this were not done, the party would lose the West entirely. The C.C.F. would sweep everything. Garson, of Manitoba, was strongly for inclusion of this extension of power. Gardiner doubted if all provinces . . . would agree to legislation. It would not become law without their concurrence. It was also felt that, under the terms of the legislation, the Department of Justice would have to rule on what could be done. It was thought advisable not to raise these questions – to have these questions raised in the House rather than to deal with them in advance. Howe who is, as Minister of Trade and Commerce, fathering the legislation, is strongly opposed to it as is also the Minister of Finance. They both feel it may further socialistic aims and lead to state marketing of goods, etc.

"I had to give the decision; in doing so, I stated that I thought the Cabinet could not, on a matter affecting Agriculture, go contrary to the strong views of representatives of three Western Provinces. Howe immediately said: carried, and that ended the discussion of one of the most difficult matters we have had to deal with. MacKinnon said to me later he marvelled at how I managed to get these matters through Cabinet in the way I did with so little friction.

"It is by being patient and waiting for all sides, and using best judgment that one can bring things to bear."

As usual, the early months of 1948 were not without occasional distractions. On January 27 the Prime Minister, in his capacity of Honorary President, attended a dinner meeting of the Ottawa branch of the University of Toronto Alumni Association in honour of Vincent Massey. He "was asked . . . to join the President in receiving the guests. I went early but in some way or another, missed the Masseys when they came into the room. I met the Governor General and Her Excellency but did not see the Masseys until afterwards. When I explained how sorry I was I had not seen them come, they made some slight reference about noticing I was in another part. There was no nice feeling about their attitude.

"Later, when photographs were being taken, I insisted on having Vincent and his wife next to the Governor General though His Excellency had asked me to stand there. I felt that the dinner was in his honour. Bracken and his wife were at one end, and I was at the other. . . .

"The evening was an interesting one though the programme was unnecessarily long. I found myself seated to Her Excellency's left with Mrs. Massey to my left.

"At the beginning of the evening, Mrs. Massey was quite cold. I could see she did not know whether to call me Rex or what, part of the time, but as the evening went on, I talked with her about some of the personal things

that were of interest to her. She warmed up considerably. I also spoke
nicely of Vincent's speech which I thought was very good. Alice told me
that Vincent had written a book on 'Being a Canadian' – now in the hands
of the printers. I was also glad to learn that her daughter-in-law was
restored in health. I spoke of being sympathetic with the suffering they
had had. I also let her know and Vincent that I had today passed an Order
which was going to His Excellency to make Vincent Chairman of the
Trustees of the Art Gallery. Each of them acknowledged this in a word.
Not with any appreciation or thanks but as something they would be
interested in.

"I had a little talk with Vincent on the way in to dinner and on the way
out. He was quite pleasant but very formal. No really personal interest. I
think he had been hurt in learning that I would not be at the meeting and
was a bit surprised when he found I was there. I asked him if he had an
engagement for tomorrow night. He was dining at Government House. I
said otherwise I would have been glad to have him come to Laurier House
for dinner.

"It was half past 10 before the dinner was over. I was glad that I had
gone particularly as I am the Honorary President of the Association, and
I was re-elected to that office."

Mackenzie King attended another dinner on February 10 given by
former members of the Department of Munitions and Supply in honour
of C. D. Howe. "Over 100 of the leading industrialists and business executives were present. Most of them had come down to receive decorations
at an Investiture at Government House this afternoon. (This I was unable
to attend.)" For the Prime Minister, a particular "feature of the evening
was a quite pleasant talk I had with Ralston who looks very much thinner,
especially in the face, than when I saw him last."

Before the Cabinet meeting on February 6, Mackenzie King had received word that Barbara Ann Scott had won the Olympic figure skating
championship. He immediately sent a telegram of congratulations. "Was
asked in the House if I had noticed about the young lady, etc. Replied that
I had had my eye on her for fifteen years past and then gave the substance
of the telegram sent. I do not think there is any single individual whose
life and art and talent has been watched as closely by the Canadian people
as Barbara Ann Scott, or who has brought as much of a thrill to the entire
nation as she has in what she has achieved, and the way in which she has
carried her honours."

On February 16 the Prime Minister began to think "of suggesting that
the first award of the Canada Medal be given to Barbara Ann Scott. . . .
This is not only for her skating but because of the fine example she has set

to others as a young woman in self-discipline, etc. I have spoken to no one of this but P. Told him to look up the particulars re the Medal.

"When I came in, I found a letter in the evening mail, unsigned save by some woman of Manitoba – the letter is from Brandon – opposing the idea of a stamp to commemorate Barbara Ann's achievement. Spoke of the Canadians who had given their lives. Of Banting having given insulin – no stamps for them, etc. Asking whether Canadians were losing their sense of values. This has caused me to reconsider the wisdom of giving the first Medal for sports though I think there is much to commend it. Were it possible to give it for what would best serve to recognize sacrifice of life in war, etc., that might be preferable. I know the original difficulty of making the Award was to agree to whom it should go. That is the great injustice of all Honours where honour comes to one, there are more deserving who are never heard of." This idea was not followed up but Mackenzie King participated, with some degree of exuberance, in the civic reception for the skater when she returned to Ottawa on March 9. "The Mayor took matters into his hands or rather Barbara into his own arms," he wrote. "I presented my cheek for the purpose requested. It was something I would have preferred to escape but there was no escaping in the circumstances."

As the session continued, the Prime Minister showed no weakening in his resolve to retire. On February 14 he noted that, in a letter to Beaverbrook thanking him for an invitation to spend a holiday in the West Indies, he had written that his colleagues had been "most considerate of me and I must seek not to embarrass them more than is possible, especially as these are certain to be my last few months in office." On February 20 he complained again about "the hopeless indifference of everyone" to problems of political organization. "In B.C. no one in particular is following the situation seriously. Howe who is the one to be looked to is allowing it to drift. The same is true of Ontario. The Liberal Office has no control there or real knowledge of the situation. In Quebec, the situation is worse than anywhere else. Gouin was telling me that he thought Duplessis was certain to be returned. That there was no real organization in Quebec. That members used to look to Lapointe and to Cardin. Since they had gone, no Quebec Minister had really taken an interest. Power is out of it. St. Laurent not in. The others, not trusted. Claxton, writing letters but doing nothing. Godbout has no real organization. The chances are the Liberals may get a very serious defeat. One that will tell against the Federal Government when our turn comes.

"I am truly glad that I have made my announcement to give up the leadership in the summer before announcement has been made of provincial elections in either Ontario or Quebec, or indeed in any of the other provinces. It cannot then be said that my decision has been made in the light of prospects that are not too good for our own party federally."

Two days later he spent some time reading the 1947 diary "from the opening of Parliament on January 30 up to the end of February. I can see that throughout the whole of that month, I was really thoroughly exhausted. Down with a very heavy cold. Suffering from influenza; taking very great chances with my health.

"As I look at it now, I feel to have really been able to enjoy a bit of that period, I should have been out of the country altogether or to the South. I was not doing work for the country that was worth anything, and the effort to overtake correspondence that had fallen into arrears, prepare memoranda and the like was really something quite beyond my strength. . . .

"By comparison, I can see I have been in infinitely better shape all this past month than I was a year ago. I wish, however, I could bring myself to taking the rest and following a normal day-to-day procedure which I should be doing to get the best out of my days and life. What I have read and what I continue to feel of strain today causes me more than ever to believe that I have been wise in arranging for the Convention in August. Very wise, too, in announcing at present the adjournment of Parliament at the end of June. As I see myself in the picture one gets from reading the diary of February of a year ago, it is like a man being dragged along instead of walking like a man, enjoying the life and freedom he ought to possess, to be of use to himself or of service to others."

For Mackenzie King, the most irritating issue in the House during this period, both personally and politically, was a revival of the controversy over the despatch of two Canadian battalions to Hong Kong in 1941 shortly before the colony fell to the Japanese. A report on the fall of Hong Kong, prepared by Major General Maltby, the officer commanding British forces in China, and dated November 21, 1945, was published in the London *Gazette* on January 27, 1948, and led to questions in the House. On February 18 the Leader of the Opposition introduced a motion asking the government to table the evidence taken by the Commission headed by Sir Lyman Duff, then Chief Justice of Canada, which had been appointed on February 12, 1942, to examine the circumstances that had led to the government's decision [see volume 1, pp. 298, 315–16, 325, 351–52]. Responding to Bracken, the Prime Minister undertook to inquire whether the British government still objected to the publication of confidential inter-governmental communications which had been included in the Commission's statement of evidence. He discussed the situation with C. G.

Power that afternoon. "He told me that while it was true that our men were not too well trained, that our situation was nothing as to what the British was like. That at British headquarters, when they were told the Japs had already landed, the reply came back they better go to sleep and allow others to have their sleep. Spoke too of some of the regular army there being so diseased and used up they were good for nothing. Altogether it was an appalling account he gave of the situation.

"He said if the British are going to comment on the state of our men at the time, he will say something in the House about not letting British Generals in the future have anything to do with men of our army. It is a great pity this question has been brought up by the Tories."

A reply was received from London on February 19. The British government stated that the substance of telegrams relating specifically to the despatch of the Canadian forces could be published but that others dealing with the international situation in the Far East at that time must remain confidential. A related question was whether the government should table a letter which George Drew had written on July 11, 1942, attacking the Commissioner's report. Drew had acted as counsel for the Leader of the Opposition during the inquiry. At the time, the government, acting on the advice of the Commission's counsel, had refused to table the letter on the ground that it contained references to confidential communications from the United Kingdom. At the Cabinet meeting on February 23, there was "a discussion of some length as to whether the evidence should be tabled or not. That part of it, at least, which the British Government were agreeable should be tabled. As Claxton remarked to me afterwards, he had seldom seen the Cabinet more divided."

The Prime Minister "saw it was going to be very difficult to decide between these groups so suggested I leave the matter over till tomorrow. I felt the statement which had been prepared needed revision and recasting and I wanted time to weigh the pros and cons in my own mind. This I kept doing through the luncheon hour.

"After luncheon at a quarter to 3, I had Bracken, Coldwell and Low come to my room. I read to them the telegram from the British Government declining to allow much of the material that had been used in the enquiry to be tabled. Such telegrams as were from the U.K. and related to our forces going overseas at the start would have to be reproduced in paraphrase. Also there were other restrictions on the production. I felt in my own mind that we ought not to allow Drew's letter to be tabled. In fact, we could not do so without a breach with the undertaking given the British Government when they allowed the Commission to have certain evidence. I felt for a minute that if this were held to, we ought perhaps to agree to the tabling of such evidence as was recorded, and not subject to the restrictions the British had imposed. Not to do this would look as though there was something we had to conceal. It would also lead to continual prodding of the Government for this and that, charging us with being arbitrary, etc. Against this was the feeling that to table the evidence was to give Drew a chance to have someone picking pieces here and there, publishing them from time to time. Also that it might be unfair to the Chief Justice, Duff, though having agreed to withhold the Drew letter, I did not feel anxious on that score.

"After Orders of the Day, I got P. to come down to my office and suggested recasting all that had been drafted in accordance with this line of procedure. It took from 4 till 7 to do this and to get a draft in proper shape. I then 'phoned Chief Justice Duff and said I would like to let him look at it and get an opinion from him later as to whether he approved. Claxton is to see General Crerar; talk with his own Chiefs of Staff. It was pointed out that even the production of routine stuff meant a good deal in the way of disclosure to enemies – much that related to secret matters connected with the war. Of course, I think the worst feature is the reopening of wounds but I believe that once we bring down the material, if the papers start that kind of thing, the public's feelings will be roused against them.

"At 9.30, I 'phoned Sir Lyman about the statement. He said to me he thought it was most effective. In fact, used the word 'deadly' in speaking of parts that refer to Drew. . . . He did think that if we did not table the evidence, the persons would think there was something which we were holding, and he saw no reason that we should withhold. I kept stressing that I did not wish to make any statement that would be embarrassing to him. He said there was nothing that could be such. That he noticed that the Toronto Globe and others had been taking shots at him, but no man could do anything in life that was worthwhile without someone misconstruing things. He spoke of the radio misrepresenting things. He said when they had been citing Maltby's report, the broadcaster had ended with the statement: it looks as if Drew had been right. He said he had not heard this himself but that his sister had. He thought the C.B.C. should be spoken to about giving these interpretations of their own to matters of the kind. He emphasized several times that he was quite satisfied with the statement. Thanked me for giving so much time to going over the matter. I feel now quite at ease in my mind about giving the statement as it stands.

"I believe in the end, it will make less trouble for everyone to give what there is of recorded evidence. Duff did say he thought the Government were a much better judge of what would be a wise thing to do as respects public opinion than himself. That he was not in a position really to judge of what was best. It was plain, however, from what he said that he regarded the statement as satisfactory."

The next day (February 24), Mackenzie King read to the Cabinet "what I had written last night mentioning that they were free to alter the last – subject to tabling the evidence. Claxton had completely reversed his position. He had been all for tabling this evidence. This morning was against it. Several other Ministers seemed to change their point of view when it became apparent that the evidence would bring out some reports that officials had made which were really confidential.

"After a considerable discussion, back and forth, it became apparent that the weight of the argument was for tabling the evidence but preserving certain portions for security reasons and protection of officials.

"Council left it to Claxton and myself to draft what we thought best. In my office, Claxton, P. and I took a run over this part of the material and worked out final clause along the lines that seemed to be most generally accepted.

"I had intended to return to the Cabinet with the statement but colleagues had left before it was concluded.

"At 3, in the House, I read the statement. There was a hushed silence. No interruption save when I said the Government thought it would be better if the Hong Kong question had not been revived. There was a sort of spontaneous snort of disapproval from the Tories but not too much of a demonstration. No other parties in the House joined them.

"When I came to the end, made clear we were not tabling Drew's letter and we were tabling the evidence with certain questions and reservations. There was first lot of applause from our side of the House. Bracken had a statement prepared which he had to modify in the light of what I had said. It was clear from his statement that they had not anticipated tabling of the evidence. Were going to make a fight for democratic parliamentary control. Now the war was over. They would have been supported by Coldwell and his party but opposed by Low. Power fortunately made a statement in which he expressed the hope that I would ask the British Government to review the situation and table everything. I did not wait a moment before saying I would be happy to make known his representations to the British Government and support it on behalf of our Government. That took the wind out of the sails of the Opposition. I could see that all my colleagues were pleased with the way matters had gone. Graydon and Diefenbaker tried to have it appear that I had been seeking to influence the British Government to have them decline to have Drew's letter made public.

"I was emphatic about not having sought to influence the British Government one way or the other but found it a little difficult to say just what I meant. However, from a subsequent statement, I made clear that the Tories were trying to insinuate that I had been trying to get the British Government to get us to hold back the Drew letter. I answered that back effectively. What might have been and would have been, had we not agreed to table the evidence – a prolonged and bitter debate – petered out with assurance that when the motion comes before the House for the production of the evidence, it will carry without a division. . . . It really required careful manoeuvring to bring about sufficient agreement in Government to enable the matter to be settled without any formal division.

"The Cabinet would have taken my decision whichever way might have been made."

On February 27 the Prime Minister noted that he would "be unhappy indeed if at the end of my public life, the Tories were able to pin on me, as they seek now to do, responsibility for the fate of our battalion at Hong Kong. A damnable sort of effort in the light of all that Canada has done in the war." He was particularly annoyed by Graydon's part in the revival of the Hong Kong controversy. "I am coming to have a very strong dislike for Graydon who, at best, is of the calibre of a basketball fan."

During the day he reviewed the debate in the House in 1942, the letters from Drew and the relevant despatches between the Canadian and British governments. "Was immensely relieved to find that there was nothing in all of the correspondence that would in any way reflect on either myself or run counter to the judgment of Chief Justice Duff. There is, of course, much that would indicate that our men were sent far too quickly, insufficiently trained, etc., but there is enough in the telegrams from the United Kingdom to make clear there was no reason to expect they would be involved in any engagements as soon as they were.

"One thing which was characteristic of our Department of Defence. They were asked only for one or two battalions but deliberately decided on two. I recall at the time taking the stand that this was unnecessary in the light of what we were doing for Europe, but encountered the usual opposition where one seeks to exercise due restraint with Government departments. It really has been a waste of an entire day, having to go over all this material which belongs to six years ago but which comes up now in ways to occasion embarrassment.

"It is this sort of thing which makes one increasingly weary of public life."

Mackenzie King informed the House on March 1 that "the British Government were not prepared to change their decision re Hong Kong telegrams. This evening's [Ottawa] *Citizen* contains Drew's letter. Evidently the Tories have decided to take chances. The whole business is most unfair. The effort now is to make a battle between Drew and the ex-Chief Justice though I can see the Tory plan is to seek to make me the scapegoat by Drew's assertion that I knew there was a certainty of war against Japan three days before our troops left.

"I have taken part of the afternoon to go over correspondence again. I think the Chief Justice is absolutely right in his decision. I am glad tomorrow to have the opportunity of raising a question of privilege and saying that Drew is quite wrong in his assertions. Of course, we shall be embarrassed at not being able to produce telegrams which support the truth of our position."

"Nothing exhausts me more than contention over a matter like Hong Kong," the Prime Minister wrote the next day (March 2), "where one realizes that it is only adding to the problems of the day to be discussing Hong Kong and that the whole purpose of the Opposition is political. It is particularly exasperating to be dealing with the types of persons that Drew and McCullagh are. If I were a wealthy man, I would sue the Toronto Globe and Mail for libel in an editorial which it has today insinuating that I might have known myself about certainty of war but may not have told it to my colleagues or to the general staff. Truly the father of lies is the devil.

"I prepared a very brief reply. In the House, this afternoon, in a few words on a question of privilege, I took exception to what appeared in the Citizen of last night. Wish very much I had supplemented it by a statement from the Maltby report but that will come in at some later time. However, it would have come in most effectively today. The Opposition has, as I anticipated it, sought at once to begin to make demonstrations to attract public attention."

On March 3 Mackenzie King considered a draft reply to statements in the press by Drew which had been prepared for him. He "felt the dignified thing was to say nothing. I held to this in the afternoon. There was not a reference to Hong Kong matter on Orders of the Day. The fact that no one spoke at all, I think, must have impressed the House. It was equivalent to Parliament saying we have perhaps gone far enough in this matter.

"I was disappointed that Power did not speak seeing that Drew had mentioned him last night and had quoted what he had said about thinking there might be war, specially as Power has in his possession the evidence he gave and which shows that Drew only quoted part of the evidence and not the part related to whether he meant there would be immediate war. He answered that question by saying he did not think there would be immediate war in reference to the charge Drew has made against me. I think Power lost a chance in not bringing that up today at once. He may speak tomorrow but at any rate what will happen is that once the evidence comes down, that statement of his will be there. The Tories will then begin to attack the Department of Defence or else drop the subject altogether. I am quite positive that, while they try to make as much trouble as possible, trying to make it appear we are trying to refuse evidence, they will gain nothing with the public by trying to keep up attacks on these lines."

The Prime Minister continued to be disappointed on March 4 that Power had not entered the debate. He felt the former Minister "could so easily have answered Drew's statement which seemed to gain strength by a quotation from part of his evidence but not the whole. The whole evidence shows he said exactly what I have said and what the Chief Justice said. He did not think there was any immediate danger of war."

The following day he "was particularly pleased . . . when quite unexpectedly on the Orders of the Day, some little time after they had been called, just when I thought we were going to resume the debate on the Address, Power rose to a question of privilege and read the statement made by Drew that I had been heaping falsehood upon falsehood and citing in support of his statement an alleged statement by Power in which he had said that he expected war with Japan. Power then said that Drew had not given the full statement; that in the very next sentence, in answer to a very specific question as to whether he thought there was immediate war, Power had replied he did not think war would be coming immediately. It was a body blow to the Tories. Not one had a word to say.

"It was the best possible answer to Drew and all the better coming as a blow in the silence of the present moment.

"Smith, of Calgary, then got up and asked when this Hong Kong business was to go on – whether we were going to get the whole evidence and when we were going to get it. Power rose and said he agreed with Smith, that we should wait for the evidence but that is what he felt Drew should have done – not piece by piece. I think this will be quite a silencer to Drew. There remains still to bring in discussion of the Maltby report which I wish I had alluded to the other day but which undoubtedly will come in well before the last word has been said on Hong Kong.

"I 'phoned Chubby later and thanked him. He has been quite upset as to what to do. I could tell from his voice in what he said to me on the 'phone that he seemed just a little upset still. He asked if I supposed there would be something more on Hong Kong. . . . I told him I was very grateful to him for having made the statement today. That I thought he had said just the right thing and that it had come at the right moment. Smith had given him a splendid opening. Repeated I was grateful to him and he thanked me quite warmly. It evidently took some courage on his part, knowing that the Tories now will try to turn on him in connection with the Hong Kong matter. I am so glad he has taken this step in defending my position – before he has had to take it in defending his own. He would have made a terrible mistake if he had allowed Drew's statement to go unchallenged too long."

The government clearly regained the initiative on March 10. "If ever in my life I helped the Government to save itself from the wolves that would devour it, I did today," the Prime Minister wrote. "Bracken has had two motions, both of which call for papers – some regarding Hong Kong; some regarding the Maltby report, etc. Bracken had put them there clearly expecting that all Opposition parties would vote together condemning the Government for refusing the correspondence called for. . . .

"I had prepared, some days ago, to meet the situation by asking Beauchesne to give me an opinion on both. He prepared two careful statements. I thought it would be much more effective to have me give an authoritative statement from Beauchesne instead of giving the same statement from myself. I took care to secure Beauchesne's agreement to my making it known that the opinion was given by him. P. told me he seemed quite pleased to have me do so, quoting him as an authority.

"While I read the opinion in Council and Cabinet, Ilsley who is usually of some opposite opinion, was all for giving out the information that the Tories were asking for. Did not see why we should not, etc. Claxton who had been the one that had pressed the more strongly for making public the evidence at the start, and but for whose pressure at the outset the Government would probably have declined to produce any at all, seemed to waver considerably as to whether we should not agree to give some of the material asked for. It is true that if we had made it all public, it would only have verified what I have said, but to have agreed to the request, would have been to create a precedent that would have blocked out the way in many subsequent motions. In declining many subsequent motions, I would have been quite wrong. . . .

"I made it pretty clear to the Cabinet that what they were proposing would make it impossible for our Government to carry on confidential communications with our own [High Commissioners] or with the British H.C. here. I pointed out, too, what I think Ilsley saw in a moment that, if we granted this motion, we would have to equally tell what instructions we were giving our representatives at the U.N. I pointed out practically all the business they did there was a matter of drafting statements, modifying them, changing, going back and forth, until some finality was reached.

"The Minister [of the Crown] took the responsibility for the final matter. Finally, Cabinet agreed unanimously. This afternoon, when the matter came up in the House, I very quietly read the opinion that Beauchesne had given me. The Tories were so sure that they did not try to raise any question but at once Bracken rose to urge a division. He really was so surprised he really did not know what or how to go about it. Asked the Speaker what his ruling was, which showed they were anxious to appeal against the Speaker's ruling. Instead the Speaker pointed out if they did not accept the Government's refusal, they could divide the House on a motion. They divided. To their amazement, while they voted as a solid body, the C.C.F. and Social Credit voted solidly with our party. The nondescripts on the Tory side voted with the Tories. We got a majority of something like 80 [146–61]. They had not expected we would get more than about 8 or 10. It would have been so had all three parties voted against the Government.

"When it came to the next motion, I followed a like procedure. They were afraid to vote and called 'on division.' We might well have embarrassed them greatly by forcing a division but I thought it best to let them beat a complete retreat in this way.

"At the opening of the House, Claxton tabled the [abridged] evidence on the Hong Kong Commission. Bracken made it clear by two questions that they were going to make capital out of our not printing the evidence, etc. He pointed out that Quebec Regiment was French, Manitoba English – were we only to table the evidence in English? Claxton replied it only existed in English. He was not asked specifically in regard to printing but that question will probably come later but I made clear we were tabling the evidence itself. That was all we had. I think now we can meet further situations by pointing out it has all been before them. I think the minds of the Tories were so full with the fact that the evidence was coming down today, and they would get two rulings against the Government on Bracken's motion, that they were completely knocked out when the C.C.F. and S.C. voted with us on the latter. I have never seen a party look more stunned or surprised.

"They tried to take exception to my reading Beauchesne's opinion but I made clear that it was because they would not believe me. He was authority on rules and procedure and when final exception was taken, that I was giving opinion of an officer of the Government, I pointed out that Beauchesne was an officer of the House – not of the Government. These preliminary victories – for they were such – prepared the ground splendidly for what followed." He added at the end of the day: "Tomorrow will come the answer to the question in the British House [put by a Conservative M.P., Quintin Hogg] which will prove that all that I have been saying – but which the Tories have been seeking to misrepresent – is entirely and wholly true. Had this material come before today, it would not be half as effective as it will be coming tomorrow.

"Today's whole proceedings have been a real answer to Prayer."

Next morning (March 11) Mackenzie King was "satisfied with report on the radio on the Hong Kong matter. I am beginning to doubt if the Tories will go much further in that situation.

"Yesterday's proceedings seemed to have settled the matter – by placing all the evidence on the table. The press finding that it bore out just what we had been saying. Two political parties – C.C.F. and S.C. – declining to join with the Tories in a vote against the Government in its refusal to produce other documents, has pretty well silenced the business.

"I was looking forward throughout the morning to getting word of a question which had been asked in the British House by Quintin Hogg and a reply made to it. It had not been answered two days ago. When word came over the 'phone that it had been answered, I devoted some little time in preparing what I would say in the House in placing it on record on Hansard.

"When I reached the House, I was amazed to have P. tell me that an extraordinary thing had happened. Robertson had 'phoned to say that Quintin Hogg was not in his seat when the question hour came and also that the question had been withdrawn. However, whoever was answering on the Government's side, not knowing that the question had been withdrawn, gave the answer so that the whole thing would be forthcoming in the press. I had to give up saying anything today on the Orders of the Day as I intended in this matter but feel it is all the better the reply appearing in the press before I say anything about it. I shall speak on it tomorrow."

In the House on March 12 the Prime Minister read the exchange in the British House which confirmed that the British government would not agree to the release of communications dealing with the international situation in the Far East in 1941 and 1942. "It was interesting to note how silent the House was as I read the statement," he wrote, "I thought the Conservatives looked ashamed of themselves. There was not a word or exception taken or question raised on their side. Our men were also quite quiet which I was glad to see as, had they applauded, it might have brought forth some further comment. Coldwell said to me later he was glad I had put on record the statement I did. It helps to disclose the contemptible tactics of some of the Tories."

Practically, this was the end of the controversy. On April 19 Mackenzie King was very pleased to receive a cable from Attlee which "completely answered Drew's charges." To the Prime Minister on April 28 "the significant event of today was that the Joint Printing Committee of the two Houses decided by a vote of 39 to 1 not to print the Hong Kong evidence. The one man who voted for it was [W.A.] MacMaster [Progressive Conservative M.P. for Toronto High Park] who is in the same constituency as Drew.

"Nothing could have been more effective as an answer as to how the public feel about Drew's action bringing this matter forward in the manner he did.

"I decided today was a good day to get on record in Hansard the telegrams which I sent to Attlee and his reply; mentioning that I did not wish to bring it up while the Printing Committee was still making its enquiry. The House listened in complete silence to what I said. No exception was taken at all excepting at the end Graydon tried to, in some words, give occasion for Opposition papers to comment adversely. I noticed in the *Journal* not more than a paragraph of what was said."

In the early months of 1948, a growing fear of the consequences of Communist expansion in Europe resulted in agitation for the exclusion of Communists from Canada. On March 1 the Cabinet discussed a report, prepared by a cabinet subcommittee, "proposing that we should not allow any professed Communist into Canada. This had been held over for my being present. Without knowing how the Cabinet had been divided, I said I agreed with Claxton in the view that it would be a mistake to prohibit persons just because they were professed Communists. That I was agreeable to keeping out those who were labour organizers coming into mines and industries to create trouble there but would not, for example, oppose the secretary of the Communist party in England – Pollock [Pollitt?] – coming to Canada when he was allowed perfect freedom in the United Kingdom nor would I prevent Gallag[c?]her, a Member of the British Parliament, from being admitted to Canada. I felt pretty sure that we could not go to such lengths by prohibiting the Communist party in Canada. I thought the way to fight the Communists was in the open, as they do in Britain.

"To my surprise, all members present, – St. Laurent was not present – Ilsley was quiet – spoke a little both ways. Were in favour of complete exclusion of Communists. I said I was sure action on that part would create headlines in the press who would begin to win for Communists here, large number of sympathizers who did not like the Government. Try to prevent people thinking as they pleased.

"As I saw no agreement could be come to, I held matters over until St. Laurent was here. I am perfectly sure that we would make a mistake to make this one of the leading issues at the present time. Much better to let sleeping dogs lie. I was surprised Gardiner was so strong for the prohibition. Also Mitchell, Chevrier, Fournier, Bertrand and others; also

McCann. Howe, I expected, would be. Gregg said nothing. I shall be surprised if he would have the view of the others."

The question was considered again the next day and Mackenzie King reported that "Claxton and I were alone in our opposition to having the Government support a report of the Committee that this should be done. St. Laurent, however, saw the situation pretty clearly and suggested that a Committee of the Cabinet – the Ministers being Mines and Resources, Labour, and External Affairs, should decide on what persons, if admitted to Canada, were likely to create Communistic strife and inform Immigration officials that these persons were not to be admitted. This saved the division of the Cabinet and really meant that the position taken by Claxton and myself was the one to which the Cabinet finally agreed."

The Prime Minister derived great satisfaction from the annual meeting between the Cabinet and the Trades and Labour Congress on March 4 in the Railway Committee room. Most of the ministers were present. "I was glad to have the Labour representatives hear those who will likely be candidates for the leadership. I wound up the morning proceedings with a short address which got a very warm reception. I spoke of it being the privilege of years to reminisce a little and commenting on the paragraph in the memo of Labour that Congress had been appearing before governments for the past sixty-five years. Pointed out that of that sixty-five years, I had been present at meetings about fifty years ago – forty-eight to be exact. . . . I thought about thirty-three of the interviews or half of the interviews. I drew attention to the statement which said that Labour legislation had been slow but pointed out that most of what we had done in that way, had come since 1900 which, when one considered it, included unemployment insurance, old age pensions, family allowances, fair wages, etc. Did not seem to me to be too slow. Mitchell had a somewhat long and discursive speech. Mentioned that personally all the legislation that had been introduced, had been originally proposed in resolutions of the Trades and Labour Congress. I told him I thought that single sentence was worth more than all the rest of his speech put together. It was something I thought they should remember and which should bring great encouragement to Labour. I pointed out how it had all practically come since the Department of Labour was created. That there had not been any Department prior to 1900, and that, at that time, there were many prominent men in the country who thought Labour should not be allowed to organize. Today we saw what a tremendous thing it was for the country to have Labour properly organized and directed. I spoke particularly of the paragraph which said that the Congress would like the establishment of an all-embracing social security programme on a contributory basis. I said it had been one of the main purposes of my life to try and bring that about. I hoped to see it complete before my days in Parliament were over. That most of it was already there, having regard to what had been achieved in the provinces and Dominion together. That the health measures took time but that I believed that many of those present would see the accomplishment of that programme. I said it was a source of joy to me to feel that in an humble way and to a limited degree, I had been able to further that great end but I came back to the point that it represented not so much that those who were in Parliament had the privilege to say the last word, but rather to Labour itself who had presented the first word, and had sought to influence public opinion in a reasonable way, that the success of the programme was due. I spoke of looking to the future of Canada and saying I felt a definite confidence in the future because of this report of Labour in the past. That I felt as long as the Congress continued to conduct its affairs along the lines it had followed to date, constructive lines – lines that helped to keep the nations steady, our country would hold a place of leadership among nations in the world.

"I then said I did not know whether I would have the privilege of again meeting with the members of the Congress at another gathering such as the one we were all sharing because as I had been sitting there, looking over the large body of representatives, I could not but feel amazed that of the number that I knew when I first met representatives of the Congress, I doubted if there were more than one or two, indeed if there were that many who were present at the first interviews of the Congress with the Government at which I, myself, had been present, either as Deputy Minister or Minister of the Crown. I said that I could not but recall the services rendered to Labour by such old leaders as Dan O'Donoghue, Paddy Draper and Tom Moore. That I liked as Prime Minister of Canada to recall their names and those of many others, and pay a tribute to the services they had rendered the nation in their day and through their work in organizing and directing organized Labour. That I wished to say that among the friendships that I had made in the course of my public life, there were none that had meant more to me, had been more intimate in some respects, and which I valued more than those of members of the Dominion Trades and Labour Congress.

"I was happy today to meet many of those who were friends. That I would like to extend to them my best of wishes for the future of the Congress and its work and for their own futures. Evidently they were much moved by this little address and responded strongly.

"Bengough, the President, got up and made a very nice little speech in which he thanked me for having been present and presiding and for what I had said. Thanked me for the services I had rendered to Labour and hoped I would be spared for years to continue to interest myself in the affairs of Labour. His remarks were also well received.

"It was a moving affair. I found my own voice wavered just a bit as I spoke about probably not meeting the Congress again but I could not help thinking what a fine gathering it was as the concluding one, should it prove to be such."

Later in the day, the representatives of the Railway Brotherhoods were received by the Cabinet. "A. J. Kelly of the Brotherhood of Trainmen presented their memorandum which was of considerable length and which he read remarkably well. . . . Here again were some memorable little incidents; Kelly, I thought, was having trouble with his throat and I had some water brought in but he managed without it. When he got through, I said would he like to have a drink with me. I had been given a glass of water as well. He then said in the presence of all the others: Well, I would never refuse a drink with you.

"Chevrier replied to the delegation in a very good speech, taking up the different points they had mentioned. Mitchell spoke rather too discursively as he usually does. Abbott, rather briefly. Howe, quite well. Ilsley, a few words and St. Laurent, also briefly. When I replied, I said I hoped I might be allowed to speak particularly of Mr. Best who was there but who was not appearing as representing any organization. That he and I had met together at similar interviews before all the others who were present had ever appeared in their representative capacity. That he had now earned a well earned retirement but I was glad to see that his old associates were pleased to have him come with them. That I was hoping to get my retirement as well but hoped my colleagues would be equally kind and give me the pleasure of honouring me by asking me to join them in a similar way when my days of retirement would come.

"I then spoke of it seeming to me that all they had asked for in the memo was in accord with the phrase I had heard which had been used a good deal of late – namely, just and reasonable. I thought every one of their demands was just and I thought every one was reasonable, which is true. The presentation was remarkably moderate and fair and convincing. I think all the Ministers felt the same way. I did mean to say something about the tremendous place the railway industry holds but forgot to speak of that. I referred to the presence of Côté as Parliamentary Assistant. What it means to have these younger men present at these delegations. They had been getting large experience in dealing with these problems in the future, and then spoke again of the pleasure it had been to me to have had the association I had had with members of the Railway Brotherhoods. Wished them well through the future.

"To my surprise, Kelly got up and made a very nice little speech, thanking me for my reference to Best and saying that they shared the hopes that my colleagues would always do with me as they had with Best. Spoke of regretting that I was thinking of retiring and was hoping I would have years of useful life and service. Altogether made a most touching speech.

"When Kelly finished, we all rose but I stopped them to say that I wished the world would look upon the little gathering we were having in this particular room to see what it expressed of relations of government and Labour, [what] good-will and co-operation there was. The different representatives came up and shook hands very feelingly. I was quite moved by the evident way in which they disclosed their feeling toward myself as one whom they had trusted throughout."

The next day Mackenzie King and his colleagues received a delegation from the Canadian Congress of Labour. After welcoming them, he asked A. R. Mosher to speak. "When he got up he referred very nicely to myself, saying they were glad that I was present. Glad to meet the Government. Glad I was looking so well; also that if it were true that I was thinking of dropping out of the leadership, they hoped I might be spared for many years in health and strength. There was good applause to his words of introduction.

"Pat Conroy read their memo which was quite long but very differently phrased than the one of the last two years. There was cordial reference at the outset and approval of the Government's action in regard to the U.N., E.A. generally and policy of helping Europe, etc. There was criticism of rising prices, etc., but all moderately phrased. The whole communication was different than those of other years. I asked Mitchell to reply first. He made one of his general statements, many platitudes. Not too helpful; brought in unnecessarily I thought references to Communism in Europe and Canada, not permitting developments here.

"Then I called on other members of the Government. St. Laurent spoke well. Ilsley very well, dealing with aspects of External Affairs. Howe was well received. Spoke well. Abbott was direct but made one slip, I thought, where he told them that wages were still ahead of prices in the uprise. There was a general outburst at that. Chevrier spoke nicely and Paul Martin made an excellent speech on what had been done in the way of social legislation. It really is phenomenal what has been done by our Government and indeed what Canada is paying out by way of redistribution of wealth. I was quite amazed myself to hear the story. It all illustrates how completely we have buried our light under a bushel and if we don't win, it is because we have had no organization either for organization or canvassing purposes.

"We ran about forty-five minutes over the time but I thought everything was going so well. Ministers were speaking in a sympathetic way: were in sympathetic mood. It was better to have it and let the interview continue. I concluded with a few words, first of all, saying I had chosen Ministers they were particularly anxious to hear because of what they had mentioned in their report. All of them had spoken about the tone of the memo and I did not hesitate to let them get away with compliment. I thought all present would remember what I had said two years ago about how I had felt in the way the report was presented. I thought I was more responsible than anyone for the different attitude and tone of today's report. I pointed out how different the whole meeting was when we got together and when we tried to make clear our position to each other and to co-operate instead of to coerce.

"I pointed out we would see from their statements what their difficulties were. They could see from ours some of the problems of government. We had to have regard for all classes – they presented in special forms those of one class; those largest in the community. I spoke of the wisdom of having more meetings of the kind where each could address the others and discover our common interest and then spoke of Canada's future depending on relations between the Government and representatives of organized Labour.

"I then thanked Mosher for his kind words of introduction which I said were greatly appreciated. I said that the last two days respecting meetings I had with Labour organizations had been particularly interesting to me, and not a little moving when I reflected that I had gone into politics, not because of politics but because of my interest in Labour. That I had found since the war that I had not the same strength that I used to have. That the years were telling and that I thought it was only right that younger men should take control of present day situations and that I should seek an opportunity – a little period of retirement at the same time. In a way, it was rounding out of the circle of my life's interests. They had begun with my interest in Labour rather than Politics. As I gave up politics, I hoped I would still have a chance for studying and reviewing in a larger way some of the great trends of our day which were affecting the well-being of masses of people, particularly Labour. If spared, I hoped to give much of my time at viewing these larger matters. It was not possible while one was in active politics.

"I went perhaps further in speaking about getting out of active politics than I have at any time up to the present. Heretofore I kept it confined to leadership. However, I felt that I would like my public career and in rounding it off, to have a special reference to Labour. I then wished them all well and hoped they would keep on constructive lines and see development through the years.

"I was loudly applauded by the gathering when it concluded. One after the other of the leaders came up and shook hands. Most of them, as I was going out of the room, came to shake hands. Conroy introduced me to his wife, then to other members. Altogether there was the kindest of feelings. I did refer to the joy it was, having in mind the years I had been in public life, to feel the attitude of friendship and good-will which had been expressed at the meeting, this morning. One after the other kept speaking about what a good morning it was. How well everything went. Insisted on my being photographed with them. I thought at first of hesitating but felt it was better. I had not wished my last photograph with Labour to be with this particular organization. However, there was no photograph taken yesterday; so they all seemed to want me to come down into the front row, which I did."

Throughout this period, the Prime Minister's approach to policy and political problems seemed to be almost wholly conditioned by his desire to avoid commitments on issues which might divide either the Cabinet or the party. On March 8 St. Laurent spoke to him about Pearson's interest in a political career. "Pearson had told him about conversations he had had with me previously about going into politics. St. Laurent would like to see him in public life. The problem was where to get the where-withal to give him the means of livelihood. St. Laurent asked me what I would think of having Pearson appointed to the Senate should he, St. Laurent, come into the Premiership; let him be Secretary of State for External Affairs. Claxton, he thought, should hold on to the very important Department he has in the light of the world's present conditions. I said of course I felt that External Affairs had become so important that the House would probably wish to have a Secretary of State for External Affairs in the House but as he himself had been Secretary of State, he might well say that he could handle the Commons end whereas it would be well to have the other House made a special centre of discussion of External Affairs. He thinks Pearson himself is anxious to get into politics. He wants to have somewhere where he can speak out his own mind fully and argue out questions himself. I told St. Laurent I certainly would like to see him in politics.

I thought he was leaning more and more in that direction. It would perhaps be wise his not doing too much speaking while he was Under-Secretary. What interested me particularly was to see with what confidence St. Laurent is already looking forward to taking over the Prime Ministership and being able to carry on. He is already working over the construction of his Ministry. I am glad of this but I feel pretty sure he will encounter difficulties that thus far he has scarcely dreamt of. Our majority is so small that it is going to be hard to keep the party together.

"Gardiner now wants to go to England at Easter for some ten days to deal with the wheat matter and it may be necessary to have him go. Reid is going out to the West for three weeks. Ilsley plans to be in British Columbia during the Easter Season. I shall be away for a few days. Anything may happen in some of these absences. However, I have no doubt we shall weather the storm until at least after the Convention. How soon the party may have to go to the country thereafter is a question. I rather imagine the election will come sooner than most expect and certainly sooner than I myself would like to see it come."

At the Cabinet meeting on March 18, the Minister of Agriculture sought approval for "a Bill to provide for the marketing of agricultural products in interprovincial and export trade. All Council excepting Gardiner, in previous years, have fought an attempt to bring in legislation of this kind. No one more strongly than Ilsley, both when Minister of Finance and Minister of Justice. When Gardiner said he should make clear that this did mean marketing legislation of the character to which some exception had been taken but that it had been narrowed down to a very small point and after all it was only authorizing legislation; that it meant control in the hands of the Federal Government. I looked over the measure with care and spoke out quite emphatically about it being I thought very unwise, and contrary altogether to anything we had consented to hitherto. Ilsley then spoke of what we had agreed to on coarse grains and that the principle of this measure was just the same. He could not see consistency between allowing the one and not the other. It appeared almost immediately that the whole purpose of the Bill was to enable the apple growers of Nova Scotia to have a monopoly in the sale of their products. That there was an effort to have it appear as related to British Columbia and some reference was made to its likely proving of effect in British Columbia elections. I was perfectly astounded when I heard Ilsley taking the line he was but, through the whole of his time in the Cabinet, there is one thing he has allowed to control his judgment regardless of his convictions on other things – that is the apple growers in Nova Scotia and his own constituency. Years ago, he fought the arrangement with the United Kingdom on the score that it would affect them adversely. He was not going to go to the League in case something might be done in his absence. He has got large subsidies through to help them. Now he is prepared to go any length, no matter what precedent it may be setting or to what it may lead to protect this special interest.

"I spoke as quietly as possible. First asked Abbott a question as to whether the Government had in mind possibly further agreements on trade with the United States and asked if this might not embarrass the situation. There was some general comment that they did not think so. Clearly that aspect had not been looked into. Howe was the one who spoke out emphatically against the Bill. He said if this was to be done for apple growers in Nova Scotia, why could not the potato growers in Prince Edward Island be entitled to some protection and monopoly. I asked about the fishermen. Someone said they had not a co-operative union. . . ."

To Mackenzie King, the sole objective of the legislation was to create a monopoly. "I was a bit surprised at St. Laurent who had fought almost viciously earlier this year as to why we had to pay a cent a piece for apples or more, when apples were in such abundance and they were rotting in other parts of the Dominion. That he should have spoken about co-operative work in the maple sugar industry as having greatly improved the quality, etc. A means of giving partial help to what Ilsley was saying. I at once pointed out that this was exactly what Mr. Motherwell [a former Minister of Agriculture] himself had boasted was the great achievement of the Department of Agriculture and that it was their duty to see that marketing of products was done by having them properly graded and no special virtue of any one concern.

"St. Laurent did say a little that was questioning as to the legislation but it was clear that some understanding had been reached whereby because of coarse grain concessions having been made to the three Western provinces, that Ilsley would get some help on this measure. Abbott seemed to me to speak just off the bat. Was impatient to get legislation out of the way and was prepared to let it go through on the score that it did not go too far. The rest of the members of Council were perfectly silent though I could see they were agreeing with me, particularly MacKinnon but all seemed afraid to say a word. I then repeated some of the arguments I had made before and pointed out that the world of today was seeking to remove restraint of trade and to establish greater freedom. We were backing the Geneva Agreements for this reason. Moreover there was a possibility we would wish to make further agreements with the United States. I thought anything of this kind would be most embarrassing. That the B.N.A. Act had established principle of freedom of trade as between the provinces. This was wholly contrary to the letter and spirit of the Act. It was doing by other means the very thing it was sought to prevent and to guarantee against when Confederation was formed.

"I pointed out if this was allowed in one industry, it would lead to all industries seeking like monopolies. It was wholly contrary to the whole doctrine and principle of Liberalism. I said moreover it clearly was helping to foster combines in restraint of trade. As I was the author of the Combines Investigation Act, I certainly could not support a measure of the kind. I added that I was not anxious, however, to have a difference with any colleague; that if I happened to be present when Council decided, I would have to ask that my name be recorded against the legislation. I thought it was preferable it should be brought up, if Council were determined on the matter, on some day when I was not present. I would of course have to take responsibility for not being present but I certainly could not support a measure of the kind in the light of what I knew to be Liberal policy and what had been followed by the administration right along.

"I then gave the Bill to Heeney to put back on his files. I find Ilsley extremely difficult. Nothing, however, could better illustrate the workings of his mind and conscience than his attitude on this measure. I shall be surprised if Council deals with it in my absence.

"I don't know where we would be in the House of Commons if a Bill ' of the kind came in at this time when Geneva and other agreements are to the fore. . . ."

These policy differences with some of his senior colleagues Mackenzie King found "more trying . . . than anything else, specially when in the back of my mind is the necessity for the greatest kind of consideration on the part of colleagues in the light of what they knew we may have to carry at this time. Clearly I have been very wise in having announced when I did my intention to retire in August. A clean cut, I believe, will be the wisest course to take. Gardiner is becoming increasingly socialistic and by professing to be Liberal, above all else, is really responsible for more in the way of furthering some Conservative policies than other members of the Government."

On March 19 the Prime Minister had a talk with Walter Tucker who was leaving for Saskatchewan to assume the provincial Liberal leadership. He was considerably impressed. Tucker had "developed into a fine man and an able leader. Tried to give him words of encouragement. Spoke of how well he had presented matters in the House. Advised him to save his strength all he could; not to allow them to have him go hither and thither in the province. Take all the rest possible. Not to try to answer what the people will say in their method of attack. Keep dignified. Advised him to have his men do the same, and on the last day of the campaign, he could draw attention to the mud that had been thrown and make capital of asking people if that was the kind of thing they sanctioned in the Government of their province.

"I told him I thought he had made able representations in Caucus. Been most helpful and had a splendid career before him. He is a real loss to us in the federal field. However, he may be back again. He has played a very chivalrous and fine role. He spoke exceedingly nicely about what it meant to him to be under my leadership, as he called it, and he added he was certain it was going to be very difficult for me to get out of the leadership if times became serious. I told him on no account would I stay on indefinitely. I wished him well in all his work."

Two days later, Gardiner came to see the Prime Minister about his own leadership ambitions. "After a short conversation about regional pacts, etc., he said to me he was thinking of going to the Convention. I did not know just what he meant. I said: What Convention? He said: the Liberal Convention in August. He then said to me: Are you going to stay on? If you are, I would not on any consideration become a candidate but I am considering it. Some of my friends want me to, and I may decide to be a candidate. I said to him there was no chance in the world of my considering staying on. That of course if war or something came, there might be circumstances which would make a difference but otherwise I was anxious to get out of leadership, out of Parliament, and out of the House of Commons. I was feeling pretty weary when I spoke to him. I made no comment on the wisdom of his being a candidate but said: As you know, Gardiner, I am taking no sides as between any of my colleagues or otherwise. It is true the people say that I want St. Laurent to be elected. What I want is every member of the Government to feel that as between my colleagues, I am taking no part. It is for the Convention to make the choice. He said he understood that. He was going to Saskatchewan tonight. I must say I was rather amazed at his thinking of running for the leadership of the party though I have been told that he has had that ambition right along.

"I cannot believe he would carry the Convention though he might make serious division in the ranks of the party. I would have thought he would be behind St. Laurent but apparently he is not. That might mean a contest in which race and religion would play a part that I would be sorry to see come up."

The imminence of his own retirement and the party's slim majority in the House of Commons obviously coloured the Prime Minister's attitude in one of the strangest episodes during the early months of 1948, a series of secret negotiations with the United States about a reciprocal free trade arrangement between the two countries. On January 13 Mackenzie King had prepared a memorandum summarizing an interview he had had that day with the Minister of Finance. Abbott reported that "on his last visit to Washington, where he had met Harriman, Lovett, and several others, the Americans themselves had brought up the question of complete reciprocity treaty with Canada. He and the officials of his Department, Clark and Deutsch, had been working on the extension of the present treaties, and the increase in the number of the articles there are in them. The question of a commercial union had come up. I do not know by whom. At all events, it was discounted at once, certainly in Abbott's mind, and I told him would be equally so in mine. That the word 'commercial' would soon be dropped in political discussions and the campaign be on the question of union with the States. However, if a treaty of complete reciprocity, such as in Sir Wilfrid's day, was before the country, [it] would, I told him, . . . meet with a different kind of reception. The country had learned they had made a mistake in not accepting the treaty in Sir Wilfrid's day. What we had since achieved in reciprocity would have prepared the public mind for a complete reciprocity.

"Abbott wanted to know if I would be agreeable to a discussion going ahead on the official level on complete reciprocity. I told him I would, but by all means to lose no time in furthering it. I think he said that Clark, of the Finance Department, was very strongly for it, and would welcome negotiations, which I imagine McKinnon would also share in. What Abbott emphasized was that the proposal was not his, but had come from the Americans themselves. He spoke of the talk with Harriman and of Harriman sending warmest remembrances to me. Abbott himself pointed out that this would be the answer to all our present restrictions. If we could get complete reciprocity, he felt we would no longer be dependent on uncertain markets of Europe, which are bound to be uncertain for some time and that this would give what was needed to maintain, as far as could be maintained, the prosperity of our country.

"Abbott felt sure, of course, there might be opposition from manufacturers and especially in Ontario. I said he need not mind that. Our industries were holding their own pretty effectively with larger industries. Could expect one hundred percent approval all along the line.

"The real points were:

(1) the matter having been suggested by the United States;

(2) his own discussion with leading men in finance; and

(3) strong feeling in Finance Department – Clark, Towers and Deutsch, who were all favourable;

(4) approval of proceedings on official level. My own approval strongly given. It is clear to me that the Americans are losing no opportunity to make their relations as close as possible with our country."

Writing on February 13, Mackenzie King referred to a conversation with Abbott a week or ten days earlier "in which he spoke of very secret negotiations with Washington of a Treaty with Canada which would give us wide entrance into the United States market. He had been asked if it would be all right if the United States went ahead – with the possibility of the Treaty coming before Congress before the summer. Both Abbott and I agreed that the measure was of such advantages to Canada that we should not risk the chance of [not] having an agreement of the kind made. I told him he could say that he and I were agreed, that our Government would be prepared to ask Parliament to support a Treaty of the kind, should it be negotiated before mid-summer."

The Prime Minister's next reference to the negotiations was on March 6 when Abbott called "to give me further particulars of the progress being made in trade negotiations with the United States. He said that today the United States officials are bringing the matter to the attention of the Under-Secretary of State, Lovett. The proposal now is that Lovett will bring the matter up to Marshall and it will later go to the President but the United States will try to secure the support of the leading Republicans in the Senate before giving publicity to what is proposed. Taft of the Senate still holds to his father's view as to greater freedom of trade with Canada and will support a measure of the kind. From what Abbott told me, it now appears that the United States are prepared to make an agreement, if need be for twenty-five years, abolishing all tariffs between Canada and the United States. They, on their part, will reserve the right to fix a certain quota on cattle, fish, potatoes and on other commodities. But the quota in each case would be larger than those at present are, that we would have under increased quotas under the Geneva Agreements.

"We, on our part, would be given the right to restrict for a period of time certain of the commodities which we are now securing from the United States. This would be for a transitional period.

"As to wheat, there would be some special agreement. We would be free to offer the same conditions to the United Kingdom. We might even consider were it not for butter, etc., offering similar conditions to all the nations of the Commonwealth. The Agreement represents a tremendous advance toward freedom of trade throughout a large part of the world. Instead of proceeding by resolution of both Houses, the Americans would probably proceed by the concluding of a Treaty. They would like to get the matter before Congress in April.

"Abbott said he had mentioned the matter to no one in the Government other than St. Laurent and that but slightly. I told him it would be well for him to tell St. Laurent the whole situation before Abbott's officials, Deutsch and McKinnon, return to Washington tomorrow.

"I strongly advised Abbott to let us clear up all matters concerning the United States trade as rapidly as we can, so as to have them out of the way before this new transaction comes up in Parliament."

Mackenzie King discussed the matter with Abbott again on March 16. "Told him to read with care what *Life* has on a suggested commercial union. I was relieved to hear him make clear that what is being criticized and what we had agreed to in our previous talks together, was not any immediate complete free trade but rather trade so arranged as to make possible the gradual integrating of our systems along lines of the Hyde Park Agreement."

At another meeting on March 22, St. Laurent, Howe, Clark, McKinnon and Deutsch were present. "Deutsch outlined to myself and other Ministers what had taken place at Washington in the way of exploration of possibilities of further trade relations with the United States," Mackenzie King wrote. "McKinnon and Deutsch have been in conference with opposite numbers on the official level in the State Department. They had worked out a tentative agreement along lines previously mentioned in part to me by Abbott. In a word, the picture was ultimate free trade between Canada and the United States. During the interval in the next five years, Canada maintaining the restricted measures she has found it necessary to place to enable her gradually to get an equal financial balance in trade matters. The thought, however, was that there would be certain quota arrangements which the United States would retain but which would be larger than those granted us by [the] Geneva [negotiations] and really larger than we would be able to fill. These quotas would affect such articles as cattle, potatoes, a certain kind of fish in the Maritimes, and other articles. One question over which there had been considerable difficulty was wheat, but now that the international wheat agreement had come into being, it could govern the question of wheat export. Canada was to be free to accord the same treatment to the United Kingdom as Canada was according to the United States.

"Deutsch made an excellent presentation. What I have recorded here is the barest outline. Other features where agreement could be for twenty-five years; also if Ministers agreed to what was proposed, the matter would then be put up to the Secretary of State and the President. Up to the present, it has not got beyond the Assistant Secretary of State. Two or three of the United States Ministers would be brought into the secret first. The

President would be the one to approach the Secretary of Agriculture Anderson who would be a difficult person to deal with. The idea was to have agreement by Party in the United States, that is to say Republicans as well as Democrats would have to agree to it, or matters would not proceed further.

"It was thought that Vandenburg and Taft of the Republicans would favour such an agreement. The United States would wish to have the matter public by the 15th of May."

To Mackenzie King, there were "two important aspects I felt I should speak of; one was . . . the question of timing. I admitted that the agreement, if it could be brought into being, could be of tremendous benefit to Canada. The point to be considered still was the element of timing. That my experience in politics had taught me that no matter how good a thing might be, if the people were taken by surprise in its presentation, there was bound to be opposition to it. That they had to be led gradually into the appreciation of what it would mean. I felt perfectly sure that if this agreement were announced in the House of Commons, something which had already been arranged, and had to be approved by Parliament, there would be instant opposition from the Conservatives, and they would keep up that opposition very strongly. The cry would be raised at once that it was commercial union that we were after. So far as I was concerned, I would be a liability rather than an asset in the picture inasmuch as the Tories would say this is Mr. King's toy. He has always wanted annexation with the States. Now he is making his last effort toward that end. The press would not grasp the details. I doubted myself whether I had mental energy and physical strength to make an explanation in the House of Commons such as had been made to us by Deutsch. If that explanation had to be gotten over to the public from the Commons, I did not know how that would be done with the details what they were. The size of the agreement what it was, etc.

"It would be represented that we were seeking to separate from Britain. I said I would feel no matter what happened that we would have to offer Britain the same rights in our market as we were offering the Americans. All present agreed that it was so.

"I concluded by saying that if the matter had to be settled in so short a space of time in relation to trade alone, I certainly felt it pretty doubtful that we should give our consent to it."

The second aspect, the Prime Minister continued, was more "far reaching" and "might make not only possible but easy of realization what was being sought on this extension of trade – on the line of this increase in reciprocal trade. I said I would have to swear three members of the [civil] Service present to absolute secrecy and to tell them that, at the moment, negotiations were on at Washington for the establishing of an Atlantic Security Pact – negotiations between the United Kingdom, United States and Canada. The stage, at the moment, was on exploration only. That I felt trade proposals might be made to fit as it were into the larger Atlantic Pact. That if, for example, the Atlantic Security Pact were agreed upon and were brought before Parliament and be passed as it certainly would be, we might immediately follow thereafter with trade agreement as being something which still further helped to further the object of the Pact, namely the removal of restrictions to trade within the area arranged by the Pact.

"It might even lead to the United States and United Kingdom coming to more in the way of greater freedom of trade between them. I felt that both the United States and the United Kingdom would go very far in the direction of anything that would disclose a closer unity of interest between them. That, later, certain other countries, France, for example, might be brought into a larger, freer trade area, etc. All three – Clark, Deutsch and McKinnon – were strongly taken with the idea. They had not known of what is being considered in the nature of a security pact though Deutsch mentioned that the Americans had asked them if some security feature might not be added. They said they could not speak of this. On the other hand, the fact that the security had been mentioned seemed to suggest that the Americans who proposed it did have some knowledge of what was going to be worked out for security purposes and might be thinking of combining the two. Armour, Hickerson, Under-Secretary of State Lovett, and one or two others would have a knowledge of both.

"I suggested it might be well for Clark to get in touch with Pearson at once and have a word with him about possible consideration of the two matters in relation to each other as I had indicated them. All present agreed with that.

"I then told those present that I felt I should make clear to them not only that I was likely to be a liability rather than an asset as I had indicated that the Tory attack would be that I had wanted annexation, and this could mean separation from Britain, etc., but that I was really not in any shape to aid a movement of the kind in Canada. That I had not the mental power. Was feeling fatigued and exhausted, now I was incapable of another general election campaign. That I could not do justice to the situation in the House of Commons and that this was a factor which would have to be taken into account. I said I was even beginning to doubt my own judgment on many matters. I found myself much too cautious and conservative in international matters to feel my views were shared by some of the younger men around me.

"I had great difficulty in being prepared to go the lengths they wished to go in the time they wished to take. I felt I should not be counted upon for a battle of the kind much as I believed in the wisdom of what was proposed. I simply had not myself what was needed to put it over. I said I might come to have a different view after a bit of a rest and change. Just at present, I was anything but equal to international negotiations of any kind. I said I thought I ought to say that I believed the Americans in their attitude were carrying out what I felt was really their policy and had been so over many years, of seeking to make this Continent one. That I thought they had long seen that a conflict likely to come would be between Russia and themselves, and that they had felt that their position would be strengthened if they controlled all of North America. That I myself frequently felt I knew they did not want to bring this about by any conflict but that it was simply a farsighted view as to what would be wisest in the changes that would come with them. If I were an American, I might easily share that point of view. I said that, while I had recognized it, I had never allowed it to gain any headway in my own dealings with public affairs. That personally I would rather have Canada kept within the orbit of the British Commonwealth of Nations than to come within that of the United States. That all my efforts had been in that direction. It had always been said that any change that would come on this side in matter of political allegiance would be due to what happened here instead of other parts of the world. I thought we could keep all of this in mind in anything that was done at this time to see that all British considerations were taken into account."

Talking alone with Hector McKinnon after the others had left, Mackenzie King was informed that "the Americans had said they did hope, if the matter came to where it was one of political parties, that I would head the movement in Canada. That my name and long public career would give a lead to the situation; nothing else could. I mentioned to Hector that the President was coming to Williamsburg to say he was there to pay a tribute to me and my years of public life. That I had never allowed occasions of the kind to go to my head. That I knew the President was not coming to Williamsburg on my personal account. It was to help to further the larger ends which the United States had in view. That I thought my strength had lain in the fact that I had seen clearly the significance of moves of the kind in all my relations with the President and others. That that had really helped me in continuing to hold the position I have for so long. Hector said that he was sure the people realized that. He said that the trouble was that most of our men who got into new arenas, suddenly believed it was they, themselves, who were so important.

"Later, this afternoon, I told Mr. St. Laurent quite frankly as I saw the proposal on the trade matter, it was certain once it was introduced in the House, Conservatives would block it steadily until the end of June when Parliament would adjourn. If we came back at the end of the summer, they would block it again. That I did not think the Government could use closure.

"Also that I felt the blocking would go on until Parliament would have to be dissolved and a general election take place. Mr. St. Laurent said that he thought so far as our chances and the electorate of Canada were concerned, we did not need this issue to help us win. The public felt we were the best Government that Canada could have, and that the Government would be returned on that score. To make a new issue was not necessarily going to be an aid to us as a Government. This, I think, is very true. I told him, however, that if an election came, I would have to ask the Governor General to call on him to take office. I could not be induced on any score to go through a campaign. I mentioned having seen Taussig who was a strong man physically at Harvard come down suddenly and be in a wheel chair for one or two years after. I could not take risks of the kind. I made it quite clear that I could not take on these greater responsibilities at my age.

"Speaking all together in the morning, I dwelt strongly on this. I said I just could not see clearly or think clearly on some of these matters after a certain amount of time of the day was gone. That Hughes, the Chief Justice of the United States, had told me at Banff he could work in the morning and a certain length of time in the afternoon but could do nothing after that; if he did, he was not in shape for work the next day. I said that I was finding myself in a similar condition. It was not the burden of years merely but the burden of cares and the reviving of old issues which was making it more difficult for me to get through anew what I had experienced before in the way of strain."

Later in the diary for that day he reflected that he was "really so depressed and weary in my head that I wanted to get away from everything. What has been suggested to me today is almost the largest proposal that, short of war, any leader of a Government has been looked to to undertake. Its possibilities are so far reaching for good on one hand, but possible disaster if project were defeated that I find it necessary to reflect a good deal before attempting a final decision."

On March 24 the Prime Minister "had a talk with Wilson of the Financial Post of Toronto who also was anxious to get my views on greater freedom of trade or total freedom of trade between the United States and Canada. He was going to talk with a group in the States. I asked him whether he had been invited to talk to them or was going down to talk.

He told me it was a group that was studying these matters. He was anxious to get my views as to the line the Government would regard as most appropriate. I was most careful to indicate to him there were considerations such as the present condition of the world, the position of Britain at the present time. Her effort at rehabilitation. Many other considerations which will have to be taken into account in studying the tariffs. Gave him nothing in a final way but gave him to understand that I would not favour such a thing as commercial union, etc.

"I now want to record a quite extraordinary experience which I took to be a perfect evidence of guidance from Beyond. This morning, apropos of nothing but feeling I ought to look at some book, I drew out from my shelves a volume entitled 'Studies in Colonial Nationalism' by Jebb. A book I have not looked at in twenty years. Did not like the title – either Colonial or Nationalism and had forgotten having read it with care. Looked first at page 124 – reference to Sir Wilfrid. I found myself looking with interest to the last chapter of all which was entitled 'The Soul of Empire.' Was amazed to see how completely the views there expressed accorded with my own. The desire for fuller independence of the Commonwealth, at the same time preserving the unity of the Empire, etc. . . . A true picture.

"When I had read them, I had felt they were significant in reference to the proposals being made to me to support the programme of complete freedom of trade between the United States and Canada which I have felt to be exceedingly dangerous, specially at this time, as calculated to raise an issue that would be very serious. In the first place, I do not believe it could be successful but for me to be placed in the position of being the spearhead of furthering a commercial union as the last act of my career would be to absolutely destroy the significance of the whole of it. The Tory party would make out that from the beginning my whole vision had been to further annexation. I was really at heart anti-British, etc. Everything opposite of the truth. Strangely enough, this afternoon, thinking on the importance of this question, I began to discuss some phases of it with P. without revealing what has been under way. To my amazement, I found he had been giving a lot of thought to this question and had been terribly concerned about it. He volunteered the statement that he knew Clark of the Department of Finance felt it was the only way we could come to balance our accounts with the States and was pressing very strongly for something of the kind. He used the expression that we would absolutely be selling the soul of the people, meaning the whole relationship with Britain and the Commonwealth. The use of that word brought at once the title of the chapter I had read in the morning. The fact that one of the men I talked with spoke of Cockshutt brought back to my mind that Abbott had referred to Cockshutt as evidence of how some of the big employers had completely reversed their early position and were now favourable to freedom of trade.

"Each thing that happened today in the interviews seemed to bring confirmation of what I had felt about the whole business when I read the article on Colonial Nationalism. I felt wholly convinced that the taking out of that book, and reading that chapter was no matter of chance but had been inspired from some source in the Beyond. I would no more think of, at my time of life and at this stage of my career, attempting any movement of the kind than I would of flying to the South Pole."

Next day he had a further talk about the problems with Pickersgill and later with St. Laurent. "Told him I thought the whole proposal had come from Clark of the Finance Department but that, while it might be sound economically, I believed it would be fatal politically. Quite impossible of carrying out at this time in the limited time that was being suggested. It was the sort of thing that would require months, if not years of education. It would be most unfortunate if an issue of that kind came in a year of the Convention, such as the present – a year of threatening peril. I could think of nothing that would destroy my name and reputation more than to be made the spearhead of a political fight which would be twisted into a final endeavour to bring about economic union with the United States, which would mean annexation and separation from Britain. I said I doubted if Ilsley or Gardiner would support a proposal of the kind. St. Laurent said that he himself had felt when he learned of what was suggested, that the proposal was hardly likely to be feasible. That he had thought it might have been developed between now and the time of the Liberal Convention and make a plank for the platform there. He also agreed that Howe and Abbott were very strong for it because of the concrete problem they are dealing with, and as believing it to be the one and only solution. I am afraid they would create a still larger problem. He was not too sure how Quebec or some other parts would view giving Britain the same freedom of trade as the United States. That there were sure to be misrepresentations there. I let him know I was giving him my views because I would be absent and did not wish anything settled on this matter without having a final say."

Before leaving for Williamsburg on March 29, Mackenzie King had lunch with Pearson. "I was glad P. was present. It is apparent that he [Pearson] had come to arrange to have further explorations made of the trade matters at the instance of Clark and others, that negotiations at Washington might be further developed. I told him quite frankly I doubted very much the wisdom of attempting anything that had to be brought on within the next month. Did not think this matter should be brought before the public at this time with the situation what it was. To have that situation in American elections, proceedings in Parliament and Canadian elections probably forced, my thought is it would be a terrible mistake and would defeat its very ends. I said I had a strong feeling I could not possibly undertake the kind of campaign that would be required nor did I think it was in Britain's interests and our own at this time. The campaign to which it would give rise would be a vicious one. Not at all the kind I would wish to have to do with myself."

In Washington the next day, the Prime Minister "brought up the trade matter" in a conversation with Hume Wrong. "Pearson evidently had given him the impression that I was not favourable to proceeding on account of the limited time in which decisions would have to be made. Conversation was kept for the most part on the matter of time. I pointed out my experience in Laurier's Cabinet re reciprocity; also the fears that would be aroused if the matter was sprung suddenly and would have to be settled within a limited time. I added [that] if agreed to by both political parties in the United States, fears would be greater than otherwise. Would have old questions of commercial union and annexation, etc., brought up again. With conditions in Europe what they are, that would be most deplorable if a matter like this added to the confusion of the present year and in the House as well. I referred to what would happen in the House of Commons where the Conservatives would hold up everything until the end of June, again in the Autumn and would force an election in which the party might be badly defeated.

"Wrong said the suggestion I had made about leaving a clause in the pact for economic, social and other considerations had been agreed to. That Hickerson had gone over the draft and included something that was pretty certain to be agreed to at tomorrow's meeting. Wrong pointed out that the trade thing might evolve out of that in time. He said that he, himself, had been doubtful from the start about the possibility of getting anything of that magnitude through in so short a time. . . . But it was doubtful if conditions in the United States would ever be as favourable as they are at the moment.

"Wrong said even if we did give England the same advantages, he could see where there might be difficulties in time. I pointed out that the issue was very large. That unquestionably came back to what the future of Canada either in the British Commonwealth or as a part of the United States will be. I said I felt sure that the long objective of the Americans was to control this Continent. They would want to get Canada under their aegis. If I was an American, I would have the same view specially considering Russia's position, etc. On the other hand, I did not feel we would be as well off . . . [as] a State of the Union as we will be possibly as the greatest of the self-governing portions of the British Commonwealth of Nations. At any rate, I would not want myself to take a position contrary to this. Wrong replied that certainly our form of Government was much better than that of the United States. But it seemed to me, however, in talking, as if both Wrong and Stone were a little disappointed that matters were not likely to be proceeded with. I had the same feeling in talking with Pearson. I am afraid most of External Affairs have become imbued with the attention they have received from the Americans and the place the Americans have allowed them to take in the foreground of international affairs. I said quite frankly I thought the United States was using the United Nations as an arm of their foreign office just as the French Foreign Office had used the League of Nations for a similar purpose in their country. . . ."

On April 21 the Prime Minister met with Abbott, Howe, St. Laurent, Pearson and McKinnon. "The two latter were anxious to get final word from the Government as to whether they could proceed with the tariff negotiations which were being conducted on the official level. The time they thought had come when matters should be brought to the attention of the President. The Acting Secretary of State Lovett, and the Secretary of State Marshall, and Harriman, Secretary of Commerce, being already in the know. Pearson read a carefully prepared statement of exactly what was proposed. There were two features in the statement to which I drew attention.

"I kept fairly quiet so as to let others speak out. Abbott did not hesitate to express very emphatically the fears he had come to have about the impossibility of getting an agreement through in the time that was suggested and with the hope of being able to get the Canadian public sufficiently informed to ensure approval of a treaty based upon it. Howe was more inclined to urge very strongly going ahead but before the afternoon was over, conceded that it would perhaps be impossible in so short a time to effect a satisfactory result.

"St. Laurent made clear that he too had great concern about the possibility of getting anything through so quickly. Mike Pearson had read his memo and drew attention to certain of its features, on the time within which matters as now proposed would have to be completed. I conceded that the logic of the argument was strong, and that if economic grounds alone had to be considered, there could be little doubt that arrangement proposed might be most helpful in meeting Canada's problem. I said, however, that my first concern was of necessity with the political end. Pointed out we had only a little over two more months before Parliament would be adjourned. That I could not imagine the form of a treaty being brought in without the Conservative party blocking its progress. That we would find we would get nowhere before the end of June. If we came back in the autumn, we would continue to be blocked by obstruction and would have to dissolve and go to the country on the issue. Between now and June, there would likely be five provincial elections in Canada, this year. Ontario, one already announced. In addition, there was the Liberal Convention. I thought that would be the place where the party would have to agree on a clause which would govern all matters of trade relations with the States. I stressed strongly that regardless of what the economic facts might be, the issue would turn on union with the States and separation from Britain and this at a very critical time. I also pointed out the possibility of war. All great anxiety in the course of ensuing months. Pointed out, too, that the fact that it was proposed both political parties in the States would join, would be a detriment rather than an advantage in getting acceptance of the treaty in Canada. . . . I said the proper way to proceed would be by general resolution in the House which would get acceptance of the principle, first, and later bring in the treaty. Pearson and McKinnon kept speaking of it being unfortunate if the Americans got the impression that they had made an offer and were turned down. We pointed out that no offer had come to the Government thus far. That we would have to take all our colleagues into our confidence before giving an answer. It was felt that this would be too dangerous at this stage. That to get an agreement through between now and the time of the general election in the States, was simply out of the question. All were finally agreed that this would have to be made known to the Americans, and that, at once.

"Curiously enough, they were saying that the final decision would have to be made within two weeks. I pointed out that never before in international relations, had it been thought that a transaction of such a size would be consummated in so short a time. It is an interesting fact that on this particular day, it should have fallen to my lot again to take the stand I have from the outset in this matter. I am sure in so doing, I have made one of the most important decisions for Canada, for the British Commonwealth of Nations, that has been made at any time."

Apparently convinced that the matter had been settled, Mackenzie King on May 5 "was astounded to receive a memo from Pearson enclosing a letter from Hume Wrong to him in which Wrong stated that, when Howe was at Washington, he had informed Lovett that senior members of the Cabinet had been attracted by the trade proposals and would be prepared to make an agreement on the basis of what had been suggested. A little later on, indicating the possibility of our dissolving Parliament to go to the country on the agreement. . . .

"I spoke to Mr. St. Laurent about the matter. He had seen the memo but was somewhat non-committal. Said there must be some exaggeration or misstatement but seemed hesitant about saying much concerning it. He agreed, however, when I talked with him later that there had been no undertaking with respect to an agreement [and] that the whole business had been pretty much confined to the question of the wisdom of proceeding at all, seeing that a certain limited time had been fixed within which negotiations would have to be concluded.

"At six o'clock, I had Howe come to my office. Read him over the statement. He took instant and sharp issue with what was set forth in Wrong's letter. He began by saying that Wrong had taken him to see Lovett. He was not anxious to go to see him and did not altogether wish to. Wrong had expressed a desire for it and had gone. He said he never made any suggestion of our being ready to make an agreement at any time. He had said something about the procedure that would be necessary, etc.

"My own opinion is that in matters of the kind, Howe is almost an innocent abroad. Bases conversation on what he has heard without regard as to whether he should be imparting the information to others. For bargaining purposes, etc., nothing could be worse than what he appears to have said. I don't think Wrong could have misunderstood what Howe was saying though I do think he may perhaps have been over-anxious to get the negotiations pinned down to a certain point, and that in a way that would commit the Government to a point from which negotiations would have to proceed later on."

Next day the Prime Minister told Pearson of his talk with Howe, "and suggested he, himself, should have a talk with Howe. I said to him I thought I would write him a memo as I did not think there should be any misunderstanding on the matter. I did not try to pronounce judgment as between Wrong and Howe but said to him that clearly the alleged statement was wrong and the whole government would get into a terribly false position if it were to go unanswered in the form in which it had been set forth in writing. Also I thought the American Government should be advised at once of the true position. I confess I get alarmed beyond measure at the casual way in which a few officials take it into their hands to try and settle the great national policies; force the hands of the Government, etc. without having the least knowledge of the political side of matters of the kind or the least kind of political judgment. A measure of the kind proposed, if proceeded with by other than the most careful, educational effort in advance, and sounding out of all parts of the country, might throw the Liberal party of Canada into oblivion.

"I told Pearson that while I might miss to be the head of the Government, I would never cease to be a Liberal or a British citizen and if I thought there was a danger of Canada being placed at the mercy of powerful financial interests in the United States, and if that was being done by my own party, I would get out and oppose them openly. It is only too clear that Clark with McKinnon and Deutsch and Towers of the Bank of Canada have all got it into their heads that this is the only way to balance trade with the United States.

"Howe has got the absurd idea that what complete freedom of trade would mean is that Canada would be piling her manufactured goods into the United States. . . . I wonder what is going to happen when this comes up for discussion anew.

"Yesterday I had the feeling I might like to stay on in the Cabinet as the President of the Council as has been suggested so as to assist the members of the Government until the election is over without contesting any seat myself or entering the campaign to any extent.

"I begin, however, to debate anew whether, if situations of this kind are likely to arise, I would not be wiser to get out of politics altogether. Take no further part even in the House of Commons. The last thing I want over the years I have worked with fellow members of the party is to end up with any real disagreement with colleagues.

"After returning to the House this afternoon, I wrote a letter and memo of some length to Pearson that the whole situation might be in writing without the possibility of any misunderstanding. But for taking this step, I am sure real trouble would arise in the future." There are no further references to this episode in the diary and the discussions with United States officials appear to have been broken off at this time.

# CHAPTER SEVEN

# Pre-Convention Preparations

WHEN THE PRIME MINISTER went to Williamsburg in April 1948 to receive an honorary degree from William and Mary University he planned to be away from Ottawa for about ten days. Though he enjoyed the visit, particularly the brief meeting with President Truman, he decided on Sunday, April 4, that "it was my duty to return to Canada without delay. I would not be happy being away from there with the situation what it is in Berlin at the moment, Cabinet without myself present and Parliament reassembling tomorrow. While I need a rest and will try to take some days off this week in Ottawa, I am sure I can get more of a rest by being in my own rooms at Laurier House or at Kingsmere than anywhere else at this time. I felt too it was fitting that I should return with the Governor General and that really to stop off at Washington or New York was more for little social pleasure than for aught else. Accordingly, I gave definite plans to start off in the morning."

As he was leaving for the airport the next day, Mackenzie King was informed that Mrs. John D. Rockefeller had died just after returning to New York from Arizona. The flight to Ottawa was without incident. At dinner that evening, St. Laurent told the Prime Minister about an increase in freight rates which had been announced that day by the Board of Transport Commissioners. Although anticipating a political furore, they agreed that nothing would be gained by reversing or otherwise interfering with the decision.

The meeting of the Liberal caucus on April 13 was devoted to discussion of an Opposition supply motion objecting to the increase in freight rates. The Cabinet had already decided, after "a good discussion in which Chevrier made a first rate presentation," not to intervene. At the caucus, the Prime Minister reported, "Chevrier outlined his position which he repeated later in the House, this afternoon. I was suffering from a very heavy cold and had to send to get my overcoat because of the change in the atmosphere of the House. Temperature in the Committee room. I told the party I had come to make clear the position we were in. There were two matters we had to consider. One, the question of our individual views on freight rates. How they were to be expressed, etc. The second was our attitude towards motion if carried which would mean the defeat of the Government. I pointed out that the motion before the House was not to go into Committee of Supply. That up to the present, not a dollar of supply had been voted. No Government could carry on without supply. Mr. Coldwell had moved to strike out the motion to go into supply. To substitute for it a motion which meant there was no confidence in the Government. I said that motion could only be carried as a result of the attitude of our own men. If our majority was small and if men stayed away, or voted against the Government, we would be defeated and defeated by our own Members. There would be nothing left then for me to do but to go immediately to the Governor General.

"Would point out that the Government had been defeated by its own followers and other Members in the House. I should then tender my resignation. I would be asked who I would send for. I would reply it was no use sending for Bracken, he could not form a Government. No use sending for Coldwell, he could not form a Government. The only advice I could give would be to grant a dissolution in Parliament. I said dissolution would certainly be granted. My next step would be to come back. Call the party together and tell them what had been decided. Let them know that Parliament would be dissolved, and an election take place. I would then have to ask them to select the leader that was to lead the party through the campaign. I must make very clear to them on no circumstances would I undertake to lead the party after its defeat, or indeed through another general election. My decision on that score was irrevocable. They would then have to choose their Leader. Have an election at the worst possible time for the party. Time when question of prices was at its height. Question of freight rates to the fore. Other matters that had arisen out of the war creating complication and with no definite programme.

"I then said consider what is the alternative. The alternative was to be sure that the Government got through with this Parliament. That at a Liberal Convention, the leader would be chosen. New platform set out. New leader would have a chance to go through the country; would have the backing of the party from one end of the country to the other. A good chance of winning the election.

"I added that I doubted very much the wisdom of allowing an election at this time, while conditions were so serious in Europe. I said that anything might arise, even in the course of the present week. I then said quite openly in Caucus when I had come back last November I had told the Cabinet but had not told the public, that I had gathered that when the spring of this year came, around the beginning of April, the Russians would begin to try to make it impossible for the Americans and the British to get into their own zones of Berlin. This might occasion some active conflict and that while I am not hoping for war, someone might be killed and in no time a conflagration would start in Berlin itself which would lead to the Russians immediately taking a step that would enable them to sweep across Europe through France and the other countries to the sea. Take possession of the whole of Europe.

"I said I did not think members of Caucus took much stock of what I had said at the time. Seemed to think it was fanciful but now it had all come to pass, almost literally as I had outlined it. I then said I would feel tremendously relieved when this week was over. If the Italian elections went through without incident, there might be a breathing space. Something of a very serious nature might happen this week. I then repeated that Members must realize that it was for them to decide themselves what it was right to do. I said every man in the room owed his position, in part, to the party. If there had not been a party helping them – any of them would have been nowhere. Any man who voted against the party or was absent at the moment of defeat would be a marked man for the rest of his life. It would not be a question of how he had voted or why he had voted re freight rates – the question would be why had he defeated the Government of which he was elected to be a supporter. I said any man who would do that would deserve nothing from the party. It was a pretty blunt talk. Members listened very solemnly. They gave me a good round of applause at the close."

Several of the members "spoke of it being excellent talk. Howe came with me [to a Canadian Club luncheon] and said I was the only one who could have done it. Pouliot even said it was a splendid talk. They and others seemed to feel it would settle the question of wavering of the Members."

Seven of the provincial governments appealed to the Cabinet against the freight rate increase and the appeal was heard on April 26. According to Mackenzie King, six of the premiers were present, Macdonald, McNair, Manning, Garson, Jones and Douglas. "Most of the Cabinet, excepting St. Laurent and Mitchell, were present. The Premiers made their representations regarding the findings of the Railway Board. Macdonald spoke on behalf of the others. I thought they made out a pretty strong case for some revision of the whole situation. They took the position, unless we could order some change, they might have to make our Government accept responsibility for the findings of the Board. . . . They made it pretty evident that it would be impossible for the Government to act as a court of appeal; that the whole business would take a year or more. I was rather amused to see how most of the Premiers excepting Garson seemed to look upon the Government as enemies, as if we were responsible for the Board's decision. Jones said nothing but acted as though he had been injured in some way.

"McNair's manner was not dissimilar. Macdonald was rather better than the others. Garson was wholly frank and really helpful. . . . I made clear to them that we could not consider reverting to political decisions in the making of freight rates. . . . At one stage, I suggested a possible further conference between us thinking we might work out something but immediately McNair said he had to leave at once. This was a matter of politics. We could not have indefinite delay. Others spoke of having to leave at once. I finally told them, when speaking of what should be said to the public, they might be free to make known their own representations, that the Government would consider them carefully but I would not guarantee as to the time within which our decision would be reached. The interview lasted two and a half hours."

The Cabinet discussed the freight rate appeal on April 28. The Prime Minister "spoke at length . . . on the importance of not allowing a situation to develop between seven provinces and ours. We must recognize that their people and ours were the same. I pointed out I thought their representations had been most effective. There was need for complete revision of some of the things that had been done. That the Board needed strengthening; possibly there were things that the Royal Commission [on Transportation] should take up but generally the line was not to get committed until the whole brief had been carefully studied and then an effort made to do something constructive.

"I found Chevrier much more determined in his own way than any of the other members of the Government. They are pretty much agreed that the Commission had made some shocking admissions with regard to some of the matters that they had not taken into account in their judgment. There was confusion in their own statements which made some revision essential. We discussed the matter for a considerable time."

The problem was discussed in Cabinet again on May 18. Mackenzie King told his colleagues he "thought the situation demanded a major operation. There could be no confidence established as long as the present Board and personnel remained what it is. . . . We could get a first-class man for Chairman and one or two additional representatives and give the provinces as well as the Dominion a board they could have confidence in. Then we could decide how matters were to be dealt with by experts as their advisers. My view met with general acceptance by the Cabinet. Gardiner was not present. It was recognized he might fight for a continuance of Cross as Chairman but all were agreed that Mr. Cross was a sick man and some suitable provision would have to be made for him. Judge Rand of the Supreme Court was mentioned as possible Chairman but it was felt he could not be expected to give up that post. Another name suggested was Archibald of Nova Scotia who was Chairman of the Conciliation Board during the war. Seems to have made a great success of his work. His name met with instant approval.

"After discussion, it was left to Ilsley to begin to see if he could secure him. Matters later will have to be taken up with Cross and others." Archibald, a judge of the Exchequer Court, was appointed to the chairmanship of the Board of Transport Commissioners on July 1.

Shortly after returning from Williamsburg, the Governor General left for a visit to the United Kingdom. Mackenzie King saw Alexander on April 9. When the Governor General asked if he had any message to send to the King, the Prime Minister "told him to assure the King that all was well in Canada [;] in the event of any situation developing in which the United Kingdom and United States would be involved in the preservation of freedom, to count on Canada. I also sent greetings to the King and Queen and others. He spoke of possibly having a talk with Attlee. If he did, it would be just as a private individual. I said I did not know that it mattered very much whether he saw him as Governor General or as an individual but perhaps seeing him as individual, would not raise any question concerning the position of Governor General.

"I then spoke to him about the title of Governor General. I said to him that when I had been in England, last year, at Chequers, someone in the Commonwealth Relations Office had suggested, when we were discussing the title, the possible use of the words 'King's Lieutenant.' He turned to me and smiled, and said I rather like that title. I pointed out to him that the term Governor was really obsolete, as being appropriately applied to the post as it now exists. That I had noticed at Williamsburg, the President of the University had spoken of the Governor General as representative of the British Government which of course was quite wrong. I said a term like King's Lieutenant would keep the close association with the King. Would be better than the term King's Representative which had been thought of. He said he did not altogether like the word 'representative.' Was a little clumsy but returned to the point of liking the designation 'King's Lieutenant.' I said if he thought well of it, it might be worth while having a word with the King concerning it. I would like to see the change made while he was holding the position of Governor General here."

By April 13 a severe cold the Prime Minister had acquired in Virginia had developed into influenza and he was ordered to bed. Two days later he was thoroughly depressed, a mood "which caused me to feel that the whole of my public life has been pretty much a failure. That I have lost at its close what I had hoped for most, namely, the real respect of the nation for my years of public service rendered genuinely for that reason – not for self-aggrandizement, records and the like. Along with it seems to have gone even desire to wish to write Memoirs of any kind. To be satisfied now with getting papers together and due disposition made of them."

He returned to this theme on April 16. "More and more, I feel that I would like to get out of office before any new schemes are brought forward which I shall have to endorse or oppose. There is more than enough to handle at the present without creating more machinery, giving the bureaucrats everywhere more in the way of power without responsibility. What most of these schemes come to is allowing a body of men who have the most favoured positions in the Civil Service become a world law making and governing body without having in any way to gain office through the will of the people themselves. Civil servants are special representatives and political favourites being exalted into Ministers, with Ministers becoming less and less the masters of their own homes, and having loaded onto them more and more obligations with the creation of which they themselves have had little or next to nothing to do."

Mackenzie King equalled Walpole's record tenure of office as Prime Minister on April 20 and received a flood of congratulatory messages. Still not fully recovered from his illness, he "really wondered once or twice whether I was wise in attempting to go to the House at all. I felt terrible depression and sadness. I could not get my mind to work at all. However, at 10 to 3, went along to the House. The three o'clock bell was ringing as I went in so I had to wait until after prayers. When I went to my seat, I received a great ovation from the men on our side of the House but I noticed that there was little or no applause from the Opposition benches, either Conservatives, C.C.F. or S.C. I felt in a moment the damage that had been done by the article that had been sent to the Press Gallery from the office, and which was all too evidently in the minds of M.P.s. It was clear to me that they were sick and tired of those indifferent recognitions of occasions and, heaven knows, I felt that way very much myself.

"Neither Bracken nor Graydon were in their seats, nor were Macdonnell and one or two others. Immediately after prayers, Ilsley rose and drew the attention of the House to the significance of the day in relation to my years in public life. He spoke very nicely from some words that he had prepared and was followed by Mr. St. Laurent who spoke in French.

John McNicol, of the Opposition, then rose and said he had only a moment before been asked by his leader if he would speak on behalf of the Opposition. That he was ill prepared. He went ahead, however, in a most kindly way and then came a reference to the friendship between his mother and my own. I was afraid he was going to find it impossible to get through. He was too deeply moved but made his reference in a most kindly way. He was followed by Coldwell who spoke clearly and to the point as he usually does. Then, Blackmore, in the absence of Low, spoke and made a kindly reference. To my surprise, Tommy Church then came forward. Made a very kindly reference particularly to the family in Toronto. He was followed by Pouliot who contributed one of his quasi-friendly, quasi-satirical speeches. It was a difficult group to follow, specially with the members of the Press Gallery looking on and having in mind as I am perfectly sure they all had, the material that had been sent in bundles to the Press Gallery. It made me break out into a perspiration as I tried to think of what I should say. I doubt if a public man has ever been more bitterly wounded in the house of his own friends. I went ahead without notes and without really being conscious of what I was saying. Finally I came to what was written out and read it quite boldly but with a consciousness that I was saying the right and appropriate thing. It was quite clear that it was so regarded by the House as the Opposition, I noticed, applauded quite generously when I concluded.

"The whole business was, however, a very trying ordeal – one, I hope, I may never experience the like of again in my life. One of the first notes that came across the floor was from Douglas Ross, of Toronto, who claimed our grandmothers were related and wishing me well. I am glad he did not attempt to speak."

The British High Commissioner called on Mackenzie King later in the afternoon with a "letter in Mr. Attlee's handwriting given in England to bring to me. It was a letter . . . extending congratulations when I would exceed the years of office of Walpole, and making me a present of a beautifully framed old original print of Sir Robert Walpole with an inscription beneath indicating that it had been presented to me by Attlee. A successor of Walpole's in the list of Prime Ministers in the United Kingdom at a time when I had exceeded Walpole's record."

In a talk with Wishart Robertson on May 7, Mackenzie King learned that Senator Lambert "was suggesting that the Chairman of the National Convention should be chosen from the premiers of the provinces and spoke of Macdonald of Nova Scotia as the one who should preside. I said nothing but listened to his statement. It was that he had since talked with St. Laurent and I think one other Minister who doubted the wisdom of this but advised that he have a talk with me. I instantly said that I thought it was entirely wrong to get someone to accept the position of President and Vice-President of an Association. Give them all the work of drudgery to do through the years and when it came to one important occasion, to deny them full rights of their office. For my part, I felt no one else was entitled to preside but Fogo and Blanchette, then President and Vice-President. He told me that Fogo had felt it a body blow when Lambert had suggested this. He also talked about Ilsley's going to the Supreme Court. He believed that was what Ilsley wanted more than anything else. He knew he was planning to get into private practice before the Convention. I told him that I would support Ilsley for the Supreme Court. Thought he would make an excellent judge and merit that position. He says Lambert and one or two others are expected to be working on the platform but none of them are doing anything. It really is a tragedy that younger men of the party like Claxton, Abbott, Martin and others should not interest themselves in the future of Liberalism, through the necessary work of organization and in other ways. They are throwing away their future and the future of their party for giving their time so exclusively to the side of the work which relates to their work in the Ministry. They owe it to the party to watch the party's interests outside.

"When I came back to Laurier House, I was very tired. Went to bed for over half an hour's rest, and then had tea and dictated a letter to be read at the meeting of the Reform Association, Montreal, tomorrow night at a dinner celebrating the 50th anniversary of its founding. I understand between twelve and fourteen hundred persons will be present, including several of the Cabinet Ministers. I have never had any real word about the meeting other than that there was to be such an occasion. Claxton extended an invitation verbally through P. but the significance of the occasion had not been made clear to me. I feel very strongly that I really should have planned to be at this gathering. It will probably be my only chance to appear in Montreal or the province of Quebec before leaving the office of Prime Minister. I would certainly get a great reception and being present would help to give spirit and courage to our members. If I were not so very weary and did not feel that I would have to have an address worthy of the occasion, I would still decide to go down. I have really talked with no one about the affair and I imagine it is now too late. It does seem to me, however, that I am burying all my talents and allowing such lights as have helped to gain me position and prominence in Parliament and the country to be extinguished one by one. It is most disheartening and depressing. Whether it is fatigue, exhaustion or what it is, I cannot say but it seems impossible for me to rise above it.

"H. brought in a man named Girouard with a little Irish Terrier pup. A dear little creature – but only about seven weeks old. I looked into the little fellow's eyes and have been seeing them in my own ever since. The little chap's face recalled old Pat. It has made me long to have another dog with me but, with all that has to be thought of in the next few weeks, I doubt if I should let anything else burden my mind. May be that something may work out."

Next morning the Prime Minister decided to attend the dinner and, on the train that afternoon, he dictated a speech after reading over "the speech made at St. Laurent banquet in Quebec and part of the speech at the National Federation. I had earlier read the speech made at Ernest Lapointe's banquet. I got in half an hour's rest before reaching Montreal. I would have been wiser to have done less reading and had an extra half hour.

"Was met at the station by Claxton's secretary and accompanied by P. went direct to the Windsor. Was shown into the Royal suite where a few minutes later Claxton came to take me to the large dining room of the Hotel. I was perfectly astounded to see the room crowded with guests. A head table splendidly arranged to one side and the room immediately opposite as well as the Gallery filled with other guests. . . . I was given a great reception when being shown to my seat and after sitting there for a moment was given another great ovation. The same thing was repeated in a surprise way when Mr. St. Laurent, in speaking, made his first reference to myself. The entire audience stood and sang 'For He's a Jolly Good Fellow' and later when I rose to speak and concluded my remarks. It was clear that the audience were delighted I had come to the gathering and that there was a feeling of real affection toward myself. Unfortunately, despite the rest, I was feeling very tired. My mind seemed to have a sort of metallic quality as against a flow of spirit which made it difficult for me either to experience real feeling of emotion, joyous or otherwise. My part in the evening seemed to me throughout, more or less mechanical. . . . I really condemned myself very strongly for having, at the outset, shirked the business altogether. Fortunately, at the end, I did yield to being present under the stress of conscience which seems to me had been almost buried in the last little while.

"With all my heart, I rejoice that I did go down. With all my heart, I wish I had done just a little better and also once there remained until the evening was over instead of hurrying away. I must cease this business of incessantly trying to cover arrears and give myself up all in all, or not at all to those matters which are the important ones and make their immediate demands.

"I felt that the dinner itself went very well. It was over some fifteen minutes in advance of the time for the radio but the period of waiting was splendidly filled in by suitable songs and music.

"Claxton made a good introduction – a little long perhaps. St. Laurent had his speech written out which otherwise detracts considerably. He had too much on his thoughts the question of language and race at the beginning. But the rest of his speech seemed to be well received. I could not help thinking, however, while he was speaking that his appeal is far different than that of Sir Wilfrid's. He has great charm but has the fault which I have been guilty of right along of being, if anything, too thorough, and not having sufficiently the right touch. As I listened to him, I could not help thinking of what Gardiner's feelings (he was nearby) might be in sizing up the problem that will come inevitably to the fore before the Convention is over, and even more later on of the cleavage that may come between the French and English-speaking, Catholic and Protestant – in large part because St. Laurent finds it impossible to leave this emphasis alone. He is supersensitive in some ways. It might make for greater unity if a much younger man were chosen.

"Abbott has much charm. Whether he has the physical strength or the breadth of vision and knowledge is another thing. Claxton is very able. I fear . . . his recklessness in the matter of expenditures and his tendency to extremes of publicity. . . . (P. told me that Hume had told him that Gardiner had said he had spoken to me about whether I would run again. That I had told him definitely on no condition would I be ready to stay on as Prime Minister. He said then that he himself was definitely in the contest for leadership. That if he won, he did not think St. Laurent would stay. He would try to persuade me to take the External Affairs. That this was where Hume had got the notion that I might stay on in the Cabinet as President of the Council.) I cannot see Gardiner as Prime Minister of Canada. He would antagonize many of the Liberals who do not like the C.C.F. because of many of his policies being really C.C.F. He would antagonize the C.C.F. because of his jealousies of their leader. That would soon lead to a most appalling confusion in seeking to get any unity on economic policies.

"All I really wish to note here is what I saw of the difficulties ahead as we all sat at that head table tonight. It made me wish that I really had the strength to continue on but I saw more clearly than ever as I thought over ideas for the speech, and more particularly as I found difficulty in speaking, etc., how impossible it would be for me to think of continuing on.

"What was particularly noticeable about tonight's gathering was the evident unwillingness of the party to let me go and the great hold I have on its confidence. That is a truly remarkable thing. I was truly battling for permission to give up the Prime Ministership of the country and it was clear that the audience last night would have had me hold on to it at any cost had I been willing to do so. This is something that few men in public life have ever experienced. Certainly none after the length of time that I have been in office."

The Prime Minister had received word on May 4 that Joseph Atkinson, the publisher of the Toronto *Star,* was seriously ill and "could hardly hope to survive a fortnight longer. . . . During the morning, I had dictated a letter to Mr. Atkinson expressing the hope that he might live to enjoy another summer at Muskoka. I believe, however, his heart is now very weak. I shall miss him greatly. He has been an exceedingly true and loyal friend."

Atkinson died on May 9 and Mackenzie King left for Toronto the next day to attend the funeral. He was "tremendously impressed with the announcement of Mr. Atkinson having established a Foundation to which all the profits beyond a certain point of the Star were to go for charitable purposes in Ontario. He told me of this a year or so ago but the project seemed to be on a vaster scale than I had realized. The more one looked at his life, the more one is impressed with the help he has been to fellow men and how marvellous his attachment to causes relating to human betterment. It was all a bit of a surprise but made me very happy to realize how close our association had been, and how kindred its foundations. His desire to give back to the country all that he had earned from it, parallels the thought I have had over years, of wanting to give back to the country in the end, if possible, all I have secured in salary, etc. I told John Buchan of this when he was Governor General. I hope I may be able to realize that ambition. My mind has felt much relieved at what has been covered in today's work, and particularly at having, this morning, suddenly thought of making my theme to the press gallery on Saturday night – a word as to my retirement, to make clear the method of it, and the time that may be involved, in working out what is best for the country and the party."

On Saturday, May 15, Mackenzie King attended for the first time one of Norman McLeod's annual luncheons at the Rideau Club. McLeod was the British United Press correspondent in the capital. "I had not expected to speak but, being called upon, found it very easy. Said some things that were on my mind in reference to my getting out of office and the reasons for it; relations with press, etc."

The Prime Minister returned to Laurier House in mid-afternoon to prepare for the Press Gallery dinner that evening. "Took a rest of an hour and a half, being pretty tired and feeling this to be the best possible investment. Then tried to block out anew what might be said tonight. Felt increasingly that rest would be more valuable, so went back to bed for another half hour.

"Left Laurier House about twenty to 8. Was met in my office in the Commons by Hardy, the President of the Press Gallery, and conducted by him to the large Railway Committee Room where different things had been worked out to illustrate in a humorous, if not ludicrous way, some of the things related to my career, for example, portrayal as a pugilist who had won out on records. Also a coat of arms – composed of Industry and Humanity in one square; 5 cent piece in another square; then conciliation, etc. As a matter of fact, I was too tired to pay much attention to what there was in the way of display. I confess I was amazed at the numbers present. After this preliminary meeting which had been in the nature of cocktail party over previous half hour, we went up to the Restaurant. The head table had been arranged at the far end which, in some ways, I liked better though I imagine it is not as good for the audience. I thought the performance on the whole was much more dignified and restrained than that of previous gatherings of the kind, while the whole thing seemed to be focussed on myself. The humour was kindly. There was also a good deal of fun over the question of appointment of a successor. I was a bit surprised to find that Hardy and myself were the only speakers on the programme. That meant they really expected me to deliver quite an address. Fortunately I had settled in my mind what I thought of saying and as it turned out, it proved to be on the whole most successful. I spoke a little at the outset of the earliest recollections of the Gallery dinners – of Sir Wilfrid speaking of the journalistic careers of members of the Gallery. How little I thought that years hence, I would be doing the same thing at similar gatherings. I referred to having thought of speaking on three subjects: (1) the art of holding on to office; (2) the art of quitting office; and (3) making a living when out of office. I linked what I had to say on that kind of a thread. What I dealt with most was my intention to leave office; that this was the last press dinner I would be addressing as Prime Minister and making clear that I had called a convention to get free of responsibilities. That after new leader had been chosen, I would still take my time to give up the Premiership but did not intend to hold it beyond a few months at the outside after the Convention. I made clear that I would not treat the selection of a new leader as though it was a notice to get out of office at once, saying I would give him time to prepare his Cabinet; would wish to have time myself to remove a few pictures from the walls. Take papers away. Spoke of desiring to visit different parts of the country. Thanked others for suggesting that I might possibly feel that a trip to Rome and

Greece might be in the public interest. All this by way of humour but making clear that I intended to remain until the end of the present session, even if it ran over to the fall. I intended when getting out of office, to do so in a way which I thought would be befitting of years during which I have served.

"At the end of the speech, I spoke of having mixed feelings at the thought of leaving. Then made presentation of the little framed picture of John Bright and read the letter to Mr. Hansard written 100 years ago. Reference to speeches, etc., seemed so appropriate that it received a great round of applause. I was amazed when I sat down to see the ovation I received from all present. I had not found it too easy to speak. Indeed had difficulty in seeing the audience very clearly and getting my mind in the position of sharpness – in making sharp the divisions of what I was saying. However, I seemed to have got into what I said something of the feeling that I experienced, and something of the real feeling of the occasion.

"What pleased and astounded me most was the fact that men came up to speak afterwards, some of them on the *Globe* staff apologizing for the way the paper had treated me; a man from the Army apologized for having ever written a line against me. Others moved almost to the point of tears by what I said. Indeed each one who spoke, making some exceedingly kind reference and extending best of wishes. I think the gathering was moved at the thought of a man voluntarily giving up position and a career in the sense of what was owing to the country, the party and himself. Not waiting until the last moment to enjoy the finest position in the gift of the country. They all sensed it was an historic occasion and as one of the men said to me, closing of an epoch so far as Canadian politics were concerned. Many of those present were particularly nice in the way they spoke, as were also Bracken, Coldwell and Low who really were appreciative in their words.

"The whole evening went off much better than I had anticipated it. I did feel that it was a fitting close to my relations with the press. What I think pleased them as much as anything was reference to having begun my so-called career in association with journalism and thanking them anew for having made me a life member of the press gallery which would give me a permanent association with the House of Commons just as being member of the Privy Council did with Parliament to the end of my days.

"Few men in any country at any time found it possible to say some of the things that I was able to say last night. (This being dictated Sunday.) I wish I had added as it was in my mind to do at the moment that I was leaving the office without a feeling of antagonism to anyone. I did say that

I was astonished I had a friend left after all the years, and at the welcome they had given me – expression of goodwill for the night which would always be remembered as one of the great rewards of public life.

"I was kept shaking hands for some time. Hardy invited me to come back and rejoin the party in the Railway Committee Room but I felt quite sure it was best to leave which I did and to come home direct.

"I got back to Laurier House a little before 11. Again I thanked God on my knees that all had gone as well as it had. Enjoyed looking at the photograph of members of the family and sharing thoughts of the evening with them. Felt a great peace of mind and clearness and freedom of mind as I quietly thought over the events of the past week in my library and made certain decisions which I felt were helpful.

"When I looked at the clock in the library, just as I was about to go down, I was astounded to see both hands exactly together at 12. Today and yesterday have been important days in my life."

In the House the day before, the Prime Minister had outlined the federal government's health programme, basically a series of annual grants to the provinces totalling $30,000,000 for various health services and hospital construction. On his way back to Ottawa from the Atkinson funeral on May 11, he had "read over some correspondence from Martin about health matters and also cuttings from previous Throne speeches on our health policy. I am determined to make a strong fight tomorrow to round out the policy of a national minimum of employment and security which I have sought to have in its entirety made Liberal policy and identified with my life's effort to that end. I have already spoken privately to the Minister of Finance and one or two others about the importance of our taking this step, this year."

On May 12 Mackenzie King "saw Martin in advance and told him of what I had in mind. Indicated to him how I thought it would be best to proceed. Before going to Cabinet, I had a word with both St. Laurent and Wishart Robertson. Told them that I felt the health matter was all important and would like their assistance in the Cabinet. I stressed to St. Laurent the importance, if we were to carry the country in the next elections, that our appeal should have a human side to it; not to rely on railway rates, trade, statistics and the like. To see that we made the health matter the outstanding one as part of our programme of social security. I stressed the fact that we had a record of many years identified with measures that I had brought in, or had been part of my life work, and that the party could make real headway with the electorate in giving the undertaking that it was carrying on this policy. I think my name will stand in good with the people in relationship with true Liberalism for some little time to come.

"In Council I pointed out we had left the health matter over for some time – years in fact. That now we had come to where I thought we should reach a final conclusion. Before beginning the discussion, I said we had better consider the strategy of the matter. The party would be having its convention in August. The alternative lay between our having a programme already presented to Parliament which the Convention would endorse and which would become the big programme in the election campaign, or leaving the matter over until the Convention at which time the Convention would shape the programme. It would be, in all probability, the same one that we would put through Council ourselves. The decision might even be to go much further. I pointed out, however, that the Conservatives would have their programme presented in advance. We would be left in a position of having to follow them and also follow the C.C.F. who already have announced their programme in full.

"I then spoke of what I had aimed at myself in the direction of national minimum. Pointed out that by concentrating on health aspects, we would perhaps obviate having to take up other bits of social reform at present.

"I did not want the party to do more than it really should. I then left the matter to Martin to outline. He set forth various special health grants. Toward this part of the programme, there was no opposition from any source.

"Next came grants for hospital construction. Here there were different views but the Cabinet was pretty solidly favourable.

"Abbott, as Minister of Finance, fought to use great care in not loading the Department with expenditures that would be recurring and which it would be hard to meet when we had not the revenues we had today. Howe was less favourable than anyone to health grants, as I expected he would be, but spoke particularly as Dr. McCann did, about what has taken place under the British legislation. I spoke at once against any attempt to follow what had been done by the Socialist Government in England; that rather we should preserve the principle of private enterprise and initiative and separate our view of social legislation from that of the C.C.F.

"Dr. McCann made a very able presentation pointing out particularly how little today people were inclined to give to hospitals, charities, etc., because of the taxation though the need for hospitalization was greater than previously because of the difficulty of getting the poor classes to make ends meet. Wishart Robertson followed strongly along the same lines.

"Gardiner was favourable. McCann was favourable. St. Laurent had been the one to suggest changing loans for hospital purposes to outright grants to aid in construction, the reason being it was impossible for hospitals to secure necessary labour and material at anything like the earlier cost.

"Claxton also supported the idea generally. Abbott said at one stage he recognized he was defeated before he had begun. Indeed was not unduly critical but did his duty as a Minister of Finance. There were eighteen of us at the Council table. I made much of the fact that this was the moment we should get everything settled, before Martin left for the West next week. If we are going to do anything, we might as well do it while by-elections were on. At any rate, we were getting near the end of the session, and must have this programme settled. Martin suggested I should make a statement in the House myself of what we intended to do. This seemed to meet with the general approval of the Cabinet. I think we could have put the whole thing through but it meant a rush at the end as some of us were going to luncheon with Dr. King. I now feel satisfied that the programme Martin had hoped to secure will go through and my programme for a nationwide social security minimum will be established before I leave the Government. It will, of course, include the programme for health insurance though this may take some years to bring it into existence. It is quite interesting, with Mr. Atkinson's life work coming as it has, to the fore, at this moment. It could not be better."

Next morning the Prime Minister discussed strategy for that day's Cabinet meeting with Martin. "I told him of the efforts I had made in seeing individual Ministers and in reviewing the whole situation carefully.

"I secured from P. the statement which had been prepared by Martin, Davidson [Deputy Minister of Health and Welfare] and officials of the Health Department, based on what had been generally agreed on in Council yesterday.

"When I went into the Cabinet, I took this statement with me. I had not had time to read it over. I told my colleagues, however, how it had been prepared. It was based on discussion of previous day and I would read it to them. When I went through the statement, I gave my own criticism of it; pointed out I thought it was necessary to build up the early part in a way which would make it clear that what we were doing now was part of the programme outlined in previous Speeches from the Throne. I also stressed not placing too much emphasis on a national insurance scheme but rather on a nation-wide health insurance to be worked out in co-operation with provinces. Pointed out I thought I could improve these parts if Council would leave it with me to go over the statement. This was agreed on and I got complete acceptance of what we had gone over yesterday, unanimously by the Cabinet with such members as were present."

Later on May 13, while he was revising the statement for the House, Mackenzie King "received an exceedingly kind letter from Paul Martin making of record what he felt was owing to me in making the programme as extensive as it is and getting it through. He and his staff have done the major work, of course, but I am quite certain that without following the methods I have, both in the matter of timing and planning, etc., it would not have been possible to get the programme through this year. I think, too, it has been brought along just at the right time.

"I went to bed feeling very happy at what had been secured through the Cabinet. Feeling very strongly that it was the rounding out of a great health programme of which I had laid the foundations, and on which any subsequent development will be based.

"The chief changes in the statement as it now stands and in what had appeared in previous Speeches from the Throne was using the phrase 'nation-wide' instead of 'national' rather to get over the objection that we were trying to centralize at Ottawa."

"This has been one of the great days of my life," Mackenzie King wrote on May 14. "A day in some ways unparalleled in what it means of achievement in the way of bringing aid to those most in need. Alleviation of suffering and to the building up of a stronger and healthier nation." Continuing to revise the statement, he noted that Martin "had urged strongly bringing in reference to Pasteur's law of Peace, Health and Work, even if it were on the sentimental side. I felt this might be developed into a speech. It was better for the statement to be kept on practical lines. . . ."

At the meeting of the Cabinet that day, he told his colleagues he "had revised the entire statement which I had read to Cabinet yesterday but had not added anything which was not in the statement other than some statements of policy which had appeared in previous Speeches from the Throne. The work on today's statement was really the work that was done in 1943–44–45. I then said I would read over this portion which I did and also the conclusion. I did not re-read the statement of appropriations to be made. What I read was accepted without a comment but with entire approval. I must record here two facts which are of real significance – the first is that Mr. Atkinson's death should have occurred as it did on Sunday last. His known attitude on health matters and what was known of the views of the Star, both the Toronto Star and the Montreal Star. What the Ministers had felt in what they had read of Atkinson's life, and what they knew was owing to our association in these social matters. All helped to create just the atmosphere that was needed to bring the whole health programme to completion in the short time this was effected."

"What I should record, above everything else," he added, "what has been most on my mind in dealing with these matters, was first my own brother's struggle with tuberculosis. My father's blindness. The struggle with sickness in our family from time to time. My sister Bella's frail condition. Max's long illness and his bringing Pasteur's law of Peace, Work and Health to my notice. My grandfather's struggles, etc. All the family life, as it were, seemed to be working together with me on these matters. In other words, the programme was born in large part out of trials experienced in my own home. The whole of it is but a part of the large programme which began with the creation of the Department of Labour.

"P. has been most helpful as we talked matters over together. I know he felt very strongly what it had meant to be in the Prime Minister's office in the way of helping to effect great social reforms. Much is owing to his zeal in these matters. Suggestions he has made and how he has followed up with Martin and others what was necessary to this effect."

The Prime Minister read his statement in the House that afternoon almost immediately after the opening. He was "received with marked applause when I mentioned I was going to state the Government's policy on health and health insurance. When I came to the paragraph stating that we were not going to delay longer the health grants because of two main provinces [Ontario and Quebec, neither of which had signed tax rental agreements], I was given a great reception. Also as mention was made of the different grants, there was considerable applause on our side and with the C.C.F. and S.C. The Tories really looked dismayed as I was proceeding.

"Finally when I came to the matter of hospitalization, that part of the speech received very strong approval. Indeed from all parts of the House at the conclusion of the speech, there was real ovation. I felt we had scored a triumph. I believe, as I told St. Laurent, that this programme will probably ensure the return of the Liberal party at the next election.

"I did not think people were being swayed by matter of tariffs, railway rates. What they were thinking of was their own battle. Having a fine carefully worked out programme, one which we can point to as having been developed over the years, ought to give to the Liberal party its chance of being the one to continue to implement it as time goes on. It gave me tremendous satisfaction to read the programme to the House. I felt fully conscious that it will prove to be one of the most memorable statements made in Parliament. I felt, too, that it was the rounding out of my work and could be regarded as such by future generations.

"Coldwell was quick to recognize this, and I shall always be profoundly grateful to him for the fine, straightforward way in which he said he could not think of a finer monument that I could have left to my lifework in Parliament than what I had brought forward today. That it would be so recognized. Low made a similar assertion on behalf of the Social Credit. Bracken did his best to say something. He fell, however, to the level of having to read his own party's programme on health and to try to make out that our programme had been based on what the Tories had done. It was so flat that it got little recognition. It was only too obvious that the words used had been taken from previous statements which have appeared, of Liberal policy in Speeches from the Throne and elsewhere.

"I felt very happy. Our men were delighted at the programme. Everyone in our party seemed tremendously pleased, I think. St. Laurent, Ilsley and others were more than surprised at how splendidly all had gone. Abbott spoke over and over again of how perfectly timed everything was, and what a help it will be to him in the presentation of his budget to have this statement made today."

Accompanied by three members of his staff, Mackenzie King celebrated the day by going to the Capitol Theatre to see the film, *Iron Curtain*, which was based on the Gouzenko affair. "I imagine that no four spectators have had in a way a more intimate association with the whole business so far as the Government is concerned than the four of us who were present," he wrote. "It had a special interest to Laurier House. The play was preceded by a quiz – teams of the Bank of Canada and of the Bank of Toronto. Young women and young men. The first time I have seen a quiz. Enjoyed it immensely.

"An amusing and rather extraordinary happening took place when a young lady from the Bank of Canada was asked to give the names of the last four Prime Ministers of Canada. She mentioned my name but could not think of any of the others. The Master of Ceremonies made public the fact that I was in the audience. I mention this as all being significant in reference to this particular play and its bearing on Communists' attitude toward it. I am wondering in how many parts of the world, one could have a public announcement made of going to a play which sets forth a complete disclosure of Communist intrigue – have it publicly announced that the one who was responsible for it was in the audience and then feel no concern in mingling with crowds who were present. Indeed after getting out of the Theatre, people were watching me getting into our car. There was some cheering. One man shouted: You are a true man – among men. There was no comment of an adverse kind. People seemed to approve of what they had seen. This was out in the open, out on the street. It was an amazing thing when one considers what might have happened in any other country, under like circumstances. In the other states, one would have been obliged to go under a police guard.

"I found the play extremely interesting. Well done. What pleased me the most was the restraint shown in different features of it. There was nothing melodramatic about it. All was remarkably true to actual occurrences. Single exception being the picture which disclosed Gouzenko being encountered directly by the officials from the Embassy, escaping death at that moment. It was justifiable shortening up of the actual final happenings. There was, too, a reversal of the order in which he took his papers to the newspaper office first and then to the Government. It would have been better if they had held to the correct order there. I think the play will do great good. I was particularly pleased at the little pictures of the Ottawa Capital as it appeared from the photograph. What impressed me most of all was the way in which the screen had disclosed how the Russians had gone about organizing a spy system, the minute they moved into the Embassy which we went to no end of pains to secure for them.

"When I think of the welcome I gave to Gousev, his wife and children at the time of their arrival, how we secured this Embassy for them, etc., and all the time they were planning out means of having Canada subsequently seized by Russia, it all seems quite beyond belief. I will have quite a story to tell there if still spared. Certainly it is a little short of providential that we have made the discovery we did and were so successful in handling the whole business through the Supreme Court, etc. While I always felt worried and sorry for the delay the investigation took, and also thoroughly disapproved of some of the methods adopted by the police, I do think events justify what was done. I really felt immensely interested in the play."

During the preceding week, the Prime Minister had also found time to discuss the proposed budget with the Minister of Finance. In a conversation with Abbott on May 13, he had "stressed the point that our present generation has had to bear the load of the war. I thought we should require future generations to carry the load of paying off the debt. That I felt it would antagonize the people if, with a large surplus, we devoted it all to reducing the debt. I expressed cordial appreciation of efforts to make obligations for people getting on in years easier. Urged very strongly that he bring together the increased expenditures we were making this year on veterans' pensions, health, etc. Pointing out that these were means of helping those most in need by distributing wealth through taxation. There were two ways of assisting those in need: (1) reducing their taxes. The other (2) giving them more in the way of spending power and what would save them expenditures on the needs which they had to meet. I thought the budget this year should stress particularly what we were doing in that way through health grants." At the Cabinet meeting later that day Abbott outlined his budget proposals and Mackenzie King found the ministers "divided on the question of whether there should not be more in the way of tax relief.

"Abbott was strong for reserving this for next year, making rather a good showing next year, better than cutting things into two – one half this time and the other, next year. He is wise in making clear that the surpluses today are artificial rather than real. They are based on money that has been loaned and much of which we may never recover.

"The discussion was in good spirit, on all sides, and I felt at the end of the morning that Abbott had been very fortunate in getting the degree of unanimity he did. There are some other features to remain over until tomorrow."

After concluding the discussion of the health programme on May 14, the Cabinet "took up tariff changes that are to be announced in the budget speech and other matters which will be dealt with there. I congratulated Abbott on getting through with so little in the way of contention. I think I have been fortunate in having different parts of the Cabinet work together toward that end – kept a good spirit throughout."

In his diary on May 17, Mackenzie King reflected with some satisfaction on the developments of the preceding weeks. He noted particularly "how immensely relieved in mind I have felt since Saturday night's meeting. In the first place, there is the satisfaction of knowing it had all gone so well and that the impression left, which is most important in saying farewell to the press, was a favourable one, and that will be frequently and favourably recorded in years to come. There was too the continued satisfaction at the outcome of the health programme. Editorials in both [the] Citizen and Journal this morning were strong in their praise of it. Almost unqualified, and each seemed to emphasize the discretion used and the proportions given to the programme and to the conciliatory attitude I had disclosed toward the provinces of Ontario and Quebec. I said to P. later I hoped that out of this might grow a settlement with Ontario and Quebec in regard to financial agreements. I would like to see that out of the way before I leave office. If spared, I shall also see Newfoundland and the Confederation issue decided one way or the other. Whichever way it goes, it will be to the credit of my administration. We have done the best we possibly could. These are great matters.

"What, however, has given me the greatest pleasure is the relief of mind that has come with having forecast the programme from now on to the end of the year and having included in it the possibilities of a trip across Canada as Prime Minister and also a possible trip to Europe. My own feeling about the way the latter may work out will be that there will be a British meeting of Prime Ministers probably in October at which I will be present. The trip through Canada may take place in September. I may go to Europe in October – possibly to Britain . . . then a trip to southern Europe taking in Italy and Greece and, if possible at that time, which is very doubtful, . . . a trip to the Holy Land as well, and then back to Canada with my retirement thereafter. Meanwhile, it will have been possible to make during the summer months the readjustments necessary at Laurier House and to get the period following carefully planned. I have indicated my intention to stay on in Parliament for Glengarry until the general elections. That will secure me my indemnity, transportation, franking, etc., at least until the beginning of the summer of 1949, without too much extra strain and exertion until that period, and a chance to get will made, letters and papers sorted out at Laurier House. Having a little in the way of writing possibly anticipated in the meantime. Man proposes and God disposes. Something may completely alter all these plans but at least it precludes speculation on the part of the public as to my real intention and purpose. It also prepares the party and the public for what will take place so that there will be no unnecessary disappointments or surprises along the way.

"It will, too, I think, be a fine example to the world of how public men should hold and cease to hold the trust which may be theirs when giving up office. That of itself is disclosure of one's spirit and purpose.

"I felt really more rested in mind and body after dressing and breakfast than I have felt for a long, long time."

Later in the day he added: "In letting my mind run over possible days of retirement, I had thought once of the 15th of September, the anniversary of my father's birthday. In thinking of the larger programme, I felt that I might make it the 11th of November, or the 15th of November – the former my brother's birthday; the latter, my sister Isabel's birthday. Most likely the 11th of November which was Armistice Day after the first war, and which I spent with my brother in Denver, as a day of recognition of what his life has meant to mine.

"It was through his suffering and from him direct that I secured the passage of Pasteur's Law of Peace, Work and Health which became the thesis of my Industry and Humanity. Indeed, it has been the basis of most of my work since. A sort of guiding star along my work since. The war of blood and death through the period of the war versus the law of peace, work and health which has had to do with my efforts to improve conditions for the working classes, and has led above all to a Liberal programme for a nation-wide system of health insurance.

"I sought to care for my brother when he was ill. What has come since from the sacrifices that had to be made and which were real sacrifices at the time has all been in the nature of reward. All in accordance with what I believe to be most fundamental to all the law of God, that it is only as we give that we receive. That it is [in] what we do for others that our own lives are truly blessed, and blessed I believe in that way as in no other. It is the law of sacrifice and the true meaning and significance of sacrifice. Nothing is lost in the economy of God."

Abbott presented his budget the next day, May 18. Forecasting another large budget surplus during the 1948–49 fiscal year, the Minister introduced few tax changes. An additional exemption of $500 was granted to taxpayers over 65 years of age and tax credits granted to mining, oil and gas companies for exploration and drilling expenses were extended for another year. There "was little enthusiasm about the Budget," the Prime Minister wrote. "There being no income tax relief was a natural disappointment. Also using large surpluses to reduce the public debt was anything but popular. It had not been possible for Abbott to bring out the real significance – of so framing matters to ensure continuous employment, by making doubly sure of Americans placing orders in Canada in connection with the E.R.P. programme [European Recovery Programme] which they might well hesitate to do if we allowed them to make vast expenditures from their Treasury and we were depleting our Treasury by allowing our people to get the tax relief.

"There was appreciation of the allowances made for people over 65 in estimating income; also in the Dominion raising from $5,000 to $50,000 the exemption level on estates for Dominion succession duties. Also appreciation of getting rid of taxes on food but, apart from these small items, the budget was not one to cheer for. Indeed the greatest applause was given to Abbott's last paragraph in which he made the kindliest possible reference to myself. I doubt if any Prime Minister when in office has had a comparable tribute paid him in the presence of all his fellow-members in the House of Commons in the way it was received. It amazed me beyond belief. Unfortunately, as it related to myself, I could not very well shake hands and compliment Abbott on his speech at the close as I have done with previous Finance Ministers. It is going to be a difficult budget to rally our men around but I feel pretty confident we shall more or less have unbroken support."

The Liberal caucus the next day was largely devoted to a discussion of the budget. The Prime Minister noted that "the proceedings were opened more or less by Ian Mackenzie who spoke from his seat in the audience and made a real onslaught on the budget saying it was in no sense a Liberal budget. He stressed strongly what I had done through the years trying to have budgets brought in which would help to give relief to the poor. He thought this was a thoroughly Tory budget. No budget to the poor. We could not win an election on it. It would lead to the defeat of the Government, etc. . . .

"A splendid speech was made by young Loran Baker, of Yarmouth – one of the best short, helpful addresses I have heard made by any Member of Parliament. A fine level-headed type of man. There were criticisms back and forth. Finally I had to take the floor and bring matters to a conclusion.

"I spoke of the reasons I had called a caucus. Said the discussion I thought had justified my judgment. I then took up Mackenzie's words that we could not win an election on this budget. I said that might be perfectly true and was the strongest of reasons why we should not permit an election to come until we had brought in another budget. That this was entirely in our own hands. I was trying to have Members see the necessity of holding together in the House. I then said while it might not be possible to win election with the present budget, we might win the next election with the next budget, and this budget would help us to win it. I thought what the Minister of Finance had in mind was shortness of memory of the public and the wisdom of giving a full loaf to the public at election time rather than half a loaf now and a half loaf later. Neither giving the satisfaction which they might wish to have. I then said that Mackenzie had talked about the budget not being one to help the poor. Therefore not a Liberal budget. I said I would not take second place to anyone in wishing to help the poor. I thought all present had become members of the Liberal party through a desire of the kind. I said there were more ways of helping the poor than simply taking off a certain amount of income tax. There were times and seasons one had to consider this aspect. We had been making a great battle against inflation. It was recognized during the war, and since, that we had waged a splendid battle in this connection. We were now getting rid of controls. To bring a budget which would increase inflation at a time when our problems were growing out of inflation would not be helping the poor. It would be making their lot more difficult.

"I pointed out that the Government was spending large sums of money at this session on giving increased purchasing power to war veterans and their dependents. Also in connection with the health grants and in other ways. That all of this was helping the poor. The health grants and hospitalization were helping most of all in that they gave money at a time of need and that to those who were most needy. That was the most effective way of helping the poor. I then pointed out what we had done in family allowances; said it was not what one budget had done, but we must look at the whole series of budgets in Parliament. Electors would have to run over not this year alone but show relationship of this budget to the others.

"I then drew attention to the problems we were seeking to meet at this time. Had been faced with as a result of shortage of American dollars, etc.

It came to the real point which was that the best of all ways to help the poor was to see that there was plenty of employment. What hit the poor the hardest of all was unemployment and depression. I then pointed out everything was related to the present situation in Europe. Referred to contributions already made. Said Congress in the States was being asked to take vast sums of money out of the public treasury to purchase commodities to send to Europe. We, in Canada, were trying to get a share of that purchasing power which would last over several years. If the United States saw that some people were being deprived of tax relief because of taxes being required to purchase commodities for Europe – while Canada was relieving her people of taxation – they would very soon hesitate to place large orders in Canada for articles to be grown or manufactured here to be sent to Europe. That we might lose all that purchasing power. That our people must remember that much of our prosperity was due to our having taken money out of the Treasury and loaned it to have commodities purchased with these loans. That these loans were drying out. If we did not have demand for our commodities which would salvage employment at high level, that more quickly than anything else would destroy a party at a general election. What we had to make doubly sure was that we had plenty of employment next year or the year after at whichever time the elections might come.

"It was a difficult matter to explain but I got the main thought across in pretty clear fashion. I said the Minister of Finance could not very well come out in his budget and state all this. Much better to have these thoughts seep through by the press and through discussion that would all come to the fore; I then spoke of another way of helping the poor which was the kind of thing done in granting relief to older people.

"I spoke of my feeling that the two classes that needed help by the Government were those who were just beginning the race of life to see that they were given a fair start, and those whose day's work was done, that they should not have to carry burdens at the time their strength was diminishing and they were no longer able to work. I thought one of the most cruel things in the world was that older people should, after a life of work, see their savings disappear and deprived of leaving part of their estates to their children, having their money gobbled up by the State. I thought this should be stressed to the people. That Abbott had in this particular begun a reform which was tremendously to the credit of the Government. I said I thought that we were helping the industrial classes when we relieved the older people of certain obligations they had to meet as, for example, through ill health and through payment of taxes on their incomes and succession duties. That this was not merely old people who were being helped but sons and daughters who would have to be making provisions for them as well as their own families.

"I found myself in speaking very tired and was afraid, at one stage, I would not be able to make clear what I was most anxious to explain. Indeed I found my mind not too free and active. Also a little difficult to speak. This all due mainly to the unrest of last night. Up so late and wakeful afterwards. However, several of the Ministers and Members told me afterwards it was a most effective speech. Ilsley told Claxton he thought it was the most effective speech he had heard me make. I certainly think it did help to change the whole outlook of members of the party and to give them what they needed by way of supporting the budget."

The Prime Minister learned on Saturday morning, May 22, that J. L. Ralston had died during the night. He wrote that "when word came of Ralston's death, I felt quite weak myself for the moment. Have got now where hardly anything impresses me at first, I am so tired." He found it particularly difficult to prepare a tribute. When it was completed he observed that it was "anything but what I would like to have written but I realized it was more important to get something in the press at once, than to wait for a carefully prepared statement. I then had to prepare a telegram to Mrs. Ralston and to her son Stuart. I know Mrs. Ralston will feel bitter toward me. Indeed will say – may even feel that I am in part responsible for the strain that has brought Ralston's life so quickly to its close.

"There is no doubt in the world his sudden death is part of the deferred reaction from the strain of the war. It is however mostly due to constant work with no relaxation. He was a tremendous worker; very fine and noble character. I let go what had been written both for the press and telegrams feeling incapable of attempting more."

On May 24, when the House opened, "John Hackett of Stanstead, as President of the Canadian Bar Association, paid a tribute to Ralston of some length. He had carefully written out what he had to say. I had thought over the matter of a tribute but felt as he was not in the present Parliament, and as there had been no precedent in paying tributes to Ministers of previous Parliaments, I had better not establish a precedent, so had said nothing. I had spoken to Graydon who was acting Leader of the Opposition in advance of the House opening and told him of my view. Hackett had not spoken to him about his intention. However, I followed immediately Hackett concluded telling him I had considered the matter and then went on to pay a tribute to Ralston. Spoke of his services to the country at the time he was Minister of Defence. I had not prepared a careful statement but said just what I felt as I was speaking. I should perhaps have prepared a careful statement but think I am right in having not set a new precedent which might be embarrassing to the Parliaments in the future. It was clear that Ilsley had intended to speak. He had a very carefully prepared tribute which he read. This occasioned others to speak. The Member for Prince which Ralston had represented for a time, spoke. . . . This being Empire Day, Graydon proposed singing of the National Anthem in which all joined."

The next day Mackenzie King was in Montreal for Ralston's funeral. He "went with Mr. St. Laurent, Claxton and Gibson to the church where crowds were gathered – a simple but impressive service. I thought the two Hymns were beautifully and appropriately selected. The words in 'the sands of time are sinking', seemed to me most appropriate to fit Ralston's life and its reward at the close. The other 'Lead, Kindly Light' is always suitable where there has been the element of faith. There was no eulogy save what was incorporated in a very suitable prayer.

"In looking at the pall bearers: Macdonald (N.S.), Ilsley, Crerar, I could not but recall how strongly these men had joined together to try and secure conscription and also to get Ralston at the head of a Ministry. Ralston himself I do not believe had any real ambition for this. I thought Dunning had grown considerably older in appearance.

"The service at the cemetery was to my mind deeply impressive. The grave was on a hillside of a beautifully wooded grove. The sun lighting up the leaves of early spring. A firing squad stood on the far side of the grave, and after a simple service, fired the salute. The Last Post was also sounded. The Government had offered a military funeral. The family wisely rejected display to that extent but were glad to have the military salute at the close. I think all this was in accordance with what Ralston himself would have wished.

"During the service, Chubby Power sat next to St. Laurent and myself. The gathering brought back many remembrances of years that were past. I would have thought of the number assembled there from former Ministers, that Ralston would have been the last rather than the first to go."

He added that "at the cemetery, I was the first to shake hands with Ralston's son immediately after the burial. Later had a talk with his two brothers who spoke of the message I had sent them at the time of their mother's death. One of the brothers told me when I enquired about the circumstances of Ralston's death, that he had, after dinner, felt tired. Said he thought he should go to bed. Had gone to his room. They had heard no further sound. In the morning, it was discovered that he had not been to bed at all. It looked as though he had passed away while saying his prayers. It is a very beautiful ending to a good life.

"Ralston was really a very fine character. Had those around him used a little more judgment, the situation which occasioned his resignation might have been saved. I have no doubt in my own mind that the right thing was done so far as the decision of the Cabinet was concerned."

During the morning on May 29 the Prime Minister "looked over an article by Grant Dexter which appeared in the Journal of yesterday on what was alleged to have taken place at the time of Ralston's resignation. It was the kind of material that those of the Cabinet who were supporting Ralston for conscription tried to make out for purposes of record at the time of Ralston's resignation. I was surprised at Dexter having lent himself to an article of the kind at this time but I remembered that the Free Press was all violently for conscription. The report, however, makes clear that its inspiration has been [T. A.] Crerar. Indeed it admits that Crerar was the one who is alleged to have taken in hand the case for Ralston. The article is far from true. Some day, I shall, if spared, give the true story. The article takes no account of the effort that had been going on for weeks to crowd me into the position of accepting conscription when no other member of the Government was prepared to take the responsibility to carry on the Government under that policy. Of course, there is nothing yet known of the real reason that the measure of conscription was agreed to by McNaughton to save a 'parlour revolution' at the time of war itself. An open defiance of the civil power by the military at the time of war itself. The reviving of these things at this time is anything but decent."

Mackenzie King had noticed in the evening papers on May 20 a story that "Attlee was trying to arrange a Conference of Prime Ministers for the Autumn. I imagine this is now quite certain as a probability. It should be possible to work in a trip to Greece and Italy. This may delay the Canadian tour unless it can be arranged before the others." Four days later, Clutterbuck brought him a message from Attlee which "proposed a meeting of Prime Ministers at the latter part of June with a possibility of further meetings in September. Suggesting that perhaps St. Laurent might come with me though representing that they were particularly anxious that I should come. I told Clutterbuck, if this proposal had related to the first week of June, I might have been able to meet it but as Parliament was to adjourn the last week of June and it might be the last time I would be in Parliament as Prime Minister, I did not see how I could well leave. I pointed out we had several by-elections. If we were to lose those and, with Tucker having just resigned, our majority might be down to three or four. . . . If I were absent, a situation might arise which might lead to the defeat of the Government. I felt this was too great a risk to run. I promised to think the matter over carefully but I doubt if I should consent to go until the autumn. The reasons which had made the British Government agree to a meeting early next year or a meeting in the autumn of this year, must remain pretty much as they were.

"I cannot think of anything that has happened since that would make it imperative to have the meeting in the latter part of June rather than mid-September or October. It remained also to be seen whether Smuts will get a majority over all in South Africa.

"I told P. of the messages received. Asked him to have someone secure sailings so as to see what ships there were but indicated that I doubted if I should consider going. He had no suggestion to make. I shall have to think the matter over very carefully."

Returning to Ottawa from Ralston's funeral on May 25, Mackenzie King and St. Laurent "had a very intimate and helpful conversation together. I showed him the memo Clutterbuck had brought me last night. He was instantaneously and emphatically opposed to my going to a Conference in England in June. He pointed out how much we had to do in the interval and how impossible it would be in a week's time, over there, to really effect anything. He also realized immediately the problems that were to be considered – very thorny ones – the whole situation was the result of pressure from those who wished to develop the Empire idea. He spoke of Menzies having made a speech recently of all parts speaking with one voice, etc. I think he felt what the problems would be like himself, should he become Prime Minister. That it would be the same situation that Sir Wilfrid had had to meet. He thought the Tories were looking for a real issue. That if we won the present by-elections, the Tories would probably get rid of Bracken and seek to bring Drew in his place and would then raise some issue of an Imperialistic character. They might seek to have Duplessis carry seats from Quebec at a general election first. I said I thought they would – we both agreed that it would be bad day for Canada, as seems altogether probable – should Drew come into the federal House. I dislike the man so thoroughly that I doubt if I could stay in the House looking at him from day to day. St. Laurent was strongly of the view that I should not resign after the Convention for some little time. His idea – and he suggested it himself – was that I should go to England to a meeting of Prime Ministers in the autumn, leaving whoever was chosen as Leader to be Acting Prime Minister while I was away and to give him a chance thereby to get about the country himself. He, St. Laurent, had no desire to go to a Conference or the U.N. in Paris. He thought I should perhaps put in an appearance there. His view was that I could attend the meeting of Prime Ministers in London, discuss all phases of the situation brought up but point out that, as a new leader was to take over, it was only fair that I should make no final commitment but present the situation to him on my return. He also took strongly the view that I ought to make the appointments to the Senate. Not leave them to my successor. That this would be fairer to whoever succeeded. He thought that letting the new man come in about the end of October or November would be preferable to anything else. He then said to me that he rather hesitated to say it but perhaps he might be putting it too strongly – but that he really felt I should be prepared to stay on in the Cabinet if only nominally, to let the country have the feeling that I was helping to guide and shape policy. I told him that I had naturally thought of that aspect. Personally I would rather get out altogether, not even continue as a Member so as to have the time free to make a disposition of my possessions, etc. Leave what records I wished, etc. He then said that he thought on patriotic grounds, I ought to be prepared to stay, say as President of the Council, until the present Parliament was over. That that would give the people more confidence and would certainly be helpful to the party itself. I told him all of that would have to be thought over carefully. That my own personal wish would be to quit though obviously the financial question would present itself in another year. He said there was no reason why I should not give most of my time to my own affairs, simply attend Council for purposes of giving advice. I said that what I felt was that the Leader might rather resent having it appear that I was still at the helm. He argued that it would be quite the reverse. He said Harris has the view that Gardiner would get quite a few votes in Ontario. That probably Ilsley would get more than anyone else in Ontario. He said Ilsley had within the last day or two thought of taking the chairmanship of a revised Railway Commission but that he had changed his mind on that score.

"I told St. Laurent that at all costs we must get the House over by the end of June. Spoke to him about the Ottawa developments. My desire to have something considered in that relationship. Personally I feel too tired to pilot a bill through.

"We had tea together on the train. On arrival at Ottawa, I went to call on Clutterbuck and told him the result of our conversation together. He said he had partly prepared the British Government on what would be coming, from what I had said yesterday. He also said he agreed it would not be fair to myself to take on this additional burden."

On May 28 the Prime Minister "was amazed and I confess a little saddened to receive the word that Field Marshal Smuts had suffered defeat in his own constituency and did not have a majority over all. A few minutes after receiving this word, came the further message that he had tendered his resignation as Prime Minister.

"I feel very sorry for Smuts personally. This certainly would have been his last election and with his fine service, it was owing to him to have won his own seat triumphantly and to have carried the country. However, there is a great lesson to be learned from the results. It is one which accounts for both him and Menzies being out of office today and myself still being in office. I told Menzies when in Ottawa that, on returning to Australia, he would find he may have felt he had been playing a big part in Britain but he lost his own country to which he owed his opportunity in Britain. When he got to Australia, he never unpacked his bags but was going to return within a few days to England. The Australian members thought they had had enough of the Imperial statesmen and he lost office before there was a chance to return.

"Smuts has always been looked upon as being a strong Imperialist. Of finding in Britain rather than in South Africa, his spiritual home – notwithstanding that he was a Boer. Some time ago, he agreed to accept the position of Chancellor of Cambridge University and was to be installed in the month of June. This certainly meant in the eyes of others that he was quite sure of being returned as Prime Minister after the election. It must have meant in the eyes of many South Africans that the moment the elections were over, Smuts was leaving Africa for Britain. The fact that the elections in South Africa were being fought on lines which served to bring out the nationalistic feeling very strongly would make an incident such as Cambridge University one just about enough to turn the balance. However, the acceptance of the Chancellorship was a mere symbol. It stood more or less for what Smuts has been most interested in all his life – namely being what Lord Willingdon termed him: the blue-eyed boy of the Tory party in Britain. Until the last Conference or two in England, he has more or less consistently taken the Imperialistic role, etc. At the end, he has received from his own people the verdict that he had, in their eyes at least, been more Imperialistic than nationalistic. He was subordinating South African policies to the larger ones of the Empire. This would particularly appear to be the case by the results in his own constituency. The fact that the cities backed him in the first returns would be natural for that is where the British interests are the strongest. That the country seats went against him would indicate he had lost the confidence of the people of his own stock. It is interesting to me to realize that while I have been the one that has had to stand most in the way of condemnation from British sources in earlier years, as being anti-Imperialist, etc., I should be – and particularly as contrasted with some of the other Prime Ministers – the only one now left in office of those who were leaders either in Britain or in any other Dominion during the last war. As a matter of fact, I have been for some time the only Prime Minister who was Prime Minister prior to the war and who has continued as Prime Minister since. That is another record. This I put down to having taken just the opposite view to that taken by those of an Imperialistic outlook. I recall during the war stoutly refusing to be made a member of an Imperial War Cabinet. I stoutly opposed going to Britain, at different times, for conferences, etc., where I felt my real duty was to Canada first, and resolutely setting myself against anything which would weaken the position which I had with our own people here. It is interesting that Smuts' defeat should come just at the moment that another great effort is being made to start anew an Imperialist drive. Unquestionably the meeting recently suggested of Prime Ministers in London in June or July has been due to the expectations that Smuts would be present and that he would arrive after a victory in South Africa. The whole scene is now changed in a matter of hours.

"Smuts' fall confirms, I think, the wisdom of my decision not to run another general election after the number I have already been through and my age being what it is, and also not having waited until within the last year of a Parliament to make that decision known. It shows the wisdom of having called a National Convention not later than the beginning of the present year. Were it being called tomorrow, it would be said that my decision had been reached as a result of Smuts' defeat in South Africa. I have had the evidence since [the calling of] the Convention that the party is more strongly behind me than ever, and also that Canada is itself in a better position than she has been at any time both in herself and as seen in the eyes of the world.

"Smuts would have been much wiser to have taken a course similar to my own, and pleaded his years, as he might well have done, as a reason for not entering another campaign. He told me, however, that he felt quite sure he would win this election. He thought he would retire shortly after but would make the decision then.

"I am not sure that it is going to prove for the best that he has been defeated. I am afraid the nationalist opinion may go too far in an opposite direction. It will, however, make a great difference in the kind of battle that whoever represents Canada at the next Conference will have to wage in London. There will be again a tremendous drive for centralization, etc. Canada will have an ally in South Africa against an extreme of that kind. I think it may now be assumed we shall hear nothing more of a meeting in London in July though telegrams received yesterday from Robertson would indicate that Attlee and Bevin were still hoping for this but would send word in a day or two. Without doubt, they have been waiting for the results in South Africa. I think this too will open the door for my going to London in September or October; if I am spared and should go, I will be the only Prime Minister at the Conference of all of those who have held office over the greater part – if not the whole war. Certainly I will be the elder statesman. It is, by the way, interesting to see how the British papers always refer to Smuts as the elder statesman of the Empire though he has been a much shorter time in office than I have been. What a complete change from the position as it was in my earlier years of office! – with the London Times trying to drive me out and its correspondents doing all possible in that way."

After several exchanges of messages, the Prime Minister received a cable on June 4 from Attlee confirming that the conference would be held in October. "I have sent him a reply tonight and given the assurance that I believe I could fit in that meeting before laying down office. It would look now as though I might hold on to office until an autumn session opens at the beginning of November and that, meanwhile, there might be a chance not only to visit England but also to take in Greece and Rome as well, or, if not, a tour of Canada. I imagine by that time I will be quite ready to let the new leader take over the obligations of Premiership as well."

In the House on May 26, Mackenzie King had "listened with great interest to a rattling good speech by Ilsley on the budget. He has developed very much. Is much happier since he has been in the Justice Department." Two days later, Ilsley came to Laurier House to inform the Prime Minister that he had decided to leave public life and join Ralston's law firm. Mackenzie King told him that he "had assumed when I heard of Ralston's death that there was a likelihood of his taking Ralston's place in the firm. ... I was therefore not surprised that he had reached the decision he had ... but I was hoping that no final action would be taken until after the by-elections. That his leaving the Government might be made the subject of controversy in them. He then said he would like to read to me what he had written out which he did and which indicated that he had reached this decision months ago; had been negotiating since; that the reasons were personal. He might like to say they were to make provision for my family and myself, but to what he had written added that he was completely in accord with the Government's policies and there was no difference of any kind. That he would be staying on until the end of the session. He based the article on the rumours that had been going about in the press to which he wanted to put an end. I asked him if he did not think the statement should be made in the Commons. He asked me whether I really thought that would be best. That he felt it was hardly the thing for a Minister to announce his intentions in regard to the future in that way. It would be better to have the matter handled through the press. I said I thought he was right and, in all probability, questions would be asked the day after in the House which we would have to be prepared to answer. I then said to him that my thought had been that what I would have liked to have seen was he would have become a member of the Supreme Court. His eyes filled with fire and he said instantly that I would like better than anything in the world, but that is impossible. I said to him that I had talked over this matter with Wishart Robertson.

"I had known that Rand was anxious to get back to New Brunswick and might take the Chief Justiceship there. I was quite prepared to make that change if he, Ilsley, were agreeable. He then repeated that he would like the Supreme Court better than anything but that it was just impossible. That McNair did not want Rand back in the province. McNair was anxious to get the judge on the Court of Appeal made Chief Justice in case he himself should encounter some defeat or wish to leave politics shortly and might like to have that position for himself. That the one he wanted appointed was not likely to live very long. . . ."

The Prime Minister then suggested the chairmanship of the Board of Transport Commissioners but Ilsley said he "did not feel he would care for it. I said to him I thought it would be too monotonous as dealing with one question all the time. He said that was exactly the way he felt. He then said that the Montreal position would be not only lucrative but highly interesting and exciting. He thought it would mean very heavy work and he might share Ralston's fate as a consequence of undertaking it. But that if he was to get out at all, now was the time that he must do so. He said it was improbable that the party could continue forever in office. If he stayed longer, and till the party were in opposition, he might then find that he had gotten so out of touch with the profession and with legal matters that he would be too late to pick up a practice anew. He then spoke of his financial position which meant that when he had paid his life insurance with all that there were of taxes, etc., his life insurance was not large – he had really nothing left for savings. I agreed the position was unendurable for a Minister of the Crown who was not a man of means. One of the serious things democracy was facing was to get men into public life whose interests were in public service primarily. Not position or power. The highest form of service. Ilsley agreed that a rich man like Howe would find it possible. Others might take the position for what there was in it. There was a real danger along the lines I have indicated. I then said to him had he not considered the possibility of his being chosen the leader of the party at the Convention. He said that he had gone into that carefully too but did not think there was a chance. That Gardiner would likely pick up most of the votes of those who might be opposed to St. Laurent on the grounds of race or religion. He was getting a lot of letters suggesting he should consider standing for the leadership as a Protestant and English-speaking and as being preferable to Gardiner. He thought this was making his position extremely difficult. That it might come to the Convention where he would be gathering support for quite a time and he would then be turning his support over to St. Laurent to ensure his election. He did not wish to be put into that position. He felt that St. Laurent was preferable to Gardiner. He spoke of him in the highest terms. He then said: but if I wait in making this statement, it will be thought that I am dropping out because I think I would be defeated at a Convention. I don't want that thought to prevail. I said to him I could understand his desire to make the announcement before the Convention but had hoped he would wait until the end of the session. I then said I could understand his feelings. That I myself had given the long advance notice that I had so that there would be no mistake about my reasons for getting out, not being due to any change in the tide, or any fear of defeat. . . .

"I then came back to the date of the announcement; not making it on Monday at a time that would reach Yale before the polls closed. I said I thought he should give it to the papers in the evening, so that it could appear in the morning papers. He could give it before the Yale announcement was made. That would remove any question about results in Yale having had a bearing on his decision. He said: all right. He would do that but he could not think of delaying any longer. I then told him that I was very sorry that he was leaving the Government though I fully understood and appreciated his position. I said to him that I thought he was deserving of any position on any Bench in Canada which he might wish to have. That I thought possibly it would come yet to his being appointed to the Supreme Court and that if, in the future, any influence of mine could be of assistance toward securing him any position he might wish to have, he could count upon it. That I thought his abilities were of the highest but I need not say how great his public services had been and how completely he possessed all the qualities of integrity, industry, etc., which were those that were most necessary in high position. I spoke without reservation and I am sure from the quiet way in which he received what I said that he felt the sincerity of my words and was greatly pleased by them.

"I felt it was in every way due to him to say what I said. I then went with him down the stairs to the front door and, in saying good-bye, wished him all that was best. His last question was did I think he should stay on until the end of the session. I said by all means but he should make that clear in his announcement. I also said to him that I thought we should arrange to bring on a by-election in his constituency at once. I said I assumed there was no doubt we could elect someone there. He said he thought we certainly could. I said: you know, it is going to be pretty hard for my successor and for the party to keep the majority that we need in the Commons until the time of an appeal to the country.

"Throughout his whole conversation, he made perfectly clear that he liked public life. Would enjoy continuing on in the Government were it not for what was involved in the way of financial risk for the future with uncertainties of public life what they are. That he told me was his sole reason for finding it desirable to make this change at this time. It was really what he had said to me earlier in the year and also to Howe and St. Laurent whom he had taken into his confidence."

The provincial election in Ontario took place on June 7. "I shall be surprised if Drew does not have almost the same majority as he had before," Mackenzie King wrote. "A little less perhaps. This because the C.C.F. and Liberal votes will help to make possible the return of many Conservative candidates by minority vote.

"Tomorrow we have our two by-elections [in Vancouver Centre and Ontario]. I think we will have a very close run in both. Indeed I should not be surprised to see the C.C.F. carry both. As Johnson [the Premier of British Columbia] said today, the Governments are blamed for everything whether they be floods or fires; prices, lack of housing, etc. This is all great ground for the C.C.F. They too will get all the Communistic and S.C. votes and those of discontented Liberals. The outlook is not too hopeful for our party. This because of total lack of organization or anything resembling it, except at the moment of campaigns themselves, while the C.C.F. are working all the time. They have really a splendid organization."

"During the evening," he wrote later, "the results kept coming in from Ontario elections. It would seem that results had been just about what I predicted prior to the polls being closed. Drew has not quite the same number of representatives. The Liberals are one or two fewer than they were. C.C.F. have made gains. Drew has lost his own seat to the C.C.F. My first thought on getting results was to what lengths responsibility rests on Hepburn's shoulders and those who were associated with him, for destruction of Liberalism in Ontario. It may lead to – if not the destruction – at least the crippling of Liberalism throughout Canada in the general election. He certainly opened the door first to the Tories and now to the C.C.F. to power.

"My next thought was how unfortunate it is that none of the members of the Government would heed my request to bring on the by-elections as soon as possible. Had they been brought on at the time that I wrote Howe, they would have been over before the budget was introduced, before the floods [in Manitoba and British Columbia], before these provincial elections in Ontario. Now it would look as though, through lack of organization, the C.C.F. have been given the best of chances to win in Vancouver and in Ontario constituencies tomorrow. The C.C.F. given a great chance to hold their own in Saskatchewan and a chance to make great headway in the next federal election. In addition, Duplessis will probably announce the date of his election on Wednesday and will be given an exceptional chance in Quebec as the strong man allied with Drew in Ontario to hold the federal government in check and save the autonomy of Quebec. The results in Ontario will almost certainly lead to a very strong alliance between Ontario and Quebec in the next federal election and, in all probability, to Drew becoming the successor to Bracken. Probably immediately after the Dominion elections, should they not be delayed beyond June of next year. I am afraid our own Members will become restive and increasingly difficult to hold in line. I would think that this may be a terrible discouragement to St. Laurent. It is difficult to say how the whole scheme of things might not be considerably altered when the Convention comes on, from what at the moment is anticipated.

"I really do not expect victory in either Vancouver or Ontario. Should we win, it will be by a small margin. The Tories in both constituencies will be at the bottom of the polls though today's results in the province of Ontario may give the Tories quite a run in the federal by-election, than would otherwise have been the case."

After dinner on June 8, the Prime Minister noted, "returns of the by-election for Ontario constituency began coming in. I said to Howe at afternoon sitting that I did not think we would carry Ontario. . . . He thought we would but I have felt all day that it was highly improbable. I also doubt very much if we will carry Vancouver. Howe seemed to think that we will also carry that seat. I don't believe it. H. brought in first returns which show C.C.F. leading and Liberals next. P.C. 3rd. Fortunately a little later, while the relative position remained the same, the showing of the Liberals considerably improved. I then said I thought we would win, believing that the first vote would be from the town of Oshawa where C.C.F. is very strong. The last vote to come in would be the rural vote where I think the Liberals are stronger though I am told the C.C.F. is as well pretty strong in the rural. As far as I would go at the moment – 8.20 P.M. – I would say we may win but still doubt if we will.

"Tucker's resignation was read by the Speaker in the House today which means that we lose one on division there. If we lose Ontario and Vancouver, that will mean four on a division. Lacombe [Independent M.P. for

Laval–Two Mountains] always has voted with us and in any emergency. He is out for an appointment as a magistrate from Duplessis which means one more on a division. In other words, six less than we have had. Normal majority being somewhere around ten. That is a serious position for the Government to be in. It all goes back in part to the very long delays in bringing on by-elections and ineffective organization. I feel sorry for Tucker in Saskatchewan who is putting up a splendid fight [in the provincial election] but who seems to get the worst of it while the C.C.F. get the best at almost every turn.

"Returns that have come in since dictating the above indicate that Canadian Press concedes the election of [A.] Williams, C.C.F. This return will get to Vancouver two or three hours before polls close there. I shall certainly be surprised if we win Vancouver. I think it will be lost also to the C.C.F."

Confirmation that C.C.F. candidates had won both by-elections came the next morning. In the House, Mackenzie King reported, the C.C.F. "were in a jubilant mood. Coldwell seemed to take the matter in the right spirit. His public statement was a good one. Knowles was inclined to be demonstrative. I know our men were disappointed but not crestfallen as the Tory party appeared to be. Poor Bracken was not in the House. I think he must wish by this time he had never accepted the job of leader.

"I had a long talk with St. Laurent whose first word was that what was needed was organization from the roots up. I told him I had been trying to get that across for years past. I said to him that I thought I ought to take Mayhew into the Government at once so as not to leave British Columbia without a Minister. He spoke of having a word with Tom Reid [M.P. for New Westminster] first. I felt he seemed to think that Reid should be recognized. There is no doubt in my mind that Mayhew alone of the British Columbia members commands the respect of all. He would be only [in the Cabinet] until a general election when another could be chosen, if need be, and perhaps just after the election rather than before. I said I would ask Glen to resign Mines and Resources. Give that to MacKinnon. Let him drop the Fisheries and give Mayhew the Fisheries. This should be done without delay."

After arranging for Glen's resignation, the Prime Minister "talked with MacKinnon. Told him what was on my mind. He was quite cordial in his approval. Thought I was right in all the steps. Thought there was no chance for him to drop out until elections. He said he would be very happy to take that post.

"Tonight I 'phoned Howe to thank him for his help in the campaign. Also Senator McKeen at Vancouver and Tom Reid. All seemed most appreciative of my giving them a special word of thanks. Sent telegrams this morning to Gifford, our candidate in Ontario, and to Campney in British Columbia. McKeen says we did not get out half the vote. Why, he does not quite know. Some of the men working on flood relief, etc. The real fault is the delay in bringing on the campaigns. I told Howe tonight I thought we should come on at once when Ilsley resigns. Also as soon as Saskatchewan elections are over, with Tucker's. I am far from believing that this shake-up may not do a lot of good coming as it does before the Convention and bearing out as it does what I have said as to the need of party organization. Howe was right in saying that some younger men should be in charge."

On June 10 Mackenzie King completed twenty-one years of service in the office of Prime Minister and had a typically active day. Just before noon, he summoned Mayhew and told him "I had decided to appoint a Minister from British Columbia at once and would like to have him come into the Government. I knew he had not thought of running again but it seemed to me that he might. I felt he should come in at least until the end of the Parliament. That that honour was due him and that I hoped, when the time came, he would see his way to continue on as Minister for British Columbia. I said I thought his presence in the Cabinet would be appreciated by the province, and our members. He was very pleased. . . . Felt, however, that Tom Reid might feel that he had some claims. He mentioned he would not wish to stand in his way. I said there could, of course, be no doubt that the people of the province would look to Mayhew as to natural successor. Sinclair [M.P. for Vancouver North] was young and had his future. . . ."

The Cabinet met at noon and the Prime Minister outlined the changes in the ministry, Glen's resignation, Mayhew's appointment to Fisheries, and MacKinnon's transfer to Mines and Resources. In addition, a number of Parliamentary Assistants were appointed or transferred. Robert Winters went from National Revenue to Transport; Reid replaced him in National Revenue. L. A. Mutch, M.P. for Winnipeg South, was appointed to Veterans Affairs and J. W. MacNaught, M.P. for Prince, to Fisheries.

That evening, Premier Johnson of British Columbia came to Laurier House to dine with Mackenzie King. "I like Johnson very much," the Prime Minister wrote. "A fine fellow. Nice looking man. Fine character. Icelandic descent. During the evening, had a talk with Hamber, of British Columbia, re flood situation getting even worse; now threatening whole communities with risk of lives. Hamber wanted martial law declared but martial law means absence of all other laws which cannot be carried out. However, Claxton is watching Defence end. 'Phoned him about doing everything. [A state of emergency had been declared in British Columbia on May 31 and on June 9 a joint federal-provincial scheme for relief and rehabilitation of areas where flooding was particularly severe was announced.] Johnson enjoyed seeing the house and having a talk. He remained until 9.45 P.M. I had had P. come intending to go over the Hospital speech but felt it was a mistake to tackle it tonight. Came to bed and got the news in bed. Afterwards, dictated diary for today to H. until 20 to 11 P.M. Quite a heavy day with what remains to be done tomorrow. However, I believe that all will be well.

"I again am thankful to God that I have reached the milestone of 21 years in office. A record that will not be equalled, I imagine, for a long time to come, I almost doubt if ever again in Canada. I am grateful for the strength that I have today. Grateful for the opportunities that the past years have given. Grateful for what opportunities may still lie ahead. At least, I have been able, I believe, thus far, to do honour to the names I bear."

Mackenzie King spent Saturday, June 12, in Toronto where he attended the official opening of Sunnybrook Hospital and a civic dinner. The next day he was in Dorval as a guest of J. W. McConnell. He enjoyed his "talks with McConnell. Find him exceedingly pleasant. A man of fine noble purpose. I noticed he always tries to pass on a nice word about others. He is not given to being critical – is rather kind."

During June, the Prime Minister became concerned again about the effects of the budget and continuing inflationary pressures on the government's political prospects. On June 15 he had an "interview of some length with Humphrey Mitchell about reduction of interest on annuities and pointing out necessity of not allowing the Finance Department, by its economic theories, to help to destroy the Government which I think it is already succeeding in doing by its policies over last year or two.

"After the Co-operatives delegation, had a meeting of Cabinet which lasted until nearly 2. Discussed among other things the problem of rises in prices of bread, meat, etc. through situations that have arisen. Mayhew was in the Cabinet for the first time today. I can see he is going to be a helpful addition. However, it was apparent that even if it [Mayhew's appointment] was harmful politically, it was the right thing to do. He has been getting the finance point of view which carries the risk of being harmful and the certainty of defeat on some of the matters that were being discussed. I feel very anxous about this situation which I think is one of the most serious the Government has faced yet. Possibility of increase in price of bread, meat, soap and much else. I stressed the need of saving the political situation even if it meant something that was not orthodox from a finance point of view. Unfortunately Abbott was busy with a Bill down-stairs. Howe held out for line being advocated but himself admitted we had made a real mistake in applying all the surplus in reduction of debt instead of giving half at least in the form of tax relief."

At the Cabinet meeting the next day, "much time taken up first with the question of annuities. Interest rates thereon. Really important part with a long discussion on the action to be taken with respect to continuing or removing certain subsidies, and action to be taken to prevent rise in the cost of bread, soaps, etc. With regard to meats, it was clear rise could not be prevented but some steps might be taken to keep down the rise. There was a discussion at some length about removal of cattle embargo going in to the United States. It looks as if Gardiner had deliberately made the statement that embargo would be removed later to help an immediate rise in prices in Saskatchewan which is most unfortunate as it makes the whole situation for the future very complicated. Nothing was to have been said of a possible rise until on into August. The whole situation on prices is very threatening.

"I spoke out very strongly in the Cabinet about the necessity of our considering very carefully the whole situation from the political point of view. I said if we lost more by-elections and antagonized the people any more on taking steps which will send up prices, where it was possible for us to avoid so doing, I thought the Government would be defeated at the next elections. I said quite frankly – perhaps too bluntly in Abbott's presence – that I thought the budget had been a mistake. That the whole surplus should not be used to wipe off the debt. That some relief should have been given consumers. I thought now we might well say the time had come where we were using part of the surplus that we were bargaining for, to prevent a further rise by re-imposing certain subsidies. I pointed out there were four events of which we must take particular note: first, what will happen at the end of this session. I believed we would be confronted with debate in the House in which an effort will be made to show to what small proportions our majority had been reduced. Might even meet with defeat or all but defeat at that time. Certainly if steps were taken which would cause consumers' position to be made more difficult. Secondly, there was a Convention at which we might find that instead of the Government gaining general acceptance of its policies by the delegations that would be present, we would discover that delegations were coming from all parts of the country, ready to talk to the Government and tell us wherein they thought our policies needed a change. Thirdly, there was a general election which we have to consider. I thought it was now a matter of Liberals or C.C.F. Our job in the meantime was to make as certain as we could that all of our people, especially the women, would not be taken from our ranks to join the C.C.F. We might expect some movement in Quebec which would be upsetting there and no one could tell what the outcome would be, unless we regained some strength meanwhile.

"I then pointed out that the matter above all else that had to be watched were the pending by-elections. If we could win the seat which Ilsley is resigning, and the one Tucker has resigned from, and two Quebec seats where Independents are resigning, in order to take Government appointments from or join with Duplessis – we might reinstate ourselves in the public mind. If, however, we lost those elections, I would not like to say what might happen when Parliament reassembles for another session. I pointed out that we were no longer before the country in the position we were before the recent by-elections and the Ontario provincial elections. I felt it necessary to speak out very strongly as I feel that the Finance Department policies are getting us into no end of difficulty from our political point of view. I tried to point out that unless we wished to have the C.C.F. come in and put through vast subsidies, restore controls, etc., on different items, to say nothing of other measures that we were introducing, we might have to make some expenditures on a considerable scale which would prevent further rises in the cost of living at least for some little time to come. It is a hard situation to meet as no doubt the strictly economic point of view will tend in other directions, but they would be directions which would lead to the defeat of the Government.

"I was tired this morning from not having rested too well last night. Felt that I was speaking a little more sharply and critically than I should have done. I felt, however, that matters had been too completely left to Abbott, Howe and St. Laurent and the three of them do not really see where their views are leading the Government as a whole. I would think that all the rest of the Government excepting Mayhew who is, I know, of Abbott's point of view, and Ilsley who was not present would be of my view and that pretty strongly.

"Martin and Bertrand are the most outspoken. Too many of the others are silent."

On June 17, a delegation of Ontario Liberal members, with Louis Breithaupt as their spokesman, saw the Prime Minister "about the situation of the party as a result of the by-elections and particularly the strong feeling which exists against the budget having given no relief to taxpayers, etc. Breithaupt said the Government were getting the reputation with the people of being icy cold; really not being in touch with the people at all. He said he knew what my own attitude was but the blame was placed on the Finance Department and leaving matters too completely to officials there.

I told the deputation I was glad they had come and spoken their minds freely. I gave them the reasons which caused us to agree to the budget in the form in which it was presented. Said I would immediately make their representations known to the Cabinet. This I did at the meeting between 12 and 2 in my room 401. I was amazed on looking at the evening Journal tonight to see that Breithaupt had apparently talked with the reporters and told pretty much the whole story with the twist that the Journal gives these matters in the press.

"This makes increasingly difficult the attempt to get the Government to do the things that yesterday I was urging its members so strongly to do and which today I felt they were coming nearer to agreeing to. I still feel that Howe and Abbott impose their own will much too strongly on others largely through having a knowledge of certain matters respecting finance and trade and relations to the United States, etc., which are not possessed in equal measure by other members of the Cabinet. I spoke again today very strongly against what I believe to be the feeling of the members and stressing anew how dangerously near we might be to defeat before the session is over. How impossible our situation will be next session if in the interval something is not done to let the people see that we are sympathetic, particularly with those who are finding it increasingly difficult to meet continued rise in cost of living.

"Martin appealed pretty strongly for action on lines of prosecutions of combines. I found a readiness to have excise removed. Also I think something to prevent the rise in price of bread. There seemed to be difficulties ahead with respect to meat."

He added: "I am greatly concerned lest the inevitable divisions between those who view matters from the financial standpoint and those from the human, will bring cleavages that are too wide."

Next day (June 18) Mackenzie King had a talk with Abbott who "naturally had been very upset by Breithaupt's interview. Was inclined I think to feel that I had sided with the Liberals who were protesting and had not backed up his policies. Pointed out to him that Breithaupt had said that I had said their projects were wise. Drew his attention to the fact that 'wise' would not be the word used in relation to project. They would either be right or wrong or desirable, etc. 'Wise' related to procedure which is what I had dwelt on three or four times. That they were wise in coming to talk over their difficulties with me instead of making protests in public. The very thing that Breithaupt did immediately after the interview.

"Abbott drew attention to the Montreal Gazette's report which said that I had spoken about the Bank of Canada people, officials, and the

Price Board people throwing about their weight, etc., during the war. I was able to say I had not used any expression of the kind. No mention had been made of the Bank of Canada or the Prices Board – all straight lying on the part of Blakeley, the reporter. Fortunately the concluding paragraph of the Gazette article said there had been a turbulent scene in the Cabinet and that Abbott was the target of the attack. Abbott was in the Cabinet himself and therefore knew what took place there. As a matter of fact, it was one of the best meetings we have ever had and one which had led almost to all but complete agreement to make some of the changes that the Members had been asking for. Abbott said to me he would find it very difficult now to carry out these changes. I said it certainly had made the situation embarrassing but not to make any decisions at present. I can see that he had been quite hurt and rightly so. He said that Breithaupt's action had been just because someone in his own riding had been affected adversely. He was like Euler, German in his disposition and very selfish, etc. I think the whole business was just that Breithaupt had been talking in four walls of a room; when he got up, he was still underway with steam and had said more than he had intended to say. I tried to get him today to talk with but could not locate him.

"The interview was a most unfortunate one and has been most embarrassing."

At noon the Cabinet met. "Meeting lasted again until about 2. I began by referring to Breithaupt's statement. Told them how the Members had come to my room. Mentioned that I had given the Cabinet the full information yesterday; sought to explain Breithaupt's action by what I have just dictated. Suggested we should not discuss today the questions of prices and that it would be unwise to make any decisions at once.

"Abbott accepted the position very well I thought. Said no more than he would be expected to say in the circumstances."

Mackenzie King "found the members of Council and I myself like the others much depressed. Breithaupt has brought home to the party the significance of losses of the by-elections and the narrow margin by which we are now holding on to power. I am amazed at the feeling of certainty that most of the Ministers seemed to have; that we are running no risk of serious embarrassment before the session is over. I look forward to a rather disconcerting time in the last week."

Later that day he had a talk with St. Laurent, first about Ilsley. "Talked of Ilsley's resignation. St. Laurent thought he should hold it back until after the Convention. Then a word about the Convention proceedings. St. Laurent agreed I should come on with my address before the resolutions, etc., were brought in. Also that I should open proceedings myself and turn them over to Fogo and Blanchette. He agreed with me too it was inadvisable to have a row of premiers making speeches. I said I thought I would make one important speech and one at the close congratulating the new leader.

"We talked of the Breithaupt incident. I spoke of the precarious position the party was in. Individuals making all kinds of difficulties for us. He seemed to not be concerned about that. Also spoke of being amazed at progress he thought would be made in Quebec against Duplessis. I am very doubtful about that.

"The trouble is, in talking with Ministers and others, people say to them what they think they would like to know rather than, too often, the truth. Ilsley is agreeable to staying on until the next session of Parliament but will not stay past that time. I can understand his position and told him so. I advised strongly his being present at the Convention. His first idea was not to be present. I said I thought he should be and should make a speech. I said I thought perhaps the by-election could be brought on immediately after, so as to ensure our having an extra vote in the House. He thinks there is no doubt about our winning the seat. Paul Martin, on the other hand, says he has evidence from Gillis, the C.C.F. are already at work and expect to be able to carry the seat. Howe would prefer to have no by-election. I think that would be a mistake and would cost us a seat in the general election. However the thing now is to wait and see what happens in Quebec and New Brunswick, and how things shape up at the Convention.

"I talked at length with Paul Martin about the Prices Committee work and asked to be shown their report, being given particulars of it before it is brought down. I suggested pressing for some form of board to which complaints could be referred. He repeated his suggestion as to the possibility of the Tariff Board being used for that purpose until regularly established board similar to that of the Railway Committee, be established. I am sure the Ministers are too tired to tackle anything in the way of new legislation. Most of them are getting pretty weary."

The Abbott-Breithaupt controversy was magnified by the press and raised in the House of Commons. On June 22, the Prime Minister saw Breithaupt who "looked very downhearted. Said the last thing he had meant to do was to cause me any concern. Told his wife he would regret that more than anything. Could not believe his eyes when he read the account in the press (which I felt sure would be the case). Showed me a wire he had sent Abbott to deplore what had appeared. Agreed that our whole conversation had related to the future; that there had been no agreement on anything. Had his little notes there. Showed me some telegrams he had sent to organizers about the elections. He explained that this was because he wanted to be sure of his case before he stated it. This was in reference to budget having hurt us in the last campaign. I think practically everyone admits that. His whole attitude and utterances however were just what I expected, that he had really not meant to hurt or to embarrass the Government but to help in regard to the future. That there had been no agreement on anything.

"When I saw Abbott later, and told him this, he said I was more charitable with Breithaupt than he would be. He thought he was personally interested in radios, washing machines, leather goods, etc., which had been affected. This had occasioned him to feel as he did. I don't think myself it would have occasioned him to talk with the press. I am sure that was just because he was caught off guard and being pursued by reporters who I had not even known were waiting about the time the group came into my office.

"I agreed with Abbott as to what he had in mind saying in the House and which he did actually say. I was glad when Knowles asked a question which gave me a chance to clear up misrepresentation as to what had been 'agreed to' at the talk I had with Breithaupt and his group and the rumours about differences between them and myself."

At the Cabinet meetings on June 22 and again on June 24 there was a good deal of discussion about rising prices and the report of the select committee of the House of which Paul Martin was chairman. Mackenzie King reported that "St. Laurent was helpful in meeting the opposition of Abbott and Howe to some measures of subsidy and to keeping on certain controls at one or two courses of action along Liberal instead of Tory lines. Of the two, Abbott is much more Liberal than Howe. I tried to keep the proceedings calm and collected and succeeded in this.

"Martin has a poor way of presenting his case. He gets too impatient and is at times inclined to be rude. He of course is very fatigued and weary. When I saw that we were not likely to get a favourable decision along the lines that I thought we should have without embarrassing Abbott and Howe in the presence of others, I suggested Mr. St. Laurent, Ilsley, and Martin should remain after Council and let them sit down with me and see if the four of us could not work out satisfactory clauses.

"I tackled the one on subsidies and controls and got agreement of all four to what subsequently became part of the report. Ilsley worked out a clause regarding taxation of profits. St. Laurent was helpful in both and on other clauses. They were all tentative. Martin had still his problem to get them into the report just as I had the problem of getting the Cabinet to accept them.

"I took a very strong position on our not allowing the price of bread to increase at any cost and some subsidy arrangement would have to be worked out to that end. We got a decision favourable to that. Both Howe and Abbott said they did not like it but saw the rest of us were against it, and they would agree. The trouble is they have a greater knowledge of the facts of situations than others and others are handicapped in debating with them.

"I stayed on until half past three without any lunch to get this matter straightened out. It was intensely hot and humid but I felt we were helping to make a programme for the Liberal Party Convention and also to get policies introduced which would help to save our people from going over to the C.C.F. and eventually help us to win out in another campaign."

The following day (June 25) the Cabinet reached final agreement "on arrangement that may be necessary to keep down a rise in prices of bread; also to postpone action with regard to withdrawal of subsidies on oils and fats which will affect some commodities until the autumn.

"Martin got his report on Committee on Prices into the House at 3. Its summary is in the press tonight. I think what he has achieved is remarkable. A lot of work has been done on the report and that in the right direction by members of the Committee. I think he has done a fine service to the party in getting matters through as he has. He says he was up all night, battling to get the final consent of the Committee.

"I regard this as an achievement which would not certainly have been brought about but for his persistence and also had I not been present to handle the situation in Council and, I might add, without St. Laurent's assistance. He has kept saying that if we ever admitted that a situation existed that we could not deal with while others were prepared to say they could, we might as well look forward to certain defeat."

Mackenzie King was greatly pleased by Martin's speech closing the debate on the report of the Committee on June 28. He noted that the Minister "was in exceptionally good form and was going at the Tories with an oldfashioned off-hand style. He was not too careful in some of his assertions but paid little or no attention to objections taken. Did particularly effective work in taking up each resolution in the report and challenging the Tories to vote against it. The C.C.F. had evidently been wholly sympathetic to the report as finally made. At the end, he was given a great ovation by our men and when it came to vote on the resolution, not a single Member in the House was prepared to vote against it. The Tories did not rise to demand a vote, indeed they were most anxious that none should be called. I felt very inclined to make them vote but on reflection, I felt that they had something of a real grievance in the way they had been treated in committee and after all we were winning the battle and it might be just as well to leave matters there. They had had their talk but when it came to action, were ready to quit. There seemed agreement among the Ministers who were around me that it was just as well not to call for a vote. It really was a triumph. The work of the Prices Enquiry has been a difficult matter, particularly concluding part of its work and indecision as to almost the very last to whether a report should be made or not. And then hesitation on the part of the Government itself as to a clear cut statement of its own policies. The chances are while the Breithaupt incident was an unfortunate one, because of being so unusual and contrary to matters of confidence, it really did help to force an issue in a way which, in the end, has helped to bring a clear definition of Liberal policy and a definition along lines of the real Liberals who were anxious to support. It would help to shape the platform for the Liberal Convention."

The Prime Minister's spirits had been lifted considerably by the Liberal party's gains in the Saskatchewan provincial election on June 24. Next day he noted that "the morning papers announced the Liberals had carried 18 seats. Tucker, of course, has gained his own seat by a big majority. That is a splendid victory he has had with all the odds against it – federal by-elections won by C.C.F.; provincial success in Ontario seats by C.C.F.; Drew's victory; trouble over railway rates; and Heaven knows what else. By his steady fighting and fine leadership, he has raised the Liberal following in the House from 5 to 18, and very great contest in other seats. He has put new heart into the Liberal party across the continent. Only one Tory has been elected and he is likely to join the Liberals.

"I sent a telegram to Tucker this morning and tonight 'phoned him personally. He sounded remarkably fresh after the campaign. Told me how easily they might have defeated the Government but for certain things that happened here and there. In the course of the campaign, the entry of the Social Credit did us a lot of harm but not one of these men carried his deposit. It means that from now on, the fight in Saskatchewan is likely to be between Liberals and C.C.F. I think the results of the Liberal fight have put a militant spirit into the party of which it has been in great need. I now feel entirely confident that we will win the next federal election. It is pretty certain that New Brunswick on Monday will return a large Liberal majority in that province."

As Mackenzie King expected, the McNair government was re-elected on June 28. He described it as "a Liberal sweep. I drafted a wire to Mc-Nair the Premier and later got him on the 'phone. He told me at the time that it was doubtful if Conservatives would get more than 4 or 6. They got 5. C.C.F. and Social Credit did not win a seat. He also told me that the young people had also helped very much in the winning of the victory which had been due to organization. It was a tremendous achievement and will be most helpful to the federal Liberal situation. It should also help the Liberals in Quebec. If they could only defeat Duplessis, another victory for Liberalism in the federal field would be as certain as day follows night.

"Bertrand said today he believed that if the elections were at this time, they would win. I very much doubt that. I think our Quebec organization has been practically nil though the province itself is unquestionably Liberal.

"The Conservative party is in an appalling condition. It is rapidly becoming extinct."

Before he retired, the Prime Minister was very anxious to ensure that the national capital plan would continue to be implemented. His diary for the first six months of 1948 contains repeated references to this subject. On March 19 he reviewed the plan with Jacques Greber and "told him I hoped they would get something under way in regard to the outlook from the Hill [Gatineau Hills] beyond which gives the view of Ottawa. To have plinths carry the record of the battles of the war just as the last war of 1914–18 was recorded inside the peace tower. Significant facts could be recorded on the stones to be cut in the mountainside.

"There could be a platform from which all the main points of view of the City would be seen and which could be designated by arrows.

"Later tonight, I 'phoned Bronson. Told him of my talk and strongly advocated getting something under way this summer. Both he and Greber said they would see that this was done. I also stressed to Bronson the importance of keeping the centre of the City open as a common, as I did to Greber. Not allow any City Hall to be built in the centre. Build a City Hall in another place. I liked what Greber showed me of sketches he had made for the war veterans building. A great improvement on what had been suggested before. Linking in two buildings together with an arcade. He has some real sense of classical beauty."

After reviewing outstanding legislative proposals on May 26, Mackenzie King told "the Cabinet that I would like to bring in a bill on the improvement of the National Capital. I said, as the Ministers knew, I had taken a special interest in the development of the Capital. We had now reached the point, however, where, if progress was to be made, the Government would have to make clear its decision to appropriate money over a term of years. I said I wanted the Ministers to feel free to speak critically. That, while I was interested, I knew there could be some objection and did not wish to press for the measure unduly. Pointed out to Council what was proposed in the way of removal of the tracks, arranging for many thoroughfares. What was thought of as a Memorial in the Laurentian Hills, disclosing

Ottawa skyline and necessity of a bridge over the Canal to lessen traffic around the Chateau, etc. I then took the suggestion that Bronson made of appropriations of 10, 15 millions – over the next ten years. St. Laurent was very helpful in suggesting that it might be well in any bill to make what was done subject to the approval of Parliament each year – by having the amount to be used for that year introduced in the form of supplementary estimates.

"Dr. McCann was particularly helpful in pointing out that he thought the amount proposed was too small. That at least 25 millions ought to be appropriated over the next 10 years. To my surprise, Council seemed prepared to go that far. Abbott took no exception. Others, while not participating much in the discussion, indicated clearly their readiness to bring in the bill. Ilsley was not in Council at the time, nor was Howe, but I had authority to go ahead and made the announcement in the House at 3.

"I must now take care to get a bill carefully drafted and a speech carefully prepared. It will be my last measure as Prime Minister and I shall be surprised if with this background, the Commons does not support the measure. Taken in conjunction with the health programme of this year and labour legislation based on my Industrial Disputes Act, will make a fine conclusion to my record in Parliament on constructive measures that will run far into the future, affecting the well-being of the people. I can see I am very tired but far from being sufficiently rested, this morning, to urge the matter in Council. I must now get sufficiently on with the task to make the bill a real success.

"With what the City has been doing in the way of arranging for the annexation of areas round about, the Ontario Government to assist; also what has been planned by Greber, etc., brings all these things together in a way that should make possible a first-rate story. It is going to take a lot of concentration to get it worked out in time."

The Prime Minister presented a draft bill to the Cabinet on June 3. "Some of the Ministers spoke of possible effect that the mention of 25 million dollars would have in other parts of Canada. Ilsley, for example, of what would be said in Nova Scotia with the limited amounts being voted for the marsh lands. What would be said in British Columbia of limited amount we might be giving for floods. Anything involving smaller expenditures for smaller purposes would be compared with this vast amount. Also I thought the amount being asked for Ottawa for the first year, 4 million dollars, was excessive. I agreed with the criticism, felt that it would not be helpful to the party. That it would be much better to have just a measure that would declare intention; be in earnest of what should be done over the years and vote sum for one year only at a time. Not mentioning any total over a period of years. That I felt would remove necessity for any resolution in advance, and debate. When I spoke to P. of this, he suggested resolution without a bill. This seemed to me to be preferable. I have decided to bring in only a resolution and to arrange a sum in the estimates, this year. The whole matter should be put on basis of improvements that will be necessitated through Ottawa being a Capital City and which the City and municipalities themselves would not be expected to undertake."

A resolution was drafted and on June 17 Mackenzie King "took up the subject anew in the Cabinet. It was like going over ground that had never been agreed to or thought of before. At least, it so seemed to me. Heeney was of the opinion that there was more sympathy in the Cabinet for the resolution than I had imagined. Later I asked for supplementary estimates for this year – 2½ millions. He thinks I would as readily get 3 millions were I to ask Council for it. I may do this tomorrow. The Resolution has been recast along lines I indicated to H. after the talk in Council and is now I think in very good form. I am sending the draft to be placed in today's Votes and Proceedings of the House. I am pleased to have the Resolution connected with the 17th of the month. I believe it is one that will find its place in the History of Canada and be quoted many times in the course of years to come. The thing now is to get a good speech for the occasion of its introduction in Parliament. That is going to be difficult to do with the pressure what it is; our having three sessions a day including Saturdays which was agreed to this morning and with other inevitable engagements. I must pray for strength and guidance."

When Mackenzie King arrived at the House of Commons on June 28, "there seemed to be uncertainty as to what it was best to begin with, this morning. I decided, however, at the last moment, to go on with my Resolution on the Capital and so informed the House at the outset. When I got up to speak, I found great difficulty in speaking loudly enough to make myself heard. In fact, it was one of the few occasions where Members asked that I should speak louder. I went ahead in a mechanical sort of way without really being too sure of the order in which I should take up some of the topics that were in my mind. Indeed I drifted into an explanation of the projects that have been advocated. As I proceeded, I found myself getting very tired and very indifferent, as to what I ought to say further or as to the manner of saying it. The result was that what might and should have been the occasion of a great speech, one worthy of being quoted from in the years to come, was a very commonplace statement of a few obvious things which should be done immediately in the way of necessary developments in the Capital. I made no reference whatever to the improvements of the Capital being in the nature of a memorial to the soldiers in the last war. This I did more or less deliberately as I knew that when the matter was taken up during my absence in England, the Conservatives strongly disapproved of voting money for Capital improvements in the way of doing something to commemorate the services and sacrifices of the men in the war. I felt that to bring that topic in would create immediately a controversy which might cause an unpleasant debate. The main thing was to get the Resolution passed by both Houses and then later, as headway is made in the developments, and people are brought to where they can understand what is proposed as a Memorial, to then bring forward the project in that larger connection. I am sure that from the point of view of tactics, this is wiser though I would like to have stressed the war memorial feature of it all in relation to the second. McIlraith fortunately said the right words at the close of his remarks.

"I was glad to get through with the Resolution. A bit humiliated making such a poor fist of what ought to have been one of the best speeches of my life, with the knowledge however that the thing itself was all important and had been done, namely, the last measure introduced by me in the House of Commons was one that had relation to Canada's future and the future of its Capital.

"The resolution carried at the hour of adjournment – 1 o'clock."

On June 24 the Prime Minister had joined other members of the House listening to the proceedings of the Republican convention which chose Thomas Dewey as leader of the party. He "much enjoyed being seated . . . with members of different parties. Could not help thinking what a mistake one made in not mixing freely with the Members. Gathering my information from talks with them rather than following the secluded, cloistered sort of life in my library at Laurier House doing hack work where I should really have been making no end of friends as can be so easily made at this time. All Members of the House feel pleased when the Prime Minister talks with them and one would find it a very easy thing literally to make hosts of friends by just a little more of the personal touch. That has been one of the several mistakes of my public life. Part of it comes from not being married, not having anyone to help me in my home. The other, the lack of organization in my office which should have been five times the size it is and ten times as efficient. I have had to do far too much. What other Ministers regard as staff work rather than their own. It gave me a feeling of real sadness as I sat there and thought I was giving up all this just because I had found myself growing unequal to the task when, had my life been differently planned and my office work differently arranged, I might have been gaining instead both in body and mind and spirit from the kind of associations which a position of Prime Minister enables a man to enjoy. I wondered very much if I had not perhaps made a mistake in deciding to give up all that I have in the way of position and means, to retire at a time when I am now beginning to feel my normal strength again. I think the decisions were made when I was more or less affected by over-fatigue, influenza, etc. Nevertheless, this I know is a matter of feeling. My reason tells me I am taking the sound and sensible course."

Still in an introspective mood on June 28, Mackenzie King called on the Governor-General who had just returned to Ottawa from a visit to Brazil. He told Alexander about the plans for the Convention in August and "of my resigning a short time thereafter. He used the expression: that is a little sad. I said that, in some ways, I felt that myself. I did not like the severance of the happy relations I had had with him, my colleagues and others, but I felt I was following the wise course. He said something about my having plenty to do in the way of writing, etc. I told him I did feel, if anything was to be done in that direction, it should be done before I became unequal to the task. Moreover, I simply could not contemplate going through the strain of another general election, without organization that would be needed to have it conducted properly. I told him of the cables from Attlee [concerning the proposed conference of Commonwealth prime ministers]. He said they would certainly want you there, with your experience. Hoped that I would go. I said I thought it would result in that. It would make probably a good rounding out of my years of office. He said: you have had a very great career."

Later that day, the Prime Minister had a talk with Gardiner who had come to recommend the appointment of a Senator for Saskatchewan. He "told him no appointments would be made until after the Convention. Gave no promise. He told me that he had spoken to St. Laurent some time ago of his thought of entering for leadership. St. Laurent had told him – and Howe had told him – he ought to do that. St. Laurent had said it was better that there should be a contest. I spoke about bringing on by-election at once in Rosthern. He told me that he thought it was better to hold that seat until after the Convention. We might want it for some purposes in the reconstruction of the Cabinet. He then said I will tell you what I have in my mind; if I were chosen leader, I would ask Gordon Ross to be a Minister from Saskatchewan. I told Gardiner later that Gordon Ross had good claims for a Senatorship. . . ."

In the House on June 29, Mackenzie King was questioned about Canadian representation at the Conference of Prime Ministers in London. He found it "quite amusing to see how eager Macdonnell was to see what answer I would give to Graydon's question as to whether I, myself, would represent Canada at the Conference. The answer I gave left the door open for whatever situation there may be. St. Laurent seemed quite pleased with the answer I had given. I think the feeling of the House, as indicated by a remark by Pouliot, was that I should go. It will be interesting to see how the press views the matter. It will be a great victory on top of all the criticism there has been as regards my attitude to conferences in London that the press of the country should be more or less united in my being the one to represent Canada at this time. Some will say that the new leader ought to have that experience but I imagine most will take the view that, with the experience I have, I should be the one to be at the Conference."

Late that evening Ilsley came to the Prime Minister's office in the House of Commons with his formal letter of resignation. He told Mackenzie King "he would like me to see it before it was signed and asked when he thought it should be regarded as received from him. He had already dated it: June 30. I read the letter over and said to him that nothing could be kinder. That I wished to repeat again how very deeply we all felt at his retirement from the Government. I said I could truthfully say I knew of no one in the course of my public life who had been more conscientious, continuously industrious, whose time and thought had been given more completely to public affairs or who had been more honourable in their discharge. That I felt his service had been of the highest possible order and could not thank him too warmly for what it had meant to the Government and to the country. I wished him the best of everything in the practice of his profession. He seemed quite moved when I finished speaking, and said he was deeply grateful to have the words I had expressed.

"With reference to law, he said he already saw how intensely interesting it would be. He had not realized until working on the case that he is preparing for the Privy Council, how many matters there were of which consideration had to be taken, of the things he had to contemplate being obliged to answer in a moment. He spoke of the competition with great minds. Said to him that he need have no fears; that his mind was of the highest order. That he had in addition what many others had not, a long experience in Parliament, and public life and experience in the office of Minister of Justice. That all this would stand him in great stead. I implored of him not to work too hard but to give himself a little more freedom than he had while in office. He asked what he had better do about the letter. Said he might as well sign it at once, and walked over to my desk and attached his signature and then handed the letter to me.

"I told him I would give him a reply tomorrow. I wanted him to know that it was a letter I regretted deeply having to accept, bringing as it did his resignation from the Government.

"As he was to be in the House tomorrow, I did not say good-bye but we parted at the door, each with a look of happiness and a thought that if these separations had to come, this one had been of the character it was."

At the Cabinet meeting on June 30, Mackenzie King spoke "of this being Ilsley's last day in Cabinet. Turned to him. He was sitting in a corner just in a chair beneath the bronze bust the party had given me. I spoke quite strongly of how deeply we all felt in losing him from the Government. Of what we all felt his services had meant to the country and the Government in particular, specially to us all. Of his integrity and industry. Thought and judgment, etc. Of his exceptionally conscientious, earnest discharge of public duty. (I had said to him yesterday that I did not know how many millions of dollars he had saved the country or how much money I had saved but I wondered what might happen now that he was going and not having him to assist me in my resistance to vast expenditures. I said I felt so tired I found it almost impossible to battle. He had said that was only too true.)

"When I had concluded the remarks, I went over to his chair and shook hands with him, extending to him the best of wishes for his future and using the expression: May God bless you, at the end of what I had to say. Ilsley seemed genuinely touched by what had been said. He said it made him feel particularly after what I had said to him last night, as if he were shirking a real responsibility in getting out. He went on to say, however, he had felt this was necessary. Spoke of having to separate from colleagues with whom he had been so closely associated, etc. It was quite a moving little scene."

Amid the many preoccupations of the day, the Prime Minister managed to prepare his reply to Ilsley's letter and deliver it to him in person. At the end of proceedings in the House, Howard Green "made a very kind and pleasant reference to Ilsley. That occasioned something more by Coldwell and a word by him in reference to myself. Hume had sent me a note from the Gallery that Coldwell was going to make some reference. Hoped I would stay in the House. There were one or two other references so I then decided to read to the House the letters and to add a word about Ilsley. To say just a word of thanks to Coldwell and others. This gave me a chance to say a final word of good-bye. I did so in just an expression of pleasure it was to be giving up office after so many years with the knowledge that I was leaving with the goodwill of Members of all parties. I thanked them one and all. There was a great round of applause to this. I noticed that Macdonnell had come down to the front seat. He was the only one in that row at that time. He pounded his desk approvingly and turned to whoever was to his left and I could see was remarking on the appropriateness of what I had said. Evidently the House was moved. It was somewhat of a dramatic scene – all unpremeditated, unplanned, but brought into a perfect setting by Pouliot's action which was intended to be that of an enemy."

The speech by Pouliot had been made earlier in the evening on the Prime Minister's Estimates which, according to Mackenzie King, "would have passed without a word had not Pouliot intervened. He made an extraordinary speech which revealed the resentment he had cherished as he said toward myself over eighteen years. He tried to have it appear that he had the true Liberal doctrine. Had not paid attention to followers but was indifferent to their views and more or less doing things on my own. He sought to have it appear I had followed his advice on some matters of administration – all nonsense. Also completely wrongly interpreted some remarks I had made to him about Europe being mostly in one's thoughts when one was there, and not Canada. What I really had told him was necessity of our Ministers paying attention to Canadian affairs, not spending too much time abroad.

"I could not make out what he meant about my stating what I intended to do as to carrying on as Leader. His references to the Convention. Indeed I could make so little out of what he said beyond that I saw he was in one of his resentful moods and liking attention drawn to himself that I found it difficult to know what to say in reply. It was apparent that our party, indeed the House – both thinly seated – resented very much his remarks and tried to stop him. I kept thinking that he had intended to attack either Heeney or Pickersgill from what I had heard from others but apparently it was myself he had been nursing a grudge against. I began to see that what he evidently was feeling was that he had not been made a fuss over; called into consultation, etc. I never dreamt until later on when it was pointed out to me that he had really felt he should have been in the Ministry. A perfectly impossible man for any Government.

"I had not intended to speak on the estimates at all. Indeed my whole feeling through the day was to avoid anything in the nature of a valedictory or anything of a sentimental character, at leaving the desk I had occupied for over twenty-one years. I really felt therefore that I owed him thanks for giving me a natural excuse to speak. What I said appears in Hansard. What, however, does not appear there is the guiding hand and Providence behind even Pouliot's action which gave me a chance in a very natural way to make clear my own position in the office of Prime Minister during the past years and to remove some wholly erroneous impressions which have gained nationwide, if not still wider current. Having dealt in a light way with Pouliot, I spoke of the staff of the Prime Minister's office; what I have felt most keenly about the inadequacy of its organization and staff. This should give my successor a chance to really build up what will be necessary, if he is to carry on in any orderly fashion. It also enabled me to disclose something of the office of Privy Council which might serve a useful purpose, should circumstances make this advisable a little later on. If, for example, war should come and I were to hold, as I would wish to, to what I had said about not reappearing in the House as Prime Minister, I could take that office [President of the Privy Council] and still give the Government the benefit of my experience. It afforded me, moreover, a further chance which was to say something about Laurier House. I have had very strongly the impression that once I gave up the office, an effort would be made to have it appear that Laurier House was a gift of the party and that it should go to my successor in the leadership. I felt sure that this would be the case on the part of our Quebec friends which would be natural enough if St. Laurent were chosen. On the other hand, I think I owe it to myself, having hardly had the use of my home for my personal life, to look forward to the enjoyment of it for the remainder of my days, not to be left without a home of my own.

"Pouliot's speech also gave me a chance to make very clear my intention not to resign the Prime Ministership immediately after the Leadership was determined. I felt, however, in speaking of this point that I was not making myself any too clear and regretted the clumsiness of it. I keep forgetting how people really think out these matters; most people seem to have the impression that the Leadership of the party and Prime Minister-ship necessarily go together. I made clear my intention to stay on for some weeks and possibly months; also that I recognized in this intention what I have had in mind from the beginning, namely the world situation which might make it advisable for me to hold on to office at least until the situation in Berlin has been decided one way or the other, with freedom to act as might seem advisable by the outcome.

"I had really not thought of saying anything at this time about having had to meet all the expenses of the upkeep of Laurier House myself but while on my feet seemed to be impressed by the advisability of doing this, and let the country know that I had had to carry this financial obligation all along. This gave me a chance to make clear that the house was my own; that it had been furnished with the help of personal friends. I was happy to place on records of Parliament Mr. Larkin's name in that connection and to make clear that I intended to continue to live at Laurier House, once I had given up the office of Prime Minister or Parliament. This will save no end of pressure later on. St. Laurent was sitting at my side when I was speaking. I had said nothing to him about what I intended to say. I did feel that this was the moment to make it possible for an official residence to be secured for him or whoever might be chosen and for future Prime

Ministers. If in the House another year, I could follow it up in some way myself.

"From all sides of the House, I was given a very warm reception when I concluded what I had said. Members were evidently thinking of the occasion as one related to my last appearance as Prime Minister in the House. Throughout the day, members of the press gallery seemed to be watching every moment."

When he sat down, the Prime Minister "spoke to St. Laurent about what I had said. Told him I had in mind trying to ensure a residence for himself, should he come in as Leader. I spoke to him about the Edwards property as being the finest I thought in Ottawa for the purpose. Exceptional site; fine appearing house, etc. He evidently had been exploring the situation or been talking it over with Murphy who told him there was a lease of a couple of years and the whole place would have to be torn down inside, etc. I told him the lease could be arranged in a minute. That I doubted whether Murphy was right in his view. There might be some need for alterations, probably what was most needed were additions which could easily be made. St. Laurent said he had heard there were plans for a new building which contained quarters for the Prime Minister. I told him there were indeed plans. He said to be located on the old Supreme Court area. I said there were plans; I had had them made but they were for office purposes rather than residential. Prime Minister's office, Privy Council and External Affairs. They had provision for a dining room and for a private garden as was arranged in most of the capitals of Europe but they were not meant for living quarters. I said I thought in many ways a man was better to be removed a bit away from the Parliament Buildings. To have his home away from the Buildings. It was something of a change. St. Laurent then said to me it did seem extraordinary we should spend the enormous sums we do in salaries to Ministers and Ambassadors abroad, expensive dwellings, allowances and the like, way beyond what a Prime Minister received. I told him I was glad he had come to take that view. It was something I had been citing as an absurdity over the years. All of this kind of thing I can bring out if necessary in Parliament in advocacy for another where I could not say a word in reference to myself. I felt a real sense of relief and satisfaction to have this situation which has been a torment all along the way, made perfectly clear."

He added later: "I had never intended to say what I had said in the nature of a valedictory. Indeed had no intention to make a valedictory but rather to have matters the other way about. But for the rest that I took between 3 and 4 when I was very tired, the thought might not have come to me at all of speaking on an official residence for a Prime Minister which led of course up to Laurier House. Again but for Pouliot's speech, his having waited in his secret vindictive way to say what he did, I would not probably have said what I did. In fact, all of it came to me while on my feet. I would have hesitated particularly to the reference to Laurier House but have derived a feeling of satisfaction at that utterance, much greater than almost any I have made in relation to my own affairs in a long time."

Next morning (July 1) Mackenzie King was pleased by the press reports of the closing day of the parliamentary session. He was surprised by the prominence given in the Montreal *Gazette* "to my last hours as Prime Minister in the House. Later when the *Citizen* came, I was much pleased with the front page – Mr. King says Farewell to the Commons. Karsh's picture of myself in a standing position under which Valedictory – Rt. Hon. W. L. Mackenzie King, o.m. who at 10.50 P.M. Wednesday waved a last farewell as Prime Minister to his House of Commons colleagues most of whom stood in respectful tribute to him. It was an historic occasion and in many ways the end of an era. Nothing really could be finer than this. I don't believe any Prime Minister ever left office with all so favourable at the close. 'His smiling farewell' – that is the way I should like to leave this world itself. Indeed it seemed to me through a good part of the evening that it might well be that at the close of life, I would experience a sense of gaining a larger freedom in the fuller life.

"I read the press accounts. Pouliot's speech, of course, was featured but, on the whole, the general impression was kindly."

During July, operation of Canada's major railroads was threatened by a strike. At the Cabinet meeting on July 13, the Prime Minister reported, "most of the morning was taken up with a consideration of the strike situation. Mitchell reported on the attitude of representatives of organized labour making it clear that they were very determined not to yield unless given a wage rate which they believed to be owing them.

"Their argument is that during the war, they did everything they could to meet the wishes of the Government. Did not seek to take advantage of the chances to get increases at the time. Cost of living had gone up considerably. Gardiner had looked after the interests of the producers. They thought that their interests should be given equal consideration. They have been holding out for 23¢ an hour increase. The companies still holding to around 10.

"Abbott was not in the Cabinet nor was Claxton nor Fournier nor Ilsley, or one or two others but Howe, St. Laurent, McCann, MacKinnon, Bertrand, Chevrier and Mitchell and Gibson were present. After a general discussion, I went around the Cabinet making each Member express his views. I confess I was surprised to discover that without exception, all seemed to take the view that the strike must be prevented. That the men were entitled to an increase. That the Government should lend its good offices to get the nearest compromise possible. That there was great difficulty in getting any decision as to what that figure should be. Mitchell had proposed himself 15½¢ but the men had stated absolutely they would not accept that as a settlement. They were holding out for 23 cents. It was generally admitted there was no bluff and they had matters in perfect shape for a strike. When it came to one o'clock I suggested that before three they should all think seriously over what the position would be in Canada once a strike took place, as to what we could [do] to remedy the situation. St. Laurent had an opinion from Justice that we could take the technical view that the war was still continuing and use a sort of War Measures Authority to take over the railways, if need be, and operate them. I said I thought we should not stand on any legal technicality. Least of all should we seek to invoke any measure that related to the war. That was a measure entirely of the past.

"I stressed, too, the position of Europe and what it would mean if a war were to come on at a moment when the transportation system of Canada was tied up. Also what it might mean in causing Russia to take some precipitate action if it were seen that Canada was tied up in the way she would be with a transportation strike. I thought it was well to have this sobering picture at work."

When the Cabinet meeting resumed in the afternoon, the Prime Minister "immediately renewed the consideration of the strike situation. Mitchell had meanwhile been in touch with the men, who were still holding out for 23 cents an hour. I had previously read a letter to the Cabinet from the President of the C.P.R., indicating what the costs to the railway companies would be if wage increases of a certain amount were granted. Howe and Mitchell finally suggested that they thought the best way to have the situation met would be for me personally to see Hall, who is representing the men in the negotiations. He had an interview with the press stating that the men were holding out for 23 cents and making clear they were prepared to strike unless the settlement were effected.

"I said I was quite ready and willing to do this, but wished Council to know what I would be free to say. I said I proposed to point out that we were all anxious to effect a settlement and appreciated the position of the men. Particularly their loyalty at the time of need. That I thought the settlement should be based not on figures for compromise, but what was just. In that connection we should have regard for their position. The last time an increase had been made and how the cost of living had gone up in the interval. Also the relation of the Brotherhoods to the other trades.

That I would tell them we thought that Mitchell had gone perhaps further than he should in proposing 15½ cents, but that I would wish to know whether they were prepared to settle at a figure that the Government could defend on the ground that I had indicated, or would keep on pressing further. I said if the latter were to be the situation I would not seek to urge my colleagues to trouble with the matter further. We would have to leave it to the men and the Cabinet to settle themselves. Mitchell had asked for authority to propose 17 cents. I had taken exception to this, but I could see that the Cabinet would be prepared to go to 17 or 18 cents an hour."

At 4.30 P.M. the Prime Minister arranged for Frank Hall to call at Laurier House. "I was there before 5 o'clock. He arrived at 5.30. I had arranged for us to have tea together in the morning room, and to go, after tea, to the library to talk over the situation there. I had met Hall before with some delegation, and quite liked his appearance and manner as soon as I saw him.

"We had scarcely begun tea when he surprised me as a result of something that came in conversation, when he asked whether I was familiar with William James' writings. I told him I was not only familiar with the writings, but I knew them very well. I had them in the library. Mentioned a variety of religious experiences, etc. He also spoke of the book by the French Count de Mortigny, which he liked very much. I was speaking about leaving the office I was in. He said to me: 'Mr. King, the railway men are all very sorry you are ceasing to head the Government. We not only have a great respect for you, but a great affection as well.' I said that nothing could please me more than that. I had entered public life and tried to be of assistance to Labour. I could have no reward greater than the goodwill of Labour at the end of my days of public service. I spoke of the fine letter I had received from the delegation of Railway Brotherhoods who waited on me recently. We talked a little of the world situation. I then told him a bit about Laurier House. We went together to the library. I took out William James' book, showed him the writing on the front of it being a gift from my brother, Max, and I let him see how it was marked. He spoke about my having a philosophy of life which would help me to meet situations. I gave Hall the circular chair which faces my mother's picture. I took my seat at my table.

"I said, 'As you know, I am anxious to have a word with you about the strike situation.' I then told him what Mitchell had told us in Council. Said I wanted him to know that Members of the Cabinet were all kindly disposed, that none of us had forgotten the assistance that the railway employees gave to the Government at a time of war and since. They had not sought to take advantage of difficult moments to press claims which it would have been hard to meet then, and we all felt they should not be permitted to suffer on that account. I said perhaps the companies have been slow in not getting the settlement some time ago. Hall mentioned they had followed all the processes of the Industrial Disputes Act. He then told me about the railwaymen believing that was good legislation and had come to appreciate it. . . . He spoke of the delays there had been under the Act by the company, and said they should not have to suffer on account of the delays. This came up in connection with his asking me whether we had considered the retroactive feature. I told him no. We thought the main thing was the settlement of the rate. This other could be worked out. He indicated that that was a pretty important feature. Men did not like to feel they had been strung along and done out of so much as a consequence. I said I agreed that that was a correct point of view. Companies have been slow in acting and have put off things far too much.

"I spoke to him of the responsibilities that we felt rested on us on account of the European situation, and pointed out what an appalling thing it would be if Canada were tied up with a transportation strike at a time when there might be some movement in Berlin by Russian armies. That I personally would not be surprised to see the next step in Berlin that of German armies under Russian direction now in Potsdam move into the city of Berlin and take possession of it for the Russians. No one could say, but I had learned what the situation was last autumn and had been fearful of it ever since. It had all been developing along lines then foreseen by members of the British Commonwealth. I pointed out that a great transportation strike in Canada would put this country in a condition of chaos, and might be just the factor which would cause the Russians to take a step that they otherwise might not take. This was the real reason why I felt, as Leader of the Government, that we must exercise our good offices to prevent anything of the kind, to say nothing of what, in our own immediate interest, we should do.

"I then said to Hall that I would really like to know whether I should try to persuade the Cabinet to think of anything beyond the rate agreed to. I said my own opinion was that probably Labour knew I was sympathetic with them and they had felt if they could get things where I would have to take the last word, it would probably throw it their way. I wanted them to understand that I could not and would not do this beyond what I believed to be on a basis of justice. I was not concerned with particular figures. I was with what their rates had been so many years ago and what difference the cost of living had made since. But there was something that should be defended. I also spoke of what it involved in increased rates, and the meetings of the Premiers who were coming here next week. Of the companies' profits and their financial position. That we had to be considerate of all these factors. Also of the effect that large increase would have on increased purchasing power, and the effect on demands that would come from other industries, and the increase in the spiral of the cost of living. All of this made it necessary for me to know whether there was any use in my exercising my influence further to prevent a strike.

"Hall spoke of their demands for 23 cents, etc. I said there was no use speaking of that. Their own representative on the Board had given the figure 20 cents. No government could be justified in going beyond that figure, and indeed I was quite certain we could not think of recommending an increase of that amount. Hall then turned to me and said: 'You have been very frank with me, Mr. King. Have you any figure in your own mind that you feel you could support?' (These are not the exact words.) I said: 'Mr. Hall, I cannot say as to that. You say the strike will come if we do not go further than 15½ cents. I would not say that I would stop at half a cent, or a cent, or, for that matter, a cent and a half, though I don't know that I could get support in going that far. But I certainly would not feel justified in thinking of anything beyond an increase of 17 cents.' Some other words came in, and he later spoke once or twice of 17½ cents. I turned to him and I said: 'No, not 17½ cents, 17 cents would be the outside figure.' I said I would see what I could do, but could not promise that it would be accepted. It might be less, but it would not be more.

"I said 17 cents had come into my mind because of associations of the past. We had been looking at a picture of Old Pat. He had asked me how long Pat had been with me, and I had told him, seventeen years to the day. I also mentioned that my birthday was on the 17th. 17 seemed to be a number that was mixed up with my life in different ways, but that, of course, was no reason why it should be thought of in this connection. But might account for my having it in my mind as a sort of mystical factor.

"He then brought up the question of retroactive feature in connection with what he spoke of – in connection with the 17 cents. I told him that, of course, the retroactive feature would have to be thought of. There might be some point at which this could be reached.

"He spoke of Humphrey Mitchell having a better place with the Labour men than he had formerly. I mentioned Howe had spoken of finding him reasonable to talk with, etc. He said he could expect that of Mr. Howe.

"I thought it best not to seek to exact any direct promise from him. I had said to him at one stage that this talk was to be entirely between ourselves. It was for my own guidance. That I wanted the negotiations to be as they had been through Mitchell. He said he understood that. I said Mitchell had done well. I said he should be the one to make the settlement. That what he was saying to me and what I was saying to him was only to let him see how my mind was working.

"I then said I assumed that he would perhaps wish to talk matters over with some of his own men. I could not expect him to give me any definite word. I thought the best thing would be for me to let Mitchell know that I had been talking with him, and for him to have a talk with Mitchell in the morning. He seemed to appreciate that.

"As we walked together toward the door of the library I said to him that I was so glad we had had the talk we had together, and I wanted him to believe I had given him the best word I possibly could. That I thought something along the line we had talked over would be sound and just, and could be defended, though I could give him no assurance as to how far the Cabinet would feel justified in going.

"When we came to the foot of the elevator he asked if he could get a taxi. I told him my car would take him to the hotel. He shook hands very pleasantly and said he had much enjoyed the talk we had had together, and thanked me for it. I felt the talk had done real good, and I believed it would have the desired result."

The Prime Minister then telephoned Mitchell and told him the substance of his talk with Hall. "He asked me, did he talk strike? I said, no. There had been no threat in that way at all. I told him about his having brought up the retroactive feature when I had spoken to him about no possibility of anything beyond 17. Mitchell said: 'I think we will get a settlement then.' We both agreed it was best for him not to see Hall tonight, but to meet him and the men in the morning."

Next morning (July 14) the Cabinet met again and "Mitchell outlined the talk with the men this morning. Said it was evident that the talk I had had with Hall yesterday had had a good effect. That he, Mitchell, had told them that he thought it possible a settlement might be effected, that the Government might support an increase to 17 cents, but that there would be no use his going back with anything else. He would still have to find out whether this figure could be accepted. He said that he had spoken about the retroactive feature. He himself had made no commitments. We took up in Council what the retroactive features would amount to. Found it was quite an addition. St. Laurent, Howe and others thought that even if we had in one way or another to make up the amount to the railways it would be in the public interest for us to do it. The few millions it would cost would be little compared to the cost of a strike. St. Laurent thought that we could refund the amount of the tax collected from the railway companies as being a contribution from the public to the railways in helping to make the agreement. This would cover what loss had been incurred to themselves. We discussed possible procedure with the company representatives, but this only in a tentative way. By 20 past 12 Mitchell was finally authorized to see the men and tell them that the Government was prepared to support 17 cents and retroactive payment still to be worked out. Council was to meet again at 2."

When the meeting resumed, "Mitchell said the men had accepted the 17 cents retroactive to March 1. He had previously rung me up in the office at about 20 past 1 and told me that so far as the men were concerned the strike was off at that figure.

"The question then came up about meeting the representatives of the companies. They had been asked to come to my office at 2.30. We decided in Cabinet not to make any commitments of what the Government would do beyond that the Board of Railway Commissioners would have to decide what was fair and right in the matter of rates, etc., in the light of what the public would be owing to the companies should they accept a settlement at this figure.

"I was interested in seeing how positive Howe and McCann and Mac-Kinnon, and also St. Laurent, were not only in the matter of making concessions to either of the railways, but to have the matter one on which the railways would be told what the men had agreed to, and would have to say whether they would take responsibility for refusing the amount, thereby having the responsibility for the strike.

"At 2.30 P.M. Mr. Crump and Mr. McNeill, of the C.P.R., Mr. Walton and Mr. Johnson, of the C.N.R., came to my office. I had asked Mr. St. Laurent, Howe, Mitchell and Chevrier to join me. Four of the representatives stood immediately opposite my table. The others were grouped on either side. I opened the interview by thanking them for coming, saying they knew that the Government had been discussing the matter with both parties to the dispute. I thought perhaps I should ask Mr. Mitchell to let them know what the present position was. Mitchell then spoke of the 17 cents with the retroactive feature until March 1st. I thought I could see at once that all were prepared to accept. Mitchell told me privately before that Crump, the representative of the C.P.R., had said when he was told privately of it, as Mitchell had at the office, that it was a good settlement. Crump stated that he would be in a better position to say what his company would do if he knew what was being done for the C.N.R. I had to reply we were only concerned with the question of the strike, that we did not wish to be involved in this question of rate-making. The Board of Transport Commissioners were there for that purpose. We could not make any commitments of any kind. All we wanted to know was whether the proposals of the men were acceptable to the company, and if not, to be in a position so to advise the men and the public.

"Crump, I could see, felt he was in a very difficult position, as indeed he was. I thought he handled himself very well. In a word, what he said was, and they all agreed, that there was no bluffing on the part of the men. That a strike would come tonight if that figure were not accepted. He said that already he himself was concerned about getting people out of Banff, etc., and would have to act very soon. He then said he could not take the responsibility, as a Canadian, for allowing a strike at this time. He realized how serious a strike would be, but he did present to us the figures which had come in a letter from Mr. Mather yesterday as to what the cost would be to companies, etc. I did not comment on this beyond saying that I felt everyone had a grave responsibility at this time, that I was sure the Board of Railway Commissioners would feel that they should consider the attitude of the company in helping to meet the situation and do what was just in that matter.

"I then said I thought I ought to let them know that I did not favour the Government interfering in disputes between managers in private industry and employees. That we did not desire to intervene in this dispute except that we had seen lately how serious the matter would be and we would be held accountable by the people if we did not lend whatever good offices we could. In the circumstances the Government had, notwithstanding, been acting as intermediary, and seen both parties. I thought we were much indebted to him for the way he had managed negotiations thus far. I then said that what was most in my mind was the situation in Europe at the present time. . . . I spoke of what I had gathered when I was in England last November.

"I told them my own colleagues did not believe me, but they had gradually seen the whole situation focussing up in Berlin exactly as I had told them. I personally felt that perhaps the next step would be a German army under Russian direction marching into Berlin and taking possession of the city. I added that St. Laurent knew, from cables received from the Commonwealth Relations Office, how very seriously the British viewed the situation. I spoke of the trouble in Palestine, in Greece, in Malaya and China. If to all this was added complete paralysis of Canadian industrial life and economic life it might just give to the Russians, if it was their intention to strike, the moment that would count most for them.

"I noticed that both Walton of the C.N.R. and Crump of the C.P.R. nodded approvingly to these remarks. It was quite clear that Crump was basing his position on what was the patriotic thing to do at this time. He also spoke of the millions that would be lost once a strike was under way, etc.

"I asked Howe and St. Laurent if they wished to speak. Howe had spoken about how the C.P.R. had, a couple of years ago, forced the Government to intervene to get a settlement. I had asked when it was that the men of the C.P.R. would not work together. I had thought in the past they had. But they apparently had complained and had been ignored. The reason for ignoring was, I said, of the company. St. Laurent came up quite strongly, making clear that each railway would have to take its own responsibility for the strike. The C.P.R. would have to say whether it was prepared to allow a strike to take place, by not accepting the rate the men were offering or willing to accept, and this regardless of anything that might be related to the Canadian National. He put it squarely to Crump that the C.P.R. would have to say now what it was prepared to do. I asked twice whether Mr. Mitchell should be authorized to tell the men that each company was prepared to accept the 17 cents plus the retroactive feature to March 1st. I did not get an answer the first time, but I came at it again, and after listening to some further discussion I said I understood from the discussion that Mitchell would be authorized to go and tell the men that each company would accept the 17 cents and retroactive feature. I asked if I was right in that, and all four representatives of the companies agreed. Mitchell then left to tell them.

"I thanked the representatives of the companies for their attitude, which I said I thought was right and shook hands pleasantly with all of them. When they left we returned to Council, much relieved at the strike being off, and also not having made any commitments ourselves, having left it to the two parties to work out an agreement in the light of the rate that had been fixed. They seem anxious to have a contract for two years. Nothing has been fixed as to that. Mitchell pointed out how the motor people had made plans that will [raise] the cost of living, and which will embarrass the situation. All seemed anxious not to lose a moment's time.

"While we were waiting for Mitchell to return, a draft statement was prepared for me to give out. It had been prepared in part in the Labour Department, talked about Mitchell and myself doing this and that. I took the view that we ought to refer to the Government lending its good offices, crediting the strike settlement to the two parties concerned. I pointed out that credit would go to Mitchell without saying it, and that I could perhaps say a word about it. One of the Ministers was quite strong in saying that something ought to be said to the public. They hardly realized what had been saved. I think that is very true, and more true of the world if we got through the Berlin situation.

"When Mitchell came back he told us that the men were tremendously relieved and pleased. All had spoken very nicely of both himself and myself. That they had all made kind references. The amusing part is that while no mention has been made of my talk with Hall in the press, the men have all been informed of it by Hall himself, who expressed appreciation of Mitchell's services and mine, etc. Howe and Chevrier and Dr. McCann all said in Council that they thought my talk had helped to save the situation. I told them I thought it had helped, in a way, but that the whole credit should go to Mitchell and the Government generally.

"I then suggested to Mitchell that we have the press come to my office and then give out the statement to them. We rounded up about 25 or 30 in about ten minutes. When they came in I told them I thought they would like, perhaps, to get a statement from Mr. Mitchell. He read it over to them. I then took matters in hand so as to prevent too much discussion of what had taken place this way or that. I took care to speak of the Government lending its good offices, to have done so through Mitchell, and praising him for the way in which he had handled the whole business. Said we were all, as colleagues, greatly indebted to him. I think the public should be made aware of it.

"I then said I did not like to have the Government intervene in private industry, and enlarged upon what the situation might have been in Canada. . . . I stressed that all parties concerned, the employers, the men and the Government, felt the great responsibility there was in the light of the world situation today, and the relief there was now, speaking also of the spirit, which had been good throughout, etc.

"When the press men had left, Mitchell turned to me and said: Mr. King, I am not given to flattery, but I say to you that I think but for you this would not have been settled. Your background with the men is what has saved the situation. I said: Mitchell, I really believe that the men have not forgotten that I have played square with them throughout. The railway men particularly have not forgotten the treatment they have received from myself in getting back their pension. I think they have felt they would go very far not to disappoint me, and they would believe what I said to them. He said: there is no doubt of that. It is your life and the background of your life which has saved this situation. I thanked him for his part again, and congratulated him on it. I told him to tell Mrs. Mitchell it proved what it was for a man to have a good wife.

"Later I rang up Mr. Hall to tell him how pleased I was. He told me he was greatly pleased. Had very much enjoyed our talk yesterday. The men all appreciated what I had done, what Mitchell had done, and also what the Government had done. Also the attitude of the Cabinet. I said I believed it was all just and sound. I also told Hall I hoped to have some talks with him again in the future. He could not have been nicer in the way he spoke."

The Prime Minister was "immensely pleased and relieved at the prevention of a great railway strike. The first work that brought me into public notice in Canada was the settlement of a strike – perhaps the greatest service rendered to Labour in that regard and the country was the settlement of the Grand Trunk strike years ago. The justice done Labour at that time has borne its fruit today. In some way or another it seems to me that the hand of Providence has so shaped matters as to cause me to have had to do with the prevention of this great strike as one of the last acts of public service, one which would link the close of my career with its opening and make the circle complete. I have felt so happy and moved about this that I could at moments have easily found it difficult to restrain a certain emotional feeling arising from delight, but I have in no way yielded to this. I confess, however, that a public service such as this makes me feel a little sad at the thought of giving up the position I still hold, and which might continue to mean very much to the country. Few, if any, will know what my life's work has meant to thousands of homes today, and possibly even to the world. This is the opportunity that comes with power. However, it looks as though I were being given the strength to complete the task in a way that Providence alone could arrange. The years are there – seventy-four. There remains the getting of one's own house into order before the end comes. I feel sure that with the contacts with nature which I will have in the country more of enduring worth may be accomplished in the end."

The formal hearing of the provincial appeal against the freight rate increase was held on July 20 at 11 A.M. The premiers of Nova Scotia, Prince Edward Island, New Brunswick and Manitoba were present. McIntosh represented Saskatchewan and Wismer British Columbia. Mackenzie King found the Maritime premiers "more like three antagonists in their attitude than three members of the same party. Macdonald was very self-opinionated. Jones, of Prince Edward Island, is a man of no judgment. Trying to be antagonistic with everybody. Macdonald made a long presentation on behalf of the others, some of whom simply fell in line with what was being urged. I had a good many of the Cabinet with me and, at one stage, after listening to a lot of argument, I said I was only a lawyer as a sort of compliment, but was I not right in believing that powers could be given the Board of Railway Commissioners which would enlarge their authority in whatever way was desired. Garson immediately said that I had put my finger on the crux of the whole matter, and that was the way out. I then said I felt very pleased with myself as a member of the profession.

"In closing, I mentioned to the Premiers that in their first presentation they had stated the crux of the whole matter was the Chairman of the Commission. I pointed out that in what they had now read there was not a word of thanks for what we had done [the appointment of a new chairman on July 1]. I thought it was something that should have been mentioned."

The last major problem Mackenzie King considered before the Convention was the question of the entry of Newfoundland into confederation. On February 5 the Cabinet discussed a memorandum from the Department of External Affairs on the extent of Canada's interest in the referendum on the future of the colony being prepared by the British government. According to the Prime Minister, the memorandum "rightly stated that we did not wish to interfere in the question of whether or not Confederation with Canada should be put on the ballotting paper by England – on the referendum paper which was being prepared by England for Newfoundland people to vote on. However, it had in the latter half of it suggested statements to our High Commissioner, Robertson, in England which would give the British Government reason to believe we would welcome having the Confederation matter included. I said I did not think we ought to, specially in the light of the first part of the statement, say one way or another what we were or were not to do. That was their responsibility.

"I pointed out that sooner or later, it would be known that Canada had mentioned certain things; that would defeat the very thing that those in Newfoundland wished to achieve in the way of Confederation. The very thing our High Commissioner in Newfoundland felt should not be done, namely, they never thought we were anxious to have them in Confederation. I could see that St. Laurent was unwilling to do other than press the matter as it had come from External Affairs. He refers to the body there as though it was some council of learned men so much wiser than anyone else, so he does not profess that he himself has had to do with the matters advocated. Seeing this, I left the discussion to other members of the Cabinet, particularly Wishart Robertson, McCann, Abbott – all of whom thought it would be wrong for Canada to express any opinion on what . . . Britain should do.

"Robertson pointed out quite emphatically that what they should do is to decide between responsible governments and other governments and when they had found responsible governments, come to negotiate with them. That is the position I have taken from the beginning.

"St. Laurent was inclined to feel that all that had been done up to the present, should not have been attempted if that was the view taken. In this, I think he is quite wrong."

On May 19 Mackenzie King "had a talk of some length with Scott Macdonald [Canadian High Commissioner in Newfoundland] who thinks Newfoundland almost certain to come into Confederation but agrees with me it is going to be a source of trouble for some time to come. The only thing to do to save the Island from drifting into the hands of Americans. Specially important to Canada."

The first referendum was held in Newfoundland on June 3 and "word came of Responsible Government leading . . . with Confederation second in returns from St. John's. It looks as though the two will be very close. Personally I would prefer to see responsible government carry and then an agreement made between a government that was responsible with the Canadian Government. Come what may, we have advanced in a very real way in relations between the colony of Newfoundland and the Dominion."

In the House of Commons the next day, the Prime Minister announced the vote, 14.32 per cent for Commission Government, 41.13 per cent for Confederation, and 44.55 per cent for Responsible Government. He reported that he "heard Ilsley say to Abbott that he hoped the vote for Responsible Government would carry but he was afraid it would not. That is also my feeling. . . . We at least have moved the whole matter forward. When Confederation does come, it will have been our Government which will have taken the great step to bring this about."

A second referendum was scheduled for July 22. Two days earlier Mackenzie King had discussed the situation with St. Laurent. "He personally feels, and I agree, that unless there is something more than a poor majority, we should not take the Province into Confederation. I said it was necessary to look ahead and see what would come if we had a poor majority. The estimate the Department [of External Affairs] have is that Confederation will carry, but with a very small majority."

In his diary for July 23, the Prime Minister noted that "in Council on Tuesday (July 20) St. Laurent mentioned that our advice was that Confederation would carry by a narrow majority. He thought, and Council agreed, that if it was very close we should not consider Confederation. It was agreed we would decide the matter finally on Tuesday night. Thursday was the day of polling. The first returns, which would be St. John's, were against Confederation, as one would expect. Then, as rural districts came in the balance turned, but all too indecisively to say what would be done. I issued a small statement of a character to hold off any final word until the next meeting of Council. Today's results indicate Confederation having carried by a small majority, but all returns not yet in. – It looks now with a majority of 5,000 or thereabouts. If the referendum had carried with a sufficiently large majority to admit Newfoundland, my own feeling is that this step will add very much to our problems for some little time, that the Maritimes will become more difficult to handle. At the same time, I believe that the bringing in of Newfoundland is the logical end to it, and probably in the course of time it will be among the accomplishments of the administration of which I am the head. It will be that of the rounding out of Confederation by the addition of a tenth province. This will be completing the nation in its physical boundaries as it has already been completed in its complete autonomy and its position as a nation within the British Commonwealth of Nations."

Again the vote in the referendum was close; some 84 per cent of the eligible population voted, 52.34 per cent for Confederation and 47.66 per cent for Responsible Government. The Cabinet discussed the results on July 27. "Decision reached definitely to regard the majority secured as substantial enough to justify the decision to proceed now with the next stages required before getting consent of Parliament and the Government's intention to recommend Confederation to Parliament. I had never dreamt that my name would probably be linked through years to come with the bringing into Confederation of what will be the 10th province and quite clearly the last. Having relation to my grandfather's part in laying the foundations of responsible government, it is interesting that it should be left to me as practically the last of the completed task before giving up the Leadership of the Party. To have been the one, as Prime Minister, to announce the entry, within a few months' time, of Newfoundland into Confederation. It is wholly probable that, if spared, I shall have something of significance to do with the event itself when it comes to pass. Might even be listed as one of the Fathers of the larger Confederation."

On July 30 Mackenzie King had Pickersgill come to Kingsmere during the afternoon. He noted that "much time was taken up in the morning about the statement regarding Newfoundland which I dealt with over the 'phone and again in the afternoon, making further revisions, redrafting telegrams to be sent to Newfoundland." That night on the news broadcast "the first words were that Newfoundland was to be brought into the Confederation: 'Prime Minister King announced today that the old Colony of Newfoundland', etc., was to be taken into Confederation. The broadcast was very good. Was one I might have given myself. Explained what the Confederation meant. I could not help but realize that this act rounds out the Dominion and its ten Provinces, bringing to completion the work that had been begun by the Fathers of Confederation so many years ago. It was gratifying that it was possible for me to make this decision and to welcome the Newfoundland electors while still in the party and Prime Minister of the country."

The next day (July 31) the Prime Minister visited Maxville in his constituency of Glengarry to attend the Highland games. In his speech he referred to his "desire to make the last speech I would make as leader of my Party before retiring in the constituency that had honoured me with representation in the federal Parliament. This was well received. I then spoke of Newfoundland joining the Confederation, outlining the negotiations and explaining the present position. I said I had the honour of being the first public man – and that in the presence of the people of Glengarry – to inform the public, in an address of welcome, of the decision of the people of Newfoundland to join the Confederation. I made it clear that Parliament had still to approve, but indicated I thought this would be done. The people were clearly quite pleased with this reference. They are very proud of their constituency, and its association. This will add one event of real significance to the history of the riding."

# CHAPTER EIGHT

# The National Liberal Convention

ONCE THE SESSION concluded on June 30, Mackenzie King began to make his preparations for the forthcoming convention which would choose his successor. Some time earlier he had agreed to make a recording of a statement to be given to each of the delegates as a souvenir of the occasion. After a great many revisions, the statement was finally recorded on July 14. He "made two recordings of the speech. I had made a few changes last night and this morning. The second reading I thought was very good. They then let Pickersgill and myself immediately hear the record. I was greatly pleased. Only two defects I noticed, one the 'S' sounding too sharply, the other the whole record a little too fast. I had been speaking slowly, but might have been much slower to advantage. The record ran about seven and a half minutes."

The Prime Minister learned on July 19 that John Bracken "had resigned the leadership of the Conservative party. It was stated by some of the press authorities that he had lately had an examination which had revealed a serious condition. His own secretary had said that for a year or two past he had had grave trouble. I confess it made me feel quite sad. Bracken's life as leader has really been a tragedy. He should never have left Manitoba. Was never fit for leadership in Ottawa. Has been a failure in every way, but to have him not merely kicked about by his own party, but suffering from what may be an incurable disease, made one feel a profound sympathy. I wrote a short note for the press and sent a telegram of sympathy to him. Later word confirmed the reported resignation, though not to take effect until the National Convention of the party to be held later. This will mean that the Conservatives will not put their programme forward until after ours. I always thought they would have been foolish to present it shortly before.

"I should think Drew is the most likely person to be chosen leader, simply because he has a dominating way with him. Can secure good finances and press support. If, however, he does become leader, I think it will mean that the Tory party will be out of power for good, and that the chances of a Tory party being returned or of ever being returned again will be nil. He has an arrogant manner, worse than either Meighen or Bennett, and has a more bitter tongue than Meighen. This helped to destroy these men and the party. Having that type of man as an opponent has been the best asset I have had. Certainly, I have been fortunate in arranging to get out of the leadership this year. I could not stand having Drew as an opponent. I would find too much of perpetual antagonism. . . . Bracken has been very decent in the years of his leadership. I would think that Fleming, of Toronto, might be a good chance. Fulton, but for certain limitations, would make, to my mind, a much more impressive type of leader than almost any other. Graydon, had he measured up in the House, would have been the natural successor, and having taken a dignified stand, would have had a good chance. He, however, is poor stuff – a schoolboy. Diefenbaker might well be the choice. He is a second Arthur Meighen in style, satire, etc. Also very hard working and informed. His name will be against him as the party leader.

"It was interesting to know that Bracken was not in the House the last couple of days. Not there when Parliament adjourned, an unfortunate close to his career as a leader. Between my leaving and Bracken leaving, etc., the House of Commons begins to change its complexion in my mind's eye. From the country's point of view it makes me sad to see the sort of confusion that I think will be more or less inevitable in the next few years. Bracken's departure has made me feel my own giving up of office even more before this general break-up. One thing is certain: Bracken is leaving because his party has no chance under his leadership. Were I to decide to stay on I think there is little doubt that we would again, as I believe we would in any event, win the next election. I am not getting out either from fear or defeat, or any dissatisfaction of my party."

Mackenzie King spent most of the next afternoon on "the draft of the resolutions for the Convention. It was a strange agglomeration of matters gathered from different sources, but far from being what was really required for the Convention, or of a character to help the party in presentation to the country. I suggested that the committee in charge of this work, of which both Claxton and Paul Martin are members, should try to make out a brief statement of principles and policies of the party and to get them in concise form, not to try to be too specific, like setting out concrete measures, but to make general statements which can be well defended. I pointed out that what had been shown us was another evidence of the lack of proper organization of the party. I shall be surprised if the Convention goes through. Howe says he doubts if Fogo is strong enough to really carry through what would be expected of him. Blanchette certainly is not equal to presiding. I am afraid much difficulty will be experienced in finally settling all arrangements. What is really needed is some effective manager. The men who should be looked to for these positions are younger people. Had I not arranged matters to the point where they are I doubt if the resolutions would be ready when the Convention meets."

After the Cabinet meeting that day (July 20), St. Laurent told the Prime Minister that "he would give anything in the world if he could be relieved from becoming a candidate. I asked him why, and he said he had come to see that the problems were much greater than he had ever dreamed they would be. He said he did not feel equal to the responsibilities. I said he would be chosen, no matter what he felt, and that he could not think of dropping out now. He asked me if I would think of going to the United Nations Assembly at the head of our delegation in Paris in September. I told him I would have to think that over, but could not decide on it until after the Convention. We would see how matters would go then."

Mackenzie King spent several hours on July 27 going over the revised resolutions, "the work being under the auspices of Claxton and Martin. On the whole, they had done remarkably well but there were some matters I did not like – one seeking to link up the policy of Canadian unity as something enacted by Sir Wilfrid and carried on by myself; as though the Liberal party had a monopoly of what is a part of every party's effort, though their means to attain that end may differ. I said that if a resolution went before the Convention in the form in which it had been drafted, it would be said that I had had to do with the drafting to help to glorify myself and more particularly that the draft had been prepared to help St. Laurent as a successor to Sir Wilfrid and myself.

"I finally spoke of the matter in Council, referring only to the first aspect. I had in mind that Gardiner might be the first to raise this point. Was surprised to find that he rather favoured keeping that part. Claxton himself had prepared it.

"In talking later with P., I pointed out I felt it was a mistake for the party at this Convention in choosing a new Leader, to be looking too much into the past. Let the whole programme have relation to the future. I said for example that if the Tories began to speak of Sir John Macdonald and his utterances with reference to present day affairs, it would be said they were half a century behind. I think these things are well enough in speeches but the object itself should not be inserted as an aim of the party.

"Martin and Claxton had apparently hoped to put through a series of resolutions under the heading of Charter – the Charter of Liberalism. I thought that would be a great mistake. Mentioned that Liberalism was something that was rather an expression of attitude toward different problems that might arise. Its principles and policies could not be confined in a charter. The principles might remain the same but their application and policies would have to change with the times. The idea of a charter was a confining thing; limiting, restricting. All I think came to see and agree to this. I was a bit surprised to find out how poorly the question of labour and social security had been handled. I felt there was far too much of detail and effort to include far too many concrete projects. I suggested and I think all present felt that if the whole programme could be reduced to half its size, it would be better.

"There were omissions – for example, in record of the Government not a mention had been made of six years of war and the achievement it had been for the Liberal party to have carried the country through that period as a united nation. Also the contributions that had been made toward the recovery of Europe. It shows how men's minds lose perspective in thinking of the immediate question."

Reading the *Globe and Mail* that day, Mackenzie King was annoyed by an article which attributed his election as Leader of the party "to my having greeted Lady Laurier on her arrival at the Coliseum and given her a seat on the platform, thereby identifying myself with Sir Wilfrid whereas . . . [it] said this awful Mrs. Macdonald . . . [had said] that it was Sir Wilfrid's wish that Fielding should succeed and I would follow later on. As a matter of fact, Lady Laurier was not on the platform. I never greeted her or spoke to her at the Convention. She came in and sat at the far end of the gallery. When she came in, the delegation stood up. She was greeted with applause and that is all there was to it.

"I have heard that, after Sir Wilfrid's death, she herself, a bit old and sympathetic, thought of Mr. Fielding as an old man and that it would be nice to give him a complimentary appointment for a year or two with me to follow. I was as surprised to learn that after the Convention was over as anyone else, but it had nothing to do with Sir Wilfrid's own wish. The writer says it shows Sir Wilfrid's sagacity; that he thought by having Fielding chosen, he could bring the conscriptionist Liberals back into line. If Fielding had been chosen, the real Liberals might well have left the party altogether. Joined the Progressives, because their real feeling was so strong against conscription and the way Laurier had been treated by those who left him. I was chosen because I stood by him."

The Quebec provincial election took place on July 28 and Mackenzie King began to receive returns just before dinner. "They indicated from the start that there was likely to be a Union Nationale sweep. Before the evening was over, it was apparent that the Liberals had only about 8 or 10 seats out of the 92, Duplessis having swept everything before him. There are three reasons for this. The first is the mistake that was made at the time of the Dominion-Provincial Conference, unfairly trying to concentrate too many of the taxes in federal hands, the unwillingness to make concessions to the provinces at that time. Ilsley's ill-health, which made him afraid to over-rule Clark. Clark's illness, which made him less reasonable than he otherwise would have been. Had Ilsley not been so narrow, and conceded a few points at the time, I believe we could have got a Dominion-Provincial agreement. As it was, from then on, the Premiers from Ontario and Quebec both saw that we had handed over the Liberal ground to them on provincial rights, and they have fought on it ever since. It gave them a good chance to combine their efforts against the Government.

"The next thing, unquestionably, has been the increase in the cost of living, etc., the additional taxes that have been put on, etc. Again the Finance Department's insistence on having a so-called cyclical budget, taking vast surpluses to use to pay off the debts, and not giving any reduction in taxation at this time.

"Finally – and I think this, perhaps, most important of all, the organization that Duplessis had built up, based on moneys derived from liquor licence sources, and the immense amount of money used by his Government, his promises, patronage, etc., – straight corruption. Against this, the lack of any real organization by the Liberals until the last minute; indecision as to who their leader was, etc., etc. Pickersgill said he was thoroughly discouraged. Curiously enough, I had a sort of feeling that while it would affect us somewhat federally, in the end the province would stay with the Liberal party in a federal election. I thought it meant Drew coming in from Ontario as federal Conservative Leader. If that is done, I doubt if Quebec will give him its support, even with Duplessis' help, and this should assure the return of our party to power."

The following morning Mackenzie King telephoned St. Laurent who "felt a bit discouraged. I told him I did not feel that way at all. I hoped he did not for a moment think it was affecting his chances in any way. As a matter of fact, last night I was afraid he might wish to retire from the contest for leadership altogether. I spoke to him about speaking to a motion on National Unity [at the Convention]; also about having Cabinet speakers come on in the order of their precedence. He said he was grateful for my 'phoning him and relieved at the optimistic view I had taken.

"At noon, I got Godbout on the 'phone. Found him terribly depressed. His voice was like a man who had spoken to the last minute. He seemed particularly disgusted about losing his own constituency by about 80 votes to a man who is a good-for-nothing type. It shows that there must have been much money used in the constituency."

The next few days were almost completely devoted to the preparation of the Prime Minister's speech for the Convention. It was virtually finished on August 3 and, that afternoon, Mackenzie King went over the entire speech with his secretaries. Certain sections were removed to shorten the text and he "got the last part into final shape so that the whole speech could be down to the printers before the afternoon was over. P. said he would read the proofs at night. I would like to have had a little longer on the last part but was determined that the whole should be brought within an hour's time without allowing for applause. Felt at the end there was nothing to do but just let it go without further revision."

It had become clear that the only serious challenge to St. Laurent's election at the Convention would come from the Minister of Agriculture. On August 4 the Prime Minister "felt so disturbed over what I have learned of Gardiner's tactics in seeking to win the Convention by all kinds of machine methods that I decided I would 'phone to one or two of my colleagues and make suggestions to them which I have felt to be necessary and in the interests of the party and the country. I got Howe first: suggested to him that he should allow himself to be nominated, and then before the voting, announce that he was withdrawing. That everyone knew he was supporting St. Laurent and would not wish to take away a vote from him. He was very pleased that I had spoken to him. Said he would gladly do that. Was terribly put out by what Gardiner had been doing.

"Later I spoke to Abbott in the same way. He told me he had practically come to the conclusion to let his name go before the Convention though he did not want the position. Disliked what Gardiner was doing. I said to him I thought he, Howe and Claxton owed it to themselves to be among the number nominated if Martin and others as well as Gardiner were letting their names go. He agreed and said he would be happy to do this. A little later, said he would withdraw his nomination, making clear he was doing so with what he felt for St. Laurent, etc. I had already spoken to Claxton. Advised these three to get together and decide on their tactics in this regard.

"Howe spoke of names for St. Laurent's nomination. He had Senator Gouin as one. I told him I thought it would be unwise. Suggested one of the French Liberal Members in the House of Commons instead. Also spoke of Ilsley and, of course, agreed to Garson.

"Next, spoke with MacKinnon. I was shocked to find that he had been holding back too strongly [his support] for St. Laurent, though saying nothing. Apparently he was not too sure whether he would get the Senator-ship he wants, if Gardiner should be chosen. He wanted to know whether I was sure I would be staying on for a time and there would be a chance of his getting the appoinment before I left. I said, as he knew, if there was a by-election, with what was involved it would mean another risk, and I thought nothing should weigh against the good of the country. I said to him that, as he also knew, and this I had said to the others, there was no one that could hold the present Government together, even up to the time of the session, but St. Laurent. The selection of anybody else might mean the whole Government going to pieces before another session. He must think only of the interests of Canada as a whole. He then said he would do as I had advised him. Frankly I thought MacKinnon had a higher sense of loyalty and more courage than he appears to have."

In the afternoon, Mackenzie King "had a short talk with John Hart who told me that he and Wismer would support St. Laurent. I urged upon him how important it was that this should be done in the interests of the country and the Government.

"Tucker came in later. I had a long talk with him. Was astounded at what he told me of Gardiner's action. Of his insistence on not allowing by-election to take place in Tucker's own constituency. He wanted the seat there for a Cabinet Minister later – Minister of Agriculture. He had not told Tucker who it was to be, nor had he consulted him about the by-election. The executive in Tucker's riding had felt they should manage their own affairs and nominate their man notwithstanding what Gardiner had said. Yet Tucker said he had to stand for Gardiner. Did not want to create a civil war in Saskatchewan though he spent most of the time telling me how Gardiner had treated him over the years. I was astonished at Tucker, to discover he was not courageous enough to come out and follow his own conscience. He admitted to me that St. Laurent alone was capable of holding a Government together in Canada's interests and that under Gardiner, the party would go to pieces. He was a purely machine politician. Now Power had come out and said he was going to support Gardiner. Evidently Power had been promising portfolios. I think somebody said he had. Colin Campbell today is in town. He has come out for Gardiner. It is the same combination that some years ago met with Hepburn to which Gardiner was a party and were going to try to oust me. A machine group. If the Government ever gets into their hands, we will have a Hepburn gang in control of Dominion affairs – an appalling prospect. An exceedingly dangerous one. It would be difficult for me if matters go too far, to refrain from letting the party know for whom I stand. I wish to hold back choosing as between colleagues but the interests of the country may demand a final word. I am letting it be known through other sources just how I feel about the importance of St. Laurent being chosen.

"I was shocked to learn of the way Martin has been not only allowing himself to be nominated but using the press to further his ends and getting a section of Western Ontario worked up in his interest. He thinks that he has a chance – now or never. That the party would not appoint a second French-Canadian. I suppose he means also a Catholic if St. Laurent gets in. He, Martin, has no chance of winning himself and it can only help to make possible a win for Gardiner. If necessary, I shall see him and have a personal word with him. I could do this, if necessary, helping to save himself and his future. I think they should stick to what all these have said at the outset that they would support St. Laurent and had no other thought or feeling. I am afraid offers of position, money and all the rest of it are being used and that the campaign has been silently framed up over months by Gardiner and his gang. As a matter of fact, he has made the position for all of us more difficult than any other member of the Government by arrangements he has made for helping producers at the expense of consumers in Britain and other countries at the expense of Canada itself."

The Convention opened on Thursday, August 5. To start the day, Mackenzie King "had little Pat brought up to the library for a good morning greeting. It was interesting to think of how different the little chap looks today from when I first saw him in the library. It is interesting that he should have made his re-appearance here today.

"I wore my grey flannel suit. Put on delegate's badge of the Convention of 1948 just before going downstairs. The library looked very beautiful with the lovely roses; magnificent with quantities of red roses and white lilies which Lily Hendrie had sent and which I received last night. They made the library glow with life. Throughout the morning, I confess I felt a great peace of mind and heart. Very near to the invisible world of reality. Had a strong sense of being close to those I love. I prayed earnestly for God's guidance through the day and that he send me strength.

"When I drove from Laurier House, I felt very happy. Not even fatigued, rather with a feeling of triumph that I had at last reached this stage in my career. I shall not soon forget the drive to the Coliseum grounds. P. had called and was with me in the car; also H. The morning was a lovely, bright and beautiful one."

When he reached the Coliseum the first person he "recognized was Hugues Lapointe, which seemed to me most appropriate in relation to what took place at the last Convention. It was to Lapointe more than anyone else that I owed my nomination and indeed much of the success of my career. When we stopped, the first person I met whom I was delighted to meet – was Mr. St. Laurent. He was wearing a grey suit, like myself. I shook hands with him. Said I was pleased that the person with whom I shook hands, should be my successor. We had to look about for the place of meeting.

"Went over to the reception building where members of the Government, a few Premiers, and others began to assemble. Had talks with them all who came in. Was presented with a red rose. Later signed the register. It was interesting to see the line of those who are members of the Government at present and those of the past. To think that all of them were all ones with whom I had had a close association over the years. Ilsley was missing from the number and there were, of course, one or two others, Dunning, etc. Cyrus McMillan looked very much older. He spoke about being prepared to publish a book of annotations of my speeches in Parliament. He is going to write me of that later. We were delayed some time preparing to line up to go to the Coliseum. I was disappointed at this as I had hoped we might meet sharp at 11 – instead of 11.30 A.M. Two pipers, Cameron Highlanders, headed the line of the procession as we marched from the reception building to the Coliseum – they played Bonnie Dundee. I confess I felt very proud and very happy as I walked at the head of that line. In a strange mystical sort of way, there seemed to come into my mind thoughts of my grandparents on both sides. My father and mother and sister and brother, and young Lyon; other members of the family connection. Sir Wilfrid and Lady Laurier; Mr. and Mrs. Larkin, Sir William Mulock; Bureau; Béland and others. As I dictate, I should have thought of Dandurand; Rogers and others. I felt there was a real cloud of witnesses but there was not time for more than fleeting thought. My thoughts were more of them rather than of anything else, and of having faithfully discharged my duties over the long period in office.

"My thoughts came back to the struggles of my grandparents and home. It was a great moment marching through the aisle. Only a man who has marched at the head of a procession where he feels he would be the first to be stricken down where he felt it would help the cause, can experience the sensation that one does at such a moment.

"When we entered the Coliseum, there was tremendous cheering by the assembled gathering. The Coliseum was well filled – all but the arc at the far end. When the platform was filled, there was first 'God Save the King' and then 'O Canada.' Then without waiting very long, advanced to the front of the platform in front of the microphone and said I would ask all present to join with me in repeating the words of the Lord's Prayer. The microphone was not working well with the result that I doubt if the audience caught the words for I found myself left reciting the prayer alone without anyone on the platform or the audience joining me. There was, however, a perfect silence. It made me happy to make that profession of my belief, and what was wholly fitting for a Convention.

"When the Lord's Prayer was completed, I then immediately began on the opening address which went I think very well though had I had time to prepare the speech myself as I would like to have done, I would have made it much more colourful and of a character to arouse and enthuse the audience. As it was, it was merely an outline in the nature of an historic setting of the Convention itself in relation to others – of the time and place of meeting, and to those who were assembled."

Most of the forenoon "was taken up with routine proceedings which advanced much more rapidly than had been anticipated.

"After the session had concluded, delegates began to come on to the platform to shake hands – for forty-five minutes or thereabouts, I stood greeting those who came for this purpose. It was really very touching to see how sincere the men and women from constituencies all over Canada were in their expressions of regret at my retirement and their expressions of goodwill for the future. One notices a note of genuineness and sincerity in so-called 'people' – in contrast with the kind of thing one meets with in sophisticated circles. My heart warms to the man who comes straight from his work; from the plough, from the factory, the locomotive and the like.

"P. and H. drove with me back to Laurier House. We had a glass of sherry and I looked over the latter part of my speech for tomorrow which I had not had a chance to see since its last revision. Made out a title page and then we had lunch in the dining room. The house looks exceedingly nice; everything polished and bright. Flowers everywhere."

The Prime Minister did not return to the Coliseum until nearly four o'clock in the afternoon. He found that "one thing that occasioned some concern was the decision . . . to give the candidates time to make addresses to tell what their platform was. Except that it would create a scene, I would take strong action for Gardiner framing a platform of his own while he is in the Government. He has no right in expressing a platform. He should leave the Government first if he intends to criticize. I did not feel it was right to create a scene at this time as it looks now pretty certain that St. Laurent will carry the day and shall refrain from saying anything. If there was a chance of St. Laurent being defeated, I should be careful to see whether I should not explain responsibilities of Ministers of the Crown vis-à-vis the Government while he remained a member of the Government. It is a mistake to allow an unconstitutional act of the kind to pass unchecked and unnoticed.

"St. Laurent told me that he felt considerable embarrassment. That he was not going to enter a contest on oratory. Planned to speak on national unity. He would have to speak in English and French. He did not like to be cut down to fifteen minutes in English where others would have twenty. I gave him my opinion on Gardiner's action and how his delegates had worked out this change. I do not think that Fogo is very strong in controlling situations. He might have fought for holding this rule of the Convention and explain that we were adopting methods of previous Conventions – not the American.

"I advised St. Laurent to draw attention to the fact that he was not advertising himself; also that he as a member of the Government was not criticizing but supporting Government policy and then go ahead with his talk on national unity. Not confined in any way, as indeed he would not [be], on a basis of new platform. The Government's policies stand; resolutions of the Convention are to be our guide. Not some newly manufactured programme by a member of the administration. Gardiner has taken, in the last few years, far too much in his own hands, and got his way far too easily by his rough methods.

"I have been, however, immensely relieved today seeing pretty clearly the tide is sweeping strongly to St. Laurent. The most important step in this direction was Martin's declaration today that he was supporting St. Laurent. P. had much to do with this in conversation with Martin last night. Martin had at least consulted him as he has been in the habit of doing. The statement is an excellent one and will do much to ensure St. Laurent's election. Someone sent me the statement. I thought it was Martin and beckoned to him to come and speak to me on the platform. He was at a loss to know where I got the statement. Said he had not sent it. Knew nothing about it. Did not know whether it was right or wrong. I said to him I was glad to hear of what he had done. Then he added quietly: I have done it. I was surprised to see how earnestly he took himself. Someone said to me today, which discloses how everything is thought of, that the one thing that might have helped to ensure Gardiner's election would be if four candidates that were determined to stand: St. Laurent, Power, Paul Martin and until the last moment Angus Macdonald, who were all Catholics, and Gardiner – the only Protestant. It would probably result in a religious division, in which Catholic vote would be divided, and Protestants coming together as one. This could not possibly have happened but it is the kind of thing passed around the delegates, and shows what considerations account has to be taken of in times like the present. Power clearly will get very few votes; not more than a handful. I think Gardiner's lobby started a little too soon. St. Laurent's modesty will be an asset. I am told that Quebec is now virtually solid for St. Laurent.

Maritime Provinces will support him strongly, and Manitoba. He will get support from British Columbia. Ought to get many from Saskatchewan and Alberta, but I imagine Gardiner has these two provinces in his hand. The fact that the West is so strongly Gardiner will operate against him in the other provinces. It now seems to me pretty certain that St. Laurent will win.

"I spoke to Chevrier today about letting his name go up and withdrawing and supporting St. Laurent in so doing. In this way, the delegates will see that all the leading members of the Cabinet without exception are for St. Laurent and none of them for Gardiner. That will have an effect."

The Convention adjourned just after 6.00 P.M. "I got back to Laurier House at 6.30. Had an hour's rest before starting out to a garden party at the Farm. It was a lovely afternoon. It seemed to me that most of the delegates were there. Wives of the Cabinet Ministers received in a tent where a few refreshments were served.

"I did not move out of this tent but shook hands steadily for over an hour with delegates. Had a cup of coffee on two occasions; one alone and another with some lady much to the amusement of photographers and others. Here again I was deeply touched by the remarks of the different delegates and so many old friends. I missed too a large number. Just before the garden party was over, the grounds became lighted up with the most glorious sunset that I think I have seen in my life. I have never seen the western sky so completely aglow with fire coloured light. It was a wonderful sight driving away from the grounds.

"I quite enjoyed the drive home but kept regretting that I was so completely alone in sharing the great events of a day like today. I could have wished that some members of the family might have been down with me but still more that I might have had a family of my own. I felt that particularly today. However I cannot say that I feel really lonely. I feel a sense of the fullness of life, tremendous satisfaction and pride in the fact that all has gone so well. What is most remarkable of all is what comes to very few public men – that I have been spared to see how people feel and to know how the country will view through time to come, my part in the affairs of the Government. I expect tomorrow's meeting will produce a real effect."

Next day Mackenzie King spent the morning on the platform at the Coliseum, lunched at Laurier House with Handy, and returned to the Coliseum about 2.20 P.M. where he was met by Gordon Fogo. He was given a great ovation. The household staff from Laurier House were all present as well as a few personal friends. He noted that, "when Fogo called on me, it was half past 2. He pointed out there was no need of an introduction and I started in as soon as the applause ceased. I was given a great ovation. It really was a tremendous ovation, long continued. I felt that my speech was likely to be flat and uninteresting at the beginning, particularly as I had asked Hume whether he thought it was on the right lines. He rather demurred. Did not seem to approve too much. (These men always read into things that are said, their own ideas.) In the nature of things, there was not much to applaud. As soon as I touched the second sentence that I would be in the 30th year – if it would be next week – there was tremendous applause from then on at different intervals. Also great applause when I got to the part that related to the achievements of the party and my own record as Leader. Equally great applause on the mission of Liberalism when I was dealing with that part relating to social security. When I came to international matters, there was a dead silence. Very tense. Remained so until the close and I then received a great outburst of applause. People standing on all sides, and continuing applause over five minutes without any effort to do so.

"Curiously enough, I hardly noticed what was taking place. The applause did not seem to make any impression beyond that I felt a sense of tremendous relief and happiness that all had gone well and that the speech had had the effect that I believed it would have. I felt a tremendous satisfaction at having got the record complete. One that will last through time and having met with the tremendous approval it did, by delegates from all parts of Canada. At no point was the applause louder and stronger than where I said I believed I had the confidence of the party today in greater measure than I had ever possessed it. That was a tremendous thing to say at the end of 29 years. It was the more remarkable to have it applauded in a way that would leave no doubt in the minds of anyone. That was the way the party felt toward myself.

"When I had finished, Senator Farris introduced a resolution in reference to myself and to my years of leadership. The speech was very fine. What I appreciated most of all was his reference to no scandal in the period of administration, though we were in the greatest of all wars, and also reference to character being the basis of my success. I thought he did all this remarkably well. Then it pleased me very much that Hugues Lapointe, the son of my dear friend Ernest, should have been the one to second the resolution. I could only follow him in part as he spoke in French and I was behind him, not well situated to hear, but could tell the kind of references he was making. There was a tremendous reception given what was said by these two gentlemen. I felt that I had had my day in my speech but I rose to acknowledge what had been said in these two speeches – the first in English, and the other in French. I said: Fellow Liberals – Senator

Farris, Mr. Lapointe, Ladies and Gentlemen: I can only thank you but this I do with all my heart. And then in French: Mesdames, Messieurs: Je vous remercie de tout mon cœur. These were my last words. It was interesting they should have been in French. I had not attempted anything of the kind in my speech purposely as I was not aiming at any dramatic effect. It was apparent from the way members of the party spoke and those in the audience, that they were tremendously appreciative of the speech. I felt I had put Liberalism in its true and right place, with its emphasis on those in the humbler walks of life and the need of giving them security and freedom. Indeed the whole Convention has been dominated by the words: Unity, Security and Freedom, which I liked better than those that carry with them the note of progress which to me related more to spiritual things and to material things than to those pertaining to human life and the things of the spirit. I was glad to get in the statement I did about being possibly called upon to defend our country with our lives as well as our policies. Also particularly to conclude with quotations from Pasteur. That was where I began in the writing of Industry and Humanity which has carried me through as Leader of the Liberal Party. I shall never forget what I owe to my brother Max. It was what he gave to me in return for what I tried to do for him. One sees the powerful working of spiritual laws in all this."

The Prime Minister stayed on after his own speech until nearly 6.00 P.M. and returned in the evening about 9 o'clock. He "unfortunately missed Claxton's address. Smallwood of Newfoundland was speaking when I came in. He gave a humorous address. I had, too, unfortunately, missed Bradley. I don't know how they both came to be speaking but I think it would have been wiser if they had not appeared on the platform. I sat between the two of them. Had pleasant talks with each. Explained I thought it would have been better for our Convention not to pass any resolution on Newfoundland. It might raise the question of provinces claiming their right to have a special say. Both agreed with me it would be unfortunate were any adverse comment to be made. I quite enjoyed sitting between these two men at that time and felt there was something quite significant about this little feature of the evening.

"I stayed on until after the Convention adjourned after 11 P.M."

When Mackenzie King arrived at the Coliseum, on August 7, he "found that Abbott and Claxton were doubting whether they should let their names go forward in nomination. I told them by all means to do so. Also Chevrier, to make sure that his name appeared, and later Garson who thought of having his name not go forward as he was nominating someone else. I said to each of them it will let the country and Convention see how the men in the Cabinet really felt toward St. Laurent. I confess I have felt increasing indignation at Gardiner's behaviour in working up a lobby of the disgraceful side of machine politics. I was justified in the interests of Canada to prevent anything of the kind. He is a ruthless, selfish individual. When I heard that he had promised a parliamentary assistant he would take him into the Cabinet, after hearing what he had told Gordon Ross – I felt a feeling of almost anger, that a member of the Cabinet could begin to replace his own colleagues before he had any authority to do anything. I came away about 12.30 realizing I would require a little rest before going back."

The Prime Minister returned to the Coliseum about 2.30 P.M. "The afternoon had been reserved for nominations. There was quite a little time before it got under way. Names were put in and one after the other of our colleagues withdrew making it quite clear that they had already indicated where they stood. It left only Power, Gardiner and St. Laurent. When the names came to be chosen, luck again seemed to go against St. Laurent who was placed in second position for speaking. Gardiner came last – immediately before the vote. He had been counting on this more than anything else. That his speech should be the one that would sweep the Convention. Power stayed in to give emphasis to what he wanted to say about Liberal principles. I confess I approved very strongly of most of what Power said. I thought he made a remarkably good presentation. What I disliked about it all was that it was begotten really of his having left the Cabinet, thereby thinking that whatever was done thereafter was not good Liberalism, but worse than that, [after] having indicated that he was going to stand by St. Laurent. . . . I could not help thinking what a pity it was that Power had spoiled his own chances. This leaves St. Laurent without having him in his debt in any way.

"It was evident when St. Laurent spoke he was not willing to lend himself to the kind of tactics others had been adopting. Made it plain he had no intention of entering any oratorical contest. Spoke of national unity. I felt he was under great strain. Much fatigued. The only exception I would have taken to his address was that I wished he had wedged in his French speech between two English speeches. He was sure enough of his own people. Leaving off with the French was putting himself at a disadvantage. However, he made it plain he was not seeking the position but that the position had to come to him.

"Then came Gardiner who did not do too badly at the start but who made it quite plain as he went along he was hoping to win on the score he was a great organizer. He tried to have it appear his organization had won Saskatchewan in the last election and he was ready to start tomorrow with the organization of the party. I have been trying to get him and others for years to try and do something on that score while members of the Cabinet. I have never been able to have them take that task in hand. I was particularly pleased to see the way the Convention went when suggestion was made about the need for organization; and also to see the concrete action they have taken under the resolutions. Gardiner made a great deal of his friendship for me. I took that with a grain of salt. I thought of the time he was prepared to join with Hepburn and Power, and one or two others, to form an administration leaving me out altogether. At the same time, I would have overlooked all this had it not been that when he came to speak of St. Laurent, he spoke of him as being a great lawyer and having knowledge of certain questions but seemed to stress that to win elections, one had to be a great organizer which, by inference, St. Laurent was not. When I heard that reference to legal ability, I said to myself this is getting down to a contest on basis of personalities, knifing a colleague. At noon, I had decided I would not vote at all particularly on the first ballot. P. was going to hold my ballot and not let me have it but I thought that perhaps it would be well not to vote on the first ballot and be perfectly neutral between all three candidates. When, however, I heard Gardiner's speech and these references in particular, my feelings changed considerably. I spoke to Howe and said I had a mind to vote. He said he thought I ought to. Claxton in the morning had said he thought I should vote. After all, I was a delegate from Glengarry. Was supporting St. Laurent, as they all knew, and felt that it would be much against the country's interests to have either Gardiner or Power elected. That it was well to make it clear that St. Laurent had a good substantial majority. I felt he would be elected but with Gardiner's speech, that made me decide to vote while I had previously decided not to do so. It was embarrassing in that photographers were watching me to see me mark the ballot and place it in the box. I would have preferred letting them see I was not voting at all. I did. After I had voted, for some time wished I had not. I kept thinking this was perhaps one mistake I had made in that it was unnecessary. I could have waited for the second ballot, which, as a matter of fact, never came. After all, Gardiner will remain a colleague in the Cabinet. He had been speaking of me in a frank way but again it seemed to me a question of principle – country's interest and showing one's colours. The arena was crowded. The order was remarkably good. The afternoon's proceedings were very tedious, while waiting for scrutineers to count the ballots. It was getting on toward 6. I suddenly remembered that I had been chosen Leader during the afternoon, at an earlier hour than 6. I recall I was back at the Roxborough about 7 but had been about the grounds for some time after being chosen. I remarked to Fogo that evidently I was now in my 30th year of

Leadership. He passed the word on to Blanchette who got up and announced that I was now in my 30th year of Leadership.

"Finally the scrutineers came, ready to make the announcement of the returns. I looked at my watch. Hands in a straight line at 6 P.M. I had previously suggested that the returns should be given in order in which names appeared on the blackboard, alphabetically, but they announced the figures in accordance with those that were highest in the vote. They announced St. Laurent: 843. It was apparent he had a majority on the first vote. All began to cheer. I could not make out the other figures. Apparently they were: Gardiner 323; Power 56. Different members got up and shook hands with St. Laurent. Madame St. Laurent came on the stage at the time and I had her sit beside me. I did not attempt to go over to speak to St. Laurent who was sitting at the end of the platform. Gardiner and Power fell in line in front of the microphone to make the election unanimous which they did in a very nice way. St. Laurent then came forward. He was quite filled with emotion. Kissed his wife affectionately and then shook hands with me. I congratulated him warmly. Said I was delighted. He then spoke for some little time in English and in French. Did remarkably well under very trying conditions.

"I enjoyed a little joke with Madame St. Laurent telling her I was right when I said at Quebec that the nigger was drafted for the duration. She looked remarkably happy. She had a little sentence which she read over the microphone. I had been wondering whether I should speak. Extend a word of congratulations. While sitting there, thought of how St. Laurent had come into the Cabinet at the time of war from a high sense of duty and of the help he had been through the war after Lapointe had passed away. I decided that I would tell them of that incident. That they might see what St. Laurent had meant to me and to the country and know the reasons why I was so pleased to have him succeed.

"I then got up and asked to say a few words. I told them that while I was sitting there, I had remembered how Ernest Lapointe had passed away. I had been thinking how I had felt; that perhaps I, too, ought to give up. I had lost the one who had been at my side and meant everything to me. When we were coming back from Lapointe's funeral, I asked Power who we could get to replace Lapointe. He had said without question: Louis St. Laurent was the best. I then spoke of having telephoned him and how he came to Laurier House and into my library. How I told him I wanted him to come and help in the war. How he had said no man should refuse at a time of war. Asked for time to have a word with his wife. Told him I had never had to put off anything on that account. When men were a success, it showed what it was to have a good wife. I then came back to where he came within no time at all saying he would enter into the Government. All my colleagues knew the great part he had taken and what we all owed to him. I then said how delighted I was; they would therefore understand my delight at his appointment. I felt I should have brought in Gardiner's name at least to extent Gardiner would be the first to say what a strength he had been, but somehow or another something kept saying to me he had been really shameful in his whole behaviour. I did not think there was any need to mention his name at this time. I thought he quite deserved the lesson he was getting. I thought of the statements he had been sending out to the press; of the attacks on the Government and of his trying to boost his own material, of the gang he had around him. Fellows like Colin Campbell and others and of the money that was coming from some sources which would give him a control of affairs of the country. All that was in my mind when I was speaking and I left him alone. I was sorry to have done so. If I had thought of his mother before rather than after, I might have brought in his name. He owed everything to her but his ambition left him indifferent in many ways to family obligations.

"Later I met his sister who was present. A very nice person. I spoke to her about his mother. What a fine woman she was. When I had made my few remarks which I was grateful to God for having thought of at the time, it was just what was needed at that moment – St. Laurent and Madame St. Laurent then left to go to a reception in the hall where numbers were going to congratulate them. I remained behind to watch the proceedings. To my amazement, people began coming up to shake hands with me. I stood again receiving for quite a long time. It was very pleasant receiving the kind congratulations of those who came. I was pleased that among the number was Angus Macdonald who spoke in a very nice way. I was surprised not to have had any greeting from Ilsley. Did not see him throughout the whole Convention. Members of the press gallery gathered around to have a word. I fortunately was on the platform when Blanchette and Fogo were each presented with a silver gavel commemorative of their presiding at the gathering. I thanked them both warmly. . . ."

It was about 7.45 P.M. when Mackenzie King drove home to Laurier House. Handy remained to dine with him and while they "were having dinner together, Handy told me that little Pat was a gift from Norman through himself and that it was to have an association with today. I cannot say how deeply I was touched by this expression of deep affection. Nothing could have given me more real pleasure than a thought of the kind. It is truly wonderful how all has worked out to bring it about on this day.

"I have in my hands licence – Ottawa – No. 1, 1948, which was purchased at the beginning of the year in the hope that I would have a little dog before the year was out. Now it goes to Pat III. The licence is all the more welcome in that it is heart shaped. It should be dated August 7, 1948.

"I spent the evening after dinner writing this diary to date."

Before leaving for Kingsmere about 11 P.M. he wrote: "I can truly say as I leave that I do so with a much lighter heart tonight than I had 29 years ago. A happier heart and a more peaceful mind. I have no regret – only thankfulness to God that all has gone so well, and that this chapter of my life has closed at the beginning of my 30th year of leadership of the party which came to me through my loyalty to Sir Wilfrid and which has been handed on to St. Laurent today through his loyalty to me."

He "looked up the record of the last Convention at Kingsmere to see the time at which I actually was chosen Leader. The voting had begun apparently around 3. I had the lead from the start. This might give a certain justification to my having been Leader from that time and therefore in my 30th year before retiring at this time. It was in fact, however, nearer 8 o'clock before the final vote was declared. St. Laurent was declared Leader a few minutes after 6 P.M.

"I then began reading parts of the 1919 Convention. Noticed that I had been mistaken about it being the same days of the week. It was in fact Tuesday, Wednesday and Thursday – though the 6th was the day on which I made my speech in 1919. It was the following day that Lady Laurier came to the Convention. The record shows she was in the gallery, not on the platform, and that Murphy was the one who drew attention to her being there. I myself had not occasion to make any allusion to Lady Laurier's presence. This apropos of the false statement by McAree in the Globe.

"Read over the speech made at the time; also part of the speeches made by Adamson and others telling of the treachery of the Union Government during the elections of 1917 and what occasioned the Liberal defeat. It is the worst chapter of Canadian history. I confess much of my thoughts through the day were of the action of some of the men of our party in whom I have been greatly disappointed. Chief of all was Gardiner for entering the race the way he did; trying to knife St. Laurent, putting out little praises of himself, etc. Propaganda regarding himself, etc. His sole emphasis on machine politics. No statesmanlike outlook.

"Next I think was Martin. I was amazed to find out both in what I read and what he said in conversation to discover how eager he had been for the leadership at this time and the belief that he could have carried the Convention. He told me on the platform that he even yet was not sure whether he was right in not standing. Told me he had a terrible time with himself for days deciding what he should do. Power I was not surprised at.

Indeed I thought his speech the best of all at the Convention. Great justification for much that he said. A tragic figure he appeared there and looks in the pictures of himself which were taken. Tucker I am disgusted with beyond words after the way he spoke to me in my office of Gardiner, to see him standing and leading the cheer in the Convention when Gardiner's name was read out as a candidate – nominated before he made his speech. It is something I shall never forget. Like a man with no moral centre.

"Gordon Ross is another man I feel contempt for, having supported Gardiner whom he loathes and hates and talks against, because of promise of a position in Gardiner's Government and going back on St. Laurent whom he knows to be the best of all possible leaders. He will get no Senatorship from me. I imagine he knows it by now for I have said nothing to him. Of the other colleagues who let their names come forward, and of Garson who acted and spoke like real men.

"I could not help feeling reading the account of the last Convention how appallingly wicked was the whole treatment of Sir Wilfrid and how underneath all what he must have suffered with his sensitive nature. I read part of Graham's speech at the Convention. It, too, filled me with disgust. His effort to win on the strength of Sir Wilfrid's name and his friendship with Sir Wilfrid. Yet at the time of crisis, he could not show where he stood. I confess for Borden I felt an equal contempt; also Meighen and specially those men of our own Government. Men who called themselves Liberals, who joined the Union Government. Men like Rowell, Crerar. That they could have lent themselves to the tactics used at the time."

When Handy arrived at Kingsmere on Monday, August 9, Mackenzie King "felt a certain right" to look at the morning papers "while the matter was still one of real interest. This I did with regard to the Journal and Citizen. On the whole, enjoying accounts of both. I think it is apparent the press is of the opinion that I have achieved another victory re making certain of St. Laurent's election. There was no doubt the fact that I was so strongly for him though I kept much in the background throughout, was a factor for ensuring his election. I am the more delighted than ever that his influence will all be in the direction of high statesmanship. I like the expression that one reporter used, of rounding out of the circle in the day of my taking over as successor of Laurier, turning the successorship to one of French Canada. The one thing that has pleased me very much has been the absence of any open discussion of race or religion at the Convention, and I doubt if there was much of it behind the scenes. I was right when I told St. Laurent not to speak of either again."

During the day, Ilsley telephoned "of his own accord. He said he wanted to let me know it had not been intentional on his part that we had missed each other at the Convention. He said he had started to make his way toward me a couple of times but was held up. Was sorry we had missed. Said he hoped I did not feel it had been an oversight. I said no such thought had entered my mind. I confess I was a bit surprised. I then spoke to him about his trip to England. He said it had been quite a strain but that they had won their case, which was fortunate. I said to him at one stage where I thought if he had allowed his name to go before the Convention, he might have been chosen Leader, specially where there was uncertainty as between Gardiner and St. Laurent. From the way he spoke, I saw that he himself had felt that way. He said he believed that that might have been possible. I could see that he would have welcomed the opportunity had it come. To my surprise, however, he spoke particularly of Angus Macdonald. Said he never saw anything more absurd or pathetic than the way Macdonald kept debating with himself as to whether he should allow his, Macdonald's, name, to go before the Convention. That in a committee, he was saying he did not know what he should do; whether he was right in not allowing it to go; whether he should go. Ilsley said it was the most absurd thing he had witnessed.

"I guess Macdonald knew he would have been snowed under. Was regretting that his course had been such as to make this inevitable."

On Wednesday, August 11, the Prime Minister returned to Ottawa and had a "conversation of two hours with Mr. St. Laurent. He greeted me very warmly. I had received a charming letter from him. He thanked me for what I had said after his election. He was evidently much touched. I told him that I was so pleased with the result and would welcome every opportunity to help him in any way I could. He said that he knew that. There was no need to give him any assurance of that. When he sat down, I could see what was weighing mostly on his mind were the problems that had to be considered. I said to him I would like at once for him to know that I was prepared to do whatever would mean most to him in the matter of time at which I would ask the Governor to accept my resignation. If he would like me to do this within the next few weeks. I should be only too happy or I would be prepared to wait whatever time he might wish to take in the interval for himself to get matters in readiness before taking office. He at once said that he would wish me to go to the United Nations and to London Conference. He then began to speak of the problems that were on his mind. It was clear to me that he had been thinking mostly of what it would be best to do as regards the future. He seemed most concerned about the filling of vacancies of Justice and External Affairs; wondered if he would be justified in trying to induce Pearson to come into the House. Give him the portfolio of External Affairs. I told him I would favour that very strongly. He mentioned the constituency that he thought he could run in successfully by our appointing the sitting member to the Senate. The Member in question is one I would wish to honour in that way in any event. He said it would be a big responsibility as Pearson had no guarantee for the future. I told him I had none when I made my venture into politics. That was the real test of the man.

"My own view, though I did not express it, is if Pearson does come in, he will succeed St. Laurent when he gives up the leadership whether in office or in opposition. I would like Pearson to come in, and think him quite the ablest man for that post. Indeed if he could have been induced to come in at the present time, that would have been all to the good in many ways but I am glad to have St. Laurent, above all others, succeed me.

"We spoke of Abbott. I said I thought it was worth considering whether Abbott might not be made Minister of Justice. He said he would himself think that excellent but feared that Abbott might be hurt if he were not given a chance to carry out what he has in mind as Minister of Finance in connection with the next budget. I agreed with that and said I would not for a moment urge a transfer without it being in accordance with Abbott's own wish. I suggested, if it were made, that Claxton might be the best man for Finance as he has human sympathies and would be very able in a portfolio of the kind. I doubt, however, if that change could be made.

"The next question that came up was getting a new Minister for Nova Scotia. Winters seemed to be the most likely person but as St. Laurent said, neither of us have been able to measure him up. Nothing would be done without conferring with Isnor first. I know he would like a Senatorship. I strongly advised bringing on by-elections soon; not letting Ilsley's by-election stand too long. St. Laurent said he had not had any talk with Ilsley. I told him of the conversation we had had together. To my amazement, he inquired as to whether it might not be worth while bringing Angus Macdonald back from Nova Scotia. It might be a way of placating the provincial premiers. I told him it would be most unwise. That he would not find Macdonald loyal. That it would antagonize others to regard anyone who had occasioned embarrassment for us. He said at once he would not give the matter a further thought. He doubted if he would accept as he was thinking of getting the Chief Justiceship of the Province. I told him what Ilsley had said to me about Macdonald at the Convention, taking it as a matter of state as to whether in the country's interest, he should not allow his name to be put up, etc. He spoke of Walter Harris as being one of the best. I told him I agreed with that. Believed he would make a good administrator. Might handle defence very well. I said I thought it would be well to take plenty of time to think of these matters.

"We then had a talk about the Convention itself and how disappointing had been the attitude of some of the men. I expressed my surprise at the way MacKinnon had held back. Refused to show his colours until after I had talked with him pretty plainly. I spoke of Gardiner's conduct as being wholly contemptible. I thought he had hurt himself in his own speech when he tried to knife a colleague by referring to St. Laurent as being a skilful lawyer but by implication no good as an organizer, etc., which was what the party needed. It was one of the worst scenes that I had ever witnessed. All of Gardiner's behaviour was thoroughly bad. Tucker's was most disgusting as well.

"St. Laurent said he thought Chubby's speech was the best of the three. I told him I thought it was very good. What was said in it was in large part very true. He agreed it was along the lines I myself had been protesting against in Council from time to time. What worried him most was the knowledge of the questions that would have to be decided at once and their effect. The most important being decisions that would have to be made today on the admission of cattle into the United States. That would send up the cost of living still further. He felt sure the cost of living had been the one thing that had helped Duplessis more than anything else. This was something no government could meet – but indeed the first act under the period of new leadership would be a further increase.

"He spoke, too, of the embarrassment there would be over the question of oleomargarine; difficulties with provinces over railways, etc. As he went over these matters, I said to him that he would have to remember what someone had said about the pyramids; when we looked at them from a distance and saw them as a whole, it would appear that no one could attempt to reach the top. As however one drew nearer, one discovered there were a series of steps and it was in that light he would have to view meeting the obligations that were before him. I advised strongly not to decide too soon on the date of an election."

They also talked "of the conference of Premiers in London. I said I really was not anxious to go to the U.N. [in Paris] and I would only go to the other because I believed the British Government really wanted me because of the nature of questions that were coming up which affected India, Ceylon, etc. Smuts would not be present and they were counting on my years of experience to help them. St. Laurent was very strong in saying it would be the worst thing that could happen to him so far as Quebec is concerned were he to start over as soon as he assumed office. It would mean taking office too soon and would be used against him that he had left Canada at once. On the other hand, he spoke of an article in the Journal which is a contemptible one. I told him I would pay no attention to any newspaper; do the thing that was right. All would work out in the end. That had been my view.

"We talked of some of the other matters. He said to me two or three times, I shall need to have your advice and counsel. I am counting on that. He also spoke of how overwhelmed he was with letters, and of knowing little about the office. He also asked whether we would see the press at once and let them know what the plans were. In this connection, he asked if I would be making what is referred to as a grand tour, visiting Italy and Greece. I told him that while it would be pleasant to have that opportunity, I had never counted on it and felt that I should return to Canada right after the meeting of Prime Ministers – within a week or so. That I was definitely decided on that. I spoke of wishing to take P. with me. While he said nothing, beyond saying that Robertson was one External Affairs seemed to regard as a good man, left the matter there but I had in my own mind I would not take P. if it would embarrass him.

"When I 'phoned P. in the morning, spoke of his coming, he made no comment one way or the other which caused me to feel that he would probably prefer to stay here and be with St. Laurent and Claxton so as to get a foot in before St. Laurent took office. I was ready to give him the chance but felt if he were really not keen about it, I could make some other plan. This recalls that I was surprised St. Laurent had not spoken of Claxton for Paris. He himself said he thought Claxton ought to take on the work of organization. I advised him very strongly to put it in his hands. Get freed of any control by Gardiner in any direction and let Claxton understand that if we were to win, the organization would have to be properly attended to. That is most important of all.

"We were both pretty tired at the end of the talk together. I confess I felt sort of selfish in not being able to do more for St. Laurent. I know how terribly heavy is the load already and is certain to be. He is pretty tired but has been under a great strain. He is very modest. Very much in earnest. I believe he will yet surprise them all."

At the Cabinet meeting that afternoon the Prime Minister "at once said they would allow me to say how pleased we all were with Mr. St. Laurent's selection as Leader of the Party. That I would like to renew the congratulations to him and extend best of wishes. That I thought we had reason to be pleased at his selection. This was said in Gardiner's presence. Gardiner at once said he would like to second what I had said.

St. Laurent thanked me quite warmly. Said he felt what a responsibility it was. Would try to do the best he could. Would rely on my always giving him the assistance that he needed. I then said I would like to say before we went any further that I thought we should now return to a due appreciation of collective responsibility of the Cabinet. Some of us had been off more or less on our own. Different Members of Council had been in connection with the Convention, speaking their own mind on different matters of policy. I thought we should remember the Cabinet was one and that no declarations of policy, etc., should be made without having matters first settled in the Cabinet. What I said was so pointed at Gardiner that I felt it necessary to add that I was not speaking of anyone in particular though I had noticed that Chevrier had, according to the radio, said there was to be a Royal Commission to deal with freight rates matter. That I thought this was unfortunate. When we looked up press references later, it was apparent he had spoken this way but was giving it as a personal opinion. I pointed out that members of the Cabinet could not speak on these matters personally as distinct from the Cabinet as a whole."

On August 13, Mackenzie King received Sir Norman Brook, the Secretary of the United Kingdom Cabinet, "who had come from Mr. Attlee to talk over matters to be discussed at the Prime Ministers' meeting. Clutterbuck was with him. I had Pearson and St. Laurent join us. We talked in my office from around about 5 until 7 when they left. St. Laurent, Pearson stayed on until 20 to 8 and then St. Laurent and I drove together to the Country Club.

"In conversation, Sir Norman said that the British Government felt that India might wish to become a republic. Give up association with the Crown. The question would come up whether India could be kept in the Commonwealth of Nations and how. The British Government thought every effort should be made toward that end. The first step would be to seek to have the Government of India appoint its own Governor-General by whatever name they pleased. Same for all the Dominions. Could be called King's Representative or by whatever name they wished. The main thing would be to allow same thing as in Ireland, of maintaining the King's authority in external relations. A third thought was to have the Prime Minister of India made a Privy Councillor. What would be done being something still to be explored. Similar question came up with regard to Eire.

"Apparently Costello, the present Prime Minister, who is believed to be even more inclined to effect closer relations with the Crown, has made a speech or two in which he declares that the present status of Ireland is that it is already an independent state and had only a sort of association – one of appearances rather than reality – to the Crown.

"Ireland may therefore wish to pull out. There is the question, too, of what may be best in regard to Czechoslovakia. Brook said there would be no effort to make a new constitution. The point of view would be rather that of declaring a certain position as already established. I pointed out that is what we maintained as regards the Statute of Westminster.

"Brook spoke of what had already been done regarding citizenship in Commonwealth; same British subject, etc. I shared the view it would not be wise to make any new constitution. Also it was desirable to keep these countries within the Commonwealth. I thought that matter ought to be considered from the side of the use of certain terms as, for example, British subject; also the use of the possessive by the Crown – such as in Speeches from the Throne – 'My' people; 'My' Ministers, etc. I said already we had tried to get away from that usage in several Speeches from the Throne. I noticed Sir Norman made a note of this.

"I thought the Privy Councillorship idea was that it would make intense difficulties for the man who was accepting it. St. Laurent said it would give constitutional significance to those who were Councillors now in other parts of the Commonwealth and would not wish any such significance to be given.

"At one stage, Sir Norman spoke of recognizing the King as the King of the British Commonwealth. I at once said that that would be I thought wholly objectionable. Its significance would be deemed to be that of the Commonwealth being the unit – with unitary policies, etc. Just doing the very thing the Tories have been aiming at right along. I said that perhaps that would split up the Empire quicker than anything else. I thought we should keep to the view it was a community of nations. The emphasis of union should be to institutions which we have in common, based on certain fundamentals of justice. I pointed out too that having a loose association with India might cause South Africa to seek that relationship rather than the one she now possesses. They rather expect in England that South Africa may wish to fall away from any closer union – even from the closeness of the relationship she now has.

"Sir Norman was quite emphatic about not having any additional centralized machinery; also abandoning the old idea of Imperial Conferences but favoured rather special conferences on special subjects with different parts of the Commonwealth. I could see, in all he was saying in this connection, that the views I have expressed in these connections from time to time, have won acceptance.

"Other questions likely to come up would be situation of Berlin and

Europe, Australia and New Zealand likely to raise the question of [effect of the] Western Union on trade relations between Britain and Australia. I asked about the present view in regard to the possibility of war.

"Sir Norman said that the feeling had changed. That Bevin did not seem to be so fearful of conflict. That at least they were beginning on negotiations.

"I stressed the importance of the British Government letting it be known before the meeting of Premiers that it was for an exchange of views and that conferences, in their nature, were private. In no sense was the meeting to be one of laying down policies. I thought all this should be made clear in advance of the time and date finally arranged.

"I suggested too that there might be different meetings between individual Premiers and only occasionally bringing all together, so as to avoid too much formality and equally not to attract attention to the older countries being together, when problems related to the new countries came up.

"The question of Communism also came up. St. Laurent, Pearson and I were together later and discussed further the personnel of the delegation to the U.N. Agreed to put on Wishart Robertson and Chevrier as well as myself. McNaughton and Vanier, other delegates. As alternatives, Wilgress and someone from External Affairs. One or two parliamentary assistants.

"Then, too, the question of delegates to the Empire Parliamentary Association. St. Laurent expressed surprise that at least half a dozen premiers of provinces were going. . . . To me, it is all part of what I call centralized Empire conspiracy. A sort of effort to bribe the provinces by taking these leaders for trips to Europe, etc. Decided to let Wishart Robertson choose two persons from the Senate. I had favoured Gibb Weir as Whip, and Tremblay from the House of Commons. Not to give anything further to Mackenzie. Spoke specially of Golding. Fauteux will be going as Speaker.

"We went out to the Country Club for dinner. St. Laurent spoke of how heavy the whole job appeared to be. Said he had never realized the kind of load I must have been carrying over the years. Just could not understand how I managed it. I talked with him about taking rest at periods; not letting himself be driven too much. Also suggested instead of taking a house, to stay at the Roxborough quietly, and do the entertaining at the Country Club, where it was for visitors, at government expense. Said I had made a great mistake, I thought, of loading myself so heavily in a personal way. He had been to see the Perley house. Thought it very large. I suggested at the next session if we can get the leaders together, we could agree on purchasing and furnishing a house. Would be all the better for him to wait and see what developments there were through the years. I think he was rather glad at this suggestion. It is clear he is worrying a bit about not taking a house which would be regarded as a Prime Minister's residence. The trouble with the Roxborough is they serve no meals on Sunday.

"At the Country Club, we had an exceptionally pleasant evening. St. Laurent and I immediately after arriving joined Sir Norman Brook and Sir Alexander Clutterbuck and were joined later by Pearson and Pickersgill. We had cocktails in front of an open fire and then a round table dinner party. Light wines. Nice service. Stayed and had our coffee there.

"Had an extremely interesting talk about matters connected with the war. Sir Norman Brook told of its beginnings and about its last days when Churchill was trying to decide which day ought to be fixed for V.E. Day. Unable to get in touch with Russia and finally settling the matter by 'phoning America. He had told Sir Norman to hold back the six o'clock news. As a matter of fact, they could not be held. Got the statement out about 20 to 7. Pearson told of how they had all been in the cellar at Canada House when the war began; how the basement had been fitted up at great expense and was the only part that really suffered damage when a bomb came and let water in from outside. . . .

"It was 11 o'clock when we broke up. St. Laurent and I drove back together. I did my best to encourage him in some aspects of the work, for which he seemed really grateful. Told me he was profoundly impressed with the magnitude of the problems."

That night Mackenzie King left for Seal Harbor, Maine, to visit John D. Rockefeller, Jr. He arrived just before midnight on August 14 and the next afternoon talked to Rockefeller "about my own plans. I told him I was frankly in doubt as to what it was wisest to do – as to going into St. Laurent's Cabinet as President of the Council and remaining in the Government until the elections were over. This subject he pursued himself as we went up the mountain together. He asked me whether I would be free to withdraw at any time if I felt tired, or would I be bound for a definite period. I explained that I would be free to leave but could hardly do so without a political question arising. Withdrawing would be construed as some difference with colleagues. Also I said there might be questions arising in which I might not be able to agree with some Members of the Government. It would be most unfortunate if I had to leave because of a difference. I also spoke of what I had still to do by way of getting my papers together, making a will, etc.

"When I spoke about leaving Laurier House to the state, he spoke of the difficulty of these places being kept up afterwards. I said I had no doubt the state would keep up Laurier House. If it were a private group, I would not feel so sure of that. But I mentioned that most of the things that I had there were historical in their way; had been given to me while in office. Told him of Mr. Larkin's contributions, etc., and that I did not feel I would distribute any of these things among the family or relations but would try to have them preserved for the state. I also told him of Kingsmere; of the extent of the land there and what I had in mind. I said these things I could keep as a guarantee until the end of my days. He seemed surprised when he learned there was no pension of any kind after so many years of service. I told him I had no doubt, that I had put aside quite a little and said I could dispose of life insurance, etc. Had no doubt the state would, if I ever was in need, see that I was looked after. As one got older, one would be happier with smaller quarters, etc. I had no fears on any of these scores. Also that I could do some writing, etc. I did say, however, that I thought I would like in a way to stay on for another year or two because of the income which I would derive and making easier the transition from being head of government to being a private citizen. At the same time, I felt as one got older, one did not know at what moment one might find one's strength failing or sight, etc. It was well to get all things cleaned up while one's memory was still intact."

The Prime Minister remained at Seal Harbor until Friday, August 20, and returned to Kingsmere the following day. During the day he discussed with his friend Mrs. Patteson "the pros and cons; wisdom and otherwise of my planning to stay on as President of the Council should this be desired by Mr. St. Laurent. I told her I had come pretty well to the conclusion that the wise thing to do would be to drop out of the Government altogether after returning from England, regardless of the embarrassment that might be created through a drop thereby of some $14,000 in salary. The main consideration is that to stay on is almost certain to be embarrassing to Mr. St. Laurent as well as myself. The Opposition press and members would be certain to continually assert that I was directing affairs. That mine was the Master's Voice, etc. In the Government itself, I would find it increasingly difficult to oppose views of colleagues such as Howe, Claxton, Gardiner and some of the others, without making it difficult for St. Laurent to side with one or the other. I am far from believing that I would be able to agree with some of the policies which I know certain of the Ministers intend to press.

"In the House of Commons, too, I should find it very unpleasant to be facing Drew as Leader of the Opposition. I have such contempt for the man that I would find his arrogance unbearable. I had my fill of that kind of thing under Meighen and Bennett and do not see why I should voluntarily incur the sort of insulting behaviour to which I would have to submit if in opposition to him as a member of the Government. I can have my say wherever it is necessary as a Member of Parliament. It would be extremely embarrassing to the Government if for any reason, whether because of impaired health or otherwise, I should have to withdraw before the election. It would also be embarrassing if I were in the Government at the time of the elections and did not take an active part in relation thereto.

"All of this ignores what one's own feelings might be from day to day through being continually reminded of a lack of authority which I have had over all the years.

"J. said that she and G. had been talking over the situation together and they both feel that I would be wise not to stay on. They both spoke particularly of the possible embarrassment to St. Laurent which is what I have thought much of – the use the press would make of divided authority. They also pointed out that no one could possibly have had more in the way of appreciation of his services than I have had, or left public life under more favourable circumstances than those of which the Convention was a sort of climax and final expression. That anything from now on, so far as my own reputation is concerned, would almost certainly be an anti-climax and might easily help to destroy much of what I have already achieved."

The next morning (August 22) Mackenzie King spent some time "drafting a statement for submission to Mr. St. Laurent re my attendance in Paris at the opening of the U.N. Assembly and also at the meeting of the British Prime Ministers. I have made it perfectly clear that, in these matters, I wished to do entirely what [in] Mr. St. Laurent's judgment will most accord with what is in the public interest and his own wishes. It is, I think, important that the public should know that if I go, it is not because of my will or wish in the matter. I increasingly feel that now that Mr. St. Laurent has been chosen, the sooner I turn over responsibilities of office to him, the better."

On August 23, the Prime Minister met Lord Mountbatten at Government House and they had a talk about the situation in India. Mountbatten "said he thought India would stay in the Commonwealth. That Nehru who was much opposed to the British, had come around very much in the time that he has been in office. That the attitude to take toward India would be that it was of course for them to say if they wished to remain in the Empire. If they did, we would give them the warmest of welcomes. I pointed out this had been our attitude. The attitude we had taken toward Newfoundland. I said that in talking with him, I might have the trump card in being able to say something of my grandfather's part in the rebellion against Britain in 1837 and my attitude toward the British. He thought Nehru was mostly afraid of the United States. Coming into the Empire because of the United States and some influence that Canada might have; of danger of being drawn into the war. I could not quite follow what he had in mind but told him of how I had brought Canada into the war by refusing to make any commitments in advance and having our own Parliament decide.

"When His Excellency joined us, Mountbatten said that no words could describe the hate which the people of India had of Britain. His Excellency seemed a bit surprised at this. Mountbatten stressed it and also said privately that both he and Ismay had said they would rather infinitely be in the war with its dangers, than in the situation they found in India when they were there. He said it looked at one time as though there would be the most terrible civil strife and massacre. He said there was only one thing to do and that was to lose no time whatever in giving India self-government. He said Churchill had been wrong in his whole point of view. His whole attitude was a very democratic one. On the other hand, he, too, in my mind, has a good deal of English self-confidence about him. He it attractive looking; very able, I think. Full of self-assurance. Less inclined, I think, to give credit to the Government and others than to take a great deal of it to himself."

During the afternoon the Prime Minister "spent quite a long time with Mr. St. Laurent first going over statement I had prepared which I suggested he should change as he thought best in conference with Pearson.

"I said I had written it as from my point of view purposely with a view to having made quite clear it was his wishes that I wished to have followed. I made it wholly clear I would approve of any wording he might wish. He suggested bringing in collective responsibility of our colleagues for the decision."

Mackenzie King found St. Laurent "very positive about my going to Europe and to London. The discussion on this matter gave me opportunity to make quite clear to him that while I was ready to help all I could, that I was decided I should not think of continuing on save as a Member of the House; that any advisory assistance that I could give might best be given at Laurier House where he could come and dine with me at any time, and we could talk matters over together. I said I thought it was desirable to let the country know at once that I intended to retire, as soon as I got back from England, and that I was giving up all tasks of Government, leaving the situation as completely to himself as possible. I said I did not think it would be fair to him to have people given any chance to say that I was still directing matters. That the hand that was governing was not his. That would be a fatal mistake in relation to the elections when they came off. It would then be said that I was no longer available, etc. That he should form his own government. He had stressed to me very strongly on the train one day, before the Convention, that I owed it as a patriotic duty to stay on in the Government, whoever might be appointed Prime Minister.

"I had led him to believe at the time that if he were chosen, I would be ready to consider this. I felt, therefore, it was doubly necessary for me before he goes further in arrangements for the Ministry, to let him see clearly what my decision has been and feeling is.

"He said very little – in fact, nothing at all in reference to my remarks in this connection but brought up the question of necessity of getting a Minister of Justice and Minister from the Maritimes without delay. He said he had talked with Claxton who did not want Justice. Thought it had come to be looked upon as a sort of secondary portfolio. That Defence was all-important in the public mind and he would wish to keep that post. I said it showed wherein Claxton's ambition was defeating his judgment. That Defence was the last portfolio in which people of the country were interested, important as it might be, should war arise. I said I had told Claxton I thought for his own future he should have taken the chairmanship of the committee that Martin had taken. Also that I regarded Justice and Finance as the two most important portfolios next to Prime Minister. He said he thought he could get Garson to come into the Ministry. I said if he could, by all means to arrange that at once. As he talked, I came to the conclusion that it was due to something Claxton had said. I told him I doubted if Garson would come. He raised the question in connection with the constituency.

"We then had a talk together about Pearson of which I shall make a note elsewhere."

"I next had a talk with Pearson who is much concerned as to what he should do. He knows Mr. St. Laurent's wishes but has many considerations of which to take account. He agrees that St. Laurent would make a fatal mistake in going to Britain within a short time after assuming office. In Quebec, they would use it against him from now until the day of the elections.

"I told Pearson what I had said to St. Laurent about my getting out altogether. Said to him I felt that the press were stressing the end of what they were terming the Mackenzie King era, and that the new era should begin with Mr. St. Laurent whose position should not be weakened through the possibility of it being said that I was still a directing force. I felt that for me to stay on would make it exceedingly embarrassing for him, and

also exceedingly embarrassing for me. Pearson did not say much one way
or the other but I could see that he agreed with what I was saying."

After the dinner that evening for Mountbatten, Mackenzie King "had
St. Laurent drive back with me on my way to Kingsmere. I dropped him
at the Roxborough. I feel increasingly that he is finding the burden very
heavy. He told me too many people are already after him for different
things, to free them from penitentiaries, to get them appointments, etc.
I stressed to him very strongly the need for him to get a Deputy Head of
the Department. Someone who could relieve him of all that kind of thing.
Take his mail and distribute it, be responsible for what was done in
different directions. That unless he had that, he would not last any time.
He would need someone who could keep others away and be a brake
between him and those seeking to get near him, but particularly someone
who could handle all his correspondence. He said he sees that already
but I am afraid he will find like myself that he will never have enough
time to do anything for himself in the way of meeting that situation."

On August 25, the Prime Minister read to the Cabinet the statement
he had prepared for the press "which had been revised by Mr. St. Laurent
and Pearson as to my attending the meetings in Paris and London, and at
Mr. St. Laurent's request, my intention to retire on return from the London
meeting, should that suit his convenience. I told the Cabinet that I wanted
them to know that I was quite prepared to retire at once. That I would
prefer, above everything else, having the enjoyment of Kingsmere for the
months of September and October preparing a will and other matters
that I should have been doing long ago, than to take on obligation of going
on to Paris and London. That I would not enjoy the U.N. Assembly, and
as regards the London meetings, they were always difficult affairs for me.
However, I was prepared to do what would best assist Mr. St. Laurent
and then read the statement. Said it carried responsibility on all who were
present. I could not help but notice the appearance on the faces of the
Members of the Cabinet. They all looked a little tired.

"I was met with a question at the end, that they hoped it did not mean
I would not be in the House. I told them I had said I would stay as a
Member of Glengary until the elections because of the limited majority we
have though I frankly would prefer giving up altogether at once, and would
do so were it not that I knew of the difficulties we were all facing and
wished to help in so far as I could. With the consent of Council, the statement was given to the press at noon. It appeared in the afternoon papers.

"I have in mind retirement about November 11 which is Armistice Day
and my brother's Max's birthday. Curiously enough, I noticed in the
evening press that Hume had suggested that date as a probability."

Mackenzie King had a dinner that evening at the Country Club for the Governor-General and Lady Alexander and the Mountbattens. Most of the evening he "talked with Lord Mountbatten whom I found once we began to converse, in an intimate way, most pleasant and charming. Gave expression with genuine feeling to his democratic point of view. Said Churchill was wholly wrong with regard to India. That the people were all right if their confidence could be gained. Spoke about his own work. Thought it was best for him to go back to the Navy at present, not to take on anything else until later. That everything he had taken on had come to him. He had not tried to take a particular post. He spoke of his eldest son who is just preparing to run for Parliament and with a good deal of pride, the young fellow had refused to sign certain papers which would have committed him to a particular stand in his campaign. He said he would tell me confidentially what he had only mentioned to one or two others, namely he had strongly advised his nephew, the Duke of Edinburgh, husband of Princess Elizabeth, to take a very democratic stand. Not to try to argue the matter with the King and Queen and to cause them to change their views, but to use his influence on his wife to have her just as democratic as possible in regard to the changes that were now taking place as being in the right direction."

Arrangements for his trip abroad caused Mackenzie King some minor anxiety. On August 26 he told Pearson that he "thought I really should take P. with me as the one person I have been accustomed to working well with. I cannot, as long as I remain Prime Minister, be left without necessary help while abroad." The next day he "learned from Pearson that he (St. Laurent) was terribly disappointed at the possibility of my taking Pickersgill to Europe. He feels P. is one person who knows the Department. Knows where my papers are and knows the line that I would probably wish to have taken on different measures, and also how the business of a new session is to be made ready. I just had a word with him tonight on that saying that my reason for wishing P. along was that I could not forget I was still going abroad as Prime Minister with the responsibilities of a Prime Minister in meeting any questions that might arise either at the Assembly or while in London, and felt that I should have with me someone with whom I was accustomed to talk on these matters, and who could help in the drafting of the speeches I was prepared to make. However, when I saw how really distressed he was, though he recognized that I had every right to take P. with me, I practically made up my mind to make some other arrangement, having much in mind the sacrifices that he, Mr. St. Laurent, had made for me at the time of war and coming into the Government."

After the Cabinet meeting on September 1, Mackenzie King had a talk with St. Laurent about the prospects for bringing Garson into the federal Cabinet. "Pickersgill had a personal interview with Garson on his way west and Garson has apparently expressed his willingness to come into the Government if he can get Glen's seat in Marquette. St. Laurent suggested he might write Glen asking if he would be prepared to make way. I told St. Laurent that I knew Glen wished for an appointment in External Affairs more than aught else. There is a chance for him to go to Australia. There are other possibilities as well. I doubt if Glen will have the strength to take on anything else at his age. He may, however, be prepared and would I am sure but for financial sacrifice, to make way for Garson. I would feel if matters cannot be arranged otherwise, means should be found to assure to Glen what may be necessary in the way of compensation for what he would otherwise have received for attendance in the House of Commons.

"I agreed with St. Laurent that the thing to do was for St. Laurent to write him at once, putting the position before him. St. Laurent naturally feels much elated at the possibility of securing Garson."

On September 3, the Prime Minister discussed the problem of finding a seat for Pearson with St. Laurent who "mentioned Farquhar's seat in Algoma. Farquhar is now 73. I had objected strongly to this some time ago but having regard to our great majority in the Senate, and particularly as it is a seat in which Pearson might get an acclamation, I said to St. Laurent if Howe could guarantee the nomination, and the election of Pearson in Algoma, I would forego the rule I have made of not recommending anyone over 70, doing this on the ground of finding a seat for a Cabinet Minister. I agreed with St. Laurent if this step is to be taken, the sooner the election was over, the better. He has been talking with Castonguay about proclaiming the new Act and Castonguay as usual is behind times, and will take a couple of months for the by-election. I said if St. Laurent wished it, I would take Pearson into the Cabinet just as soon as he could arrange for a seat. I suggested that Howe should go immediately to the constituency and, if possible, let us be in a position to take the step on Wednesday of next week.

"St. Laurent referred to my wish to have Pearson in London for the Prime Ministers' meeting. I replied that should not stand in the way of getting him elected without delay. That I would manage somehow to get on with Norman Robertson's aid and without anyone else. I received word today that Malan of South Africa would not be present, neither would Chifley of Australia. St. Laurent is in much the same position as Malan. It is doubtful if Ireland will be represented by Costello or anyone.

"St. Laurent has also Garson coming in. He could get Glen's seat – Marquette. I suddenly thought of the vacancy in the chairmanship of the International Joint Commission. Told St. Laurent if he liked to offer that post to Glen, I would be prepared to appoint him. He has been Minister of Mines and Resources, would be quite suitable for that post if his heart condition permits it. St. Laurent says he understands Glen went to the office once but found he had to drop the effort. It may be that he will of his own accord be prepared to give up the seat. I am afraid financial difficulties might prevent this.

"I should have recorded at the time of the talk I had with Pearson, after he had talked with St. Laurent – some days ago – he told me that St. Laurent had talked with him as had been agreed between St. Laurent and myself he would, and that he Pearson felt he would be ready to take the risks involved if a seat could be found for him. Said he had not taken any part in politics but was and had always been a Liberal and would have no difficulty in maintaining his Liberal outlook. He recognized the risk there was in giving up his present post. I told him that I did not think he need fear for the future. Were he to resign, I would not fill the post of Under-Secretary until the election was over. If he was defeated, would reappoint him to the post. I did not see there was any reason why this should not be done. I mentioned that Sir Wilfrid had had that same idea with regard to myself when I gave up the Deputy Ministership though I had not known it until after the elections were over and I had carried the seat. I told Pearson he delighted me beyond words in being prepared to make the venture; that I thought in regard to his future, he was wise. That it would be a good thing for Canada to have him in public life and if I was not mistaken, he would be at the head of affairs some day. I wished him all that was best."

Before going to the Cabinet meeting on September 8, the Prime Minister discussed the problem with St. Laurent and Howe. "Howe has arranged over long distance 'phone (pretty risky methods) to get assurance from leading Liberals and also some Conservatives that there will be no opposition to Pearson if he runs in that seat. Farquhar has agreed to resign. I agreed to appoint him to the Senate. Despite his years, I believe this to be justifiable to make certain of a seat for a Cabinet Minister, having regard to large numbers we have in the Senate.

"Have arranged to have all this done on Friday of this week. Strongly advised St. Laurent to lose no time in getting Garson in if he is coming. He said Garson wants to be sure of certain matters of policy. I feel very doubtful if Garson will give up his position as P.M. of province for that of Minister at Ottawa, though he would be a real acquisition to our Parliament. To help in this, I again agreed to appoint Glen to the Senate though he is in ill health and may not last long if vacancy thus created could be sufficient to induce Garson to come in at once.

"St. Laurent left me with the purpose I thought of arranging to have Garson here on Sunday but I doubt if there will be any chance of having him sworn in before I leave for Europe."

Norman Robertson was in Ottawa at this time and he and Pearson saw the Prime Minister at Kingsmere on September 9. Before leaving Robertson raised the question of remaining in Ottawa for a few days to discuss financial relations between the United Kingdom and Canada. Mackenzie King told Robertson "I really needed him in Paris. That I had given up taking P. with me. That I knew very little about procedure of these Conferences. I would not mind personally but as Prime Minister of Canada and as the oldest Prime Minister to be present in Paris, I felt I needed what guidance and protection I could get. I could see that Pearson was most anxious to have Robertson stay. He now is not likely to be in London to help at meetings there but will be campaigning I assume in Algoma. I told him on no account to risk any defeat by not staying on the ground and making as sure of his election as possible. Howe thinks it will be unanimous but there may be a C.C.F. as Coldwell is for fighting all by-elections."

Next day (September 10) Mackenzie King told his Cabinet colleagues that, as they "had all seen, by the press, mention of the possibility of Pearson's coming into the Cabinet, I was glad to be able to tell them he had consented to give up the present position and take his chances in an election. I thought they would agree we were fortunate. He would be a strength in the Government. The stronger the administration, the better for every member of it. Taking the chances he was at this time shows the kind of stuff he was made of. They all knew something of his record but did not know some of the things he had declined, among others Secretaryship of the U.N. and Presidency of the Rockefeller Foundation. I asked that this latter information should be kept secret. I spoke of his career in other ways. Then went on to say that some of the Members, on learning he might be coming in, had offered to vacate their seats. Then spoke of Farquhar and read his letter to the Council and the reply that I had sent to him. I then told them that the order was ready to be passed for his appointment at once; also order fixing the date of the elections. Then asked St. Laurent if he would not like to say something. I made it clear he and I had talked the matter over and were in complete agreement as to Pearson's coming in at once.

"St. Laurent said there might be some feeling on the part of some of the

Members in the House, that choice should have been made from them but agreed with all that I had said. He was greatly pleased that Pearson was coming in. I said that I thought being a Member of Parliament was a great distinction in itself. Would be a serious mistake if Cabinet Ministers had to be chosen from Members just because they were Members. Other things being equal, they should have preference. Agreed that some might be nasty, thinking they were more entitled; if they were, they only showed they were not the type that ought to be in the Government. I then put through several Orders. Immediately after, went to Pearson's room to tell him that the Orders had gone through."

The Prime Minister added: "When I went in, Pearson was sitting at his desk. I went over and extended congratulations to him on the Order having been passed for his appointment and saying that I was greatly pleased. I was sure he had taken the right step. Believed that some day he would be holding the office which I was holding at the present time. Pearson thanked me and said he would endeavour not to disappoint any hopes one cherished for him. Hoped he would not let any of us down (although this is not the exact expression used). He said at once he was so glad his appointment had come under my administration. I told him that was added pleasure to myself. We then had a word or two about the constituency. I advised him strongly to centre everything on that. I spoke to him about possible successor. Mentioned possibility of Norman coming back which he thought is what he wanted. Doubted the wisdom of bringing Wrong from Washington. Talked of one or two other arrangements that might be made for London which seemed to me fairly good. I then had him come along with St. Laurent and Arnold [Heeney] over to the Supreme Court where he was sworn in before Justice Kerwin. There I had the pleasure of renewing congratulations after he had taken the oath and Kerwin had signed it. Just before Kerwin extended congratulations to him, I congratulated St. Laurent. Said to him that I hoped Pearson would be the help to him that he had been to me. St. Laurent seemed to appreciate those words. They expressed my deepest wish.

"We then came back to the East Block. I had asked the press to meet us at 5 and then had a pleasant interview."

Early in September, John A. Costello, the Prime Minister of Ireland, visited Ottawa. Mackenzie King gave a dinner for him at the Country Club on September 7. He found the evening "one of the most difficult in some respects I have ever had to face. One difficulty filled with dynamite which might have occasioned an explosion which would have been far reaching indeed. If anything ever bore out the wisdom of checking to the last detail oneself, it was what was witnessed in the menu cards that were placed on the table.

"I had not seen the evening papers but apparently Costello had given a press interview in the afternoon in which he had said Ireland had severed its last link with the Crown [Costello had announced plans to repeal the External Relations Act of 1936, Ireland's last formal constitutional tie with the Commonwealth]. No longer are they prepared to regard themselves as being in the British Commonwealth of Nations. . . . That the link is the association of free nations having similar ideals, way of life. I had known that this question was coming up at the meeting of Prime Ministers but had not anticipated anything of the kind would be announced in Ottawa, and certainly not on the day of the Government giving the Prime Minister a dinner. I had Her Excellency to my left. . . . Immediately opposite was Mr. Costello and Mrs. Howe. I could see Her Excellency was quite excited about what she had read in the afternoon papers. It took me a moment or two to make out what it was she was feeling so strongly about. She had said how much she had enjoyed Costello's presence at dinner at Government House Saturday night. Thought all was going well but did not know what to make of this statement this afternoon. I then got her to tell me about it.

"What astonished me was that when I looked at the menu, I found that Measures had, without saying anything to me, inserted two Toasts: one to the King and the other to the President of Ireland. I had spoken to Measures about there being no Toasts included the night that the Mountbattens were here. He had evidently taken it into his head to have Toasts on this occasion. Had I been consulted, I would have given The King and the Prime Minister. Made no mention whatever of any president of Ireland. This was equivalent to regarding Ireland as an entirely separate country with a President as Head of State. A state as much independent of the British Crown as the U.S.A. There was nothing to do excepting to try and meet the situation as best [it] could be met without creating a difficulty. So I got into conversation with Costello. Asked him to tell me what he had said in the interview. I then told him we had at the table representatives who felt strongly this North of Ireland position and others. That I was anxious at this gathering, which was a social one, nothing should develop which might create a controversy which if it got into the press would be most unfortunate. He explained what he had given to the press. Regretted they always make heavy headlines. I then directed attention to the Toast. Said I was wondering what I should do. I hoped he would know – if I used the expression Eire instead of Ireland – Eire being the one we were accustomed to think of as representing what had been represented by the Irish Free State. Also that I should perhaps propose both Toasts or would he like to propose one. Costello at once said he did not wish to embarrass me in any way. If I wished him to do so, he would be pleased to propose the King. I thanked him warmly for this and said I would then propose the President of Eire. This got over what might have been an extremely embarrassing situation.

"I can only pray that these particular menus, though they will be kept by those who were present at the dinner, do not become the subject of controversy in Parliament. I would have to take the whole responsibility, though I had no knowledge of what was on the card. I had approved the front part but had never been consulted re the Toasts.

"Of course the Deputy Minister and Minister of External Affairs are the more responsible as Measures is the Protocol Officer, and should not have ventured to place anything on a card which was not in accordance with what was strictly written and approved. Nothing of course could have suited Costello's book better than the menu card as arranged. Equally nothing could be more full of explosives than just what that card might produce. This may well be related to the vision I had re danger of explosion. I said in speaking I had to keep in mind the whole situation as it has developed, and deal with it as skilfully as possible.

"When I came to speaking, I found speaking very easy. On the whole I may be mistaken, but it was one of the best speeches of my life. I spoke very much from the heart. Began by saying I had just been thinking this might be the last occasion on which I would be speaking as Prime Minister to my colleagues and other friends at a public gathering in Canada. In one way, it made me sad that such should be the case but that was really over-balanced by the sense of new freedom that I saw coming as a result of lessening of responsibilities."

The next day Mackenzie King wrote: "Thinking over what I had said last night, of what Costello had said of Ireland – relations to the British Commonwealth, I began to see very clearly that the great question of the future is whether Communism with its materialistic interpretation of history is, by means of material force, to destroy those countries whose civilizations are built upon the spiritual interpretation of life. I began to feel that my real mission might be that of having to do with keeping together the communities that today are part of the British Commonwealth. Once more to save the Commonwealth in spite of the Tories who will put all their emphasis on the Crown and symbols and be prepared to let the nations that will not give allegiance to the Crown cease to be members of the Commonwealth.

"My own feeling is that reality is more important than appearance.

That we must look beyond today and its problems to a larger menace and, at all costs, keep, if possible, the nations that have been – or are – associated with the Commonwealth, still in that circle of community of free peoples that may act as one in time of great emergencies. It is apparent to me that the Irish will not adhere to any doctrine of allegiance to the Crown. It is doubtful what India may do. South Africa too is becoming increasingly Republican in its point of view. The larger vision is one that must be kept to the fore."

On September 9, the Prime Minister had a luncheon for Costello "and High Commissioner Hearne, Norman Robertson and Pearson. . . . We had a very nice talk together at luncheon and after. Had a good hour and a half's talk with Costello who outlined fully the present Irish position toward the Commonwealth. It gave a chance to find out exactly what is proposed. He reviewed the whole case from the time of Cosgrave's government up until the present, the most significant part being what De Valera had done in getting free of the oath of allegiance in making provision for the election of the President by the people under proportional representation. He said to all this the British Government had not objected. At all events, had acquiesced. He spoke of the intention to abolish E.A. Act. Said if his Government did not do it, a private member would bring in a bill and it would carry. Costello said he thought he had the goodwill of all five parties in his Government. He believed by a certain amount of talk, he would be able to get them welded into one party. His aim was to end bitterness between parties in Ireland. He told us confidentially that he had talked with persons about Ireland's position in the matter of giving assistance at a time of war. He wanted to bring about a situation where Irishmen, wherever they were, would be prepared to fight to maintain a Christian civilization. Ireland would not, however, remain in the Commonwealth on basis of allegiance to the Crown. She would like to continue as a nation associated with the Community of Nations that were known as the British Commonwealth. He thought India, Pakistan, Ceylon, and possibly South Africa might be held by a kind of association but doubted if they could be held under any doctrine of allegiance to the Crown.

"I brought up this matter in Cabinet yesterday when we had finished discussing what was to be dealt with at the U.N. and pointed out that it might raise a more serious question than any that had come up thus far. I could see that St. Laurent, Martin and one or two others at first were pretty strong on the idea of no severance with allegiance part of the Crown but in discussion they began I think to see that taking the long distance view, it might perhaps be better for peace-loving nations of the world to hold together on some kind of basis that would not, for the present, be too clearly defined. I think here Lord Morley's maxim of events helping to determine evolutionary trends is a wise one.

"Costello made quite clear that his aim was to keep on friendliest terms with Britain and to further friendliest relations. Wanted to trade with Britain. He seemed to feel that the preference would be defended, whether they were under the Crown or not, having in mind the association there has been over the years, but said Britain had more to lose than the Irish by not giving them preference. He made it clear that he would like to keep the association as indicated but that, if the British insisted on a Crown condition they would be quite ready to be out of the Commonwealth altogether. It seemed to me that Costello was quite sincere in his whole argument and that his statement was logical enough.

"I put the matter in this way, that at the time of the Balfour declaration it set forth what was then established, the position of the nations of the Commonwealth; that it included the words 'allegiance to the Crown.' That, according to him, there had been so far as Ireland is concerned, no allegiance to the Crown; that allegiance to the Crown had been cut out deliberately by De Valera. That in the election of the President, without any reference to the King, no exception had been taken by the British in either case. That, in fact, allegiance to the Crown did not exist today. If the position were to be registered anew, it would have to be that of association with the Community of Nations, that recognized the Crown as the Head, naming specifically the four: Australia, New Zealand, Africa and Canada. Costello made it clear that he could not take any other position and that no other political party would for a moment support any continued link with the Crown. He said that the Crown to the Irish meant something quite different than it did to other countries. It stood for the role of the Castle in Dublin and the kind of treatment of the Irish that that signified in their minds.

"I asked him a deliberate question – if he was going to the meeting of Prime Ministers. He said that Attlee had asked him whether he was coming, without extending any formal invitation. He said at the same time Noel Baker was talking to one of his Ministers – had taken out his watch and said: At this moment, Attlee was inviting Costello to come to the meeting, but he says up to the present, he has no invitation. He has left the door open with his colleagues to go over when certain matters affecting Ireland may be discussed. He would not go to any Imperial Conference. That work, he thinks, is done for, forever. I made it clear that I was going on the understanding it was not an Imperial

Conference but meeting of Prime Ministers, more to afford them opportunity to talk together. Robertson put in – as we were talking together in this room about many matters we had in common. Not with the intention of making decisions to be formally reported to Governments or Parliaments. There was some talk about the status of High Commissioners. I avoided that pointing out they had no problem. From now on, they would be making their own appointments by the Government. The King would not appear in them. In our relationship, High Commissioners represented governments as contrasted with the King as representing the country in foreign relations.

"Costello drew out a memo from one of his Ministers to ascertain if Canada would make a basic treaty with Ireland with regard to trade and some other matters. My reply to this was I liked what he had said about Canada and Ireland being close together, as helping in a European situation but just as I thought Canada and America should be close together in helping similar situations. That I thought we would be as ready to consider making a treaty on trade matters, etc., with Ireland as we would with the United States. I asked Pearson what he thought. He said subject to the views of his Minister it might be well to explore the situation with a view to seeing whether matters could be carried the length that when it came to formally dealing with the matter, they would be sure of success. A point I brought out most strongly and which I feel is of real value is that with the world what it is today, there is a parallel between what happened prior to the war with Hitler. That, at that time, there were certain nations like Holland and Belgium who thought they could be neutral, where they could not and would be crushed. I said in the war with Communism, the same thing was true. Nations might think they would be neutral but that such a thing was impossible. That we had better all have our association so strong and clear that we would be a united power. Costello drew attention to a very remarkable fact, brought out in August number of the New Statesman – that the British Empire now has ceased to be mainly Christian. That with populations of India, Ceylon, etc., included, their populations would outnumber ours. The total of other of the nations of the Commonwealth. It is clear that some great questions and changes are ahead."

Before leaving for Europe, the Prime Minister's interest in his memoirs and in the disposition of his papers revived. For some time he had been considering the appointment of W. Kaye Lamb as Dominion Archivist. At the Cabinet meeting on September 8, "he brought forward recommendation to appoint Lamb of Victoria to the Archives in succession to Lanctot. No announcement to be made at present. He quite clearly is the best man in Canada for a post of the kind. Might never have been known to our Government but for the day that he came to make a presentation to me of the microfilms of Mackenzie's paper 'The Gazette' – 'Colonial Advocate', at which time I saw in an instant the exceptional qualities he possesses and his grasp of the whole situation. [Fred] Gibson has since gone into his record very carefully and taken up the matter with St. Laurent. They both agree no better appointment can be made." Mackenzie King "had a talk with Gibson of the Archives regarding the Memoirs" on September 13. "He is much pleased at Lamb's appointment and also said good progress is being made in the work of Memoirs. P. also said that Acland has made good headway with chronology from press cuttings. P. has been helpful in all of this. Indeed he has done his very best to help in every way."

Two days earlier the Prime Minister had discussed his future plans with Pickersgill, "giving him particularly the reasons why I felt I should not think at all of staying on in the Government. . . . He thinks I am right. I spoke about arrangements I had made for [Sir Robert] Borden to have [Loring] Christie and such stenographic assistance as he needed at the Archives for a year after I came into office. I told him I would expect the new Administration to see that I was supplied with necessary help until I got my papers well sorted and foundations laid for their distribution, etc."

Mackenzie King left Ottawa on Monday, September 13, and sailed from New York on the *Queen Mary* two days later, on what was to be his last visit abroad.

# CHAPTER NINE

# The End of an Era

GEORGES VANIER, Canada's Ambassador to France, met Mackenzie King when he landed at Cherbourg on September 20, 1948. They travelled together to Paris by train and the Prime Minister told Vanier of "the possibility of his going to London if Robertson came to Ottawa. He said he would be delighted beyond words at this. He feels he has been long enough in France. He says all France is in a very unsettled condition. We may see a very unfortunate and serious development here in the next few weeks. He rather believes a general election is inevitable and that de Gaulle will come in.

"As to the Berlin situation, like others, he hardly knows what to think though he says that the last war would be nothing as compared to a Russian invasion. That the whole of France would disappear. That the Russians are really barbarians. They would take all of the individuals who are of the elite, educated, carry them off to Russia and make them work in the mines, the rest of the population becoming slaves of Russian conquerors. He feels very deeply concerned."

The Third General Assembly of the United Nations convened in Paris against the background of a tense and potentially explosive situation in Berlin. In addition to the Prime Minister, Canada's delegation included Senator Wishart Robertson and Lionel Chevrier with two Parliamentary Assistants, Hugues Lapointe and Ralph Maybank, as alternate delegates. General McNaughton and General Vanier headed a strong group of officials which included Norman Robertson, Dana Wilgress and R. G. Riddell. Norman Robertson had dinner with Mackenzie King on September 20 and, like Vanier, expressed concern "about the possibility of war. Thinks it might come. Also thinks that France might collapse altogether very shortly. No one seems to be able to really keep the country together or to give a lead out of its present situation. Apparently he and others have been getting the organization of our delegation under way.

"Chevrier and Wishart Robertson came over to the Hotel to tell me of their meeting of this morning. I had made it clear to all that, except for speeches I have to make, I would find it very difficult to do much else. As a matter of fact, I am quite tired.

"In conversation with Robertson, I gathered that he would like and is quite prepared . . . [to go] back to Ottawa, and that at once rather than a year hence. He thinks Pearson and St. L. might like to have Désy or Dupuy come and be deputy [minister] until the elections. They do not either of them wish to come back to Ottawa. My own view is that if Robertson is to return to Ottawa, he should return at once and be of help to the government there. What is needed is someone to guide them on a variety of policies rather than only on E.A. [External Affairs]. He himself sees that necessity. I did not say anything to him of possible successor in London. I am glad to think that he is prepared to return at once if need be."

After lunch the next day, the Prime Minister, accompanied by Norman Robertson, Gordon Robertson and Jules Leger, went to the Palais de Chaillot for the first session of the Assembly. He "was surprised at the number of representatives of different countries I met in the hall and . . . had met at previous conferences and most of whom I had entertained at one time or another in Ottawa. The whole proceedings were very simple, ran very smoothly. Evatt was chosen President. Canada has, however, a representative on the Committee of Credentials – in the course of the afternoon, Wilgress was elected Chairman of one of the committees. He alone of all the committee leaders by acclamation. It seemed to me the addresses by the President of France, Auriol, and by the Foreign Minister of the Argentine, who presided, were largely platitudes. But many delegates had become almost professionals. On the other hand, there did appear to be something of real value in men of many nations coming to know each other personally and working co-operatively together."

During the next week, a good deal of Mackenzie King's time was absorbed by preparation of speeches for the Assembly and for his reception as a member of the Institut de France. Characteristically, he was unhappy about his farewell address to the Assembly on September 28. "When my turn came to speak," he wrote, "I found myself very short of breath and indeed wondered as to whether I would be able to get through. However, by keeping calm and going ahead, I managed all right. I was given considerable applause at one point and where I made reference to Canada's contribution to devastated countries in reply to Vishinsky and, in conclusion, was given a good reception. Applause continued until I took my seat. As soon as I sat down, I was amazed to learn I had missed one of the pages – page 13. Strangely enough tonight H. [Handy] brought in an envelope to me. Said it was No. 13 – the one that was missing. It contained two letters of no importance. It was a page relating to the atomic energy commission. I was sorry, particularly on McNaughton's account, that I had left out this page which really helped to complete what I had wished to say on that subject. Personally, I was very disappointed not being in good shape and doubly so as I felt, if I had declined the invitation to go to the dinner at the Vaniers or left it until the end of the week, I would have been in really good shape today. However, it is a relief to have the speech over. Personally, to my mind, it is far from being what it should have been, and what it might have been, had I really had time to prepare with care."

In his diary for October 1, the Prime Minister noted that he had wakened during the night with difficulty in breathing and feared a recurrence of influenza. This was to be a frequent entry in succeeding days and weeks. Despite his concern about his health, he attended the opera that evening, occupying the box of the President of the Republic. To him, the fact that he was so honoured made it a great occasion. The following day he reflected on the news from Canada. "All through today, I have been conscious of feelings of things happening in Canada which I cannot but regard as most unfortunate. I am quite sure that Drew will be elected as leader of the opposition. I cannot, however, [but] feel that his election will change the character of our Parlt. and equally of the country. I really feel sad at heart at what it would all mean, what instinctively I feel is coming.

"I am anxious, too, about Pearson taking no chances on his constituency. It gave me a special pleasure on coming in to find a message from Pearson saying he had been spending days in his constituency. Liked the people, etc. He was quite pleased with the address to the U.N. which, he said, had received a very fine press in Canada. His telegram mentions that he had been asked to accept honorary chairmanship of the University of Toronto Mackenzie King Scholarship Committee and wished my approval in advance. This made a pleasant close to the week as well as the day."

Mackenzie King received word on October 3 that George Drew had been chosen as leader of the Progressive Conservative party the day before. "Two thoughts have come to my mind: first, one for Canada. I cannot overcome a feeling of sadness of what I fear as a consequence of Drew becoming leader of the Conservative party. He will revive all the old Tory spirit in its hatefulness and bitterness, something I have been able to prevent in my years of office. He will be worse than either Meighen or Bennett. He will centre above all else on a centralized Empire which will make St. Laurent's position very difficult. He may try to carry along in a friendly way with Duplessis until the elections are over, but I doubt if he will be able to conceal his real feelings and motives that long. There will be raised anew the old prejudices of race and religion. If the international situation develops along more dangerous lines, it will be hard to say if something approaching civil strife may not develop in Canada. He will have behind him the powerful Tory machine. Will not spare efforts or money in seeking to gain power.

"The other thought in my mind is again how a kind Providence has been inspiring my thoughts and guiding my way in my resolve to get out of the leadership of the party and of the government at the time I have. Drew's appointment adds one more to the list of the leaders of the Opposition I have had in the course of my day. I thanked God, however, that I will not be one who will be obliged to follow him in the speech on the address at another session. My parliamentary career is drawing to its close just at the right moment. I have a record which for length of service and in service in other ways . . . will secure my name in the history of the nation for all time. That place will not be marred by the kind of conflict that I would have to face if, at my age, I were to return to the H. of C. with a man like Drew. If ever I showed wisdom, vision and judgment in my political life, it was in selecting the time I did to announce my intention to retire and the time fixed for retirement itself. All of which had taken place before it was known that Bracken was dropping out, before it was even known that Drew would be a candidate. With my health what it is, I could not have gone on."

Later that day, the Prime Minister dictated a telegram to Pearson "strongly urging his concentration on the constituency. Also one to St. Laurent letting him know he was in my thoughts in the light of the new responsibilities that would be his with Drew in opposition; also stressing the importance of Pearson staying with his constituency until after the by-election. I learned from Robertson that Pearson had talked with him over the long distance 'phone and had very much in mind that he should come over here at once, notwithstanding the by-election and that St. Laurent was of the same opinion. The trouble is going to be that St. L. will be inclined, with his good nature, to echo anything that Pearson might suggest or that others will urge upon him.

"It was fortunate I had talked with Robertson before saying I thought this very thing would happen. He was able to tell Pearson not to consider coming until after the campaign."

Before leaving for London on October 5, the Prime Minister had "a most secret and important" talk with Ernest Bevin at the British Embassy in Paris. "Bevin opened the conversation by saying that he wanted to let me know the full particulars of the situation but had waited until it was rounded out and he could give me a complete picture. He said he felt much better and happier today than he did when we talked together in London. He had felt pretty discouraged at that time. Now felt in a quite different mood. He would give me the whole picture of the Berlin situation. He reviewed much that appears in communications I have received from Attlee. Said there were times when the situation was getting dangerous. That he thought the Americans had not understood the real position. That Clay, the [American] General there, was much too arrogant. . . . He himself had had to speak about the extreme utterances that Clay was making. That he had been brought back to Washington and told he must not interfere with political side of matters. That things had quietened down a bit since then, that we were particularly fortunate in Robertson, our General. He then went on to say that Marshall himself had not grasped the situation at first. Once he did, things improved materially. That in England they had had, with their little strength, to do the best they could in feeding the population until the Americans became more apprised of what was required. They had then begun to send additional planes. . . . That now, since they had all met in Paris, they had been taking stock as to what they could be sure of in the way of equipment, etc., to meet the military requirements of the Benelux countries. Apart from this, he thought that from now on the U.S. would be prepared to take on about 80 per cent of what was needed to take food into Berlin. After a conference with Schuman and officials, etc., they were now confident they could keep on the supply of food for the Berlin population for an entire year. More than that, they would be able to give the people some coal for their homes.

"There was not much employment in Berlin. The standard of living would be lower, but not too bad. They had figures on what would have been needed in the worst winter possible. That was the case two years ago and they had made their estimates on that basis.

"He then said that America was ready to help to equip the Benelux countries' Navy, Army and Air. That they [the Americans] thought they would be able to raise altogether some 30 divisions in Europe, which was quite a force. He described what the morning papers set forth of the arrangements as to Montgomery taking charge and the French having to do with the Army and Navy. The apparent upset that was reported in the press was due to the fact that [General] Juin, who is in Morocco doing good work there, did not wish to be transferred. Therefore, another French General would have to take his place. He said Montgomery was too much of a prima donna and talked too much. He was intending to tell him he must tone down a bit. He wished the British had Alexander instead of Montgomery, that Churchill had let us [Canada] have Alexander first. He thought Alexander would have made a much better Chief of Staff. I said to Bevin at one stage that, if Alexander were really needed in the European situation, so far as our Government was concerned and we could feel that the situation demanded it, we should not stand in the way of his being replaced by some other Governor-General, though I could not say what his own feelings and wishes in the matter would be.

"He then said he thought the Russians had come to view the situation quite differently of late. That up to a very short time ago they were going on the assumption that no administration in the United States would permit . . . the use of the atomic weapons. They had come to believe that, if a war came, the American people would allow the Government not only to use atomic weapons but any weapons that would help to ensure a Russian defeat and they would have to face a long period of war. He thought the Russians could gain a quick victory in Europe as things now stand, but would not be prepared for a long war. With [John Foster] Dulles' talks with Dewey, Marshall's with Truman, the head groups of the two parties had a perfect understanding between them and were in agreement on attitude toward Russia.

"He said what was most important was that the U.S. would now take all the money that had been appropriated this year by Congress and have it used immediately to help to build up the situation in Western Europe. As soon as Congress made further allocations, they would get further appropriations of still larger sums to go on throughout the year. Marshall put it in a word, that the equal of one day's expenditure on war was not too much to pay for the prevention of war. It was better to pay out these large amounts at once and save the day before it was too late.

"Bevin asked me if I had looked over the report of the defence suggestions of the British Government. I said I had. I thought the document was a moderate one. I approved of it generally, though I would point out it went on the assumption of a Commonwealth policy. I thought it would be wiser not to speak of it in these terms. That each nation had a right to have its own foreign policy as well as policies on domestic affairs. That we should seek to harmonize these various policies. I told him how we had succeeded in getting Canada into the war quietly. I found Bevin most receptive to that point of view. He said the military were hard to convince, that they were rigid in their lines. He had to send back the plans they had proposed to have [them] revised. They looked only to the strategy and not to the political [considerations]. When I spoke to him about Berlin and the risks there might be through an incident, he admitted quite frankly that it was still a possibility. He said he had still to admit that the risk would always be present. They would be most cautious in everything.

"Bevin then spoke of the situation in India, but I had to leave to keep an engagement at the Foreign Office. I said to Bevin that I really was not familiar with the Indian situation, as I should be. . . .

"He referred again to how different he felt today from when I saw him last year. Indeed, he looks much better. Says he is feeling much better. I could not but greatly admire his quiet way of speaking and of developing several points as he went along. It is fortunate for Britain at this stage that she has a man of his experience, ability in affairs, etc."

After this talk with the British Foreign Secretary, Mackenzie King attended a luncheon at the Quai d'Orsay given by the French Foreign Minister, Robert Schuman. When the French Prime Minister arrived, Mackenzie King was quite embarrassed when he saw that both he and Schuman were "in morning clothes, black sack coat and striped trousers. I had on a double-breasted blue [suit]. I had asked Vanier if I should not change. Felt I should until he persuaded me not to. This is one real mistake I shall always regret.

"It was apparent that both Schuman and the P.M. were seeking to pay every possible tribute to Canada in what had been arranged. I mentioned to Schuman what Marshall had said to me about finding it such a comfort to talk with him and the confidence he had in him, Schuman. Schuman said Mr. Marshall had said the same thing to him. I mentioned that this was said before anything else when Marshall spoke to me.

"The P.M., Queille, came in. As we proceeded into the dining room, the Foreign Minister and the P.M. made me precede them. A small fire was burning in the grate. Mr. Schuman, passing toward the fire, asked me to sit to his right. Vanier sat opposite myself to the P.M.'s right. Mr. Schuman mentioned that this was the first fire they had had in the Foreign Office this year. He spoke of the little gathering being more intimate and permitting more in the way of conversation – a closer contact than if he had given a large dinner.

"The conversation at the luncheon table turned in particular upon strikes. I told them the story of our Industrial Disputes Act. Also the settlement of the Railwaymen's strike. It was interesting to note from what others said of the parallels of the French situation. The great difficulty is the inflation. Prices and wages, of course, are the problem, but, as the latter go up, up go prices, etc.

"I thought both Schuman and the Prime Minister seemed remarkably calm, neither seemed to have immediate fears, but Schuman did say two or three times to me that their security lay in the U.S. and the atomic bomb, that but for that he felt the Russians might precipitate war. That is a momentous truth. It is interesting for me to recall that I had to be one of the three, Attlee and Truman the other two, to decide that the secret of the atomic bomb should not be disclosed until some system of control based on confidence was established.

"The luncheon was a particularly delicious one, trout and partridge, as well as a special type of ice cream being on the menu, with wines, etc. At the end of the luncheon, Mr. Schuman, without rising, lifted his glass and said that he had wished to express his feelings of personal affection and regard for myself, equally feelings of affection and regard of France, to thank me for all that Canada had done for France during the war, and for the present relationships.

"In reply, I thanked him for the honour of inviting me to luncheon and especially the honour of the P.M. coming to be present. Said I thought the people of Canada would be greatly touched when they learned tomorrow that this honour had been paid to myself as Canada's representative. There was a little more said along the same lines. We then adjourned to the room in which we had met at the outset. Before taking our seats for coffee, Mr. Schuman stopped along with the P.M. and Vanier and myself, and said in French that the Government of France would like very much to confer upon me the highest class of the Order of the Legion of Honour as a tribute both personally for my part in public affairs and as a tribute to Canada. That he hoped I could see my way to accept. They knew I had not accepted honours generally, but that I had accepted the O.M. They would be prepared, I thought he said, to have the King agree in the first instance to my accepting the honour, which he said he very much hoped I would accept while I was still in office.

"I replied in English that I was much touched by the honour and the thought that it should have been proposed by himself in the presence of the P.M., and realized how great an honour it was. I hoped he would not misunderstand my appreciation of it, of what had been suggested, if I mentioned that, throughout my life, I had rather taken a stand against acceptance of decorations and titles, etc. That I wanted it to be clear to the people that I had entered public life and was giving what service I could because of the love of service in itself and not for the sake of recognition or decoration. That I had declined similar honours in the past from other countries, and I might have added from the French Government itself. That I felt it might be misunderstood now that I was in Paris to accept this honour. That, as long as I was in the office of the Prime Minister, I preferred to hold to the position I had taken. I added it took me three days to make up my mind to accept the O.M. and I accepted that honour only because it was so personal from the King himself and because I was the only one of his Prime Ministers in the Commonwealth who had been Prime Minister from the very beginning of his reign. . . . I then thanked the Prime Minister and himself again, and mentioned that I hoped they would allow me to forego the acceptance, at least for the present. Mr. Schuman translated himself what I had said to the P.M. Vanier also added a word or two. I asked him to note particularly the reference to 'at present' in case I should be in Paris some time in the future when I am no longer a Minister of the Crown. Mr. Schuman replied they had noticed the words 'at present' and hoped that would still leave the way open.

"As we had coffee, Mr. Schuman went to another part of the room and came back with a beautiful, large, exquisitely printed volume, a reproduction of Virgil. Referred to the special type, etc., and expressed the hope that I would accept this as a souvenir of the occasion. I asked if he would not inscribe the volume. This he did, both himself personally and the P.M. The inscription read as follows:

> Presented to Mr. Mackenzie King, Prime Minister of Canada, a great friend of France, in testimony of our affectionate gratitude. Paris, October 5, 1948.

> H. QUEILLE,                           Robert SCHUMAN,
>   *Prime Minister*                    *Minister of Foreign Affairs*

"In thanking Mr. Schuman for this gift, I told him that I would treasure it at Laurier House as long as I lived. I would see that it was left there as a national possession to Canada. In presenting it to me, he spoke very affectionately. In fact, I do not recall anyone ever having spoken in a more tender way than he did toward myself. I reciprocated warmly his affectionate greetings and said I would reciprocate them according to the French method. I then kissed them on each cheek. It was really a most touching moment in my life. I said to him that the occasion had been a great reward of my years of public service and was a crowning honour."

Leaving the Foreign Office, Vanier accompanied the Prime Minister to the Institut de France. "There was an air of great distinction in the entire building," Mackenzie King wrote. "We were shown the libraries. I have seen nothing comparable to them in my life at any of the universities. They stand as they stood two or three hundred years ago. The librarian had placed on the table books relating to Canada, one going back prior to the founding of Quebec. Vanier was surprised, as I was, that such a book was in existence. It is interesting to see how early French explorers had been able to visualize the location of the Great Lakes, etc. Interesting, too, to see a description of areas of New France. The entire building was most fascinating. One felt one's self in an atmosphere, the highest, the rarest in some ways, that a country could possess. One of the interesting studies was one of Voltaire as he appeared quite naked. It would have been prepared by sculptors who knew Voltaire himself. The emaciated look of the man was an interesting study. One of the most interesting rooms was a small circular room copied from one in Rome where certain meetings were held. One felt the inspiration of such an environment. Again, I felt that here was a further crowning honour, the highest gift that France could make to any individual or any representative of any country – to be a member of the Institute – higher than even that of possessing the Legion of Honour. Here again was pointed out to us the beauty of the scene, etc."

In London on October 6, Mackenzie King had tea with Attlee at Downing Street. "Everyone round the door, police and others, seemed most friendly. To my great surprise and delight, as I went in the corridor, I met Lord Addison, looking very cheerful and happy but a little bit older. We had a very happy exchange of greetings, after which I went to Attlee's apartment on the top floor. Attlee was sitting in a chair with his two feet on a rest wearing carpet slippers. Mrs. Attlee was seated behind a tea tray. Both got up when I came in and spoke very warmly. Attlee resumed his reclining position. I spoke at once of feeling so deeply for them in the difficult times they had had through ill-health. Mrs. Attlee referred to her own illness for some little time as well as Attlee's. He did not seek to make light of his trouble, but said he thought that it was improving. To tell the truth, I was quite shocked at his appearance. It looked to me as though he was a sick man. Very doubtful if he will recover his strength while remaining in office.

"I referred at once to his kindness in sending me the engraving of Walpole and the letters sent at that time. He seemed quite pleased at what I said but was most modest in his reference. I also told him that I hoped they both appreciated how I felt for them. It was clear they did have a feeling of true friendship. I then spoke of the different members of the family. Michael has had a birthday recently and is now again on a trip. Felicity is assisting at a school. There are two other girls, one, or both, married."

Discussion then turned to the agenda for the meeting of Prime Ministers, particularly relations between Ireland and the Commonwealth. "The first subject brought up was the position of Ireland and Costello's speech at Ottawa," the Prime Minister wrote. "As Attlee said, his own Government had had no knowledge he was going to make it. I told him of the whole occurrence of the night of the dinner, and also of the talks we sub-sequently had. Attlee spoke in a friendly way of Costello himself as a man. Also, how delighted he was with the Irish during his visit to Ireland and spoke of being greatly concerned as to what should be done when they claimed they were no longer part of the Commonwealth, of the way of keeping them in the Commonwealth. He was quite open-minded whether to have them come at the latter part of the proceedings or not. Did not wish to embarrass the situation. He spoke of the grievance that they kept referring to in the past, also the same being true of America.

"Referring to myself, he said 'You have taken a quite different line.' I then spoke about India. He said he was sure Nehru wished to stay in the Commonwealth. I said if I could be helpful in any talks with him just to let me know.

"I went on to speak of really not knowing much about the problems which were coming up. Asked about the opening proceedings. He said he did not think they would wish speeches. He thought the danger was that some things might be said at the start which it would be difficult to over-come later. All he was planning to say at the beginning was to extend a word of welcome. We would then have a television picture taken, he thought in the grounds. Mrs. Attlee thought it would be better on the ver-andah. We would then have a little meeting to discuss procedure. I men-tioned the King's invitation for 1.15 P.M. He said he would see that there would be no difficulty there. Would make sure I would get away in plenty of time.

"I spoke of the defence report. Mentioned about the talk on Common-wealth policy. He said he understood completely that there would be no effort at a common policy, would make that clear. Re the harmonizing policy, etc. I said I agreed as to the general plan in commitments. I spoke about the situation in Europe. He agreed that the thing seemed to be im-proving. That there was no cause to fear for immediate war, but that the Berlin situation was dangerous.

"I must have remained for about 40 minutes. Attlee was given some of his medicine by his wife. While she was away, he told me that trouble had developed between his toes. He thought it was some infection during the war. He had gone to Ireland, being told that being near the sea would be helpful. Unfortunately, it increased the rash and extended also to his hands as well. That part he had been freed of. The other was subsiding. He then pointed to the side of the stomach and said there was some internal trouble there, but he did not think it was serious.

"During the evening, to my surprise, in reading the press I read an article on his intended retirement and of the contest already taking place for his successor. I shall not be surprised if he remained throughout this conference and his retirement were to come before the end of the year."

The King's private secretary, Sir Alan Lascelles, called on the Prime Minister on October 8 "to speak about the dinner at the Palace on Monday. He said the King was particularly concerned about the relations with Ireland. I felt he was pressing me strongly to take the position that Ireland could not hope to stay in the Commonwealth unless she were to repeal the External Affairs Act. He doubted if the Irish realized what the consequences would be. It would mean that every Irishman in England who went to Ireland would be a foreigner. That Ireland would become a foreign country. Also he doubted if they understood the implications of the Statute of Westminster. I told him a little of Costello's visit, but stressed my hope that some way would be found not to have the Irish drop out of the Commonwealth. I said we had to look ahead to our particular friends in the future. That I thought, if we had difficulties with Russia, it would be over Communism. It would be well to have the Irish fighting unitedly with us."

Mackenzie King's health had not improved. He saw Lord Moran, Churchill's physician, on October 7 and 8 and was advised that there was evidence of considerable heart strain. During Moran's second visit on October 8, "he brought up the question of nurses. I protested against that as unnecessary and very costly. He said, however, that it would be a great advantage to him to have someone who could check up on matters related to the effect of the pills he was giving me – they are digitalis, I think – and also on the sleeping, etc. He thought that if I had them for a couple of days it would, perhaps, in the end, let him proceed with more certainty and benefit. This I agreed to finally, and the nurses are to come tomorrow night. He had, however, arranged to have a nurse come tonight to give me an injection of morphine, which he hoped might cause me to sleep. He seemed to feel that the continuous loss of sleep was something that had to be overcome as quickly as possible.

"We talked a little of what announcement could be given out. He thought it would be best to discuss that further in the morning. He asked me on the way if he could speak to [Norman] Robertson wholly confidentially. I gave him that right. He said he would see Lascelles and would have matters explained to the King, and would also see Rowan, who would explain matters to Attlee. He evidently did not wish to speak to Attlee himself. He apparently thought this would be quite enough. Lord Moran was attending a dinner in the Dorchester in an adjoining room.

"Robertson was also having a dinner for the Masseys [who were visiting the United Kingdom]. . . . He himself came up at my request for just a word. I had to tell him in a few sentences that it meant not attending any meetings of Prime Ministers. I could see at once that this was a heavy blow to him. His thoughts were of who should come over. He rather favoured Pearson, but I told him I rather thought St. Laurent would be preferable as it was a meeting of Prime Ministers, and secondly, as I had indicated in a statement to the press that he would come if necessary when the conference was on. I was surprised to learn that both were in Algoma.

"Moran, he and I began to discuss statement for the press, etc. But I decided it would be best to leave matters until tomorrow. . . . He had brought a nurse, who gave me an injection of morphine. He then left that I might have a good night's sleep."

His inability to attend the meetings of the Prime Ministers greatly concerned Mackenzie King. He told Moran he had come to London because of "my years of experience to deal with these serious questions of Ireland, India, etc., in the Commonwealth, and felt it would be a great disappointment to Attlee and others if I were not there. I said I might give an example of the kind of advice that I could give. That sitting quietly there waiting for them I had been thinking over the talk with the King [scheduled] on Monday. That everyone was emphasizing keeping Ireland out unless she would agree to recognizing the King as the head, and thinking of what this would mean to the Irish and to other people purely in relation to the relation of Ireland to the Commonwealth, etc. I said in my own mind that a far greater question would be raised, and that was one which would affect monarchy itself. That I would have to tell the King I felt it would be raising a terrible issue if it was once said that, because of the unwillingness of India to accept the King as head, they could not take a place in the community of nations. I said that I would raise the whole question of the Commonwealth being based on sovereignty.

"Lascelles had rather indicated that this was the case, as set forth in the Statute of Westminster. I told Lascelles I thought we should try to work out something that would relate to the community of nations having certain ideals, etc. I can see that I am right in this. Strangely enough, I said to myself, is it left to me again to try to save the Empire in spite of itself? How strange it is I should be at this stage trying to save monarchy, having relation again to monarchy's attitude toward my grandfather in 1837, when we were struggling for the liberties of the people."

On October 9 the Prime Minister decided definitely that St. Laurent should come to London as soon as possible to take his place. He dictated a memorandum "to send to Pickersgill to transmit through him to St. Laurent and Pearson. Robertson later got in touch with Pearson over the long distance 'phone. He had already received my wire. This will probably mean that St. Laurent will be here early next week. I am sorry to bring him on in this way, but perhaps it will meet the situation in Canada as well as here in the best possible way." St. Laurent and Pearson were campaigning in Algoma East that weekend but on Sunday, October 10, Norman Robertson received word that St. Laurent would arrive on Thursday, October 14, accompanied by Pickersgill.

Despite his illness, Mackenzie King continued to receive visitors in his suite at the Dorchester. On October 12 he discussed the problem of Ireland and India with Lord Addison, the Lord Privy Seal. Addison told him that "the last memorandum he had read before leaving the office was the opinion of Lord Chancellor Jowitt that we must not be too legalistic in dealing with Ireland. He spoke of Attlee's feeling that they could not belong to a club and not pay their fees. I told him I thought the great issue would soon be Commonwealth versus the Crown and, if great care were not taken, if Ireland were crowded out because of not subscribing to the Crown relationship, it might raise a very serious issue, not against Ireland, but against the Crown itself. It was on the words 'Community of Nations' and what was common to the community, rather than the symbolism of the Crown, that the Commonwealth should be held together. . . .

"Lord Addison seemed really impressed. Asked me if I had talked with the Prime Minister about it. I told him I had sent word by Norman Robertson. He said Evatt seemed to share views akin to my own. He was seeing him and others tonight. He had not thought about the Crown becoming the issue rather than the Commonwealth by an action that would assert the Crown relationship as a sine qua non. I pointed out how my plan had left the door open for other parts to become republican or not, as they pleased."

The following day Prime Minister Nehru called on Mackenzie King. He "enjoyed Nehru's visit very much. He reminded me a little of Sir Wilfrid Laurier in his fine, sensitive way of speaking, using his hands, etc. He gave me his views about India. Thought it was best to have the Constitution passed without raising any question of relations within the Empire. Once the Constitution was established, they could then, he thought, work out the relationship of India to the rest of the Commonwealth on the basis of the Citizenship Act. Lord Jowitt had been talking with him along that line, maintaining an independent citizenship in each country, Canada, etc., but acknowledging a Commonwealth citizenship which brought with it certain obligations of co-operation, etc. I gave him my views on the emphasis being placed on Community of Free Nations, rather than having emphasis upon the Crown which would almost certainly be drawn into controversy if it were made the main issue. He saw the point at once and said he regarded it as quite important. I also outlined to him what I had thought of as regards member nations of the Commonwealth qualifying under the Statute of Westminster, etc. This, he also said, was worth carefully looking into.

"He spoke of the terrible situation they had had in India this year. He explained the situation in Pakistan as an effort on the part of those in authority to restore an old theocratic form of government. That Jinnah, while he did not believe in religion, or care much about morals, had used religion as a weapon, with the result that the people had become fanatical and serious crimes had taken place through an effort on the part of some to claim that the day was passed for an old order which would prohibit women from taking part in public affairs instead of being kept aloof and veiled. He said that that was not an original custom. . . . He thought there would be troublesome times in Pakistan. He promised to send me a copy of his life. He spoke very highly of his sister's references to myself. He spoke very highly of the Mountbattens. He said he had seen Kearney [Canada's High Commissioner in New Delhi] occasionally. Did not say much about his work.

"He thought some advantage might be gained by having the Foreign Office send their despatches direct to the High Commissioners for sending on to Governments, instead of the Commonwealth Relations Office, as a matter of saving time. I emphasized the importance of pretty direct communications and care being taken to have them considered in the atmosphere of one's own country rather than in London. I think care has to be taken not to give too much authority to High Commissioners, but to retain the agency character of their work.

"The talk I had with Nehru made a most favourable impression on me, having regard to his own imprisonment, etc. I gave him a little account of my grandfather's life and the times in Canada in 1837/38, and later."

Just after lunch on October 14, St. Laurent and Pickersgill arrived at the Dorchester, "having left Ottawa yesterday and having crossed in a few minutes over twelve hours. The plane had been diverted. They stopped at an airport near London. I thought St. Laurent was looking very well. I was delighted to have a good talk with him. He reviewed happenings in the Cabinet and recent meetings in Manitoulin [Algoma East]. Seemed sure of Pearson's election. I gave him particulars of my own condition. Begged him to stay in bed until tomorrow, which he is wisely doing.

"Had a talk of equal length with Pickersgill. Gave me particulars of Ottawa happenings. . . ."

That afternoon Attlee called to tell the Prime Minister "about a meeting they intended to have with the Irish at Chequers on Sunday, along with some representatives of the other Commonwealth countries, to see if they couldn't work out some solution. The main difficulty, he says, is that after having taken Holy Orders they have renounced them. The difficulty was to see how they could get them back.

"About India, he mentioned that they were now working on the question of Commonwealth citizenship. On the High Commissioners' business, I said I thought the British Government precedence list should be revised and give all Government members precedence and then follow with foreign countries and High Commissioners. He indicated that the British plan was to interweave the latter, giving them, as it were, equal status. The real point is, I think, as mentioned by Pickersgill, that the arguments of Lord Curzon that they represented the King, or the Head of the State, and were the guests of the country they visited, were out of date. That, in reality, all had come to represent the governments of other countries, and foreign ambassadors were not in different relationships [with the British government] than High Commissioners. However, something will be worked out on that line during the conference.

"Attlee himself looked remarkably well considering he had had a busy day yesterday and was at the Palace until late last night. As he talked, he kept working away on the top of his head with the fingers, which has become a habit of his over the years. I told him of how distressed I was at his condition. I was glad to note how much better he was looking. I felt a little ashamed at not having written a personal letter to him before he came to call. I should have answered his personal letter to me at once. Apparently, he had the same nurse, Miss Downer, at St. Mary's, as I have here. He thought I was right in following Moran's advice.

"When Lord Moran came in tonight he said Mr. St. Laurent was wishing to see him. He asked me if he might talk freely to him. I said to tell everything.

"After Attlee left, Sir Girja Bajpai [India's High Commissioner in London] called. I had an exceptionally interesting talk with him of about an hour, during which time he reviewed matters in India. He told me of his close friendship with Nehru. He spoke of Nehru being wholly free from bitterness despite his years of imprisonment, of his desire to keep the British connection. . . . He spoke nicely of Kearney. He is anxious that the High Commissioners' position should be improved in London. That they should deal direct with the Foreign Office itself as the Foreign Office does with foreign ministers. The Foreign Office should keep the High Commissioners informed. I told him there was a danger of High Commissioners becoming a sort of government unto themselves and also developing a secretariat here but he is anxious, apparently, to get some closer means of consultation. He spoke of Nehru visiting Paris tomorrow to see Marshall. He thinks the Americans are not interested in India. Did not realize how important that side of the world is. Nehru has the impression that the Americans have world conquest ideas in mind. He would like to see a strong Europe built up as a sort of mediator between the States on one side and Russia on the other, not allow either colossal power to control the situation. He told me in great confidence that Nehru would give an assurance to Marshall that, if matters ever came to a war, he thought that India would be with Britain and the U.S., but they were strongly opposed to talking about trying to build up strength in case of another war. . . ."

On October 15 the Prime Minister spent a few hours with his old friend, Violet Markham. They "talked a good deal about the present world conditions. She is deeply concerned about France and, of course, rightly concerned about Russia, though not fearful of immediate war, but feeling how unjust it is that Britain should have to suffer in this way after her part in two wars for freedom. She is not keen about having India or Pakistan become part of the Commonwealth. Thinks their problems are so vast and different from our own, that their remaining in may be too much of a burden in the end. My own feeling is that members of the Commonwealth shall need all the friends they can have in what before long may be a test as to who is to rule the world. Great care will have to be taken not to repel either the Indians or the Irish.

"Violet told me of other chapters of her book which I asked her to let me read. She also offered to let me have a large room at Wittersham to come and stay there for a week, to bring staff with me. I mentioned that I would speak to Lord Moran of this but thought it might be impossible.

"In the course of the conversation, she said that, among other things, she was at present disposing of her wealth. That she thought it well to do this both for selfish as well as personal reasons. As a matter of fact, getting rid of some of it would net her less in taxation and prove a gain in the end. She said that, through her broker and counsel, she was really better off than before the war.

"She then told me that she had left a sum for me in her will. Also a like sum for Lady Tweedsmuir and other friends. Mentioned what she was doing for relatives, etc. She said that she would like, however, to give me the amount rather than have it left until later on. It might be helpful at this moment in tiding over a situation. I told her I was much touched by her thought of leaving anything to me. Her reply to this was: you are my oldest friend. She then said that, if given at once, it might help to tide over a difficult time. What she was concerned about was how to make the gift without violating some law prohibiting money from leaving England. She suggested I talk the matter over with Robertson and see how it might be arranged. She was extraordinarily nice in the way she referred to the matter as one which could mean nothing to her financially but which gave her very great personal pleasure to do.

"I told her that I had no fears about the future. She said, however, one never knows how long another may live, or how short a time. 'I think this is the time to arrange these things,' she said.

"When we spoke of the Masseys, she seemed to think that Vincent's chief grievance was not having been given anything to do. Not having had recognition for the work he had done over here. She said being Chancellor of [a] University meant nothing. I told her about having appointed him to the Art Gallery. I said younger members felt that the diplomatic positions etc. belonged rather to them. I might have added he has done nothing to help win the friendship and good-will of the party.

"She spoke of their kindness to her throughout the period of the war. She is deeply concerned about who may succeed Attlee. Thinks he is the best of the govt. group."

After Violet Markham left, the Prime Minister had a long talk with St. Laurent and Pickersgill. "We talked about the position vis à vis Ireland and India – some talk of the situation at home, etc.

"Lord Moran gave St. L. the whole confidential statement last night of my condition.

"This morning, when I asked Lord Moran about it, he told me that the influenza, shortness of breath, etc. were aggravating causes; had just served to bring some condition to the surface and aggravate it. That the real nature of the trouble was cumulative. That there had been impairment of the heart through strain over the years. Each had been getting worse, particularly through pressure. He says I will have to learn to live within definite limitations.

"I was glad to have had the talk with St. L. as I gathered in our conversation he might be more extreme about having Ireland and India kept out unless they subscribed to the allegiance to the Crown. He seemed to feel that there must be something that would make the Commonwealth a unit. That it would become little more than a cluster of countries if the Crown were not made the symbol of it all. I stressed my point of the symbol being secondary to the substance. That, in reality, there was no such thing as a Commonwealth – as an entity – with policies of its own. The whole plan here was to bring that to pass. In reality, there was a community of free nations held together by kindred ideas, etc. . . . The Crown was merely an outward symbol. I agreed, however, that we, in

Canada, should leave it to the others to work out their relations, to take the position we were quite satisfied with [the] relations which existed between ourselves and Britain and between ourselves and other parts of the British Commonwealth. If Britain wished to make other relations, etc., we could consider their effects later on. Above everything, I advised against any attempt at finality. I strongly advised Pickersgill to get the article from 'The Times' of a few days ago, setting forth the exact nature of the present meetings of Prime Ministers."

The Prime Minister had two more long talks with St. Laurent on October 16. On Sunday evening, October 17, St. Laurent called on Mackenzie King to report on the discussions that afternoon at Chequers with two representatives of the Irish government. "They had had an interesting talk over the relations of Ireland to the Commonwealth," he wrote. "The fact that Ireland herself has definitely declared she is out of the Commonwealth makes it difficult to find ways for her continuance in the Commonwealth. St. Laurent himself had put forward the interesting suggestion that Ireland, notwithstanding the repeal of the Foreign Relations Act [*sic*], wished to remain associated with the nations of the Commonwealth. This might permit of her people not being regarded as foreigners, and of relations respecting citizenship, etc., continuing as they are. He had spoken of this to me before. I think it is quite an ingenious idea, and one which the Irish may be prepared to consider. He said he had made it quite plain that in Canada we were as anxious as the Irish or any of the others to have it known that we were the complete masters of our own house. He mentioned that many were quite prepared to have the Royal Standard on our own flag to make it clear that we were under a monarchy, that ours was a monarchical form of government, whereas the Union Jack was regarded as the flag of the United Kingdom, its presence signifying to many something of the colonial relationship.

"St. Laurent seemed to feel that it would prove an advantage later on to have Attlee, Jowitt, Noel-Baker and others realize what the attitude toward the United Kingdom and other parts of the Commonwealth would be."

Turning to the political situation in Canada, the Prime Minister reported that St. Laurent was "most hopeful about the winning of Algoma East, and of Rosthern. Feels if we do, writs should be issued at once for by-elections in Laval-Two Mountains [the sitting Independent member, Liguori Lacombe, had resigned on July 15, 1948] and in Marquette, Manitoba where Glen will resign later. After he has taken office [as Minister of Justice], Garson will be chosen as a candidate. He told me that, instead of having to persuade Garson, . . . [he] seemed quite keen to come in. He went on to say that, evidently, they all recognized that he himself would not be long in office and that, if Garson wished to come at all for the leadership, now was the time he would have to come in.

"I said I doubted if he would ever win against Pearson. St. Laurent agreed, but said naturally they all had their own views.

"I think his talk with the others at Chequers today was most helpful. In every way it is a good thing that he is participating in the conference. Also, as he himself strongly affirms, he has been spared having to be away from Canada except for the few days absence."

Each day Mackenzie King received reports on the Prime Ministers' meetings from St. Laurent, Robertson and Pickersgill, as well as from numerous visitors. For example, on October 20 St. Laurent told the Prime Minister that, during a talk with Nehru, he had "stressed the necessity of having some link with the Crown to be part of the Commonwealth. I told him I did not agree with that at all. It would only bring the Crown into a world controversy if that were given as a reason for keeping Ireland out or not having India stay in. I repeated what I have said to others of the wisdom of finding a way, through the Statute of Westminster, of letting nations that had ever had and who would continue to meet obligations of other nations of the Commonwealth, qualify as members. I can see that the whole battle here is the Commonwealth against the Community of Nations. The whole purpose of the conference is to force the latter position. I doubt if St. Laurent . . . sees where he will be driven to when he gets back if he lets anything slip by rather than keep up constant pressure. He is not strongly maintaining the position that we are satisfied with things as they are. He is troubled a little with a cold. I gave him a box of cough mixture that Maude Salisbury gave to me. I advised him strongly to try and take days of rest at the end of each week. I think Pickersgill has been somewhat helpful at the conference in trying to oppose extremes advocated by Australia and New Zealand."

King George visited the Prime Minister at the Dorchester on October 21. "The call by the King was an extremely pleasant one," he noted. "The King looks quite youthful and slender. He was wearing a light grey suit, a turned-down collar with a grey and black small check tie. Nicol introduced him at the door. I had asked Norman Robertson to meet the King at the door, with the manager of the hotel, Mr. Leigh. His Majesty came in by a side door and was accompanied by Sir Alan Lascelles and a Scotland Yard man. When he came into the room, we shook hands very warmly. . . . He began speaking by regretting that I had been laid up, not being able to be at the meetings or at the party. Was glad I was making good headway. I thanked him warmly for his kindness in calling and for the honour and pleasure it was for me to have him do so. Spoke of the flowers the Queen had sent me, and pointed them out to him. I also remarked how well the flowers had kept. He said: 'It was on Friday last, was it not?' It really was on Monday. He then told me that the Queen had shown him the letter that I had written to her myself. I said I regretted I never knew how to address Her Majesty or himself. I hoped I had not made too many mistakes.

"He then spoke about some of the members of the conference. He spoke of Nehru in particular. Said that he had been sitting one night with Nehru on one side and Jinnah on the other. This was at a dinner. One of them, I think it was Jinnah, did not say a word. Nehru had been seated between Queen Mary and himself. He spoke about Nehru having to take back some of the things he had said in his book. He asked me how I liked him. I said I liked him very much. Told him of the talk we had had together.

"He asked about one or two of the others. Told me of some of the things that he had said to them. He spoke of India and of Pakistan, of the people wanting to be out of the Empire, arguing for it, and, when the time came, really did not want the British to withdraw. They could not really believe they meant to withdraw. Also now they did not know exactly what they wanted, whether to stay in or not. I told him I gathered, from what Nehru had said, that they were busy with their own constitution and wanted to have it settled first, establishing their position, and that he hoped some way would be worked out for their remaining within the Commonwealth.

"In regard to Ireland, all the King said was he was sorry they took the position they did. That he himself would like to visit Ireland. He said that most of his jockeys and racing horses had come from southern Ireland. I said to His Majesty I thought great care should be taken not to allow it to be said that the reason Ireland was not a member of the Commonwealth was because of some requirement that related to the Crown. That it would be a great misfortune if the Crown were the subject of controversy – as a reason why certain nations could not be kept together in the Commonwealth. He did not question this in any way. He said something to the effect that, of course, that was something that should be carefully watched.

"I spoke of Alexander. What a good Governor-General he is making. The King did not make any comment on that.

"He referred to Attlee as being far from well, he thought. He did not himself like the possibility of having someone else as Prime Minister from the [Labour] party. He spoke particularly of not trusting, or liking, one member of the Administration who was thought of for the post.

"He spoke of the High Commissioners and of the desire to make them Ambassadors. He said that nearly all his time was taken up receiving Ambassadors and Ministers. That the whole lot of them changed every six months, and there were about fifty changes. It took a terrible amount of time, and he had no time for reading. He said he was signing papers all the time. He said: 'They keep me working always.'

"Spoke of the American elections. He thought Dewey would win from what he gathered.

"That led him to speak of his [proposed] trip to Australia. He said he was working on the return trip by way of Hawaii and the Panama Canal. It was impossible to say now whether it would not be wise, or not dangerous, for them to return by the other way. He had been trying to impress upon Attlee that it might be desirable, when he was coming through the Panama [Canal], to have the [American] President-to-be visit him on the ship. That would be a gesture that would be helpful vis-à-vis Russia, but he supposed they would be busy changing their plans for turning over the Government. I said I thought it would be desirable, if there was a change of Government, for both leaders to pay him a visit. The President in Office to visit him first and the President-elect also to visit. That would please both political parties in the States and would make a deeper impression on the Russians. I could see that he felt that was something that would need thinking over.

"He asked if St. Laurent had been sworn in [as a United Kingdom Privy Councillor]. I told him I thought he had. I was not sure. He himself said he was holding Council on Monday and St. Laurent could be sworn in then, if necessary. He said he would be seeing him at 5.30. I spoke to him of what a splendid man St. Laurent was. Spoke to him also of Pearson, whom he knew.

"Speaking of the two leaders from India and Pakistan, he said he had told them to get together in a room and settle their difficulties. He did not know whether they had accepted his suggestion or not.

"He spoke of the years having been difficult years. Anxiety through them all. I spoke of how splendid his example, and that of the Queen, had been. Of the feeling of affection and of loyalty which the Canadian people had for them both. How much their example had helped in the morale.

"I then referred to my having been Prime Minister since his accession to the Throne. I would like to say how much I had felt the many marks of kindness shown by the Queen and himself towards myself in these years. That all along the way I could see only complete confidence and great kindness. My relationship with him as Prime Minister had been one of the happy rewards of public life. That I had been so glad the period had been marked by Canada's prosperity, and place in the war, and position in the world.

"The King made one remark that I expressed a doubt about. His Majesty thought that what we ought to have here [in London] was a Minister of the Crown from the different Dominions. That they would be able to give the background of situations, etc., to their Governments. I said they had had that arrangement when necessary during the first war, but the danger I saw in an arrangement of that kind was that the several Ministers from different parts of the Commonwealth, all residing in London, would begin to form a little government of their own, and imagine they were determining Commonwealth policy and that their whole point of view would be chosen from London. I thought myself the communications were so effective today for cabinet consultation, I questioned if they could be much improved upon.

"I said I thought the idea of calling Canada's representatives in London Ambassadors would be considered in Canada as an endeavour to make Canada more of a foreign country than part of the Commonwealth. I agreed it was desirable that precedence should be improved. That I doubted the wisdom of changing the title, at least for the present. The King spoke of the list being now so long that, in giving parties, they had to divide the numbers into two to make two parties. He hoped the U.S. Ambassador who is now here would stay for some time. That otherwise it meant that the U.S. would again be at the bottom of the list and would always have to come in the second party. He said that Harriman had only been here six months. He said the result was it looked as though the U.S. was at the foot of the list, which he did not like.

"The King seemed to me, in appearance and manner, to have developed very much. In conversation he did not hesitate in the utterance of a single word, except once when he was seeking to repeat a word that began with a 'd.'

"It was a quarter past four when the King came in. When it came to 5 o'clock he looked at the little clock and said he did not wish to tire me and then came over and shook hands. I thanked him for his visit and spoke once more of what his example had meant to the world and of the honour and pleasure it had been to me in public life to have had the position of being his adviser for so many years. He expressed the hope that I might be well soon and then enquired about when I would be leaving. My last words as he went out and looked back in a kindly, smiling way were 'God Bless you, Sir.'

"As the King was here, I went back and thought of the years of 1837 and thought of mother being born in exile. The picture in the little frame was beneath the flowers which the Queen had sent to me, and the one picture in prominence in the room. I drew the King's attention to the fact that the flowers were just above my mother's picture. My father's picture was also on the dresser nearby."

Later that day, Sir John Anderson called on the Prime Minister and they talked about the international situation. Mackenzie King asked him "how he figures out that the Russians had not the atomic bomb. He told me there were two evidences: one was that they had not the uranium and other materials needed; that we knew from the frantic efforts they were making and the kind of material they were using that it was of very inferior quality. They had nothing comparable to what Canada possessed. Secondly, that the processes in the United States were fabulously costly and took so many years to complete. The Russians could not possibly carry out a process of the kind for a considerable time, despite what they might have come to know through German scientists, etc. He thought it was a blessing that the U.S. possessed the bomb.

"I told him I did not like the way the Russians were changing their police in Berlin. That it looked to me as if something might happen there at any moment similar to what had taken place in Prague. He thought that was quite possible. He spoke of the times as being really very dangerous and the situation having its origin in the belief that man had come to have in force, the inferior types that were controlling affairs. He thought public life had never been as low in England. He spoke of his years as a public servant, not having cared to ever put in writing much that he had seen or known. He might leave something for others to read after he had gone.

"I was pleased to discover that he is the directing head of the Opera Company here. His whole attitude was an extremely friendly and, indeed, delightful one. I said to him that Lady Anderson had asked me why I did not call her Anna. I said I did not want to get into trouble with her husband. Sir John had quite a laugh over this, and said: 'You need not be in any way bashful.'

"I thanked him for their kindness in inviting me to come to dinner with the King and Queen of Denmark and Churchill next week. He thought the latter would be coming round to see me. He said he had seen him today and he looked much older. Some days he looks quite different. I said I doubted if he could get through five books of the war. He said he has all the material of the last three collected and classified. Mentioned certain persons whom he had helping him. Said subsequent volumes would be much less difficult to write than the first. He said the second was now ready and he thought it was better written than the first."

As the conference continued, Mackenzie King became concerned that Canada's position would not be adequately reflected in the final communique. On October 21 he "had a talk with Pickersgill, who seemed to have given up trying to battle further to make the report of the meetings representative of Canada's feelings, and inclined to let some aspects of it go. He spoke of the rudeness of Evatt and Fraser and, indeed, of the unpleasantness of the whole meeting in the last two days.

"St. Laurent and Norman Robertson are at Attlee's dinner tonight. After the dinner, they are to get on with a further effort of completing the draft. I sent a short letter to Attlee before dinner."

Next day Mackenzie King went through "the latest draft of the final statement for the conference and made three or four changes. I found later from Pickersgill that all had been made in the discussion at the conference table in the morning. As I read the final draft, it is, I think, innocuous in many respects. What the British have got out of it is talk of a Commonwealth government as though there was a complete entity of Commonwealth with so many governments, exactly as there is in the Dominion of Canada with so many provincial governments. They have been focussing up to a Commonwealth government by seeking to get regular meetings of foreign ministers and frequent meetings of Prime Ministers. Agreed to by all. Both St. Laurent and Pickersgill got tired of taking exception to some of these things which may be interpreted differently, but did not oppose them. I personally do not think it matters much but believe the British will get a real shock some time when they discover what they are doing for appearances sake in the hope of everything being ultimately finalised on these lines, . . . may react and effect just the opposite.

"I have been reading an editorial in 'The Telegraph' or some other newspaper speaking about my being opposed to conferences, etc., because of my leanings towards the United States. Nothing could be further wrong than this. It is because I think that too frequent conferences are the cause of trouble in the end. Much better to have individual relationships. We have found that out with the provinces in Canada. Britain will find it out increasingly with the Dominions.

"This morning's meeting at Downing Street was anything but pleasant. I gathered that Beasley [a Minister in the Australian government] . . .

accused Attlee at one stage of what was equivalent to bad faith. That Attlee had finally to say he could not tolerate language of that kind and that it would have to be withdrawn. Attlee is one of the mildest of men. Even Fraser told me tonight that Beasley had gone too far. St. Laurent and Pickersgill felt really embarrassed and were really shocked. What apparently has happened is that Evatt has left the conference and telephoned over his instructions that certain words were to go in, no matter what happened. Others could not agree to them. Moreover, if they were refused, he [Beasley] was to break up the conference. This fellow Evatt has become a regular Hitler. It is a question of power going to a man's head. I am glad I was spared all this at the conference as I certainly would have been very outspoken and this to a degree that would have offended some part of the Commonwealth.

"I had a nice talk with St. Laurent after lunch. I think it is fortunate he has been here. If he gets back alright without being overtired, he will be able to speak with authority and not as the scribes. I also had a talk with Pickersgill in the afternoon."

Later that day Prime Minister Fraser of New Zealand visited Mackenzie King and told him he thought "things had gone a little too far on Australia's part at the conference. He was more concerned about finding a formula for India and Ireland. He likes my idea of those who had been members of the Commonwealth to continue to be such, etc. Seemed most anxious I should have further talks with Nehru. Said he had learned from Mountbatten and someone else that my talk with Nehru had made a great impression on him, a greater impression than anything else except his talks, of course, with Mountbatten."

In a talk the next day, October 23, Madame Pandit confirmed "how pleased her brother was with the talks we had together." The Prime Minister also received a visit from Eric Louw, the South African Minister of External Affairs. "He told me the scene at Downing Street was really a disgraceful affair. . . . I have been looking over the newspaper comments on the conference. To one who knows what has taken place, they are more or less whitewash – a make-believe that everyone has been united and that the conference has meant much etc. My own feeling is that the British Government will find increasingly, as the numbers, etc., continue [to grow], that they will be creating more and more in the way of friction between the nations of the Commonwealth instead of furthering what is their chief ambition, to be known as a Commonwealth policy. They emphasize dropping the word 'British' but they gained their point by substituting a single policy for Commonwealth defence, trade, foreign affairs, etc. Louw, I think, helped to keep the record straight. He told me he had had to say several times they would have to count him out where they insisted on putting phrases in the report he knew his Government could not support.

"I found, [in] the conversation with him, much more in common in some things than I could begin to find in views of the British Ministers. I am more happy than ever that I was not drawn into the conference and the attendant meetings. Louw said he was nearly dead. He was up until 12 each night and thoroughly done out with the gatherings and the discussions. I have gained more, I think, that will be useful and of benefit for the future by quietly reviewing the whole business here."

In a conversation with Lord Jowitt and his wife on October 24, Mackenzie King "found Jowitt's views were very similar to my own re High Commissioners not being called Ambassadors, as indicating further separation from the Commonwealth. He had shared the feelings of disgust that the others had at the last day's proceedings in the meetings. He thought his talks with Nehru had been of no avail. I told him I thought Nehru would not make any commitment of any kind until after their constitution had been established, but my talks with him had led me to feel that he was sympathetic to remaining in the Commonwealth but had to consider all that he had said in the past. He would find it easier to deal with the Commonwealth question later on. I then put forward to him my views about regarding any part of the Commonwealth which had been under the King at any time as being qualified for membership in the Commonwealth provided they would carry out from then on the same obligations as the others. He thought this afforded a very good basis of arrangement. Seemed quite impressed by it. Said he had hoped to make something out of the common citizenship but that had not apparently worked as well."

The next day, October 25, was an eventful one for Mackenzie King. He received Prime Minister Liaquat Ali Khan of Pakistan in the morning and found him "quite clear in his own mind of the wisdom of maintaining relations with the Commonwealth." He later saw Nehru who "spoke of being pleased he had come to England, more particularly to have met the different Prime Ministers. He spoke particularly of the pleasure of our coming to know each other, also of the visit of his sister on Sunday. He brought with him a letter from the two little girls [Nehru's nieces], and a metal box made in Kashmir with the top of jade. I noticed he seemed particularly pleased in referring to the visit they had had. The little note is a sweet one from the two of them. He extended a warm invitation to me to visit India. I did the same to him to visit Canada. Because of the short time he had and the fact that he had still to say goodbye to Attlee

... and as the ceremony of the University of London function was coming on we had only a chance for a further word. I told him that whatever decision India might make, Canada would always have a place for India. He himself had spoken of the helpful relationship he had felt we might have."

The Prime Minister "had to dress rather hurriedly to be ready for the ceremony of receiving the Degree of Doctor of Laws from the London University. Sat in the front room for a time, waiting for others to arrive and to robe, which they did in my bedroom. At about 6.30 P.M. Lord Athlone, as Chancellor, came in. He was accompanied by the Vice-Chancellor, Miss Penson, and by the Principal of the University, Dr. Logan, and the orator, Mr. Evans. Also Lord Moran and Norman Robertson. The first four were all gowned. I was told to remain seated....

"By request of the University, 'The Times' photographer was permitted to take pictures. Lord Athlone read a short adress. . . . The Orator, Mr. Evans, was then called on to speak. He read an exceptionally kindly and historically valuable address in presenting me to the Chancellor, who then placed the hood over my shoulders. . . .

"While it was understood that I would not have to speak, I felt I should say something. I began by thanking the Chancellor for what he had said, sharing the memories he had recalled of our years in Canada together, and of Roosevelt's visit. I then thanked the orator for what he had said. Mentioned it all seemed difficult to understand, as I listened to the recital. Recalled how I had lived at Passmore Edwards Settlement, Tavistock Place, passing London University on my afternoon walks. How little I had dreamed of any such development over the years and spoke of it as the rounding out of the circle of my associations with London and parliamentary life here, my introduction to the latter having been through the Harvard Fellowship which took me to the Passmore Edwards Settlement to live. I thanked the University again for the honour."

Even after the conference had concluded, the Prime Minister's stream of visitors continued and he seemed to spend a good part of each day on the telephone chatting with old friends. On October 28 he had a telephone conversation with Nancy Astor whose husband "apparently has the same trouble I have and has been resting for the past month or so. She spoke of the talks she had had with Mr. Rockefeller who, she said, loves me dearly. I let her know that I thought he would like to come to England. She said to tell him she would give up everything to take him to Europe or elsewhere if he would come; also she and her husband would be going to Tucson in February. She suggested that I should come along and all of us would take a good rest there. She talks in a rough and ready way but is most interesting. She had offered to let me come and stay and make use of their house during convalescence.

"Also received a pleasing telegram from Mr. McConnell and a letter from Mrs. Churchill. . . . Yesterday, I had a nice talk over the 'phone with Mrs. Chamberlain. She is disappointed in the book about her husband. Says the writer has very little about his real personality or personal side of things. Feels too the book was published too soon, etc.

"Received word this afternoon that Churchill himself would be coming in the morning on his way to the country. I should have been sorry to have missed him on this trip.

"Sorry not to have got off letters to McConnell and Mr. R. [Rockefeller] today. Also am beginning to be anxious about farewell letters to H. M. [Her Majesty], Mrs. Attlee and others.

"Kept busy through the morning on correspondence with H. [Handy] and Mrs. Black. Also continued after luncheon doing some 'phoning. Did not get a chance to rest before Bevin came at 3.15 P.M. He seemed relieved that the conference was over. . . . Told me confidentially he was not altogether sorry they might not be able to have the Big Four work together until the spring. He thought the Russians were beginning to see they had made a bit of a mistake. Perhaps by March or April they might wish to discontinue the blockade of Berlin and be ready to discuss some other matters.

"There was a good deal of dissatisfaction. He said the Russians had an army of 40,000 ready to come into Europe. The French had a number of trained men in Africa; their spirit was quite different now to last November when there was defeatism on every side. He said, in touching any question, it was like plucking plums off a tree and finding they were rotten. He could not get any definite help anywhere. The Americans were working splendidly with him. He likes Marshall very much. Felt they could get what was needed of equipment . . . [for the] three-power armies. Last year could get nothing very definite from the States. Altogether felt much more encouraged. He told me about his own condition which alarmed me very much.

"Bevin said after Tuesday he must have a rest of some time. Went on to tell me how he was suffering from shortness of breath; pointed to a place . . . [in] his chest where he felt a pain. Felt some time when he took off his shoes at night that his feet were greatly swollen. In fact, he described all the symptoms that Lord Moran has been telling me are of the most serious kind.

"When I spoke to Moran tonight, he said he never spoke of anyone who was his own patient. Bevin was not so he could speak of him. He had felt disgusted at Bevin taking too much to drink at times, actually drinking Vodka, etc. He would go to dinner and after dinner might feel that he was gay like a young man and, of course, the next day would be done for. He thought he had got beyond where anyone could really control him.

"Bevin told me he would take a month off if he could. Said he must. When I said he ought perhaps to come out to Canada, he said he would like to do that. . . .

"Moran said that Bevin was not particularly interested in his home or wife. Was just wrapped up in politics from day to day. Thought he and Attlee were the best of the govt. Really stood for the British workman at his best. Felt it would be a great loss if Bevin were to go. If anything were to happen to him, the party was likely to go still further to the left.

"He [Bevin] seemed to me to be very patient, to be smiling notwithstanding the knowledge of the serious condition which he knows he has. As he went, he shook hands a couple of times. As he looked back going out of the door and smiled, I had the feeling we might not see each other again though I would not like to carry that thought too strongly. He has left me with the impression that they would be able to prevent a war for at least two years. That something like what happened in Prague may happen in Berlin. Our people may be able to get enough force in to meet such force as may seek to get control of the city. It is all a terrible situation.

"He said that Schuman was a splendid man. Had told him today he thought the Communists had made a serious mistake in bringing on the coal strike [in France] at a time when the Chamber of Deputies were not sitting. It enabled the govt. to take stronger measures and they would likely be able to get the better of the strike. If the Chamber of Deputies had been sitting, the Communists would have roused a good deal of trouble there. He thanked me for the part I had taken in helping him in the difficult situation over Palestine and said he was delighted with the splendid work that McNaughton had done. He had written McN. a letter thanking him. He said nothing could have been better than his work at Paris in connection with the atomic bomb matters.

Later in the afternoon the Prime Minister saw Victor Sifton, who was visiting London, and then Sir Campbell Stuart, a former Canadian who was director of the London *Times*. "In speaking of memoirs," Mackenzie King wrote, the latter "said not to trouble to speak to anyone else. He would come out next summer and arrange for publication through some of the big papers in the States and the Times here. He thought he could bring about a situation which would bring me quite a lot of money. I accepted all his offers with thanks. Told him I was doubtful if I would get anything written for publication. He kept on saying what he would like to do in that connection."

Before leaving on a visit to Turkey, Lord Moran saw Mackenzie King for the last time on October 29 and asked him "to let him have" any "thought I had on matters particularly related to Churchill" to "be published after his [Churchill's] death." Winston Churchill arrived for a visit shortly after Moran left and Mackenzie King summarized their conversation in a private memorandum included in the diary. "When Winston came in the room, his words of greeting were: 'Well! Mackenzie, my dear friend, I am sorry to see you here. You were greatly missed at the conference. We all wished you were there.' I remarked how exceedingly well he was looking and how pleased I was to see that. I also said that I had seen where he had been making great changes in the Conservative Convention and in the House yesterday. In regard to the latter, he said he hoped I would read the Hansard account of his speech. That he had spoken for an hour and a quarter and had not felt any the worse for it. He called out once or twice 'I have brought you my book' and then went back into the other room and autographed it himself. He said I have already given you the American edition. This is a copy of the English edition.

"Without following the order of the conversation, it was somewhat along the following lines. Churchill spoke about the word 'British' and the word 'Empire.' I told him also I noticed that the word 'Confederacy' had been used in speaking of Canada. I told him, in Canada, we did not like particularly the word 'Empire.' He said he had used the expression 'Empire' and 'Commonwealth of Nations' so as to permit different persons to take their own choice. He certainly would never wish to see the word 'British' disappear. As to 'Confederacy,' I told him we had seldom seen or heard the word used in Canada. He spoke to me of the possibility of coming out to Canada in the spring to get his degree at the University of Toronto. He hoped I would come to Toronto to see him while he was there. I mentioned that I hoped he would visit Ottawa. He said he hoped he may also be able to stay a few days with Alexander. He would want, however, to make no engagements and to have the time for writing and quiet.

"Speaking of his speeches, he literally beamed with pleasure. It is amazing how his countenance expresses his inner feelings of delight, and how quickly he responds to words of appreciation and approval. There is an equally rapid change where objection is taken to his own point of view or views. This was noticeable when I mentioned about the word 'British' having a different significance in different parts. . . .

"I said to Winston I was anxious to ask him one question on which I could have his answer [as] a matter of record. I asked if, during the time that I had been in office, he had ever asked for anything that it was possible for our Government to do which we had not done or if I had failed him in anything. He instantly said: 'You have never failed. You were helpful always. There was nothing that you did not do that could be done' (or words to this effect). He spoke two or three times of the tremendous help Canada had given in the Air Training Plan and in the air. He also said you helped me with Menzies. He was referring there to Menzies' desire to have the Commonwealth Prime Ministers take a bigger hand in directing the war and to control Winston. . . . Speaking of the Bomb, he said it is our only shield. He spoke also of the time that I communicated with him at Fulton after his address there. He said what he had said had been borne out. He mentioned that he knew Dewey and liked him.

"I told him I liked Truman, found him very straightforward and doing his best. He also spoke of my having been helpful at the beginning of the war when the question was whether the British fleet should be moved to the U.S. What might have happened, for example, had Mosley been able to get the control of the British House of Commons and make a settlement with the Germans. He said the Americans were very difficult at that time. That I had been helpful in getting the true position understood. He meant the constitutional procedure and his own position at the time that he would do anything rather than let the British fleet fall into German hands. He said he was going to deal with this matter in one of his books. He also asked if he might have permission to use despatches between us. I said to feel free to use anything. He said you have already given consent, through Attlee, for some that will be appearing in the next volume which will come out shortly.

"Winston asked me when I was going to retire. I told him on returning to Canada. He said, you have had a great career. He repeated that once or twice. When I said that he would be sorry to have learned of the death of Smuts' son, he answered that he had wired Smuts. I was a bit surprised, however, that he did not enlarge upon his feelings for Smuts. His reply that he had wired him seemed to me to reveal a certain self-centeredness which is undoubtedly a trait of character which reveals a good deal.

"In the course of conversation, he used many fine expressions. As he was going away he said, you have built a bridge between the United States and the United Kingdom. As I referred to his great services to the World and to Freedom, he used the last expression and I said, God bless you, as he was leaving. He came to my bedside and his eyes filled up with tears. He shook my hands very warmly and affectionately.

"As he went out of the door, I could see that he was restraining feelings of emotion. We could not have had a pleasanter talk together.

"I was a bit disappointed later when I learned that, as he had been leaving the hotel, he had told Robertson who went to the door with him that he would like the press to know that he had called.

"He mentioned that we were old friends of some forty years, close together in the war, etc. This desire of publicity being given to the call was noticeably different from Attlee's attitude, for example. Attlee has called three times and, each time, has been so modest as not to indicate any kind of desire to have publicity given to his calls."

After Churchill left, the Prime Minister saw Violet Markham again and then Harold Macmillan. Attlee arrived later in the afternoon and they "had tea together. Attlee looks much stronger than when I saw him last. He was pleased with the way the conference had gone. Thought it had been helpful. He felt very much pained at the speech which Churchill had made yesterday. Said it was mischievous. Would do harm in different parts of the Commonwealth and upset much of what had been done. Churchill used to be the leader of the Tory party when they talked of Empire and the rest of it. He had since dropped out of that position. Now, he spoke as a Tory politician, nothing more or less. I said I had noticed what he had said about Conservative governments in different countries. I said that was the first time anyone from England had tried to control elections in other parts of the Commonwealth. Attlee was quite annoyed at this and much else. He said that he himself had arranged meetings at Chequers.

"I said that I had asked Churchill in the morning if my Government had ever failed him at any stage of the war, either before or after. He had replied 'Not in anything.' He had spoken of the great services we had rendered. . . . I asked if my Government had ever complained of any relation with Britain. He said never. I said those are two things I wanted to remember. I told them to Attlee this afternoon. It was quite plain that Attlee had not liked Churchill's speech yesterday at all.

"I talked a little to Attlee of Bevin. He agreed that he was much in need of a rest. Also Noel Baker. He spoke of two weeks. I am afraid Bevin will need a longer rest or will not live very long. Attlee thought he would have a very busy time until Christmas. . . . I said I got the impression from all I talked to that it was felt he was the one who restrained his party from going too far, he and Bevin. He said, on the contrary, the party were pretty much of one mind – and pretty solid together.

"He seemed less concerned about Europe. Made it clear that he did not know what might happen at any time. Had to be prepared to meet any kind of a situation that might arise. . . .

"The conversation was very general. He could not have been friendlier. He poured the tea for both of us. We had a couple of cups. He stayed quite a little time. . . . I wished him well personally and thanked him warmly for our friendship and also for the kindness of the British Government, etc. He then came back and shook hands twice before he left the room. We wished each other well.

"Noel Baker came in. We had a further cup of tea and a pleasant talk together. He seemed well pleased with the meeting. I thanked him for his gift and kindness and also wished him well.

"Noel Baker was followed by Dulanty, the High Commissioner of Ireland, who brought messages from Costello to say how sorry he was I had been ill and could not visit Ireland. I told him of having written Costello. He himself said he thought it was unfortunate the partition question had been brought up at this time, that the question of separation had been brought up at all. He is a very humorous fellow. He told me some good stories. . . . Was most pleasant.

"Mrs. Norman Robertson came in and we had a nice little talk together. I spoke of the name that Norman had made for all of us here and how well he had done. She was very modest about everything. She said that Norman liked England but she thought his heart was really in [the] External Affairs Dept. I said he was more than a departmental man. That he was a Government man – very helpful for policies generally. I said that we had missed him very much."

Mackenzie King left London on October 30 and motored to Southampton to board the *Queen Elizabeth*. Just before he left the Dorchester, the Prime Minister was about to write "a word of good-bye to the King and Queen" when Sir Alan Lascelles arrived. He volunteered to take back a message "which would save me writing. I thanked him for this but said I would supplement what I had said by a word which I would write from the ship. I asked him about the style of address in writing a private letter to the King and Queen. He referred to beginning with either Sir or Madam and using Your Majesty only once in the letter and at the beginning of the letter of using the words 'With my humble duty' or words to that effect, and concluding with 'Your obedient servant.' He said he did not use the word devoted or loyal himself in a letter to the King. He did not stress the word 'loyal' which he did not use himself. Said much less attention was being paid to styles of communication now. He brought up Churchill's speech himself. Said he thought it was unwise and troublesome.

That he was losing his grip in the use of words, etc. I said I had not liked the reference to the Tory Governments throughout the Commonwealth. . . . He said himself he could understand why others, like India etc., would not wish it. He said he did not think it was wise to discuss labels. To let usage decide what was best. That I think is the real mischief of conferences. They lead to questions being asked which it is difficult to answer. If not answered, they create additional difficulties. I remember Edward Grey expressing that view.

"Lascelles seemed to think that the conference had been, on the whole, successful. He spoke of the pleasure he had in looking forward to seeing Pearson and his wife. They were coming over that afternoon. Word had been received shortly before that Pearson's plane had landed and that he was on his way to London. It appears that at one stage it was thought they might have to turn back to Shannon Airport because of the fog. However, they managed to get along splendidly.

"I spoke of the King's trip. Mentioned about His Majesty seeing leaders of both parties in the United States. Lascelles said there were some difficulties about the Panama Canal. Question of whether it was wise to have anyone go there to see Their Majesties. I asked if their ship could not be brought up into the Atlantic but he doubted that. On reconsideration, he thought there was much to be said, if the opportunity was favourable, to having the King see both the Republican and Democratic leaders. He, Lascelles, took it for granted that Dewey was going to win. I must say it looks to me that way, not because of any particular fault of Truman, but rather because of his misfortune in the divisions of the party through [Henry] Wallace's candidature; also loss of support over the negro issue.

"When I told him how much I had appreciated the visit of the King and the flowers and the letter from the Queen, [and] that, while I appreciated being thus honoured, I recognized it was a tribute to Canada, Lascelles said no, it was intended for myself – intended as personal."

As the Prime Minister noted, Pearson had arrived in the United Kingdom that day fresh from his victory in Algoma East on October 25. Shortly after Lascelles left, he called at the Dorchester. "He looked wonderfully well, bright and cheerful," Mackenzie King wrote. "Has a fine intellectual and spiritual look. One could feel that he had been participating in a campaign which gave him a commanding look. He was very cheerful and pleased. I told him how delighted I was to shake his hand. I congratulated him on his election and wished him all that was best for his future which I knew was going to be a great one. He spoke at once about how glad he was [that] he had accepted my advice in the matter of devoting his time to the constituency. He repeated this two or three times.

Said it had enabled him to know some friends in each polling booth. There had been little political organization and that old Farquhar [the former Liberal member] had been perfectly marvellous, taking him all over and introducing him personally, etc. He now feels he has the constituency for the next campaign.

"I suggested his sending a cable or two from Paris to the constituents. One could see he liked the thought at once. I spoke to him about Claxton's speech which I said was ill advised, his continuous references to Russia and our preparations for war against Russia. Said I thought he should use general terms of our wishing to do our part with other nations in being prepared against aggression from whatever source it might come etc. Claxton was really helping to focus Russia's enmity on Canada. I feel there is great danger of this in the way in which some other policies are being handled. I do not like Canada attempting to assume position and take on responsibilities greater than those which belong to the U.S. and the U.K., not to speak of other nations greater than our own though less fortunate perhaps.

"Pearson spoke of the greetings he brought from the Cabinet. It was particularly nice to hear him refer to our colleagues and discussions there. I told him of how pleased we all were with St. Laurent's part and with the by-elections [the Liberal candidate had also held Rosthern, Saskatchewan, in the other by-election on October 25]. He thought the latter had made a real impression. I said I thought the results of by-elections would determine the fate of the Government. It was clear from his actions in entering the Government and the results of the by-elections that I had not been leaving a Ministry that was weakening but rather a strong Ministry at high tide. The results were also the best endorsements of St. Laurent's selection as leader. I had a few words with Mrs. Pearson – both looked very well after their night flight. I advised them to take a good rest until tomorrow morning."

The *Queen Elizabeth* sailed early in the morning on October 31 and, during the voyage, the Prime Minister spent most of his time relaxing, musing and reading. On November 1 he noted that, "in my reading last night I saw where Arnold Heeney had been addressing the armed forces at Washington in a secret session. It was mentioned he was the Secretary of the Cabinet, etc.; this I think is entirely wrong. The Secretary of a Cabinet should not be speaking anywhere. I noticed where Mackenzie, Deputy Minister of Trade and Commerce, had been speaking on the U.S. trade matters. They are more technical etc. At the same time, I think this is dangerous; if Deputy Ministers are going to usurp the position of Ministers, the Government is soon going to be in trouble. The Civil

Service cannot expect to be immune from attack in the House and, at the same time, make speeches either in one's own country or, more seriously, in another country. The opposition have a right to know, for example, what Heeney disclosed regarding the armed forces. These are ministerial responsibilities. This has arisen largely from Pearson speaking in different places. Now, Heeney gets his chance to speak, to travel, etc., through that example. Unless St. Laurent takes a firm stand, he will find . . . a bureaucracy running the Government and not the Government controlling a bureaucracy."

Later that day, Mackenzie King speculated about the organization of his memoirs. They "might well be made up of chapters such as 'My friendship with Ludwig' – bringing out its significance. 'Relationship with Sovereigns of Britain' beginning with Deputy Minister – at the time of Queen Victoria's reign, CMG from Edward VII etc., down to the letters written on this voyage.

"This chapter should have its beginning with my grandfather's life and Queen Victoria's proclamation. Increasingly, I see the Book of Memoirs taking shape in the form of chapters which will be under individual headings, developing the subjects from beginning to close instead of by years, as for example, home and its influence etc."

November 2 was election day in the United States. George Fulford, the former Liberal member for Leeds, was on board and joined the Prime Minister for a talk. "George began speaking of being so pleased that Canada was taking such a lead in international questions," Mackenzie King wrote. "I gathered that he had in mind what he had read about our wishing to have in Canada the conference regarding the Atlantic Pact. I told him there was great danger of our getting beyond our depth in some of the international obligations that we were assuming, and that we would be well advised to have the Great Powers – the U.S. and the U.K. – accept the main responsibility for initiating matters of major and world wide significance. We would get little thanks if they succeeded but would get plenty of blame if they were a failure. Above all, we were running the risk of making Canada the first target for Russian aggression.

"We talked of the elections in the U.S. I said I thought they would be very close. That my preference was for Truman but I felt the handicaps that he had, through the Democrats having been in office so long succeeding Roosevelt, the loss through Wallace's third party, also the feeling that Wallace had occasioned in the southern states through his advocacy of the negro cause, also the opposition which John Lewis had sought to raise against him in labour requests – that these might prove too much for him to overcome."

Mackenzie King was delighted on November 3 when he received news of President Truman's re-election. He noted that "during the day it was touch and go as to whether he would get the required number of votes in the electoral college but, by noon, it was apparent that both the House of Representatives and the Senate would be Democratic so that if the required number of electoral votes was not obtained by either Dewey or himself he would be sure of election by decision of Congress.

"By four this afternoon, Robertson came to bring in word that Truman was assured of a substantial majority in the votes of the electoral college and that his election was conceded by Dewey. I cannot say what a relief this is to my mind and heart. Had Dewey been returned, I would have had great fears for the return of Republican policies dictated by the big interests. Also a certain jingoism which might have made the threat of war even greater than otherwise it might have been.

"One begins to see that, while it may not have accorded with diplomatic usage, Truman was not unwise to let the American people know that he was prepared to send a member of the Supreme Court to see Stalin personally on his – Truman's – behalf. That he was all for prevention of war by mediation. I rejoiced at Truman's victory in particular because I believe it has been so well earned. He assumed the task under the greatest difficulties. He has fought bravely all along and I believe is thoroughly sincere and honest. I am also delighted he has a majority in both Houses of Congress. He will now be able to govern with a firm hand. That of itself will have a tremendously steadying effect in the United States. Altogether, the result of the elections will, I believe, lead to the removal of much uncertainty and to a vast improvement of conditions. It is fortunate for Canada that Truman has been returned. Our relations are of the best. It might have been quite difficult had the results been otherwise."

The Prime Minister reached New York on November 6 and was back in Ottawa the following day. He was "delighted to reach Ottawa with the sun shining brightly as we came into the city. The hands of the clock were in a straight line a little after half past twelve when I took a last look at them. I looked at Mother's picture and then came into the sitting room and looked at further park improvements and also got glimpses of the Parliament Buildings.

"When we reached Ottawa, Harry Letson represented the Governor-General and came aboard the car with a letter from His Excellency, then Mr. St. Laurent came on board and later Pickersgill. The car was switched around to save a long walk. There was quite a little gathering at the siding. I did not try to say more than that I was glad to be home, feeling much better than when I left London. I was also glad to see Tassé [a barber at the Chateau Laurier Hotel] at the station, also Matte and several others but I was too fearful of becoming shaky on the platform to try to pick out individuals. Fred MacGregor was enthusiastically nearby when I got into my car. I felt a little lost and embarrassed when I found I was driving home alone."

At the station, Mackenzie King told St. Laurent he "would be quite ready to tender my resignation on Thursday or on Monday. My thoughts were to be governed by his wishes. Matters were left over for us to have a talk together further later on in the week."

On November 8 the Prime Minister discussed the date of his resignation with Pickersgill, who told him that "St. Laurent thought that Thursday would be too soon. Hoped I would wait until Monday. Monday would be the best of all as it would enable Garson to be here and get back in time for nomination in Marquette; also would enable St. Laurent to go to the Maritime Provinces later in the week to be present at a dinner in honour of Ilsley. That suits me admirably. I felt, during the day, I would have to give up thought of attending the Armistice Day Service.

"The next problem is that of the Cabinet positions. St. Laurent feels he should take in a Minister from Nova Scotia. Will take in [Robert] Winters. I told both he and Pickersgill that I thought this was imperative. They must not leave Nova Scotia without a Minister.

"We then discussed senatorships. . . . Was relieved to find that St. Laurent was quite prepared to leave over any appointments to the Senate. That I think is best. It lets him have a number to work out future contingencies with.

"I learned to my great surprise that Glen is thinking of accepting the International Joint Commission. I am afraid that will be severely criticized and also be harmful to him. He may be here this week."

Mackenzie King saw St. Laurent later in the day and they "agreed to Monday [November 15] for my tendering of my resignation. He mentioned his daughter had spoken of some kind of reception at which ladies could extend greetings. I advised him to make the relationship strongly one between the Prime Minister's Office and Government House. When the Cabinet was formed, to return to the East Block and meet them there in a formal meeting. I said I would like to attend a meeting on Friday, if I could, or possibly before the ceremony at Government House, but that remains open. I asked him to take in the ceremony at the Cenotaph, etc., on Thursday.

"We discussed the Cabinet situation. I advised strongly for a Minister from Nova Scotia at all costs. He wanted me to help him in the readjustment of the others. To make suggestions. We agreed it would be unwise to have by-elections, to take no chances in that way until at least the existing ones are over.

"I spoke of the danger of some of the things which I have been thinking of; for instance, Claxton talks so much of Russia, also the over-doing of expenditures, useless preparation for war in the North etc., not having any meeting in Canada for the regional pact business. He said there was no justification for the inspired article in the Sunday Times. He told me he is having much trouble with Gardiner who hardly attends Council at all. He comes and tells them that he has to go here and there. I said, in that event, he should make the decisions without him, let him know that the Cabinet would have to decide matters without him. St. Laurent said he really thought Ilsley would still be with us but for Gardiner. That he had been responsible for Ilsley's illness, his constant conflict, etc.

"I also spoke about being careful [in not] making too many commitments, not to put too much reliance on the United Nations. I think he is beginning to see already what is involved in absences of Ministers and officials, making matters altogether too difficult. He told me, by the way, that the Cabinet had decided against some of the matters that had been passed on from the Conference of Prime Ministers, particularly regarding annual meetings of Prime Ministers or Foreign Ministers. He said the despatch had been sent before I got back so that it could not be said that it had been due to any action of mine, which is true."

Still concerned about his health, the Prime Minister began to worry that he would be unable to call on the Governor-General. However, on November 9 he received word that Alexander proposed to call on him at Laurier House. The Governor-General arrived late in the afternoon and was "exceedingly pleasant and kindly. We talked together somewhat of the conference – of India and Ireland, of the dinner at the Country Club the night Costello was here, . . . of procedure for Monday next. Told him particularly . . . of having wished to be present at Remembrance Day ceremonies but of doctors advising against the cold. Of thinking it wisest not to take the risk. He was quite emphatic that that was wise. We then discussed the procedure for Monday and definitely decided that would be the day on which I would tender my resignation. He told me he would like to give a dinner for me. Had intended doing so before I resigned but would arrange for it later on. Brought very warm greetings from Lady Alexander.

"I received His Excellency in my bedroom having felt it advisable to stay in bed all the afternoon."

Mackenzie King decided on November 10 to announce the date of his resignation in a letter to the Canadian Legion. "I had been looking forward to the National War Memorial ceremony as being the last public appearance," he wrote. "As I had been invited to luncheon by the Legion, I felt that to make the announcement of the date through the Legion would be a fitting tribute to them since I could not pay the tribute to the dead of the Great War at the Memorial itself. Accordingly, after morning reading, I spent the forenoon drafting a letter by hand to send to Baxter, the President, who oddly enough is a distant connection. Unfortunately, it took until after noon until the letter was finally revised and then sent, which would leave to the press very little time. I felt, however, that the letter was an historic one – one of the most important of any I have written.

"I was told that the letter was given a warm reception at the luncheon and that its reading was followed by some kind remarks by Mr. St. Laurent. It really was the rounding out of my period as Prime Minister. The strain of the war years is really the reason for my present condition and for my not being able to be at the Memorial Service itself. I was disappointed in reading the evening Ottawa papers to find they had only used a paragraph or two of the letter, the ones giving the date, but left out altogether the reasons for the part that I attached the most importance to, namely the reasons why I had chosen the Legion and was now choosing the 15th for the time of my retirement. I certainly have been unfortunate in the public relations of my office."

The following morning, Mackenzie King "was disappointed not to see the letter to the Legion in full in either paper and particularly disappointed at Mears' statement in the Gazette which indicated that my statement had been given to the Legion in the first place instead of to the press. It was also clear from other evidence that the press were resentful of my not having given them the word first. They disliked my announcing the date of my retirement through the Legion, missing altogether the real significance to be attached to the communication. However, some day that letter will be regarded as one of the most important and significant which I have ever written."

The Prime Minister attended his last Cabinet meeting on November 12. He "felt a certain slight emotion as I saw the coats and hats of the Ministers hanging in the hall and what looked like a complete cabinet. When I went into the ante-room, Jean was telephoning and I shook hands with him. On entering the Council chamber, all the Ministers stood up. When they were seated, there seemed to be a tense silence. I said immediately I was glad to be back again, very sorry not to have been able to attend the meetings of the Prime Ministers in London. I said that as all were Privy Councillors and friends I perhaps should tell them just exactly what had taken place. I mentioned I was tired out when I left Ottawa and had rested up on arrival at the Harvard Club [in New York]. On board the ship, I had had little sleep. On reaching Paris, I had developed trouble in the matter of breathing and lack of sleep . . . [and] had told Vanier I did not want to get into the hands of doctors there who would keep me in France and immediately had decided to see Lord Moran on reaching London. Spoke of his having taken me to see Sir John Parkinson, a heart specialist, and of the two telling me I must give up any thought of attending the conference as there might be a failure – that I might collapse and that the danger that was developing was what was known as cardiac asthma which would be a very serious business. They had advised my going to bed immediately. I hesitated. My purpose in seeing them had been to get something to carry me through the conference but I had felt I should perhaps follow the doctors' orders. Consequently, I had followed the advice given. Moran had seen the King and explained the situation to him; also had seen Prime Minister Attlee. I mentioned that Moran had subsequently explained the condition to Mr. St. Laurent, that the long rest had done me good. I felt now on the way to complete recovery. . . . I had to take it easy during the winter but would hope to attend Parliament part of the time at least.

"I then thanked Mr. St. Laurent for having taken on the obligations of acting Prime Ministership as he had. I said to Mr. Howe I had been pleased to notice that he had been Acting Prime Minister [during St. Laurent's absence in London]. Howe replied saying acting long enough to see that the job was not one for him. I then told the Ministers that I had no regret and intended to see the press later. I would like to say to them what I intend to say to the press, that I had no regrets on being relieved of the responsibilities of office, but that I was leaving with a feeling of gratefulness and gladness in my heart at the position that Canada had achieved etc., and the larger freedom which I hope now to enjoy. I said that I hoped it would afford me a chance to see each one of them as friends. Said that I had for each one feelings not only of friendship but of deep affection and that I would be interested in their lives and work so long as this was permitted to me. I said that I had enjoyed my years of office and was sure that I was right in not staying on longer. I said that my task in the Office of Prime Minister was completed. I said there was one matter I would like to bring up in council as they knew I had been personally deeply interested in the work of the Federal District Commission. Had meant to fill up the positions required by the Act before leaving for England but had been unable to get a complete slate. I said I had, after conference with the Ministers, now a complete slate and I read over the names and occupations of those recommended. In speaking of Ontario, I said I had myself communicated with Sandwell. Mitchell asked if it was [B.K.] Sandwell of *Saturday Night*. I don't know whether he has some feeling or not. I asked him later if he had any question about Sandwell. He said no. I said I thought he possessed the kind of interest which would be of great help. When we came to Sanderson of Saskatchewan [a leading Liberal in Prince Albert], I spoke of him as having had to do with the National Park for a longer time and more intimately than most of the men there. I recalled it was his father who presented me with the house on Lake Waskesiu.

"I then asked if there was any discussion. All agreed on the order to be passed.

"I next asked if there were any matters which members of Council would like to bring up. Mr. St. Laurent said there was not anything in particular but he would like, on behalf of all his colleagues, to say how much they regretted my leaving the Ministry and how greatly they would miss the guidance I had given over the years to public affairs. He spoke at some length of the outstanding features of the ... Government's achievements during the years that I had been at the head of the party, referring to keeping both the party and the country united, referring also to the period of the war, to the fact that there had been three epochs in Canadian history dominated by personalities of Sir John Macdonald, a shorter period dominated by Sir Wilfrid Laurier, and what he spoke of as the Mackenzie King era. . . . He extended good wishes to me for the future etc.

"This caused me to make a little further reply. I said that, while there had been a Conservative era of 25 years under Macdonald, there had been over 60 years of the Liberal era under Sir Wilfrid Laurier and myself, that all his years and mine combined were over 60 years in the leadership of the Liberal party. That I hoped the Liberal regime might continue on to round out 100 years which I thought should be possible if they were true to Liberal principles. That I thought the test of endurance of anything was whether it was capable of perpetuating itself more or less indefinitely. I did not think Conservative reaction could do this nor did I think extreme radicalism would effect it either. But I did believe that Liberalism, standing on the principles of private initiative and control of some aspects of business etc., was capable of giving the country what was needed in way of rightful direction. I said I thought they would have an unpleasant time with the new leader of the Conservative party but the more unpleasantness there was the better it might be for the Liberals. I then wished them all, as a Government and as individuals, every success and referred again to my affectionate regard for one and all. I then rose and shook hands with each member of the Cabinet and with Heeney. There was something very sincere in the appearance of all while I was speaking at the table and in their manner in saying Good-Bye. Just as they were leaving, Heeney brought the formal Order-in-Council in regard to the Federal District Commission. I went back to my own seat to sign it while most of the Ministers were standing. I then rose and said I wished to remind them that we were all Privy Councillors and that I hoped as such they would continue to keep me informed from time to time of what was happening in Council.

"I then went to the door and out by the door of the ante-room but turned back to say the words: 'God bless you all.'

"St. Laurent came to the door to ask me if I wished him to be with me at the meeting with the press. I told him that was what I was counting on. He said he would be along in a minute. I can honestly say that I felt no emotion whatever in saying good-bye and in realizing that this was my last meeting of the Cabinet.

"Later I felt a sense of great relief and happiness at the thought that all had gone so splendidly and that I was parting with my colleagues with only the kindest feeling on their part and on my own. I doubt if a Prime Minister ever left office under happier conditions. Certainly, few have left of their own volition."

Mackenzie King then met the press in his office. "It was the largest gathering of press representatives that I have seen in the room. I remained seated until all were in the room and then mentioned that, as they knew, I was retiring on Monday. I said I had just said goodbye to my colleagues at the last meeting of the Cabinet and that I wished now to say goodbye to members of the press. I told them I had prepared a short statement which I thought would answer what the public would wish to know, namely why I should be retiring at this time but before reading it I would like to say a word about my having announced the date of my intended resignation through the Legion. I said that, reading some of the papers, I gathered there was a feeling that this was an unusual method and that I should have made the announcement possibly through the press. I then stated pretty much what I had said in the first part of my letter to the Legion. I told them I was very happy to have had the opportunity to make that announcement in the way that it had been made; having been deprived of being present at the National War Memorial and making it my last public appearance, I was glad to have the opportunity to identify what was most in my mind in leaving office with those who represented the men and women who had taken part in the war, more particularly those who had been killed or lost their loved ones. This would always be the period that was outstanding in our history.

"I then read a statement. . . . After that, I spoke of the interest which they knew I had always taken in the work of the Federal District Commission improvement of Ottawa as the capital of Canada and stated that the Order I had signed in Council today and that the Cabinet had passed today was an Order bringing the Commission up to full strength through the appointment of representatives of different provinces. I then read the names of the nine representatives. I said I hoped they were all to take their duties earnestly and would have the work of the Commission furthered as much as possible. That I thought Ottawa and surrounding district would be made the most beautiful capital in the world. Nature had made provision for such and we were still young enough to make plans that were not only necessary today but would suit the capital of the country in years to come. That Canada would be a great country and that her capital should be planned accordingly. I then asked if there were any questions which they would like to ask. Someone spoke about further appointments to the Senate. I said I was leaving those to my successor. I was asked about the procedure respecting my resignation and appointment of the new Prime Minister. I outlined what has already appeared in the press from the memorandum prepared by Letson for the Governor-General. Asked about photographs there. I said that was a matter for the Governor-General to decide. Then someone asked if I were to go South for a winter. I said no I hoped to spend my winter at Laurier House enjoying the Canadian air and enjoying my own home. Something too was said about Kingsmere. I then stated, perhaps more emphatically that I should have, that I really wanted to at last enjoy my home and see something of friends in it. Someone also asked whether I thought a residence should be provided for the Prime Minister. I said that I had said in Parliament that I thought a residence should be provided, staff, servants etc., and allowances for entertainment which would be appropriate. I said many of our Ministers and Ambassadors were much better provided for than the Prime Minister; that was alright for them but was not fair to a Prime Minister. I also said that an impression had been created that Laurier House belonged to the party or was being maintained by the Government. I said neither was the case; that I had had to meet the taxes, the cost of maintenance and all matters connected with supplies etc., cost of garage, motor cars, repairs, etc. I said when these outlays were added to the deductions of the taxation from the Prime Minister's salary, it left very little to carry on with. Then I said I perhaps ought to mention that, in addition, where members of the public service received a pension, there was no provision for a pension for a Prime Minister. If he did not put aside part of his salary, he would have nothing to live on, unless provision had been made in other ways, when his period of service was over; that I thought provision should be made for a pension for future Prime Ministers. I was asked if I thought that should be done for Cabinet Ministers. I said there were different views on that; that I knew in England, for instance, they made provision for certain of the Ministers, depending on the length of time, etc., [but] that I did not wish to enter on a discussion. There were different points of view and I would rather leave that question for the moment.

"At the beginning of the interview, I said I had been advised to avoid political controversies at present. I did say that I hoped Parliament would without delay make provision for whoever might succeed as Prime Minister. That this would be not only for the immediately succeeding Prime Minister but for those who might have office in years to come. I said, in regard to Kingsmere, that I doubted if I would have lasted as long but for the rest and recreation that I had been able to take there. I had not had what is called a real holiday in twenty years.

"Bird [John Bird, then a correspondent for the Southam Press] asked what I regarded as the most memorable moment in my political life. I replied that I did not think of any moment in particular, but I would say that certainly I regarded having helped to keep Canada united through-out the war as the main contribution I had made. That I thought our policies in that regard had been fully vindicated and the war effort and other efforts depended upon the unity of the country. Something was said about getting on with the memoirs. I said I had not begun a line as yet; had sent my papers to the Archives a year or two ago to be looked over there and had not looked at a letter before sending them down. I had of course in addition, private papers and special communications which I would like to go over and make disposition of and set my own house in order etc., but what the future plans might be depended on Providence.

"Hardy of the Press Gallery then spoke on behalf of the members. He referred to our pleasant associations and extended best of wishes for my health and strength for a long time to come. He also referred to my being a member of the Gallery. When he had finished, I said I had meant my last word to the press to be renewed thanks [for membership in the Gallery] which I regarded as one quite exceptional and to let them know that I had hoped to take advantage of it, not only in the Gallery at times, but in the more sacred precinct of their own quarters.

"The members of the Gallery then came up one by one and shook hands. Each greeted me cordially and many with kind personal remarks."

On Saturday morning, November 13, Mackenzie King said goodbye to the staffs of the Privy Council Office and the Prime Minister's Office. He noted that both Pickersgill and Heeney "spoke nicely. Their remarks

were greeted in a splendid way by members of both staffs. I was surprised
to see that, with the exception of a few of the men, there were hardly any
of the staff whom I recalled having seen in the years I have been going in
and out of the East Block.

"It was exactly twelve when I had said good-bye to the two staffs."

He then attended a meeting of a cabinet committee which received a
delegation from the Canadian Legion. "On the committee were St. Laurent, Claxton, Gregg, Abbott, Mitchell. There was a large representation
of the Legion executives. Baxter [the President] presided.

"After shaking hands with all the members, I told him [Baxter] I had
just seen the staff and had remained over for the meeting, wished to express regret again at missing the luncheon and not being able to be at the
War Memorial. I told him of what I had in mind. Spoke of the war and
of what it will always mean to me – the feelings, the . . . relatives of those
who had lost their loved ones etc.; wished to pay a silent tribute with
them.

"I then spoke of Mr. St. Laurent. I mentioned what he had meant to
me and to the Government when Lapointe passed away. Of his family
participating in the war. Told them that they could feel assured of his
fullest sympathy and understanding.

"Baxter spoke with great appreciation of the letter I had sent to the
Legion and of the announcement being made and of the date of resignation given through them. He then spoke in quite exceptional terms of my
service to Canada through the years.

"It gave me particular satisfaction to say to the Legion that I felt pride
in having helped to keep the country united during the war. That, of
course, those who deserved recognition were the men and women who
actually served and that I believed that our policies had been wholly
vindicated. There did not seem to be the slightest exception to this statement on the part of anyone.

"Before Baxter concluded, he said he thought my services to Canada
and to the cause of freedom would be such that the sons of those who
belonged to the Legion – their children and their children's children
through generations to come – would honour my name for the part that
I had taken and the service I had given Canada etc. I have not listened
to a statement delivered in a more clearly or beautifully expressed manner or any finer word of appreciation. It was more surprising in that I
have always thought of Baxter as a very strong Conservative and I had
not expected from him any words of special recognition. When he had
concluded speaking, he read the statement to the committee and was followed by two other members of the Legion. Gregg replied. There was
very little said in addition. Claxton then mentioned a few words."

Baxter had asked to see the Prime Minister alone. "When the interview was over and the representatives and the Ministers had left, he and I were alone in the Prime Minister's office. We sat together side by side in one of the rows of chairs behind the table. Here I had one of the most remarkable experiences of my life. I had known that Baxter was a distant connection but I have never realized how close the relationship was.

"I opened the conversation by repeating again about regretting not to have been at the War Memorial service. Also saying to him how sorry I was to learn he had not himself been well. When I had asked him to sit down when reading his brief, he said he would be glad to do this, as he had not been out for three or four months.

"When I spoke about his illness, he told me that he had coronary thrombosis about four months ago. Really should not be out at this time. . . . I was waiting to see if he had something to bring up but apparently he had not anything.

"I then spoke to him about our relationship and mentioned to him that my mother's mother was Miss Baxter who married William Lyon Mackenzie. And that George Baxter who had come out to establish a school in Kingston, which school had been attended by Sir John Macdonald and Cartwright, was a brother of my mother's mother. I asked him if he was a relation of George Baxter. He said he was a great grandson. I have never had that association clearly in my mind. He then told me that he was named after William Lyon Mackenzie, my grandfather – the L. and M. in his name stood for Lyon Mackenzie – his full name is Lyon D. Mackenzie Baxter.

"I then asked if he had known the Sir George Baxter in Scotland. He told me he had visited him twice during the war, had been through the streets there. Had recently received from him a copy of a volume regarding the family. He understood that I had a copy as well which I recall I have.

"I spoke of Mackenzie being a remarkable man. He said that when the bounty was put on Mackenzie's head and they were searching for him, George Baxter, his great grandfather, would not allow the search to be made in his premises and, for this reason, his school was taken away from him. He then took up insurance or some other business of the kind. It was all quite an interesting revelation to me. I was much impressed with Baxter's appearance – his whole nature. It really made me quite proud of the connection. Now, what is so remarkable is that, over the last few days, the Baxter relationship in different ways has asserted itself

very strongly. Within the last couple of days, there has been a letter from
Mrs. Baxter Anderson of Kingston who is of the same family. A letter
from her son who is named William Lyon Mackenzie Anderson and who
is now in Chicago. . . . There were one or two other Baxter communications which I at the moment do not recall, but I remember yesterday
making a note of being impressed to note carefully these communications
as being significant – so many of them. It is now to my mind wholly apparent that all that has happened, particularly including this morning's
talk, makes clear that I am being impressed with the significance that
the talk today had in relation to my mother's family. Pickersgill remarked
to me two or three times that Baxter was a relative. I had not had this
thought in mind when I wrote him. What is so interesting is that the last
conversation I would have had in the office of Prime Minister will have
been between Baxter and myself, he representing one branch of my
mother's family and I representing the other, each in relationship [to]
my grandfather. Baxter himself spoke of the pleasure it had given him to
address me across the table. He had hoped we might meet at this time. I
remarked upon how singular it was that he should be the last person in
that room with me, having to do with Government affairs. The last interview should be between the two of us, he representing the Legion and
I representing the Government, and our talk having been of the men who
participated in the war."

Immediately after his morning reading on November 15, Mackenzie
King wrote a letter to Lord Alexander which he completed just before
going to Government House at 11.00 A.M. "I had asked Handy to accompany me," he wrote, "and we also took with us little Pat whom
Handy held on the way down. This being an historic occasion, I was
anxious that it should have associations with Handy and was glad also to
have Pat in the car.

"When I went out of the front door, a reporter and a photographer
were nearby. . . . Before leaving Laurier House, I said goodbye as Prime
Minister to members of the staff. Went into the kitchen to shake hands
with Mrs. Gooch. . . . On reaching the car, noticed two little boys who
were standing on the sidewalk near the car. I shook hands with them as I
got into the car.

"As we reached the Government House grounds, I pointed out to
Handy that the hands of the clock were together at five to eleven. We
noticed that the grounds were covered with snow. Snow was falling quite
freely. It was a beautiful sight – the first of the change of the season.

"At Government House door, photographers were there in numbers.

I was met according to plans by Chichester [a member of the Governor-General's staff] and General Letson. I went immediately to the Governor-General's apartment – to the circular room where His Excellency was waiting. When announced, Lord Alexander came forward and shook hands very warmly. He lead me over to near the fireplace and asked me to take a seat and to be comfortable.

"I thought it well not to sit down but to begin at once to speak of the purpose of the visit. In conversation, I said pretty much what I had written in the letter – that, as His Excellency knew, I had for sometime been anxious to retire; that I had come this morning to tender my resignation as Prime Minister and hoped it might be accepted.

"I added I shall miss very much the official and personal relations I had been privileged to share with him in the time he had been in Canada. But apart from that and some natural regret at breaking other old associations, I really would feel a great relief once I was out of office. I thought this was the right time to have a successor appointed. His Excellency said something to this effect: 'Well! Mr. King, I need not tell you how sorry I am that you feel it necessary to tender your resignation but, knowing what the circumstances are, I shall as the King's Representative be prepared, as it is your wish, to accept it. Who would you advise me to send for to form a new administration?' I replied without question, Mr. St. Laurent. He, as Your Excellency knows, was chosen Leader of the Liberal party by a very large majority at the convention. He, I believe, is able to command the majority in the House of Commons and will be able to do so more effectively than any other member of the House. Mr. St. Laurent, as you know, has exceptional qualifications for the position of leader and I would feel that Your Excellency could have no better advisor in the position of Prime Minister. His Excellency then said: 'I shall act on your advice and send for Mr. St. Laurent and see if he is prepared to form a ministry. I would like, however, to ask you to continue in office until I have ascertained from Mr. St. Laurent what he is prepared to do. I shall send for him at once. He may wish to consult others before giving me a final word. If so, I would let you know the time at which I will be able to inform you officially that Mr. St. Laurent is prepared to assume the responsibilities of office. I will hold your resignation meanwhile. Later when Mr. St. Laurent is here and prepared to take office. I will formally accept your resignation.'

"His Excellency went on to say: 'I did not say to you how much I regret that you have found it necessary to retire. Our relations have been exceptionally pleasant nor do I forget at this moment that it is to you that I owe my appointment as Governor-General. I shall hope we may continue to see much of each other. You will always have friends here at Government House,' and more to the same effect. I said: 'I thank Your Excellency very much for what you have just said. There is only one thing you have said, if I may be allowed to say so, that I must take exception to and that is, that you owe your appointment to myself! I added, 'you owe your appointment to the fact that you are Lord Alexander of Tunis. My colleagues and I felt our Country would be honoured if you would accept the appointment, that it would meet with the approval of the people of Canada, generally.' Alexander replied: 'You pay me a very high honour in what you have just said. I thank you very warmly.' I did not wait to sit down but said I thought I should withdraw. When Lord Alexander went to press the bell for Letson, we had a word about the arrival of the young Prince yesterday. The GG brought up the subject himself by speaking of the joy of the announcement given out from the Palace which he thought must have been in the form used many years ago, at the time of Queen Victoria and perhaps others. I said I thought there would be great pleasure at the fact that the child was a boy. He said he had expected it would be a girl. I said I was glad the event had happened at the time it had. I felt glad that I was still in office and able to send a note of congratulations from the Government. I remarked that St. Laurent and I seemed to be running a neck and neck race as to which might be the one to have that honour. His Excellency then said he would like to accompany me to the front door. He had sent word earlier to the photographers that he would appear there. Just before we had left the room, I asked for Lady Alexander, if I might have the pleasure of seeing her before giving up the office of Prime Minister. His Excellency remarked that she would be at the reception this afternoon. He then told me he thought of inviting Madame St. Laurent but not the wives of the Members of the Cabinet. That St. Laurent's wife would, so to speak, balance his own. He would later have the wives of the Ministers and of the High Commissioners for the purpose of a Commonwealth reception to mark the birth of the son of Princess Elizabeth and of Philip of Edinburgh.

"When we reached the stairs which lead to the outer door, the photographers were lined up at the foot of the stairs, taking some snapshots. I was asked to shake hands with His Excellency.

"I should add that before coming away when our formal conversation had ended, I withdrew from my pocket the letter I had written and handed it to His Excellency. I said I had written a short note this morning which I would like to hand to him and I handed it to him unsealed.

"At the door I was asked to shake hands with His Excellency. We then shook hands. We were asked later to do so again at which the Governor replied 'I cannot shake hands too often with Mr. King.'

"After the photographing was over, I put on my coat and rubbers. As I went out of the doors, the photographers asked a question or two. I told them that I had tendered my resignation but that His Excellency had asked me to continue on in office until sometime in the afternoon, until Mr. St. Laurent was prepared to take over.

"One reporter remarked you are still Prime Minister to which I acquiesced. He asked me what my future plans were. I said that remained to be seen, but intimated that I was very happy and already felt the joy of the new freedom. It was quite apparent I am sure from my manner that this was no affectation. I did feel a tremendous relief.

"Photographs were then taken anew of Handy and myself in the car, and then we drove off with Pat back to Laurier House.

"On coming in to Laurier House, hands of the clock were in a straight line at 11.25."

Mackenzie King first telephoned Mrs. Patteson "to let her know how relieved and happy I felt. Pickersgill had mentioned that the Canadian Broadcasting Corporation were anxious to have a short broadcast, and he submitted a draft which had been prepared. It has been prepared as if the broadcast was being made at night. I told Pickersgill I would like to read it while I was still Prime Minister. He thought there might be some constitutional difficulties in telling anything that had passed between the Governor and myself. I said I thought I could so word the message that any difficulty on that score would be avoided. What I wanted to do was to send a message to the people of Canada, to let them know that my last thoughts were related to the confidence that they had expressed in myself and colleagues over so long period of time.

"I was at work on this when Stuart Garson arrived. He had asked to see me while I was still Prime Minister and before he was sworn in [as Minister of Justice]. He came at twelve and we talked together in my library before the fire. I told him how pleased I was at his having agreed to enter the Ministry. That I believed that he had taken the right step. That it was necessary to have experienced men in government at Ottawa. That I thought the Government would be greatly strengthened by his presence and that of Pearson. Garson said he was much concerned about the situation as he left it in the province. That he did not know how the coalition would keep together. He had witnessed one of the roughest scrapes between some of them after he had left which he felt he could have settled in a moment if he had been still at the head of affairs. I told him that was inevitable where men were seeking position; that they would soon get together. . . .

"I spoke of the address he had given on Communism. He said I hoped he would use that to explain the position in an intelligent way. I also spoke about the wisdom of avoiding too much in the way of commitments. I felt that was one of the dangers; that our government was being drawn into world affairs to an extent that I questioned the wisdom of. He said to me that he had, all the years he had been Premier, never made a commitment in advance. He had always watched against that carefully. He agreed there were real dangers along the line that I had indicated. I also spoke about watching expenditures and extravagance in administration – not trying to do more than we could do in the right way. He said to me that he would have liked to have made the severance he had earlier – would liked to have been a member of my government but that he held back through fear of the consequences of his leaving the government of Manitoba. He emphasized that two or three times he really would have liked to have come in and to have been a member of my administration first.

"This was doubly interesting in view of something that appeared in Saturday Night news items that he had not entered the Government sooner as he may not have wished to come in with me. What mischief makers men are!

"He then spoke about hoping he might come and talk over matters with me from time to time. I told him I should be delighted to see him at any time. While we were talking, a typewritten note was handed to me to the effect that an announcement had come over the Press that a scholarship of $1,000 . . . had been established by friends of mine at the University of Toronto who wished the scholarship to be known as the "Mackenzie King Scholarship" etc. This was really a delightful surprise. . . .

"Later in the afternoon a box of three dozen roses was left at Laurier House with greetings from the Federation signed by Fogo.

"During the morning a large box of chrysanthemums and other flowers came from [Baron] Silvercruys in Washington. Still later, there was another lot of chrysanthemums delivered at Laurier House. . . ."

The Prime Minister "continued a draft of the broadcast until about a quarter past one when I had luncheon in the dining-room. I was glad to have this period in that room with its associations and paintings.

"After lunch I dictated the broadcast to Handy and at 3 o'clock I delivered it in the dining-room. Meanwhile, I also sent a telegram to the President and Secretary of the Glengarry Constituency to let them know they were in my thoughts in the last hours as Prime Minister.

"I also sent a telegram to Violet Markham whose interest in my political career had been longer than that of any other friend.

"I phoned to Sir Lyman Duff to thank him for an exceptionally fine letter which came from him yesterday. . . . I then dictated a letter to President Truman.

"Pickersgill had arrived in time for me to go over the broadcast with him and Handy in the dining-room. . . . They were present when I delivered it. Little Pat was also lying under the table. I was glad to see the little fellow there. The other Pat was in the same place on a previous occasion.

"While we were arranging the broadcast equipment, something was said about it being an interesting time – the birth of a baby etc., and I added the passing of a Prime Minister. Altogether, all of us felt very happy.

"In broadcasting I had the picture of Sir Wilfrid behind me. The broadcaster had so arranged it and I was able to enjoy the other paintings from where I sat. I said good-bye as Prime Minister to Pickersgill, as I was just about to go up in the elevator, and thanked him for his help over the years. I only had time for about 7 minutes' rest before leaving to go to Government House.

"I went down alone and was met at the door again by a barrage of photographers. I was met by General Letson who took me to the Governor-General's room.

"When I entered the Governor-General and St. Laurent, who had been seated near the Governor's desk, both rose and came over and shook hands with me.

"His Excellency said something about Mr. St. Laurent being prepared to take over the Government but before he said anything further, St. Laurent said himself that it was with great misgivings. He began to speak to the Governor and myself of what it would mean to others not to have me continue in office. He spoke of my experience etc.

"I replied that I had no misgivings. That I knew the Government was very fortunate to have him at its head. His Excellency then said that, as Mr. St. Laurent was prepared to form a Ministry and had submitted his slate, he would as the King's Representative accept my resignation, but he spoke again of my long service to the Country and also brought in a reference to the Commonwealth and our happy relations.

"When my resignation had been accepted, I looked toward His Excellency to see if he was not about to shake hands with Mr. St. Laurent. This he did. I then shook hands with St. Laurent myself and wished him all that was best. I thanked him for relieving me of the responsibilities of office and said to His Excellency that I would like to congratulate him on his first Minister.

"The three of us had a very pleasant talk together. Heeney was then brought in to arrange the books for the Ministers' signatures. While this was being done, something was said about a residence for the Prime Minister, that I hoped that would be arranged at once. The Governor then said to me, he certainly thought that should be done without delay. He then asked me whether he could not be of help in that direction, as to who should bring the matter up, whether it should be the Leader of the Opposition or not. I said to His Excellency you will have to ask Mr. St. Laurent who is your adviser. I assumed much depended upon how the spirit moved those concerned in Parliament. He pressed me a little further and asked whether it would not perhaps be the Leader of the Opposition. I said I really could not say. That perhaps a committee of Parliament could take the matter up. I said also I thought there should be some provision for a pension for the Prime Minister. I said, take my position; if it had not been for personal friends and Lady Laurier who left me Laurier House and personal friends who furnished it and gave me a sum to help maintain the House and to meet the situation that might arise once I was out of office, and but for a bequest or two that I have received, I would be leaving with practically nothing. What had saved the situation for me was that, when I was given assistance to maintain the House, Mr. Larkin had said that he wanted me to be able to keep up the position that I had as Prime Minister when out of office, when I might, as would be inevitable, leave office. I said I thereupon treated the money that had been given me as a trust and put it in a separate account and never made any withdrawal upon it. I allowed it to accumulate interest and kept it apart from what the Government had provided – took what was provided for a Prime Minister. I could not, when the taxes were taken off, begin to meet all the obligations; if I had attempted to meet all the obligations that a Prime Minister should on what was provided, I would simply not have been in a position to do so.

"I said certainly there should be a house which should be furnished – maintained and provided with servants etc. His Excellency seemed quite concerned about the situation and much in earnest. I should not be surprised if he would inspire something. He then said: 'Will you still obey orders?' I said yes, if they came from him. He said: 'Well, there is a seat for you. I would like you to sit down and not to remain standing.' He had an armchair placed at the side of his desk from where I would be facing Mr. St. Laurent and the Ministers as they were being sworn and also to be near the rest of the Cabinet as they came in.

"Members of the Cabinet were then brought in. They all came over and shook hands with me. Afterwards, I remained seated through the swearing in ceremonies. The Governor then asked me if I would sign as a witness the swearing in of St. Laurent as Prime Minister and of the two new Ministers. He gave me a particular pen to sign with.

"Later when the signing was all over, he handed me the pen in a case, saying he would like me to have this as a souvenir of the occasion. I thanked him saying he had always been so kind and saying this was the last of his kindnesses. I really meant the latest. Someone there said there would be a good many more. He mentioned that he had had the pen engraved. I later thanked him personally very warmly.

"His Excellency then asked me if I would join Mr. St. Laurent and himself to go and have a photograph taken. The three of us were to have been photographed together. All the other Ministers then followed. The first photograph was taken in the nature of the three — the Governor, Mr. St. Laurent and myself being seated. Then other photographs were taken with the other Ministers standing, some partly seated. A photo was taken in front of the large painting of Queen Victoria. There were several pictures taken. Finally, one with the Governor-General, St. Laurent and myself again. Later on, one with St. Laurent and myself. His Excellency then took me over to the drawing-room where the Members of the Cabinet were being photographed. In the drawing-room, I met Madame St. Laurent and extended warmest congratulations to her; the new Lady-in-Waiting — a very pleasant young lady — was also present. I had a few moments' talk with her. I was also delighted to meet St. Laurent's three daughters.

"Her Excellency and Madame St. Laurent sat on a sofa and talked until the Cabinet began to come in and their wives. The table was arranged in a corner of the room with refreshments, sandwiches, champagne etc. After all were assembled, His Excellency said he had two toasts to propose. He then proposed a toast to myself in which he spoke of the regret felt at my relinquishing office, of the years of service and referred in the nicest possible way to the latter. He then proposed a toast to the new Prime Minister, Mr. St. Laurent, in which he spoke in an equally felicitous manner of his taking on the responsibilities of office. A little later in the afternoon some of the representatives of the nations of the Commonwealth and their wives came. There were only three I think, Lady Clutterbuck and her husband, Mr. and Mrs. Hearne and the Australian Ambassador and his wife. His Excellency then proposed another toast which was to Princess Elizabeth and the Royal Prince to wish them health and happiness etc.

"Shortly after Mr. St. Laurent and the Ministers withdrew to attend the Cabinet meeting. I remained for a short time having a pleasant conversation with the wives of my former colleagues. I then said good-bye to Their Excellencies. I felt remarkably happy having had this little reunion with my Colleagues and their wives, and with friends at Government House."

After his retirement as Prime Minister, Mackenzie King lived quietly at Laurier House and at Kingsmere. Though occasionally consulted by his successor and members of the Cabinet, he seemed to take relatively little interest in most domestic political issues. His attendance in the House was irregular and he was seldom seen in public. Virtually no progress was made on his memoirs and what energy he had was absorbed in keeping up his voluminous personal correspondence. Following a short final illness, he died at Kingsmere at 9.42 p.m. on July 22, 1950. The Mackenzie King era had ended.

# Appendix

## CHANGES, MACKENZIE KING MINISTRY
## JANUARY 1, 1947 – NOVEMBER 15, 1948

| | |
|---|---|
| August 10, 1947 | H. F. G. Bridges died in office as Minister of *Fisheries* |
| August 14, 1947 | Ernest Bertrand appointed Acting Minister of *Fisheries* (ceased to act on September 1, 1947) |
| September 2, 1947 | Milton Gregg appointed Minister of *Fisheries* |
| January 18, 1948 | Ian A. Mackenzie resigned from the ministry |
| | J. A. MacKinnon resigned from *Trade and Commerce* |
| | J. J. McCann resigned from *National War Services* |
| | Milton Gregg resigned from *Fisheries* |
| January 19, 1948 | C. D. Howe appointed Minister of *Trade and Commerce* |
| | J. A. MacKinnon appointed Minister of *Fisheries* |
| | Milton Gregg appointed Minister of *Veterans Affairs* |
| June 10, 1948 | J. A. Glen resigned from the ministry |
| | J. A. MacKinnon resigned from *Fisheries* |
| June 11, 1948 | J. A. MacKinnon appointed Minister of *Mines and Resources* |
| | R. W. Mayhew appointed Minister of *Fisheries* |
| June 30, 1948 | J. L. Ilsley resigned from the ministry |
| July 1, 1948 | Louis S. St. Laurent appointed Acting Minister of *Justice and Attorney General* |
| September 9, 1948 | Louis S. St. Laurent resigned from *External Affairs* |
| September 10, 1948 | Lester B. Pearson appointed Secretary of State for *External Affairs* |
| | Louis S. St. Laurent appointed Minister of *Justice* |

## THE MINISTRY, NOVEMBER 15, 1948

| | |
|---|---|
| *Prime Minister and President of the Privy Council* | W. L. Mackenzie King |
| *Minister of Trade and Commerce and Minister of Reconstruction and Supply* | C. D. Howe |
| *Minister of Agriculture* | James G. Gardiner |
| *Minister of Mines and Resources* | James A. MacKinnon |
| *Secretary of State of Canada* | Colin W. G. Gibson |

| | |
|---|---|
| *Minister of Justice and Attorney General* | Louis S. St. Laurent |
| *Minister of Labour* | Humphrey Mitchell |
| *Minister of Public Works* | Alphonse Fournier |
| *Postmaster General* | Ernest Bertrand |
| *Minister of National Defence* | Brooke Claxton |
| *Solicitor General* | Joseph Jean |
| *Minister of Transport* | Lionel Chevrier |
| *Minister of National Health and Welfare* | Paul Martin |
| *Minister of Finance and Receiver General* | Douglas C. Abbott |
| *Minister of National Revenue* | J. J. McCann |
| *Minister without Portfolio and Leader of the Government in the Senate* | Wishart McL. Robertson |
| *Minister of Veterans Affairs* | Milton F. Gregg |
| *Minister of Fisheries* | R. W. Mayhew |
| *Secretary of State for External Affairs* | Lester B. Pearson |

With Mackenzie King's resignation from the ministry and St. Laurent's appointment as Prime Minister and President of the Privy Council on November 15, the only changes in the cabinet were Robert Winters' appointment as Minister of Reconstruction and Supply and Stuart Garson's as Minister of Justice and Attorney General. C. D. Howe retained the Trade and Commerce portfolio.

*Parliamentary Assistants* (not of the Cabinet):

| | |
|---|---|
| *Agriculture* | Robert McCubbin, October 30, 1947 – November 15, 1948 |
| *External Affairs* | Walter E. Harris, October 30, 1947 – November 15, 1948 |
| *Finance* | R. W. Mayhew, September 25, 1945 – June 10, 1948 |
| | Gleason Belzile, October 30, 1947 – November 15, 1948 |
| *Fisheries* | Thomas Reid, April 22, 1948 – June 10, 1948 |
| | J. W. MacNaught, June 11, 1948 – November 15, 1948 |
| *Labour* | Paul E. Côté, October 30, 1947 – November 15, 1948 |
| *National Defence* | W. C. Macdonald, September 25, 1945 – November 19, 1946 |
| | Hugues Lapointe, September 25, 1945 – November 15, 1948 |
| *National Health and Welfare* | Ralph Maybank, October 30, 1947 – November 15, 1948 |

| | |
|---|---|
| *National Revenue* | Robert H. Winters, October 30, 1947 – June 10, 1948 |
| | Thomas Reid, June 11, 1948 – November 15, 1948 |
| *Reconstruction* | G. J. McIlraith, September 28, 1945 – December 31, 1945 |
| *Reconstruction and Supply* | G. J. McIlraith, January 1, 1946 – November 15, 1948 |
| *Trade and Commerce* | G. J. McIlraith, February 3, 1948 – November 15, 1948 |
| *Transport* | Robert H. Winters, June 11, 1948 – November 15, 1948 |
| *Veterans Affairs* | W. A. Tucker, September 27, 1945 – April 21, 1948 |
| | L. A. Mutch, June 11, 1948 – November 15, 1948 |

# Index